Strategic People Management and Development

Sixth Edition

Strategic People Management and Development

Theory and Practice

Edited by Gary Rees and Ray French

Publisher's note

Every possible effort has been made to ensure that the information contained in this book is accurate at the time of going to press, and the publishers and authors cannot accept responsibility for any errors or omissions, however caused. No responsibility for loss or damage occasioned to any person acting, or refraining from action, as a result of the material in this publication can be accepted by the editor, the publisher or the author.

First published as *Leading, Managing and Developing People* by the Chartered Institute of Personnel and Development
Sixth edition published in Great Britain and the United States in 2023 by Kogan Page Limited

2nd Floor, 45 Gee Street	8 W 38th Street, Suite 902	4737/23 Ansari Road
London	New York, NY 10018	Daryaganj
EC1V 3RS	USA	New Delhi 110002
United Kingdom		India
www.koganpage.com		

Kogan Page books are printed on paper from sustainable forests.

ISBNs

Hardback	978 1 3986 0762 0
Paperback	978 1 3986 0760 6
Ebook	978 1 3986 0761 3

British Library Cataloguing-in-Publication Data

A CIP record for this book is available from the British Library.

Library of Congress Control Number

2022038341

Typeset by Integra Software Services, Pondicherry
Print production managed by Jellyfish
Printed and bound by CPI Group (UK) Ltd, Croydon CR0 4YY

CONTENTS

List of figures and tables **ix**
About the editors **x**
List of contributors **xi**
Acknowledgements **xiii**
Walkthrough of textbook features **xiv**
Online resources **xvi**

PART ONE Strategic people management and development **1**

01 Introduction 3

1.1 Overview **3**
1.2 Introduction **7**
1.3 The structure of the book **12**
1.4 Conclusion **12**

PART TWO People management and the strategic context **17**

02 The scope and nature of people management 19

2.1 Overview **20**
2.2 Introduction **20**
2.3 Definitions of personnel management, human resource management
     and human resource development **21**
2.4 The scope and nature of HRM and HRD **23**
2.5 Models of HRM and strategic HRM **25**
2.6 HRD and strategic HRD **27**
2.7 The shape of HR **30**
2.8 Capability building by the HR function **35**
2.9 Strategic HRM and human capital management **38**
2.10 Future trends for people professionals **41**
2.11 Conclusion **43**

03 People management: strategy, culture and values 45

3.1 Overview **46**
3.2 Introduction **46**
3.3 The scope and nature of strategy **46**

3.4 The importance of culture 49
3.5 The interplay between strategy and culture 53
3.6 Branding and organisational values 53
3.7 The competing values framework 56
3.8 Good work as examined by the CIPD 56
3.9 The customer and the organisation 59
3.10 Customer alignment 60
3.11 HRM and RISK 61
3.12 Conclusion 63

04   HRM contributions in different settings 66

4.1 Overview 67
4.2 Introduction 67
4.3 HR in different contexts 68
4.4 HR roles as the organisation grows: SMEs 73
4.5 Expanding our borders: the growth of internationalisation 77
4.6 Strategic international HRM 78
4.7 Conclusion 86

05   Professional and ethical people practice 89

5.1 Overview 90
5.2 Introduction 90
5.3 Professions 91
5.4 The purpose of business 95
5.5 Introducing business ethics 96
5.6 Approaches to ethics 97
5.7 Sustainability and HR 102
5.8 Equal opportunities and ethics 103
5.9 Data, technology and ethics 106
5.10 Embedding ethical practice – the role of HR 108
5.11 Conclusion 109

PART THREE Strategic people management
and development effectiveness 111

06   Recruitment and selection 113

6.1 Overview 114
6.2 Introduction 114
6.3 Effective recruitment and selection 118
6.4 Validity of selection methods 122
6.5 Contemporary themes in recruitment and selection 125
6.6 Fairness in recruitment and selection 129
6.7 The extent of professional practice 131
6.8 Recruitment and selection: a contingency approach 134
6.9 Conclusion 136

07   Talent management and developing employees for performance 139

7.1 Overview **140**

7.2 Towards conceptualising talent and talent management **140**

7.3 The growing importance of talent management for individuals and organisations **142**

7.4 Context matters **143**

7.5 Key talent management stakeholders **148**

7.6 The talent management cycle **151**

7.7 Employee learning and development: a key element of talent management agendas **154**

7.8 Conclusion: reshaping talent management agendas to enhance organisational performance **160**

08   Engagement, wellbeing and inclusion 164

8.1 Overview **165**

8.2 Introduction: recognising workplace dynamics **165**

8.3 Engagement **167**

8.4 Wellbeing **174**

8.5 Inclusion **182**

8.6 Conclusion **190**

09   Managing the employment relationship 193

9.1 Overview **194**

9.2 Introduction **194**

9.3 The contract of employment **195**

9.4 Conflict and the employment relationship **203**

9.5 Diversity at work **208**

9.6 Conclusion: Reflections on managing the employment relationship **215**

10   Performance and reward: a strategic approach 219

10.1 Overview **220**

10.2 Introduction **220**

10.3 Perspectives on performance management **223**

10.4 Monitoring progress and measuring results **224**

10.5 Performance management as a process **224**

10.6 Motivated to perform? **237**

10.7 The links between reward and performance **240**

10.8 Arguments against the use of performance management **246**

10.9 The role of HR and best practice within PM **246**

10.10 Conclusion **247**

11   Organisational design and effective working practices 251

11.1 Overview 252
11.2 Introduction 252
11.3 Key terms 253
11.4 Models of structure 260
11.5 Approaches to job design 265
11.6 Smart and agile working 271
11.7 Conclusion 273

12   Organisational development and change 276

12.1 Overview 277
12.2 Introduction 277
12.3 Types of change 278
12.4 Analysing the change context 282
12.5 Choice of change intervention 286
12.6 Leading change 298
12.7 HR value added and change 303
12.8 Change and performance 305
12.9 Conclusion 308

PART FOUR Conclusion 311

13   Summary themes and future trends 313

13.1 Overview 313
13.2 Key trends 314
13.3 Conclusion 324

Bibliography 326
Index 380

LIST OF FIGURES AND TABLES

Figures

FIGURE 2.1	The hard model of HRM	25
FIGURE 8.1	Facilitating wellbeing: A plan-do-check-act model	181
FIGURE 8.2	Women and parenting responsibilities – a live debate	188
FIGURE 9.1	Some possible sources of the contract of employment	195
FIGURE 9.2	The relationship between the contract of employment and collective agreements	199
FIGURE 10.1	The people and performance model	221
FIGURE 10.2	Some of the activities which could maximise ability, motivation, opportunity, satisfaction, commitment and engagement (AMOSCE)	222
FIGURE 10.3	HR supporting mechanisms	223
FIGURE 12.1	Child's approaches to organisational change	279
FIGURE 12.2	Model of change momentum	281
FIGURE 12.3	Combination of concurrent change interventions	282
FIGURE 12.4	The iterative nature of change and planning for change	283
FIGURE 12.5	Lewin's force-field analysis	288
FIGURE 12.6	A systems approach to change	295
FIGURE 12.7	Systems intervention strategy	296
FIGURE 12.8	The expertise of the change agent	301

Tables

TABLE 1.1	CIPD qualifications map	13
TABLE 7.1.	Coaching vs. mentoring	156
TABLE 8.1	The distinction between characteristics of psychological contracts	166
TABLE 8.2	Relational and practical factors within inclusive working practices	185
TABLE 8.3	Processes of inclusion and exclusion	189
TABLE 10.1	Performance management as a process	226
TABLE 10.2	Pitfalls of target definition	231
TABLE 12.1	PESTLE framework	284
TABLE 12.2	The TROPICS test	287
TABLE 12.3	The key features and methods of SIS	296
TABLE 13.1	Human capital at multiple levels	319

ABOUT THE EDITORS

Dr Ray French is a former Principal Lecturer, Associate Head and Head of Undergraduate Programmes at the University of Portsmouth Business School, where he taught in the areas of organisational behaviour and cross-cultural awareness. Ray has a long-standing and deeply held commitment to international higher education and is the author of three editions of *Cross-Cultural Management in Work Organisations*.

Professor Gary Rees is Head of School of Organisations, Systems and People at Portsmouth University. He is a Chartered Companion of the CIPD and Member of the British Psychological Society. He has written numerous textbooks covering Strategic HRM and Management and Organisational Behaviour with Paul Smith and Laurie Mullins respectively. Gary also serves on the CIPD's Qualifications Advisory Group.

LIST OF CONTRIBUTORS

Dr Matthew Anderson is a Senior Lecturer in Business Ethics at the University of Portsmouth and teaches undergraduate and postgraduate courses in the areas of organisational behaviour, human resource management and sustainable business. Matthew's research interests focus on the intersection between civil society and business. In particular, his work explores business engagement with fair trade and transitions to a circular economy.

Kerry Collier is a Principal Lecturer in Human Resource Management and Associate Head of Organisation Studies and HRM at the University of Portsmouth, Faculty of Business and Law. A CIPD member, she has over 25 years' experience as an HR practitioner and has worked predominately within the private sector but also in the public and voluntary sectors.

Dr Liza Howe-Walsh is a Reader in International Human Resource Management at the University of Portsmouth, following a successful commercial career in PwC. She has published widely including journals such as *The International Journal of Human Resource Management*, *Journal of Business Research* and the *Journal of international Management*, and is on the editorial board of the *Journal of Global Mobility*.

Dr Foteini Kravariti is a Senior Lecturer in HRM/OB at the University of Portsmouth. She holds key roles in international institutions and sits on the Editorial Advisory Board of the *International Journal of Contemporary Hospitality Management* and on the Steering Committee of the Research Methodology SIG of the British Academy of Management. She is an accredited academic member of CIPD and a Fellow at Higher Education Academy (HEA). Her current research interests fall under talent management.

Dr Victoria Pagan is a Senior Lecturer in Strategic Management and Director of Equality, Diversity and Inclusion at Newcastle University Business School. Her research interests coalesce around knowledge – its generation, uses, and violations including epistemic violence and epistemic injustice. Her current work is an exploration of the impacts of the uses of non-disclosure agreements in a range of workplace contexts.

Charlotte Rayner is Emeritus Professor at the University of Portsmouth. She is interested in all aspects of human resource and people management, with a current focus on ethical challenges in maintaining individual motivation and purpose in a world seeking to work in algorithmic sets. She lectures worldwide and publishes in the field of workplace bullying and harassment, and was the first President of the International Association on Workplace Bullying and Harassment (IAWBH).

Dr Peter Scott is a former Senior Lecturer in Employment Relations in the Faculty of Business and Law, University of Portsmouth, teaching human resource management, employment relations and diversity. His research interests include the political economy of employment relations, disability and employment, technical change and employment and research ethics.

Dr Emily Yarrow is a Senior Lecturer in Management and Organisations at Newcastle University Business School, UK. Emily's scholarly work focuses on and contributes to contemporary understandings of gendered organisational behaviour, women's experiences of organisational life and the future of work. Her research interests broadly include organisational theory, gender and inequality regimes, and impact and governance in higher education.

ACKNOWLEDGEMENTS

This sixth edition of our book contains new topic areas, research findings, case studies and other examples, intended to reflect topicality and enhance relevance for readers. The book has been written to meet the needs of the CIPD 7C002 module on People Management and Development Strategies for Performance for both the CIPD Level 7 Advanced Diploma in Strategic People Management and Strategic Learning and Development qualifications.

We are dealing with a fast-moving area of both study and practice, strongly influenced by the wider economic, social and, on this occasion, global health context. Nonetheless, some classical insights and findings continue to underpin the subject matter and we have built on earlier editions of the book. Thanks are due to Charlotte Rayner and Derek Adam-Smith who edited the first two editions and all other previous contributors. We welcome new chapter authors: Kerry Collier, Foteini Kravariti, Victoria Pagan and Emily Yarrow. We wish to thank, finally, staff at Santorini Restaurant Chichester, where several key planning meetings took place in a most pleasant setting.

Gary Rees and Ray French

WALKTHROUGH OF TEXTBOOK FEATURES

Learning outcomes

LEARNING OUTCOMES

After reading this chapter, you should be able to:

- identify important themes within the area of managing and developing people through an analysis of three case studies;
- appreciate the ongoing importance and topicality of core issues involved in strategic people management;
- familiarise yourself with the learning features within this book;
- understand the structure of the book in relation to the CIPD People Management and Development Strategies for Performance unit (7CO02);
- map the People Management and Development Strategies for Performance unit (7CO02) learning outcomes to particular sections and chapters within the text.

Case studies

 Case study 3.2

How VisitBritain/VisitEngland devised a new people strategy during Covid-19

The government body used the hiatus in the tourism sector as a golden opportunity to carry out significant change work. Devising a brand-new people strategy is a huge undertaking at the best of times. And it's even more of a huge undertaking against the backdrop of a global pandemic. But that's exactly what Debra Lang, director of HR and professional services at national tourism agency VisitBritain/VisitEngland, a government arms-length body, took on during 2020 – a process she describes as 'like trying to fly a plane and build it at the same time'. But, despite tourism being one of the sectors worst hit by Covid, and the government-funded organisation unable to furlough staff, the timing turned out to be fortuitous.

Review questions

 Review questions

1 Indicate with examples three ways in which recruitment and selection policies and practices can be used by an organisation aiming to develop staff as part of a talent management strategy.

2 Evaluate the evidence regarding the potential validity of biodata and personality assessment as tools for selecting employees.

3 What do you understand by the contingency approach to recruitment and selection? Provide two examples, from academic sources or your own experience, to illustrate this approach.

4 Evaluate the effectiveness of social media and online recruitment methods in comparison to the employee referral scheme. In what circumstances might the social media route be a more effective way of attracting applicants?

Reflective activities

 Reflective activity 10.2

Analyse the targets or objectives that you have been set during a PM process. To what extent do the pitfalls listed in Table 10.2 apply to these? How could your targets be improved upon?

ONLINE RESOURCES

This textbook is supplemented with PowerPoint slides, sample essay questions and an instructor's manual. These can be found at **koganpage.com/spmad**.

PART ONE
Strategic people management and development

01
Introduction

RAY FRENCH AND GARY REES

LEARNING OUTCOMES

After reading this chapter, you should be able to:

- identify important themes within the area of managing and developing people through an analysis of three case studies
- appreciate the ongoing importance and topicality of core issues involved in strategic people management
- familiarise yourself with the learning features within this book
- understand the structure of the book in relation to the CIPD People Management and Development Strategies for Performance unit (7C002)
- map the People Management and Development Strategies for Performance unit (7C002) learning outcomes to particular sections and chapters within the text.

1.1 Overview

Managing and developing people forms a key part of everyday life in work organisations. While topics and issues covered in this book may fall within the formal remit of a specialist human resource management (HRM) function, there is equally a strong sense in which managing and developing employees infuses all aspects of working life. There is value in taking a strategic approach to this area of work, aligning people management and development practices with long-term organisational objectives (CIPD, 2021a). Many HR professionals go further, seeking to link people management strategy and practice with an organisation's culture, brand and values.

Whether at the strategic or operational level, managing people is no easy task and anyone engaged in this activity will seek to improve performance and outcomes based on evidence showing which approaches are likely to bring success. Prior evidence can also, conversely, help us to identify and avoid misaligned strategies and policies. In this book we aim to provide evidence-based material which, while never guaranteeing success, can point to positive outcomes in people management based on sound principles.

Research in the area of managing people has a long history of over 100 years. There are still classical findings which remain valid, while knowledge develops at pace and there is continuing and rapid emergence of new findings. The trick is to appreciate what is changing and what is enduring within the subject area, and we aim to guide readers in this respect within our book.

Strategic people management is critically affected by the external context and there is a need to remain responsive and be aware of topical issues. In previous editions we focused upon recession and post-recession aspects of HR and how these were manifested in practice. Since 2016 the UK has left the European Union and been hit by the Covid-19 pandemic, during which the closure of many places of work led to a questioning of basic working patterns. At the time of writing, the invasion of Ukraine is causing a humanitarian catastrophe, mass movement of refugees as well as significant uncertainty for the world economy. Seismic events cast doubt on our ability to foresee the future and the impact of such torrid times on the people profession. Nonetheless, we still plan for a hopefully brighter future. What will the next ten years bring for people management professionals?

In 2020 the Chartered Institute of Personnel and Development (CIPD) published a report *People Profession 2030: A collective view of future trends* (CIPD, 2020a). The report identified likely 'drivers of change' over the 10-year period, together with a summary of what these trends mean for skills capabilities of people professionals and how they can add value.

1 **Internal change: evolving organisational models, structures and processes**
   Under this heading the report notes that HR professionals can lead the way in organisational change, design and development. This can involve scanning the external environment to anticipate shifts, adapting people functions for more agile ways of working and taking the lead on strategic change, and considering people needs from the outset.

2 **Digital and technological transformation**
   HR professionals within this heading should develop skills for a digital world, ensure engagement with employees throughout change programmes and challenge other business areas to consider the impact of technological developments on people, including crucial ethical considerations.

3 **Changing demographics and diversity and inclusion**
   To thrive in 2030 and beyond, the HR profession can use expertise to develop effective strategies by influencing senior leaders to champion equality while ensuring good practice is embedded throughout the organisation. The report notes that this is a complex and evolving area, so there is a need to refer to evidence when forecasting and understanding demographic change.

4 **Diversifying employment relationships**

This driver of change focuses on how wider social change plays out at work in terms of moving away from a 'traditional' employment relationship. HR professionals are advised to develop line managers so they can work effectively in multiple types of employment – for example, when managing virtual teams. It would also be important to balance the needs and expectations of customers and employees within new working arrangements and relationships.

5 **Sustainability, purpose and responsible business**

Within this heading, people professionals have a role in championing a strategic approach to responsible business, working beyond organisational boundaries with external stakeholders and communities. The report notes that HR is perfectly placed to influence positive change, especially in diversity, inclusion and equality.

There is little doubt that the future challenges facing HR professionals will be substantial, with the demands of managing and developing people (both upward and downward) in organisations becoming potentially even more demanding and complex. The 2020 report summarised above identifies the need to take a strategic approach while embedding good practice throughout what are rapidly changing workplaces.

We hope that insights contained within this book will help you both to manage people effectively and support other managers with people responsibilities.

Individual chapters within this book identify and discuss the core topics that make up the study and practice of managing and developing people. We have organised the chapters into discrete areas – for example, engagement wellbeing and inclusion, managing the employment relationship, and performance and reward. However, managing people is a broad area of work, and day-to-day events and challenges are best understood and acted on by taking an overview that goes beyond any one sub-division of HR work. This can be seen in Case study 1.1 below, which deals with a single theme, but one that has broader ramifications for managing and developing people.

 Case study 1.1

HR in a time of crisis – a role across borders

Within hours of the invasion of her country on 24 February 2022, Maryana Kiverska, HR manager at Impressit a Ukraine-based digital agency, was on the phone to her boss, co-founder and CEO Roman Zomko, discussing how best to provide safety for, and communicate with, their staff. On that call, as well as others with leadership team members – conversations backdropped by disorienting news of missiles striking across the country as well as updates on invading troops and tanks entering Ukraine across multiple border locations – it was agreed that tools would be downed for the next 24 hours and Impressit's management would try to get the workforce to convene later that evening on Zoom.

As Zomko told *People Management*, HR was central to their agreed-on priorities. 'I gave the mission to our HR manager to go one-by-one through everyone [on that first company call] to make sure they are fine [as] we kept track of who joined.' With about a dozen staff members missing from that check-in it would be Kiverska's job to follow up and check that they were as okay as they could be.

In the first week or so Impressit had to figure out a way to manage working in a war. The business had to determine what being flexible meant in an extreme situation, settling upon a 'do what you can' approach. The importance of continuing to work, to ensure both business and job security and to keep money flowing into Ukraine, was impressed upon staff. In this regard HR had a central role.

Other tasks falling to HR at that time included offering accommodation and relocation expenses, as well as logistical support, to staff who needed it and could take it. Later down the line, people-focused tasks would involve ensuring that the two Impressit employees who were conscripted had bulletproof vests, helmets and tactical equipment. Worst-case scenario payouts from the business also had to be sorted out for their families. We can only hope for the best outcomes for Maryana, Roman and the staff.

Meanwhile, in the UK a coalition of 40 large companies formed to help Ukrainian women and children displaced from their home country following the invasion (Nimmo and Chambers, 2022). This consortium was co-ordinated by entrepreneur Emma Sinclair and included retailer Marks & Spencer, recruitment companies Robert Walters and FDM, as well as the talent provider Impellam group. The consortium aimed to help migrants secure visas and also provide accommodation and language training should they enter the UK (Cave, 2022).

The supermarket chain Morrisons contacted the Home Office to offer assistance in providing jobs for refugees, saying that it could provide hundreds of jobs in positions ranging from butchers and fishmongers to shop-floor staff and warehouse operatives. 'Morrisons will welcome refugees with open arms,' a spokesperson said. In March 2022, Tesco made 1,400 roles available for refugees in its central European business arm, establishing a Ukrainian language recruitment helpline plus providing language training for successful applicants. Tesco was exploring a similar scheme for the UK.

Other companies seeking to offer jobs to refugees included Vodafone, the online fashion retailer Asos, Sainsbury's, the pub chain Greene King and cosmetics retailer Lush.

1 What do you think that the immediate response from managers at Impressit in Ukraine tells us about the core role of HR management?
2 If you were an HR manager involved in offering Ukrainian refugees work in the UK, what aspects of people management would you need to consider? You may wish to look ahead at our chapter headings in this book to frame your thoughts.

SOURCES: Nimmo, J and Chambers, S (2022) UK firms open doors to refugees fleeing Ukraine, *Sunday Times*, www.thetimes.co.uk/article/uk-firms-open-doors-to-refugees-fleeing-ukraine-fgjgbk9fb

Cave, D (2022) How Ukrainian HR is working through war, *People Management*, 6 April

1.2 Introduction

This chapter introduces the purpose, content and structure of the book. This sixth edition has been written to meet the requirements of the CIPD People Management and Development Strategies for Performance Unit (7C002). We have updated our book to include new chapters reflecting topical subject areas, recent research and survey report findings, and have also devised relevant and topical reflective activities and case studies.

A consistent rubric has been developed for each chapter, which includes the following key features:

- a set of learning outcomes
- an overview
- an introduction
- short reflective activities
- critical reflection
- a conclusion
- case studies
- key learning points
- review questions
- explore further (suggested further reading and references).

The text introduces a balance of theory and practice, drawing upon major research work, including theoretical and conceptual models through to major survey research findings. A combination of learning activities, including reflective activities, case studies, vignettes and links to relevant articles, is intended to bring the subjects to life and offer you scope for self-reflection. See section 1.3 'The structure of the book' for more details.

Managing and developing people is fundamentally a topical area that can draw debates and actions from every possible aspect of a business environment, from strategic decision-making to the number of car parking spaces that are available to staff and customers. Case study 1.1 addressed an extreme scenario, where unintended consequences of such a singular event could be life-changing. This is, of course, a highly unusual situation; nonetheless, employers do need to consider their duty of care to employees as part of their everyday work.

One important recent development affecting HR professionals is an increasing need to take decisions based on valid evidence which can serve as the basis for accurate predictions. In our book we address the current trend for using HR analytics in a number of chapters. Alongside this trend we find an accelerated usage of artificial intelligence (AI) as part of decision-making in a range of people management scenarios. Case study 1.2 shows how AI may need to be used carefully, with continuing human intervention needed to optimise its value and avoid critical failures.

Case study 1.2

Can you use artificial intelligence to sack workers?

AI is now very much a feature of the workplace but HR specialists need to be alive to the risks it presents. Unintentional consequences of AI decision-making can include bias, discrimination, unfair treatment and an inability for employees to fully understand and accept decisions. Failure to mitigate these risks can lead to employment tribunal cases being brought and associate reputational risk to the employer.

One recent case centred on a subsidiary of a beauty products company in which three make-up artists claimed that they had been unfairly made redundant because of an automated decision generated by AI software. The three employees were informed that they had to reapply for their jobs following video interview. The AI software analysed the content of their answers and facial expressions, together with other metric data on their work performance. They were subsequently informed that they were being made redundant, in part due to algorithmic decision-making (ADM).

The company defended its decision, citing that the algorithm assessment only accounted for a quarter of the marks awarded and that the AI software was used in tandem with human decision-making processes, which, overall, produced a fairer outcome. The result of the tribunal's deliberations was that the three workers received an out-of-court settlement.

While there is some doubt that AI is currently robust or reliable enough to make a case for its use in complex HR work, the promise of time saved and its use for mundane work is accelerating its deployment in the workplace. It is legal for employers to make decisions without human intervention, although these are in limited circumstances and require transparency. In this case the employer was unable to explain the basis for the redundancy situation, while the workers' case was brought partly on the grounds of lack of transparency.

1 In what ways did the use of AI contribute to the events set out in this case study?
2 How could HR professionals ensure that such an outcome is avoided in future?

SOURCE: Gregory, M and Hawkes, C (2022) Can you use artificial intelligence to sack workers? *People Management*, 30 March

While developments in technology are an ongoing and inevitable part of the context of people management, there is also inevitably scope for the role of wholly unanticipated events. The Covid-19 pandemic was one such event. We have chosen not to overplay the pandemic by use of constant examples studded through the book; nonetheless it is, of course, highly significant and we examine some elements of its lasting impact in Reflective activity 1.1.

Reflective activity 1.1

Why the new hybrid working is a win–win

Changes to working practices have brought advantages for both businesses and employees, but we need to continue to adapt, argues Perry Burton, Head of People and Culture at Grant Thornton UK.

For many of us, the pandemic has caused a fundamental shift in how we work, with work no longer a location, but simply what we do. As offices across the UK continue to open, many companies are starting to embed new ways of working with a hybrid working approach – where people split their time between the office and home – seeming very much the norm for those in office-based roles. A Grant Thornton Business Outlook Tracker Report found that 88 per cent of the mid-sized businesses surveyed were adopting a hybrid working approach in December 2021. However, this employer, along with others, was faced with a decision on hybrid working when the UK Government allowed office premises to re-open as part of their plan for post-pandemic economic recovery.

The end of daily commuting after March 2020 and increased flexibility made pandemic working arrangements very appealing to some workers. Effective digital tools for virtual working also enable employers to make the most of the benefits it offers such as reduced spend on office space and a more agile workforce. A UK Government survey showed favourable results in terms of productivity among hybrid workers, with output per hour in the last quarter of 2021 exceeding pre-pandemic levels despite the return of work-from-home guidance during that period.

In Grant Thornton's case, the future of working patterns will involve people deciding for themselves the best approach to take for the type of work they have to do, balancing what works best for the individual worker, their teams and clients. A framework for how we work was intended to support people in making decisions about when and where they work. A variety of working patterns had resulted.

Perry Burton notes that 'there is no one size fits all approach' (this will be a recurrent theme throughout our book). He also cautioned that 'it is too early for approaches to be set in stone'. However, the overall conclusion based on Grant Thornton's approach was that 'moving away from the idea of presenteeism and trusting your people to decide how, where and when they work, enabled by an effective use of digital technology, will enable you to get the best from each other, deliver genuine value to clients and make your business more inclusive'.

1 Identify four jobs where hybrid working would not be appropriate and give reasons for your choices.
2 Before reading subsequent chapters of our book, conduct research on the term 'inclusivity at work' and identify ways in which hybrid working may make an employing organisation more inclusive.

SOURCE: Burton, P (2022) Why the new hybrid working approach is a win–win, *People Management*, 21 March

The issues brought out in the Grant Thornton example above, show again the topical nature of HR work and the need for HR professionals to adapt to sometimes rapidly changing circumstances. In 2022, with the early phases of the pandemic receding, there is a need to re-evaluate effective working practices in a fundamental way. The topic of hybrid working requires understanding across several areas of our book, including the notion of flexibility and the management of change, which we will examine in depth in Chapter 12.

HR professionals are required to seek out ways of improving performance, even in hitherto successful organisations. There is also, inevitably, a maintenance element to HR work in which procedures and records are updated and kept fit for purpose. At other times though, HR will be required to trouble-shoot and deal with major problems. Work organisations can exhibit pathological or dysfunctional behaviours which need diagnosis and resolution. This quasi-medical role for HR can be seen in Case study 1.3. In this case the negative symptoms exhibited are rooted deep within the organisation's culture. Changing such a culture is challenging and may involve tough decisions, although there is a sense in which culture change should ideally be a positive process with 'buy-in' from all parties. Here there is no choice but to address the situation with urgency, given both the reputational damage accruing to the organisation and, most importantly, the need to ensure that all employees are treated in a decent fashion with dignity and respect.

 Case study 1.3

Spiteful and vindictive – and a failure to apologise

In 2022, Natalie Tawse won over £2 million in compensation from her previous employer ZNF Bank. The payment was awarded following a successful claim in 2020 under the categories of direct sex discrimination, victimisation and equal pay. This award, which attracted much media coverage, was made up of retrospective equal pay, personal injury, loss of future earnings, plus additional payment for aggravated damages. The employment tribunal when making their decision noted that the bank was guilty of an unreasonable failure to follow the ACAS code on disciplinary and grievance procedures. This failure resulted in a further £317,000 being added to the compensation.

Ms Tawse was employed by ZNF Bank from 2012 to 2016. She became aware that a male colleague who had been appointed within a few months of her on the same job was paid 25 per cent higher. The bank's position was that despite the same job titles and job description, one worker was 'senior' while the other was 'junior'. Interestingly, the tribunal found no notes of interviews, 'very limited' records of recruitment processes more generally and no assessment of candidates against job or person specifications. This once again points to the links between different parts of the HR role – in this case recruitment and selection and remuneration. The bank also claimed that the male employee who Natalie Tawse used as her comparator had earned more in a previous job, hence needed to be enticed away. The tribunal rejected this argument.

A note written by a manager involved in selecting the two workers referred to Ms Tawse as 'too light', however there was deemed to be no objective basis for the comment. The tribunal recommended that the manager in question would benefit from unconscious bias training or more HR input on selection and pay decisions – Ms Tawse was also found to have experienced sex discrimination in the award of bonuses.

Natalie Tawse was also found to have been victimised by her employer. When approaching her manager, he repeatedly used the phrase 'not now, Natalie,' which then became a 'catchphrase' in the office. The tribunal's finding here was that her treatment was very negative and belittling, and therefore an act of victimisation. The tribunal found that managers at the bank had behaved 'spitefully and vindictively'. The judge noted that the employer should issue an apology, however Natalie Tawse did not request an apology as she doubted whether it would be 'genuine and heartfelt'. A perception of an unapologetic attitude was cited as reason for compensation in respect of injury to feelings. There had been a total breakdown in relations during her term of employment which was reflected in the tribunal proceedings.

Several alleged incidents of harassment were deemed 'out of time' by the tribunal, so no formal findings were made. However, they were made public during procedures, attracting significant media coverage and consequent negative publicity for the company. These included male colleagues' discussion of sexual activity in Ms Tawse's presence. On one occasion a black Halloween-style witch's hat was placed on her desk. It was alleged that this had been carried out by drunken male employees. The striking image of a witch's hat featured prominently in media reporting of Natalie Tawse's case and make it easy to locate the story several years later via internet search.

The witch's hat incident is emblematic of the culture present in the bank at that time. An organisation's culture, including taken for granted assumptions and routinely used language can be a powerful driver of performance. However, it can equally turn toxic. In later chapters we will examine the potentially important role of HR in fostering culture, which includes monitoring and design of recruitment and remuneration policies.

It might, finally, be noted that the widespread publicity given to this case was sparked by the very high pay-out awarded to Natalie Tawse – itself a reflection of her earnings in a highly paid sector. A failure to provide a respectful work environment and to treat workers in a fair and dignified way is a failure in all workplaces, including less high-profile settings that may not attract this level of publicity.

SOURCE: This is a real-life case study. Names of the participants have been changed. Jonathan Ames' article 'Banker who had witch's hat left on her desk awarded £2m,' in *The Times*, 31 January 2022, provides an overview of the events depicted here. A number of law firms have also commented on the case which can be found online.

Questions

1 Summarise the HR issues set out in this case study. What could an HR professional do to minimise the chances of a similar situation occurring?

2 Before reading subsequent chapters of our book, outline the potential difficulties an HR professional may encounter in attempting to change an organisation's culture.

1.3 The structure of the book

The learning outcomes and content for the People Management and Development Strategies for Performance unit are subdivided into four areas: aligning people practices within organisational strategy and culture; people practices linked to organisational performance and employee experience; understanding current practice in major areas of people management and development; and understanding the role and influence of people professionals in different organisational settings.

Our book reflects these learning outcomes presented in four parts; although unit learning outcomes are embedded within individual chapters' content.

- **Part One** introduces the book and the scope and nature of strategic people management and development.
- **Part Two** examines the strategic context and addresses HR's link with strategy, culture and values and also considers the aims, objectives and contribution of HRM across different types of organisations. We conclude with a reflection on professional and ethical practice.
- **Part Three** addresses the core areas within managing and developing people and how they can aid strategic effectiveness. In each chapter we show how relevant and valid theory can be put into practice to add value in terms of worker and organisational performance.
- **Part Four** comprises a summary of themes contained within the book and identifies future trends based on various research findings and reports.

Chapters 1 and 13 introduce and conclude the book through the use of integrated arguments, case study illustrations, and contemporary thinking and research.

1.4 Conclusion

The nature of strategic people management and development make this is a highly challenging and integrative area, but also a very rewarding one. Having a good grounding in managing and developing people is core knowledge for those working in HR. We trust that you find the following chapters informative, thought-provoking and a useful framework for understanding the management and development of people and the contribution that HR professionals can make at a strategic level.

At this point it is appropriate to introduce brief clarification on terminology. As we will see in Chapter 2, tasks involving managing and developing people often fall to specialist HR managers within work organisations. In an important sense, however, general or line managers need to be involved in managing people too in their day-to-day work. The term 'HR manager' therefore denotes anyone who takes a role in managing and developing people. In some cases, HR work is outsourced to specialist providers beyond the actual organisation. In view of this complex picture some writers use the term 'human resource practitioner' to encompass anyone whose work touches our subject area. For our purposes, though, the terms 'human resource manager', 'human resource practitioner' and 'HR or people professional' are sufficiently close for all three to be used interchangeably and you will find examples of each term throughout the book.

Although we hope our book will prove useful for a wide readership, there is a particular link to CIPD unit 7C002 People Management and Development Strategies for Performance. The following table shows how the learning outcomes of that unit are covered within specific chapters of this book.

Table 1.1 CIPD qualifications map

Learning content		Chapters												
		1	2	3	4	5	6	7	8	9	10	11	12	13
1 – Understand the benefits of aligning people practices with organisational strategy and culture														
1.1	Explain the major objectives of people practice and the ways achieving these may benefit employers and employees		Y	Y	Y	Y	Y	Y	Y	Y	Y	Y	Y	
1.2	Explain the advantages associated with aligning people management policies with organisational strategy and risk		Y	Y	Y	Y	Y					Y	Y	
1.3	Evaluate ways in which organisations integrate people management practice within their culture, brand and values			Y									Y	Y
1.4	Critically evaluate models of systemic thinking and how they underpin the interconnective nature of people practice work		Y	Y								Y	Y	
2 – Understand how the development of people practices improves organisational performance and employee experience														
2.1	Examine the merits of different models of people practice management, linking them with effective business performance		Y	Y			Y	Y			Y	Y	Y	

(continued)

Table 1.1 (Continued)

2.2	Critically evaluate research that links people management practice in organisations with improved employer outcomes	Y	Y	Y			Y	Y		Y	Y	Y	
2.3	Critically evaluate best practice, contingency and resource-based approaches to the development of people practices	Y				Y				Y	Y		
2.4	Explain how high-performance work practices are associate with positive organisational and employee outcomes	Y	Y			Y		Y		Y	Y	Y	Y
3 – Understand current practice in major areas of people management and development work													
3.1	Discuss major areas of responsibility in people management work in organisations	Y	Y	Y	Y	Y	Y	Y	Y	Y	Y	Y	
3.2	Evaluate current developments in the fields of resourcing and performance management					Y				Y		Y	
3.3	Evaluate current developments in the fields of learning and development and organisational design and development		Y				Y				Y	Y	
3.4	Evaluate current developments in the fields of employment relations employee engagement and diversity and inclusion							Y	Y				
4 – Understand the role and influence of people professionals in different organisational settings													
4.1	Examine the merits of the various ways in which people practice activities are organised, structured and evaluated in different organisational settings	Y	Y	Y						Y	Y	Y	

(continued)

Table 1.1 (Continued)

4.2	Critically assess the nature of professionalism in people practices and the role of the CIPD	Y	Y		Y	Y			Y	Y		Y	
4.3	Analyse the advantages of partnering with customers to understand their current and future needs from a people perspective		Y							Y			
4.4	Assess the value of facilitation, coaching and mentoring, and consulting in different people practice contexts						Y					Y	
4.5	Critically evaluate how data analytics and technological developments present practical and ethical challenges for people professionals				Y					Y		Y	Y

PART TWO
People management and the strategic context

02
The scope and nature of people management

GARY REES

LEARNING OUTCOMES

After reading this chapter, you should be able to:

- have an appreciation of the role and function of HRM and HRD

- explore approaches to, and models of, HRM and HRD

- be aware of and evaluate models of strategic HRM and HRD

- consider the links between organisational strategy and HR strategy

- understand the interrelationship between line management and HRM/HRD

- identify recent research findings about how HR equates into practice

- assess the value and contribution of HRM and HRD

- highlight probable future trends which would shape HR.

2.1 Overview

In Part 2 of this book, we examine some of the factors influencing the nature of human resource management (HRM) and human resource development (HRD). The aim is to lay the groundwork for subsequent sections in which we first identify core themes in strategic people management and development (Chapters 3 and 5), and then go on to examine effective practice in selected areas (Chapters 6–12). In Chapter 4, we will highlight the ways in which managing and developing people may vary across different types of organisational settings. In this chapter we will discuss some even more fundamental questions, including how HRM and HRD are defined, who does – and who should – take responsibility for managing and developing people, and whether HRM and HRD can be regarded as strategic activities. Underlying these questions is the concept of HR practitioners adding value, possibly by taking on the role of business partner.

It is useful at this stage to clarify the relationship between the two terms HRM and HRD. They could be considered separate aspects of an overall HR function, while one of these sub-functions may take precedence over the other at any one point. Within academic models, HRD is typically subsumed within HRM when functional aspects are taken into consideration. In this chapter we will explore the HR function in terms of HRM and HRD, without making judgements as to how these two areas converge or separate themselves. Dependent upon the context, some organisations may combine the HRM and HRD functions into an HR function, while other organisations may have a predominance of HRM within the HR function.

HR requires the collaboration of line and senior management. We attempt to pinpoint the value of HR and, within the overall aims of our book, look at key research findings from recent research, which inform current debates.

2.2 Introduction

HR has gone through a plotted journey with its nomenclature, from Industrial Relations to Personnel, to Personnel Management, to HR to HRM and to People Management. Each of these terminologies attracts a potentially different perspective, approach and interpretation.

This chapter will explore aspects of HR and HRD, including the definitions, role, various HR models, the shape of HR, and how we measure and value HR.

 Reflective activity 2.1

Despite the change of name from 'Personnel' to 'HR', it could be argued that the HR function is still suffering from a lack of status and, like Cinderella, does not get invited to the ball (or top table).

Why could it be that HR, on the whole, lacks the reputation to make strategic contributions to organisations and establish a strong reputation for itself?

We will argue that the role and function of HR has transformed itself over the last 50 years or so. However, there will no doubt be examples of the full span of traditional personnel and modern HR in contemporary UK organisations. To what extent can HR be pigeonholed into structural or functional compartments, thereby limiting its scope and impact?

Ulrich, quoted by Brockett (2010, p 11), stated that, 'I think that HR people should see themselves as a professional services group within their own organisation, being a key account manager for the most important clients. Their job is to assess the resources available and use their knowledge to determine how best to transfer those resources to client productivity.'

However, before we look at contemporary HR roles, some historical perspective is useful, and it is important to consider the transition from personnel management to HR, and to address definitions in order to make appropriate contrasts.

2.3 Definitions of personnel management, human resource management and human resource development

2.3.1 Personnel management

We begin by considering a widely used definition of 'personnel management' from several decades ago: 'Personnel management aims to achieve both efficiency and justice, neither of which can be pursued successfully without the other. It seeks to bring together and develop into an effective organisation the men and women who make up an enterprise, enabling each to make his/her own best contribution to its success both as an individual and as a member of a working group. It seeks to provide fair terms and conditions of employment, and satisfying work for those employed' (IPM, quoted in Hendry, 1995, p 10).

As we can see here, personnel management was perceived as occupying a neutral position, placed between employers (in the form of management), and other rank and file employees. Its role was reinforced by the development of policies and procedures indicating professional independence and objectivity. An emphasis upon standardisation and equal treatment would often underlie such policies.

2.3.2 Human resource management and human resource development

Any brief consideration of definitions of HRM elicits a set of definitions which differentiate HR from personnel, in academic terms at least. Storey (1995, p 5) defines HRM as: 'a distinctive approach to employment management which seeks to achieve competitive advantage through the strategic development of a highly committed and capable workforce, using an integrated array of cultural, structural and personnel techniques'.

However, definitions of HRM are by no means identical, or even especially similar. Boxall and Purcell (2000, p 184) argue that 'HRM includes anything and everything associated with the management of the employment relationship in the firm. We do not associate HRM solely with a high commitment model of labour management or with any particular ideology or style of management.'

While a universal and generally accepted definition of HRM is lacking, the same could be said for defining HRD. HRD has been defined by Stewart and McGoldrick (1996, p 1) as follows: 'Human resource development encompasses activities and processes which are intended to have impact on organisational and individual learning. The term assumes that organisations can be constructively conceived of as learning entities, and that the learning processes of both organisations and individuals are capable of influence and direction through deliberate and planned interventions. Thus, HRD is constituted by planned interventions in organisational and individual processes.'

While defining HRM and HRD may prove to be a tricky task, the nature, scope and objectives of HRM and HRD may change considerably in differing contexts. The historical background, senior management philosophy and practice, external forces and internal forces may shape different outcomes as far as what HRM/HRD actually does within the organisation.

In terms of what HR typically 'does', we could include the following as typical: HR planning, job and organisational design (see Chapter 11); recruitment, selection and induction (see Chapter 6); developing employees and talent management (see Chapter 7); managing the employment relationship (see Chapter 9); pay, reward and performance management (see Chapter 10); ethical treatment of people including equal opportunities and diversity management (see Chapters 4, 8 and 9); health and safety; knowledge management; mentoring; and disciplinary and grievance-handling, to name some.

2.3.3 *The move to people management*

It could be argued that the CIPD Profession Map launched in 2020/2021 expanded the scope and nature of HR Professionals' knowledge, skills and abilities. In contrast, 'People Management' has been considered to focus on recruiting, training, engaging and retaining employees to optimise their talent and maximise their productivity, and is a subcategory of Human Resource Management (Hi Bob, 2022). Some people might argue that little has changed except the title (the old wine in new bottles analogy).

While many senior HR leaders have had their job titles change from HR Director to Chief People Officer (CPO), does this mean that the previous HR Director is more strategic in their role, actions and outcomes? Similarly, does the CPO now concentrate more heavily on human capital management to enable the organisations' strategy to be enacted? This chapter will unpick many of the key debates and issues around the role and the evolving role of HR/People Management.

2.4 The scope and nature of HRM and HRD

In understanding what HR does in an organisation it can be useful to take a historical perspective. Who actually started the HRM process in an organisation (eg a CEO deciding that, due to growth of the organisation, an HR function and HR manager needed to be brought in) can provide a starting point from which to trace its subsequent development. The question of why the HR function was started (perhaps with specific goals in mind, such as identifying training gaps, dealing with increased specialist recruitment, etc) is also highly relevant. Following this, identifying key milestones in the history of the HR function may provide further understanding of how HR has evolved (eg the introduction of a performance management system). While each organisation evolves in its own inimitable fashion, generic models of the goals of HRM can, nonetheless, be considered.

2.4.1 HRM goals

While the academic debate surrounding the defining of HRM goals continues, Boxall and Purcell (2008, p 20) suggest that there are four underpinning motives in HRM:

- *Cost-effectiveness* – maintaining stakeholder loyalty and trust is essential here, and this may mean running the business within budgetary constraints or maximising profits.

- *Legitimacy* – in essence, the allocation of moral legitimacy and ethical standing in society (see Chapter 4).

- *Flexibility* – in order to cope with change, organisational flexibility is vital for survival. It incorporates both short-term responsiveness and long-term agility (see Chapters 9 and 11).

- *Autonomy* – particularly managerial autonomy and the power to act. The political context may bring about change in managerial behaviour, which may need some regulation in terms of corporate social responsibility.

The goals of HRD could be defined simply as developing and improving the performance of individuals and organisations, and we might also include team performance at this point.

In addition to this, 'the most obvious role HR has to play is as the expert on ethical employment practices (which is a core strand of corporate responsibility)' (CIPD, 2013a, p 5).

While the various goals of HR may differ across private, public and not-for-profit sectors (see Chapter 4), there will also be some similarities. Current UK public sector HR goals may tie in with strategic initiatives linked to the Gershon Efficiency Review (HM Treasury, 2004), the post-pandemic efficiency in government report (2021) and any other key governmental initiatives; for example, Agenda for Change, commissioning, private finance initiatives and best-value-type initiatives. Ultimately, efficiencies (savings) are sought, with the stated goal of maintaining, or even increasing, service-level quality, which means that employees will ultimately have to work harder or, more euphemistically, to work 'smarter'.

Managers in the private sector will already be familiar with the imperative for efficiency gains and, as we will note in the next chapter, the third (or not-for-profit) sector is also facing pressures in this regard.

↪ Reflective activity 2.2

To what extent can an organisation exercise duty of care to all its employees and at the same time drive towards the highest level of cost-efficiency? How can HR balance these potentially conflicting goals?

In order to move HR from a mere internal function, we need to analyse the broader strategic context within which it operates to consider whether HR can be strategic in its intent, actions and contribution.

2.4.2 *Strategy and HR*

Strategy in its most basic sense is a plan of where the organisation would like to go. Although a strategy may take the form of a statement, it is also likely to be supported by strategic plans and imperatives that make up the building blocks required to meet its planned destination. A strategy should not be envisaged as an end in itself, as there may be a requirement to change course, or to embark on several journeys. One metaphor for business strategy is that of travel. For example, your strategy might be to travel in a northerly direction. At some points in time people might observe you travelling toward the south. However, your long-term strategic intent is still to move northwards and your apparent change of direction might be a short-term retreat or tactical manoeuvre.

De Wit and Meyer (2004, p 50) define strategy as 'a course of action for achieving an organisation's purpose'. Taken in its broadest sense, this may not automatically mean profit generation and maximisation, or market domination. Strategy could be determined from more of a bottom-up approach, for example in a workers' collective, than a purely top-down approach; or alternatively a range of key stakeholders/shareholders can be involved in making strategic decisions.

There may also be a vision or mission statement to accompany a strategy. The vision is sometimes a means of providing employees with a notion of where the organisation is heading and the values associated with it. The mission statement should reinforce to employees where the company is intending to go but is often directed at shareholders or customers.

Possessing an organisational strategy and HR strategy is not enough. Strategic fit between HR strategy, HR practices and organisational strategy is paramount (Wang and Shyu, 2008). So, how is such strategic fit accomplished? One method is to consider the vertical and horizontal integration of HR policies and procedures. The vertical fit is important in terms of achieving organisational goals through ensuring the alignment of HR activities to strategy. Horizontal fit plays an essential role in making use of these resources. Horizontal integration of HR activities includes aligning different HR activities such as recruitment and selection, performance management and reward so that each activity supports (rather than contradicts/ interferes with) other HR activities. Vertical integration includes the way in which these activities fit into and support overall organisational activities, including the organisational vision, mission, etc.

The CIPD (2021a) define strategic HRM as 'the overall framework that determines the shape and delivery of the individual strategies, systematically linking people with organisations by integrating HRM strategies into organisational strategies to deliver organisational success'. In order to assess the extent to which HR as a function can be strategic in its thinking and actions, we need to consider the various approaches/models of HR and the extent to which these align with strategic intent.

2.5 Models of HRM and strategic HRM

Hall (cited in Gilmore and Williams, 2009, p 144) defines strategic HRM as 'not any one particular HR strategy, but is a framework for shaping a number of people management strategies'.

While the analysis of the employment relationship and context is important, Beardwell and Claydon (2017) argue that two other issues affect the definition of HRM. First, the significance of HRM is variable, sometimes with emphasis upon people, strategy, employment relationships, etc. Second, HRM is derived from a range of antecedents, and depends on the stance and philosophy of the analyst (see Figure 2.1).

Figure 2.1 The hard model of HRM

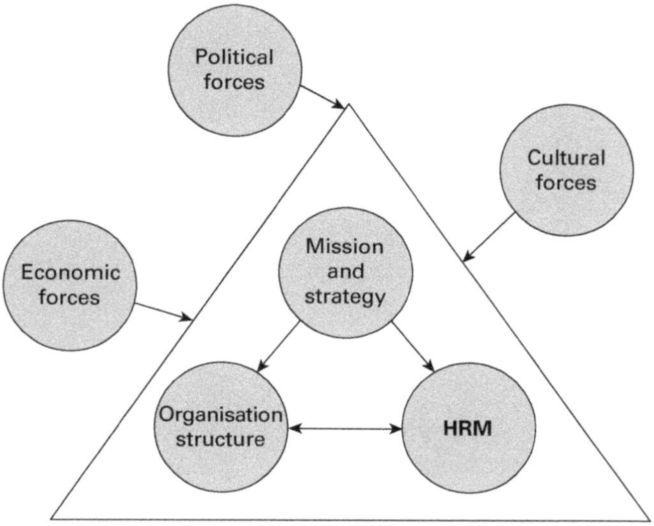

SOURCE: Fombrun, Tichy and Devanna (1984, p 35)

These definitions also ally themselves to the hard and soft models of HRM (Fombrun, Tichy and Devanna, 1984; Beer et al, 1984). Hard models emphasise using employees to gain competitive advantage and focus on business and employment strategies by linking HR to business systems. Soft models, contrastingly, emphasise employee commitment and engagement, and attempt to align the interests of employees and management (see also Chapter 11). Devanna et al (1984) suggest that within the organisation there needs to be an alignment of mission/strategy, the organisational structure and HRM. External to the organisation are forces (eg political, cultural and economic) impacting upon the organisation. This approach assumes that HR emerges from the other factors, with strategy as the primary driver, and that HR needs to seek a 'best fit' within this context.

Another approach found within the field of HRM is the resource-based view of the firm; namely one 'that focuses on the resources and capabilities controlled by a firm as sources of competitive advantage' (Barney and Hesterly, 2008, p 74).

Another approach used in HR is that of the 'best practice' model, often referred to as 'high commitment' or 'high involvement' HRM, in which managers consider how bundles of effective HR practice merge together.

Beer et al (1984) incorporates human resource flow, rewards and the work system within a soft model of HRM. Pivotal to these three concepts is employee influence. The interchange of these four concepts helps us understand the role and function of HR within organisations.

2.5.1 Critique of best fit and best practice models

A major criticism of the best fit model is that it may ignore employee interests and be ignorant of some of the important aspects of the psychological contract (see Chapter 8). The focus of the best fit model may be the pursuit of economic performance to the detriment of everything else. There may also be academic criticisms when addressing the measurement of various HR practices. How do we assess the validity of best fit practices?

The transient nature of strategy and the need for constant change also makes alignment of current and future needs difficult. When considering the best practice model, it is difficult to argue that HRM can apply across all organisational settings at all times. To what extent do HR practices transfer from the United States to Eastern Europe or the Indian sub-continent, for example? Another central concern is the extent to which organisations can adopt a long-term approach in reality.

In order to assess whether the 'fit' has been appropriate, it may be necessary to gauge this against some sort of measure. One possible approach may be to consider the balanced scorecard.

2.5.2 Balanced scorecard

Another model that helps to assess the contribution that HR makes to a business is that of the balanced scorecard. The CIPD *Human Capital Reporting* survey (2004a) argues that the central focus in this model is upon vision and strategy, with four key supporting elements that require targets and measure taken, namely:

- *Learning and growth* – relating to how we sustain our ability to change and improve (see also Chapter 12).

- *Customer* – how we should appear to our customer (see also Chapter 4).
- *Financial* – how we should appear to our shareholders.
- *Internal business processes* – to satisfy shareholders and customers, what business processes must we excel at?

This model assumes planned and effective communication (internally and externally) to be a key imperative. The question arises as to what level HR can become involved in developing and measuring the balanced scorecard.

While the scorecard takes into account important aspects such as customers, contextual factors may be omitted. The Bath model, which we now go on to analyse, may be useful in providing an understanding of such factors.

2.5.3 The Bath model of HRM and innovation

The concepts of human, social and organisational capital are not new. The Bath model adds extra understanding by providing contextual issues such as climate, trust and culture as the platform from which innovative outputs can then emerge. Where traditional human capital approaches have addressed inputs and outputs, the context is often overlooked. There is now an appreciation that employees work within teams and contexts, relying upon successful working relationships in order to add value to the organisation, with less emphasis upon the measurement of an individual's performance (CIPD, 2012a).

2.6 HRD and strategic HRD

However, as we noted at the start of this chapter, 'mainline' HR may not necessarily include HRD and strategic HRD. HRD may be considered to be a sub-set of HR, and strategic HRD a sub-set of strategic HR. But the field of HRD has grown rapidly in the last 30 years and 'development' as a theme cuts through many traditional HR areas. The current heightened interest in talent management (see Pilbeam and Corbridge, 2010) includes a great deal of debate and research around talent development; see also Martin (2012).

The definition of development carries with it a series of different connotations and meanings. Thomas (2001, p 184) defines it as 'a process of competency attainment and of self-differentiation in the sense of progressively distinguishing oneself from the environment and from other people in order to create a unique self-identity'.

Gubbins and Garavan (2009) argue that the primary responsibility of HRD professionals traditionally focused on identifying, selecting and evaluating training programmes. In effect this equates to transactional HR. However, Gubbins and Garavan contend that the role of HRD includes the consideration of environmental forces, and how the development of employees can add to competitive advantage.

Beer and Spector (1989, p 25) define strategic HRD as 'a proactive, system-wide intervention, linked to strategic planning and cultural change. This contrasts with the traditional view of training and development as consisting of reactive, piecemeal interventions in response to specific problems.'

Perhaps the question of where HRD sits as a discipline is a moot point. On a micro level, can HRD be aligned to adult learning and associated psychological theories? On the other hand, at a macro level, where national policy and HRD will be linked, the influence of educational policy and societal impact should be investigated. Wang and Sun (2009) argue that economics, psychology and system theory constitute foundations of HRD.

McCracken and Wallace (2000) devised a model depicting nine key characteristics of strategic HRD. Underpinning these characteristics are a strong learning culture, strategic change focus and a highly mature organisation in HRD terms. These nine characteristics bear similarity with the strategic HR theory outlined above. The first characteristic that McCracken and Wallace identify is that of shaping organisational missions and goals.

Second, there is top management leadership (including support). Third, the environmental scanning by senior management is in HRD terms. Fourth, there are HRD strategies, plans and policies in place. Fifth, strategic partnerships exist with line management. Following that, sixth, there are strategic partnerships with HRM. The seventh key characteristic is that trainers act as organisational change consultants. The penultimate characteristic is the ability to influence corporate culture. Last, there is emphasis upon cost-effectiveness evaluation.

To what extent are skills, knowledge and core competencies the drivers of innovation and the key sources of competitive advantage (Gratton, 2000)? If core competence leads to organisational capability and competitiveness, then developing employee competence will be a strategic priority.

With regard to considering a HRD strategy, post Covid-19, the CIPD Learning and Skills at Work Survey by Crowley and Overton (2021) highlights some key issues for people/learning and development professionals to consider:

1 Pressure on organisational resources for learning and development (L&D). There is little question around the impact of the pandemic in less use of L&D metrics, plus reported reductions in budgets, L&D headcount, the use of external consultants and learning budgets.

2 Sudden changes and no going back, where three quarters of organisations changed their L&D strategy in response to the pandemic. There are obvious concerns as to whether the previous investment in L&D will return.

3 Rush towards digital delivery but use of experience-rich tech still low, with a seismic shift to digital learning, with in-person L&D scaled back or halted. Surprisingly, the take up of emergency technologies remains low, perhaps because organisations have not thought through or had a chance to think through the best form of digitalised/blended learning and choice of best learning delivery methods.

4 Greater sophistication yielding greater engagement and demand, where organisations that adopt a more sophisticated approach to technology create a virtuous circle and an increased appetite for learning and perhaps a more supportive learning environment, but at the same time are more likely to report barriers to delivery.

5   Increased opportunities to better align with organisational need, where the pandemic has created increased opportunities to align better with business need. So senior leaders value learning more and also having a clearer understanding of how learning adds value to the organisation.

6   Relationships and human connectivity are crucial. The report highlights that there are large falls in the majority of formal and traditional forms of learning, but also that with the switch to digital, the ways in which individuals support and trust each other has increased.

7   Visibility of skills gaps and how we tackle them are key to success. Workforce agility has been driven up by demand as is the need for reskilling and redeployment. Changes in the impact of automation and redeployment and how roles changed, plus reskilling were found in the majority of organisations surveyed.

8   Are learning professionals equipped to meet the skills agenda? The report suggests greater agility is needed to meet future needs. The existence of a suitable mixture of specialist roles, like online facilitator, learning technologist, etc was varied and sometimes absent.

9   Desire to demonstrate impact hampered by barriers to evaluation. Despite a slight increase in evaluation methods being used, only a small minority of organisations are considering the wider impact on the business or society, or assessing behaviour change and transfer of learning into the workplace. Hence barriers to evaluation have intensified mainly due to other business priorities.

10 The majority of organisations surveyed do not use evidence to inform programme design. Continuous feedback is the most common method of adding value, but only a third of organisations report that they are productive in identifying the performance issue before recommending a solution.

⤴ Reflective activity 2.3

The recommendations from Crowley and Overton's 2021 survey are, first, for organisations to Build Back Better – considering what has worked well and then what can be adapted to ensure success going forward. Second, embrace digital innovation, by targeted investment on a clearly defined business case. Third, co-create organisational value by considering how business functions (often siloed) can work better going forward. Fourth, harness the wider learning environment by purposeful building of relationships and connections across the whole organisation, with a clear understanding of the role of the line manager in L&D provision. Fifth, be future-focused by considering the skills and capabilities required in the future, and make a plan to build for future skills, while creating learning pathways and career choices for employees. Last, make evidence-based decisions by using evidence gathering to underpin decisions in design and delivery and thereby define the desired performance outcome and engage key stakeholders through both quantitative and qualitative evidence.

1 The recommendations posed seem highly plausible. Why would organisations

not be able to implement these recommendations?

2 What advice would you provide to an L&D/people professional in dealing with resistance to change encountered when incorporating these recommendations?

The HRD function can play an important part in developing an organisation's culture to learn and its aspiration to be a 'learning organisation'. However, caution needs to be adopted here, in that we need to continually strive to link learning with performance (Henderson, 1997).

The interplay of HRD and HRM will continue to prove challenging to organisations. In some cases there are obvious structural divides in organisations; for example, HRM and HRD departments that don't particularly work well together and deliberately separate out the functional aspects. In other cases, there is a strong synergy of activities that seamlessly integrate with organisational practices, and add value, and are seen to be adding value.

2.7 The shape of HR

Harrison (2009) provides a useful framework when deciding the shape of the L&D function, which can then be extended to HR more generally. First, there is the line-managed function, where line managers are handed the main responsibility for HRD/HRM. Second, the HR and HRD function could be outsourced.

Third, there is the three-legged stool model proposed by Ulrich (1997). Within the line-managed function, there is very much a devolved approach, handing over the majority of responsibility to line managers. The outsourced model may work well for specific aspects of HR and HRD, for example, assessment centres and competence development. Some of the key determinants in deciding whether to outsource include cost-efficiency, added value, control and partnership.

Previous work by Harrison (2005) cited three other shapes that HRM/HRD could adopt: as a cost or profit centre; as a consultancy; or the traditional centralised function. Operating as a profit centre may prove more attractive to an organisation than viewing HR as a cost centre, which does not necessarily generate its own revenue and therefore is a drain on corporate budgets. The argument of accountability may be less profound if a profit centre is generating sufficient funds. It could be argued that an HR function that can 'sell' its services successfully exhibits a level of professionalism within the market. However, the converse argument could also be true. HR operating as a consultancy service may bring into question the internal/external fit, and to what extent the 'consultancy' aligns with corporate culture and values.

In a CIPD survey (2013b), just over half of HR professionals reported that their departments outsource some activities. This recent trend offers another perspective on the shape of HR and shows again the importance of contextual factors, for example developments in technology which enable activities to be outsourced, possibly to another country.

2.7.1 HR business partner model

Perhaps one of the more talked-about current models is that of the HR business partner.

Ulrich's original work in 1997 emphasised four key roles that HR need to adopt:

- strategic partners
- administrative experts (shared services)
- employee champions
- change agents.

If HR adopts a more business-focused approach, as advocated by Ulrich, Younger and Brockbank (2008), then the emphasis upon customer focus, cost efficiencies, innovation and the ability to respond quickly to changes is highly important. Business partnership describes the relationship between HR managers (partner) and line/functional managers within an organisation, with an emphasis upon outputs and performance measures, and a view to increasing effectiveness and efficiency of the organisation as a whole.

A research report produced by the CIPD (2007a) found that less than 30 per cent of respondents had introduced the model in full, with another 30 per cent having partially introduced the Ulrich model.

Perhaps larger organisations are more likely to adopt the Ulrich model, commonly known as the 'three-legged stool', whereby three functional areas of HR include (CIPD, 2010a):

- Shared services handling transactional services, such as absence monitoring, payroll, etc. The emphasis here is upon low-cost and effective HR administration.

- Centres of excellence, consisting of small teams of HR experts with specialised knowledge of leading-edge HR solutions. Competitive advantage is sought through HR innovations, such as reward, learning, engagement and talent management.

- Strategic business partners working with business leaders to influence strategy formulation and strategy implementation. Some activities include organisational and people capability building, resource and talent planning, intelligence gathering, etc.

A report from Henley Business School looked at the factors behind successful HR departments and asked how others could do better. The Henley report found that the majority of non-HR professionals believed that getting the operational side of HR right was more important than the function understanding business strategy; and while chief executives and board-level colleagues valued strategic skills more than operational, this was never as much as HR did. It also suggested that: 'Some functions operate in victim mode, which isn't conducive to securing investment or confidence in the function' (*Personnel Today*, 2012).

2.7.2 business partnering: the counter arguments

Pitcher (2008) argues that the business partner model had not resulted in strategic thinking and was primarily only a change in title. He cites the example of Elizabeth Arden, where the HR director, Gabriele Arend, disagreed with any model that split HR professionals into recruiting, training and employee relations experts. Her company is moving towards a traditional structure, where HR employees are trained to develop generalist knowledge.

A CIPD Factsheet (2015a) recommends exercising caution when adopting the business partner model, suggesting that there is a danger of creating silos when the HR function is segmented because one size does not fit all.

Perhaps the key question comes down to credibility and contribution, summed up succinctly in a Deloitte report (2009, p 8): 'The business partners' greatest failing has been their inability to convince senior managers that they have the necessary business acumen to contribute to the strategic debate.' The CIPD Factsheet (2015a) supports this argument by stating that the HR function needs to focus on both short-term financial goals and maintaining longer-term objectives, such as organisational health and long-term people performance issues. In addition to this, the HR function must support the organisational strategy and maintain credibility, particularly from board level members.

Ways of strengthening partnering

The CIPD (2015a) argues that the HR business partnering relationship should be regularly reviewed and strengthened by:

- adopting an analytical approach to business performance measures through people metrics
- ensuring that business partners are involved from the outset in the planning process, are prepared, and also spend time exploring the broader aspects of the business context
- being able to communicate through business language, particularly through HR metrics and their links to business performance
- setting personal objectives for strategic HR partners aligned to those of managers who share their business area
- using tools to obtain a broad-ranging view of the HR function, including business partners, to see the extent to which they are fulfilling their role.

 Case study 2.1

Severn Trent to supercharge its strategy

Although it might be more synonymous with Ross Geller's futile attempts to get a sofa up a flight of stairs in that episode of *Friends*, the word 'pivot' also unexpectedly became a buzzword for Severn Trent in 2020, after it was forced to rethink on its plans to improve employee experience when the pandemic hit.

The water company's work had been in the offing since 2018, yet just a month before it was due to start delivering, Covid-19 reached UK shores. Rather than waver or deviate from its plan, the firm instead worked to 'supercharge' it and bolster support for its 7,000 employees.

'It really helped people during that time to know that, while everything outside was uncertain, when they came into work, we knew what we were doing,' explains group HR director Neil Morrison, who said the company's approach remained steadfast: 'This is the plan, no excuses. We're going to deliver this.'

As a regulated company, Severn Trent presents a business plan every five years explaining how it will deliver for its customers and employees. For its HR department, the 2020–25 submission was focused on engaging colleagues and allowing them to feel like they own the company's targets.

Part of this planning process was its 'Bike on the Boat Tour', the concept of which was inspired by a New Zealand team that competed in the America's Cup race with bikes on their boat: lateral thinking which revolutionised its performance. 'The whole point was to look at a problem in a different way, with creativity and innovation,' Morrison says. 'We wanted to ask all our colleagues how we should approach the way they think about the service we provide differently.'

The firm's CEO hosted nearly 80 hour-and-a-half-long events over eight weeks, under the 'Bike on the Boat' project, speaking to employees about the innovation they wanted. Having set its KPIs and presented them to 1,000 senior management team members at an event held in an airport hangar, the company hosted another event to kick off the plan in 2020, only – mere weeks later – to be forced to 'pivot' as lockdown measures were introduced.

With 40 per cent of staff unable to go into the workplace and the other 60 per cent deemed 'essential' workers, Morrison describes how this split the organisation into distinct groups – but that the company managed to make it work. 'Very early on, we decided not to furlough anyone and not make any redundancies,' he says. 'We would still pay bonuses if we hit our targets, and that was also really important because people's partners were being furloughed or losing their jobs.'

As the pandemic developed, Severn Trent ran a regular CEO video blog, a cross-company news bulletin and communications distilling government messaging on restrictions. 'We tried to create experiential learning and communications to help people process information in a way that made sense for them,' Morrison explains. But because much of its staff are frontline workers who do not spend their working day in front of a computer, not everyone was able to receive the emails, so Severn Trent also introduced 'Comms Cells', an area on the walls with information employees needed to know.

During the first year of all its changes, despite the challenges of the pandemic, employee engagement increased 2.5 per cent, with an average employee rating of 8.3 out of 10, putting Severn Trent in the top 5 per cent of utility companies globally. According to Morrison, this achievement has continued steadily, remaining at this high level. The company's impressive work in this area also ensured it took home the trophy for 'Best employee experience' at the 2021 CIPD People Management Awards. 'All of these measures indicate that people are enjoying what they're doing,' Morrison says. 'The quality of feedback shows staff are invested in making things better and helping to deliver, which, to me, is a sign of success.'

Prior to the pandemic, Severn Trent had also launched employee inclusion and diversity advisory groups for LGBTQ+, ethnic minority and disabled staff, and they too were 'supercharged' after Covid's emergence, quickly becoming key to the firm's response. 'We recognised that everyone was going through a different kind of experience in the workplace, so it was quite easy to take our "lunch and learn" sessions or Black History Month celebrations virtual, for example,' Morrison explains. 'The groups created communities working together to talk about what was going on, so people could share things that matter to them, rather than us telling them what to do.'

But when restrictions were lifted during the summer of 2020, Severn Trent was quick to bring as many people back to the workplace as possible. 'Our performance is better when we are collaborating because of the nature of our business: a 24/7, 365-days-a-year essential service,' he explains. 'Having people together is really important to be able to solve problems.'

So, what next for Severn Trent? Excitingly, the company will be contributing to the Commonwealth Games, hosted in the Midlands later this year. Employees will be volunteering during the event but also act as baton bearers in the run-up. 'This is a major sporting event taking place on our doorstep that should be something we're all really proud of,' Morrison says.

But, despite impressive data and award wins, the firm isn't done pushing employee experience further. 'We've had real co-creation with our colleagues and our communities, feeling very much connected to what we're doing, and I don't see that changing at all,' Morrison says. 'It's a fundamental part of our DNA.'

1 Critically consider how Morrison created a "we are all in this together" inclusive approach.
2 To what extent is employee engagement an ownership and "bottom up" approach?

SOURCE: Powell, C (2022) Covid enabled Severn Trent to supercharge its strategy, *People Management*, 28 February

---

 Reflective activity 2.4

The changing nature of HRM

Using the analogy of management of the transformational process, four key themes emerged from the CIPD Research Report, Leading transformational change: Closing the gap between theory and practice (2015b):

1 Relational leadership – transforming change achieved through relationships and social interactions with organisational members rather than authority and control.
2 Building trust – delivering the enabling conditions in which significant change can thrive.

3 Voice, dialogue and rethinking resistance, where labels of resistance are replaced with understanding of employee voice as legitimate and enabled through dialogue.
4 Emotion, energy and momentum, by managing the change process by maintaining levels of energy and momentum within the change process.

If we turn the emphasis away from change management and focus this approach to the HR function, how could HR operate within the spirit of the change process? How could HR operate in the way described under these four principles?

2.8 Capability building by the HR function

Another view is presented by Deloitte Consulting LLP and Bersin in their report 'Global human capital trends 2014: Engaging the 21st-century workforce' (2014), which identifies three key areas of capability for business-oriented HR professionals. These are:

- HR and talent skills, including technical HR skills such as training, recruitment, employee relations and compensation strategies, which need to be refreshed each year as new technologies and strategies emerge; a deep understanding of the labour market in the area and sector in which their organisation operates; the ability to manage a service operation; and high-level skills across multiple technologies and with data, statistics and analytics.

- Business, industry and global skills, including a deep understanding of their organisation's business, sector and global reach, covering, for example, how their organisation makes money, what drives long-term competitive advantage, new product development and how to drive innovation.

- Leadership, management and change implementation skills, including the ability to achieve practical results through change management.

Their research found that less than 8 per cent of the HR leaders who responded to the global survey thought that their HR team had the skills needed to meet the challenges of the global environment and consistently deliver innovative programmes driving business impact. While 27 per cent of business leaders responding to the survey rated HR as excellent or good in delivering HR and talent management, 42 per cent believed that their HR team was underperforming or just getting by. This survey indicates that improving HR capabilities and skills may be desirable for many organisations, and can be both an objective for HR transformation where the required skills are lacking and a means of transforming the HR function in practice.

For further discussion regarding the future implications for HR, see Chapter 13. The shape of the HR/HRD function may evolve through historical developments, or may be deliberately changed to meet the needs of key decision-makers. Perhaps the important factor here is how HR can constantly adapt its HRM and HRD activities, services and interventions to suit critical needs in that particular situation. Flexibility, adaptability and survival of HR remain the key determinants of HR's ability to transform itself to differing contexts. HR does not operate in isolation and requires management support – sometimes senior management support, but more often, line management support and engagement.

2.8.1 HR showing added value

For HR to maintain its credibility, it not only has to be seen to be adding value, but also needs to provide evidence through appropriate measurements that it is. The use of HR metrics and other indices like human capital management measures continue to be an aspect of HR. Warech and Tracey (2004) believe that HR is far more than a cost centre, and that being able to communicate assertively affects HR's collective impact on the company's bottom line.

The role of the line manager cannot be overplayed, and both HR and HRD specialists need to engage with line managers in order to establish and maintain a successful business partnership. Cantrell and Benton (2007, p 360) state that their research 'shows that the more involved managers are in employee development, learning and performance appraisals, the better the financial performance of the organisation'. These authors also emphasise the important role that line managers have in active involvement with selection and development of employees.

If we consider the results of the IRS survey (2010, p 5) on HR roles and responsibilities, 'most employers measure the effectiveness of their HR functions, with 72 per cent rating their HR function as very effective or above average based upon their evaluation'. Here HR has contributed towards managing cost-cutting exercises, an increased role in developing strategy (with senior managers), and reorganising and restructuring work (in order to save costs).

When it comes to creating a learning culture in organisations, where will this emanate from? Who will be the custodian of knowledge management (including knowledge creation and share)?

With regard to HRD showing added value, there is some similarity of arguments presented from HR material earlier. In a study of Indian companies, Rao and Varghese (2008) found that:

- HRD managers need to recognise stakeholder expectations and understand the overall business and strategic context of their function.

- The HRD function should focus on intellectual capital generation activities and ensure good return on investment on training and other interventions.

- HRD practitioners need to equip themselves with capacity and competencies needed to build the HRD function, and become proactive strategic partners.

- HRD practitioners need to strengthen their partnership and credibility among stakeholders through involvement with policy-making.

Ulrich and Smallwood (2004) argue that HRD can create value through building organisational capabilities such as talent, speed of change, shared mind-set, accountability, collaboration, learning and leadership.

2.8.2 Linking the HR function with performance

The HR function can only operate through others (akin to line managers too). So, the question arises as to the compatibility and sometimes shared goals and practices of these two key roles.

Also, the issue of how much line managers are expected to contribute towards implementing people management activities and practices is a moot one. What should the level of intervention from HR's perspective be when they spot errors and mistakes in the way in which line managers operate? If HR is purely acting in an 'advisory' capacity, whereby managers can ignore advice, then by definition, does this not spell the denigration of the HR function?

In an IRS survey (2009), it was found that in some cases HR took the lead (eg providing specialist knowledge or expertise surrounding a tribunal claim). In contrast, policies that needed to be applied across every individual employee in the workforce involved greater focus on the role of the line managers (eg performance appraisal reviews). The survey found that in 87.3 per cent of tribunal claims, HR took the main responsibility compared to 5.5 per cent who reported a shared responsibility between line managers and HR. The other two areas where HR took on a significant role were equal opportunities and employee relations (see also Chapters 6 and 9). It may be presumptuous to assume that the three key areas avoided by line managers could be considered to be 'dirty work', ie tricky areas that can be drawn out, complex and potentially damaging to the reputation of the individuals concerned. In the IRS 2008 survey on line managers' roles in people management, the key findings included:

- Line managers are increasingly expected to implement people management policies, with duties ranging from managing flexible working requests to handling disciplinary and grievance procedures.

- HR practitioners are not always impressed with the way that line managers carry out these responsibilities and assess their performance as poor in some areas. Line managers are judged ineffective in training and development, absence management and maintaining personnel records.

- HR practitioners believe that training for line managers should be compulsory, and that levels of training and support on offer are inadequate.

- Two-thirds of organisations predict the role of line managers to change further in the next three years, and this means taking on more HR functions.

Despite the IRS survey finding that HR use a number of techniques to support line managers in their people management role, such as coaching, meetings advice and support, training and posting information on various channels, the attitude that line managers possess can sometimes inhibit outputs. Some of the problems here may be quite simple, for example the line manager is taking on too much, which may detract from what they perceive as their core function or contribution.

 Reflective activity 2.5

Consider how a formal arrangement can be made so as to secure a strong working relationship between HR managers and line managers. What key aspects would this arrangement include and how could they be evaluated?

2.9 Strategic HRM and human capital management

Human capital management (HCM) can be defined as the collective knowledge, skills, abilities and capacity to develop and innovate through company employees. At the core of HCM is an integrative and strategic approach to the management of people. A CIPD Factsheet (CIPD, 2015c) states that HCM strengthens strategic HRM by:

- drawing attention to the significance of 'management through measurement', so as to provide objective linkages between HR interventions and organisational success
- providing guidance on what to measure, how to measure and how to report on the outcomes of measurement
- proving that superior people management is delivering superior results and indicating where HR should proceed
- reinforcing attention on the need to base HRM strategies and processes on the requirement to create value through people and achieve organisational goals
- defining the link between HRM and business strategy
- strengthening the HRM belief that people are assets rather than costs
- emphasising the role of HR specialists as business partners.

While operating strategically, an organisation will typically undergo several change initiatives in order to meet these objectives. The concept of HR transformation helps organisations to progress both the organisation and the function itself.

Organisations need to decide their objectives for HR transformation. The most common reasons for organisations to embark on HR transformation are to:

- meet a business goal, such as cost reductions, or refocusing on changed priorities, for example improving the organisation's capacity to recruit and retain the right people
- respond to cost-reduction pressures in a strategic rather than an incremental or piecemeal way
- align HR more closely with the organisation's business strategy in relation to people management
- improve the match between the skills and competencies of the HR team and the future needs of the organisation
- increase the effectiveness and efficiency of operational processes
- focus on a business-critical people issue such as a recruitment, skills or performance challenge
- change the balance of ownership of/responsibility for people issues across the organisation in relation to the HR function, senior managers, line managers and employees.

Case study 2.2

Swiss Re putting HR front and centre

The people function can be an afterthought during times of upheaval, but the reinsurance giant decided purpose should start at home. A sprawling township in South Africa, where 70 per cent of the population live in shacks, and the 41-floor Gherkin building in the City of London, home to the UK head office of global reinsurance firm Swiss Re (and several others). The two seem worlds apart.

Yet the former is the subject of the video James Hartley, Swiss Re's managing director and regional head of HR EMEA, points to as demonstrating the power of the firm's #TellOurStory initiative, which launched at the beginning of 2019.

The video features Bongiwe Mncube, HR partner MEA, describing the transformative effects of Swiss Re's Middle East and Africa Underwriting Academy, not only on a business location beset by skills shortages, but also on the life of one particular 28-year-old South African township resident, who – before being taken on by Swiss Re – was "totally lost… hanging out on street corners".

He says: 'I now can afford my children's school fees, I can afford stationery, I can afford transport for them to go to school, I'm able to take care of my siblings and elderly mother,' Mncube relates in the video. It's powerful stuff – and just one of many stories shared as part of an initiative designed to reconnect members of the 100-strong EMEA HR function with their individual purposes.

Given Swiss Re's wider context, it had become increasingly apparent, explains Hartley, that the function needed to provide a very particular kind of support, and role model certain key behaviours for the rest of the business.

Founded in 1863 and headquartered in Zurich, Swiss Re has 80 offices globally and 14,500 employees. It offers corporate solutions to mid-sized and multinational corporations and life capital insurance. But its largest income stream comes courtesy of its status as the world's second largest reinsurer, with the firm's B2B offering ranging from cutting-edge telematics-based products for the automotive sector, to insurance against crop failure for African farmers.

However, despite its size, the business is far from immune to challenging market conditions. 'In reinsurance, margins have been squeezed, and we've had to come up with innovative ways of retaining revenue. Corporate solutions has had a tough couple of years so is in a turnaround phase,' says Hartley.

'So if we're going to have leaders adept at managing ambiguity and a changing landscape, we need an HR function that's courageous enough to push the boundaries.'

The first step was to get all leaders within EMEA HR to discuss with their teams what inspires them about what they do day to day. Then smaller groups were brought together to debate various behaviours identified as common themes, such as putting 'purpose and pragmatism ahead of process and perfectionism', combining 'commercial and emotional impact' and acting 'with courage'.

'I was talking about my own personal purpose, which broke the dam a little bit,' says Hartley. 'We held an HR-wide town hall event, which got people to start to tell their stories. Then there was a kick-off event where we ran masterclasses on telling stories.'

Colleagues sharing their stories via video on dedicated #TellOurStory calls, in team meetings and in town halls continued regularly throughout 2019 – as did storytelling training. An 'Our Little Book of Why' was also produced, including details of each member of the EMEA team's purpose. Stories include highly personal accounts – such as one colleague discovering that her smiling at a stranger had stopped them attempting suicide – and span across all levels.

'Historically, you find the most senior people get this kind of thing, but my litmus test was: does it resonate with a payroll adviser in Bratislava?' says Hartley. 'I wanted the business to experience something different from HR. This for me is where the storytelling element comes in. If we sit with the business and say "here's the process, here's the tick-box, here's the form", we will drive a certain reputation.

'Inevitably there is a bias in HR to immediately go to the "what", sometimes the "how", but rarely the "why". But if we can start talking about a personal story or context, it just changes the dynamic.'

The business's shift to ratingless performance management to encourage quality conversations is an example of where HR has been able to role model the kinds of 'courageous' human conversations line managers should be having with direct reports. 'It just moves that whole thing from being a very corporate, left-brain, intellectual exercise, which can be the tendency in our sector,' says Hartley.

And a more energised, purpose-driven HR team has been critical to supporting Swiss Re's overall transformation and reorganisation agenda. Quickly creating HR project teams to support particular aspects of the change programme is much more effective where new team members have already connected on a personal level, says Hartley.

The EMEA HR team also enjoys top quartile engagement scores, with this going up 17 points since 2015. Crucially, the function has maintained high levels of client satisfaction, up 32 points from 2015.

It will now be important to sustain the momentum, and to roll the initiative out more formally to the wider business. Regarding why #TellOurStory wasn't kicked off with non-HR colleagues, Hartley is adamant of the value of starting with HR – something many organisations fail to do, he says, with the function (ironically) something of an afterthought when it comes to change programmes or L&D, for example. 'It absolutely can't be HR for HR in an insular way. But I think there's real power in starting a movement within HR that can engage, inspire and challenge the business. I don't think the business has sole mandate on innovation and creativity,' he says.

'I do think we have an opportunity at group level. The group exec committee is now saying "do we need to connect more emotionally?"'

'We already have a wider cultural shift. Our CEO starts town halls, not with share price, but by saying: "We've helped rebuild communities devastated by hurricanes and wildfires. And in doing so we've fulfilled our purpose of making the world more resilient."'

1   To what extent does the 'why' come into HR professionals' dialogues, or not, as is the case?
2   The concept of HR professionals inspiring line managers can be a challenging one to say the least – but why is this the case?

SOURCE: Roper, J (2020) Why Swiss Re put HR front and centre of its change programme, *People Management*, 20 February

2.10 Future trends for people professionals

The CIPD report *People Profession 2030* (2020a) highlights the following future trends:

1 Internal change, with evolving organisational models, structures and processes (see also Chapters 3 and 12).

2 Digital and technological transformation (see also Chapters 12 and 13).

3 Changing demographics and diversity and inclusivity strategy (see also Chapter 8).

4 Diversifying employment relationships (see also Chapter 9).

5 Sustainability, purpose and responsible business (see also Chapter 5).

Within this report the authors emphasise the need to 'better understand the strategic long-term direction of the profession, which requires us to understand the issues that will be faced by workforces in 2030 and beyond' (p 8). There is a question as to the predictability of major global events, like a global health pandemic, a global economic recession, a global ecological crisis and specifically how these events change the world and specifically the world of work.

 Reflective activity 2.6

Given the highly unpredictable nature of events external to an organisation, to what extent is the onus upon people professionals in organisations to direct employees and functions towards specific strategic initiatives and goals? When does employee wellbeing have to become the highest priority in an organisation? To what extent are data metrics and evidence the driving force for keeping alignment with external changes?

 Case study 2.3

Although many of us still work for a single employer, we increasingly experience work in a much more networked way than in the past (Marchington et al, 2009, Swart et al, 2007, Kinnie et al, 2006). Think about the last project team in which you were involved: the chances are the members were drawn from both inside and outside your organisation. Despite this, we know very little about the management of human capital in a cross-boundary, or networked, context.

Indeed, we might go further and say that much of current HR thinking, strategy, structure and practice is predicated on and reflects more traditional hierarchical structures. We therefore need to develop our understanding of these contemporary ways of working and how organisations use innovative forms of organising to manage human capital across boundaries.

A prominent way of working across organisational boundaries is to organize work in projects. Such arrangements are widespread, both within and between firms, in sectors such as pharmaceuticals, car manufacture, advertising, marketing and media and consulting. Complex, so-called 'mega-projects' or integrated project teams (IPTs) are the principal way in which large-scale major construction projects, such as Terminal 5 at London Heathrow Airport and the London Olympic Park, and IT integration projects, such as the change to online self-assessment tax returns for HMRC, are designed, developed and then operationalised.

These changes reveal an interesting paradox: potentially fragmenting changes, which could mean that organisations may not be able to maximise the value from their human capital, are taking place at the same time as greater emphasis is placed on the central role of human capital in organisational success (Takeuchi, Lepak and Swart, 2011).

Increasingly, we are faced with the task of managing employees across organisational boundaries. In more traditional organisations we tend to equate employees with the people whom we directly manage; but more and more we are finding disconnect between those whom we employ and manage. We may, for example, employ people but not manage them on a face-to-face basis because they may be providing outsourced services on a client's site, as in the recruitment process outsourcer Alexander Mann Solutions (AMS). Alternatively, the clients of AMS find they are interacting on a daily basis with staff who are not their employees but are central to their success. Indeed, Paul Fielden, Associate

Partner in IBM, said in a recent interview for our research, 'I can draw on over 150 IBM people to staff projects for my clients, but I only directly manage three of them.'

These innovative forms of organising have multiple benefits because they allow firms to leverage the knowledge, skills and experience of staff they do not employ, but there are also various challenges. The financial services firm which outsources its call centre operations to India achieves both cost and expertise advantages, but it knows these call centre workers are perceived by their customers as the public voice of their organisation. These innovative ways of working in 'adhocratic', project-centred, knowledge-intensive networks (see also Chapter 11) throw up challenges for achieving the traditional HR aims of integration, alignment and consistency (Marchington, Rubery and Grimshaw, 2011).

The consultant will have to display commitment not only to her employer, but also to her client, team and her own professional development. Indeed, many of these HR practices sit more comfortably in an environment where there is a single focus of commitment rather than the potentially multiple foci of commitment found in the networked way of working where employees are habitually working across organisational boundaries (Kinnie et al, 2012).

We need to consider the consequences for HR if the source of competitive advantage shifts from the single firm to the complex network involving literally thousands of firms. This means that the classic HR practices for recruitment, talent development and retention are no longer solely the property of an individual firm.

2.11 Conclusion

HR needs to operate effectively at strategic, tactical and operational levels. Rees and McBain (2004, p 25) argue that in order for HR to maintain its importance, it needs to:

- participate in strategic decision-making, demonstrate added value and act as a business partner
- move from assuming full responsibility for all HR managers and engage with line managers (and develop the capability of line managers)
- shift the focus from internal to external, including benchmarking against other organisations and collecting data on competitors. This includes keeping in touch with business trends and how these impact upon people management practices within the organisation
- become more anchored in, and central to, the contribution to business, thereby building commitment from employees
- move away from reactive supporter to proactive strategic adviser, anticipating required changes.

This model echoes the principles of business partnership but is less concerned with structural issues and focuses upon the role and contribution of HR more. This 'internality' argument on meeting customer needs is explored by Jenner and Taylor (2007, p 8), where HR views employees (and potential employees) as internal customers, and 'anticipating, identifying and satisfying customer requirements'.

Perhaps the final word needs to come from Boxall and Purcell (2015, p 275):

Strategic HRM should help researchers and practitioners to recognise models of HRM, to understand how they have evolved and the strategic tensions that characterise them, help them to measure their impacts and develop ways for how they might be improved.

The HR function will continue to evolve with the onset of increased globalisation (or even post-pandemic deglobalisation), technological enhancements, etc. Perhaps the focus should not be on whether it is 'strategic enough' (post-Ulrich), but more on its practical value added, with an eye upon continuous improvement and customer focus.

🔒 KEY LEARNING POINTS

1 The HR department or function has changed considerably in the last 40 years and currently tends to adopt a managerialist (corporate) position. The question now arises as to whether the emphasis upon people management has provided a stronger emphasis upon employee wellbeing and nurturing and appreciation of employees' contributions.

2 HR needs to take time to evaluate and justify itself as a function or face attack or possibly outsourcing or replacement.

3 Where HR sits within corporate planning is pivotal to its involvement with strategic and mainstream business activities.

4 HRD and strategic HRD play an important function in the development of employees to adding to business success.

5 The HR business partner model carries with it a series of potential benefits and limitations, and should therefore be adapted according to the organisation and context, and possibly face up to the fact that it simply won't work as a model.

6 Despite the theory, there is a great deal of evidence to suggest that HR does receive the attention and support that it requires as a key function within organisations. The interplay between line management and HR is crucial in obtaining the right business outcomes.

? Review questions

1 To what extent can there be a 'perfect shape' to an HR function in an organisation? Consider the arguments both for and against this proposition.

2 Does the HR business partner role sit most comfortably within private, public or third sector organisations? Support your answer with practical benefits.

3 How can the HR/HRD function build relationships with line managers so as to put improved working practices into effect?

4 What is meant by 'strategic HRD'? Evaluate the major components of strategic HRD.

Explore further

Aston Centre for Human Resources (2008) *Strategic Human Resource Management: Building research-based practice*, CIPD, London

Boxall, P and Purcell, J (2015) *Strategy and Human Resource Management*, 4th edn, Palgrave Macmillan, Basingstoke. This textbook is strong on theory surrounding strategic HR.

Caldwell, R (2008) HR business partner competency models: Recontextualising effectiveness, *Human Resource Management Journal*, **18** (3), pp 275–294. This article provides useful arguments around the business partner model.

Rees, G and Smith, P (eds) (2021) *Strategic Human Resource Management: An international perspective*, 3rd edn, Sage Publications, London

03

People management: strategy, culture and values

GARY REES

LEARNING OUTCOMES

After reading this chapter, you should be able to:

- have an appreciation of the importance of strategy and culture in organisations
- explore the interplay between strategy and culture
- explore the importance of organisational culture – branding and underlying values
- have an appreciation of the competing values framework and its application
- gain an understanding of the CIPD's approach to good work
- consider the customer and their links and alignment to organisations
- explore the links between HRM and risk.

3.1 Overview

This chapter builds upon the underpinning provided by Chapter 2 on the nature of HR and people management. Various HR models were explored, but these can only truly be evaluated by considering how they link with the organisation's strategy as well as culture. Organisational structural issues are considered in Chapter 11. The importance of organisations' values and how they impact upon organisational culture and performance will be explored using the competing values framework. As a means of integrating the linkages between strategy culture and HR practices, the CIPD Good Work Index shall be used as an exploratory framework.

3.2 Introduction

Organisations often provide bold statements within their vision and mission statements around their expertise and future direction, sometimes to the point of ambiguity and over-reaching strategic intent. 'We aim to be the world's greatest producer of ...' may be a statement or comment too far, so this begs the question as to who and what mission and vision statements are for. In Chapter 2 we defined strategy as 'a course of action for achieving an organisation's purpose' (De Wit and Meyer, 2004, p 50). Vision statements provide words describing what the future looks like for a successful organisation, while the mission statement answers the question: How do we get to this successful place as an organisation? The overarching purpose is to motivate employees towards specific goals or visions. Research by Kaplan and Norton (2005) showed that 95 per cent of company employees in their sample were either unaware of or didn't understand its strategy. This chapter will start by exploring the concepts of strategy and strategic thinking before considering culture and then the interlinkages between these two critically important concepts.

3.3 The scope and nature of strategy

3.3.1 Strategy, HR and customers

The need for organisations to plan ahead in an uncertain and complex world is obvious. Organisations need to devise a corporate strategy in order to move from analysis to actions. Pisano et al (2021, p 39) argue that there are three core areas of corporate strategy with all three being interlinked:

1 Strategic analysis includes the organisation, its mission and objectives which provide value for people involved with the organisation (stakeholders).

2 Strategic formulation where strategy options have to be formulated and selected in accordance with particular skills of the organisation and the special relationships with those outside of the organisation (suppliers, customers, government, distributors, etc).

3 Strategic implementation consists of the selected options and their development.

The balance of assessing the external environment (and its potential instability) together with the internal decision-making processes (have we taken everything of importance into account and is our timing right?) will determine strategic planning and implementation time scales.

'Strategy is a rational decision-making process in which the organisation's resources are matched with opportunities arising from the competitive environment' (Hseih and Chen, 2011, p 17). The constant analysis and weighing up of how the organisation fits within its current and changing environment remains the remit of senior management, but how does this link with HR strategy?

According to Hsieh and Chen (2011, p 17), 'An effective human resource strategy systematically coordinates all individual human resource systems and implements them so as to directly influence employee attitudes and behaviours in a way that helps a business achieve its competitive strategy.' This means that both the corporate strategy and HR (people) strategy need to be constantly aligned.

However, HR strategies need to be aligned to business strategy in organisations. While there are numerous authors on business strategy bringing together key aspects of corporate/business strategy (Johnson et al, 2019; De Wit and Meyer, 2004; Ansoff, 1988, etc), two specific strategic perspectives and analysis that place the customer as a key component shall be discussed – Kim and Mauborgne (2005) and Porter (2004).

3.3.2 *Blue Ocean and Red Ocean strategy*

There have been a range of factors that have impacted upon organisations' strategies after Covid-19, with many organisations changing the way that they conduct business, supply chains altering dramatically and some organisations growing exponentially while some have disappeared beyond trace. Changes to technological advances has resulted in improved industrial productivity and suppliers producing a significant array of products and services (Del Giudice et al 2017). Kim and Mauborgne (2005) argue that many consumer brands have become more alike and that in overcrowded industries differentiating brands becomes more difficult, and this leads to two potential types of strategy being adopted: Blue Ocean and Red Ocean strategies.

Red Ocean strategy is typified by organisations competing in existing market spaces, trying to beat the competition by exploiting existing demand and making the most of the value/cost trade off. Under this strategy, there is an alignment of the whole system of a company's activities with its strategic choice of differentiation or low cost.

On the other hand, Blue Ocean strategy considers the creation of uncontested market spaces by making the competition irrelevant as well as creating and capturing new demand and breaking the value/cost trade off. Under this strategy, there is an alignment of the whole system of a company's activities in pursuit of differentiation and low cost.

This model has obvious overlaps with Porter's Generic Analysis model, providing further insights into attracting customers through products and services, and we now go on to examine that well-established model.

3.3.3 *Porter's generic analysis*

Customers are faced with greater choice of products and services from a global supply of these products and services in a highly competitive marketplace. When organisations are determining their strategy based upon a competitive analysis of the competition, Porter's model (2004) discusses a two-by-two matrix model, with scope (narrow or broad) occupying the vertical axis, and the source of competitive advantage occupying the horizontal access, with either a cost or differentiation focus.

Porter (2004) highlights three key strategies available to organisations. First, a cost leadership strategy, where an organisation reduces costs (while charging industry-average prices) to increase profits, and also increases market share by charging lower prices whilst maintaining a reasonable profit. This approach is normally associated with a low-cost base for employee costs, as well as other resources, facilities, etc.

Second, a differentiation strategy which involves making an organisation's products or services both more attractive and different from other competitors. This approach requires effective sales and marketing that can communicate effectively this unique offering as well as delivering in this service together with intelligent research to support assertions made.

Third, a focus strategy includes a good understanding of markets so that niche markets can be identified and exploited. Underpinning this is the need to secure brand loyalty from customers.

Porter (2004) argues that a clear and well-defined strategy needs to be adopted because ambiguity can lessen the impact and effectiveness of adopting one of these three approaches.

While strategic models like Porter (2004) and Johnson et al (2019) focus on the internal organisation dynamics adapting to the external environment, attention needs to be drawn towards the ultimate goal in organisations – the perceived stakeholder value and how that determines decisions around both strategy and HR – see also the Beer and Nohria (2000) model in Chapter 12. While much of the focus is upon single organisations and customers, there is a need to go beyond that when dealing with supply chain issues, which have taken a higher level of priority post Covid-19.

3.3.4 *Supply chains, customers and strategic HRM*

A supply chain is 'a set of three or more entities (organisations or individuals) directly involved in the upstream and downstream of product, services, finances, and/or information from a source to a customer' (Mentzer et al, 2001, p 4). Organisations 'have adopted a supply chain orientation (SCO)' (Mentzer et al, 2001), when integrative and collaborative supply chain management activities are explicitly the result of an emphasis upon customer focus, customer value creation, coordinated marketing and profit generation (Lengnick-Hall, Lengnick-Hall and Rigsbee, 2013, p 367). Ketchen and Hult (2007) argue that there is a substantial and largely untapped source of potential competitive advantage through effective supply chain management. These authors highlight the extent to which HR systems align within an SCO context and state that their relationship with high performance is contingent upon three factors:

1 the degree of differentiation among the supply chain partners
2 the degree of integration needed among supply chain partners

3 the extent to which a supply chain orientation has been adopted among a dominant proportion of supply chain partners.

Consideration needs to go beyond a focus on systems linking to HR practices to performance. A range of governance issues around choosing appropriate partners within the supply chain may be critical; namely, ones that share similar corporate values and will be low risk when it comes to branding and association with brand reputation of any of the suppliers within the supply chain.

3.4 The importance of culture

We shall start by trying to hone in on the meaning of organisational culture, differentiate it from national culture and then explore organisational sub cultures too.

3.4.1 Defining organisational culture

The search for a universal definition of organisational culture remains as problematic as the search and finding of the Holy Grail. Schein (1992, p 12) defines culture as: 'a pattern of shared basic assumptions that the group learned...that has worked well enough to be considered valid and therefore, to be taught to new members as the correct way to perceive, think, and feel'. However, Watkins (2013) argues that 'there is little consensus on what organisational culture actually is, never mind how it influences behaviour and whether it is something leaders can change'. Martin (2006) suggests a more pragmatic approach in the understanding of organisational culture, by stating that organisational culture 'determines how an organisation operates and how its members frame events both inside and outside of the organisation'.

Szydlo and Grzes-Buklaho (2020) provide a useful set of descriptors that capture the essence of organisational culture:

- organisational culture is a social creation, it is created and maintained by a group of people who form the organisation
- organisational culture is holistic, it encompasses the phenomenon in its entirety, which is more than the sum of simple components
- organisational culture is the beliefs shared by members of an organisation
- organisational culture is something that unites, stabilises, reduces uncertainty, leads to internal integration, enabling employees to adapt to a changing environment
- organisational culture is linked to the subjects of anthropological studies, such as rituals and symbols
- organisational culture is shaped and developed in the process – it is an inertial (ongoing) and, at the same time, self-developing phenomenon, it is the result of the learning process by means of dealing with environmental problems and internal coordination
- organisational culture is historically determined
- organisational culture is passed on in the process of socialisation, it is rarely consciously taught

- organisational culture changes, though it is difficult to change – the processes of cultural evolution are gradual and slow
- organisational culture 'hides' largely in employees' minds, feelings, perceptions and reactions.

The descriptors above capture the complexity of organisational culture and also in identifying the attitudinal and behavioural aspects that embed themselves in organisational culture.

Schein (2009) provides a useful conceptual model that breaks down the key components of organisational culture based on three levels. First, the 'artefacts' which are visible in the organisation and reflect organisational structures and process. Examples include hierarchical indicators, like a large office, ornate name plates on the office door, etc. Second, what Schein terms 'espoused values' which surround the strategies, philosophies and goals of the organisation, for example an organisation may focus all that it does on attracting and retaining good customers, with the mantra that 'the customer is king'. Third, Schein presents the 'underlying assumptions' which are the unconscious, taken-for-granted beliefs, perceptions, thoughts and feelings of employees. This critical level is the ultimate source of both values and actions, and it resonates with the notion of culture being defined as 'the way we do things around here'. When an employee faces a difficult situation and has to make a quick decision, on what basis do they finalise their decision? Would it be based on corporate values or something else? Arguably, the culture of the organisation, with its roots firmly entrenched in values and beliefs, may play a prominent role in decision-making.

3.4.2 National versus organisational culture

When we consider national culture, Trompenaars and Hampden-Turner (2004) argue that the culture of a nation is defined by the shared values, expectations and behaviours learned by a group of people which are transferred across generations. The potential overlap between national and organisational culture is worthy of consideration when analysing organisations. Sometimes national culture may have a dominating effect on organisational culture but it is unlikely to be the other way around. There are also potential pitfalls in potentially generating – or perpetuating – national stereotypes when analysing organisational culture.

 Case study 3.1

Blood Cancer UK: culture change

The charity moved to a culture focused on outputs and objectives rather than where and how staff work.

As people return to some form of post-pandemic normality, many organisations have moved towards a more hybrid working model, investing in technology and staff to create an environment that promotes flexibility.

While the general trend among workers seems to swing in favour of more flexibility, many smaller businesses and third sector organisations lack the HR resource and funds to be able to adapt swiftly. However, Jessica Badley, Head of HR and OD at charity Blood Cancer UK, says it is still possible to create an agile working environment without a big budget. 'We know most of our staff prefer much more flexibility,' she explains. 'So we've told them that we trust them to make their decisions on where and how they work based on our mission and our values.'

When she joined the charity in November 2019, Badley says there was already a 'vision to move towards a real flexible way of working,' but the pandemic simply accelerated that. 'We already had the building blocks in place – we knew that, for us, agile working meant being focused on people meeting objectives and outputs, and not where they worked or what hours they did – which really helped us when we all had to work from home,' she says.

Prior to the pandemic, the charity had worked to a very traditional pattern, Badley explains. Everybody went into the office from 9am until 5pm all week, with some people 'occasionally' working from home on Fridays. 'So we had to shift the culture and people's mindset,' she says.

In order to address this, Badley held meetings with different teams and asked their thoughts about flexible working, as well as what they needed to make it work. Their responses, she says, included, 'we can't do it because we need to sit together to get the job done,' or, 'I'd get really distracted and just watch TV'.

For others, it was as simple as IT equipment, and some managers also raised concerns about managing performance 'if they couldn't see their team'. This led to the charity changing its performance management system entirely – moving from traditional annual appraisals to setting and reviewing objectives every one to four months – and developing internal training programmes.

These training programmes include one for line managers, which explores any unconscious beliefs they may have, explains Badley. 'For example, when addressing concerns around not knowing if someone was actually working, we would say, "you don't know what someone's doing even when you do see them at a computer – they could be on Facebook all day" – so that's not a true assumption.'

In fact, the organisation ended up having the opposite problem – staff were working too many hours, 'so we had to tell them not to,' says Badley. Instead, she and her team linked the charity's flexible working policy with wellbeing and, to avoid reaching the 'burnout stage', encouraged people to adjust their hours accordingly if they did extra time the week before in order to meet a deadline.

Since introducing its flexible working policy, Blood Cancer UK has noticed a significant improvement in its retention rate; in November 2018, the 12-month rolling average rate was 70 per cent, whereas the most recent figure from September 2021 is 94 per cent. Additionally, a quarterly pulse survey also revealed a huge increase in employees recommending the charity as a place to work, jumping from 41 per cent in December 2018 to 93 per cent in September 2021.

Badley puts this positive feedback down to not only the charity's approach to flexible working, but also its new wellbeing provisions, which were developed alongside its agile working policy and have seen sickness absence drop to an average of just 1.3 days per employee. 'We wanted to be a world-class wellbeing organisation,' she said. 'And that means people thriving at work, not just managing.'

Other strands of the charity's work on wellbeing focus on employees' mental, physical and financial health, including a specific initiative on menstruation and the menopause. 'We know some people really struggle with their periods – for example, if it makes you really tired or unwell, we're saying that's okay, just start your day later or even do fewer hours that week,' explains Badley.

The move has, she says, come as a welcome surprise to many staff. 'But there's no point struggling through if you don't feel well – the cause doesn't matter, it's still impacting you,' she adds. 'We would rather people were well because then they'll work better. Bringing this in has been quite a culture change.'

But, importantly, implementing these significant changes to the organisation's culture is not just a one-time thing, Badley points out. The agile principles are a 'practical framework' which is reviewed every six months, and all staff are included in those discussions.

'It's about continuous improvement,' she explains, adding that the organisation has also recently undertaken a benefits review, and is looking at ways to improve its internal communication in a bid to keep attracting and retaining talent.

'As a charity, our pay rates are not as high as the private and public sector,' Badley says. 'So if we want to diversify our workforce, be more inclusive and keep our retention levels high, this is our best chance to try and be competitive.'

1 Explain the reasons why Badley's approach to employee wellbeing was so successful.

2 To what extent is this case study a little different in that employees appeared to be working too long hours and too hard. Would the intervention that Badley brought in have happened had the employees been working shorter hours and more flexibly?

SOURCE: Rambhai, J (2022) Blood Cancer UK – cultural change www.peoplemanagement.co.uk/article/1746561/blood-cancer-uk-implemented-truly-flexible-culture-better-retain-talent

3.4.3 Organisational sub-cultures

Sub-cultures are created when a specific group of employees within the organisation have a common set of beliefs, values or experiences that differ from the existing dominating culture. This group are therefore a subset who share similar values and obligations. When we consider organisational behaviours such as Groupthink (Janis, 1972), the impact of team behaviours can override individuals. Janis (1972) refers to the *Challenger* space shuttle disaster in 1986, where the position for NASA on whether or not to launch a rocket was always 'a launch should be cancelled if there is any doubt of its safety' (Hirokawa, Gouran and Martz, 1988). How then did the problem with the O rings faults and launch get overlooked? Janis (1972) argues that when team cohesiveness is high, there is a strong team need to maintain relationships within the group (group harmony), and this is at all costs. This concurrence-seeking tendency of a close- knit group can result in inferior (and disastrous) decisions being made. We should not under-estimate the power and influence of sub-cultures and consider them by using the competing values framework (see also Section 3.7) as well as other appropriate analytical models.

3.5 The interplay between strategy and culture

McKinsey's classic 7S framework provides some explanation of the dynamic inter-relationship between strategy and culture, with culture (shared values) linking to strategy, systems, structure, style, staff and skills. While culture is all pervasive, this model may not shine a great deal of light on the intricacies of how strategy and culture interact and affect each other. Similarly, if we consider the extended model of this – the 8S's (Higgins, 2005) – where the inclusion of strategic performance as an output measure is included, the connection between strategy setting and strategic performance is highly interlinked but again may not indicate how these are as we may be comparing input measures and output measures and potentially missing out on some of the variables that impact upon input and throughput measures (see also Chapter 12).

The emphasis upon shared values suggests that shared values and culture are one and the same. Hays (2022) defines organisational values as behavioural guidance for employees, as they are the principles and beliefs that provide a cohesive vision and defines who the business is as well as defining the organisation to employees, stakeholders and customers, and crucially reminding employees of the preferred way of achieving outcomes at work. These values serve an important purpose in setting the organisational identity about what matters most and helps employees make the right decisions. Hays further argues that values-based recruitment can improve retention as well as differentiating your organisation from its competitors.

 Reflective activity 3.1

A study done by faculty members at Duke University found that leaders, by and large, get the notion that culture is important and is an important determinant of performance. Over 90 per cent of leaders said that they could probably improve their culture. Fewer than 20 per cent said that they had actually done anything about it. People get it; they just don't do anything about it.

1 Why is this the case and what makes culture so difficult to manage and potentially change? (See also Chapter 12 on culture change for consideration of various change interventions.)

SOURCE: Heskett, J (2022) Columbia Business School Publishing www.mckinsey.com/featured-insights/mckinsey-on-books/author-talks-how-to-gain-a-competitive-edge-with-organizational-culture?cid=other-eml-alt-mip-mck&hdpid=1b9a121d-6c2d-43cf-b56a-7e4e63004c6c&hctky=2872684&hlkid=23001334a3ba4871bf3be093293115ee

---

3.6 Branding and organisational values

According to Edwards (2010, p 6), 'Employer branding is an activity where principles of marketing, in particular the "science of branding", are applied to HR activities in relation to current and potential employees.' Edwards (2010) also argues that employer branding considers current and potential employees as branding targets.

Herman and Gioia (2001) discuss some of the benefits of incorporating the strategy of building an employer's brand; namely to reduce marketing and recruitment costs, attract higher quality and quantity applicants for jobs, improve retention and increase employees' loyalty, increasing efficacy, effectiveness and profitability, optimise results, and having higher attractiveness to customers and investors. The 'cost' of maintaining this high branding reputation is something for debate too, owing to the turbulent and uncertain nature of the business world.

Martin (2007) argues that employer brand image is strongly linked to corporate identity through organisational culture together with a range of issues associated with employer brand – reputation, attractiveness to outsiders (impacting upon recruiting talent), as well as insider identification with employer brand, and all of these then align with organisational performance.

 Case study 3.2

How VisitBritain/VisitEngland devised a new people strategy during Covid-19 The government body used the hiatus in the tourism sector as a golden opportunity to carry out significant change work. Devising a brand-new people strategy is a huge undertaking at the best of times. And it's even more of a huge undertaking against the backdrop of a global pandemic. But that's exactly what Debra Lang, director of HR and professional services at national tourism agency VisitBritain/VisitEngland, a government arms-length body, took on during 2020 – a process she describes as 'like trying to fly a plane and build it at the same time'. But despite tourism being one of the sectors worst hit by Covid, and the government-funded organisation unable to furlough staff, the timing turned out to be fortuitous.

A self-described 'lifetime civil servant' and having previously worked in the Department for Work and Pensions, HMRC and the Cabinet Office, Lang is currently seconded to VisitBritain/VisitEngland from her role as Director of People and Workplace at the Department for Digital, Culture, Media and Sport, having initially been drafted in January 2020 for a year (now extended to two) to shape and enact the organisation's vision for a future-proof people strategy.

Lang's main remit, she says, was to create a more transformational HR function and to develop a people strategy to support the company's 300 staff, a third of whom are based across 19 countries, with a new approach to engagement and a particular commitment to improving L&D and I&D – two areas a deep dive into staff survey data revealed were lacking. 'The team didn't have the capacity to look further ahead,' she explains. 'The people function should be there to curate the people experience, not police it.' After getting the green light to create the new approach, Lang spent a month talking to a cross-section of staff about their experiences, discovering 'what they enjoyed and what hacked them off', as well as commissioning an all-staff engagement survey and becoming 'best friends' with the data analysis team to truly understand the results.

From this listening work was borne a host of staff networks, each run by passionate groups of employees to drive the organisation's work in their particular area. What began as one mental health network is now eight, including seven in I&D, which have allowed Lang to tap into 'latent energy' within the workforce. 'As a small organisation, we don't have much resource centrally, but these groups have found untapped enthusiasm none of us knew was there,' she says.

And although undergoing a significant change project while dealing with a pandemic sounds less than ideal, Lang is adamant the timing has been a bonus. Morale, she explains, has been particularly low during Covid, with some staff, including Lang herself, even contracting the virus, so the new strategy has 'energised' the workforce and given them something to focus on. 'Obviously things have been awful, which made me question whether it was the right time,' she says. 'But while you need a people strategy in good times, you need it even more during bad times.'

A particular success of the change work has been VisitBritain/VisitEngland's youth network creating a virtual week-long work experience programme for more than 200 students considering a career in the sector – something more than three in five say they're now keen to pursue. As well as benefitting the students, Lang says the scheme was a positive experience for those who organised it. 'I wanted to encourage more young people into the sector, and the youth network has blown my mind,' she says. 'The team got a lot out of working with these young people.'

And where some areas of the organisation have seen the 'volume turned down' because of Covid-19, other teams have been able to put that spare capacity to use via a workforce interchange network and shadowing (WINS) portal, where departments can advertise their requirements for short-term help, and staff from elsewhere in the organisation can apply to take it on. 'We wanted to utilise all our resource across the globe in a positive way,' Lang explains. 'Some projects have been started in the US, passed to Europe and then picked up in Australia as the day has gone on.'

But despite the limitations of the pandemic, the change work has boosted the organisation's people metrics. Its latest staff survey surpassed each of the Civil Service People Survey's five benchmarks around employee engagement, including a nine-percentage point increase in those who say the company inspires colleagues to do their best. And Lang is particularly proud that the initiative has cost nothing. 'You don't need to buy in an expensive consultancy for something like this – you just need a good HR professional,' she says. With lockdown measures hopefully being lifted soon (then 2021) and the tourism sector tentatively considering how it will reopen, as well as the organisation itself considering what its model of hybrid working will look like after Covid, Lang is certain it will be in a much stronger place to support the industry as it rebuilds: 'The whole company, at one stage or another, has been in total lockdown, and yet we've done this fantastic thing. We've got a great HR team and an engaged workforce who are passionate and committed to working in tourism, and that will be reflected in how they support the sector.'

1 Why was the VisitBritain/VisitEngland initiative so successful?
2 To what extent was understanding organisational and national cultures a factor in Lang's thinking and approach in dealing with the changes?

SOURCE: Whitehouse, E (2021) *How VisitBritain/VisitEngland devised a new people strategy during Covid*

3.7 The competing values framework

The competing values framework (CVF) comes to diagnose an organisation's cultural effectiveness and to map the percentage of human and financial resources, to understand the dominant culture of an organisation, the level of contradiction between values, and the harmony between the organisation and its leadership or initiatives (Abbett, Coldham and Whishnant, 2010). Cameron and Quinn (2011), created a four-box culture conceptual model that they used in categorising organisational culture, with the vertical axis focusing on stability or flexibility of the organisation and the horizontal axis considering whether the organisation is more inward or outward looking. The four resultant quadrants lead to a particular cultural category. Inward and flexible leads to a clan culture, with a close-knit community, the outward focus and flexible quadrant resulting in an adhocracy culture, an entrepreneurial, innovative and risk-taking culture. The stable and inward quadrant leads to a hierarchy culture, where the focus is upon efficiency, process and control, and, finally, the outward focus and stable quadrant leads to a market culture, which is an action driven, competitive and win oriented culture.

While this model has created great coverage and usage in organisation, there are some limitations to its usage. Quinn acknowledged himself that, at certain thresholds, the contradictory functional requirements (conflicts) might become exaggerated and may lead to major reconfigurations of the coalitional structure and the dominant perceptions of what is success, with this often leading to culture change.

 Reflective activity 3.2

Consider Cameron's OCAI measurement tool, where six aspects of culture are being assessed, (see www.ocai-online.com/about-the-Organizational-Culture-Assessment-Instrument-OCAI). While an individual may identify a particular dominant culture, how does this diagnostic tool work in an organisation of 1,000 employees from very different socio-economic and ethnic backgrounds?

Second, to what extent could we identify clan, hierarchy, adhocracy and market cultures to align more with functional areas, like marketing, Finance and HR? Why is it that these quadrants align to functional areas?

3.8 Good work as examined by the CIPD

3.8.1 Good work

The CIPD's purpose is to champion better work and working lives by improving practices in people and organisation development for the benefit of individuals, the economy, and society.

The CIPD 2021 Good Work Index (Norris-Green and Gifford, 2021) states that good work is fundamental to individual wellbeing, supports a strong, fair society, and creates motivated workers, productive organisations and a strong economy. The CIPD's definition is:

- Good work is fairly rewarded and gives people the means to securely make a living.
- Good work gives opportunities to develop skills and a career and gives a sense of fulfilment.
- Good work provides a supportive environment with constructive relationships.
- Good work allows for work–life balance.
- Good work is physically and mentally healthy.
- Good work gives people the voice and choice they need to shape their working lives.
- Good work should be accessible to all.
- Good work is affected by a range of factors, including HR practices, the quality of people management and by workers themselves.

It would be difficult to argue against any of these points from an employee perspective, but the question arises as to whether employers fully embrace all of these aspects of good work, and if not why not?

According to the CIPD, across each of these areas of activity or influences, employers need to develop an effective people strategy that includes:

- values, culture and leadership
- workforce planning and organisational development
- employment relations
- people analytics and reporting.

3.8.2 The CIPD seven dimensions of good work related to job quality

1 Pay and benefits. Subjective feelings regarding pay, employer pension contributions, and other employee benefits.
2 Contracts. Contract type, underemployment, and job security.
3 Work–life balance. Overwork, commuting time, how much work encroaches on personal life and vice versa, and HR provision for flexible working.
4 Job design and the nature of work. Workload or work intensity, autonomy or how empowered people are in their jobs, how well resourced they are to carry out their work, job complexity and how well this matches the person's skills and qualifications, how meaningful people find their work, and development opportunities provided.
5 Relationships at work. Social support and cohesion. The quality of relationships at work, psychological safety, and the quality of people management.

6 Employee voice. Channels and opportunities for feeding views to one's employer and managers' openness to employee views.

7 Health and wellbeing. Positive and negative impacts of work on physical and mental health. Often considered as an outcome of job quality.

3.8.3 Good work and performance

Finally, the findings in the 2021 report add to the evidence from previous CIPD Good Work Index exercises that have demonstrated a relationship between multiple dimensions of good work and self-reported job performance.

In line with previous iterations of CIPD Good Work Index research, workers who report more positive relationships in terms of job design and employee voice appeared more likely to have positive perceptions of task performance and contextual performance.

There is a need for further, more targeted research on the specific drivers of performance in different roles and sectors, and also a need to broaden the evidence-base on performance outcomes to avoid reliance on the self-reported perceptions of workers.

But the 2021 data nonetheless offer some support for the business case for investments in job quality and work engagement and voice strategies as a means of supporting wellbeing and performance.

3.8.4 Implications for people management

The questions asked and the data gathered by the 2021 CIPD Good Work Index to some extent provide an important snapshot of the UK workforce and workplace in the midst of the Covid-19 crisis, but, as noted in this publication, the 2021 report may well be capturing the calm before the storm.

The report argues that we should also note that this report, by definition, does not capture the experiences of some of the most vulnerable people who may have already lost their jobs. The apparent stability of Good Work Index indicators may well come under even more severe pressure during 2021–2022 as the economy opens up, government support is reduced and withdrawn, and employers are left to rebuild their operations post-Covid-19.

The pressures and demands for work reorganisation that the next year will bring may have profound consequences for the job security and conditions of workers across sectors, as well as impacting much more broadly on work intensification (with implications for work–life balance and wellbeing), opportunities for development and other aspects of job quality. There is an urgent need for policymakers to consider the impacts of Covid-19 on the workplace, jobs and the wellbeing of workers.

Given the existing evidence base that poor job quality in some sectors hampers national productivity performance, it is even more important to refocus on the quality of jobs as the UK economy builds back from the Covid-19 crisis. This report provides a clear picture of the multiple dimensions of good work as experienced (or not) by a representative sample of the UK workforce. As such, the report adds to the evidence on occupational, gender-based and other inequalities in access to good work that pre-date Covid-19 but may be exacerbated by the continuing crisis. It is therefore equally important that policymakers, sector stakeholders and employers give full consideration to the impact of decisions made in response to the current crisis on the jobs of different groups within the workforce, so that we can use building back from Covid-19 as an opportunity to address disadvantage among vulnerable worker groups by improving access to purposeful work, better contractual conditions and opportunities for employee voice.

This CIPD Report recognises the timing and considerable influence and impact of environmental factors, but stresses the need for policymakers to consider the positive opportunities that may arise post pandemic recovery. There is scope to give considerable attention to homeworking and the benefits of a healthy work–life balance for employees.

 Reflective activity 3.3

Stephenson Harwood, a London law firm, stated that it would allow staff to work remotely, but pay them 20 per cent less than their current salary. In a report written by Meierhans (2022), the BBC was told by Stephenson Harwood that it had recruited some remote workers from outside London during the pandemic on a lower pay package, reflecting the lower cost of not commuting into London. This law firm also stated that they were extending this remote working option to existing staff, and also apply the salary difference between the two packages. The firm stated that it didn't expect many people to take up the offer to work remotely full-time.

1 To what extent will perceptions of the value of hybrid working change in this organisation?
2 What sort of message does the organisation send out to employees on how they are being valued?

3.9 The customer and the organisation

If we consider the success of organisations, it could be argued that those organisations that keep their customers close and specifically those that can anticipate customer needs and deliver to customer expectations will surely thrive. In the last few years, communication, social media and various feedback platforms have changed the ways that companies have had to operate. As Slater (2020) commented, 'As companies grow in scale, maintaining focus on meeting customer's requirements at speed becomes more difficult as other business imperatives and pressures (e.g. cost, infrastructure and competition) arise. But the necessity of understanding your customers' needs and desires, and rapidly inventing solutions that meet those needs, is more critical than ever for companies looking to remain innovative in an increasingly uncompromising business environment.' The underlying assumption here is that the organisational culture can switch to a faster sense of urgency and subsequent delivery of customer needs.

Reflective activity 3.4

'The customer is always right.' If this statement was applied literally, then businesses would certainly collapse. A customer might feel that an item they wanted to purchase was too expensive and only willing to pay a third of its stated price, so a sensible compromise is needed. When we consider the relationship between HR and its customers, we may consider colleagues to be internal customers and non-colleagues who interact with the business (potential paying customers) as external colleagues. Anyone who has worked on customer care training will recognise this arrangement. Can we really treat customers as employees and employees as customers? The fundamental aspects underpinning this is dignity, respect and trust and that there is a good bond between them.

1 When organisations draw up their stated values, to what extent do these go beyond the whole organisation, permeate through all staff and potentially through customers too?

2 Identify the potential issues associated with Question 1 and also some of the potential risks.

3.10 Customer alignment

Throughout this chapter the inclusion and understanding of the customer within the organisation's purpose has been a central tenet. The heightened level of global competitiveness strengthens the case to include a core requirement of an organisation's employees to have a very strong understanding of customer needs and, more importantly, customer values and beliefs, and in particular those values and beliefs that are very important to customers that would make them break brand loyalty immediately should those values and beliefs be breached in any way.

Jamrog and Overholt (2004) highlight the need to keep customers close to the organisation, and that, in doing so, leadership and culture are of massive significance and link very strongly to organisational performance, but more importantly organisational effectiveness.

These authors highlight a 'map' of where HR fits within organisational effectiveness, with clearly identified connecting alignments of five key components:

1 Strategic alignment, where the strategic priorities are transmitted, shared and made consistent with employees' values and behaviours.

2 Customer focus alignment, where customer relationship is the focus of the strategic, performance and people approaches.

3 Leadership and talent management alignment, where leadership style, communication, motivation, commitment and behaviours lead to a productive organisational climate.

4 Performance alignment, where the processes and day-to day behaviours and activities match the strategic priorities.

5 Cultural alignment, where employees' values and beliefs as well as the processes directly linked to them enable behaviours that support strategy.

This model posits that culture, leadership and performance sit within the customer focus, which sits within the strategy, which sits within the organisation which sits within the external environment.

 Reflective activity 3.5

To what extent does the Jamrog (Jamrog and Overholt, 2004) model over-emphasise the focus upon the customer and the further alignment of strategy and cultural alignment? How feasible is this in practice within a large organisation working within a volatile, uncertain, complex and ambiguous environment volatility, uncertainty, complexity and ambiguity (VUCA) (Bennett and Lemoine, 2014).

3.11 HRM and RISK

While a great deal of HRM literature focuses upon the positive impact of HRM systems and practices (Beer et al, 1984), this has to be counter-balanced with the consideration that ineffective HRM practices (and sometimes the absence of them) may impact negatively upon the organisation, increase risk and many other damaging consequences, such as brand reputation, employee retention etc. The issue of risk is tempered against a backdrop of organisational and environmental uncertainty and unpredictability. An organisation cannot mitigate for every unforeseen circumstance and operate effectively. Risk management is considered to involve the identification, analysis, evaluation, control and monitoring of risk and uncertainty (Baker, Ponniah and Smith, 1999). 'Risk management is about mitigating risk and protecting resources. What is the most valuable resource of any company? Its people.' (Nickson, 2001, p. 25).

Post Covid-19, the risk may be staff retention, whereby the core capability (talented) employees leave, and as a double impact join the organisations' competitors. There are several key issues associated with employee behaviours and actions, and acting in an ethical manner and avoiding damage to the organisational brand. Sometimes organisational culture can mitigate extreme and unacceptable behaviours, but at the same time increase reputational damage, for example where there are instances of risky shift behaviour (Belovicz and Finch, 1971), Groupthink (Janis, 1972), and sometimes lack of actions altogether (avoiding whistleblowing of employee's behaviours and actions).

Case study 3.3

Why Companies House turned to its workforce to help transform its culture

Having existed in its present format since 1844 with little in the way of significant upheaval, to the untrained eye, Companies House isn't exactly at the forefront of organisational change. The Government Agency is chiefly responsible for incorporating limited companies in the UK, and around half of its 1,000-strong workforce have, in the words of Director of People Transformation Angela Lewis, very operational and process-based roles – staff that might typically be more difficult to see things like higher engagement and lower levels of sickness absence.

Yet, since her promotion three years ago from Head of HR and Estates, Lewis has put people front and centre of the agency's digital transformation process, exponentially increasing engagement across all levels of the workforce (90 per cent of staff now believe their role contributes to the wider organisation), reducing sickness absence (down from an average of 10.5 days per employee to just 6.49 in three years) and earning Companies House a shelf full of awards and accolades for its people work, not least the coveted Investors in People platinum accreditation.

At the start of this work in 2017, Lewis knew the first step of wider transformation was to get the organisation's culture in shape. 'If we didn't first focus on the people, how they were feeling and how engaged they were, we were never going to succeed,' she says. Her team initially held a series of workshops where employees were invited to talk about what they loved about Companies House's culture, and what they wanted to change, and of these were borne the

agency's core behaviours: adaptable, bold and curious. 'These were things we weren't visibly displaying as much as we needed to if we wanted to be truly transformational,' Lewis explains.

A culture change community was duly set up, at the time comprising around 60 staff keen to get involved, but which has now evolved to incorporate around half the agency. 'That's where we're very different to other organisations,' says Lewis. 'We're all involved in driving the change, whereas in other places I've worked the people strand of transformation has been separate.' The work also saw the introduction of Companies House's Ideas Hub, via which employees suggest ways to change how the agency does things – whether that's directly related to their role, or within the wider organisation. More than 500 ideas have been suggested to date, with one in particular resulting in savings of more than £600,000. 'If you listen to the people who know what they're doing, and you give them the infrastructure and encouragement to be able to say "we could do this better", then you see the results,' says Lewis.

When Covid-19 hit, rather than putting the agency's transformation plans on the backburner, the pandemic actually accelerated the ongoing change work, she says. Plans that were already afoot to become a hybrid organisation and introduce smarter ways of working were expedited, and 80 per cent of staff were set up to work remotely in just four weeks. 'That was already part of our five-year strategy, but the speed at which it was put in place was unbelievable,' says Lewis. Somewhat ironically, she says, running meetings virtually has in fact broken down barriers and allowed staff to challenge things more: 'We wanted to get to a point where people weren't afraid to put their hand up because of hierarchy. As a civil service department, we're living with the hierarchy of hundreds of years. People had to stop being so humble and start thinking they can achieve amazing things.'

Covid-19 has also seen other areas of the organisation flourish – in particular its 27 (and counting) employee networks. They have, Lewis says, developed and matured during lockdown, with different groups of staff with shared interests or circumstances maintaining support for one another, as well as the addition of six more networks, including working families. This has in turn provided an extra layer of support that the organisation's leadership team 'couldn't possibly have provided because we were responding to the crisis,' and helped to supplement what was being asked of line managers.

Although Covid-19 is far from over, and the wellbeing of her workforce tops her list of priorities going into 2021, Lewis is also looking ahead. With the cultural element already brought to life, the organisation will now be looking to enact the rest of its five-year strategy, although she's keen to stress that the cultural aspect is by no means over: 'You never get to an end point with culture change – you have to keep adapting to what's coming.'

But with a raft of awards under her belt, and Lewis's sharing of the agency's work fuelling both an increase in candidates clamouring to join and a queue of other organisations wanting to find out more and implement her thinking, it's difficult to see any more room for improvement. For Lewis, personally at least, this is certainly not true: 'I've worked in numerous HR roles, and every day I get a little jolt of joy from seeing how my colleagues are supporting each other. Working in an organisation with so much compassion and commitment to change is exactly where I want to be. I have to pinch myself.'

1 To what extent did Lewis's focus on changing organisational values have a contributory impact on the changes presented within the case study?

2 How can Lewis make sure that any changes remain stable and enduring?

SOURCE: Whitehouse, E (2021) Why Companies House turned to its workforce to help transform its culture, 28 January, *People Management*, www.peoplemanagement.co.uk/voices/case-studies/why-companies-house-turned-to-its-workforce-to-help-transform-its-culture

3.12 Conclusion

The impact of digitalisation and technological advances together with changes to global trading patterns, supply chain, and distribution of goods and services, and more significantly the role of the customer, combined with almost instant customer feedback and behaviours requires greater agility and responsiveness from organisations. While these extra-organisational factors are critical, the internal workings for organisations remain vital on how the systems and working practices meet the customer needs set out in the opening comment of this concluding section. A highly competitive, and possibly overcrowded global market will result in organisations struggling to balance this external/internal perspective. Information about company branding, reputation, values and much more is already easily available, so the role of the HR function is to ensure that employees feel that they have an employee value proposition throughout their duration of employment, with the quality of work and what the employee receives in exchange for their skills, capabilities and experience that they bring to the organisation being adequately recognised and rewarded. In some cases this will impact significantly on the role of the line manager and how their behaviours and actions impact either positively or negatively on the employee's value proposition.

 KEY LEARNING POINTS

1 Understanding the linkages between strategy and culture in organisations is critical. Strategies are set by people and employees help shape culture. It is all about people management.
2 The interplay between organisational sub-culture and culture can be complex and challenging, and the focus needs to concentrate on the dominant values and beliefs.
3 Exploring the CIPD Good Work framework and how it can impact positively on the operation of the HR function
4 Use appropriate models (like the competing values framework) when analysing some of the tensions within organisational culture and subculture.
5 Appreciate the interdependencies between business strategies, organisational customer and the subsequent values espoused in tandem with meeting customer requirements.

 Review questions

1 To what extent is the quality of work (as perceived by individual employees) critical when examining if someone is working for an employer of choice?
2 Does the HR function fully address the extent to which teams or groups of colleagues work together, and in addition, do the subsequent values that are formed result in effective working practices or not?
3 Building upon review Question 2, to what extent is there too much emphasis upon the HR function at organisational level rather than tactical and team level, with strategy

and culture often firmly embedded at organisational and strategic level?
4 How realistic is it to place the mitigation of risk solidly within the remit of the HR function? Are there other agencies within organisations that need to be included here?
5 To what extent should concepts like 'retention' be considered more as employee engagement, and treating the employee with greater respect and the sense that they are truly valued within the organisation? To what extent does this inclusion rely on a suitable organisational culture?

Explore further

Boxall, P and Purcell, J (2015) *Strategy and Human Resource Management*, 3rd edin, Palgrave Macmillan, Basingstoke. This textbook is strong on theory surrounding strategic HR.

French, R (2015) *Cross-Cultural Management in Work Organisations*, 3rd edn, London, CIPD Publishing. Addresses culture from a range of differing perspectives.

Rees, G and Smith, P (eds) (2021) *Strategic Human Resource Management: An international perspective*, 3rd edn, Sage Publications, London. Covers strategy and culture as well as strategic HRM.

04
HRM contributions in different settings

LIZA HOWE-WALSH

LEARNING OUTCOMES

After reading this chapter, you should be able to:

- appreciate how HR practices may differ across sector types: private, public and third sector
- recognise that delivering HR services in smaller organisations differs from those in larger organisations
- consider the ways in which the HR function may change as an organisation grows in size
- understand the concept of global HRM and its implications for practice in terms of policy and practice for localisation and control from head office
- explore the notion of strategic international HRM and the variegations in practice for staffing overseas.

4.1 Overview

This chapter takes theory from Chapters 2 and 3 and applies it to the working lives of HR practitioners (HRPs) in different contexts. While the function of managing HR is similar in most organisations, the work of the HRPs themselves varies according to the context in which they operate; this is partly dependent on the size of the organisation and also whether it operates in the private or public or third (not-for-profit) sectors. Organisations change as they grow, and although all have to be compliant with the law, small businesses may only seek involvement by HR to ensure such compliance, commonly using external consultants. Following growth, generalist internal HR managers are typically appointed and, with further success and growth, specialists, policy designers and strategists broaden the input from HR. Their continued tenure means they are perceived as adding value to the organisation to support the performance of employees and the organisation.

Public sector and third sector (not-for-profit) HR practitioners can sometimes feel undervalued in academic research, which typically focuses on those organisations seeking profit. In this chapter we argue that all HR managers, irrespective of their organisation's fundamental aims, 'add value' and support the performance of the relevant organisation and its employees. We will explore this important notion in depth using examples from a variety of contexts.

Taking the concept of context further, we explore international and global HRM, presenting the practical issues of locus of control (how far the organisation controls from head office or allows localisation), and the movement of staff overseas by the use of expatriates and other forms of staffing (Collings and Isichei, 2018; Patel et al, 2019). Some expensive techniques are used by organisations for staffing overseas, often with little understanding of the benefits accruing to the organisation. Throughout this chapter, the relationship of HR practice and the interface between line managers and specialist HRPs is discussed, as we regard this link as a highly salient issue for the management and development of people in all types of organisations.

4.2 Introduction

Chapters 1, 2 and 3 outlined the main influences on HRM and HRD with regard to managing and developing people. In this chapter the focus changes in several ways. First, we will build on the concept of HR 'adding value', introduced in Chapters 2 and 3. We re-examine the original concept of 'value-added' and the ways in which HR can contribute in this regard. As we saw in Chapters 2 and 3, discussion on the potential role and contribution of HRPs has continued over a long period of time, for example Ulrich (1997), Warech and Tracey (2004) and Boxall and Purcell (2008) among others. The debate continues in the 2020s with one recent contribution introducing the notion of HR co-creation, whereby HR works collaboratively to develop HR practices with other organisational stakeholders with a view to enhancing value to the organisation (Hewett and Shantz, 2021). In this chapter we will revisit the notion of adding value through a narrowing of focus to specific types of organisation thereby illustrating, with examples, how the nature of the challenges within HR can vary enormously depending on the specific situation.

In the second section of the chapter, we will broaden our scope to an international focus in order to examine the management and leadership of people in multi-country organisations (Bird and Mendenhall, 2016). It is not only when operating from sites in other countries that international understanding is needed. When one is sending employees abroad to work on assignments, or using staff employed by organisations based in countries offshore, there is a need to understand the HR implications of increasing geographic scope. With the success of internet-based selling and recruitment, the need for international HRM (IHRM) is now not only the province of large multinationals, but a reality for many smaller organisations and the third sector. Hence practitioners' competence in international and global HR becomes more prevalent than unusual as a means to support the performance of the organisation.

4.3 HR in different contexts

It is essential that all staff contribute to the organisational effort. The work output of some staff such as those in sales is highly tangible and their contribution to the organisation's goals obvious. But what of HR practitioners? As a service function, one needs to be explicit in order to identify the organisational benefit from their work (Peccei and Van De Voorde, 2019). HRM as a profession is connected to employees and their outputs regarding the organisation (Huselid, 1995). As we saw in Chapter 2, our understanding of how employees contribute has previously largely been driven by the resource based view (see Boxall and Purcell, 2015 and Collins, 2021). Within this perspective the value of the organisation is created from resources, including employees, the CEO and HR practitioners who are intricately involved in delivering such value (Glover and Butler, 2012). In recent years HR has seen a dramatic shift in the importance of delivering HR policy and practice changes due to the profoundly changing nature of work resulting from the global Covid-19 pandemic and also impacted by Brexit. The recently coined term 'agile HR' reflects an HR operational strategy (McMackin and Heffernan, 2021) intended to meet the challenges HR practitioners face in responding to the rapidly changing nature of work while increasing value to the organisation. Arguably, HR have been at the front line of business creating a greater appreciation for the strategic role of the HR function to enable business to shift work arrangements (in some cases literally) overnight.

The notion of 'value' in contemporary strategic thinking was developed by the strategist Michael Porter, who saw those in the organisation adding value in a cumulative 'value chain' (1985). As an economist he saw 'value' being related through performance of resources (including staff) to profits. Regardless of whether the organisation is private, voluntary or public, the importance of managing performance is of paramount focus to employees, a purpose linked directly to enhancing profits or surpluses. However, the labour market is experiencing a time of increased competition reflected in the CIPD Labour Market Outlook survey (CIPD, 2021b). The results of this Autumn 2021 survey indicate rising pay pressures may persist in difficult-to-fill vacancies creating a dilemma in terms of enhancing profits in the short-term versus the long-term gain of having resources in place.

Porter suggests that value is added in two ways: either by reducing costs (hence leading to a higher profit margin); or by adding features and benefits which clients and customers value and are willing to pay for and, although they cost more to deliver, can be charged for at a premium, hence adding to the profit margin. A similar idea was put forward by Kim and Mauborgne (2005) in their conceptualisation of Red Ocean and Blue Ocean strategies – see Chapter 3.

Applying Porter's guidance to the HR context of managing and developing people reveals a multitude of ways in which added value can be achieved. Although public sector and third sector organisations do not usually seek to make profits, they are immensely budget-conscious, especially in the strictures of austerity measures periodically implemented by governments. Hence, we need to pay attention to how they can use Porter's fundamentals of adding value. Being publicly funded, such organisations have to take care with all expenditure. Given that many public-sector institutions carry a staff cost of at least 50 per cent of their overall budget as they are usually in a service capacity, the role of HR should be fundamental (see Knies et al, 2018 for a review). Value can be added by a reduction in overall expenditure after savings are made in an area or doing more with the same staff, or by developing staff so that the service they provide outweighs the cost of the development.

Let us consider the public sector. Given that wages are such a major cost, HR can influence added value by contributing to projects which reduce staff costs. This might be through helping line managers reorganise work or job roles so that the same can be done with less. For example, local councils conduct much business using digital technology with their residents – meaning initial investment in website design, equipment and training existing staff, but eventual savings as automation takes effect such as reducing costs for electoral services by collecting annual canvass data through electronic tablets reducing data entry. Other initiatives to enhance communication with employees, often working from home, have been led by employee engagement strategies, including peer to peer recognition, facilitated by HR, enabled by greater use of technology. The Ordinance Survey office moved to a much smaller building after recruiting and training staff (over a long period) competent in technologically based mapping, reducing the need for a paper-based library of maps and bulky equipment. The organisation leveraged developments in mapping that, combined with HR practices, delivered sustainably lower-cost platform job designs meaning that this generation of staff can do more with less space. Value has been added through reducing costs.

Truss and Gill (2009) investigated the process that HR delivered in the UK public sector, exploring the issues of social capital, perceived added value and HR process through in-depth interviews at two NHS hospitals and two local councils. Their study found both value-adding and value-reducing examples. Value is reduced when extra costs are incurred that cannot be passed onto the customer, thus lowering effectiveness. Perceptions of value reduction in their study included poor union–employer relationships, which led to stagnation and blocks to change. Poor time boundaries within recruitment were an example where line managers saw HR as reducing value through the loss of good candidates (p 679), and inconsistency in HR personnel in providing their internal services was always seen negatively (p 680).

One can see how this would add to costs as line managers and senior staff sought to use the HR department members they trusted and who had a reputation for delivering processes, while avoiding those less reliable. Timely responding by the HR department in the delivery of processes was perceived as value-adding by non-HR managers in all areas.

It appeared that a visible and proactive HR leader was highly influential on how HR was perceived. In most cases the HR strategic contributions were acknowledged as solid; it was in the detail of more day-to-day process where value was not positive, and also through inconsistency of personnel. Their study included HRPs where they correlated stronger performances with a strong sense of identity and purpose such that even if HRPs were working at a level of isolation, they knew the HR strategy and understood their contribution. HR departments which were led less well and had a poor sense of identity and cohesion among members were perceived less well. These lessons are likely to be useful in non-public-sector contexts too as an under-performing staff affects the function's image in a disproportionate way and places extra burden on staff trusted to deliver.

What comes out clearly in the 2021 CIPD People Profession survey, (CIPD, 2021c), is the impact of external factors as driver for change. The normalisation of working from home, whether this is some of the time or full time has created enormous change and challenges to the way we work and the way employees are managed by the HR function. Arguably, the role of HR has never been more paramount to delivering policy and practice that has evolved at a lightning pace supported by progressive digital technology. As such HR has become key to organisations strategy and direction, linking HR practice and business outcomes.

Many local governments are considering how they embrace a hybrid model of working. The CIPD carried out a survey and interviews of employers to assess their views of the business post-crisis (CIPD, 2021d). The findings suggest the public sector will experience the biggest shift in ways of working with over a third of employees expected to work from home regularly. Studies have highlighted the impact of working from home on mental health and wellbeing. Hence sometimes financial constraints can lead to invoking better HR-related practice.

 Reflective activity 4.1

Consider the local authority challenge of supporting workforce wellbeing.

1 In what ways do you think the relationship between line managers and HR may have changed as a result of the new approach?

2 How would staff in your HR department react to enabling hybrid working through managerial discretion?

3 Discuss the strengths and weaknesses of devolving power to the line manager in the public sector.

Turning now to the private sector, the links between HR strategy and business strategy are based on private sector organisations, often taking 'top performing' organisations in a financial sense and then asking about HR practices. It is becoming clear that although researchers do find positive relationships between HR alignment with business strategy and performance, the impact of differing crisis causes further exploration of how HR leaders respond to an increasingly difficult external environment (Collings et al, 2021). The pandemic has created an opportunity to reconsider HRM strategy to adapt to the changing nature of work.

Are the better financial performers just more organised and integrated, or is there something special about the alignment of HR? With regard to costs, the need to be assured that the benefits from spending are optimal raises the issue of whether HR have the analytic skills to be able to undertake such analysis, which is inherently difficult in a constantly changing environment (Collings et al, 2021). HR professionals have responded to the changing environment through developing their skills, the People Profession survey report (CIPD, 2021c) highlights 61 per cent of HR professionals had undertaken upskilling or reskilling to support their organisations.

The need for HR to challenge all types of managers is not new. However, the spotlight on HR professionals to provide direction and value to organisations has arguably never been so prevalent. HR is uniquely positioned to add value as it reaches into all corners of the organisation. The ongoing debate regarding senior staff remuneration packages is a good example. Senior staff use skills (bringing together market knowledge from a range of sources), experience and professional judgement, contributing a key set of competencies that are central to the organisation's strategic success. A highly complex set of (often incomplete) data means the skill of senior staff in decision-making is at a premium. For any organisation in times of austerity there is an argument in favour of paying more for skilled people who will create wealth (value) far beyond the cost of remuneration. This balance has to be weighed carefully and is one in which HR plays a role, bringing its own skills in knowledge and understanding of the implications on all parts of the business.

HRD can be the lynchpin for the achievement of strategies where job redesign is an aspect of implemented business strategies. Job redesign is often at the centre of cost-saving, for example when new technology is implemented (such as picking systems to reduce the number of warehouse staff), and staff cuts where roles need to be reshaped to achieve a lower staff footprint: cost-efficiency and using high-performance work practices fundamentally add value (Katou, Budhwar and Patel, 2021). Such changes are strategic in nature and result in redeployed staff undertaking altered roles, having been retrained and probably under new terms and conditions of service. HR is involved in achieving strategic change, and although it may never serve a customer directly, adds value (Kieran, MacMahon and MacCurtain, 2021) through implementing business strategy.

The differences between the public and private sectors may not be great in many instances. All are about empowerment, learning and training so that responsibilities can be flattened in the hierarchy with cost savings. The value added might be spent in different ways; the hospital may do more with the same number of staff, the distribution firm might expand using the savings from their strategy or pay higher dividends to shareholders. But the strategy was the same, and HR has played a key role, even though the spending of the value added might be very different.

The final sector we consider is the third sector, that is, charitable and voluntary organisations, which often operate in fragile environments, vulnerable to changes in funder behaviour. Most have needed to turn their activities towards different streams of funding and meant they have had to be as nimble as any commercial organisation but are constrained in ways not experienced by for-profit companies.

The sector has expanded as government has retracted from providing direct services, such as in elderly care with provision being delivered by private and third sector organisations (Thompson, Williams and Kwong, 2017). There is a blurring between public, private and third sector (Bromley and Meyer, 2017) with far more private-sector organisations working within third sector constraints. We now turn to the challenges for HR to add value in the third sector context.

Without doubt, issues to do with recruitment can be especially tough in this sector. Many charities engage volunteers, and HR has an important role in ensuring these individuals are treated well outside of the parameters of the traditional employment contract, and that value is added (Alfes, Antunes and Shantz, 2017). It is usually the case that third sector pay at all levels, being open to scrutiny by funders and the public alike, is low (Cunningham, 2008). How does one attract and retain talent in such contexts? How does one fund training and other learning opportunities in order to develop staff when budgets are commonly connected in discrete ways to deliverable projects? How far can 'rewarding work' be used or abused? The sector is poorly researched from an HR perspective, although with the development of the non-profit sector, a trickle of research is now being published (see Bartram, Cananagh and Hoye, 2017).

Central to issues around funding and reward of employees is the relationship between the third sector group and other agencies with which it partners. In elderly care the partner might be a local council; in education, a government department; in research it may be the NHS or specific benefactors. It is common that funders impose terms and conditions on those agencies which deliver services (Cunningham and James, 2017), thus leaving the third sector provider little room for movement in some HR policy. In addition, competitive tendering for third sector contracts may mean those involved with negotiating contracts have to be very lean with their highest cost factor, that is, employees (ibid). As funding is based on contracts typically lasting one to two years, substantial long-term investment or investment in potential new areas of work through HRD can be difficult to resource.

Reflective activity 4.2

Funding HRD activities in the third sector can be problematic, especially providing learning events for the many staff who are on low wages. The Children's Society takes advantage of a strong link with the trade union UNITE. In several instances, the charity enabled a few employees (who are often workplace trade union representatives) to attend UNITE training, who then cascaded the knowledge and skills through the Society at far lower cost than external providers, but to exacting standards.

The Children's Society is quite a large charity. How might a small charity enable learning and development to be funded or delivered at low cost?

Some areas of HR add value directly in any organisation; for example, in the provision or overseeing of administrative tasks connected to people, for example wage systems, pensions, employment records, benefits and rewards systems. These are fundamental to the functioning of all organisations. However, they are often seen as 'hygiene factors' and so not necessarily valued when everything goes well, but heavily criticised when they fail to perform. Few employees are grateful for being paid on time, but most would be unhappy if wages arrived late! Their effectiveness provides value and ineffectiveness causes cost, thus reducing value.

Without doubt HR adds value through some of the roles described by Ulrich and Brockbank (2005). It is always valued for its contribution in keeping the organisation in compliance with legal requirements (the HR expert), and HR specialists have developed into providing policy advice and implementation at a strategic level (HR strategists). Moreover, HR adds value through continued evolvement with business imperatives (Ellehave and Ulrich, 2021).

The data for the performance value (financial and otherwise) created by HR professionals are difficult to study with certainty (Saridakis, Lai and Cooper, 2017) as if one uses broad-brush measures (such as return on capital employed) many non-employee components are involved, thus making a 'straight line' between HR involvement and organisation-level performance measures to be impossible to measure with. Many HR initiatives concern longer-term development where an outcome (such as learning) might take many years to impact directly (Garavan, McCarthy and Carbery, 2019) and hence shorter-term value might be perceived in more fluid terms as a function of 'return on expectations' by senior and line managers (Garavan, McCarthy and Carbery, 2019). On the other hand, HR-based initiatives which are well communicated as aligned with strategy and agile (see, Ahammad, Glaister and Gomes, 2020) can make the case through clear articulation alone. It is therefore a positive reflection on the maturing of our profession that there is recognition of learning and development professional's importance at the heart of supporting organisational challenges (CIPD, 2021e).

 Reflective activity 4.3

Consider a recent major change in your organisation.

1 Could this have been undertaken without HR input?

2 What was the nature of that input (with regard to that specific type of organisation) and did it add value through reducing costs further or achieving the change more efficiently or effectively?

4.4 HR roles as the organisation grows: SMEs

The function of HR is needed in all organisations beyond the simple formation of a partnership between two or more individuals. Many small organisations do not see the need to employ an HR specialist and, forever cost-conscious, tend not to directly employ HR assistance until it is really needed – perhaps as a result of hygiene factors not being met. Instead, HR might be outsourced to an HR consultant retained for policy and administrative tasks with their legal expertise enabling the small organisation to adhere to regulations. The small business is highly reliant on the skills and knowledge of such consultants, and is dependent on the provider being effective. Many HR consultants do excellent work with small businesses, often beginning with a limited and legalistically geared brief and patiently expanding their role into organisational development, HRD and other facets of delivery as the organisation is successful. Indeed, contact with HR consultants is sometimes the only space when owner-managers of small businesses take time away from their operational focus to consider their staff in a systematic and future-oriented manner.

The next evolutionary step is to hire an HR generalist to service the small firm, and logically occurs when it is cost-effective to do so. A small business generalist needs by default to be a jack of all trades (perhaps with the exception of legal support) and undertake (or at least co-ordinate) all HR roles. HR generalists may not be providing very sophisticated services, but it is likely they will be closely aligned with the business as their day-to-day activities are immersed with those connected to clients, suppliers and the product/service to be delivered. Short lines of communication and close contact with leadership should mean fast delivery of change. Naturally, the agenda will be limited in scope and subject to tight funding, but the capacity to add value focused on the business is very high.

Greiner (1972) suggests that as organisations grow they pass through a series of crises. Almost like a squeeze-box movement, the locus of control is central. Most small business-owners like to have control, but this can become more difficult as the organisation grows, failing to deliver optimal effectiveness as the owner-manager becomes a bottleneck of decisions and checking employees' work. In some senses many small businesses reflect the 'hard HR' model (see Boselie, Brewster and Paauwe, 2009, for a review of the Michigan approach). A resolution of this early Greiner crisis for small business sees a middle line of managers having more autonomy to enable growth.

It is possible at this time to move into more staff development as typified by the 'soft HR' Harvard school (Boselie, Brewster and Paauwe, 2009), although hard HR may predominate. But greater autonomy risks fragmentation as the organisation may grow in different ways under the direction of a team of sub-unit leaders, leading to a crisis of control. Greiner's next crisis is therefore a need to pull things back into a more coherent whole again. Even at this stage, as often SMEs do not devolve much decision-making, the HR generalist has only a few key managers to deal with. Unitarism is assumed, and the atmosphere is often still patriarchal (Legge, 2005), especially if the owner-manager is still in charge. If a full-time HR professional has not been hired before now, it is likely this crisis sets the scene to do so whether the organisation is for-profit or not (see Ridder, Piening and Baluch, 2012 for a review).

In what way can the generalist HR practitioner provide value for the SME? Boxall and Purcell (2015) are clear that beyond the standard HR administration, the focus of any HR activity, if it is to be aligned into the organisation strategy, needs to focus on areas rich in human capital. Hence, HR can provide insight on focusing effort to those who create the value which is essential for strategic success. Thus, an importer geared to growth through extending market share can focus on rewards connected to performance targets with appraisal and feedback to those sourcing and selling products as the nexus of HRM strategy. A professional firm of knowledge workers may have a different focus such as that of HRD opportunities and an emphasis on work–life balance as a means to recruit, retain and foster performance in the professional's key to delivering the organisational offering.

In the medium-sized organisation, HR professionals thinking through these 'bundles' (Selden and Sowa, 2015) for the organisation can add great value. But, as the firm grows, it is likely that so too will the number of HR professionals, with evolution into better defined roles (as described by Ulrich (1997)). However, as the medium-sized organisation works its way through the growth cycles, the final stage Greiner suggests is a 'crisis of red tape' as bureaucracy has been used to co-ordinate the organisation. Recent research suggests perceived red tape negatively impacts aspects of HR such as recruitment (Bach et al, 2021).

 Case study 4.1

Aurora's HR challenges

Aurora has 200 employees and is a worldwide leader in yacht insurance worldwide, based in Cowes on the Isle of Wight. Careful stewardship through the early years, and the retraction of mainstream insurers from the niche, has allowed steady growth. Online advertising links customers to the call centre (100 staff), which also deals with initial claims.

Each staff area has a board director. There is an underwriting and claims group (40 staff), the marketing department works with IT (15 staff), and the finance department (18 staff) is under the direct control of the CEO, who is a qualified accountant.

Aurora has a differentiated strategy – not the cheapest in the market, but reliable for reasonable claims.

The firm employs three HR practitioners who also oversee the building and non-IT facilities. One looks after recruitment – with call centre staff being a main headache – one deals with HR administration and facility issues, and the third, Elena Papas, is the HR director dealing with policy and strategic issues, and also helps out her line-reports. Call centre staff are trained by an external provider.

The Covid-19 pandemic crisis affected the company's financial standing at first, but with the return of corporate stability the retention of established customers has been excellent, and in 2021 there has only been a 20 per cent drop through customers giving up their expensive hobby. But new customers are looking for cheaper deals and 'dodgy claims' are increasing from this cadre. These dynamics have led to stagnation in sales, and internal tensions are rising in the firm as non-payment of claims has affected the company's reputation in the close-knit boating community.

Elena has been challenged that the once-positively regarded 'professional' practices in HR (e.g. clear job description, target-setting and performance appraisal systems) are tying everyone down far too much as 'belts need to be tightened'.

1 How can Elena respond to these pressures?
2 In what other ways can she and her team add value at this time of stagnation?

The larger organisation holds different challenges for HR. Diversification may mean different strategies in different sub-units and human capital investment may vary across the organisation (Boxall and Purcell, 2011). The drive for efficiencies through standardisation of processes and policies may mean over-bureaucratisation in some cases and insufficient support in others (Boxall and Purcell, 2011); in larger organisations there are many decision-makers, and co-ordination within the HR department may become paramount to gather issues and focus effort. No doubt supported by trends within the external environment, there is a growing set of commentary and research supporting the notion that HR is in danger of short-term opportunistic practices rather than adopting a long-term sustainable contribution to the organisation (Marchington, 2015). As the distance between key areas for attention and HR increases, so gaps may appear. It is perhaps not surprising that the seam of 'critical HR' research (which includes examination of dysfunction between HR effort and what is valued) is undertaken almost always in large organisations (Truss and Gill, 2009; De Vos and Meganck, 2009) and there is a gap in systematic research knowledge of what goes on in the smaller set-up. One might see that co-ordination activities within HR costs salaries, but the effect a synergistic team can provide can make a real difference (Becker and Huselid, 2006).

There has been a trend over the last couple of decades away from vertical integration (where one owns all aspects of the organisation) towards outsourcing and supply-chain management. A common technique in large organisations, but how far can HR be outsourced? The strategy literature suggests that when outsourcing, it is only those aspects of the organisation that do not contribute to strategic success which should be considered – otherwise one has competitive competency owned by others. Many CIPD surveys show that payroll administration is commonly outsourced by organisations of all sizes – a specialist firm can often provide payroll cheaper than in-house. Other aspects of HR are far more contentious. How far should training and other learning events be outsourced? If knowledge is central to the product or service being offered, surely HRD must be provided in-house?

 Reflective activity 4.4

Visit the CIPD website at www.cipd.co.uk. Look through the collection of surveys and related articles on outsourcing there. Pick one function of HR that is contentious in terms of being outsourced and show how it is controversial. At this point you may wish to look at Chapter 5 and the discussion there on professionalism and ethics in HR.

1 Are the factors to be considered the same for private, public and third sector organisations?
2 Can HR ever be entirely outsourced and, if not, which aspects of HR should always remain in-house?
3 Give reasons for your conclusions.

Outsourcing in HR is a debate that will no doubt continue (Mishra et al, 2018; Patel et al, 2019). An interesting set of data is shown by Wahrenburg et al (2006), displaying variation across the portfolio of HR activities, and is echoed in the recent People Profession 2021 survey (CIPD, 2021c). As one would expect, clerical functions are far more likely to be outsourced than senior management advice. They found variation between industries, with some commonality within an industry (they examined finance in particular). We would argue that if the whole of HR is outsourced it is seen as a commodity, adding no strategic value, then in some senses the profession could fail. However, Patel et al (2019) offer some useful insights in their attempt to investigate the effects of outsourcing and development of the strategic position of HR departments. One must recognise that some strategic advice will come from consultants who have broadened activities from being auditors and advising on finance to helping with cost and value-added. If HR is entirely outsourced, clearly the message from the architects of the organisation is that HR as a function is not seen as central to the management and leadership of people in providing competitive advantage. However, the unprecedented challenges of the external environment have created significant opportunities for HR leaders to reinforce the central role HR has to the organisation and its performance (McKinsey & Company, 2021).

The shift into and out of outsourcing has provided a highly variegated situation for HR practitioners and those seeking a career in HR. Opportunities for roles exist within all sectors, either fully employed by an organisation or acting as a consultant independently or as part of an outsourced agency. In the end the HR function is delivered. But how the value is created and by whom varies. Any internal HR function relies on the interaction with the business and ensuring HR practitioners have the skills to interact with the business is crucial (Collins, 2021).

 Reflective activity 4.5

A small law firm is having difficulty attracting and retaining lawyers in a provincial office overseas. It currently has no in-house HR function. The partner in charge has decided to introduce hybrid working in line with the larger competitors.

1 Brief the management team on how hybrid working could be introduced and managed.
2 How could they utilise HR input to assist with their goal?

4.5 Expanding our borders: the growth of internationalisation

The use of technology supported by the internet has created a connected, international framework that has changed the scope for recruitment, working and operations at a fundamental level. Such advances mean that national borders are being crossed by even small organisations who now find foreign markets offer the staff they need, or customers who might want their organisations' products and services. Thus, the portfolio of skills needed in managing and leading people is becoming an international arena, and one for which the HR professional needs to be prepared. It is to the international context that our attention now turns.

Why do we need to explore global strategy in HRM? HR as part of the strategic component delivering organisational strategy is increasingly breaking national borders (Farndale et al, 2018). With wider globalisation, HR is under pressure to deliver policies and practices that will support the business objectives of the organisation and demonstrate results in an increasingly competitive economic environment. Working alongside the other business functions such as finance, operations and corporate departments, HR have to understand how they can help to deliver the vision to the business in an international context.

Changes to demographics (North, 2019), such as an ageing workforce and the emergence of developing countries, mean that looking towards future staffing may require an international approach. We see more organisations requiring staff to be internationally mobile. Organisations compete for talent across the globe as individuals broaden their search for the best employment opportunities, globalising recruitment markets. Those organisations with sites overseas require an understanding of the complexities involved with managing staff internationally and the impact this has upon the global HR strategy.

Global staffing can play a key role in shaping the competitive position of multinational enterprises (MNEs), via individuals' transfer of knowledge across the organisation, which is often cited as one of the main reasons to undertake an international assignment. Additionally, the widely accepted reasons for transferring staff from one country to another include developing the individuals' management or leadership skills, knowledge of markets or products or to strengthen the organisation's international competencies (Vlajčić et al, 2019).

Much of the research in IHRM focuses upon the management of staff within MNEs and involves the study of expatriates, but it can also apply to small and medium-sized enterprises (SMEs) and a broader definition of international staff.

4.6 Strategic international HRM

The trend over the last few years has been to attempt to link IHRM to the strategy of the organisation in line with fulfilling the company's global objectives (strategic international HRM: SIHRM) (Fan et al, 2021).

 Reflective activity 4.6

HSBC defines itself as 'The World's Local Bank' in its marketing. Visit HSBC's websites and examine their corporate messages.

1 What effect does this international branding have on HR in the UK?

2 Given its messages, how would you approach someone in a London office of the firm to undertake an overseas assignment in a subsidiary in Detroit for two years?

4.6.1 Defining strategic international HRM

In order to highlight the context of SIHRM, a definition is needed. Schuler et al define SIHRM as:

> *human resource management issues, functions, and policies and practices that result from the strategic activities of multinational enterprises and that impact the international concerns and goals of those enterprises.* (1993, p 422)

The definition brings together a number of factors that includes literature from international business and management, as well as IHRM: 'In essence, MNEs are firms that need to be global and local (multi-domestic) at the same time' (Schuler et al 1993, p 421).

Schuler et al (1993) explore this notion through the development of an integrative framework to further our understanding of SIHRM. The development of a framework leads to including three major components: issues, functions and policies and practices, which in turn are influenced by MNEs' strategic activities. These are discussed below.

SIHRM issues

The organisation needs to decide how much control it allows the local business while considering that this may vary depending on the local environment. Cultural differences play a part in the decision as to which approach the organisation will pursue. HRM plays an important role within the organisation in terms of integrated or differentiating practices.

SIHRM functions

The function relates to human resource orientation; the time, energy and financial resources operating the human resource organisation; and the locations of the resources. There are several ways that the company may choose to manage its human resources. For example, all HR policy and practice activities are handed down from the headquarters of the MNE. In contrast, local divisions are able to tailor HR practices that are more locally accepted, such as promotion criteria.

SIHRM policies and practices

Policies and practices involve developing general guidelines on how individuals will be managed and developed within the organisation. For example, the HR policy may outline the reward structure and instruct all sites to pay the local median for certain grades of employees. However, it may be part of the company's overall strategy to take into consideration the nuances within a particular environment. For example, providing specific practices that are appropriate to the local market such as incentivised pay schemes or specific talent sectors. Indeed, there may be particular local requirements that will impact upon HR policy and practices in terms of legislation such as a minimum wage, etc. Therefore, a single policy acts as a guide while consideration is provided as to local terms and culture.

It can be seen that one thread throughout the issues, functions and policies described above is that of the degree of localisation allowed by the parent office. Organisations vary enormously as to how far this is granted, and it may not be standard across the whole organisation (Farndale et al, 2019). But how does international or global HRM differ from domestic HRM? As HR practices are complicated by the practicality of applying internationally understanding IHRM's development is useful. There are different types of employees to consider, such as host-country nationals (HCNs), parent-country nationals (PCNs) and third-country nationals (TCNs).

Let us use the illustration of IBM, where the parent organisation is based in the USA. It has offices in the UK, where British employees would be seen as HCNs. It might also have staff from the USA (PCNs) and employ specialist staff from anywhere in the world who are neither British nor American nationals (TCNs). The international context introduces different ways in which these employees are employed, such as: expatriates (the USA manager takes a two-year job in the UK, but is still employed by the parent office); inpatriates (coming from a subsidiary into headquarters – in our example a UK manager taking a two-year contract to work in IBM in the USA but still employed through the British office); hybrid arrangements or on local conditions, where a foreign national decides to be employed directly by the local organisation.

 Reflective activity 4.7

Your organisation, a UK-based telecoms company employing 100 people, wants to expand its market share in South Africa, and opens a dedicated office in Johannesburg as part of its long-term strategy. The office will provide the hub for future training of local employees. Advise the organisation on which strategy would achieve its aims to introduce the headquarters culture and ethos in terms of work practices to the new office. The current HR function is served by one consultant with part-time administration support.

Which of the following approaches would you advise and why?

- Use a two-year long-term assignment, traditional expatriate package.

- Use a short-term assignment.

- Hire someone locally and provide them with some headquarters training.

- Employ someone from the headquarters on local terms and conditions.

It is useful at this point to highlight the various staffing strategies that global organisations utilise. Influences towards staffing strategies were first addressed by Perlmutter (1969) and later extended to provide the following approaches to global staffing (Heenan and Perlmutter, 1979):

- *Ethnocentric* – strategic decisions are made by the headquarters by PCN expatriates. Therefore, it is accepted that all policies and practices emanate from the headquarters. Arguably, the advantage is that qualified managers are available from the home country (precluding any local labour shortage). However, this approach does limit the opportunity to promote HCNs to senior managerial positions, thus risking the loss of staff with this potentially short-term view.

- *Polycentric* – generally the operations would be managed by HCNs with the intention that they remain in the host country, precluding the use of expensive expatriates from the parent company. There are disadvantages to this approach in the limiting of assignments by home or host, reducing knowledge transfer and management.

- *Geocentric* – this approach seeks to resource the best person for the position regardless of their nationality.

- *Regiocentric* – some autonomy is reflected in this approach towards decision-making.

This approach is likely to facilitate more local responsiveness towards operation and form regional boundaries according to geographic location, such as Eastern Europe, the Mediterranean, the USA, etc. Both polycentric and regiocentric approaches allow for more local responsiveness, with less corporate integration. However, the danger is that there is knowledge being built in subsidiaries by HCNs which the parent does not benefit from, at a risk of losing competitive edge.

Many of these strategies ask people to work overseas. The term 'expatriate' refers to someone who is temporarily assigned to an overseas location from their home organisation. Some organisations refer to such individuals as 'international assignees'.

Traditionally, expatriate assignments are considered to fall into either long-term assignment over 12 months to a maximum of four years; short-term assignments lasting three to 12 months; or business trips typically lasting no longer than three months.

Long-term assignments are considered to be over 12 months in duration and offer a full compensation package whereby the expatriate is provided host housing, living allowances, removal services, etc. Often in long-term assignments a partner and children will be included in arrangements. In terms of cost it is generally accepted that an assignment will cost the organisation three to four times the expatriate's salary.

Alternative approaches to limit the cost of an expatriate assignment are becoming more common. According to a PwC survey (2020a), 43 per cent of companies intend to increase international remote working. Their research highlights an increased focus on ensuring the costs and benefits are well understood by the business.

 Reflective activity 4.8

If the costs for the use of expatriates are so high, what arguments are there for such assignments to be used by organisations?

The rationale for an overseas assignment should always be considered. MNEs often favour a long-term assignment when the objective is to commence business operations in an overseas location. However, a smaller organisation may not have the resources to utilise a long-term assignment as that individual is intrinsic to the home company. Therefore, the strategy of staffing may well differ depending on the size of the organisation.

 Case study 4.2

Technologies Inc. (TI)

The move to reduce costs has seen a decline in the number of long-term assignments, with organisations utilising short-term assignments and business trips instead. Collecting data in this area holds many challenges and long-term case studies are rare.

In order to understand the cost involved in its expatriate programme, TI outsourced the administration of its expatriates. In 2018 TI had approximately 1,000 expatriates, costing over $70 million. Over the next three years, the company reduced the number of expatriates to around 300 expatriates. In order to achieve this large reduction in headcount TI looked at alternative ways of resourcing positions, favouring the local market. In addition, a review of its policy and expatriate package has seen large-scale reduction in benefits offered, to reduce costs by 70 per cent to over $20 million.

TIs example raises some interesting points. Until the company decided to outsource its expatriate programme it had not considered the actual costs; it knew expatriates were expensive but did not realise the extent. The challenge of tracking expatriates is echoed by many MNEs.

1 How would you recommend TI assess the success of its programme, other than the reduction of cost for its expatriate programme?
2 What do you think the effect of reducing the number of expatriate opportunities could have been at TI head office?
3 How would you be able to track such effects?
4 What effect might you want to look for in the various subsidiaries?
5 How might you measure the impact?

4.6.2 Short-term assignments

The move towards cost reduction has contributed towards the increase in short-term assignments and business trips. Instead of providing an expatriate package that allows the employee to take their immediate family on assignment, the organisation supports only the assignee. Costs are saved by precluding education costs as well as reduced housing costs (as the expatriate is not accompanied by their family) and further allowances associated with a long-term assignment such as family healthcare insurance. Thus, the employee is sent overseas with minimal support and cost.

Reflective activity 4.9

Consider this description: Green Inc., a provider of reusable energy systems to large industrial corporations has started sending more employees on short-term assignments. Assignments are with producers of equipment sold by Green Inc. and to install equipment systems into purchasers' sites. Typically, assignments last for six months and are managed as a business trip. The employee stays in a hotel and is reimbursed for meals and trips home every other month, eliminating the need to pay costly housing allowances and costs related to moving the employee's family.

The previous strategy placed the employee on two-year assignments accompanied by their family. The assignee would have had several projects running in this time.

1   What effect would this change have had on the type of applicants for the job?
2   What effect would the change have had on recipients of the services of these assignees in the host country?
3   Would any of these changes worry you from an HR perspective?
4   How would you advise Green Inc. to proceed?

4.6.3 Third-country nationals

A third-country national (TCN) is an individual who works for an international organisation and whose nationality is different from that of the company, and of the country, in which the organisation operates. For example, a UK manager working for a Spanish subsidiary of an American company. The advantages of TCNs from the company's point of view are that they require the provision of very limited additional assistance, such as housing, and education tax, and only for a restricted period.

4.6.4 Localisation

Another alternative to an expatriate assignment is the use of localisation. This is where expatriates move permanently to local terms and conditions, and it has seen an increase over the last decade (McNulty et al, 2019). This could be at the end of a long- or short-term assignment at the choice of the individual, or that an individual was sent on assignment with the expectation that they would localise with minimal support from the company. The move towards recruiting expatriates on the basis that they will localise from the beginning is not new, especially within the 30-year-old-plus market. However, what has changed is the push to hire employees locally and not use expatriates at all – here the local employer might take on someone who lives only miles from the parent company but who is never employed by the parent. The benefit to the organisation is the significant saving in expatriate terms and conditions, especially education and housing costs. An emerging trend of hybrid packages allows expatriates access to some of the expatriate package initially to set them up in the new country and then gradually remove the benefits during the year, such as help with rented accommodation.

4.6.5 *Self-initiated expatriates*

An increasingly explored area is self-initiated expatriates (Howe-Walsh and Schyns, 2010; Sinha, Patel and Prikshat (2021). A self-initiated expatriate (SIE) independently moves to another country for employment. As such, SIEs do not receive any additional support from their home country employer. However, there are opportunities to manage this growing pool of resources more effectively. Research has shown that self-initiated expatriates themselves note several combined reasons for pursuing an overseas appointment: career development; location of vacancy; no family ties; dissatisfaction with current lifestyle; timing (Fitzgerald and Howe-Walsh, 2008). Who manages these types of staffing arrangements can often become blurred. While the self-initiated expatriate will be treated as an ordinary new joiner, other support mechanisms can be put in place to support their initial move. There are additional considerations to explore regarding the level of support the HR function can offer during the recruitment phase. In traditional expatriate assignment services such as cultural training and language, etc would be offered prior to the assignment.

Howe-Walsh and Schyns (2010) show how different types of adjustment require the use of differing HR practices. In order to make the most of self-initiated expatriates, consideration of how the organisation can aid their initial adjustment can provide a strategic advantage over companies that do not provide support by attracting good candidates. The points below are highlighted as areas to explore in order to improve the process of recruitment and retaining self-initiated expatriates.

Recruitment strategy

Developing the reputation of the organisation as an employer of choice attracts candidates, thus assisting with recruitment of talent (Dutta, Mishra and Varma, 2021). Selecting the right candidates poses challenges for any organisation. Self-initiated expatriates offer additional benefits to the organisation during the early stages of their employment as they are already receptive to working in an overseas location. Additionally, they have chosen the organisation and the position offered, rather than 'being sent' on an assignment. Women are particularly open to becoming SIEs as a means to enhance their career (Andersen, Biemann and Pattie, 2015) at different life stages (Haak-Saheem, Hutchings and Brewster, 2021). This is partly explained due to lack of career progression in their current country of work.

Training and mentoring

While new joiners are often provided with some sort of induction training it is unlikely that an SIE will be offered any cultural training for the reasons outlined above. However, the benefits of mentoring should be considered. Differing types of support can be provided by developing a social network within the host country (Kubovcikova and van Bakel, 2022). HR can facilitate mentoring proactively to gain such a social network.

Non-work support

The types of activities that HR would traditionally support for an expatriate should also be considered in terms of self-initiated expatriates. Finding accommodation can be one of the most stressful parts of relocation. HR can provide support in terms of facilitating the search for properties as well as assistance with tenancy agreements. Other forms of support include: opening bank accounts; social security and residence registration; communication connections; and expatriate social groups. When facilitated, these types of support enable the SIE to start work faster and add value to the organisation.

4.6.6 Global/international HRM and the SME

The discussion so far has revolved around MNEs. Arguably, however, much business conducted today is undertaken by SMEs, many of whom have a global dimension, often levered through technology, but with implications for the HR function. As IHRM literature is mainly focused upon MNEs, there is an argument that transferability of HRM practices from MNEs to SMEs is limited (Crowley-Henry, O'Connor and Suarez-Bilbao, 2020). Drawing upon the research of MNE organisations, SMEs pose different challenges (Crowley-Henry, O'Connor and Suarez-Bilbao, 2020). SMEs are more dependent upon environmental situations in different countries.

- The importance of the founder/owner influences the development of HRM strategy of the organisation (Garavan et al, 2015; Flamini, Pittino and Visintin, 2021). Within any organisation there are links to how the organisation is perceived and their leader (Hubner, Rudic and Baum, 2021). Within an SME the owners' entrepreneurial style and the way they conduct business can be part of the attraction of working for the organisation.

- Recruitment, selection and retention within an SME is likely to be managed without the assistance of an HR function as much more informal processes are utilised with the owner/CEO often responsible for recruitment and selection (Crowley-Henry, O'Connor and Suarez-Bilbao, 2020).

The most striking difference between MNEs and SMEs is that the SMEs do not have the same HRD infrastructure capability, as mentioned above. Therefore, sending managers overseas to open or start new business ventures is not supported by an HR function locally or any specialists at the parent organisation. Being able to construct value-adding arguments for managing a limited number of staff overseas becomes more difficult in such circumstances (Garavan et al, 2015).

4.6.7 Who is responsible for international HR policy?

Traditionally within MNEs, IHR policy and practice is undertaken by specialists, either as part of the HR team or partially or fully outsourced, as outlined in Case study 3.2. The decision of what policies the company chooses to adopt towards its international workforce ultimately rests with the organisation's overall strategy. Thus, from the outset there are issues with retention and monitoring the expatriate's career path.

4.6.8 Devolution to line managers

With increased devolution to line managers, it is important to consider the perceptions of more than one stakeholder. We have already noted that HR delivery of international services may be internal to the HR function, a separate specialised function or outsourced. It is increasingly becoming the norm with MNEs that HR policy and practice delivery is undertaken by the line manager (López-Cotarelo, 2018). In an international context, the likelihood within an MNE is that there will be a duplication of stakeholders within the home country and host country. The multiple stakeholders involved in managing individuals across more than one country add another dimension to managing people. A greater understanding of the stakeholders highlights the necessity for clear and transparent strategy supported by HR policy and practice.

4.7 Conclusion

In concluding this chapter, one can see that approaches for delivering support for managing and developing people becoming more complex as the organisation expands in terms of the number of employees, the scope of the organisation, and its geographical reach. We have examined how the emphasis on what an HR practitioner actually does vary with the size, stage in development and sector of the organisation being served.

Adding value from HR is possible in all circumstances to support the performance of employees and the organisation. Although much is made of HR aligning with the strategy of the organisation (see Armstrong and Brown, 2019a), this becomes more difficult as the organisation grows and the physical and psychological distance between HR and decision-makers increases. No doubt an area for development in research is the political skills HR practitioners need to develop in order to influence and ensure that their value-adding ideas are tried by the organisation (Verbrigghe and Buyens, 2015), and that their work receives sufficient profile to make sure it is perceived as value-adding (Shaw, 2021).

We have seen that cutting costs through outsourcing is a common trend, and likely to continue as vertical integration is lessened. HR is not immune from these trends, but if it is to remain a strategic component of success, aspects of HR need to be kept in-house (Patel et al, 2019). The level of outsourcing provides many varied career opportunities for HR practitioners working in providers of services. There is a danger, though, that career paths in these directions may be limited to 'being efficient' only in cost-effective terms rather than adding value in more subtle ways.

International issues are no longer the prerogative solely of large multinationals. Globalised job markets, as well as the opportunities that the internet provides for selling products and services abroad, means that complexity can arrive sooner rather than later for many in the HR function. HR practitioners have to proactively monitor and work towards challenges that are created by the external environment. The past century has provided examples of crises whether for health, recession or war that are sadly often repeated globally. HR has to provide strategic direction to the business to meet such challenges to support the long-term future of the organisation.

KEY LEARNING POINTS

1 The HR function adds value to the organisation in a number of ways through delivering business strategy.

2 The HR function adds value, but how it does so, and who is perceived as adding value, is complex and sometimes a function of internal politics and the perceptions of line managers.

3 The way in which HR adds value changes as the organisation grows, and also between sectors.

4 Outsourcing aspects of HR is common but needs to be done carefully to ensure the organisation does not lose competitive edge.

5 Internationalisation is a current issue for those who recruit, and for those involved in mobilising staff between countries.

6 The degree of control from the parent company in the area of international HR presents a challenge which needs to be balanced depending on the context.

 Review questions

1 Do you think HR professionals at all levels can demonstrate value-added, or is this an issue only for people at the top?

2 What would you see as the challenges of someone changing job from being an HR business partner in the private sector to one in the public sector? How would you suggest such an individual prepares for their new role?

3 Assuming there are financial gains for providing an outsourced HR service, what other parameters would you consider when evaluating this issue?

4 Why is adding an international dimension to one's operation so challenging for HR? Use the example of a UK organisation setting up a sales office in Canada to illustrate your ideas. In this operation some local Canadian staff would be employed but need head office assistance during the set-up period.

Explore further

Armstrong, M and Brown, D (2019b) Strategic human resource management: Back to the future, *Institute for Employment Studies Reports*, pp. 1–36. This review from the Institute for Employment Studies and CIPD provides a comprehensive literature discussing the evolving nature of SHRM and its tendency to rely on academic research that precludes a multi stakeholder perspective.

Collings, DG and Isichei, M (2018) The shifting boundaries of global staffing: Integrating global talent management, alternative forms of international assignments and non-employees into the discussion, *The International Journal of Human Resource Management*, **29** (1), pp 165–87. The authors provide a review of three key contemporary areas of research regarding global mobility. They discuss the emergence of global talent, changing patterns of global mobility, and the emergence of the non-employee as the key alternative in global staffing. The paper provides future avenues of research that highlights the dynamic nature of IHRM literature.

Howe-Walsh, LJ and Schyns, B (2010) Self-Initiated Expatriates: Implications for HRM, *International Journal of Human Resource Management*, **21** (2), pp 260–73. This foundational contribution gives useful insights into the ever-developing area of self-initiated expatriates – a field which has become more important for recruiters in all organisations.

Osland, JS (2022) An Interview with Paula Caligiuri, Pioneer in global leadership effectiveness research. In *Advances in Global Leadership*, Emerald Publishing Limited, Bingley. Paula Caligiuri set the stage and, with Ibraiz Tarique, pioneered the first direct studies on global leadership effectiveness and the boundary conditions that influence it. The interview provides discussion regarding the areas of expatriate management, global leadership development, and cultural agility.

Rickley, M and Stackhouse, M (2022) Global leadership effectiveness: A multi-level review and exploration of the construct domain, in Osland, JS, Reiche, BS, Szkudlarek, B and Mendenhall, ME (eds) *Advances in Global Leadership* (*Advances in Global Leadership, Vol. 14*), Emerald Publishing Limited, Bingley, pp 87–123. Provides a systematic review of the global leadership effectiveness literature providing an inclusive, comprehensive definition of global leadership effectiveness.

05
Professional and ethical people practice

MATTHEW ANDERSON AND CHARLOTTE RAYNER

<u>**LEARNING OUTCOMES**</u>

After reading this chapter, you should be able to:

- understand the foundations of the 'professions'
- understand the role of professional associations
- critically assess the nature of professionalism in people practice and the role of the CIPD
- critically evaluate how data analytics and technological developments present practical and ethical challenges for people professionals
- understand the concept of business ethics
- explain the difference between the duties, consequences and virtues approaches to ethics
- comprehend what is meant by an 'ethical dimension' to the management and leadership of meeting corporate social responsibility (CSR) targets
- discuss the implications for professional leadership in managing and developing people.

5.1 Overview

The Chartered Institute of Personnel and Development (CIPD) is the professional body for HR practitioners in the UK and at the time of writing it asserts there are three key principles for good decision-making regardless of context. The CIPD implicitly points members towards delivering these principles. The first is to provide purposeful work with attributes such as safety, inclusivity and fair reward. The second is to place people at the centre of decision-making because they matter. The final principle concerns the need for practitioners to uphold professional standards and work with integrity and ethical values. Why should any HR practitioner pay attention to the CIPD or other professional standards? This chapter will discuss professionalism and guide the reader in the main pathways of ethical thinking.

While we expect to be able to make a clear case for professionalism and the role of the CIPD, the area of ethics is more complex. Not treating people as well as you can is clearly unethical, and such judgements are straightforward. However, different ethical approaches can lead to different outcomes, all of which can claim to be ethical. It is not only decision makers who engage in ethical judgement. Employees, trade unions and staff associations, shareholders and the public can (and will) make their own judgements. The employer and the HR professional need to have their rationale for the decision ready as it may need to be explained and defended.

Reputation has rarely been as important as it is today. Organisations with negative reputations find staffing difficult and are left firefighting problems which those with better reputations have moved beyond, with cost and productivity benefits following. The reputation of individuals and organisations rests on their ethical profile, their values and of course their actions. Are they consistently doing the best thing, in the best way, with the best motivation? We will see that ethical practice needs thought and therefore costs time and also money. Crucially ethical practice needs to be sustained and sufficiently consistent to reap the benefits of increased trust from employees, customers, suppliers and other stakeholders. Good ethical practice leads into wider societal benefit or corporate social responsibility (CSR) and is linked to mitigation of serious long-term issues such as the climate crisis, modern slavery, supply chain disruptions and resilience. Our stakeholders have choices, and good ethical practice means our reputation will be 'safe' for these stakeholders to want to be involved with us. It is worth the investment, and costly in many ways if we fail.

5.2 Introduction

Is HRM a profession? What does it mean to be a professional? In this chapter we begin by examining what is understood as constituting a profession together with the role of professional bodies such as the CIPD. We show that mature professionalism implies certain ethical standards of behaviour, which, together with systems of training, form a quality assurance system for users of the profession. Sometimes practice is not quite as we would like, and the strains on being an HR professional in contemporary organisations are examined. This initial section forms the basis of our link to the following, more general discussion on ethics.

Ethics must be understood at the conceptual level, but these principles only have meaning if they can be applied. First, we introduce the main conceptual components of ethics and use a variety of examples including equal opportunities to illustrate how ethical debates often run for some time. Indeed, ethical decisions are rarely about simply choosing between right and wrong, but rather between different pathways none of which are perfect. It is crucial that we all grasp the basics of ethics so that we are aware of our actions and the choices we are making.

The chapter then widens its scope to look at ethics beyond immediate employees and into societal, and legacy issues often associated with corporate social responsibility. It is likely that this field will see regulation increasing, hence to be aware of the nature of the major debates is important, although all employment contexts will have specialist needs as well.

This chapter engages directly with the contemporary CIPD focus on proactive HR support to make our organisations good places to work.

5.3 Professions

We need to first examine what a profession is. While the notion of 'profession' goes back many centuries to the social establishment of medical and legal practitioners, we focus here on present-day meanings. Professionals and professionalism are described by Evetts (2013) as implying the involvement of trust which she sees as applying to many occupations: plumbers and electricians as well as lawyers and doctors. Trust may include the handling of sensitive or confidential information, employing expertise and/or expert judgement. Professionals have to be worthy of that trust by acting in the best interests of their clients, not abusing the trust, and maintaining confidentiality. Evetts summarises that 'professions are regarded as essentially the knowledge-based category of service occupations which usually follow a period of tertiary education and vocational training and experience' (Evetts 2013, p781) and imply minimum standards of practice and behaviour. As such, professionalism is a process of quality assurance whereby the professionals adhere to standards and their clients are willing to trust them. The modern emphasis on education and training means that a whole mechanism needs to be in place to establish appropriate standards, communicate these standards, validate and test members of the profession and provide updating – as well as setting up and monitoring processes for complaints and remedial action. Therefore, there is a need for professional associations to coordinate these activities. Traditional professions such as engineering, medicine and the law require practice as well as academic validation such as providing evidence through practice diaries to demonstrate the application of knowledge. This emphasises that it is not just the knowledge base that is important: the application of knowledge is equally critical. The traditional professions often have differentiated branches as their knowledge base has grown too large to be managed simply, as HR practitioners who work with these groups will know.

Professions 'create and maintain distinct professional values or moral obligations … (by) encouraging co-operation as well as practitioner pride and satisfaction in work performance' (Evetts, 2013, p 785). Hence, professionalism is not just about knowledge; it is also about professional attitude and ethics. Crucially, the relevant behavioural and moral standards are set by the professionals themselves, usually working under the umbrella of a professional association adding legitimacy as a body independent from employers. The professional association has grown over years to be an organisation that sets, tests and maintains standards and regulates its own membership as autonomous from the employer. Nevertheless, it is essential the association engages employers and 'customers' to ensure that its work is relevant to need.

Professional associations continue to perform the role of providing credibility to their members through the control of membership (Farndale and Brewster, 2005), although this is a difficult path to tread as the associations are funded by their members. In the end, a strong professional association is respected by consumers, and members of a strong association are proud of their membership and careful to not compromise its reputation. The strength of affiliation felt by members to their professional association will of course vary (Pritchard and Symon, 2011). For some, being 'a professional' will be central to their identity and they will want regular involvement such as attending events and sitting on committees; for others this will be less so (eg Brown, 2015). Umphress, Bingham and Mitchell (2010) showed the stronger the bond to the organisation the more the professionalism ethical pull was ignored. Some associations (such as in the law) require evidence of involvement with the professional association to retain or continue their membership, others require professional updating evidence, while other associations grade membership so that member can choose an appropriate level of commitment.

This is a remarkably lively debate. In 2015 the sociologist Grint challenged the notion that professionalism involved ethics and behaviour codes. He suggested that modern firms wanted only the technical aspect of professionalism, not any social or ethical stewardship which traditional professionalism was associated with and he termed 'social trustee professionalism' (Grint, 2015). An academic literature has grown in recent years on how employers might be shaping (often reducing) values and the social/ethical contribution of their employed professionals, leaving only the knowledge base and raising the question of whether such workers could any more call themselves 'professionals' (eg Aven and Andreassen, 2020). Some professions such as accountancy have had such large-scale scandals that the notion of a few rogue 'rotten apples' perpetuating illegal practice lacks credibility, backing up Umpress Bingham and Mitchell's (2010) findings. If the law is breached (expertise professionalism) there is little hope for nuanced ethical standards and thus wholescale credibility is risked with concomitant drops in trust. New directions in the debate show broadening of both shape and structure, for example by Nordegraaf, (2016) who emphasises the networking role of professionals.

Let us now turn to HRM as our exemplar. Looking through UK advertisements for HRPs, it is clear that CIPD qualifications are required for the majority of posts, and in this sense the CIPD has an enviable reputation in the UK for well-regarded qualifications. Extensive engagement with practitioner members is part of curriculum planning for the CIPD where different levels of membership are linked to the passing of exams and evidence of practice. Administration of exams and provision of support for students entails a complex, effectively run infrastructure. A network of branches ensures that continuing professional development (CPD) is available to UK members. The CIPD measures well in terms of the technical expertise and training elements of professionalism. In the USA the Society of Human Resource Management (SHRM, pronounced 'sherm') is better known for CPD and the co-ordination of large updating events than for its formal qualification structure, and has been far more assertive regarding global spread.

↪ Reflective activity 5.1

Take some time to explore the CIPD website to examine the different membership categories, and reflect on how 'being a professional' includes being part of one's professional association. Read the Code of Professional Conduct too.

1 Why do you think the CIPD includes students in the Code of Professional Conduct?
2 Can one call oneself an HR professional without having CIPD qualifications?
3 Suppose a CIPD member never engages with local branch or national events – would you consider them less 'professional' than someone who does?
4 Explore the CIPD 'Professional Courage and Influence' section. Pay special attention to the areas which encourage you to lead on discussions that may sometimes have opposition, and on generating ownership for mistakes and improvement. How hard are these? What helps?

Being a member of the CIPD and 'acting as a professional' entails far more than passing exams, as indicated in the CIPD Code of Professional Conduct (CIPD, 2020b) and provides a good case study in the professionalism debate (see Roper and Higgins, 2020 for a useful review applied to the CIPD). The CIPD requires a commitment to update professional knowledge, uphold legal thresholds and behave with integrity at all times. In addition, CIPD members are required to 'challenge others if they suspect unlawful or unethical conduct or behaviour, taking action as appropriate' (4.2). It is clear the CIPD advocates no exceptions to positive professional behaviour in all aspects of working life. Those embracing such standards may use them as a frame for professional identity, where the standards become part of their working self (Brown, 2015).

For external stakeholders, a published code of conduct such as that from the CIPD signals to everyone the standards of behaviour required by members of the profession. From the point of view of ethical theories, codes of conduct contain principles or duties to be respected by members, abuse of which may mean the loss of professional status. A well-written code of conduct can be highly valuable to members. In reality, it is often difficult to forecast exactly which course of action is going to be in the best interests of the stakeholders even for individuals who are strongly committed to acting in an ethical way (Foote 2001; CIPD, 2015d). It is important to remember that a code of conduct does not stand in isolation – the process of developing and implementing the code is pivotal (Kaptein and Schwartz, 2008).

Recently, the CIPD researched its members in two anonymous surveys. The first found that members did find pressure from management to compromise their ethical actions (CIPD, 2015d). The second (CIPD, 2017a) undertook a deep-dive with a large sample. The research compared HR professionals to teachers and IT professionals and linked the pull between organisational identity and professional identity and included the individuals' strength of ethical courage too. The 2017 report is applicable to this chapter and close reading of pages 5–10 as well as the summary is highly recommended. CIPD found HR professionals thought they had a good sense of what they should do in ethical dilemmas, but (like the 2015 study) sometimes did not translate this into action. The stronger the ethical courage of the individual and the stronger the identification with the profession apparently led to higher ethical practice. This has affected the Code of Practice and initiatives surrounding it such as coaching and mentoring (CIPD, 2021f).

Ethical capitalism recognises that we must have trust between people and organisations for our economy to continue (Adler, 2001). Dips in levels of trust can be alarming and more organisations are developing their own ethics committees. Traditional in some industries such as pharmacology and other medical-related areas, some professionals will have not only their professional body's code of ethical conduct, but also their own organisation's ethical code. It is crucial that any organisation's ethical code has clear and direct links to its disciplinary procedure.

The more zealous ethical champions among us will point out that, as an internal service function, HRM has a great opportunity to influence and lead ethical behaviour through role-modelling, embedding culture change, and in daily discussions with line managers. By leading organisational change at all levels (including the board room) HR has access few professions do. We need to contribute to the bottom line in a way that is sustainable which will include protecting trust between internal and external stakeholders. If the HR practitioner can advise on and model ethical behaviour, then they can contribute to raising the standards of practice in all managers. Roper and Higgin's study (2020) found that HRPs unique contribution is managing internal conflict situations. Expertise in calming conflict should help develop trust and add to organisation ethical practice, but only if leaders at all levels are also engaged and educated on

its value. Some organisations engage board and other senior level of HR who do not have CIPD qualifications or indeed membership (Caldwell, 2008; Wiley, 2000; Wright, 2008) and may have little background in ethics. The mature organisation will want to act as well as it can, and in current times, needs to make decisions that can be defended against a critical minority. HRPs can find themselves with a strong leadership role in ethical practice. However, it can be complex!

Based on employee reports of very poor attention from HR when handling complaints about bullying, Harrington, Rayner and Wararen (2012) sought the views of HRPs on the issue. Qualitative data from a British sample found that HRPs knew that staff were not always properly supported, but the reasons for this were complex. It appeared that HRPs' dependence on line managers for their power could influence their judgement, almost always meaning that the HRP denied a situation was bullying in order to avoid challenging line managers. Several HRPs reported that even raising the accusation of bullying with line managers would be destructive to that relationship; a relationship central to their day-to-day work. The researchers concluded that while the HRPs' actions were entirely understandable, it left employees unsupported. Their findings helped to explain the cynicism of those who felt bullied, and their anger towards HR and its claim to be the guardian of the anti-bullying policy. It provides a warning for HR to only 'own' policies they can support – as perceived neglect can be contagious to others' judgements of HR's trustworthiness (and general professionalism).

Another study (De Gama, NcKenna and Pettica-Harris, 2012) examined the competing priorities for HRPs in a time of economic difficulty and downward pressure on employment. Drawing on a Canadian sample, this study found that HR managers' tendency to depersonalise staff and think of them as 'resources' resulted in an attitude which the authors argued was dehumanising to staff. However, there is also recognition that HR practitioners and managers are frequently conflicted by the decisions that they are required to take, and a suggestion that a holistic re-evaluation of professional practice may offer possibilities for an alternative, ethical, approach to HRM.

The authors of this chapter found evidence that the CIPD appears to perform very well as a professional association (eg Roper and Higgins, 2020) with HRPs very involved in ethical decision making both giving professional advice to others and as practitioners crafting policy and through leading organisation development. It is a complex field to research and well worth us exploring the conceptual side further to enable better analysis.

5.4 The purpose of business

An important factor to consider when thinking about business ethics is the aims and purpose of the employing organisation (Ellesworth, 2002). Organisational purpose relates directly to ethics in HRM because organisations can be taken to employ people in order to pursue that particular purpose.

One school of thought defines the business purpose as that of maximising owner (shareholder) wealth, on the basis that this is the aim of shareholders in investing their money. Perhaps the most well-known advocate of shareholder primacy was the Chicago School economist Milton Freidman. Freidman believed that making as much money as possible is a company's only legitimate goal, subject to the basic rules of society and legal constraints (Freidman, 1970). From the 1970s, shareholder primacy and profit maximisation became established as the dominant view concerning the purpose of business.

Chicago School economists went further and argued that the goal of profit maximisation was not only legitimate, but it was in fact a legal responsibility for company executives. This belief in the legal obligation to shareholders appeared consistent with the dominant economic paradigm and as such was accepted uncritically in both academic and business circles (Morrison, 2015). Following from this was the attitude that staff were a resource and cost. Harvard economists objected to this approach and suggested staff were a worthy investment as creators of profit.

Increasingly, academic studies have challenged the Chicago economists' belief in the legal obligations to shareholders (Stout, 2012). It is argued that while legal duties are owed to the company itself, this does not necessarily imply legal obligations to individual shareholders or to shareholders as a whole (Stout, 2012). Donaldson and Preston (1995) argued that the three aspects of stakeholder theory (descriptive accuracy, instrumental power and normative validity) were mutually supportive and that the normative base of the theory was fundamental.

A 'normative' approach to stakeholder theory recognises duties towards stakeholders that must be discharged even if those actions are not clearly consistent with maximising owner wealth. One example of the latter might be a company's involvement in local community projects, in which the expenditure cannot be shown to be maximising owner wealth. This is not to say that there will be no commercial benefits from this type of expenditure – customers may approve of the venture, for example, and so switch more of their purchases to the sponsoring company – but it may be very difficult to convert those benefits into forecast cashflows. In a normative view of stakeholder theory, an organisation will acknowledge duties to get involved in this way, even if the commercial benefits are partly unclear.

Many academic studies (Freeman, Martin and Parmar, 2007; Freeman, Phillips and Sisodia, 2020) and business associations (Business Roundtable, 2019) now define the purpose of business much more broadly, suggesting that a business has a wider responsibility to the society in which it operates and that the task of a manager must recognise additional duties associated with the needs and claims of various stakeholder groups.

The CIPD starts from a position of ethical capitalism that sees a need for trust between people and organisations and their stakeholders in the medium and longer term (CIPD, 2015d, 2017a). The HR practitioner is pivotal in leading ethical advice and practice within the organisation. But what are ethics, and why do we caveat the field as so problematic to simplify? It is to the area of ethics that we now turn.

5.5 Introducing business ethics

Business ethics is relevant to both the conduct of individuals and to the operations of an organisation as a whole. In the UK, the Institute of Business Ethics (IBE) provides support and guidance for business ethics practitioners through a range of training workshops and education programmes. The IBE website states that business ethics applies to 'any and all aspects of business conduct, from boardroom strategies and how companies treat their employees and suppliers to sales techniques and accounting practices' (IBE, 2022). Importantly, ethics goes beyond the legal requirements for a company and therefore is about discretionary decisions and behaviour guided by values. Put simply, business ethics is the application of ethical values to business behaviour (IBE, 2022).

From an academic perspective the subject of business ethics can be defined as, 'the study of business situations, activities, and decisions where issues of right and wrong are addressed' (Crane et al, 2019, p 5). Often business ethics is about the 'grey areas' of business where values are in conflict (Trevino and Nelson, 2014). Moral rules exist in all societies and recognising the existence of different values and norms of behaviour is an important dimension in understanding the business environment. Morrison (2015, p 11) usefully summarises this approach to business ethics and highlights the significance of, 'identifying, understanding and respecting the divergences, while being able to identify the right ethical approach which transcends cultural barriers'. It is important to remember that business decision-making does not take place in a value-free vacuum.

It has become increasingly common for organisations to articulate a set of values that aim to guide staff about the culture of the organisation and 'the way things are done'. Some companies provide employees with ethical tests to help them to make decisions in line with those values. These might involve a series of questions to ask, such as: Is it legal? Is it consistent with the company's code of business ethics? What would my mother think? How would I feel about it being on the front page of tomorrow's newspapers? (IBE, 2022). In the next section we will look in more detail at the ethical concepts and frameworks that underpin these ethical tests.

5.6 Approaches to ethics

The study of ethics seeks a systematic and defensible understanding of good and bad. In Western philosophy, this is usually considered to have resulted in three main perspectives on ethics:

- *Ethics seen as duties*: things that should be done or refrained from, because they are good or bad in their own right. Ethics of duty ask: 'How should I act?' 'Who do I have obligations to in this situation?' 'What would happen if everybody acted in the same way as me?' Staying within the law would be a duty acknowledged by most organisations, donating a percentage of profit to local charity through sponsorship may be more contentious.

- *Ethics seen as consequences*: good acts are those that lead to good results, and bad acts are those that lead to bad results. Ethical egoism asks: 'Is this really in my best interests?' Utilitarianism asks: 'Will my action maximize utility?', and 'Will my actions make people better or worse off overall?' The consequences of actions were the underpinnings for the Chicago/Harvard debate outlined above.

- *Ethics as virtues*: the desirable qualities or character traits that are possessed by good people and organisations. Virtue ethics ask: 'How should I live my life and what kind of person should I be?' The same questions can be addressed at the organisational level by value statements and initiatives. Virtuous people and organisations are seen as role models and their behaviour followed by others.

Strong arguments have been made to support each of these main outlooks and academics have long debated the role that each plays in day-to-day ethical reasoning. However, the question of what is good and bad in human behaviour remains complex and challenging, with the possibility of contradictory answers from the different perspectives (Crane et al, 2019).

The first, a duty-based view of ethics (known as 'deontological' ethics) see goodness or badness as inherent in the act itself, rather than in the consequences. If lying is bad, for example, it is because the act of deliberately saying something that the speaker knows to be false is bad *in itself*, plain and simple. Deontological ethical frameworks offer a set of duties or principles which must be respected, irrespective of the consequences. The German philosopher Immanuel Kant (1724–1804) has been one of the leading voices in duty-based ethics. In his view, ethics are based on the duties that we owe each other as fellow members of a rational species. For example, we should only act in ways that could reasonably be adopted by anyone in similar circumstances (which is close in meaning to the golden rule: 'do as you would be done by'). Keeping promises, for example, is required, because not to do so would render the idea of a promise absurd. Also, people should always be treated as being of value in themselves, rather than simply used as a means to achieving someone else's goals. In other words, people should be treated with respect for their equal status as moral beings and not subjected to degrading or humiliating treatment, coercion or abuse.

However, problems with an exclusively duties-based view of ethics include:

- *excessive rigidity*: this can result from taking no account of possible consequences of following a principle or duty
- *complexity*: if principles are made more detailed in an attempt to deal with the wide range of real-life situations, then the resulting algorithms can become very unwieldy
- *priority*: which principles should take precedence over which others (and what is the new principle that governs this precedence)?

 Case study 5.1

HR's role in ending modern slavery

In March 2015 the UK Government introduced the Modern Slavery Act 2015. The law requires businesses with a turnover of £36m or more to prepare an annual slavery and human trafficking statement that outlines the steps they have taken to ensure their business and supply chains are slavery-free.

HR professionals have a key role in the lines of defence against modern slavery. The most prevalent form of corporate modern slavery is forced labour, with 130,000 people thought to be trapped in the practice in the UK alone. Forced labour occurs when victims are put to work against their will without any other option. Organised criminals target the vulnerable, enticing them with offers of food, safety, accommodation and paid work. This never materialises; on arrival in the UK, identity documents are confiscated and, instead of the promising life their captors promised, victims are forced to live in over-occupied, cramped conditions, with no hygiene facilities and only soiled mattresses for comfort while controllers take their pay.

1 Marc Stanton, Director of the Slave-Free Alliance, argues that 'HR departments must champion awareness of modern slavery across the board. Initiating awareness literature and putting together training modules for employees of all levels is a great place to start. For those with a turnover in excess of 36 million that are obliged to compile a modern slavery statement, taking it as an opportunity to demonstrate and follow through with a real commitment to anti-slavery strategy with future-facing actions rather than a compliance piece is strongly recommended.' Consider the main requirements of the Modern Slavery Act 2015. What duties and responsibilities does an HR manager have towards their organisation's workforce?

2 What are the implications for the responsibility of companies with global supply chains?

SOURCE: Stanton, M (2020) HR has a big role to play in stamping out modern slavery, *People Management* www. peoplemanagement.co.uk/article/1743868/hr-has-a-big-role-to-play-in-stamping-out-modern-slavery

The second approach includes those who see ethics in terms of consequences, looking for good or bad in the results of the act, rather than in the act itself. They think that a deliberate untruth, for example, is neither good nor bad in itself – it depends on the consequences. From this point of view, the ethics of stealing, or even killing, can be judged only by asking what happens as a result of the particular act. One familiar form of consequentialism is utilitarianism, which looks for the greatest good for the greatest number. In its original form, utilitarianism tries to assess the change in happiness for everyone affected by a proposed act (later forms sought to consider the consequences for those affected if the proposed action were to become commonplace). There are two main types of difficulty in an exclusively utilitarian view of ethics:

- *Methodology*: while measuring changes to happiness may sound like a good idea, it is extraordinarily difficult to do so with any precision or consistency. Recent studies have made progress on measuring happiness (eg the UK now has a Happiness Index), but there are still significant methodological challenges with this data measurement and collection.
- *Justice*: as Mackie (1977) points out, the problem with this approach is that it can allow undeserved negative consequences for one group to be offset by positive consequences for another group, as long as the net change in happiness is positive. This can be potentially very bad news for minorities in particular.

 Reflective activity 5.2

Utilitarian thinking

Recent reports suggest that the trend for outsourcing looks set to continue, particularly in sectors such as IT. Despite the potential risks of outsourcing, a survey by Deloitte found that only 20 per cent of respondents had taken the decision to move work back to their home country. India has been a preferred site, and with relatively low labour costs and growing IT expertise it remains a primary outsourcing location.

This phenomenon provides an opportunity to explore the utilitarian approach to ethics. Imagine a hypothetical case of a large UK-based supermarket that is proposing to outsource its IT applications management software from a medium-sized town in the north of England to Bangalore, India. The UK centre is to be closed and there will be 400 redundancies.

1 Make a list of the groups of people who will be affected by this initiative and then:

- describe the likely nature of the effects for each group
- estimate the likely size of each group.

2 How useful is this approach in illuminating the ethical implications of the proposal?
3 Is it possible to judge the 'greatest good for the greatest number'?
4 What difficulties would arise in trying to make this analysis more detailed and precise?
5 Putting these methodological difficulties to one side, how satisfactory does the utilitarian approach seem to be as a way of assessing good and bad in this case? If it seems to be unsatisfactory or incomplete, what is missing?

SOURCE: Deloitte (2021) *Global Shared Services and Outsourcing Report* www2.deloitte.com/us/en/pages/operations/articles/shared-services-survey.html

The contrasting views of duty-based and consequences-based ethics are reflected in the quote ascribed to Machiavelli: 'The end justifies the means.' 'Ends' are results and 'means' are principles or methods, and the debate between the two views has been running for centuries.

 Case study 5.2

Designer expenses fraud

The former boss of a designer shoe brand worn by celebrities was jailed for more than four years after falsely claiming £500,000 in expenses.

Roy Luwolt earned £150,000 a year as managing director of Malone Souliers, whose luxury footwear was worn by celebrities including the Duchess of Sussex, Gwyneth Paltrow and Beyoncé.

Luwolt claimed expenses for trips to Paris, Milan, New York, Tokyo and the Middle East, where he stayed in luxury hotels including Raffles and the Four Seasons.

Judge Philip Bartle QC said: 'Mr Luwolt fraudulently obtained not less than £500,000 in expenses over nearly three years. He caused the company to incur huge expenses for himself and others for at least five holidays, with the bills paid by the company credit card of Mr Luwolt, who paid himself expenses.'

The judge noted that: 'Mr Luwolt's lavish spending on himself and his friends contrasts with his attitude to an assistant who was asked to flat-sit for him.'

The court heard Mr Luwolt's assistant was berated after making a claim of just £7.82 for a taxi home. Consider this case and the judge's sentencing remarks with reference to both the duty-based and consequential approaches to ethics.

1   Was it the scale of the fraud that was shocking or the action itself?
2   Would it have made a difference if Luwolt had not spent the money on luxuries, for instance if he needed to support his family or pay for medical bills?
3   While this case is perhaps unusual, think about how employees might try to justify their actions if caught inflating their expenses claims.
4   Luwolt was a high-profile fashion boss and often in the limelight. Are there ethical responsibilities that come with wealth and success?

SOURCE: Brown, D (2021) Former Malone Souliers boss jailed for £500,000 expenses fraud, *The Times* www.thetimes.co.uk/article/former-malone-souliers-boss-jailed-for-500-000-expenses-fraud-08wvkgv76

The third approach to ethics is that of virtue ethics which offers an alternative way of thinking about good and bad. Virtues are desirable character traits, exhibited by good people. For Aristotle (384–322 BC), human virtues are those qualities that allow us to fulfil our highest purpose as humans. These qualities lie between undesirable extremes (as courage lies between cowardice and foolhardiness) and wisdom is required to recognise the virtuous approach.

In the duty-based view of ethics the main question to consider was, 'How should I act in this situation?' By contrast, virtue ethics offers a more holistic approach that asks, 'How should I live my life?' and 'What kind of person should I be?' Virtue ethics argues that right and wrong cannot simply be resolved by applying a specific rule or principle. Instead, individuals and organisations need to develop knowledge and judgement on ethical matters over time through a process of active learning, much as you are doing now.

If we consider the characteristics of a good manager, or 'true professional', Dobson (2007) argues that a critical feature is, 'the adherence to certain "virtues" of character, such as honesty, fairness, prudence, and courage'. A virtue ethics approach is about how people should live their lives, in order to realise their highest potential. This takes time and experience. Rather than proposing a series of rules or principles, the main way of becoming virtuous is to study the lives of good people and learn to imitate them.

 Reflective activity 5.3

Get back to the office

People should get back to the office to benefit from in-person collaboration because the world must learn to live with the coronavirus after a pandemic that has wiped trillions of dollars off global output, Britain's business minister said on Friday.

'We should get back to work,' British Business Secretary Kwasi Kwarteng told LBC radio. 'We've got to get back to some degree of normality.'

Some bosses have urged people back to work. Goldman Sachs' CEO has called home working an 'aberration' while Stuart Rose, chairman of supermarket group Asda, said he had been working at the office throughout the pandemic.

'I cannot believe we have a nation sitting at home now cowered by this government,' Rose said. 'It is something we have to now live with.'

Commenting on the return to office working, Lord Rose said: 'Hallelujah! I've been calling for it for months.' He continued: 'I cannot believe we have sat here for so long, I am angry almost, to the extreme.'

1 Lord Rose, who is in his 70s, has also been struck with the virus twice, despite having had all three coronavirus vaccinations. To what extent do you think that Stuart Rose's leadership approach is unusual?

2 In this case, what are the ethical factors that need to be considered?

3 What should HR do in such circumstances?

SOURCE: Reuters (2022) Get back to the office, Britain's business minister says www.reuters.com/world/uk/get-back-work-office-britains-business-minister-says-2022-01-21/

5.7 Sustainability and HR

Climate change is recognised as the defining crisis of our time (UN, 2021) and businesses are increasingly expected to take positive action to support climate change solutions (Alvi, 2021). The CIPD's *People Profession 2030* report predicts that sustainability will increasingly influence the future of work and the people profession. HR professionals will need to respond to a widening remit on corporate social responsibility and increased demands that integrate sustainability, responsible business and organisational purpose and values (CIPD, 2020a). Due to their connections across the organisation, HR practitioners are in a unique position to embed sustainability policies and practices into corporate culture and help employees make better choices. This could involve strategic input to manage transitions to net-zero organisations or interventions to help staff cope with 'climate anxiety'. The CIPD has published a range of documents offering practical advice, including the following top tips for embedding environmental sustainability (2021g):

- Incorporate sustainability into job descriptions and person specifications.
- Discuss sustainability in the induction process.
- Include sustainability objectives in performance management targets and goals.
- Embed sustainability into learning and development processes.
- Align rewards and recognition with sustainability considerations.
- Assess the environmental impact of projects.
- Ensure that leaders display environmental behaviours.

In Case Study 5.3 we explore how companies are putting their sustainability plans into practice. This is an opportunity to consider the progress that has been made by some businesses and the targets that have been missed so far.

 Case study 5.3

Unilever Sustainable Living Plan

Speaking at a global virtual event, CEO Alan Jope said, 'The Unilever Sustainable Living Plan [USLSP] was a game-changer for our business. Some goals we have met, some we have missed, but we are a better business for trying. It has required immense ingenuity, dedication and collaboration to get to where we are now. We have made very good progress, but there is still more to do.' Some of the achievements over the last 10 years have included:

- Reaching 1.3 billion people through health and hygiene programmes.
- Reducing the total waste footprint per consumer use of products by 32 per cent, and achieving zero waste to landfill across all factories.

- Reducing greenhouse gas emissions from manufacturing by 65 per cent, and achieving 100 per cent renewable grid electricity across our sites.

Following on from the USLP, Unilever is committed to continuing to be a sustainable leader and has developed a new, fully integrated corporate strategy: the Unilever Compass.

The Unilever Compass is based on three core beliefs: that brands with purpose grow, companies with purpose last, and people with purpose thrive.

The Unilever Compass lays out 15 multi-year priorities that cover the full spectrum of Unilever's business and wider ecosystem. Each priority will tackle key challenges such as packaging and waste, gender equality, human rights, and fair value – as well as climate change and social inclusion.

1 Download the latest version of Unilever's Annual Report and consider the progress made on each of the priority areas. How does Unilever make 'the business case' for sustainability?

2 In which areas of the business can HR help to deliver these sustainability commitments?

SOURCE: Unilever (2020) *Unilever celebrates 10 years of the sustainable living plan* www.unilever.com/news/press-and-media/press-releases/2020/unilever-celebrates-10-years-of-the-sustainable-living-plan/

As discussed earlier in the chapter, the academic literature on HRM has highlighted the ambiguities, paradoxes and dilemmas of HRM practice particularly when addressing questions of efficiency, employee wellbeing and sustainability. HR and net-zero.

In a review of the academic literature, Kramar (2014) asks: 'Does the sustainable HRM literature represent a new approach to the management of people?' While studies of sustainable HRM do not yet represent a coherent body knowledge, Kramar's review suggests that academic work in this field has begun to provide a new focus on the purpose of HRM practices with a wider consideration of a variety of outcomes, not just economic outcomes. Paradoxical choices and tensions in relation to organisational efficiency and the corresponding social, individual and ecological outcomes need to be actively addressed and professionally managed. This approach offers the potential for a dynamic CSR–HRM co-creation model (Jamali, Eldirani and Harwaood, 2015). Aligning sustainability to HRM thinking allows for new solutions to HR problems, such as HR shortages, employee health or HR development, and extends the understanding of HRM performance in relation to sustainable business organisations (Ehnert, 2014).

5.8 Equal opportunities and ethics

In this section we seek to apply the concepts from our previous discussion into a specific area that is difficult to implement. We have chosen equal opportunities. Originally, to discriminate meant distinguishing one thing from another and strictly speaking the word 'discrimination' is ethically neutral. However, discrimination has acquired a pejorative sense, alluding to the exercise of prejudice, which is clearly unethical, and often illegal. In this sense of the word, it is unfair or irrelevant discrimination that is objectionable that people should be recruited on the basis of their ability to do the job, with no other factors intruding into the decision (Noon in Beardwell and Thompson, 2014). Discriminating against lazy or dishonest people is thus acceptable, but discriminating on the basis of gender, ethnic origin or age (for example) is unlawful, but how and in what ways is it unethical?

The principle of equal opportunity (EO) can involve both duty-based and consequentialist ethical arguments. The duty-based ethics point is clear: we have a duty to treat people fairly. To treat employees on some basis other than EO (eg, to allow ageist or homophobic elements to enter into decisions about them) is to fail to show respect for their equal status as fellow members of the moral community.

From the employer's point of view, a strong consequences-based case in favour of EO can also be made. Organisations that rule out candidates from a whole group on the basis of prejudice are depriving themselves of a significant pool of talent in the labour market, and this failure to engage with diverse groups is likely to lead to non-optimal performance (Von Bergen, Soper and Parnell, 2005; Hunt, 2007). Organisations are likely to experience reputational damage by the exercise of prejudice, well beyond any legal penalties, and the cost of this in talent recruitment and retention maybe very significant as well as affecting existing staff members pride and thus engagement and effectiveness (Hunt, 2007).

Nevertheless, anti-discrimination legislation is common, which suggests that the market-driven response to prejudice has been found to be inadequate therefore law is required. It would be wrong, however, to infer from these arguments that equal opportunities is the sole – or even the pre-eminent – ethical principle at play in contemporary HRM. In large numbers of businesses around the world, the owners or managers may regard it as perfectly normal to prefer to recruit or promote an acceptably competent member of the same family over a better-qualified stranger. This is not the place to debate the relative merits of the two principles, but rather to suggest that EO is often not the sole governing principle in HRM, however strong the deontological and consequence-based arguments in its favour.

Interestingly Boatright (2000) points out that prejudice treats people as members of groups, rather than affording them the individual treatment that they should reasonably expect. Making recruitment, promotion or redundancy decisions on the basis of prejudice is therefore manifestly unjust to those who are disadvantaged. In addition, the list of 'protected characteristics' to which EO law extends is always under pressure to be extended.

 Case study 5.4

Equality, diversity and inclusion in 2022, Kathleen Stock resigned as a Professor of Philosophy at the University of Sussex. Stock's research covered contentious issues about biological sex, gender identity, women's rights and transactivist demands. Despite support from the University, online trolling, abusive posters near the campus and a social media campaign to undermine her meant she found continuing at work difficult.

Writing on a blog, Stock explained how the situation developed: 'Since the beginning of the week, I've been subject to a campaign of harassment, explicitly designed to have me fired for my academic views. My first inkling of it came when I came across stickers all over my building talking about the "transphobic shit that comes out of Kathleen Stock's mouth". The next day I came across posters that named me, defamed me, and demanded I be fired, plastered all over my route into campus. Things escalated from there and now the police are involved and treating it as harassment.' In her statement, Stock went on to question how equality diversity and inclusion impacted academic culture: 'EDI (that is, "Equality Diversity and Inclusion") groups bombard faculty and students with initiatives: closely monitoring teaching materials for "insensitive" language, showing "kindness" and "inclusivity", issuing trigger warnings, "calling out" perceived injustice, being an 'active bystander', and other heavily moralised and nebulous instructions, which of course can each be interpreted wildly differently according to different subjective sensibilities. If, as an academic or student, you express hesitancy about any of these initiatives, then you are instantly castigated as unethical and badly-motivated. The University of Sussex could have been in a position where customers (students) felt an ethical transgression was being undertaken by a member of staff (Professor Kathleen Stock).

1 Discuss the responsibilities the University had as an employer.

2 University academic staff have to voice debates, and sometimes express views with which they personally disagree in order to help students understand elements of their curriculum. Should a university employer have any duty in circumstances where their academic staff become the target of rights campaigns?

3 What responsibilities do they have and who should undertake what actions?

4 Use a consequentialist and duty-based lens to examine the questions above. How might this inform your responses to these questions?

SOURCE: Stock, K (2021) Statement read in absentia, 'hate, heresy and the fight for free speech', Battle of Ideas, 9 October https://kathleenstock.com/statement-read-in-absentia-h/

Arguments about positive discrimination have been in evidence for several decades. For example, the Norwegian government introduced legislation that 40 per cent of main board seats in public companies should be held by women from 1 January 2008. This ruling, first announced in 2003, was virtually achieved by the deadline. The UK's top 100 companies (UK FTSE 100) were at 39 per cent on 10 January 2022 rising from 12 per cent in 2012. Chairing the Board remains rare with 16/100 in FTSE 100 (84 being male) and 32 women chairs of FTSE 250 (218 being male) according to the FTSE Women Leaders Review (Wilson, 2022). Change seems to be slow, but ethical arguments are crucial as well as financial and legal pressure.

5.9 Data, technology and ethics

The role of ethics in technology is an area of lively development both academically and in practice. Recent enactment of the Global Data Protection Regulations (GDPR) concerning the collection and use (through computers) of personal data including that of employees and customers has begun a fundamental change in mindset for HR and other people-based professions. HR performs a central role to ensure GDPR compliance (Budhwar et al, 2022), and this co-ordinating responsibility appears to be setting a pattern for other aspects of technology such as robotics and artificial intelligence (AI). The role requires ethical awareness and has led to a surge in interest in technology and artificial intelligence issues beyond data protection (Charlwood and Guenole, 2022).

Technology is affecting organisations through the use of AI (artificial intelligence), workplace automation and robotics. The existence of four reports from the CIPD since 2015, the latest is (CIPD, 2021h) show how seriously the impact of technology is being taken by the professional body. A useful scoping review (Budhwar et al, 2022) outlines the current published academic papers in the IT-HR field in the last 10 years. It reports a wide range of applications, some successes and some concerns. The term 4IR (4th Industrial Revolution) is an apt name to give the emergence of a new turn in the evolution of work (Budhwar et al, 2022).

Algorithms have been used by HR in recruitment at larger employers for many years reflecting some core issues applicable more widely. Originally developed to screen out highly unsuitable applicants, such computerised systems have brought cost savings, operational efficiencies and released recruitment staff to do arguably far less routine work and thus have more enriched jobs. A review of such processes raised issues which included accountability (who designed the algorithm based on what information), transparency (what exactly is being prioritised in the algorithm), power and the powerlessness of applicants who get poor feedback and no appeal, and social control as applicants learn the algorithm and fit into expected norms (Leicht-Deobald et al, 2019). These authors suggest that such systems evoke 'blind trust', in this example from HRPs, who might not question the inputs, process or outputs when they should.

Algorithms inevitably reflect previous understanding and thus risk lowering diversity and the concomitant decline in performance – see also Chapters 6 and 8. It appears that algorithms generally reject what are judged as unusual people or their actions and are discriminatory (in the neutral sense) and they may prolong bias and inequality, albeit unintentionally, (Tursunbayeva et al, 2021). The recent review by Budhwar et al, (2022) raises concerns that process issues relating to equal opportunities are not being acknowledged and therefore left unattended and this links to poor accountability in projects that are multi-disciplined.

Although we associate some technological change with job losses (such as new factories of robots rather than human fitters) it is the case that many jobs cannot be automated (Arntz, Gregory and Zierahn, 2016), typically those requiring high empathy or using multiple factors in complex decision-making. The CIPD found that overall the use of technology is enhancing the quality of some roles by reducing repetitive routine, thus raising the skills of a job for decision-making and unique tasks. In this sense such technology fits alongside human workers, and such is adjunct and supportive of the employee. Consider chat bots which are able to answer many routine queries, leaving the harder situations for human examination (Budhwar et al, 2022).

The employee experience of workplace technology was the focus of a recent CIPD report published in 2020. Given the shift to home working, job design has been impacted. Some employees report far more control over their life in working from home thus better satisfaction and engagement and likely better performance. Other employees found their home/work balance needed far more attention with insufficient time for home life. It is unclear why employees had such different reactions. Surveillance of screen time was accepted by workers in the CIPD report and they found managers have used such data to augment their ways of managing. Perhaps 'surveillance' for the employee may be legitimate 'managing' for their boss. HRPs will need to work across organisations to find new norms and behaviours. A stronger focus on task achievement maybe in view (CIPD, 2020c) as the desire for demonstrable fairness becomes greater.

Academics and the CIPD agree that as technological developments often directly affect jobs, HR needs to be in the planning loop to balance technology-biased leaders and find sustainable solutions with realistic implementation patterns (CIPD, 2019a; Budhwar et al, 2022). The 2019 report from the CIPD found that planning for AI/automation projects was potentially very haphazard, with the implication that HR could benefit projects by taking the initiative to get involved. Budhwar et al (2022) stressed the need for HR to push for workers to develop AI sensitive skills so that longer term role augmentation could proceed smoothly.

Gal, Jensen and Stein (2020) consider virtue ethics and the role of algorithms 'nudging' individuals through email and text so that their behaviour is affected in the way the programmer desires. Their article raises the issue of rights in AI and automation. Should humans always be told that they are dealing with a cyber entity? Are robots exempt from some ethical protection we afford human beings? Do robots have rights?

In summary, most commentators suggest that the management and ethical implementation of technological developments will occupy more HRP's time. As we know, enabling change requires good planning, co-ordination and engagement with those involved – see also Chapter 12. This is true in an ethical sense for technology, AI and robotic development as employees are suspicious of their roles being superseded (CIPD, 2019a; Gal, Jensen an Stein, 2020). Cost savings, increased customer experience and novel products from well-managed technology and AI projects will be strategically important and much sought after (Budhwar et al, 2022). Workforces will need to learn to work with AI through upskilling, job design that includes workers augmented by AI and other technology. However, fair and ethical practices will need to be adhered to for which HRPs may be the arbiter.

 Reflective activity 5.4

Review your last few days' emails. Identify up to three emails you think were generated using algorithms or artificial intelligence (AI) tools.

1 How does this use of technology affect your perception of the email content and message?

2 Are some circumstances more 'acceptable' than others to use AI generated emails?

3 What ethical principles could be used to inform a policy for responsible digital communications?

5.10 Embedding ethical practice – the role of HR

Given the importance of ethical conduct in business, what contribution can or should an HRP make to an organisation's ethical policy? There is no doubt that much of the work of HRPs involves ethical issues. All HRP roles provide opportunities for extensive ethical impact. By creating and embedding policies in areas of recruitment, selection, job evaluation linked to pay, and performance management, for example, HRPs have been highly influential in achieving equality for staff in hiring, reward and censure. HR business partners working with line managers are ideally placed at the front line to highlight areas of practice for attention and give informed advice and guidelines to operational staff and managers – see also Chapters 2 and 13. As such they can achieve an 'ethical guardian' role for the organisation (Lowry, 2006).

However, research by the CIPD (2017a) has highlighted the potential tensions between organisational identity and professional identity for HR practitioners. While HR practitioners may see their role as 'ethical stewards' they do not always follow through when it comes to challenging unethical organisational practice. This gap between the ambition to uphold ethical values and actual practice could be explained by 'pro-group unethical behaviour' (Thau et al, 2015); whereby the alignment of individual values and the risk of social exclusion leads to unethical behaviour in support of the interests of the organisation. In contrast, having a sense of authority in one's role to challenge organisational decisions, and viewing the advancement of current organisational practice as central to the role, can enable HR to raise concerns about unethical decisions (CIPD, 2017a).

By HR (co-)creating policies and working with other staff to set up systems that are ethically robust, their impact has already been seen in organisational practice (Sarvaiya, Eweie and Arrowsmith, 2018). However, boundaries between the territories of the HR and the CSR functions remain unclear (De Stefano, Bagdadli and Camuffo, 2018). The research reviewed above suggests that, for understandable reasons, asking HR to 'police' their own systems may be too much. Some organisations have compliance sections (eg in finance), and others internal ombudsman services (eg the military) so that complaints and investigations can be undertaken away from HR by colleagues independent to those more closely involved with day-to-day operations.

The Institute of Business Ethics (IBE) has highlighted the need for collaboration in order to embed ethical values into organisation culture (IBE, 2022). The IBE has explored the roles of HR and the ethics function, and recommended a number of areas for improved collaboration. Key areas identified included: developing and updating a Code of Ethics; recruitment and induction; training and performance management; staff survey and 'Speak Up' channels; ethics ambassadors and internal communications; joint presentations and reporting to the board. Despite potential challenges, many companies already have good relations between the ethics team and HR, and demonstrate a wider recognition that working effectively together helps embed a values-led culture across the organisation. Recent work by Rolls-Royce has demonstrated the power of real-life stories in developing engaging ethics training (IBE, 2021). Working with cases and scenarios sourced from the company's Speak up channels, the HR and Ethics and Compliance team turn these cases into anonymised stories. These case studies have given 'power and weight' to the ethics and compliance programme and helped to demonstrate the commitment to treating everyone with dignity and respect.

5.11 Conclusion

Professionalism sits at the core of good HRM practice. Professionalism has trust as a central tenet, and any effective professional body (such as the CIPD) is involved in setting standards and enabling CPD so that their members can remain aligned to good practice. Ethics are central to the judgements we make about what good practice is. Demonstrating good ethical practice means thinking decisions through in a careful manner and developing one's own moral compass. Rather than searching for one theory that offers the best or true view of a moral dilemma, Crane et al. (2019) advocate a pluralist approach whereby ethical theories act as a prism that throws light from different angles on the same problem. Used in a pragmatic way, ethical theories should complement an intelligent and considered response to real business challenges.

One common problem is that managers may fail to perceive the ethical implications of a decision or action at the outset. In this area HRPs can contribute uniquely across the organisation. By setting ethically screened policies, they can contribute to providing a framework within which managers can operate that precludes some unethical choices. By working with partner line managers, they can bring an independent view to bear on decisions where the manager might not have considered the ethical implications fully. Embedding ethical principles in training and learning events, the HRD specialist can prompt all employees to be more aware of the nature of their professionalism and the role of ethics within it.

Evidence is beginning to be gathered on ethical behaviour, and HR is among the professions to be studied. The dynamics are complex, and remain to be fully understood, but in the process we may see further developments in ethical approaches within the profession. Evidence suggests that HRPs, like all other professionals, need to be constantly vigilant of their own judgement.

 KEY LEARNING POINTS

1 HR and line managers have an important role to play in influencing the level and type of integrity observed beyond the law and adoption by others.

2 The CIPD plays an important role in the HR profession. Regardless of one's specialism, membership of the CIPD involves abiding by its Code of Professional Conduct.

3 In this chapter we have outlined areas that are becoming increasingly urgent in the HR field and which relate to ethical practice generally and professionalism specifically. These are not easy topics, and possibly require all staff to reflect at a deeper level than previously.

4 There are a variety of approaches to analysing situations from an ethical point of view. Sometimes these can lead to very different logic and actions.

5 Often employees do not analyse the ethical principles they employ.

6 There is a strong case that good ethics makes sustainable business sense.

7 Some issues (such as equal opportunities) are enshrined in law and regardless of one's personal feelings, one must facilitate the adherence to these rights, promoting them and leading the organisation through changing policies and practice.

Review questions

1 Think about an organisation with which you are familiar. Provide practical examples of ways in which it is operating ethically. Can you relate these examples to the duty, consequences or virtue perspectives on ethics?

2 Discuss the view that an organisation that is providing good value products or services to its customers, paying its bills and treating its staff decently over a long period of time is acting as ethically as anyone can reasonably expect.

3 How do HR decisions become conflicted in an ethical sense? Consider situations where you have felt professionally 'torn' between courses of action, and analyse your response using ethical frameworks.

4 Can one be an 'HR professional' in the UK without being a member of the CIPD?

 Explore further

Crane, A, Matten, D, Glozer, S and Spence, L (2019) *Business Ethics: Managing corporate citizenship and sustainability in the age of globalization,* 5th edn, Oxford University Press, Oxford. Written by leading academics working on business ethics and corporate responsibility, this new edition includes extended coverage of SMEs and social enterprises and a wider range of global perspectives on ethical debates and dilemmas.

Laasch, O, & Conaway, R (2017) *Responsible Business: The textbook for management learning, competence and innovation,* Routledge. This book was published as an official textbook of the United Nations for the Principles for Responsible Management Education (PRME) academic network, and a reference book for companies of the United Nations Global Compact Initiative.

PART THREE
Strategic people management and development effectiveness

06
Recruitment and selection

KERRY COLLIER AND RAY FRENCH

LEARNING OUTCOMES

After reading this chapter, you should be able to:

- comprehend the potential importance of recruitment and selection in successful people management and development

- identify aspects of recruitment and selection which are needed to avoid critical failure factors

- understand the recruitment and selection policies and procedures which are said to be associated with high performance, commitment and successful organisational outcomes

- evaluate selection methods according to criteria of professionalism including reliability, validity and fairness

- appreciate the links between recruitment and selection and other activities which integrate workers within an organisation and ensure their longer-term successful working.

6.1 Overview

In this chapter we examine the important role of recruitment and selection within the process of managing and developing people. Recruitment and selection is pivotal in this regard in certain important respects. At the most basic level our focus in this book is on people management within the employment relationship. Those charged with recruiting people to posts in work organisations take a crucial 'gatekeeper' role; only those people selected for employment can be subsequently managed and developed. In the most fundamental sense, the decision to employ (or not) underpins the whole area of managing people. Issues associated with exclusion from the workplace also highlight the need for professionalism, fairness and ethical behaviour on the part of those engaged in this activity.

Recruitment and selection also have an important role to play in ensuring worker performance and positive organisational outcomes that align with strategy. It is often claimed that selection of workers occurs not just to replace departing employees or add to a workforce, but rather aims to put in place workers who can perform at a high level and demonstrate commitment thus facilitating high performance work systems (HPWSs) (Para-González, Jiménez-Jiménez and Martínez-Lorente, 2019; Pilbeam and Corbridge, 2010). We will elaborate on the sometimes complex linkages between recruitment and selection and performance later in this chapter.

Recruitment and selection are characterised, finally, by potential difficulties and it is necessary to keep abreast of developments in research in the field. For example, at the end of the austerity period following the 2008 financial crash, a CIPD *HR Market Outlook* report (CIPD, 2015e), noted that following a 'long dark decade' the sun was finally shining for young jobseekers in the UK, with more employers turning to a wider range of younger recruits. However, the report alerted those involved in recruiting and selecting young workers to ensure the effective utilisation of their skills, as the UK had the second highest level of over-qualification in the Organisation for Economic Co-operation and Development (OECD) at that time. This brought a danger of productivity being undermined unless young people's skills were put to good use. Fast forwarding to 2021, many companies were experiencing difficulty in recruiting suitable staff, so more organisations moved to alternative ways to fulfill these vacancies such as upskilling current employees (CIPD, 2021b). These are just two examples of how an appreciation of current research can inform practice, and they also show the critical importance of the social context in which recruitment and selection takes place.

6.2 Introduction

Recruitment and selection form a core part of the central activities underlying human resource management; namely the acquisition, development and reward of workers. It frequently comprises an important element of human resource practitioner's work and, of course, designated specialists such as recruitment and talent acquisition consultants. However, importantly, recruitment and selection decisions are often for good reason taken by non-specialists such as line managers. There is therefore an important sense in which it is both the responsibility of all managers, and where human resource departments exist, it may be that HR managers play more of a supporting advisory role to those people who will supervise or in other ways work with the new employee. As Mullins (2019) notes, if the HRM function is to remain effective there must be consistently good levels of teamwork, plus ongoing co-operation and consultation between line managers and the HR manager. This is most definitely the case in recruitment and selection as specialist HR managers (or even external consultants) can be an important repository of up-to-date knowledge and skills, for example on the important legal dimensions of this area.

Recruitment and selection are often presented as a planned rational activity, comprising certain sequentially linked phases within a process of employee resourcing, which itself may be located within a wider HR management strategy. The two terms are commonly differentiated although there is a clear link between them.

Recruitment is commonly understood as a process by which a pool of capable people is generated, who then apply for employment in an organisation. Selection is the process by which managers and others identify and use valid instruments enabling them to choose potentially effective future employees from a pool of applicants. When selecting employees, those responsible will need to act in the light of given management goals within the organisation and, of course, the legal requirements in place within a specific country and any relevant pan-national institutions.

Recruitment and selection are interlinked; however, each element can require specific skills and expertise, and may therefore be best carried out by different people. It is not uncommon for the recruitment activity – although not normally the selection decision itself – to be outsourced, for example, to an agency. It is useful to treat each activity separately (see also Hook and Jenkins, 2019).

Recruitment and selection, as defined here, can play a pivotally important role in shaping an organisation's effectiveness and performance, if work organisations are able to acquire workers who already possess relevant knowledge, skills and aptitudes and can make an accurate prediction regarding their future abilities. If we accept this premise (which will be questioned to some extent in this chapter), then recruiting and selecting staff in an effective manner can both avoid undesirable costs – for example, those associated with high staff turnover, poor performance and dissatisfied customers – and engender a mutually beneficial employment relationship characterised, wherever possible, by high commitment on both sides.

Recruitment and selection is a topical area. While it has always had the capacity to form a key part of the process of managing people as a routine part of organisational life, it is suggested here that recruitment and selection has become ever more important as organisations increasingly regard their workforce as a source of competitive advantage. Of course, not all employers engage with this proposition even at the rhetorical level. However, there is evidence of heightened interest in the utilisation of employee selection methods which are valid, reliable and fair. For example, the search for rigorous application and scrutiny of employee selection procedures has seen insights derived from work psychology have increasingly significant influence on the way people are recruited into work roles. (Arnold et al, 2020). In this chapter we will examine several contemporary themes in recruitment and selection including the so-called competency approach and online recruitment.

Recruitment and selection do not operate in a vacuum, insulated from wider social trends, so as we noted in this chapter's overview, it is very important to keep abreast of current research. To take just one example, the CIPD annual survey report *Resourcing and Talent Planning* (CIPD, 2021i) found that:

- Recruitment difficulties have been exacerbated by the pandemic. More than a quarter of the organisations surveyed reported logistical challenges in facilitating socially distanced recruitment processes.

- Almost half of employers believe that competition for well-qualified talent has increased and that organisations faced increased difficulties in attracting appropriately skilled applicants.

- Some of the strategies organisations are adopting to attract new employees include appealing to experienced workers through career-returner programmes and mid-career change programmes, as well as an increase in flexible working practices, although the report suggests that organisations could be more proactive in attracting and recruiting diverse candidates.

- A more focused approach is needed in identifying recruitment needs and current and future workforce requirements.

- These findings need to be put into a turbulent social and economic context as at the time of the survey the UK was coming out of a third lockdown due to the Covid-19 pandemic, plus it was only four months after the end of the Brexit transition period.

This aspect of employee resourcing is characterised, however, by potential difficulties. Many widely used selection methods, for example interviewing, are generally perceived to be unreliable as a predictor of jobholders' performance in reality, and this could be compounded further by the need to use online selection activities (Manroop, Malik, Camp and Schulz, 2021). Thus, it is critically important to obtain a realistic evaluation of the process from all concerned, including both successful and unsuccessful candidates. There are ethical issues around selecting 'appropriate', and by implication rejecting 'inappropriate', candidates for employment. Many organisations seek to employ people who will fit in with their organisation's culture (French et al, 2015); see also the IKEA case study below. While this may be perfectly understandable, it carries important ethical overtones; for example, whether an employing organisation should be involved in shaping an individual's identity. We put forward the view in this chapter that, notwithstanding the moral issues and practical difficulties outlined here, recruitment and selection is one area where it is possible to distinguish policies and practices associated with critical success factors and performance differentiators which, in turn, impact on organisational effectiveness in significant ways.

Case study 6.1

Why work at IKEA? Part one

The following extracts are taken from 'Why work with us?' sections of the IKEA Group corporate website from 2015 and 2022.

'COME AND BE YOURSELF WITH US'

'At IKEA we are looking for down-to-earth, straightforward people who have the desire to learn and grow personally and professionally right along with our business.'

'A positive team spirit.'

'Working with us is like working with your friends. Our culture is based on the spirit of togetherness, enthusiasm and fun. And we're always looking for people who share our positive attitude and values.'

IKEA's website has also, over time, stressed the importance of the company's inclusive, empathetic, open and honest culture, before going on to identify some specific IKEA values including:

- *Lead by example.* Leadership is an action, not a position. We give people's values as much weight as their competence and experience. People who 'walk the talk' and lead by example.

- *Togetherness.* Togetherness or "Tillsammans" as we say in Swedish, is a big deal for us. In fact, it's at the very heart of the IKEA culture. We know we're at our best when we trust each other, pull in the same direction and, not least, have fun together.

- *Different with a meaning.* We are not like other businesses and we don't want to be. We want to challenge conventions and drive positive changes in our industry and sometimes even in the world. We are restless doers, driven by curiosity, enthusiasm and a desire to create a better world.

- *Caring for people and planet.* We want to be a force for positive change. Our reach gives us the possibility to make significant and lasting impact – today and for the generations to come. We will continue to offer more sustainably sourced and manufactured products and help people live a more sustainable life at home.

It is clear that IKEA as an employer is strongly driven by values and will seek to recruit and select employees (co-workers) who identify with those values and are committed to making them work.

1 In what ways could an employer seek to assess qualities of straightforwardness, curiosity and the capacity to become a 'restless doer' among a large group of applicants? How accurate do you think judgments made along these measures are likely to be?

2 What selection methods could IKEA employ to accurately assess whether potential workers can 'walk the talk' and 'lead by example'?

3 What are the benefits of a strategy of recruiting and selecting workers who embody organisational culture? Give reasons for your answer. Identify some possible negative outcomes of aligning selection with organisational culture.

6.3 Effective recruitment and selection

We have already referred to the potential importance of recruitment and selection as an activity. The recruitment and selection of employees can be seen as pivotal to an organisation's performance, so it is very important to get things right, or at the very least make justifiable decisions. Poor selection decisions reduce organisational effectiveness and can impede other strategies, for example reward and employee development. If a worker proves to be out of their depth this is also unfair on that recruit. Managers who have to deal with unsuitable employees often find this area of their work difficult, plus it takes them away from more proactive tasks – the so-called opportunity cost effect (Pilbeam and Corbridge, 2010).

 Reflective activity 6.1

A custodial offence

A senior NHS employee received a suspended prison sentence after falsely stating she had a degree qualification on her CV. Elaine Pedini, 47, worked as Chief Information and Digital Officer at an NHS foundation trust from October 2017 until November 2019. She pleaded guilty to a fraud offence at a court hearing in 2020 where she was sentenced to two years in prison, suspended for two years. She was also ordered to undertake 200 hours of unpaid work and complete a rehabilitation programme.

Pedini's employer was first alerted to a possible discrepancy in her personal records by an anonymous tip-off to its chief finance officer and local counter-fraud specialist. As part of the NHS Trust's duty to make fit and proper person checks, all of its executive employee files were checked. At this point it was discovered that there was no copy of Pedini's history degree certificate. This was because she had no such qualification.

The NHS trust stated that it had strengthened its recruitment process to ensure that it is no longer possible to avoid confirmation of applicants' academic qualifications prior to appointment and that it now verified qualifications with the awarding institution or body.

It is interesting to note that this case centred on recruitment procedures. At no point was Pedini's *performance in her role* called into question.

SOURCE: This is a true-life case, although names and dates have been changed. See Webber (2020) and other media reports for further details.

This case provides a good example of the possible consequences of flawed recruitment and/or selection procedures, or even when agreed practices, such as checking personal details, are not put into effect. Such consequences are potentially wide-ranging and encompass the trivial and comic to possibly tragic outcomes. One can certainly reasonably anticipate many of the negative outcomes which can follow when recruitment and selection goes wrong.

It is undoubtedly true that recruitment and selection strategies and practices have important consequences for all concerned, so what are the keys to maximising the chances of effective recruitment and selection? Some important factors are listed below.

6.3.1 *Recognising the power of perception*

Perception is defined as the process by which humans receive, organise and make sense of the information they receive from the outside world (Buchanan and Huczynski, 2019); French *et al*, 2015; Mullins, 2019). The quality or accuracy of our perceptions will have a major impact on our response to a situation. There is much data suggesting that when we perceive other people – particularly in an artificial and time-constrained situation like a job interview – we can make key mistakes, sometimes at a subliminal level. One key to enhancing effectiveness in recruitment and selection therefore lies in an appreciation of some core principles of interpersonal perception and, in particular, some common potential mistakes in this regard.

- *Selective perception*. Our brains cannot process all of the information that our senses pick up, so we instead select particular objects – or aspects of people – for attention. We furthermore attribute positive or negative characteristics to the stimuli; known as the 'halo' and 'horns' effects respectively. For example, an interviewee who has a large coffee stain on their clothing, but is otherwise well-presented, may have difficulty creating an overall negative impression, despite the fact that it might be their desire for the new job that resulted in nervousness and clumsiness.

- *Self-centred bias*. A recruiter should avoid evaluating a candidate by reference to themselves as this may be irrelevant to the post in question and run the risks of a 'clone effect' in a changing business environment. The phrase 'I was like you 15 years ago' may be damaging in a number of respects and should not be the basis for employment in most situations.

- *Early information bias*. We often hear apocryphal stories of interview panels making very early decisions on a candidate's suitability and spending the remaining time confirming that decision. Mythical though some of these tales may be, there is a danger of over-prioritising early events: a candidate who trips over when entering an interview room may thus genuinely be putting themselves at a disadvantage.

- *Stereotyping*. This is a common short cut to understanding an individual's attributes, which is a difficult and time-consuming process. The logic of stereotyping attributes individuals' characteristics to those of a group to which they belong; for example, the view that because Italians are considered to be emotional, an individual Italian citizen will be too. Stereotypes might contain elements of truth, but they may equally be entirely false since we are all unique. Stereotyping may well be irrelevant and, if acted on, also discriminatory.

It should be stressed that these, and other, perceptual errors are not inevitable and can be overcome. Many HR professionals study subjects like organisational behaviour as part of their career qualifications in which they are made aware of the dangers of inaccurate perception. We are also seeing more organisations implement training interventions to ensure employee awareness of unconscious bias and how this can influence decisions; however, it can be argued that more research is required to determine the effectiveness of such interventions (Paluck et al, 2020). Nonetheless, it remains the case that an understanding of this subject area is an important building block to effective recruitment and selection.

6.3.2 *Taking a staged approach*

Much prescriptive writing on recruitment and selection advocates viewing the process as sequential with distinct and inter-linked stages. This model is referred to as the 'resourcing cycle'. The resourcing cycle begins with job analysis and the identification of a vacancy and ends when the successful candidate is performing the job to an acceptable standard, that is, post-selection. It is a two-way process. Organisations evaluate candidates for a vacancy, but candidates also scrutinise the organisation as a prospective employer. In recent years there has been an increasing focus on employer branding and image in attracting candidates. Organisations that gain a reputation for treating people well, offering stimulating and secure employment with the potential to progress stand a far greater chance of attracting, recruiting and retaining good people. Conducting the process in a professional and timely manner is necessary to ensure that not only is the best candidate attracted to apply and subsequently accept the post but also that unsuccessful candidates can respect the decision made. If an unsuccessful applicant gains a favourable impression of the organisation, they may possibly apply for future vacancies.

The first step in the recruitment process is to decide that there is a vacancy to be filled. Increasingly, a more strategic and questioning approach may be taken. If, for example, the vacancy arises because an employee has left, managers may take the opportunity to review the work itself and consider whether it could be processed in an alternative way. For example, could the work be done on a part-time, job-share or flexitime basis? Alternatively, the job could be automated. The financial services sector in the UK provides one example of where technological developments have resulted in both significant job losses and changed patterns of work in recent decades.

On the assumption that a post does need to be filled, it will be necessary to devise specifications. Whether a competency-based, or strength-based approach (these concepts will be defined later in the chapter) or the more traditional method of formal job descriptions and person specifications is chosen, a CIPD overview (2021j) noted that specifications would need to reflect the duties and requirements of the job along with the skills, aptitudes, knowledge, experience, qualifications and personal qualities that are necessary to perform the job effectively. Consideration should also be given to how the recruiter intends to measure and elicit information regarding those skills. Are they essential to job performance or merely desirable and can they be objectively measured?

6.3.3 *Attracting candidates*

The next stage in the recruitment cycle is the attraction of candidates, as one important objective of a recruitment method is to realise an appropriate number of suitable candidates within reasonable cost constraints. Pilbeam and Corbridge (2010) note that there is no ideal number of applications and no intrinsic value in attracting a high volume of candidates, and neither is there a single best way to recruit applicants. The chosen recruitment medium needs to ensure that there is a sufficient number of suitably qualified candidates from which to make a selection without being overwhelmed with large numbers of unsuitable applications. Using a recruitment agency to find a small number of suitable candidates, particularly for senior or specialised posts, may prove a significantly more cost-effective and efficient method than a major web-based advertising campaign that generates a large response from unsuitable candidates. The choice of method will also be influenced by the availability of candidates; that is, is there likely to be a shortage or surplus of candidates? For example, in the highly competitive graduate recruitment market, organisations will match the choice of methods to the nature of the vacancy, the university or course being targeted and the specific sector, and other relevant factors. Small employers are more likely to carry out a targeted recruitment, while a large organisation (with a high-profile employer brand) will utilise a variety of methods to attract talent, in so doing accepting that they will receive a large volume of speculative applications (Suff, 2012a).

 Reflective activity 6.2

According to the CIPD (2021i), the most effective methods for attracting applications are corporate websites and professional networking sites such as LinkedIn. We are also seeing an increase in organisations using employee referral schemes, where existing workers are allowed – or even counselled – to recommend people they know for job openings.

How can the networking site LinkedIn aid the recruitment process, from both an employer and potential employee's perspective? Does the evidence suggest that LinkedIn is used more for particular types of job and role? Would you recommend that an organisation develop a social media recruitment strategy? Give reasons for your conclusions. Where possible, discuss your findings in a small group – either face-to-face or virtual, referring to your own experience of LinkedIn where relevant.

Taken overall, which method of recruitment should be adopted? There is no single best way, and a contingency approach involving an analysis of what might be effective in particular circumstances is advocated. In other words, 'it all depends'.

Human resources professionals should carefully consider and review which methods have been most effective in the past and which method(s) would be most appropriate for the current vacancy. They should also, critically, keep methods under review, making full use of emerging technologies.

6.3.4 Selection

Selection is one of the last stages of the recruitment process and includes the choice of methods by which an employer will produce a shortlist of applicants following the initial recruitment stage, leading to an employment decision. For most people, this is the only visible stage of the resourcing cycle as their experience of it is likely to be as a subject or candidate rather than involvement in planning the entire process. While recruitment can be perceived as a positive activity generating an optimum number of jobseekers, selection is inherently negative in that it will probably involve rejection of applicants.

It would be prudent to argue that selection decisions should be based on a range of selection tools as some have poor predictive job ability. While it is almost inconceivable that employment would be offered or accepted without a face-to-face encounter, many organisations still rely almost exclusively on the outcome of interviews to make selection decisions.

To have any value, interviews should be conducted or supervised by trained individuals, be structured to follow a previously agreed set of questions mirroring the person specification or job profile and allow candidates the opportunity to ask questions. However, the interview is more than a selection device, it is a mechanism that is capable of communicating information about the job and the organisation to the candidate, with the aim of giving a realistic job preview, providing information about the process, and thus can minimise the risk of job offers being rejected. Organisations seeking high performance in their selection processes should therefore give considerable attention to maximising the uses of the interview and, ideally, combine this method with other psychometric measures where appropriate.

6.4 Validity of selection methods

It may appear self-evident that organisational decision-makers will wish to ensure that their recruitment (and in this case) selection methods are effective. We have already suggested, however, that making judgements on an individual's personal characteristics and suitability for future employment is inherently problematic and that many 'normal' selection methods contain significant flaws. There is also the question of what is meant by the terms 'reliability' and 'validity' when applied to recruitment and selection.

'Reliability' in the context of workforce selection can refer to the following issues:

- Temporal or 'retest' stability where the effectiveness of a selection tool is assessed by consistency of results obtained over time. An individual could, for example, complete a personality inventory or intelligence test at different times over a period of several years, although in the latter case it would be important to isolate the impact of repeated practice on results.

- Consistency, that is, can the test measure what it sets out to? Some elements of IQ tests have, for example, been criticised for emphasising a person's vocabulary, which might in turn be influenced by their education and general background rather than their innate intelligence.

Validity in this area is typically subdivided into the following aspects:

- Face validity has an emphasis on the acceptability of the selection measure, including to the candidate him/herself. For example, it is possible (although extremely unlikely) that there is a correlation between a person's hat size and their job competence. However, you would be reluctant to measure candidates' heads as part of their selection due to their probable scepticism at the use of this measure.

- Content validity refers to the nature of the measure and in particular its adequacy as a tool. For example, the UK driving test had been criticised for not assessing ability in either night driving or travelling on motorways.

- Predictive validity centres on linkages between results or scores on a selection measure and subsequent outcome – most commonly job performance at a future point. Here it is important to identify when the comparison will be made, for example immediately in the case of a simple job requiring little training or, more commonly, at an intermediate point, possibly after a suitable probationary period.

We argue here that validity, along with fairness, should be the overriding indicator of a selection method for high performance organisations and that it is important to obtain sophisticated data on validity in all its forms. Pilbeam and Corbridge (2010, p 189) provide a summary of the predictive validity of selection methods based on the findings of various research studies:

1.0	Certain prediction
0.9	
0.8	
0.7	Assessment centres for development
0.6	Skillful and structured interviews
0.5	Work sampling
	Ability tests
0.4	Assessment centres for job performance
	Biodata
	Personality assessment
0.3	Unstructured interviews
0.2	
0.1	References
0.0	Graphology
	Astrology

In addition to this list could be the inclusion of 'viewer-rating' of applicants' social media activity such as Facebook, Twitter and Instagram. However, research has advised caution to be exercised if using this as a type of selection process due to the potential implication of bias and also limited predictive validity of actual job performance (Zhang et al, 2020).

In fact, looking at success of validity measures per se should be treated with caution as they can be affected by the performance indicators used and also the way the tools were applied. They indicate, nonetheless, both variability between measures and some overall degree of uncertainty when predicting future work performance during the selection process.

While it is recommended that validity should be the prime factor in choosing selection tools, it would be naive not to recognise that other factors such as cost and applicability may be relevant. How practical, therefore, is it to conduct any particular measure? As indicated earlier, an organisation aiming for high performance is recommended to adopt valid measures as opposed to merely practical or less costly ones. Again, one should recognise that recruitment and selection is contingent upon other factors such as the work itself. A 'high performance' organisation in the fast-food industry may legitimately decide not to adopt some relatively valid but expensive methods when selecting fast-food operatives. It should be noted that the oft-derided method of interviewing can in reality be a relatively valid method if structured and conducted skillfully.

6.4.1 Recruitment and selection: art or science?

Systematic models of recruitment and selection based on a resourcing cycle should not necessarily imply that this process is underpinned by scientific reasoning and method. As we have seen, Pilbeam and Corbridge (2010) note that even the most valid methods fall some way short of complete predictive validity. Thompson and McHugh (2009) went further, taking a critical view on the general use and, in particular, the validity of employee selection methods. In commenting on the use of personality tests in selection, these authors state that 'in utilising tests employers are essentially clutching at straws and on this basis will probably use anything that will help them make some kind of systematic decision' (p 285). They went on to identify long-discredited – but widely used – selection methods, such as the use of polygraphs to detect lying and other methods, such as astrology, which are deemed more appropriate in some cultures rather than others. It is indeed important to keep in mind that today's received wisdom in the area of recruitment and selection, just as in the management canon more generally, may be criticised and even widely rejected in the future.

The process of recruitment and selection continues nonetheless to be viewed as best carried out via sequential but linked stages of first gathering a pool of applicants, a screening-out process, followed by the positive step of actual selection. This apparently logical ordering of the activities is largely viewed as essential to achieve minimum thresholds of effectiveness.

6.4.2 Onboarding

It is not always the case that selected employees are immediately capable of performing to the maximum level in their allocated role(s) and important stages in the resourcing cycle occur post-selection. When selecting, many organisations are making a longer-term prediction of a new employee's capability. This accounts for many organisations imposing a probationary period in which employees' performance and future potential can be assessed in the work setting. The resourcing cycle extends into this post-selection phase, now frequently termed 'onboarding'. Any named induction period, and the early phases of employment more generally, constitutes a critically important part of both successful integration into the workplace culture and development as a fully functioning worker. The final stage of the resourcing cycle involves evaluation of the process and reflection on lessons learned from the process and their implications for the future.

6.4.3 Recruitment costs

A concern with effectiveness in recruitment and selection becomes all the more important when one considers the costs of getting things wrong. We begin with apparent costs which centre on the direct costs of recruitment procedures, but one might also consider the so-called opportunity costs of engaging in repeated recruitment and selection when workers leave an organisation. An excessive preoccupation with recruitment and selection will divert a manager from other activities they could usefully be engaged in. It is also useful to consider the 'investment', including training resources, lost to the employer when a worker leaves prematurely. According to the CIPD *Resourcing and Talent Planning Survey* (2021i) the median recruitment cost of filling a vacancy has fallen from £7,250 for senior managers/directors in 2015, to £3,000 in 2021 and to £1,000 for other employees These costs are down on previous estimates and may reflect the increased availability of labour as well as the increase in use of employee referral schemes.

Implicit costs are less quantifiable and include the following categories:

- poor performance
- reduced productivity
- low quality products or services
- dissatisfied customers or other stakeholders
- low employee morale.

The implicit costs mentioned here are in themselves clearly undesirable outcomes in all organisations. In high-performing organisations, 'average' or 'adequate' performance may also be insufficient, and recruitment and selection may be deemed to have failed unless workers have become 'thinking performers'.

6.5 Contemporary themes in recruitment and selection

6.5.1 The competency approach

Typically, decisions on selecting a potential employee are made primarily with a view to taking on the most appropriate person to do a particular job in terms of their current or, more commonly, potential competencies. In recent years this concept has been extended to search for employees who are flexible and able to contribute to additional and/or changing job roles. This approach contrasts with a more traditional model which involves first compiling a wide-ranging job description for the current post in question, followed by the use of a person specification, which in effect forms a checklist along which candidates can be evaluated on criteria such as knowledge, skills and personal qualities. This traditional approach involves, in essence, matching characteristics of an 'ideal' person to fill a defined job. There is a seductive logic in this apparently rational approach to fulfilling current requirements. However, there are in-built problems in its application if judgements of an individual's personality are inherently subjective and open to error and, furthermore, if these personal characteristics are suited to present rather than changing circumstances.

The competencies model, in contrast, seeks to identify abilities needed to perform a job well rather than focusing on personal characteristics such as politeness or assertiveness. The CIPD defines 'competency' as the behaviours that employees must have, or must acquire, to apply to a situation in order to achieve high levels of performance, while 'competence' relates to a system of minimum standards or is demonstrated by performance and outputs (CIPD, 2021k). Reference to competencies can indeed underpin an integrated HR strategy. Post-selection competencies can be linked with employee development, performance management including appraisal and also reward activities. The key question to ask is what attributes are necessary to undertake roles, or what attributes are shared by the people who have already performed best in the role? There is an obvious danger here when roles are flexible or subject to major changes.

We should note that competency-based approaches can present a barrier to achieving an organisation's equality and diversity objectives (Torrington et al, 2020). Where innovation and creativity are required, it may be better to recruit people with more diverse characteristics and an inflexible competencies-based approach may restrain this.

Competency-based models still remain the most popular method with a CV/application form and it is suggested that the competence-based model may be a meaningful way of underpinning recruitment and selection in the current fast-moving world of work and can accordingly contribute more effectively to securing high performance. However, we are also seeing an increase in the use of strengths-based interviews which are being used in one of two ways; either via a profile that has highlighted which strengths would be appropriate for the role and therefore selecting the applicant against these criteria or where the interviewer looks to tease out the applicant's strengths to determine whether they are the strengths needed for the role and whether the applicant is passionate about the job (CIPD, 2017b). For this to be effective the interviewee will need to be trained in this style of observational interviewing as well as remaining as objective as possible.

6.5.2 Flexibility and teamwork

Many commentators refer to significant changes in the world of work and the implications these have for the recruitment and selection of a workforce. As far back as 2003, Searle (p 276) noted that:

> Increasingly employees are working in self-organised teams in which it is difficult to determine the boundaries between different job holders' responsibilities. The team undertakes the task and members co-operate and work together to achieve it. Recruitment and selection practices focus on identifying a suitable person for the job, but ... isolating a job's roles and responsibilities may be difficult to do in fast-changing and team-based situations.

There is here an implication both that teamworking skills could usefully be made part of employee selection and that an individual's job specification should increasingly be designed and interpreted flexibly. It can plausibly be posited that we now inhabit a world of work in which unforeseen problems are thrown up routinely and on an ongoing basis and there is seldom time to respond to them in a measured fashion (Clegg, Pitsis and Mount, 2022). In this type of business environment, decisions made can be 'rational' in terms of past practice and events but may in fact be revealed to be flawed or even obsolete when they are made in the new context.

If we accept this analysis of work in the twenty-first century, there is therefore an implication that organisations aiming for high performance may need to use selection methods which assess qualities of flexibility and creative thinking (irrespective of whether they are using a traditional or competency recruitment and selection model). Of course, many jobs may still require task-holders to work in a predictable and standardised way, so one should exercise caution when examining this rhetoric. Interestingly, however, recruitment and selection practices should themselves be kept under constant review and as highlighted by Holbeche (2018), the resourcing model itself needs to be flexible to enable the organisation to achieve competitive advantage, especially if we accept the reality of a business world characterised by radical, rather than incremental, change. Organisations also need to ensure they do not infringe upon discrimination laws when trying to create the 'right' teams for their organisation.

 Case study 6.2

Good moral character in the air?

'We are looking for young, single ladies aged between 21 and 27, of good moral character, with good posture and appearance and weighing between 7st 12lb and 9st 8lb.'. This is part of a 'candidate specification' from a job advertisement put out by Pan American World Airways in 1961. The selection processes for air stewardesses at that time was recalled by an ex-employee over 50 years later (Riegel, 2013). Over a thousand women attended interviews in response to the advertisement. Two interviews followed which included 'a little catwalk so the applicants' figures could be checked'.

The airline's preoccupation with physical appearance and deportment continued in service for the successful cabin crew. There were weigh-ins every month and workers were suspended without pay until they had shed the requisite weight. All stewardesses had to sport a collar-length hairstyle and apply the same make of eye shadow and lipstick. Although this reportedly 'made some girls look like corpses,' they had to receive written permission to use another shade. There is no record of the physical requirements for male cabin crew at Pan American at that time.

When recalling the air stewardess role of the early 1960s in 2013, the ex-employee said: 'I'm very proud to have been one of the first generation of women to have had a career and be financially independent. I worked hard but had the time of my life. It really was the best job in the world.'

The selection and indeed work experiences of cabin crew detailed above are clearly 'of their time'. In 2022, the German carrier Lufthansa stressed 'customer-obsession, adaptability, teamwork and a safety-first attitude' when seeking cabin crew. The airline also promotes equality, diversity and inclusion, welcoming applicants without regard to gender identity or expression, marital status, age, race or religion. Nonetheless, weight should be proportionate to height, there is a reference to 'impeccable grooming standards' and cabin crew should have no visible tattoos or piercings.

1 Undertake a search of any two current airlines' candidate specifications for cabin crew. Identify the assumptions they contain regarding this job role.

2 Present arguments for and against cabin crew having visible tattoos or piercings. Give reasons for your findings.

SOURCE: Airlines Career Jobs (2022) Lufthansa www.airlinescareer.org/lufthansa-cabin-crew-jobs-careers

6.5.3 *Recruiting in the virtual world*

The rise in the use of the internet was probably the most significant development in the recruitment field in the early twenty-first century, and its effects continue to grow apace with the use of corporate websites, social media and apps. Recent surveys on recruitment and attraction strategies (CIPD 2021i) continue to show that corporate websites and professional networking sites are the most effective method for attracting applicants to organisations. However, there is mixed evidence that the internet produces better-quality candidates, and interestingly since 2019 we have seen an increase in employee-referral schemes. These schemes involve employees recommending people they know, for example friends of family for roles within the organisation. The emergence of this method (as a formal policy) may have been due to the effects of the Covid-19 pandemic with organisations needing to undertake urgent recruitment while minimising costs. (CIPD 2021i).

The benefits of online recruitment to employers include increased accessibility, speed, reduced costs and no geographical limits (CIPD, 2021j), although this does come with some challenges as the number of applications may increase from unsuitable applicants. The overall increase in applications, including those that are suitable, will in any case lead to an increased administrative burden. Suff (2013) also comments that applicants are more likely to know something about the organisation and its work if they use employers' websites. Employers value this aspect of online recruitment as it facilitates company branding and can enhance the appeal of working for the organisation. Indeed, developing a positive brand image is now seen as key to recruiting good-quality candidates, and the majority of organisations have made considerable improvements to their corporate websites. In the few years leading up to 2022 we saw an increase in organisations using diversity and inclusion statements on their corporate websites in part to appeal to a diverse range of applicants as an 'employer of choice' (Jonsen et al, 2021). Employer branding and therefore enhanced visibility as an employer of choice can also attract workers who will fit in well and perform to a high standard. Another advantage of a successful employer branding exercise is potential reduction in overall recruitment costs (Taylor, 2019).

Whatever the pros and cons, online recruitment continues to expand. Other employers, such as Microsoft, are enhancing brand visibility and credibility by having a wider internet recruitment presence. Microsoft uses its online tools to impact and influence its public image and reach a broader audience, in order to help create a diverse workplace with varied skills and talents.

In recent years gamification has emerged as part of the trend to use information technology in recruitment and selection. Gamification is the use of gaming techniques as a motivational tool by engaging applicants in organisational scenarios in which their competencies can be evidenced. The following example from the Marriott Hotel Group provides a good example of gamification in action.

Reflective activity 6.3

My Marriott Hotel – a new way to attract applicants?

The first ever culinary social media game, My Marriott Hotel, was launched on Facebook to promote Marriott International Inc. Developed in conjunction with Evviva Brands, a specialised brand consultancy, the game was designed as a tool for reaching employment candidates in countries such as China and India, where the service industry is growing, but hospitality has not traditionally been viewed as a highly sought-after career. By managing a virtual hotel kitchen, players are given insights into the world of hotels and a culinary career at Marriott. Three weeks after the launch of the game, the Marriott jobs and careers page on Facebook had received over 10,000 'likes' and the game was being played in over 100 countries. Existing employees were also encouraged to share and promote the game within their own social networks.

The game was developed in response to feedback from surveys and focus groups that suggested that the company needed to enhance its online profile. Despite appearing in a 'Best Place to Work' survey its brand recognition had been low in many countries.

Would you be attracted to a career in hospitality management as a result of playing this game?

SOURCE: Adapted from Freer, T (2011) Social media gaming – a recipe for employer brand success, *Strategic HR Review*, **11** (1), pp 13–17

6.6 Fairness in recruitment and selection

As the CIPD reported (2018a), there is a strong case from both a business perspective and moral perspective for ensuring workplaces are inclusive and diverse, therefore, when we consider what is meant by making appropriate selection decisions, other factors, including fairness and equity, are also important.

Decisions made in the course of a recruitment and selection process should be perceived as essentially fair and admissible to all parties, including people who have been rejected. There is evidence to support the view that applicants are concerned with both procedural justice, that is how far they felt that selection methods were related to a job, and the extent to which procedures were explained to them; and distributive justice where their concern shifts to how equitably they felt they were treated and whether the outcome of selection was perceived to be fair (see Gilliland, 1993). This research still holds true and supported by Wolgast, Backstrom and Bjorklund (2017) who report that structured recruitment and selection processes reduce the opportunity for potential bias and result in hiring the most appropriate person for the role. It is reasonable to suggest that employers should take care in choosing selection methods in order to maintain credibility among applicants, as well, of course, as assessing the predictive value of the methods.

Fairness in selection also extends to the area of discrimination and equal opportunities, as we saw in Chapter 5. In the UK, for example, current legislation is intended to make unlawful discrimination on the grounds of age, race, nationality or ethnic origin, religion or belief, disability, gender, pregnancy and maternity, marital status and sexual orientation. The law identifies both direct discrimination, where an individual is treated less favourably on the sole grounds of their membership of a group covered in the relevant legislation, and indirect discrimination, which occurs when a provision applied to both groups disproportionately affects one in reality, for example a height requirement. The Equality and Human Rights Commission highlights headhunting as one area in which indirect discrimination may occur. Headhunters may, in approaching individuals already in jobs, contravene this aspect of the law if existing jobs are dominated by one sex or ethnic group, for example. Compliance with equal opportunities legislation provides one example of performance infrastructure and would, it is surmised, reap business benefits, that is recruiting from the truly qualified labour pool and avoiding negative outcomes such as costly and reputation-damaging legal processes.

High-performance organisations may seek to go beyond the compliance approach and work towards a policy or even strategy of managing diversity (see also Chapters 8 and 9). As defined by CIPD (2018a, p 11), a managing diversity approach:

> we argue that organisations should understand that diversity is necessary, but the organisational context needs to support that diversity and be inclusive, in order to see positive outcomes for the business and individuals.

It is thus important to ensure such a policy is operationalised in the field of recruitment and selection, as staff involved in this activity can be said to act as gatekeepers of an organisation and the way it is perceived in the world outside.

 Case study 6.3

It really is a two-way process

Over many decades, recruitment and selection has been seen as a 'matching' activity whereby an employing organisation would chose an employee based on how it perceived they would 'fit' a particular role as well as the organisation itself. Of course, candidates always had a degree of choice in whether or not they accepted a job offer, although in reality such choice could be heavily constrained by financial and other person circumstances.

More recently there has been a renewed focus on the role of the candidate. Take this example from 2022. After graduating from university in 2020, Chloe Zielinska was preparing for a job interview at a tech company in Peterborough and decided to do some research. Zielinska, aged 23, had studied Geography at Durham University and had limited experience in software engineering, other than completing several free online courses. However, her prospective employer was offering new employees at her level a £55,000 initial salary plus a raft of attractive benefits.

Zielinska decided to look up the company on Glassdoor, the jobs review site where employees post comments. She was 'appalled' by some feedback on the company's culture leading to her withdrawing her application prior to the scheduled interview date. She was subsequently employed by Brighton-based company AVEgreen, which she said had 'a great vibe'. 'It's really important to find a company that has your own values.' Chloe Zielinska was very clear about the type of employer she valued – and those she didn't. 'With some companies, it's a work-to-the bones sort of situation. You might get paid a fortune to do it but I chose this line of work because I was interested in it, and I'd rather stay enjoying the work.'

The importance of company values for in-demand younger workers was stressed by several employment professionals. Emma Sinclair, Chief Executive of EnterpriseAlumni said: 'The workforce are so empowered that companies are being forced to be more flexible, compassionate and long-term about their thinking.' Ashley Ramrachia who runs the Academy tech training camp, said younger people were now 'very selective' about who they work for. 'This generation doesn't want to work for companies without a purpose or a mission' and Wes Rashid from Accountancy Cloud said he had tried to tackle the talent shortage by focusing on a diversity and inclusion agenda which the tech sector had struggled to improve.

At certain times, power in recruitment and selection can 'flip' to the candidate as part of variation in supply and demand in the labour market. In 2022 a 'white hot' job market in certain sectors appears to have been accompanied by a longer-term trend for certain categories of applicants taking an ethical stance towards potential employers, thereby impacting on those organisations' policies. It is clear that recruitment and selection is best viewed as a dynamic process, with in the current decade a sometimes highly significant role for the candidate.

1   Identify three employers you would wish to work for. To what extent do the values espoused by these organisations influence your choice?
2   What degree of power do you perceive that you have in the labour market in terms of obtaining new employment and why? Share your views with others in group discussion and compare responses.
3   Do you ultimately concur with the statement that recruitment and selection is a 'two-way process'? Give reasons for your conclusions.

SOURCE: Based on Nimmo (2022) War for talent hots up as workers rate firms on their morals, *Sunday Times*
Names and some other details have been changed.

6.7 The extent of professional practice

6.7.1 Small and medium-sized enterprises

There is evidence to suggest that many HRM practices often prescribed in the academic literature are more common in some sectors of business than others. In Chapter 4 we examined the situation of small and medium-sized enterprises (SMEs). We should note at the outset how much of a role SMEs play within modern economies; as noted in a 2019 OECD report, large firms are in fact the exception rather than the rule across the world. It is also important to acknowledge the wide variety of organisations contained within this category, ranging from micro-businesses with less than 10 employees to larger organisations employing up to 249 people (Harney and Alkhalaf, 2021). There has also been a conflation of smallness with newness, while small tech start-ups may have a very different culture to a sole trader garage or teashop. Nonetheless, SMEs as a grouping are worthy of close examination in the field of people management.

What is distinctive about SMEs in terms of recruitment and selection? The major finding over time saw SMEs as less likely to have in-house HR expertise and sophisticated systems in place (Cully, Woodland and O'Reilly, 1999). A study carried out by Cassell, Nadin and Gray (2002) in SMEs in the north of England, focused on both the use and perceived value (by employers) of a range of HRM procedures. In the area of recruitment and selection, only 31 per cent of firms in the sample used wide-ranging employee development and recruitment and selection procedures. Interestingly, 38 per cent of the sample questioned said that they did not use recruitment and selection procedures at all. In the companies that did make use of them, 50 per cent found that the procedures helped 'entirely' or 'a lot' in over half of the instances in which they are used. This is some way from the picture of widespread usage and the assumed universal benefits conveyed in some sources.

Therefore, is the traditional picture of partial and fragmented recruitment and selection practices in SMEs still valid? Krishnan and Scullion (2017) concluded that the SMEs they studied lacked the resources, capability and time to develop a bespoke talent management strategy. The CIPD *Resourcing and Talent Planning Survey* (2021i) found that SMEs were twice less likely to advertise jobs with flexible working which could reflect low awareness of the concept as well, of course, as the nature of their businesses. Mohdzani (2021) focused on the take-up of human resource information systems (HRISs) among 13 SMEs, finding that nine of them had no HRIS at all, while the other four were not deemed fit for purpose in those companies. The result was that many routine tasks which could have been automated were carried out manually, with people professionals tied up in routine administration rather than contributing to strategy. Responding to organisational growth through recruitment was, unsurprisingly, described as 'difficult and stressful'.

The reality of the context faced by managers of SMEs will frame their responses in an entirely understandable way. Mohdzani (2021) stressed the need for HR professionals to 'fight their corner' and get owner/managers buy-in when attempting to enhance people management policies and practices. Prescriptive 'textbook-style' approaches may be viewed as inappropriate or naïve in reality. It would, of course, be as damaging for SMEs as for any other organisation if a lack of high-quality practices in recruitment and selection were seen to inhibit performance and SMEs have been, to a degree, characterised by reactive and fragmented approaches to managing people. However, any assumption that universally applicable approaches to recruitment and selection are needed may ignore the distinctive processes and practices faced by particular organisations.

Reflective activity 6.4

Recent challenges in recruitment and selection

Prior to the pandemic (2020–2021) the CIPD (2018b) reported that the demand for labour was robust and therefore we were seeing a tightening labour market which led to a competitive market for skills and the increasing challenge of attracting suitable applicants. It had been anticipated that labour would become even more constrained, partly due to the introduction of migration restrictions on EU nationals. The more recent CIPD survey (2021i) noted that the impact of pandemic exacerbated the recruitment difficulties with additional challenges in incorporating socially distanced / online recruitment and selection processes. Many organisations (54 per cent) looked to upskill their current employees as well as offering work flexibility (54 per cent). This highlights the need to develop talent management strategies that incorporate not only recruitment but also development and retention. As highlighted by Deborah Fernon of CIPD, 'those employers who have development opportunities are more likely to stay, which reduces turnover. Secondly, a good learning and development culture will foster a strong employer brand, helping to attract key talent.' In addition, offering greater work flexibility enables the labour market to widen to include those individuals who are not able to 'work regular hours in a specific location' or to those who want more control over their work–life balance.

This research highlights the importance of referring to contemporary evidence when analysing recruitment and selection in general terms and also points to the importance of the post-selection phase in retaining staff.

 Reflective activity 6.5

Employers are from Mars, young people are from Venus

One of Britain' biggest insurers has banned the words 'energetic and 'enthusiastic' from its job adverts because it says they deter older applicants. Phoenix Group claimed that these adjectives were 'younger-age stereotypical words' that could put off over-50s from applying. Phoenix is run by Andy Briggs, who was appointed as business champion for older workers by the UK Government in 2017. He has warned that older workers have been disproportionally hit by the Covid pandemic.

Younger workers can also be affected by a mismatch between the expectations of employers and young people in the recruitment process (Stevens, 2013). This conflict of understanding hinders entry to the labour market for young jobseekers and contributes to high rates of youth unemployment, according to a 2013 CIPD report. The mismatch also fuels a 'ticking timebomb' of skills shortages for UK business, who might be unwittingly limiting their access to a diverse group of talent in the 16–24 age group.

Specific problems identified by the report were:

- 'scattergun' applications from young people who had not researched the organisation and/or tailored their submissions
- a vicious cycle of employers asking for workplace experience in entry-level roles
- lengthy and untransparent recruitment and selection procedures meaning that young applicants were unaware of the stages involved
- poor careers advice and guidance in schools, with resultant lack of awareness on how to improve chances of finding a job.

1   What steps can be taken to reduce the mismatch between employers and younger job applicants?

2   To what extent is it part of the role of HR managers to address a social problem such as the impact of Covid on older workers. Refer to both Chapters 4 and 9 of this book when devising your response.

6.8 Recruitment and selection: a contingency approach

The underlying principle that organisational policies and practices need to be shaped within a particular context is often referred to as the 'contingency approach'. The argument put forward within this viewpoint is that successful policies and strategies are those that apply principles within the particular context faced by the unique organisation.

One example of a 'contingent factor' that can impact upon recruitment and selection is national culture. French (2015) draws attention to important cross-cultural differences in the area, for example different cultures emphasise different attributes when approaching the recruitment and selection of employees. It is also the case that particular selection methods are used more or less frequently in different societies. For example, in individualistic cultures such as the USA and UK there is a preoccupation with selection methods which emphasise individual differences. Many psychometric tests can indeed be seen to originate from the US. Furthermore, in a society which emphasises individual achievement as opposed to ascribed status (eg, through age or gender), one might expect a raft of legislation prohibiting discrimination against particular groups. Here the expectation is that selection should be on the basis of individual personal characteristics or qualifications. This may contrast with more collectivist societies, for example China, where personal connections may assume a more prominent role. Bjorkman and Yuan (1999) conducted one of several studies which reached this overall conclusion. It may also be true that selection methods are given varying degrees of face validity in different societies. A CIPD survey (2004b) on graphology discovered that, while relatively few companies in the

UK used graphology as a trusted method of selecting employees, its adoption was far more widespread, common and therefore accepted in other countries, including France.

In summary, the contingency approach with the underlying message that managing people successfully depends on contextual factors – 'it all depends' – can readily be applied to the area of recruitment and selection. The increasingly large number of organisations operating across national boundaries, or who employ workers from different cultural backgrounds, can benefit from formulating policies within an awareness of cultural difference.

6.8.1 *Recruitment and selection and organisational culture*

It is unsurprising that the culture of a particular work organisation will influence selection decisions, with recruiters both consciously and unconsciously selecting those individuals who will 'best fit' that culture. In some organisations recruitment policy and practice is derived from their overall strategy which disseminates values into the recruitment and selection process. We provide an example of a culture and values-driven process in our IKEA case study which bookends this chapter. This company's focus on culture is by no means an outlier. Andersen (2022), cites the example of the streaming service Netflix which aims to create an environment in which employees are free to make their own decisions without 'managing up'. For Andersen (2022), such a mindset is identified by the company after 'an extensive and thorough hiring process' after which they 'have a person fully qualified to make the right calls'. In the current decade you should not find difficulty in identifying similar examples of culture and values-driven recruitment. However, we would stress that fitting the culture of an organisation does not always imply a search for autonomous or creative employees – see Chapter 11 for a discussion of 'McDonaldisation' where a strong culture involves work processes reducing the importance of individual inputs.

Other research has demonstrated that individuals as well as organisations seek this 'best fit', providing evidence that many individuals prefer to work in organisations that reflect their personal values. Judge and Cable (1997) and Backhaus (2003) found that jobseekers may actively seek a good 'person–organisation fit' when considering prospective employers. This, of course, provides further support for the processual two-way model of recruitment and selection. We provide a topical example in this chapter in Case study 6.3 where we encourage readers to consider how they regard potential employers and to evaluate their relative power in the selection process more generally. However, justifying selection decisions on the basis of cultural fit means that there are ethical issues to consider in terms of reasons for rejection: are organisations justified in determining who does and does not fit? It may be that practical concerns also emerge, for example in the danger of maintaining organisations in the image of current role models – which may be inappropriate in the future. Psychologists have also long recognised the threat posed by 'groupthink' where innovation is suppressed by a dominant group and a 'king's new clothes' syndrome develops, with individuals reluctant to voice objections to bad group decisions.

6.9 Conclusion

This chapter indicates the key importance of recruitment and selection in successful people management and leadership. An awareness of issues and concepts within this area are important tools for anyone involved with leading, managing and developing people, even if they are not human resource managers per se. A recognition of the importance of this aspect of people management is not new and success in this field has often been linked with the avoidance of critical failure factors including undesirable levels of staff turnover and claims of discrimination from unsuccessful job applicants.

It has been argued here that it is also possible to identify aspects of recruitment and selection which link with critical success factors in the twenty-first century context, differentiating organisational performance and going some way to delivering employees who can act as 'thinking performers'. It is proposed, for example, that a competencies-based approach focusing on abilities needed to perform a job well may be preferable to the use of a more traditional matching of job and person specifications. In addition, many organisations may increasingly wish to identify qualities of flexibility and creative thinking among potential employees, although this may not always be the case; many contemporary jobs do not require such competencies on the part of job-holders. It is also the case that organisations should be preoccupied with the question of validity of selection methods, ideally combining methods which are strong on practicality and cost such as interviewing, with other measures which are more effective predictors of performance. It is proposed finally that a managing diversity approach, welcoming individual difference, may enhance organisational performance and create a climate in which thinking performers can emerge and flourish.

However, it is proposed that a contingency approach to recruitment and selection, recognising that organisational policies and practices are shaped by contextual factors, remains valid and that effectiveness in recruitment and selection may vary according to particular situational factors. In this regard it is noted that cultural differences could be an important factor in predicting the relative success of recruitment and selection measures.

 Case study 6.4

Why work for IKEA? Part two

IKEA puts great stress upon recruiting employees who will complement its organisational culture. After reading this chapter, consider two further questions:

1 What are the potential benefits of selecting a workforce in terms of an organisation's culture?

2 What are the philosophical and practical arguments against selection based on values and work culture?

KEY LEARNING POINTS

1   Managers involved in recruitment and selection of employees have a key gatekeeper role in giving or denying access to work.
2   Effective recruitment and selection is characterised by knowledge of social science topics such as perception.
3   A staged logical approach to recruitment and selection, seeing it as a process, is recommended.
4   The validity of different selection methods should be considered for appropriateness in terms of the process and the role.
5   Fairness is a fundamentally important principle reflecting the ethically loaded nature of the activity.
6   The resourcing model should be regularly reviewed to ensure it is fit for purpose for the organisation to achieve and maintain competitive advantage.

 Review questions

1   Indicate with examples three ways in which recruitment and selection policies and practices can be used by an organisation aiming to develop staff as part of a talent management strategy.
2   Evaluate the evidence regarding the potential validity of biodata and personality assessment as tools for selecting employees.
3   What do you understand by the contingency approach to recruitment and selection?

Provide two examples, from academic sources or your own experience, to illustrate this approach.
4   Evaluate the effectiveness of social media and online recruitment methods in comparison to the employee referral scheme. In what circumstances might the social media route be a more effective way of attracting applicants?

Explore further

Arnold, J, Coyne, I, Randall, R and Patterson, F (2020) *Work Psychology: Understanding human behaviour in the workplace.* 7th edn, Pearson, London. The authors provide a clear and interesting discussion of different selection techniques and their validity.

CIPD (2021i) *Resourcing and Talent Planning Survey 2021*, Report, CIPD, London, www.cipd.co.uk/ Images/resourcing-and-talent-planning-2021-1_tcm18-100907.pdf (https://perma.cc/E8SE-SKWU)

Thompson, P and McHugh, D (2009) *Work Organisations: A critical approach*, 4th edn, Palgrave Macmillan, Basingstoke. In Chapter 19, 'Masks for tasks', the authors take a critical perspective on the topics of how we assess others' attributes and how such perceptions are used in employee selection.

Torrington, D, Hall, L, Atkinson, C and Taylor, S (2020) *Human Resource Management*, 11th edn, Pearson, Harlow. Chapters 8 and 9 of this well-established textbook are recommended as another voice on many of the topics covered here.

07
Talent management and developing employees for performance

FOTEINI KRAVARITI

LEARNING OUTCOMES

After reading this chapter, you should be able to:

- understand the conceptualisation of talent and talent management in relation to context
- discuss the growing importance of talent management agendas and how a recalibration can enhance organisational performance
- examine the various roles of key talent management stakeholders
- identify and evaluate approaches to employee learning and development including self-directed learning, coaching and mentoring, management development, career management, and continuing professional development.

7.1 Overview

Today businesses operate in a hyper-changing and volatile environment wherein quick responses are regarded as vital to their success and even survival. While business leaders are working against the clock, they are confronted with a range of profound challenges, one of the most significant being talent deficits in the market. Organisations have learnt that global demand for a highly skilled and adaptable workforce of agile employees underpins the workplace as a critical learning environment. Proactive support for talent training and development can differentiate an organisation by leveraging superior employee performance and engagement, and such outcomes can be viewed as an offensive strategy for sustainable success and industry leadership.

This chapter focuses on talent management as a key strategy for acquiring, developing and retaining individuals in pivotal positions, who can adapt through learning and expand their skill capability so as to deliver business agendas. We begin by conceptualising talent and talent management, before highlighting the latter's evolving emphasis on individual and organisational outcomes. We then turn to discuss the emerging importance of considering talent management within the country and sector contexts in which organisations operate, in addition examining key stakeholders' roles. We also review the talent management cycle; namely, talent acquisition, development and retention. We further delve into discussion of a range of work-based learning and developmental approaches that facilitate organisations in nurturing talent, including self-directed learning, coaching and mentoring, management development, career management and continuing professional development (CPD). The chapter concludes by considering a recalibration of talent management agendas for improved organisational performance.

7.2 Towards conceptualising talent and talent management

First coined in 2001 by McKinsey (see Michaels, Handfield-Jones and Axelrod, 2001), the term talent management has developed into a hyper-growing management discipline of great interest to both scholars and practitioners. From an academic perspective, HRM scholarship approaches talent from a resource-based view with the aim of demonstrating HRM's intended or actual impact on organisational performance; thus, within this body of literature talent is linked to human, social, political and cultural capital (Dries, 2013). In contrast, the discipline of psychology views talent as synonymous with giftness (educational psychology), identity (vocational psychology), or strength (positive psychology) highlighting the notion that employees should not be viewed only as resources but that their perceptions and attributes also play an important role in the association between HRM and organisational performance (Dries, 2013).

From a business perspective, there are two key approaches to defining talent – object and subject. The object approach views talent as individuals' innate characteristics or developed skills operating within a specific business environment that drive them to outperform others, whereas the subject approach views talent as personified within high-performing and/or high-potential individuals suggesting workforce segregation (Gallardo-Gallardo, Dries and Gonzalez-Cruz, 2013). Although practitioners' reports, for example CIPD (2021l) indicate that organisations are mainly interested in identifying individuals' contribution to organisational performance, thereby viewing talent from its subject perspective, recent empirical evidence suggests that the business definition of talent is more reflective of the object perspective. For example, Kravariti et al (2021) found that skills (eg communication and customer service) and personality traits (eg being kind and passionate) define who is considered a talent in Greek SMEs. Locating the conceptualisation of talent in a given business environment is important because this has implications for its management. For instance, if organisations view talent from its object perspective they would invest in knowledge and competence management, whereas if they view it from its subject perspective they would rather focus on succession planning (Kravariti and Johnston, 2020).

Lewis and Heckman (2006) identified three schools of thought on how to conceptualise talent management. The first school focuses on talent management's operationalisation through the enactment of HR practices, suggesting that talent management is identical to HRM. The second school refers to who constitutes talent pools and thus who would hold key organisational positions, whereas the third school turns its focus on talent without drawing links to strategic positions. Although talent management's definition is to a degree still ambiguous, Collings and Mellahi's (2009, p 304) definition is the most cited in talent management scholarship, according to which talent management refers to the:

> *Activities and processes that involve the systematic identification of key positions which differentially contribute to the organization's sustainable competitive advantage, the development of a talent pool of high potential and high performing incumbents to fill these roles, and the development of a differentiated human resource architecture to facilitate filling these positions with competent incumbents and to ensure their continued commitment to the organisation.*

Whether talent is viewed from its object or subject perspective, practitioners and academics have reached consensus that talents can be either holistically managed (ie inclusive talent management) or the focus might be only on top potential performers (ie exclusive talent management). In the inclusive approach to talent management, all employees have talents and organisations equally invest in all its workforce, or it might be that they would invest more in low performers with the aim to strike a happy balance (Dries, 2013). As per the exclusive talent management approach, investment is centred around a few 'A players' who hold strategic positions and who can thus support organisational performance (Gallardo-Gallardo, Dries and Gonzalez-Cruz, 2013). The paradox is that although inclusive talent management could create a healthier working environment, since all employees are encouraged to unfold their full potential (Dries, 2013), most empirical studies link talent management to the identification and staffing of pivotal positions with a few star employees (Gallardo-Gallardo and Thunnissen, 2016). Perhaps, this is the case because those individuals are seen as key for generating higher profitability and driving organisational performance (Glaister et al, 2018).

7.3 The growing importance of talent management for individuals and organisations

Talent deficits and an inability to develop future leaders have been perennial challenges for business leaders. Since 2012 an exponential growth of talent management strategies' adoption has been recorded, not only by organisations operating in the Global North or on a global scale, but also by smaller organisations functioning in emerging market economies. A survey by Deloitte (Deloitte and Bersin, 2014) showed that mature in talent management organisations – regardless of the context wherein they operate – reported outstanding results both in attracting desired-for business talent and in nurturing future leaders (Garr et al, 2017). Through talent management strategies, those organisations signal career progression opportunities as well as promoting an inclusive working environment wherein employee voice is heard and appreciated; thus, strengthening employer branding and talent acquisition. By utilising a range of technologies, those organisations facilitate two-way communication, timely information-sharing and the customisation of practices to employee needs with the aim of supporting continuing professional development and career growth (Garr et al, 2017). In doing so, a people-centred internal culture is developed acting as a booster to employee engagement and commitment. In the hospitality and tourism context, for example, talent shortages and high employee turnover are chronic challenges both for the industry's businesses and the country economies depending on them, which could be addressed by internally nurturing the industry's talent (Kravariti et al, 2022b).

Talent management becomes a necessity especially in periods of uncertainty, during which harnessing desired talent and building trust arms organisations with the confidence of dealing with an uncertain future (Stubbings and Sethi, 2020). This was highlighted after the 2007/2008 global economic recession when PwC's (2012) research showed that organisations which had invested in talent management, experienced fast increases in their productivity and revenues. Additional fruitful outcomes included reduced risk in matching skills to business gaps, sustainable succession management for key positions (often leadership positions), reinforced employer branding and innovation benefits, all of which accelerated organisational performance (PwC, 2012).

The Covid-19 outbreak in early 2020 posed several challenges to business leaders with the most important being managing employee wellbeing while dealing with financial adversity brought about by the pandemic. Talent management was the vehicle that enabled organisations to adapt quickly to the new business normal. Under these unprecedented circumstances, high-performing organisations developed flexible working teams wherein talent was deployed and equally dispersed to projects or roles that better matched their unique qualities (Foote et al, 2021). In other words, instead of withholding talent in particular business functions (usually the HR and Finance departments), some organisations recorded double performance by developing talent pools based on people's skill-set, which fostered their quick assignment to urgent business matters. A representative example is Ofwat, the UK water services regulation authority, which organised talent pools around employee skills and working background. Talented employees were requested to work on projects where their skills-set was on-demand, regardless of their assignment type (Foote et al, 2021). But even in cases where organisations did not adopt such an approach to forming talent pools, talent management accelerated employee upskilling and thus the development of agile teams. For instance, IT, supply chain and marketing leaders equipped sales' representatives with digital skills so that the latter could provide online support to customers overnight (Hancock and Schaninger, 2020). More importantly, PwC's 23rd Annual Global CEO Survey revealed that a considerable number of CEOs based in organisations mature in talent upskilling, witnessed rapid digital transformation and also foresaw increases in revenues, organisational productivity and reputation stemming from a workforce well-prepared for the unknown (Stubbings and Sethi, 2020).

7.4 Context matters

Considering the context within which talent management strategies are shaped and enacted is important, since today organisations do not solely compete with one another, but need to secure a leading position in the globalised business environment (Gallardo-Gallardo, Thunnissen and Scullion, 2020). Macro-level factors that usually affect the effectiveness of talent management strategies include a country's financial and political situation, and shifts in demographic characteristics (Khilji and Schuler, 2017), for example the 2007/2008 economic recession, during which talents were impelled to tolerate low wages and compensation. Once country economies moved closer to recovery and markets opened-up, talents started to actively look for better employment opportunities elsewhere (Kwan and Liakopoulos, 2011). This resulted in higher talent turnover rates and talent shortages, pointing to a revisiting of the effectiveness of talent management strategies. A further example is found in the changing characteristics of generations, which have important implications on how organisations should design effective talent management practices. For instance, the prime reason for Baby Boomers exiting a company is high rates of dissatisfaction with organisational leaders, whereas both Generation X and Millennials are more likely to choose the leave option when they feel that their organisations come short in offering career progression opportunities (Kwan and Liakopoulos, 2011). This suggests that in order for talent management strategies to satisfy the diverse expectations of generations, they should not only promote both trust between leadership and talents, but also succession planning opportunities.

Meso-level parameters driving or limiting the effectiveness of talent management strategies include – among others – supervisory and/or leadership support, the existence of succession planning practices, and methods to talent recruitment, retention, and reward (Kravariti and Johnston, 2020). Meso-level and macro-level parameters are interrelated. Generous financial rewards would attract for example male talent and Baby Boomers, whereas female talent and later generations are more interested in non-monetary incentives such as recognition, flexibility and light workload (Kwan and Liakopoulos, 2011). This possibly indicates that organisations could improve the effectiveness of their talent management strategies by adopting a total reward approach to talent appraisal. Organisations could also strengthen talent attraction and retention if they invest in developing future leaders and in embedding into their internal work cultures values related to employee training (Kontoghiorghes, 2016), otherwise they could experience a considerable number of talents exiting their company.

In short, a range of both internal and external parameters interplay, which suggests that particular talent management strategies might be effective or ineffective in specific country and sector contexts. In what follows, we first review the contemporary debate on talent management's practice in developed vs. developing countries, and then we discuss talent management within the public vs. private sector with sensitivity to organisational size (ie SMEs vs. MNCs).

 Case study 7.1

Talent crisis in the energy sector

The energy sector has been dealing with a talent crisis for more than a decade while trying to stay afloat. Experienced senior employees put less effort in helping the industry to recover as their someday has arrived. Younger generations lack relevant knowledge and skills, which would have enabled them to take over strategic positions.

Leading businesses such as the BP Group have been attempting to fix this talent gap with open-ended calls for recruiting talent, whereas others invest in various training and developmental opportunities such as graduate schemes; yet those tactics do not seem to suffice. Embracing technology in attracting, developing and retaining talent is timely provided that youth feels more comfortable sharing knowledge through technologies. A revisiting of organisational cultures and leadership approaches might also be appropriate, as talent would leave a company not necessarily for a bigger salary, but due to breaches of trust between management and employees.

1 What has driven the talent crisis in the energy sector?
2 If you were the HR director of a leading energy business, how would you bridge the talent gap?
3 Why could talent management be the lifeline to the sector's recovery?

SOURCE: Dupre, R (2014) Strategies to address the energy industry talent gap www.rigzone.com/news/oil_gas/a/133221/strategies_to_address_the_energy_industry_talent_gap/

7.4.1 Talent management in DEVELOPED versus DEVELOPING COUNTRIES

Talent management does not only support organisational performance, but it can also enhance an entire country's financial development. Governments across the globe have launched several initiatives to facilitate the productivity of organisations operating in their country, which in turn would support that country's competitiveness (Khilji and Schuler, 2017). Important variations exist between developed and developing countries in terms of talent management initiatives taken and their intended outcomes (Vaiman et al, 2019).

Developed countries, apart from heavily investing in their national talents' education, devise regulations, introduce talent management schemes funded by the state, and build market links with other countries with the aim of strengthening talent sourcing. Canada, for example, introduced an inclusive talent management programme which set forth to import highly skilled foreign talent, but also to prevent local talents' brain-drain (King, 2019). Australia on the other hand succeeded in attracting talents by offering generous renumeration as well as by building employment synergies with other countries such as India and China (Wiblen and McDonnell, 2019). European countries have long invested in their nationals' education and/or vocational training. Currently, they focus on encouraging diaspora talent's repatriation and on developing favourable conditions for employing refugee talent. A prime example is Germany, which over a sustained period has been the strongest economy in Europe (Festing and Harsch, 2019). Mediterranean countries which have been significantly challenged by high unemployment rates, economic instability and tight austerity measures as a consequence of the 2007/2008 economic recession, have recently taken on initiatives to reverse the high immigration of their youth talent. Greece, for instance, initiated a pilot state programme to encourage the return of national talent, in which the Greek government funds 70 per cent of the returners' salary for a year (Kalyvas, 2020). In Scandinavian countries such as Finland, a range of key talent management stakeholders collaborate to nurture home talent holistically, which has resulted in the flourishing of unique market capabilities able to support the leading position of domestic organisations like Nokia (Evans, Smale and Bjorkman, 2019).

Talent management has been less favourably appreciated by developing countries, possibly because the concept's perceived elite-centred nature contradicts those countries' often collectivist culture (Metcalfe, Makareem and Afouni, 2021). However, the concept has more recently been acknowledged as a key contributor to improving chronic talent deficits in those countries' markets (Kravariti et al, 2022a). 'Making' rather than 'buying' talent is a key objective of talent management strategies in this context, which are operationalised through creating development, learning and career growth opportunities (Glaister et al, 2018). It has been suggested, for example, that BRIC countries (Brazil, Russia, India and China) should heavily invest in their home talents' education if they wish to improve the utilisation of national graduates' talents and decrease the attraction of foreign talent (Skuza, McDonnell and Scullion, 2015). Talent management is, however, more complex in developing countries. It is mainly owned by multinationals who have experience in enacting Western best practices, while domestic organisations find it challenging to adopt and adapt strategies that often clash with their societies' egalitarian values (Skuza, McDonnell and Scullion, 2015). Talent management could perhaps better fit developing countries if viewed from its inclusive approach. For instance, although investment would primarily target key employees, employment opportunities could simultaneously be created for non-talents (Mwila and Turay, 2018). Hence, talent management strategies require adaptation to developing countries' context as a one-size-fits-all strategy does not seem to be effective.

7.4.2 *Private sector vs. public sector talent management*

World-leading organisations have digested that mastering organisational systems does not suffice for sustaining their competitive advantage in the long run; rather, it is all about having good people in strategic positions who can get the job done in the most efficient way. Managing those talented people has become a strategic priority for MNCs in particular, which have noted that high potentials/performers contribute circa 30 per cent to their organisational productivity (O'Boyle and Aguinis, 2012). In their way to greatness, MNCs come across talent management challenges imposed by a range of contextual factors, the most significant being local market deficits fostered by talent mobility, workforce diversity, aging populations and the varying expectations of new generations, all of which place a burden on acquiring and retaining talent (Vaiman, Scullion and Collings, 2012). MNCs have attempted to respond to the aforementioned challenges by assigning expatriates to their subsidiaries abroad, in this way transferring key competences, while employing low-skilled nationals for non-key roles (Sarabi, Hamori and Froese, 2019). As an alternative, they outsource talent recruitment to local headhunting companies that are better aware of the local market, or utilise networking websites, albeit recognising their questionable reliability (Sarabi, Hamori and Froese, 2019). From a resource-based view, talent management is considered the success route to attracting and retaining valuable, rare, inimitable and non-substitutable human resources (Kabwe and Okorie, 2019). In that sense, talent management does not contribute to MNCs' global presence only by filling in pivotal positions, but it also assists them in addressing their international business agendas via engaging them into a building exercise. Should MNCs invest in building both human capacity and leadership, and do whatever they can to stimulate talents, the latter would accelerate increases in financial revenues either by discovering or making opportunities in new markets. In reality, MNCs are in a constant race to secure an ongoing global talent pipeline, and hence adopt a rather exclusive talent management approach that provides differential treatment to just a few superstars who do or will hold managerial positions (Jooss, Burbach and Ruel, 2021). For instance, American, UK, Australian and Greek luxury hotels, despite promoting a friendly work environment, mainly tailor their approaches for the benefit of a few individuals (Marinakou and Giousmpasoglou, 2019). Although there is no magic list of best talent management practices widely adopted by MNCs, most of them opt for selective recruitment, extensive training and development, and managing retention. Bonneton et al (2022) found that in a North American MNC, when key individuals were identified early on with their careers 'delicately' treated, talents exerted less intention to exit as well as 'giving back' to their organisations through high productivity. Therefore, MNCs take a more exclusive perspective to talent and talent management with a view to preparing for the day after tomorrow.

Talent management is equally important to SMEs, whose contribution to the global GPD is considerable. Talent management in this context is approached from an egalitarian perspective (Festing, Schäfer and Scullion, 2013). We might anticipate this finding in view of SME's all-embracing culture emphasising that each employee adds significant value at some point (Krishnan and Scullion, 2017). In contrast to MNCs wherein talent predominantly refers to pivotal positions, talent for SMEs equates to the skills and attributes individuals should possess at a particular organisational life-stage (Kravariti et al, 2021). SMEs' competitive advantage lies in the adoption of less strategic practices, yet are yet highly adaptable, allowing high organisational flexibility (Krishnan and Scullion, 2017). For example, SMEs would rather identify and acquire talent from sub-streams such as employee referrals and university networks (Kravariti et al, 2021). To take just one example, Optiweb, a Slovenian SME providing online support services, launched a new programme to attract young talent, in which students are invited to work as practitioners for a quarter of a year (Mihelič, 2020). In addition, SMEs invest in informal and ad hoc training driven by employee and departmental needs, possibly due to a lack of huge financial budgets. Budgetary constraints do, however, impose some limitation on SMEs' retention strategies, which predominantly consist of non-financial rewards such as employee recognition and good interpersonal relationships, whereas monetary rewards are scarce (Chung and D'Announzio-Green, 2018).

Although private- and public-sector organisations share a few commonalities such as targeting service efficiency, the public sector has some unique characteristics that could restrain talent management's success. For example, equal treatment of civil servants is a key value of public-sector organisations that are seeking to employ any talented individual who does not only possess unique abilities and knowledge, but who also mirrors the sector's core value of fairly serving the community (Kravariti and Johnston, 2020). This subject and rather inclusive perspective of public-sector talent might challenge the successful adoption of talent management agendas, which usually suggest segregation of staff and investment in a few superstars. One would thus expect that more inclusive talent management practices would be promoted in this context, such as in the case of Canadian civil servants who are holistically offered the opportunity to self-assess their performance and thereafter develop personal development plans (Glenn, 2012). In reality, though, the public sector can grant exclusive treatment to particular pools of employees. For instance, ambassadors and diplomats have been offered special remuneration and benefits for their assignments abroad (Boselie and Thunnissen, 2018). Another example is found in the UK NHS where medical workers receive special treatment compared to those who hold administrative or managerial roles, as the former are in the front line of dealing with patients (MacFarlane et al, 2012). It is thus evident that in some cases public-sector talent management directs more investment in civil servants holding pivotal positions, such as those assuming high expertise. In addition, New Public Management initiatives set forth to restore the sector's efficiency and highlight collaborative public governance. As multiple internal and external stakeholders with diverse interests need to partner under the New Public Management umbrella, talent management strategies can assist public-sector organisations in identifying contemporary key positions and then match them with key people who can drive the required reforms. Considering the sector's ethos and nature, the unique selling point of public-sector talent management could be the recognition of individuals' values apart from skills/competencies/knowledge, which is rare in the private sector (Clerkin and Coggburn, 2012). Hence, although talent management's fit within the public sector has been questioned, HR practitioners could look at transferring and adapting some of the private-sector's best practices to this context thereby assisting the sector in improving the acquisition of new generations' talent (Clarke and Scurry, 2020), in nurturing leadership and in winning the battle of popularity (Poocharoen and Lee, 2013). The talent war is the war private and public organisations are currently fighting. It is complex, but it is a war nonetheless that can be primarily won by the virtues of power of organisations' ideals.

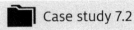 Case study 7.2

Citibank India

Headquartered in Mumbai India, Citigroup's subsidiary consists of over 10,000 employees. Citi India holistically invests in its talent pool with the aim of nurturing its future leaders. More precisely, it focuses on attracting university talent, building networks, developing management and increasing workforce diversity.

To attract university talent, Citi India organises recruitment events (eg an Innovation Challenge) in collaboration with local universities. It also organises engagement sessions in which alumni and the bank's senior leadership participate. These have facilitated the development of strong relationships with the country's leading universities and the quick identification of top talent.

Citi India has also succeeded in building strong networks with its associates. It offers a networking training programme, which consists of sessions related to team learning and to developing leadership capabilities. This training programme also sets forth to educate new recruits on the bank's products, franchises and clientele.

Management development is an additional focus area of Citi India. To prepare fresh graduates to take over strategic roles, the bank offers scholarships to recently graduated analysts so that they study an MBA course at the Indian School of Business. In doing so, it assists analysts in developing management skills.

A final aim of Citi India is to improve gender diversity in its talent tool, which could also decrease female talents' attrition. It initiated the Citi Woman Leader Award that supports women in growing their careers through mentoring and training. The bank also offers work flexibility to women who return to work from maternity leave.

1 Which approach to talent management is evident in Citi India?
2 What shapes the talent management agenda of Citi India?
3 To what degree would the approach to managing talent adopted by Citi India be applicable to Citigroup's subsidiary operating in the Global North?

SOURCE: Garr, SS, Gantcheva, I, Yoshida, R and We, M (2017) Talent Matters: How a well-designed talent experience can drive growth in emerging markets, Deloitte University Press, Westlake

7.5 Key talent management stakeholders

The design, enactment and success of talent management involves a range of stakeholders including:

- business leaders
- hr professionals
- line managers
- the state.

Stakeholders often have diverse interests and might not speak the same language in that they might neither define talent nor interpret the intended outcomes of talent management in the same way. An organisation's overall performance could be put in jeopardy if its stakeholders' motives are in conflict with formalised processes such as talent management (Thunnissen, Boselie and Fruytier, 2013). It is therefore important to understand the various roles of key talent management stakeholders.

Industrial leaders are considered organisational foreheads that observe trends in the market and inform organisations about contemporary best practice in acquiring, nurturing and retaining talent (Enz, 2009). The problem that might spring up is when business leaders have understood the necessity to introduce changes to talent management agendas, but might not be proactive in acting upon that as ambiguity may exist as to what precisely needs to be changed (PwC, 2014). Despite this, business leaders contribute to crafting talent management strategies and to aligning them to the business strategies (Hughes and Rog, 2008). Take, for example a hospitality and tourism organisation whose main strategic objective is to deliver exceptional customer service. Industrial leaders can motivate talents to deliver what is expected by strategically designing talent appraisal and reward (Chon and Zoltan, 2019).

Another key talent management stakeholder is the HR professional, who contributes significantly to talent management's effectiveness. They champion good talent management practices (CIPD, 2022a) and are involved in talent management's operationalisation (Koukpaki and Adams, 2020). Among their responsibilities is to perform talent analytics and interpret data, which facilitate the HR function's collaboration with other stakeholders in enacting talent management practices (McDonnell et al, 2017). HR professionals also add business value by strategically designing and monitoring diverse talent pools and ensuring that those are steadily available to support continuous organisational profitability (Garavan, 2012). CIPD (2022b) views talent management experts as artists who portray each business's talent, and thereafter map out methods to spot and grow talents within organisational boundaries.

Although HR professionals might design various talent management practices including talent recruitment, development and performance management, line managers are assumed to have greater accountability for talent management enactment (CIPD, 2020d). Their important role in talent management effectiveness is highlighted by recent scholarship (eg Gallardo-Gallardo, Thunnissen and Scullion, 2020), which suggests that line mangers serve as the vehicle through which intended talent management outcomes are translated into actual practices. Line managers are involved in talent identification and thereafter into adopting effective approaches to talent development such as coaching (Nyfoudi and Tasoulis, 2021), which can lead to more positive employee perceptions on the intended talent management outcomes and thus to higher performance outcomes (Kravariti et al, 2022a). This is because when a healthy relationship between employees and line managers exists, the former experience high job satisfaction which often translates into high job commitment (CIPD, 2020d). As line managers are involved in day-to-day people management, they can easily spot individuals' potential, test the degree to which employees can perform higher responsibilities, and create opportunities for them to grow (Blanco and Golik, 2021). Hence, in many industries, line managers are viewed as the key mechanisms through which talent management is appreciated by an organisation's talent pool.

The relevant national government is also considered a key talent management stakeholder, which can support sufficient talent supply with the development of employment opportunities and/or of state-funded developmental initiatives (Hussain et al., 2020). A prime example is the Vision 2030 developed by Gulf Cooperation Countries (GCC). In Bahrain, for instance, where local talent is mainly acquired by the public sector, several developmental initiatives for local talent were launched (eg the Tamkeen programme) under the Vision 2030 (Kravariti et al, 2022a). Some other governments such as the Singaporean shape regulations that facilitate talent mobility across countries and sectors, thus widening talent pools and allowing organisational flexibility (PwC, 2014). Hence, the state plays a crucial role in developing favourable conditions that could help organisations operating in the corresponding countries to address talent deficits.

 Case study 7.3

Scotland is calling: talent development programme launched

The Scottish hospitality and tourism industry was significantly hit by the pandemic crisis, with a large chunk of the industry's workforce flirting with redundancy. To support the industry's recovery, the further development of the hospitality and tourism sectors' talent was deemed necessary.

Funded by the Scottish Government and administered by the Hospitality Industry Trust (HIT) Scotland, the Tourism and Hospitality Talent Development Programme set forth to equip the industry's workforce with the necessary leadership and management skills and knowledge. The programme first ran in 2021 and reran in 2022. It was open to anyone aged 16 or above, conditional on holding a working position (either full-time or part-time) in the industry. This online programme's learning objective was to educate participants on the tools and methods that can assist them in leveraging their teams' or own performance.

The programme consisted of three training categories. The training for supervisors targeted newly or about to be appointed supervisors or team leaders, who were keen on being upskilled on matters related to managing change and team performance. The training for management was suitable for people managing teams and who were interested in developing skills related to team engagement, coaching and enhancing team performance through conversations. The upper-level training welcomed senior managers such as business owners, department heads and general managers, who already possessed knowledge on providing feedback and performance coaching, but who were keen on improving the effectiveness of their leadership tactics.

The programme was welcomed by various hospitality and tourism stakeholders with the Chief Executive of HIT Scotland David Cochrane viewing it as the vehicle to preparing the sectors' workforce for the industry's overall recovery. Marc Crothall, Chief Executive of the Scottish Tourism Alliance, highlighted that the programme had been generously funded by the Scottish Government's National Transition Training Fund, but facilitated talent development key to the industry's post-pandemic reality. The Operations Director of The Scotch Whisky Experience explained the direct positive impact of the programme on their business operations, such as the upskilled team came back with innovative suggestions on how the business could adapt to the new normal. The vast majority of the programme participants were satisfied with the training received and underscored the central role it played to their career growth.

1 What was the role of the state in the Tourism and Hospitality Talent Development Programme?

2 What are the benefits of this talent development initiative for each of the key talent management stakeholders?

3 STA's Chief Executive claimed that the programme had been generously funded by the Scottish Government. How do you interpret that and why would you fund such an initiative if you were Scotland's government?

SOURCES: Glasgow Tourism and Visitor Plan (2021) *New Talent Development Programme Launched* https://glasgowtourismandvisitorplan.com/news-and-media/2021/february/tourism-and-hospitality-talent-development-programme/

Hit Scotland (2022) *Learn Today, Shape Tomorrow: Welcome to the tourism and hospitality talent development programme – Phase 2* https://hitscotland.co.uk/talent-development-programme

7.6 The talent management cycle

Although to manage talents strategically might involve a range of practices, both practitioners and academics suggest that key practices constituting the talent management cycle include talent acquisition, development and retention. In what follows, we provide an overview of each.

Talent acquisition kicks off with identifying the most critical positions for a business and then with identifying internal talents – either through performance management or through succession planning – that is, identifying who could fill in those positions (CIPD, 2021m). The second step is to attract external talents that shall not only possess the desired skills and knowledge, but also should fit within a company's culture. The case study that follows shows how a UK-based charity adopts innovative methods to talent acquisition in order to acquire the best talent available. Although traditional methods of talent recruitment (eg online job advertisement, recruitment agencies and referrals) and selection (eg one-to-one interviews and selection tests) are still widely used (Kravariti et al, 2021), using technology in the aforementioned process has significantly benefited employer branding. Online interviews, for example, apart from being cost-effective, have improved the overall quality of the process for the benefit of both the employer and the candidate (Mejia and Torres, 2018). RetailCo is a prime example which, with the use of technology, reduced by 50 per cent the time spent for talent acquisition while significantly improving candidates' satisfaction with the whole process, thus strengthening the company's branding (CIPD, 2021n). Technology and data during talent acquisition also assist in taking informed decisions, as one can assess the extent to which investment in particular people would bring about the desired financial returns (Harris, Craig and Light, 2011). Talent acquisition is the first phase of the talent management cycle in which leading companies heavily invest, as it has been proven to double the success rate of leadership identification and talent development (Garr et al., 2017).

 ## Case study 7.4

Recruiting from the heart

Royal Mencap Society is a charity supporting individuals with learning disabilities and consists of 8,500 employees. The charity has been recruiting people who possess soft skills important to its culture, including being warm-hearted, positive and reliable. Lately, however, they have been struggling to identify the right candidates to fill in key positions.

Mencap sought professional advice to improve their recruitment campaign. A team of HR professionals centred the recruitment process around customers' profiles. For example, to attract a talented support worker, the charity advertises the profile of the people to be supported. After candidates sit a test, they attend two interviews with the most crucial being the second one where the people to be supported act as interviewers.

The outcomes of the new recruitment process were outstanding. Not only were people with learning disabilities assisted to socialise, but also they were offered the opportunity to get paid for their consultancy services. Another success lay in attracting candidates who were passionate about supporting others and who would feel proud of working in the charity.

1 What fresh methods of talent acquisition did Royal Mencap Society adopt?
2 What challenges might the HR professionals have had to deal with before launching the new recruitment process?

SOURCE: CIPD (2022c) *Mencap: Recruiting from the heart* https://peopleprofession.cipd.org/get-started/case-studies/mencap

---

As discussed in previous sections, talent deficit is a contemporary challenge; thus, retaining talent has become a critical component of talent management agendas. This is because when talent chooses to exit, important knowledge and skills are lost which are often very costly to be replaced (Holland and Scullion, 2021). The Society for Human Resource Management (SHRM, 2022) reports a number of reasons that talents often resign, including competitive alternatives elsewhere, bad experiences with their current employer or simply targeting a change. McKinsey (Chao et al, 2020) suggests a three-step approach to improve talent retention, ie:

Step 1 – Identify key employees who hold pivotal roles.

Step 2 – Develop incentives' plans and craft talent retention approaches.

Step 3 – Enact talent retention approaches and oversee the resultant outcomes.

There is evidence to suggest that talent retention practices need be tailored around the sort of talent a company aims to retain by considering the market within which it operates (Cappelli, 2000). Nonetheless, incentives can be either monetary or non-monetary – see also Chapter 10. Financial incentives include bonuses and competitive pay, whereas non-financial incentives include opportunities for learning and development, a healthy employee–top management relationship, promotions, recognition, career progression paths and flexible workload (Kravariti et al, 2021). In practice, non-monetary incentives often outweigh monetary incentives, provided that talents are already offered a satisfactory salary. In fact, McKinsey's report showed that circa 1,500 senior leaders found recognition from immediate supervisor as a more effective talent retention method compared to bonuses or pay increments (Chao et al, 2020).

Talent development has become more than ever an urgent priority given its contribution to upskilling staff, building their confidence and preparing them for the future of work. The Vodafone Business Future Ready Report (2020) suggests that talent development should be a key priority for organisations that wish to be prepared for the 'new normal', with more than 40 per cent of the surveyed executives suggesting that identifying tech skills in particular would be a key future challenge. In addition, PwC (2020b) reports that circa 75 per cent of the surveyed CEOs claim that important skills that could help companies recover from Covid-19 are hard to be identified, whereas more than 40 per cent of CEOs reported that their development schemes did not only help employees to nurture those hard-to-find skills but also improved their commitment. Given the numbers of the working population who shifted to remote working, skills such as being self-directed and seeking feedback through driving discussions with superiors or colleagues have also become important (Brooks, 2021). Providing training to talents to grow such skills internally can lead to improved talent attraction and retention rates (Vodafone Business, 2020). Additional benefits of talent development include strengthening succession planning, building internal pools of talents that could fill in strategic positions when necessary and developing future leaders, whereas in the case of SMEs, talent development might be the alternative to financial rewards which SMEs often come up short in offering due to their small financial budgets (Kravariti et al, 2021). Talent development includes a range of methods, such as coaching and mentoring, all of which are discussed in the following section.

 Case study 7.5

Cutting-edge initiative

Itsu, established in 1997, is a sushi-based organisation operating in the UK and New York. With a workforce numbering 1,500 and an annual turnover of over £100 million, it is an attractive employer especially for Europeans, who view it as a great opportunity to develop their English-speaking capacity. The organisation was challenged by high employee turnover rates, in particular in pivotal positions such as experienced fish cutters who supervise junior staff. That is understandable as such positions are socially isolating, not to mention that they are not considered 'in-fashion'.

To improve talent turnover rates, the organisation employed an external skills development provider, who designed and delivered a masterclass for junior fish cutters. Successful graduates were accredited and also offered unlimited access to material relevant to their role. To further acknowledge all fish cutters' value-added, Itsu proceeded to offer pay increments. Finally, they organised a live competition rewarding the experienced fish cutter of the year with a mini-vacation for two in New York.

After those initiatives were launched, Itsu recorded a rapid increase of experienced fish cutters, food waste savings and talent engagement. It also experienced a decrease in customers' complaints.

1 What methods for improving talent retention were employed by Itsu?
2 What could be the longer-term intended outcomes of the adopted talent retention methods at Itsu and to what extent were those achieved?
3 To what degree has Itsu adopted an inclusive or an exclusive approach to talent management overall?
4 If you were Itsu's training manager, what initiatives would you develop next?

SOURCE: CIPD (2022d) *Itsu: Cutting-edge engagement* https://peopleprofession.cipd.org/get-started/case-studies/itsu

7.7 Employee learning and development: a key element of talent management agendas

Learning, training and development are distinct concepts but interrelated, and which support talent development. Learning has to do with all the activities undertaken by an individual in order to acquire new skills, competences or knowledge, whereas training is the process through which an individual achieves those outcomes and which is led by an instructor. Development is the process and activities that lead to acquisition of the aforementioned but with the aim to support personal/professional growth (CIPD, 2021o).

7.7.1 Learning and development theories of value to the HR professional

Many theories are of value when deciding the best methods of facilitating learning, from the early behaviourist theories of the 1920s through to more recent theories of experiential, transformational and heutagogy learning. The following six are selected as particularly influential theories for HR professionals in terms of facilitating employer-provided training:

1 Cognitive learning theory (Piaget, 1964) suggests that learning is a cognitive process facilitated by the active role of instructors. It involves information interpretation, structuring, memorising and abstracting. Individuals initially learn by organising and storing learning, which they thereafter relate to new information.

2 Reinforcement learning theory (Skinner, 1974) explains that employee behaviours change as a result of their response to events. People can be motivated to repeat or not a particular behaviour if it is followed by particular stimuli, that is reward or punishment.

3 Social learning theory (Bandura, 1977) informs us that learning is an outcome of social interactions, and more precisely an outcome of observing other individuals or the environment. Trust, exchange of ideas, observation, modelling and assessment of past beliefs are key vehicles that promote social learning.

4 Experiential learning theory (Kolb, 1984) suggests that employees learn by reflecting on their past individual experiences. Kolb's experiential learning cycle consists of four stages. An individual would initially have an experience (ie concrete experience), then review it (ie reflective observation), which will lead to particular conclusions (ie abstract conceptualisation) and finally to trying out what has been learned (ie active experimentation).

5 Transformative learning theory (Mezirow, 1997) views learning as an ongoing process, which puts learners outside their comfort zone and challenges them, so that they rapidly change their perceptions. There is a constant interaction between instructors and learners, during which the former encourage the latter to evaluate issues from various viewpoints.

6 Heutagogy (Hase and Kenyon, 2007) is a relatively new learning theory, which highlights learners' interaction in the learning process and instructors' passive role. Learners are assumed to own their learning in that they independently put considerable effort to improve it driven by their personal learning needs.

Although all the approaches can be subjected to criticism, they contain relevance to both learners and trainers, as the diverse perspectives encourage consideration of different learning and training methods.

7.7.2 *Learning technologies and self-directed learning*

Technology plays a crucial role in increasing the effectiveness of learning as it reaches employees in the 24/7 globalised world. Businesses require employees to be autonomous and to have agility in day-to-day operations and a focus on developing a learning and development team who are confident and capable with technology has become a key reason for success. There are certainly some barriers that challenge learning technologies' success. As CIPD (2017c) reports, these include organisational support, employee perceptions towards learning technologies, and whether or not learning technologies are a tool to facilitate learners' interaction. If organisations are going to reap the huge benefits of future generations of mobile technologies, then these professionals need to build their own competence and confidence first to be both able to use the technology, but more importantly recognise the support needed to make sure real learning and its transfer occurs.

Another huge benefit of learning technologies is that they facilitate self-directed learning. Although self-directed learning was first highlighted in the early years of the twentieth century, it started being popular in the USA around the 1960s–1970s, whereas today about 80 per cent of learning is self-directed (Lemmetty and Collin, 2020). This perhaps indicates that individuals prefer to own their learning. Research into self-directed learning attempts to explain the benefits of self-directed learning both for employees and their employers, with the most important listed below:

- Learners are enabled to access resources from anywhere anytime (CIPD, 2021e).
- There is a contribution to employee upskilling.
- It facilitates career growth.
- Employee self-actualisation is fostered.
- People and organisations are prepared for adapting to the hyper-changing environment.
- It supports resiliency-building (Morris, 2019).

7.7.3 Coaching and mentoring

Anyone has at some point in their professional life been either coached or mentored. Coaching's objective is to help employees develop particular skills and competences, whereas mentoring refers to the informal support offered by a senior to a less experienced employee with the aim to help the latter professionally grow (CIPD, 2021f). Should organisations opt for coaching or mentoring? Merrick (2022), the Managing Director of Chronus Corporation, suggests that organisations should opt for coaching if they aim to educate people through training on particular processes in order to improve their short-term performance. Alternatively, mentoring should populate organisations' succession planning agendas should organisations wish to develop future leaders.

Coaching and mentoring are two important methods for nurturing talent, which, although they seem similar, differ in important respects summarised in Table 7.1.

Table 7.1 Coaching vs. mentoring

Coaching	Mentoring
Performance-oriented, ie a coach would help one to immediately improve a skill/capability	Growth-oriented, ie a mentor would communicate personal experiences to help one's professional development
Formal process	Informal process, ie mentor and mentee are considered partners
Short-term relationship	Long-term relationship
Bound to deadlines and scheduled meetings	Informal conversations when requested
A coach offers paid services	No formal payment involved
The coach should possess a formal coaching qualification	The mentor should possess rich prior industry-related experience

SOURCE: Stokes, Diochon and Otter, 2021

There are several benefits to coaching and mentoring, with the most important being improvement in employee wellbeing and job-related behaviours (Theebom, Beersma and Van Vianen, 2014). Additional benefits include preparing people for change or for taking over new roles, facilitating knowledge-sharing, improving performance management and managing conflict (CIPD, 2021f). For these reasons, coaching and mentoring are an integral part of the new CIPD Profession Map (CIPD, 2020b). The Covid-19 pandemic brought about several changes to employee learning and development with more than 45 per cent of organisations offering focused coaching and mentoring schemes (Crowley and Overton, 2021). This trend could be explained by the exponential growth of utilising digital tools, which facilitated e-coaching and e-mentoring. For instance, online mentoring was offered to staff at the University of Alberta via online video meetings (Koopman et al., 2021).

In practice, the most popular model used for coaching and mentoring purposes has been the GROW model. Its popularity may stem from the fact that it assists both individual learners and groups of learners to attain their set goals by following a four-step process (Whitmore, 2017).

G for goal-setting, for example where does your client want to be?

R for reality, for example where is your client now and how far away are they from the goal?

O for options, for example how should the client face obstacles to progress?

W for way forward, for example how can options be converted to actions so that the initial goal can be achieved?

7.7.4 *Management development*

In the late twentieth century, a distinction between developing employees and management was made, as the latter were considered strategic employees. Despite the importance of investing in those key employees, the 2021 CIPD *Resourcing and Talent Planning Survey* (CIPD, 2021i) showed that only 30 per cent of the sampled CEOs had actually prioritised some form of management development, albeit foreseeing an increase in relevant budgets (CIPD, 2021i).

With regard to management development approaches, Gold et al (2010) suggest three to populate the business environment. The first two approaches — informal and integrated management development – stretch managers' accountability for their development, whereas the third approach – formal management development – suggests that HR professionals are accountable for management development. Informal management development methods refer to any non-planned or non-directed method such as e-learning, development centres and action learning (Stewart, 2009). Integrated management development methods highlight that learning is an outcome of work and/or work is an outcome of learning. It is manifested as managers shadowing other managers, coaching and mentoring, and memberships of professional clubs which allow members to share knowledge and experience across their communities (CIPD, 2021p). Finally, formal management development methods refer to formal learning such as attending a university course, doing an apprenticeship, or attending formal training offered by an organisation (CIPD, 2021p). Formal management development methods are less favoured by organisations, due to the potentially high costs involved.

7.7.5 Career management

A career is a structured sequence of work experiences that promotes employee development and advances organisational capability. Three prominent career concepts exist:

- *Traditional career*: The image of a traditional career is of a pattern of jobs within a single organisation that follow a linear and predetermined path. Key characteristics of a traditional career structure are specific entry criteria linked to education and qualification attainment, a planned and co-ordinated structure of job experience, and a coherent reward strategy.

- *Boundaryless career*: The boundaryless career is multidirectional and shaped by opportunity. An individual creates a career in various organisations through a process of development along a path of experience (Sullivan and Baruch, 2009). An individual example from the past 30 years is Adam Crozier, who began employment as a graduate trainee at Mars Pedigree Petfood, and has moved across diverse organisations from the *Daily Telegraph* to Saatchi & Saatchi, to the Football Association, to Royal Mail, to Chief Executive at ITV, to Whitbread and finally to the BT Group as Chair.

- *Self-managed career*: The self-managed career emphasises the individual as master of his/her own destiny rather than the organization. Sir Richard Branson, founder of the Virgin Group, is arguably Britain's best-known example of such adaptation. Branson has directed Virgin's evolution from music to airlines, shops, telecoms, drinks and even bridalwear.

The rationale for career management is the effective nurturing of talent, specific company knowledge and the successive deployment of workforce capabilities to best serve the business. Companies such as the John Lewis Partnership, Caterpillar and the Hilton Group spend considerable time, money and effort turning fresh recruits into loyal company men and women who will internalise and promote organisational values. In addition, career development is portrayed as symbiotic, offering the potential for both individual career advancement and the enhancement of organisational capability.

The extent of the employer's responsibility in providing career development tools, opportunities and funding is debatable. Although it is assumed that HR practitioners will provide career support, this may vary in practice. Financial results or conflicting business priorities may overtake development needs. Similarly, line managers differ widely in their competence level as career coaches, and in their enthusiasm for acting as an organisational guide. There is potential ambiguity and competing expectations in the purpose of career development for the organisation and for the individual; can personal growth and development readily transfer to corporate advantage?

International career development may call for distinct approaches in managing across borders – see also Chapter 4. Expatriation is managed according to the organisational strategy for particular expertise – for example, international career structures at the oil company Shell, the Foreign and Commonwealth Office and Nestlé. Research in international careers has found that the primary motives for going to work abroad are personal interest, a search for new experiences and an interest in the external environment (Suutari and Brewster, 2000). Consequently, there may be a mismatch between individual values and organisational pressure that provokes a career crisis. For example, a BBC journalist may refuse a political assignment in Russia when the individual's interests are focused on social development in Ukraine. These individual career aspirations can change with family circumstances, educational requirements, health, financial commitments and personal interests. Moreover, for businesses in recession an increased pressure on developmental budgets may restrict investment in career development to employees identified as talent, and members of a talent pool.

A self-managed career demands high levels of self-awareness and personal responsibility (Hall, 2004). It also makes significant demands on an individual's ability to adapt in terms of performance and learning, as evidenced in this statement:

> Our graduate scheme will give you everything you need to build the kind of career you want. But it's up to you how it goes. You'll be the one in charge, putting forward your ideas, taking on responsibilities and making choices about how you get the job done.
> (IBM, 2013)

Certain individuals have a greater tolerance for ambiguity that suits an entrepreneurial approach to career invention. For others, self-directed career management is a burden resulting in mounting stress levels (Cooper, 2005). This reveals why many employees wish to keep the traditional psychological contract for the job security that it offers (McDonald, Brown and Bradley, 2005). Workers at Cadbury's chocolate factory in Bourneville may have believed their specific company knowledge and experience would secure future employment until Kraft's takeover in 2012 undermined such prospects. The unpredictability of organisational career paths shifts the emphasis to individuals' personal investment through continuing professional development.

7.7.6 Continuing professional development

There are diverse definitions of continuing professional development (CPD) which often overlap with 'principles of lifelong learning, professional education, personal development, career advancement and workplace learning' (Mackay, 2015, p 2). In short, CPD represents good practice and represents a professional value for HR practitioners. It can be argued that CPD as a product is essentially 'personal property', which offers the protection of employability for the individual, as CPD evolves there is greater recognition of the importance of professional development to support longer working lives and sustain employability.

The main benefits of CPD for the individual are updating, increasing competence and enhancing mobility (Sadler-Smith, Allinson and Hayes, 2000). Professional development contributes to greater self-confidence and competence in a job position and CPD serves as an auditable record within organisations of development activity. The potential rewards of CPD must be apparent to both the individual and employers in supporting learning development. For an individual, ongoing development can provide intrinsic motivation, elevated status as well as broader options through transferable skills (Mackay, 2015).

For practitioners, CPD knits together educational learning and work practice (Mackay, 2015). Having current skills and knowledge enriches the possibilities of a self-managed career. However, the individual imperative to update skills and acquire qualifications is often a response to job demands that will ensure contract renewal. Despite the heralded benefits of professional development as self-empowering, individuals may be entirely instrumental in learning as they seek to demonstrate career relevance. CPD is increasingly seen as an investment for employment continuity (Rothwell, 2005). An individual between jobs needs to acquire marketable experience that will differentiate them from other job candidates, such as herding elephants in Kenya. The individual works on CPD as a personal investment in learning from experience; illustrating learning agility and self-reliance through a colourful CPD portfolio. You can watch a couple of podcasts on how HR practitioners work towards their CPD here:

- www.youtube.com/watch?v=ntmpuXc77yw
- www.youtube.com/watch?v=26aZHImAWuA

7.8 Conclusion: reshaping talent management agendas to enhance organisational performance

Critical positions have always been an essential element of business-value agendas, but identifying remote talent, who can hold such positions is a new addition to the business leaders' checklist. The Covid-19 pandemic led to a significant increase in remote working with 44 per cent of the US (Mlitz, 2021) and with circa 50 per cent of the Australian, French and UK working populations shifting to teleworking during the pandemic (OECD, 2021). Those figures literally suggest that talent left the business premises. Although employee working time increased by up to 20 per cent, talents proved to be more productive outside corporate establishments and also improved their work–life balance (Frankiewicz and Chamorro-Premuzic, 2020). Perhaps this indicates that talent might be reluctant to return to the office, suggesting that the way employers will deal with this trend will define their competitive position in the market. From an individual talent perspective, this trend means that more geographically dispersed career opportunities are opened up (Vaiman et al, 2021). From an organisational perspective, this means that geographic boundaries and governmental restrictions are waived, and that businesses can reach out to global talent that can more efficiently attain their strategic objectives (Vaiman et al, 2021). Talent management strategies will thus play a crucial role in this new working pattern. They can assist HR professionals in reassessing the criticality of business roles, tracking the desired talent across the board, and developing a diverse talent pool, which would be the most suitable to compete with the leaders of their field (Kier, 2020).

The Covid-19 pandemic shared an important lesson. Should organisations wish to build resilience faster than others and benefit from 'first-mover advantage', they need to invest in reskilling or further developing their talents. Growing talents' digital skills and their capacity to adapt to a fast-changing working environment should populate recalibrated talent management agendas (Hancock and Schaninger, 2020). Organisations should also invest in growing servant leaders, who promote two-way communication and strong relationships with employees, thus fostering subordinates' higher engagement (Garrard, 2021). For instance, Microsoft's CEO during the pandemic shared his concerns about employee health and safety with all Microsoft's workforce, which was appreciated as a move of empathy and compassion (Reilly and Svensson, 2021). Developing effective leaders indeed matters and as Deloitte's survey showed, more than 60% of the surveyed employees decide not to resign due to trust in their leaders (Pelster, 2013).

Another critical element that needs to be incorporated into revised talent management systems is people analytics. The new normal underscores the development of digital talent pools, whose performance evaluation and job assignment can be facilitated with the use of people analytics' tools and technologies (Hancock and Schaninger, 2020). A few organisations have already acknowledged people analytics as a core element of their strategies, like KPMG that uses ProFinda to keep track of talents' competences (Reilly and Svensson, 2021), and the departments of an Australian professional services company which use mainly SAP to identify talent (Wiblen and Marler, 2021). Despite this, a considerable number of organisations still use basic tools and technologies (eg spreadsheet software) and perform descriptive analyses on specific HR functions (Houston and Kester, 2014). As the SHRM society highlights, the use of people analytics is conditional on organisations willing to invest in data infrastructure and in developing people's skills to perform such analyses, which might explain why this field is still immature (Kaur and Fink, 2017). The use of more advanced tools and technologies (eg data visualisation tools and machine learning) and of more advanced analytics (eg predictive and prescriptive) is necessary for organisations to take informed decisions with regard to talent selection, development and retention (Ledet et al, 2020). Advanced people analytics tools can also boost talent engagement and improve organisational revenues (Houston and Kester, 2014).

Public-sector organisations should also take a new direction with regard to talent management. Under the New Public Management umbrella, a range of talent management initiatives could be introduced, reflecting the sector's ethos of equal treatment, as well as a talented workforce who would possess the sector's values, can be acquired, upskilled and retained with a view to offering more value for money civil services (Kravariti and Johnston, 2020). This can be achieved through the design of clear career paths and professional growth opportunities for new generations, who are capable in driving necessary reforms but who currently perceive the public sector as an unattractive employer (Clarke and Scurry, 2020). There already exists evidence from some public-sector contexts, such as the Sri Lankan public banking sector and a Bahraini ministry, which suggests that increments in individual talent performance was an outcome of talent management initiatives (Kravariti et al, 2022a). Therefore, a recalibration of public-sector talent management agendas is timely to help the sector improve its accountability and thereafter have an equal share in the war for talent.

 Case study 7.6

Are you ready for the future of work?

To explore the pandemic's impact on businesses and how well the latter were prepared for

the new normal, in November 2019 Vodafone Business surveyed circa **2,000** organisations followed up by 25 interviews with business leaders in Spring 2020. The outcomes were indeed an eye-opener. All businesses had eventually recognised the value added by their human capital. More precisely, businesses understood that employees can work across borders and be productive even by working through technologies. The ability to display compassion and adaptability was considered a talent. Businesses who won the battle with the pandemic crisis had a positive view towards change, embraced technology in their working tasks, had designed a long-term business strategy, and their leaders kept them in the loop with current trends and trajectories.

Vodafone Business concluded with five key focus areas that organisations should invest in regardless of their size and location. First, organisations need to rework practices related to building resilience and come up with new business models, for example to support people inside and outside their corporate boundaries, accelerate digitalisation and welcome change. Second, organisations must learn to adapt to the ever-changing behaviours of their clients. As customers can easily compare products and prices online, they expect more than good quality or good price. Therefore, power dynamics have changed to the benefit of consumers.

Third, governmental regulations and customers are attentive to environmental issues, with youth talent expressing a strong desire to work for organisations that actively take actions upon green initiatives – see also Chapter 6. Therefore, sustainability should become a core element of business agendas. Fourth, technologies and data are shaping the new business reality. Organisations should be well prepared to handle the voluminous and important data they both collect and share with external bodies. Fifth, talents' needs and characteristics have changed. Organisations need to redefine their business talent and thereafter support career growth by offering, for example, flexible work, latest technologies, mental health support, etc. Therefore, organisations should rework on talent acquisition and development.

1   How will the five key focus areas impact organisational performance and sustainability?
2   What should be the elements of a recalibrated talent management agenda capable of addressing the five key focus areas and of enhancing organisational performance?
3   Why are data and technologies so important?

SOURCE: Vodafone Business (2020) *The Vodafone Business Future Ready Report* www.vodafone.com/business/news-and-insights/white-paper/future-ready-report-2020

 KEY LEARNING POINTS

1   There is a robust business case for investment in talent management, which can nurture future leadership and accelerate both individual and organisational performance within an uncertain future of work.
2   To win the talent race, MNCs adopt an elitist talent management approach (ie exclusive talent management) compared to both SMEs and the public sector which are in favour of a more egalitarian talent management approach (ie inclusive talent management).

3 There are various stakeholders involved in the design and enactment of talent management, the roles of whom are interdependent.
4 Retaining talents is a contemporary critical issue and organisations should invest in talent acquisition and development.
5 The individual is increasingly responsible for self-directed learning and career growth.
6 Continuing professional development is integral to individual learning.

❓ Review questions

1 What is the business rationale for talent management?
2 Why does context matter for talent management?
3 How and why should key talent management stakeholders collaborate?

4 What is the role of learning technologies, and coaching and mentoring in nurturing talent?
5 Which talent management practice should be prioritised by organisations given today's circumstances?

Explore further

Beevers, K, Rea, A and Hayden, D (2019) *Learning and Development Practice in the Workplace,* 4th edn, Kogan Page, London. This textbook draws on CIPD's new profession map to discuss contemporary approaches to learning, training and development; thus, it is an asset for learning and development professionals.

Collings, DG, Vaiman, V and Scullion. H (2022) *Talent Management: A decade of developments.* This textbook discusses the progress made in talent management research in the last 20 years and explores contemporary talent management topics such as talent retention.

Tarique, I (2021) *The Routledge Companion to Talent Management*, Routledge, Abingdon. This book is ideal for anyone wishing to get a deeper insight into the contextual nature of talent management and into understanding contemporary talent management trends such as talent analytics.

Taylor, S (2019) *Resourcing and Talent Management*, 7th edn, Kogan Page, London. This book covers a wide range of important talent management practices such as talent recruitment and succession planning, as well as exploring the stemming implications for the HR profession posed by Brexit.

08
Engagement, wellbeing and inclusion

VICTORIA PAGAN

LEARNING OUTCOMES

After reading this chapter, you should be able to:

- define engagement, wellbeing and inclusion while understanding the different meanings attached to these concepts
- understand how engagement, wellbeing and inclusion are interrelated
- evaluate the importance of the psychological contract on employees' engagement, wellbeing and feelings of inclusion
- understand how engagement, wellbeing and inclusion can link with improved organisational performance.

8.1 Overview

In this chapter we examine several current concepts and issues which are central to good and effective management of people at work. An appreciation of the concepts of *engagement, wellbeing* and *inclusion* help us in this regard in several important respects. It is, first, very important to understand current and emerging trends which affect the ways in which organisations operate. We have an interesting issue regarding terminology and language throughout this chapter. How we choose to refer to the people – as employees, workers or individuals – is context-bound, and arguably influences (or is influenced by) our thinking. Much of the current literature focuses on employees inside the organisation, yet, as we will see, so-called networked organisations rely also upon people outside: for example, freelancers, agency and outsourced workers. When reflecting on engagement, wellbeing and inclusion, it is therefore important to consider the implications of these concepts for different categories of employees.

We will also explore the psychological contract concept – essentially an unwritten set of expectations of what an individual and organisation will give to and receive from each other in the course of their working relationship (Rousseau, 1995; Tomprou, Rousseau and Hansen, 2015). Theories of the psychological contract have typically been built around full-time permanent employment, however there is increasing discussion of how the concept can incorporate the experience of contingent workers. Even workers within the organisation can fall into the contingent category (that is, working without an ongoing contract). Examples here include temporary workers, seasonal staff and interns. Overall, expectations of workers are affected by the external context; in recent years including uncertain economic conditions – for example the impact of the Covid-19 pandemic – organisations downsizing and delayering, putting more pressure on remaining employees and technological changes automating processes and shaping skill demands (CIPD, 2022e). While it can be viewed as a self-standing topic area, as well as linked to many other topics covered in this textbook, in this chapter we will consider how the level of engagement displayed by workers and their feelings of inclusion or exclusion can be related to their psychological contract (eg Soares and Mosquera, 2019). The state of that contract may also influence workers' wellbeing (eg Ahmad et al, 2018).

We also draw your attention to an intersectional approach to considering engagement, wellbeing and inclusion. Intersectionality means recognising that our identity characteristics overlap and multiply potential for discrimination and an intersectional approach is 'a gathering place for open-ended investigations of the overlapping and conflicting dynamics of race, gender, class, sexuality, nation, and other inequalities' (Cho, Crenshaw and McCall, 2013, p 788). In particular, 'for underrepresented groups, the employee experience can be heavily affected by toxic workplace culture including discrimination, bullying, harassment and other unfair treatment' (Fullilove, 2020). Throughout this chapter, we encourage you to think about the ways employees' race, gender, class, etc. impact upon how included, engaged and well they feel in relation to their workplaces.

8.2 Introduction: recognising workplace dynamics

Managing people in organisations has in recent years been carried out within a rapidly changing and turbulent environment (see, eg, CIPD, 2022e; Holbeche, 2013; Bano, Omar and Ismail, 2021). Concurrently, there are patterns towards workplaces becoming more and more flexible through a range of drivers including: accelerating globalisation and technological advance (Thomas, 2009; Thompson and McHugh, 2009); prevention of burnout and maximisation of work performance (French et al, 2015); and improving the balance of work and life (OECD, 2016). Alongside this we find further potential complications including, for example: increased imbalance of work and life because of blurred boundaries; negative career impacts of inconsistent or less visibility to managers and other colleagues; exacerbated inequalities by gender, disability and associated intersections; and the need to engage with new technologies (Soga et al, 2022).

Although questions have been raised about its meaning and value (Guest, 1998), the concept of the *psychological contract* has become a central theme of people management. Research continues to be conducted in the field (Tomprou, Rousseau and Hansen, 2015). In general terms, the concept characterises the employment relationship in terms of exchange – mutual expectations or obligations – in order to make sense of the range and degrees of commitment that flow in both directions. In other words, the 'psychological contract' is a term for describing what is implicit in terms of reciprocity and exchange within the employment relationship. It is here that organisational policy and procedures mix with individual managerial and employee attitudes and behaviours, with complex outcomes. The concept is a dynamic one. Maguire (2002) posits key differences between the 'traditional' and a more 'progressive' psychological contract related to the decreased expectation of paternalistic human resource practices, the replacement of the concept of organisational worth with 'self-worth', the substitution of personal accomplishment for promotion as the route to growth, and the decreased importance of tenure. Table 8.1 demonstrates the distinctions found by Maguire (2002).

The distinctions shown in Table 8.1 are not intended to suggest that the 'traditional' elements have been entirely replaced by the 'progressive' elements; indeed, the CIPD (2022f) record that in many ways the 'old' elements are often present. It remains the case that the psychological contract is based on employees' sense of fairness and trust and the notion that the employer is honouring the 'deal' between

Table 8.1 The distinction between characteristics of psychological contracts

Traditional	Progressive
Organisation is 'parent' to employee 'child'	Organisation and employee enter into 'adult' contracts focused on mutually beneficial work
Employees' identity and worth are defined by the organisation	Employees' identity and worth are defined by the employee
Those who stay are good and loyal; others are bad and disloyal	The regular flow of people in and out is healthy and should be celebrated
Employees who do what they are told will work until retirement	Long-term employment may be less likely; can expect – and prepare for – multiple relationships
The primary route for growth is through promotion	The primary route for growth is a sense of personal accomplishment

them. While some people may wish to move between jobs and even change careers, others continue to value job security. One other feature which remains constant as the concept of psychological contract evolves over time concerns the key importance of line managers. The most recent CIPD Factsheet on the topic (CIPD, 2022f) concludes that employees' experience at work remain strongly influenced by the quality of their line managers, and that for many their psychological contract is largely the deal they have with their direct line manager. However, and importantly, what the 'progressive' characteristics take account of is an inclusion approach, with a much more mutual, co-constructed workplace experience that values diversity, difference and personal direction.

In this chapter we will examine a range of terms which have emerged as both diagnoses of current work practices and solutions to problems of managing people in the current competitive environment. There have been significant shifts in how we think about work since 2020, for example, the Great Resignation (eg Hirsch, 2021) and broad shifting assumptions about work (eg CIPD, 2022e). The areas under consideration in this chapter continue to be academically relevant, topical and of personal interest to many of us.

8.3 Engagement

When leaders prioritize the employee experience, they position themselves to join the growing number of organizations that yield positive results including increased profitability, highly engaged teams and increased retention. (Fullilove, 2020)

The notion of engagement is certainly topical and frequently referred to, not only in business and management sources, but also more widely in mainstream news and specialist media. CIPD (2022e) states that employers should monitor employee attitudes on a regular basis to identify where action may be needed to improve performance. The same report goes on to conclude that a positive psychological contract would typically support a high level of employee engagement. Once more we have our attention drawn to the importance of the line manager in this regard, as in order to display commitment employees have to feel that they are being treated with fairness and respect at the everyday level. Engagement must be seen in relation to connections with the workplace and is defined by CIPD (2012b) as 'employees internalising and emotionally connecting to the organisation's core purpose'. This survey emphasises the role of line managers in motivating via an engaging team-management style.

8.3.1 *Defining engagement*

William Kahn first published his work on employee engagement in 1990, offering a definition of engagement as 'the harnessing of organization members' selves to their work roles; in engagement, people employ and express themselves physically, cognitively, or emotionally during role performances' (p 695). Broadly, employee engagement is therefore 'a dynamic, changeable psychological state which links employees to their organisations' (Welch, 2011). Such links can be developed individually or in combination through a sense of connection with their jobs, the workplace, and/or the organisation and a CIPD-commissioned research report (Alfes et al, 2010, p 5) identified engagement as having three dimensions:

- intellectual engagement – thinking about the job and how it might be done better
- affective engagement – positive feelings about doing a job well
- social engagement – actively seeking opportunities to discuss work-related issues.

The management of the employment relationship characterised by an 'investment orientation' towards employees is designed to elicit their commitment to the organisation. Where managers are able to achieve an engaged workforce it is claimed that this can lead to both organisational success and employee wellbeing (MacLeod and Clark, 2009). Indeed, there is now a substantial body of literature that supports this view, with practitioners and academics agreeing that the consequences of employee engagement can be positive. CIPD (2021q) suggest that managers can plan their approach to employee engagement drawing on considerations of:

- Motivation: how employees may enjoy the day to day of their work processes and content, as well as how they may work to achieve a goal and/or reward.
- Organisational identification: how employees see themselves in relation to how they see their organisation.
- Organisational commitment: how faithful employees feel to the organisation and their work.

It is important to recognise that engagement is interrelational between managers and employees – managers deliver engagement activities, and employees experience engagement. As such, for all managers can and should work to encourage engagement, it cannot be 'done to' employees. Kahn (1990) also identified three ideal psychological conditions necessary for engagement to occur:

1 Meaningfulness – employees need to find their work has purpose, relevance and is worthwhile.

2 Safety – this relates to employees feeling that they trust their organisational situation and that they can bring themselves to their work in such a way that will not be judged negatively.

3 Availability – employees need to feel that they have space to fully engage with their work alongside other aspects of their lives.

As we have identified throughout this chapter as well, there may be different organisational relationships such that engagement is a concept in which 'one size fits all'.

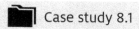 Case study 8.1

An intersectional approach to engagement

Dillard and Osam (2021) undertook qualitative research to explore the impact of identity on engagement, linked to Kahn's three ideal conditions. Some examples from their research are as follows.

Meaningfulness

Roles can bring status and influence leading to a sense of purpose ... However, this dynamic can be complicated by identity, as exhibited below in Evelyn's experience of seeking additional educational experiences to advance in her career: "He looked at me and said, "Oh, you have a degree, so you think you're something." ... from an intersectional perspective, Evelyn's experience illuminated how her identity as an educated (class), Black (race) woman (gender) intersected in ways that created oppression and not opportunity. Evelyn increased her development in order to have access to more meaningful roles. However, due to her manager's perceptions of her identities, her efforts were seen as an affront to his position in the company, particularly since he did not possess any advanced education. (p 522)

Safety

Elle, another research participant, described an experience they had:I am typically very engaged and contribute often at work. However, during a training about working with the transgender community, the trainer wasn't using appropriate terminology ... I actually texted to my manager at that time. I didn't actually say it out loud because I felt comfortable just saying it personally to somebody, rather than out in the open.

In this example, Elle did not feel safe expressing her concerns during the diversity training. As a queer, masculine presenting female, she feared that speaking up would affect group dynamics and relationship with her peers. As a result, the organisation missed an opportunity where Elle's engagement could have facilitated deeper understanding of the training content (pp 522–523).

Availability

Ada identified as a beneficiary of [a programme] that provided some relief for young and undocumented individuals living within the US ... external factors of changing legislation (which impacted her immigration status) coupled with her age (Generation Z) intersected and affected her availability at work. Her preoccupation with the impact of Covid on employment opportunities and the impending [legislative] decision ... left her with less psychological energies at work. This dynamic, coupled with being physically overworked and taken advantage of due to her age, left her less engaged (pp 523–524).

1 What does this case show us about the different ways in which identities affect employees' levels of engagement?

2 What could you do in your role to better take into account intersecting identities in relation to engagement activities?

SOURCE: Dillard, N and Osam, K (2021) Deconstructing the meaning of engagement: An intersectional qualitative study, *Human Resource Development International*, **24** (5), pp 511–32

8.3.2 *Generating engagement*

Increasing competition and changing expectations among employees have prompted a growing disillusionment with the traditional psychological contract based on lifetime employment and steady promotion from within (CIPD, 2022f). Consequently, companies must develop new ways to increase the loyalty and commitment of employees, for example designing reward systems that recognise contribution rather than position or status, continuous performance and continuous improvement rather than single events or past achievements. How else then can organisations generate employee engagement? Holbeche and Matthews (2012) suggest four 'drivers' of engagement:

- *Connection*. Employees need a sense of identification with, and pride in working for, the employing organisation; there has to be a common purpose and shared values.
- *Voice*. Managers need to keep employees informed of the organisation's progress and of organisational change, and listen to employees' views so that they feel involved in the business.
- *Support*. Employees need to be treated as individuals and enabled to do their job; they should feel they are valued and receive a fair deal from their employer, and believe their employer is concerned with their wellbeing.
- *Scope*. Work should be purposeful and provide employees with the opportunity for growth and accomplishment; it should allow for autonomy and be underpinned by mutual trust.

Alfes et al (2010) came to similar conclusions and highlighted the importance of meaningful work and employee voice to creating an engaged workforce (see also Chapters 10 and 11). Employee voice is the foundation of sustainable business performance, increasing engagement enables effective decision-making and drives innovation. To do this, organisations need to create a climate of trust in engagement that fosters opportunities for both collective and individual voice to be heard, or more simply put, talking and listening to their employees (Rees et al, 2013). Management style therefore has an important role in fostering employee engagement and employee voice. Through communication, managers can help employees place their own work in the context of the organisation's objectives. Similarly, establishing and maintaining effective communication and consultation channels can both reinforce employees' view of the value of their work and enhance social engagement. It is perhaps no surprise then that they emphasise the importance of line management style in creating employee engagement. Line managers, it is suggested, are the crucial link between the employer and employees, and their behaviour is central to levels of engagement. Their key tasks in this respect are selecting the correct people for the job, regular communication with their staff, relevant training and development, and ensuring reciprocity of effort and reward. However, what might be the challenges of this depending on the type of manager–employee relationship? For example, as Marchington et al (2005, p 78) point out: 'temporary agency workers attempt ... to satisfy their obligations simultaneously to two employers – the agency and the client.' This simultaneity raises questions about organisational commitment and loyalty.

Case study 8.2

Communication activities to promote engagement

Research in a public-private partnership demonstrated the influence of organisational communication on employee engagement through a range of management communication activities. Engagement was of particular importance to this partnership, created from two organisations already in existence, with the majority of employees being transferred into the new partnership organisation. Managers were focused on encouraging the generation of engagement with the new organisational context, specifically a culture change moving between sets of assumptions about how an organisation operates. Activities to create new terms of interaction were delivered as follows:

- Whole organisation events with presentations offering consistent strategic messages to all employees alongside breakout discussions.

- Quarterly round tables for employees from individual departments to meet with members of the senior management team, allowing specific question/answer as well as reinforcement of strategic messages.

- Monthly communications forum with the communications manager and volunteer communication representatives from each department encouraging information circulation and management actions as required.

- Team meetings between line managers and immediate team members for the development of relationships in the context of role expectations and responsibilities.

- Monthly newsletter circulated for consistent information sent to all employees, and articles can be submitted by any employee via the communications forum.

- Floor walking by senior managers offering an opportunity for everyday interaction and observation.

The response of employees to these activities was generally positive, including feeling better informed, involved and with more scope for taking initiative in their roles. There are challenges, however, particularly where employees: retain a connection with their previous organisation; feel that the new situation has not been their choice but rather an imposition; and/or feel that the new culture and working practices are not in line with how they would wish the organisation to be run. In this respect, engagement is not something that can be 'done' to employees, but rather 'give and take' is needed in the generation of employee engagement.

Managers can give time and information to their employees, then can also take feedback and observations from their employees to feed into the development of working practices. Employees therefore give their say and their involvement, as well as taking the information from their managers, reflecting on it and understanding what is trying to be achieved. The process is gradual and ongoing, not something that can be 'ticked off' as completed.

1 What does this case show us about the benefits of different types of communication to organisations and staff?

2 Is this type of engagement process restricted to public–private partnership contexts or could and should it have wider application?

3 What else might need to be taken in to account with regard to communication activities for organisations with different types of workers, eg temporary, part-time and/or casual workers?

SOURCE: Reissner, S and Pagan, V (2013) Generating employee engagement in a public–private partnership: Management communication activities and employee experiences, *The International Journal of Human Resource Management*, **24** (14), pp 2741–59

One might reasonably be reminded of the phrase that every generation holds the key to its own world, suggesting that demographics may influence the activities needed to engage employees. French et al (2015) suggest that Generations X (born after 1964), Y (born after 1978) and Millennials (Cogin, 2012; Chaudhuri and Ghosh, 2012), can display a series of distinctive attitudes towards work. These included less loyalty to the employing organisation as a result of greater labour mobility. The predispositions of these three generational groups contrasted with the baby boomers (born between 1946 and 1955) and shadow boomers (born between 1956 and 1964). The boomers and shadow boomers are, despite the removal of compulsory retirement ages in many societies, in many cases about to leave the workforce, with a consequent loss of generational memory (Dencker, Joshi and Martocchio, 2008). Papavasileiou and Lyons (2015) provide us with one further twist in the debate on the effect of demographics, concluding that millennial-aged Greeks exhibit 'some moderately unique work priorities, relative to their counterparts in other countries' (Papavasileiou and Lyons, 2015, p 2183), including a stress on intrinsic and social work values. Without going into detail on cross-cultural aspects of work values – see French (2015) for far greater detail and depth in this regard – one can conclude that culture is another potentially important influence on work values which underpin employee engagement.

8.3.3 The outcomes of engagement

Hutchinson and Purcell (2003) found that some HR policies and practices were shown to be particularly important in terms of influencing employee outcomes like commitment, job satisfaction and motivation. These were those concerned with career opportunities, job influence, job challenge, training, performance appraisal, teamworking, involvement in decision-making, work–life balance, and having managers who are good at leadership and who show respect. In Hutchinson and Purcell's (2003) framework, 'organisation process advantage'– the way these policies are implemented is what makes a difference. Put another way: it's not what you do, it's the way that you do it. There is recognition that independent of line manager leadership behaviour, the HR practices as perceived by the employees will be related to organisational commitment and job experiences, and that the outcome effect on employee attitudes will be greater when both are positive. A possible people management-causal chain emerges, which seeks to clarify the distinction between policies, practices and employees' experiences of them. It is seen as follows (Purcell and Hutchinson, 2007):

- *intended practices* – designed by the organisation
- *actual practices* – and style of leadership behaviour
- *perception of practices* – in terms of satisfaction, fairness and legitimacy
- *employee attitudes* – in reaction
- *employee behaviour* – observable responses including organisational citizenship behaviour (OCB) and attendance
- *unit-level outcomes* – organisational effectiveness and performance.

The authors conclude that the crucial link is between the employee experiences of people management, the formation or modification of attitudes towards the employing organisation and the job, and the inducements these provide to engage in certain types of discretionary behaviour (Purcell and Hutchinson, 2007, p 16).

Interestingly, it is possible to glimpse an unanticipated consequence of adopting flexible working practices that might be introduced to foster higher levels of engagement – that of work intensification. While reporting evidence that flexible workers record higher levels of job satisfaction and organisational commitment than their 'nonflexible' counterparts, Kelliher and Anderson (2010) also report evidence of work intensification being experienced by both those who work reduced hours and those who work remotely. It is certainly a complex picture, Kelliher and Anderson (2010, p 99) suggest that in contemporary workplaces, with a 'prevailing rhetoric of greater personal autonomy', employees often see themselves as responsible for their own work intensification. To some extent the professional workers saw themselves as partly responsible and therefore did not voice opposition. However, other studies have also found that employees do not always respond negatively to intensification, especially where they believe they will gain some benefit as a consequence (Kelliher and Anderson, 2010, p 99).

Where organisations are able to effectively engage their employees on the various dimensions, Alfes et al (2010) show that three important outcomes can be identified which can assist organisations in the achievement of their objectives. First, engaged employees are likely to perform better than those who are not. Respondents in the survey claimed to have good levels of job and social skills, were willing to take on extra work and tended to have high ratings in their performance appraisal. Second, engaged employees are more likely to be innovative at work. This might include searching out new methods of working, generate enthusiasm for innovative ideas and transform such ideas into meaningful applications. Third, engaged employees are more likely to want to stay with their employer.

We might expect non-permanent staff to show a more transactional approach, and show less commitment, than permanent staff. Research evidence provides ambiguous results. In a call centre environment, Biggs and Swailes (2006) found that agency workers had a significantly lower level of organisational commitment compared with permanent workers. However, this is not necessarily the case according to MacDonald and Makin (2000, p 89), who suggest 'the observance and commitment to the norms, symbols, and rituals of desirable groups is often higher among those just outside, but wishing to join, the group than it is among established members'. From the same authors we hear of higher levels of organisational commitment and job satisfaction among some temporary staff. One possible explanation, it is suggested, may lie in the short tenure of non-permanent staff within the organisation. There is a 'complexity of feelings' towards, and reactions resulting from, becoming a temporary worker, according to Saunders and Thornhill (2006, p 452), where the attractions associated with obtaining greater freedom have also been associated with greater insecurity, potentially lower control over hours of work and working patterns, and a continuing need to find new work. High preferences for temporary work would seem likely to accentuate positive feelings towards transactional-oriented psychological contracts, whereas low preferences for temporary work would accentuate negative feelings towards transactional-oriented psychological contracts' (Saunders and Thornhill, 2006, p 452).

 Reflective activity 8.1

Employee engagement – how engaged are you?

Access one of the many free employee engagement surveys available online (eg the Gallup Q12) and review the results to see if you are engaged at work. What factors does the survey measure and how do these in your opinion contribute to employee engagement? If you were tasked with improving employee engagement in your organisation what would you do? If your organisation undertakes staff or engagement surveys you could also look at the results of these surveys to help you answer this question.

8.4 Wellbeing

With the exception of a privileged few, contemporary workplaces are sites of exhaustion, stress, and overwhelm. Intersectionality imagines a world where work can be sites of collaborative ownership, personal and collective fulfilment, and solidaristic care. (Liu, 2020)

Rather than exploring legal requirements regarding employers' duty of care to their employees – see Chapter 9 for coverage of this area – this chapter section aims to signal some elements particularly in the context of engagement and inclusion and how these can work effectively in supporting the wellbeing of employees. Today's managers need to recognise that that there is no single best way of treating employees, because each one will have their own personal needs, values and beliefs, all of which interact to produce their sense of wellbeing.

Reflective activity 8.2

Generation Z and wellbeing

Are you in Gen Z (born mid-90s) and/or do you have Gen Zers in your workplace? Recent research by McKinsey (2022) demonstrates that this generation experiences lower levels of emotional and social wellbeing than other generations. Specifically, 'one in four Gen Z respondents reported feeling more emotionally distressed (25 per cent), almost double the levels reported by millennial and Gen X respondents (13 per cent each), and more than triple the levels reported by baby boomer respondents (8 per cent). And the Covid-19 pandemic has only amplified this challenge.' Workplaces that recognise this and respond with support will help them reach their goals and succeed in their accomplishments, with subsequent benefits for organisational performance.

Thinking about your own organisational context, what sorts of actions would support emotional and social wellbeing?

8.4.1 Dimensions of wellbeing

Wellbeing has been a hot topic in the UK for some time, so much so that All-Party Parliamentary Group on Wellbeing Economics was established in 2009 in recognition of the centrality of wellbeing for policy decisions (APPGWE, 2022). In 2019, the Group wrote an open letter to the Chancellor to request a spending review to increase wellbeing proposing that by foregrounding this, other objectives around economic improvement can also be met (APPGWE, 2019). They proposed six priorities for the review, including 'improved wellbeing at work' as follows:

> We know that having a job, and the quality of that job has an important impact on people's wellbeing. Employers need to measure worker wellbeing, and publish the results as standard in annual accounts. We know a lot about what can improve wellbeing at work, and employers should put policies and programmes in place, which train line managers in how to promote wellbeing, address the management of mental health problems and give people more control over how they do their jobs. They also need financial support to re-train and re-deploy workers made redundant by technological change. Reducing working hours and matching people to jobs where their wellbeing will be highest can also improve overall wellbeing for employees, whilst in turn offering benefits for employers through higher productivity.

In this, we can see that there are tasks for both government and employers and the What Works Centre for Wellbeing was established in 2018 as an independent collaborative space to provide resources to help stakeholders work towards improving wellbeing (WWCW, 2022). The dimensions of wellbeing are defined as: the natural environment, personal wellbeing, our relationships, health, what we do, where we live, personal finance, the economy, education and skills, and governance. From the workplace perspective, CIPD regularly review activities across the wellbeing dimensions of: work-related stress and mental health; wellbeing benefits provision; employee financial wellbeing; tackling 'presenteeism' and 'leaveism'; the causes and management of absence; and managing people with disabilities and long-term health conditions (CIPD, 2021r). In this respect, it can be seen that by supporting physical and mental health, finance, and offering wellbeing benefits that may also include relaxation and complementary therapies, employers are able to have a significant influence on employees' holistic wellbeing. However, this requires ongoing monitoring and evaluation given the nature of twenty-first century work and the lack of 'one size fits all' for employees.

 Case study 8.3

Work intensification and wellbeing

Research undertaken by Kelliher and Anderson (2010) includes interviewees' experiences of intensification in a number of UK private-sector organisations, with subsequent implications for their wellbeing.

Intensification affecting work boundaries
While flexible working can have some benefits for workers, interviewees in this research described why, when *imposed* on reduced-hours contracts, intensification has been a result. Their workloads did not decrease in line with their hours when they moved to a reduced-hours contract and consequently they were doing something akin to a full-time job, but in fewer paid hours. This could result in both increased extensive and intensive effort. One interviewee commented: 'There is enough workload to keep me busy for five days, but I only have three days to do it in, so I either work late, which I do sometimes, or I try and delegate some of it.' Others described that they felt the need to be available at times when they were not scheduled to be working, but when the business was operating. This took the form of being prepared to take phone calls and checking

emails at times when they were not working. For example, one interviewee reported: 'On a Monday, when I'm not at work, I'll typically put in 40 minutes to an hour just checking my emails to make sure that I'm on top of any issues that come up, or that came up over the weekend … so I check the email at least once if not twice during the Monday.'

Intensification creating energy, efficiency and feelings of value
Although there is very clearly a problem for many workers in demarcating work and non-work time, others, typically remote workers, describe that working flexibly enabled them to work more intently, exercising both greater intensive and extensive effort. For example, one respondent noted that it was far easier to maintain energy levels and enthusiasm when working for three days or four days, as opposed to working for five days. The same person noted that, contrastingly, they were more likely to sustain efficiency over three or three and a half days, rather than five (Kelliher and Anderson, 2010). The impact of commitment on effort is illustrated by a worker

who reported greater extensive effort when she worked from home. This was due to that employee perceiving that she was valued as a human being, rather than seen as a nine-to-five machine by her employer. This led her in turn to exhibit a deep-seated loyalty and greater levels of commitment (Kelliher and Anderson, 2010).

1 As an HR manager, how would you respond to employees who have complained to you about their work intensification, and the impact that it was having upon their wellbeing?

2 How might you devise a policy on setting work boundaries, including ways of monitoring the policy's effectiveness?

While there are broad-brush actions that HR managers can take towards caring for employees' wellbeing, it is often the microprocesses of work that can build towards negative impacts. For example, the issue of email overload continues to be debated, with the noted psychologist Cary Cooper (2005) claiming that 'an inundation of often unnecessary emails, and the increasing ease and accessibility to work beyond the desk without any appropriate boundaries was damaging the UK's health'. Cooper went on to claim that the nature of email communication (or how it had been adopted in many organisations) was that it demanded an immediate response leading to 'it managing us' rather than vice versa. Cooper (*2005*) reported that something like a quarter of people were at that time checking their emails on holiday and almost everybody is checking their emails when home at night, long after they've 'left' work. Lewis (2015). By 2015 Cooper noted that email overload was the biggest cause of productivity damage for the UK workforce. Also, recent intersectional analysis by Brown and Moloney (2019) 'demonstrates that the employment experiences of working women with disabilities are shaped by dual disadvantages associated with disability and gender, and that these disadvantages impact psychological well-being ... gender and disability indirectly affect well-being because of their association with numerous employment-related factors, including personal income, occupational prestige, exposure to a stressful workplace, job autonomy, and job creativity' (p 111–12).

Flexible behaviour is becoming more and more of a requirement of employees in the less predictable work roles that are a feature of contemporary working life (Foster and Harris, 2005). This can be positive for employee wellbeing in terms of increasing interest in work–life balance, the need to be competitive in the labour market, and the introduction of legislation giving parents of young or disabled children and, more recently, carers. It can also foster greater ownership of work structures through the right of employees to request flexible working arrangements (Kelliher and Anderson, 2010). In a more critical vein, attention is drawn to other aspects of the work–life balance concept by Eikhof, Warhurst and Haunschild (2007) where 'beyond working time and the provision of flexible working practices to enable child care, there is little in the debate about the need to change work per se'. These authors also comment that the work–life debate 'narrowly perceives "life", equating it with women's care work, hence the emphasis again of family-friendly policies' (Eikhof,

Warhurst and Haunschild, 2007, p 326). In this respect, this may actually perpetuate inequalities by continuing to place care/family responsibilities with women and not men. So, we can detect that flexibility, lying at the heart of the wage–work bargain, means different things to the different parties to the deal, with different wellbeing implications.

 Reflective activity 8.3

Flexible working, engagement, wellbeing and inclusion

Dr Stefanie Reissner and Dr Michal Izak note the dynamics of flexible working that face organisations and their employees. Recent crises have forced many organisations to rethink the way their workplaces operate, specifically in relation to large-scale homeworking. 'Technical obstacles, such as access to collaborative tools, that had prevented flexible working previously had to be removed almost overnight. Communication systems, security protocols, home workspaces etc. had to be tackled "in one go". Qualms about whether productivity can be maintained in flexible working were largely assuaged during the crisis. For example, Twitter announced that all staff would be allowed to work from home "forever", while Facebook executives expect half of its employees to work remotely by 2030 at the latest.' Hybrid arrangements, with some remote and some 'in-office' time 'would enable employees to plan their work more strategically, reserving collaborative tasks for the days in the office and intellectually challenging ones for their days working from home, for example.' However, there is a risk of overwork, isolation, and the exacerbation of inequalities between those with secure jobs and adequate

remote working conditions, and those with precarious jobs and challenging remote working conditions. 'Organisations that strive to profit from the advantages offered by mobile working, without cushioning its psychological and social effects, are trying to have their cake and eat it. The way that mobile working is introduced and communicated between managers and their teams influences how much internal pressure people subject themselves to.'

1 Thinking about your own work organisation (or one of your choice) reflect on how you would manage flexible working to maximise the benefits.
2 What implications might there be for the wellbeing of your employees? Think about how you might need to take into account different types of employees, different types of work, different types of managers.
3 Consider how you would strive to be equitable and inclusive in your approaches.

SOURCES: Reissner, S and Izak, M (2017) How mobile working ruins work–life balance – unless you've got a good manager, *The Conversation* https://theconversation.com/how-mobile-working-ruins-work-life-balance-unless-youve-got-a-good-manager-89182

Reissner, S and Izak, M (2021) *Swimming Rather than Sinking? Flexible Working (more than) a year into the Covid-19 pandemic,* Workwise UK www.workwiseuk.org/blog/2021/5/15/guest-blog-swimming-rather-than-sinking-flexible-working-more-than-a-year-into-the-covid-19-pandemic-by

8.4.2 *Facilitating improved employee wellbeing*

The CIPD encourages practices focused on valuing everyone as an individual – valuing people as employees, customers and clients. As such, while this section illustrates some of the different ways in which improved employee wellbeing may be facilitated, different workplaces will need to think about the applicability in their contexts and for their employees. For example, McIntyre (2021) comments from her experiences as an HR director specialising in the hospitality industry, prioritising actions to retain employees, focusing particularly on development activities, mental health support, workload and working hours. Edgell et al. (2021) researched the fire service and wellbeing particularly given the extension of working lives and the highly physical nature of the work. While gym equipment was provided to help maintain fitness, 'participants detailed a lack of systematically protected time on-shift to use them' and 'one participant detailed how this would challenge their ability to extend their working lives, especially when opportunities in non-operational/non-uniformed roles were limited' (Edgell et al, 2021 p 9). The What Works Centre for Wellbeing offers a Question Bank that can be used to design the collection of information from employees regarding their wellbeing such that employers can design responses most effectively and then repeat on a frequent basis to establish both impact and the need for adjusted interventions (WWCW, 2020).

 Case study 8.4

PWC activities to support wellbeing for employee retention

In 2001 PricewaterhouseCoopers (PwC) was described as a knowledge-driven organisation. PwC had concluded that, when its employees left, the firm not only lost the training and knowledge they had built up, but also the client relationships they developed. PwC therefore redefined its strategy based around choice for its employees, whose average age at that time was 27. Changes included a generous maternity and paternity leave scheme, childcare vouchers for returning mothers and other benefits. Moreover, most employees were equipped to be able to work from home, and almost all of them chose to do this at least once a month.

The company also launched an in-house concierge service. Employees were offered a wide range of domestic services at discount price. These included activities such as waiting in for plumbers, builders and electricians. Take-up was greatest among company consultants, who often worked offsite for months.

PwC also introduced the notion of 'paid time off', rather than the more restrictive 'annual leave'. Employees could use their paid time off allocation for short-term illness, childcare and jury service, as well as holiday.

According to the author, the strategy initially appeared to be successful. Despite skill shortages in the consultancy sector, staff retention at PwC had improved by 4–5 per cent over the previous year.

1 What does this case show us about the benefits to organisations and staff of activities that support employee wellbeing?

2 Are these activities restricted to the type of professional worker employed by PwC or could and should it have wider application?

3 More than 20 years after this case study, are the measures taken to improve wellbeing still valid and, referring to the Perkbox example later in this chapter, what new policies would you introduce at the current time?

SOURCE: Perry, M (2001) Flexibility Pays, *Accountancy Age*. In (2002) *Human Resource Management International Digest*, **10** (4), pp 13–15

In principle, the development of more innovative HR policies and practices will offer greater reciprocity in the employment relationship by addressing individual needs and supporting employees' wellbeing. Taking an intersectional approach is also found to maximise health and wellbeing, as the approach aims to offer a workplace community where all colleagues can feel valued with tailored policies and practices (CIPD, 2022g). Recent research (Pagán-Castaño, Maseda-Moreno and Santos-Rojo, 2020) demonstrates the importance of human resource practices on employee wellbeing finding, for example, that those practices that are employee-focused 'can have a more positive impact on employees than those focused on the organisation' (p 472). Interestingly, research by Hamilton Skurak et al (2018), looked at the effects of engagement on wellbeing, finding that 'to enjoy the benefits of a highly engaged workforce, organisations must enable employee detachment from work' (p 116). In this respect, it is perhaps the case that engagement needs to be boundaried in order to be most effective for both organisational performance and employee wellbeing – just enough engagement but not too much!

 Reflective activity 8.4

Resilience, wellbeing and HRM

In 2019, Cooper et al edited a special issue of *The International Journal of Human Resource Management* comprising a set of papers exploring the relationship between resilience, wellbeing and HRM. Resilience is conceptualised as 'bouncing back from setbacks combined with remaining effective in the face of tough demands and difficult circumstances, and moreover, growing stronger in the process' (p 1229). In this respect, this recognises that wellbeing can be impacted by a range of events and the ways/pace at which wellbeing recovers can be facilitated through HRM practices. The papers in the special issue highlight practices that can support resilience and wellbeing, for example:

• Focused and tailored responses at a micro-level.

• Recognising everyday triggers as well as more extreme events.

• Monitoring workload and impact on wellbeing for men and women.

• Affects of job security/insecurity on wellbeing for men and women.

• Information sharing and flow as positively impacting wellbeing and resilience.

• Creating an inclusive culture.

Thinking about your own workplace contexts, can you reflect on what might be risks in terms of demands and difficulties for employees? Are there ways that these risks could be mitigated or activities that could help employees' resilience such that their wellbeing is not so negatively impacted?

Figure 8.1 Facilitating wellbeing: A plan-do-check-act model

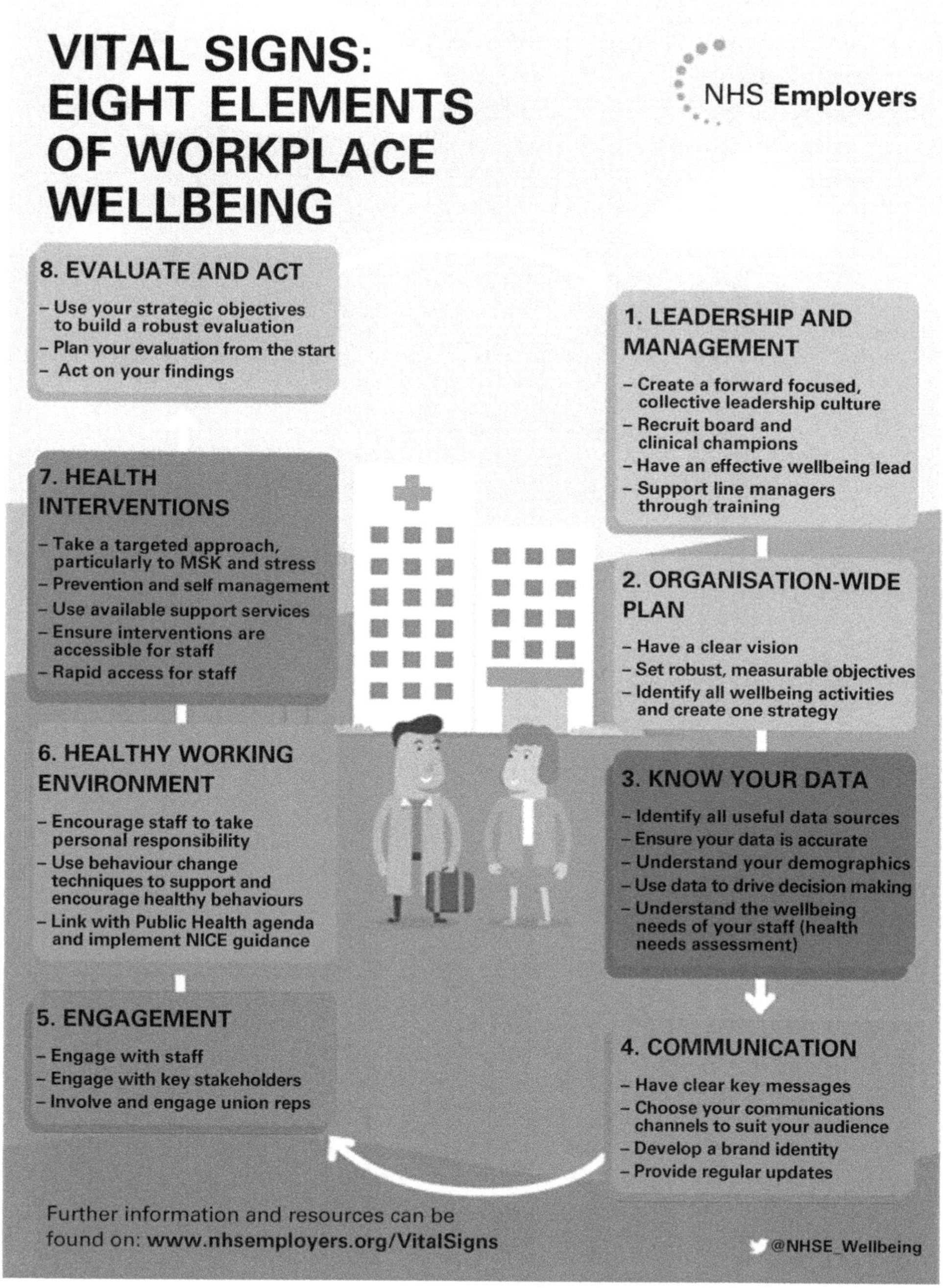

VITAL SIGNS: EIGHT ELEMENTS OF WORKPLACE WELLBEING

NHS **Employers**

8. EVALUATE AND ACT

- Use your strategic objectives to build a robust evaluation
- Plan your evaluation from the start
- Act on your findings

7. HEALTH INTERVENTIONS

- Take a targeted approach, particularly to MSK and stress
- Prevention and self management
- Use available support services
- Ensure interventions are accessible for staff
- Rapid access for staff

6. HEALTHY WORKING ENVIRONMENT

- Encourage staff to take personal responsibility
- Use behaviour change techniques to support and encourage healthy behaviours
- Link with Public Health agenda and implement NICE guidance

5. ENGAGEMENT

- Engage with staff
- Engage with key stakeholders
- Involve and engage union reps

1. LEADERSHIP AND MANAGEMENT

- Create a forward focused, collective leadership culture
- Recruit board and clinical champions
- Have an effective wellbeing lead
- Support line managers through training

2. ORGANISATION-WIDE PLAN

- Have a clear vision
- Set robust, measurable objectives
- Identify all wellbeing activities and create one strategy

3. KNOW YOUR DATA

- Identify all useful data sources
- Ensure your data is accurate
- Understand your demographics
- Use data to drive decision making
- Understand the wellbeing needs of your staff (health needs assessment)

4. COMMUNICATION

- Have clear key messages
- Choose your communications channels to suit your audience
- Develop a brand identity
- Provide regular updates

Further information and resources can be found on: www.nhsemployers.org/VitalSigns

@NHSE_Wellbeing

Perkbox (2021), a global benefits and rewards platform, suggests 20 workplace well-being initiatives that companies can consider. The list includes:

- Food provision, including healthy snack food available in the office and healthy lunches in recognition of good work.
- Emphasising the importance of breaks, including mandatory breaks at lunchtime and taking time off when unwell, sabbaticals.
- A comfortable workplace environment, including plants and natural light in working spaces, informal meeting spaces, regular team and whole-company activities.
- The availability of mental health resources.
- A programme of recognition for employees' contributions.
- Review pay and raise wages, and offer personal and professional development opportunities.

What do you think of this list? Can you see how these could be implemented in your workplaces and what challenges there might be? Overall, having a strategic approach to wellbeing is considered to be important for effectiveness, rather than having initiatives that operate in isolation. NHS Employers (2017) use a version of a plan-do-check-act model for facilitating wellbeing in their organisational contexts, as seen in Figure 8.1.

It is interesting to see that leadership and management are placed as the initiating step on this cycle. Indeed, a study in China by Huo, Boxall and Cheung (2020) that used a survey of 357 manufacturing workers, found that line managers have a particular part to play in determining employee wellbeing, particularly in relation to encouraging their motivation and their perceptions of distributive justice in relation to rewards, that it, how fair decisions were made relating to pay, bonus, and promotion.

8.5 Inclusion

Purcell et al's (2003) study on the impact of people management on organisational performance was intended to show the way in which HR practices – or what the CIPD terms 'people management', meaning all aspects of how people are managed – impact on performance. The people of an organisation are likely to represent a range of identities – for example, age, gender, race, ethnicity, marital status, caring responsibilities, disabilities – the combination of which displays the diversity of an organisation's workforce. Chapter 9 will explore the management of diversity in more detail, but here we will explore a closely related concept – inclusion. Purcell et al's (2003) study was conducted within a framework which claims that performance is a function of people's ability (knowledge and skills), their motivation, and the opportunity they are given to deploy their skills (referred to as 'AMO'). The authors concluded that a range of 11 HR policies and practices are required to turn this into action, and a model was devised, covering recruitment and selection, training and development, career opportunity, communications, involvement in decision-making, teamworking, appraisal, pay, job security, job challenge/job autonomy, and work–life balance.

Reflective activity 8.5

Understanding inclusion in your organisation

Access the CIPD inclusion health checker tool at www.cipd.co.uk/knowledge/fundamentals/relations/diversity/inclusion-health-checker-tool and review the results to receive some example recommendations to help improve inclusion in your workplace.

Think about what each question asks – what does this make you consider in relation to inclusive practices in your workplace?

Review the recommendations – what actions can you take in response to these?

8.5.1 Defining inclusion

Diversity refers to demographic differences of a group [for example] age, disability, gender reassignment, marriage and civil partnership, pregnancy and maternity, race, religion or belief, sex and sexual orientation … Equality means equal rights and opportunities are afforded to all … Equity recognises that treating everyone equally has shortcomings, when the playing field is not level. An equity approach emphasises that everyone should not be treated the same, but according to their own needs. Inclusion is often defined as the extent to which everyone at work, regardless of their background, identity or circumstance, feels valued, accepted and supported to succeed at work. (CIPD, 2019b, p 3)

Inclusion is understood both at an individual level and an organisational level. Individual inclusion is characterised by, for example: feelings that they are valued for who they are; that they can be themselves; and that they belong in the organisation without feeling they have to act in line with norms and expectations of the organisation. Organisational inclusion can be shown through, for example: fairness in policies and practices; employee voice in decision making; and leadership that models inclusion (CIPD, 2019b).

The aforementioned performance-related HR policies encourage people to exercise a degree of choice on how and how well they do their job. In other words, they help induce discretionary behaviour which makes people work better and improve performance. This happens because the HR policies and practices develop positive employee attitudes or feelings of satisfaction, commitment and motivation (Purcell et al, 2003, p ix). However, a related angle on this is the inclusiveness of an organisation – where differences between people in the organisation are both seen as beneficial and all perspectives and differences are valued such that this goes from mere presence to full contribution. CIPD (2021s) states that 'an inclusive working environment is one in which everyone feels that they belong without having to conform, that their contribution matters and they are able to perform to their full potential, no matter their background, identity or circumstances. An inclusive workplace has fair policies and practices in place and enables a diverse range of people to work together effectively.' However, what happens if the whole product or service of the organisation is exclusionary? Reading the next case study may prompt some reflections on how you would feel about this.

Case study 8.5

Inclusion or exclusion on the basis of 'looks'

An online dating community that specifically targets 'good-looking' people has now capitalised on this by launching an employment agency linked to its online dating agency: www.beautifulpeople.com/microsites/recruitment/. Greg Hodge, its managing director, argues that there are business benefits to employing attractive staff including winning more business and increased revenue generation. The employment agency, launched in 2013, allows companies who count appearance as a key factor in selection of staff the opportunity to target its 750,000 members. Employers are able to advertise their vacancies through the website to members and the assumption is that the result for the employer will be 'good-looking' applicants. Many would argue that there is far too much scope for lawful bias against unattractive employees and job applicants where their looks are frankly irrelevant to the job. There is also potential for discriminatory bias on the basis of several protected characteristics, including age, gender and race.

1 List the advantages and disadvantages to extending the current equality legislation to include personal characteristics.
2 Compare your view with that of a colleague or others in a small group and debate your main differences in your views. Then, working together, consider how you would:
   a legislate against lookism
   b incorporate opposition to lookism into HR policies and practices
   c in both cases, what do you think would be the main likely unintended consequences, and how could you overcome them?

One of the main criticisms of creating inclusion is that it requires significant resources with no guarantee of success. There is no instant formula for its achievement because it is a complex task and every organisation will approach it differently. CIPD (2005, 2007b, 2012c) suggests that, in common with other strategies for employee engagement, it needs to be led from the top of the organisation. Further, it requires systematic management action that moves from minimal legal compliance to a focus on the development of an open workplace culture in which everyone feels valued and can add value. The key is to make inclusion a mainstream issue, owned by everyone so that it influences all employment policies, practices and drivers. Enablers include:

- ensuring that initiatives and policies have the support of senior management
- remembering inclusive practice is a continuous process, not a one-off initiative
- developing a strategy to support the achievement of business goals which addresses the diverse needs of stakeholders
- focusing on fairness and inclusion, ensuring that merit, competence and potential are the basis for people decisions
- reviewing policies and update with changes in law.

Despite the apparent attractiveness of the business case, it appears that organisations may still see legislation as the main driver for making changes in practice, and view inclusion (and, arguably, engagement and wellbeing) as a cost rather than a driver of organisational success. If that is the case, it suggests that arguments for the business case need to be communicated more effectively and its profile raised as a strategic business lever (CIPD, 2007b).

8.5.2 *Inclusion-centred approaches*

Rezai et al (2020) comment that 'inclusion at work is an important social determinant of health' (p 420), echoing discussions in relation to wellbeing above. Specifically, 'feelings of inclusion or exclusion have been related to psychological developments like self-esteem, anxiety, depression and satisfaction, which can impact motivation and behaviors at work and outside of work' (p 421). An inclusion-centred approach embeds practices throughout the organisation and its culture. CIPD (2019c) offer five areas for action that HR managers can take to play their part in this work as follows:

- Set standards for respectful behaviour and provide clear routes for exclusionary behaviour to be challenged.
- Ensure line managers are equipped to foster inclusion, particularly in relation to progression/recruitment.
- Role model expectations from the most senior levels of the organisation.
- Use data to evaluate policies and practices, and adapt them to be more inclusive as needed.
- Work on the organisational culture through, for example, fair policies and practice, involvement in decision-making, and calling out exclusive practices.

 Reflective activity 8.6

Inclusion and gender

Research undertaken by Boncori et al (2019) identified factors that affect the extent to which transgender and gender non-conforming employees experience inclusion in the workplace. These are shown Table 8.2 split into relational factors, that is, factors that are cultural and interpersonal, and practical factors, that is, factors that are tangible and visible in practices, policies and procedures (p 152).

1 Reflect on the lists in the table. What actions could you take as 'quick wins' in the short term? How about the medium and long term? What strategic enablers would be needed? What are any challenges to responding to these factors?

Table 8.2 Relational and practical factors within inclusive working practices

Relational factors	Practical factors
Zero tolerance policy against discrimination	Creation of LGBT+ awareness training sessions for all staff at the point of induction
Availability of networks and groups	Visible cues of support
Visible examples of inclusion	Availability of gender-neutral toilets
Visible role models in top hierarchical positions	Availability of gender-neutral changing rooms

(continued)

Table 8.2 (Continued)

Relational factors	Practical factors
Sense of respect and belonging	Paid leave for gender-specific medical appointments and treatment
Active mentoring	Inclusive language in documents and published materials
Participation in key committees and groups	Zero tolerance against bullying and harassment
Trans/non-binary friendly policies	Flexible dress codes
Public communications regarding trans and non-binary inclusion	Provision of targeted counselling and support within the human resources unit, or via external provision
Social interaction inside/outside the organisation	Communication on legal and prodcedural requirements
'Water cooler' conversations	Use of gender-neutral pronouns
Maintenance of confidentiality with regards to ones trans history	No impositions of unnecessary requests for certificates and other forms of disclosure

It can perhaps be seen how the aforementioned actions from an inclusion-centred approach can also support efforts to engage employees and improve their sense of wellbeing at work. As discussed throughout this chapter, it is important to think intersectionally about all the actions taken throughout the organisation. Jamie Studenroth, a disability inclusion co-ordinator, echoes the CIPD actions to help HR managers take an intersectional approach to inclusion, Studenroth (2022a, 2022b), especially to commit to an intersectional approach from the most senior leadership and management, role modelling ongoing learning and helping others to learn as well, and investing resources in this work. Other recommendations were made as follows.

- CIPD (2021s) highlights the importance of data usage and Studenroth builds on this to recommend making sure to look at the data from multiple perspectives, for example what the data might mean for Black women, men with disabilities, etc.

- Employee affinity groups, also known as resource groups or networks, are a common tool to foster a sense of belonging in organisations through shared identities (see Foldy, 2019 for research on their impacts). These may be structured as single categories (eg race equality, LGBTIQ+, women) but Studenroth recommends having opportunities for these groups to overlap to allow for additional connections and associated benefits. An example of the importance of this is given as follows: 'a workplace affinity group might plan an outing that includes group participation in a charity walk. If the plans don't take employees with disabilities into account – say, by proactively offering accommodations and alternatives – some employees with disabilities are likely to be excluded. These employees might feel discouraged enough to leave the group that sponsored the event' (Studenroth, 2022b).

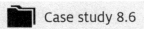 Case study 8.6

Intersections of gender, parenting responsibilities and work

One million mothers would rather leave the workforce than stay in it, says Mintel, and only 20 per cent return to work within a year of childbirth. Childcare costs, and the squeezed working and financial situation many parents report, all cause huge strain on the family dynamic, and can put parents at loggerheads. Most importantly, it is stifling inclusion and, if it does force parents out of the workforce in significant numbers, has profound implications for the future health of the British workplace. The effects are seen across both the much-discussed 'squeezed middle' of working professionals and in lower-paid positions where the economic benefits of work are lessening.

Gillian Nissim, founder, Working Mums

Your organisation started life in 2006. What's changed since?

A core of businesses have always seen the benefit of the family and flexible working, but the last few years have seen a rise in the rate of discrimination against mothers. If workplaces were so brilliant, Working Mums wouldn't need to exist.

Do working women suffer more when they become parents?

Not always. But the real problem for working mothers is that they often don't go back to the same field, which means a life-long loss of earnings. Many are working, at a loss, just to keep their toe in the door. Mothers should be able to get back to their careers.

We're seeing more men involved with parenting, but more could be working flexibly to alleviate pressure on mums. Government policy to extend paternity leave, and allow couples to divide their total leave, will put things on more of an equal footing, but men are not taking up their paternity entitlement.

Because childcare is still seen as a woman's role?

Maybe. I fear childcare is forcing family life to swing back to being female-led because of changes to child tax credits. We're hearing mothers really question their ability to continue working. It's got to the point where they're having to decide whether it's cheaper for them to stay at home. That will be bad news for families long term, as women will re-enter the workforce doing lower-skilled work.

Despite legislation, there won't be wholesale changes to family dynamics overnight. Families are at loggerheads.

In an ideal world it shouldn't be one person staying at home and the other not – it should be more of a conversation. Only when both parents have a choice will the work/family dilemma be solved.

What should employers be doing?

They must focus more on the benefits of a diverse workforce. More work is also needed around job design.

Mothers feel they have no way of resuming their roles after having a family. But women won't be able to work and have a family if there aren't more women in the pipeline.

Men need to demand more of a role in family life too, and there's nothing to be ashamed of for them in being a parent. HR shouldn't see flexibility as about gender – it's more about when and where all parents work (Crush 2013).

A recent Twitter exchange, as shown in Figure 8.2, also illustrates some of the bias that still exists around women in the workplace and parenting responsibilities.

1 What impacts on employee attitudes and organisational performance might we see as a result of these intersections in fostering an inclusive workplace?

2 How might the HR professional intervene in the interests of employee and organisation alike?

Figure 8.2 Women and parenting responsibilities – a live debate

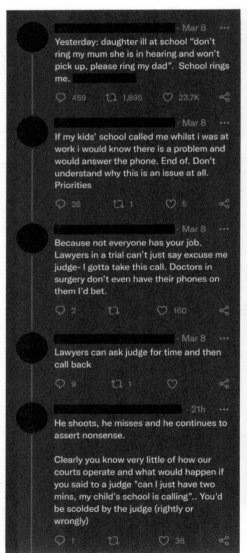

Research by Boekhorst (2015) emphasises the importance of leaders in embedding a culture of inclusion in the workplace, as has been highlighted by practitioners above. Interestingly, one finding was that rewarding inclusive behaviours with payment can play a part in others replicating them – we can all reflect on the ethical implications of this! Perhaps less instrumentally, Brimhall et al (2016) found that the quality of interactions between leaders and employees can affect inclusion, both in terms of how the employee feels and in terms of how that employee is seen by others – seeing leaders treat employees as important encourages others to accept them. More recent research by Brimhall (2019) focused on nonprofit organisations also found that 'transformational leaders help increase perceptions of inclusion, which improves employee commitment to the organization, and ultimately enhances perceived work group performance' (p 31).

While there seem to be some commonalities of the principles of an inclusion-centred approach, it is important to consider industry and country contexts that may play a part in the actions taken by HR managers and professionals. Wilson (2000) examined the influence of organisational culture on inclusion in three case study organisations – a multinational high-tech engineering company, a professional services organisation, and a company within the entertainment industry. Table 8.2 demonstrates the distinctions in terms of processes of inclusion and exclusion found by Wilson (2000).

A study of the tourism industry undertaken by Huong et al (2016) in Australia looked at the relationship between inclusion, justice and wellbeing, finding that information and communication is important in this sector. Like other studies, it also found the importance of involving employees in decision-making processes, as well as respectful interpersonal relationships between employees and between managers and employees. A study by Aldossari and Robertson (2018) examined the psychological contract in relation to inclusive experiences of employees returning to their home country of Saudi Arabia from international assignments. For repatriates there is potential for change in expectations during the time away from the organisation, and this study found that HR policies and practices in relation to the expatriation and repatriation process play a part in whether the psychological contract is

Table 8.3 Processes of inclusion and exclusion

Multinational high-tech engineering	'Efficacy of personnel processes and interventions; the use of visual images; the gendered nature of the family symbol; the [organisation] way of behaving; and time orientation' (p 284).
Professional services	'[T]he importance of clients, the attribution of gender, male networking, conformity, and time orientation' (p 290).
Entertainment industry	'[C]ustomer awareness, visual images, appearance, youth, sexuality and fun … performance, time orientation and socialising' (p 295).

maintained. Specifically, demonstrating explicit pathways for career development and promotion are particularly important. HR managers can take account of their specific organisational contexts through data gathering practices including the use of tailored surveys and focus groups or interviews that ask questions of individual perceptions of inclusion, for example feelings of belonging, opportunities to contribute, fairness of practices, perceptions of influence (CIPD, 2019b).

Overall, inclusion may be the most complex of the three concepts covered in this chapter, with multiple sources of managerial information and messages suggesting what might or should be done. There are confident, sometimes strident, assertions and claims, based on research findings and examples of what appears to be best practice, and some of these might remind us of Pollert's (1991) 'desperate search for panaceas'. Among this traffic it is possible to detect strengthening signals, describing increasing intensification of work and workers feeling pressurised. Where there is not a readily available pathway for workers to transmit signals of this sort, the alternative is to send messages through changed behaviour or attitudes. The reader, and the HR practitioner, then has the difficult task of listening and making sense of the sometimes conflicting information at their disposal.

8.6 Conclusion

To better understand the discretionary element of employment relationships, it is clear that the notion of flexibility coupled with the need to ensure engagement, wellbeing and inclusion is crucial in this regard, emphasising the need for managers who regard employees as a core asset. In 2012, the CIPD's report on sustainable organisational performance (CIPD, 2012b) concluded that sustainable organisations would need to have a balanced short- and long-term focus and, crucially, agility to adapt to challenges and opportunities. Agile response is the order of the day as timeframes are shortened, and so flexibility is sought, from collective and structural flexibility, to individual and behavioural. As organisations are re-engineered and downsized, and spans of control are increased, management attention is devoted to the increasingly autonomous worker, without losing control. There are very clear and important links between understanding the concepts, putting them into operation via effective management and subsequent organisational performance. Any activities to promote engagement, wellbeing and inclusion should have a preoccupation with the people involved and should both be implemented and reviewed through consultation with those most closely involved.

In previous editions of this book we also unravelled potential in-built contradictions within this field. The desire for organisations to integrate HR policies with business objectives may, for example, sit uneasily with the move towards Atkinson's (1984) notion of the flexible firm, characterised by decentralised responsibilities and externalised workers. The client organisation in an outsourcing arrangement could find it difficult to manage, or even influence, the policies of a labour supplier (eg Ndubisi and Nygaard, 2018). Gilmore (2013) records that flexible approaches to workforce deployment have often been coupled with an increase in part-time working, fixed-term contracts and outsourcing, making it potentially more difficult to secure organisational commitment. It has been noted that in much of the HR management literature, the typical focus had been on the remaining core activities and not on how non-core activities are provided (Marchington et al, 2009). What can be said is that engagement, wellbeing and inclusion have implications for both organisations and individuals and so organisations and individuals (including managers and leaders) will have a keen interest in the topics.

 KEY LEARNING POINTS

1 Engagement, wellbeing and inclusion have multiple meanings from both individual and organisational perspectives, with associated effects on performance.
2 There are complexities involved in promoting these, with potential challenges and contradictions.
3 Managers can usefully be aware of the concept of the psychological contract, in order to enhance worker engagement, wellbeing and inclusion.
4 A number of HR policies and practices, frequently carried out by line managers, influence worker engagement, wellbeing and inclusion.

 Review questions

1 Critically assess the respective advantages and disadvantages to organisations and to employees of the different activities to foster engagement.
2 Identify and evaluate the specific actions that managers can take that will improve employees' wellbeing within the organisation.
3 Evaluate the role of front-line managers in influencing the engagement of individuals within the organisation.
4 How might the inclusion of outsourced workers be encouraged?

Explore further

Brough, P, Gardiner, E and Daniels, K (eds) (2022) *Handbook on Management and Employment Practices*, Springer Live Reference https://link.springer.com/referencework/10.1007/978-3-030-24936-6 (archived at https://perma.cc/W3HJ-LNKW).
This 'living reference work' offers a range of chapters especially relating to wellbeing and inclusion in different organisational contexts.

Kimberlé Crenshaw's short TED Talk on 'The Urgency of Intersectionality' (TEDWomen 2016) is an important watch from the original scholar who defined the term. www.ted.com/talks/kimberle_crenshaw_the_urgency_of_intersectionality (archived at https://perma.cc/YR39-38YW)

Grey, C (2021) *A Very Short, Fairly Interesting and Reasonably Cheap Book About Studying Organizations*, 5th edn, Sage, London. This pocket-sized book offers a critical take on much management literature. Chapters 3 and 5 provide a wry commentary on the contexts underpinning flexibility and the psychological contract.

09
Managing the employment relationship

PETER SCOTT AND SALLY RUMBLES

LEARNING OUTCOMES

After reading this chapter, you should be able to:

- specify the importance of the contract of employment and its limitations for the management of employees

- explain differences in how conflict at work is viewed and some of the implications for managerial action

- assess the key implications for managers of recognising trade unions as representatives of employees

- understand the importance of management style and management practice to the effective management of employees

- understand the difference between equal opportunities and diversity

- appreciate the complexity of managing a diverse workforce.

9.1 Overview

The objectives of organisations may be expressed in different ways. In the private sector these typically relate to profitability or market share, while in the public sector account must be taken of budgetary constraints imposed by politicians. Voluntary bodies may express their objectives in terms of service delivery to vulnerable groups in society. All organisations, however, employ people to achieve their objectives irrespective of how they are expressed. Employees also have needs that they want to be met in their work, and expectations about how they will be treated. In this chapter we explore some key features that shape the employment relationship between employers and employees. Some of these elements are determined by employment law which places constraints on management action. However, there still remains considerable choice in the way that employees may be managed, and this choice is influenced by managers' beliefs and their attitudes towards their staff. One key decision that must be made is whether employees are to be treated in the same way as other organisational resources, or are viewed as a special kind of resource that can provide a competitive advantage. Much contemporary HRM literature is based upon the latter view. Either way, this chapter emphasises that the employment relationship is characterised by both conflict and consent, and a key task for managers consists of minimising the likelihood of the former while maximising the opportunities for the latter. This is important in an era where management – worker relations and the nature of the employment relationship are coming under greater strain than they have done for several decades. Further to the discussion of employee engagement and inclusion in Chapter 8, this chapter identifies two further themes that are consistent with HRM's 'unique resource' perspective: partnership working (section 9.4.2) and diversity management (section 9.5). We begin with an overview of the employment relationship and the nature of the contract of employment between the employer and employee.

9.2 Introduction

9.2.1 The nature of the employment relationship

The employment relationship is concerned with the features of the relationship between employer and employee, and the ways in which it can be managed. Thus an understanding of employment relations is important for those who are responsible for the effective management of people at work. It is, of course, true that employee status is only one of three possible types of employment status under UK law – the others being that of 'worker' and self-employed – but it is the most common, as well as conferring the greatest number of employment protections. For that reason, we focus particularly on employee status in this chapter. However, employers' use, whether legitimately or not, of forms of employment status with fewer legal rights and protections has become increasingly common, and a particular issue of public concern, with the growth in recent years of the gig economy and zero hours contracts.

In essence, employment relations is concerned with the 'wage–work bargain'; that is, what work an employee will do in return for the wages paid by the employer. The term 'wages' refers not just to the pay received, but also to other terms of employment such as holiday entitlement and sick pay. It may also refer to other rewards that the employer may provide, such as subsidised private health insurance and free childcare places. Similarly, 'work' has a wider meaning than the employee's job. Employers have expectations about both the quantity and quality of the work, and many of these expectations cannot be precisely quantified or stipulated in any employment contract. Some explicitly define specific behavioural characteristics of tasks, particularly in what are called 'customer-facing' jobs. Well-known examples can be found in the passenger airline or call centre industries, where many organisations compete on standards of customer service. This is reflected not only in their marketing policies, but also in the criteria they use to recruit, select, train and manage frontline staff. The expectations involved in the exercise of this type of work have been referred to as 'emotional labour' (Callaghan and Thompson, 2002; Hochschild, 2012).

9.3 The contract of employment

A useful starting point for our understanding of the terms of the wage–work bargain is through the concept, or idea, of the contract of employment. Each individual has a contract of employment with his or her employer, and the contract specifies the terms and conditions under which the employee works. However, the nature of the contract of employment is often misunderstood. Very few employees in the UK have a written contract which contains all their terms and conditions of employment in one document: most of us have a contract whose terms can be found in a number of sources. Figure 9.1 depicts some of the main sources of the contract of employment.

When employees refer to their 'written contract of employment', what they often mean is a formal written statement of the main terms of employment. This document is not the contract, as shown in the *System Floors* v *Daniel* case, heard by the Employment Appeal Tribunal (EAT). In its judgement, the EAT concluded

Figure 9.1 Some possible sources of the contract of employment

that 'this statement did not constitute a written contract between the parties. It was merely a document that stated the employer's views of the terms' (Sargeant and Lewis, 2020, p 52).

The written statement is important, nonetheless, since the Employment Relations Act 1996 requires it to specify the most important terms of employment, including pay, hours of work, holidays and sick pay.

The Act also allows employers to refer employees to other documents that contain these terms, or which provide more details. Thus, the other possible sources shown in Figure 9.1 may need to be examined if we are to have a clearer picture of the terms of the contract.

 Reflective activity 9.1

Sources of the contract of employment

Obtain copies of as many of the documents shown in Figure 9.1 as you can, but especially offer letters, written statements and employee handbooks.

Read through these and try to identify examples of statements that refer to employees' duties or responsibilities – that is, what is expected of the employee. Also, identify examples of the pay and other benefits that an employee will be entitled to under the contract of employment.

It is common, especially in larger organisations, for the HR department to produce an employee or staff handbook. This often contains details of employees' rights and duties. For example, it might explain what an employee is to do if they are unable to work through illness and what pay they will receive while sick. Similarly, employees who have a work roster may find that their actual times of work are provided by a notice.

Where an organisation uses job descriptions, these include the main duties and responsibilities of an employee: thus, they seek to clarify the 'work' element of the wage–work bargain. At the selection interview, there may be discussion about the terms of employment. These may cover both the work expected of an employee and the pay they will receive. For example, a candidate might ask about opportunities for overtime work and be told by the line manager how that is arranged. Although such 'spoken promises' can become terms of the contract, the problem is that it may not be easy to be sure what was said. The avoidance of such problems was one of the reasons why legislation requires employers to provide the written statement so that there is less doubt over the terms of the contract. Similarly, the need to formalise what is agreed with an employee accounts for HR departments providing letters of employment offers and specifying details in employee handbooks.

However, some terms may still not be written down. Custom and practice refers to possible employment terms that arise because they have operated for some while. For example, an office may have a custom that all workers finish at lunchtime on Christmas Eve, but this has never been written down in any formal documentation.

Suppose, then, a manager tells her staff that they will need to work till 17.30, their normal finishing time. Is this lawful? If an employee challenges this decision in a court, it may be decided that the custom is part of the terms of employment.

 Reflective activity 9.2

Custom and practice

In the example of custom and practice given in the text about finishing work early on Christmas

Eve, what factors do you think the courts might take into account to decide if it was reasonable for the employees to finish at lunchtime?

Other terms may be implied by judges to exist in a contract of employment. These are sometimes referred to as the 'common law terms' (Collins, Ewing and McColgan, 2012, pp 96–98). For example, all employees have a duty to use reasonable skill and care in their work. It will be for the courts to decide what is reasonable, but, as we have seen above, job descriptions might be used to specify the standard of work expected of an employee. Another duty of employees is to give faithful and honest service and not commit misconduct. Many organisations will produce a list of disciplinary rules which seek to clarify what this common-law term means for employees in reality, and these are often included in the employee handbook. The need to set standards of expected behaviour is both good practice and, as we see below, important in unfair dismissal claims. The important point to note, however, is that even if these are not specified in any document, the duties still exist as part of the employee's contract of employment.

Statutory employment rights refer to those that are provided through legislation, which emanates from both national and supra-national levels. The main supra-national influence comes from the social and employment legislation retained from the period of the UK's membership of the European Union (EU). Although the UK may deviate over time from EU legislation and, since Brexit, is no longer subject to the European Court of Justice's direction on how EU-derived laws are to be interpreted, the pre-Brexit body of EU law remains in force. However, it should be noted that the Brexit agreement between the UK and EU contains an expectation that the UK will retain a comparable standard of employment law to that in the EU, to prevent what the EU would regard as unfair competition through undercutting labour protections. It remains to be seen how UK governments will approach this issue in the future (see also Reflective activity 9.3). Other sources of supra-national employment legislation include international organisations' conventions, treaties and declarations, etc, that have been ratified by the UK. Choosing to ratify such instruments normally requires a country to incorporate into domestic law provisions that give legal effect to the matter signed up to. An example is the International Labour Organisation's Convention prohibiting child labour.

The purpose of employment law is to provide a minimum 'floor of rights' for all employees, and employers cannot offer terms that are worse than those provided by legislation. Some of these relate to specific parts of the wage–work bargain; for example, the UK national minimum wage and the EU Working Time Directive, which was implemented in the UK through the Working Time Regulations. The latter specifies maximum hours of work. Other statutory employment rights are concerned with the way in which employees are managed. These include maternity rights, the right not to be unfairly dismissed (see below), and thus how disciplinary action should be implemented by a manager, and legislation that seeks to prohibit unlawful discrimination on certain grounds; for example, race, sex, religion and belief. We explore discrimination in more detail later in the chapter, and also deal with the issue in Chapters 5 and 6.

 Reflective activity 9.3

Employment rights

For many managers, the growth of employment rights has become an accepted part of organisational life. However, there are critics who believe employment regulation is having a damaging impact on UK business's competitive position. This tension has been reflected in the policy twists and turns of successive governments in recent decades, particularly in the field of individual employment rights. The Coalition Government of 2010–15 undertook a number of initiatives to reduce employment regulation and, indeed, the desire to remove the impact of EU-derived social and employment legislation from the UK was a key goal of some of those who supported Britain leaving the EU. For the Conservative Governments elected in the wake of the Brexit referendum to leave the EU, an increasingly cautious approach towards the future of individual employment rights has become evident, even while legislation to make trade union activity gradually more difficult has continued. The expansion of precarious employment, return of inflation, lack of wage growth, and experience of increased government intervention in the labour market during the Covid pandemic have combined to make any obvious post-Brexit reductions in employment rights politically and electorally unattractive, quite apart from the fact that most EU-derived employment legislation is here to stay. One consequence of the urge to intervene in employment regulation has been governments' increasing attempts to politicise the setting of national minimum wage rates since 2015 (Brown, 2017).

Reacting to public concern about the precariousness of much employment, and issues such as 'gig' working, zero hours contracts and bogus self-employment, Theresa May's Conservative Government commissioned Matthew Taylor to review the issue in 2016. Although criticised for its limited proposals, Taylor's work resulted in the Good Work Plan (HM Government, 2018). The Good Work Plan proposed some relatively minor improvements to individual employment rights and remains the official framework for intended employment legislation. As of early 2022, no Parliamentary time had yet been found to put any of this into action, which does call into question how important government actually perceives it to be.

Reflecting on the above, to what extent do you think improvements or reductions in employment rights should be a priority?

The final source of employment terms, shown in Figure 9.2, is collective agreements. These can be found in organisations that recognise a trade union or unions, and where terms of employment such as pay and holidays are negotiated between the union and the employer. The outcomes of the negotiations are called collective agreements since they cover the collective group of workers represented by the trade union. A collective agreement normally covers all the employees in a particular occupation or grade, whether or not they are union members. Where unions are recognised, the employer has a relationship with both individual employees and the trade union.

Collective agreements are not normally legally enforceable between the employer and trade union. However, the substantive terms of these agreements – for example, pay and hours – are incorporated into individual contracts of employment. Where an employer has collective agreements with a trade union these agreements can be an important source of an employee's contractual terms.

9.3.1 *The wage–work bargain revisited*

The effective management of the employment relationship requires managers to understand the nature of the contract of employment. In particular, it is important to recognise that the terms of the contract may be found in a number of different sources. However, Williams (2020) points out that there are two major problems with viewing the employment relationship simply as a contractual one. First, a contract implies that the two parties come together in a free and equal way. However, those seeking work are clearly in a weaker position than the employer, who has the freedom to offer the job to a number of applicants (see also Chapter 6). Furthermore, once an employee has taken a job, he or she is then required to obey the employer's commands or orders. The second problem with a simple contractual view of the relationship is that the contract is 'indeterminate': it is not possible to specify, at the outset of the relationship, all the obligations of the parties. The contract is thus open-ended, and the relative power of the parties will be important in deciding how the relationship is shaped. Thus, it is also important to recognise that the employment relationship has a power dimension. This means that the relationship is double-edged: first, there is potential for differences, or conflict, to emerge in the

Figure 9.2 The relationship between the contract of employment and collective agreements

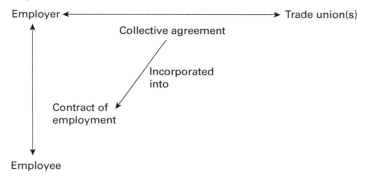

relationship. Second, however, the relationship is also necessarily characterised by some degree of co-operation between the employer and employees. The latter have an interest in the success of their employer which will help secure their jobs.

9.3.2 *Termination of the contract of employment*

If an employer terminates the contract of employment, employment legislation allows the employee to claim at an employment tribunal that the dismissal was unfair. Tribunals decide whether the dismissal was 'fair and reasonable in the circumstances'. If the tribunal determines that the dismissal was unfair it can require the employer to reinstate or reengage the employee, or make an award of financial compensation. In most cases employees will need two years' continuous service before they can make a claim.

The Employment Relations Act 1996 specifies five fair reasons for dismissal:

- misconduct, for example where an employee breaks a company disciplinary rule
- lack of capability, which is concerned with the employee's work performance and is explored in detail in Chapter 10
- redundancy
- statutory bar to employment, for example where a company driver is disqualified from driving
- some other substantial reason which might include an employee's refusal to accept changes to their contractual terms in times of business difficulty.

The first two reasons are those that are most closely concerned with managing and leading people.

The employer must show that, in addition to having a fair reason, the dismissal was handled reasonably. This can be achieved by demonstrating that the dismissal followed the principles of natural justice. In employment this means:

- the employee was made aware of the standards of behaviour expected, hence the need to explain these at the start of employment
- the employee was informed of the allegation or complaint
- an investigation was undertaken to establish the facts of the case
- the employee was given an opportunity to explain their view of the case
- the employee was offered the opportunity to be accompanied by a fellow employee or trade union representative
- the penalty was proportionate to the offence
- the employee had the right of appeal to a more senior manager.

In order to effectively manage problems with employee behavior and demonstrate that they have incorporated the principles of natural justice into their employment practice, organisations draft disciplinary rules and procedures, often including these in employee handbooks.

9.3.3 *The role of procedures*

The purpose of employment procedures is to create a 'problem-solving pathway'. They allow managers to consider an employee complaint, or, in the case of disciplinary action, provide managers with the opportunity to change or correct an employee's behaviour. Formal procedures allow appropriate action to be taken to solve a problem, rather than employees feeling they must express their disagreement with management through other means; for example, by being absent from work or performing below their capability. Procedures seek to ensure that managers deal with employment issues in a fair and consistent way, and are one of the ways in which managers seek to control or contain conflict in the employment relationship. Grievance and disciplinary procedures are the two most common ones found in organisations. However, there may be separate procedures covering specific employment matters: capability, to distinguish these issues from those related to conduct; harassment and bullying; equal opportunities; pay grading if a job evaluation scheme is used; and appeals against performance appraisal ratings, especially if this is linked to pay.

The unfair dismissal provisions of employment law have emphasised the importance of formalising disciplinary rules and procedures. The Advisory, Conciliation and Arbitration Service (ACAS) has produced a Code of Practice (ACAS, 2015) which is taken into account as a set of minimum requirements by employment tribunals hearing unfair dismissal claims. If the tribunal decides that the provisions of the Code have not been followed by either the employee or employer they can adjust any financial awards by up to 25 per cent. Although not having the same status as the Code, ACAS has also published a guide to handling grievances and disciplinary matters (ACAS, 2020). Both publications provide valuable advice to HR managers

9.3.4 *Trade unions and collective bargaining*

As suggested in Reflective activity 9.3, the election of successive Conservative-dominated governments since 2010 has ensured that the extent of labour market deregulation, including restrictions on the power of trade unions, is likely to remain prominent public policy issues. Government policies since the 1980s, together with broader economic and social changes, have had a significant impact on trade unions. To take one example, it is interesting to look at union membership figures which have declined significantly in the UK since the peak of some 13 million in 1980. At that time over half of all employees were members of a trade union, and collective agreements set the terms and conditions of about three-quarters of the UK workforce. In 2020 some six and a half million workers were union members, which accounted for just under 25 per cent of the workforce. These figures represent a significant decline, although membership has increased slightly, but consistently, in the years since 2016. Union membership remains stronger in the public sector, however, where about 52 per cent of employees were members. Overall, union membership is also more likely to be encountered among women, older workers and in larger employers (Department of Business, Energy and Industrial Strategy, 2021).

As we saw above, collective agreements arrived at through negotiation between trade unions and employers can be a major source of an employee's contractual terms. Collective bargaining refers to the process where employers and unions jointly agree the terms and conditions of employees. For the employer, collective bargaining can be an efficient means of determining contractual terms since it does not require negotiation with each individual employee, and can assist in containing the conflict that may arise over employment terms. In addition, since the union has made the agreement, it has an interest in ensuring its members (the employees of the organisation) accept the terms that are agreed. Collective bargaining, then, is a key function of trade unions, and is a process that can provide greater equality of power in the employment relationship.

Collective bargaining is concerned with both parts of the wage–work bargain. It determines important parts of the wage the employee receives. As well as pay, hours and holidays, it may cover matters such as overtime and shift premiums, sick pay, redundancy payments, pensions and health and safety (van Wanrooy et al, 2013, pp 80–82). These terms are the *economic* aspects of the contract, or 'wages'. However, collective bargaining can also determine *work* issues. For example, as well as redundancy pay, a collective agreement may specify how staff would be selected for redundancy, should that situation arise. In addition, it is not uncommon for there to be collective agreements covering staffing plans, equal opportunities and performance appraisal schemes. Thus, collective bargaining has a managerial aspect which means that these matters are determined by joint agreement, not by managers alone. This provides an example of how gaps in the open-ended contract may be filled.

As well as collectively bargaining with employers on behalf of employees, trade unions have other functions. They may provide specific services to their members as individuals. These may include legal and financial advice for both work and personal matters. Trade unions in the UK seek to represent their members outside the workplace in wider social matters. This might include lobbying for improved social policies to help eliminate poverty, for example, and campaigning to improve the employment conditions of migrant workers or those on precarious contracts. One further role of trade unions, important to those managing employment relations, is that following the principles of natural justice noted above, trade union officials typically represent their members in formal grievance, disciplinary and similar matters.

 Reflective activity 9.4

Find out more details of the role of trade unions. The easiest way to do this is to go to the unions' websites. If your employer recognises a union or unions, this would be a good starting point. If not, perhaps visit the web pages of two or three unions you have recently heard about in the news. Most can be found simply by typing their name into a search engine or visiting the Trades Union Congress website, which lists many unions (www.tuc.org.uk/unions). For each union, identify how it describes its role and seeks to achieve its objectives, the types of workers it recruits and how many members it has. From your research, consider what are the main similarities and differences between how the unions you have looked at see their roles, priorities and objectives, and what the reasons might be for any differences.

9.4 Conflict and the employment relationship

We have noted the potential for conflict to arise in the employment relationship, so how do managers view the reasons for its existence? Before exploring the answer to this question, undertake the following Reflective activity.

 Reflective activity 9.5

Conflict at work

For this activity, you are asked to reflect on the following four statements on conflict between employers and employees. For each, identify the values or beliefs of those people who hold this view. Which of these views most closely reflects your own view? Why?

Conflict between an employer and employee is:

- a dysfunctional factor in an otherwise healthy organisation

- largely preventable, provided organisations take a proactive approach to developing policies and practices which take account of employees' needs and expectations from work

- an inherent feature of organisational life, but one that can be largely institutionalised and managed through recognising that differences of interests exist between the two parties

- a reflection of the fundamental divisions and inequalities in the wider society.

Each of the four views reflects different explanations of the causes of conflict between employers and employees and how they are to be managed. These views are based on 'frames of reference': a term first attributed to Fox (1966, 1974) to distinguish between the beliefs held by managers that influence their approach to the management of employees.

Those that believe conflict is dysfunctional are characterised as holding a 'unitary' view. Often using the team or family analogy, those with unitary perspective expect co-operation from their staff since the goals of the organisation and employees are the same: employees must understand and accept their role, and also accept that the leaders of the organisation are best-placed to make the important decisions. With its emphasis on co-operation, the unitary view would see conflict as a result of poor communications, or, significantly, as the result of trouble-makers, like trade union activists, who generate conflict in an otherwise harmonious organisation.

As human resource management theory and practice has developed, some authors have adopted the term 'neo-unitary' to capture the beliefs that underpin this approach to managing the employment relationship (Farnham and Pimlott, 1995). This perspective has much in common with the traditional unitary view in that co-operation and harmony between employers and employees is believed to be the normal state of affairs. However, as the statement in the activity suggests, conflict can be prevented, but only if managers are proactive in developing policies and practices that take account of the needs and expectations of employees. Managers could thus utilise the type of solutions proposed by the human relations school of thinking to engender employees' commitment to their work and the organisation's objectives (Edwards, 2003).

Those who believe that conflict in the employment relationship is inevitable are said to hold a 'pluralist' perspective. While not disputing that there is scope for co-operation between managers and employees, pluralists point to the differences in interests between employers and employees. For example, employers will naturally wish to minimise wage costs while employees will, equally naturally, wish to maximise their pay. The key concern of pluralists in the employment relationship is to find ways to manage the conflict so that disruption – for example, in the form of strikes – is limited. For those with a pluralist perspective, trade unions are not the cause of conflict. Rather, they have a legitimate role in representing one interest group, employees, in the relationship. The task for managers is to build a relationship with trade unions, and develop procedures so that disputes and differences can be resolved through the process of negotiation. Some (eg Ackers, 2002) have extended the pluralist concept to talk of neo-pluralism, which broadens the rationale for industrial co-operation to its wider role in ensuring the cohesion of society as a whole. This is perhaps best expressed in the continental concept of 'social partnership', which has taken limited root in the UK, but aspects of it are considered further in section 9.4.2.

Those holding a radical (including, but not exclusively, Marxist) view of conflict see this as the result of workers being exploited in the employment relationship. The development of procedures with trade unions to prevent and resolve expressions of conflict is, at best, only a temporary solution. Conflict, it is argued, will be eliminated only when the distinction between the owners of capital and workers is removed.

9.4.1 Management style and employment relations

The distinction between unitary and pluralist perspectives provides a basis for understanding different management styles. According to Purcell and Ahlstrand (1994, p 177) '[management] style implies the existence of a distinctive set of guiding principles, written or otherwise, which set parameters to and signposts for management action regarding the way employees are to be treated...' 'Style', then, describes the choice that is made as to how the employment relationship is to be managed. These authors identify two dimensions of management style: individualism and collectivism.

Individualism

Two broad extremes of individualism can be identified, based on the extent to which managers view employees as individuals with needs and aspirations. Those that are described as having 'high individualism' or an 'investment orientation' towards staff would typically emphasise the following policies and practices:

- employees seen as an important resource
- a focus on internal labour markets
- employee development, appraisal and individual systems of reward
- empowerment.

This management style is based on a neounitary view where conflict and differences can be prevented, and, as we will see later, is aimed at generating employee engagement.

In contrast, managers who have a low concern with individual employees, a traditional unitary view, would adopt a 'cost minimisation' approach with the following characteristics:

- labour as a commodity to be bought from, and returned to, the external labour market as economic activity dictates
- an emphasis on numerical flexibility
- limited, if any, training
- tight control over pay.

Collectivism

Purcell and Ahlstrand (1994) also draw a similar distinction on the collective dimension of management style which seeks to capture the extent to which managers accept that employees have a right to act collectively – for example, by joining a trade union – and are willing to negotiate and consult with employee representatives. At one extreme, typical of the traditional unitary approach, there would be resistance and hostility towards trade unions. At the other end of the spectrum the relationship sought by management is highly co-operative with the union, and would include: regular consultation with union representatives on strategic plans; extensive information exchange; and the use of joint working parties to manage employment matters. The contemporary term for this approach is 'partnership', and we examine this below. Between these extremes lies what Purcell and Ahlstrand (1994) refer to as 'adversarial relations'.

Adversarial relationships may exist in organisations where unions have been recognised by the employer for many years, but where managers would prefer not to have to negotiate with them. The primary concern of managers in these firms will be to protect their right to make decisions without the involvement of unions, sometimes called the 'managerial prerogative' (Storey, 1983). Control and stability of the employment relationship, through formally agreed procedures, are important characteristics in such businesses, and the issues on which unions can negotiate are usually carefully and tightly drawn.

9.4.2 Partnership working

We have already noted the importance of collective agreements as a source of employment terms, and that these can be arrived at through either adversarial or co-operative relationships between the employer and trade unions. Since the 1990s, a number of examples have appeared of so-called written 'partnership agreements' between employers and unions that were intended to formalise a more cooperative approach between the two parties. As Williams (2020, pp 190–94) observes, partnership working is intended to benefit all parties in the organisational employment relationship by putting the principle of cooperative relations onto a structured footing. In practice, however, such agreements have been subject to criticism as often somewhat vague and aspirational, more concerned with mechanisms of enabling employees to 'have a say' and other such 'process' issues, rather than giving guarantees about employment security or similar substantive matters (Williams, 2020, p 191), and their sustainability seems to be reliant on a supportive managerial and wider political context for harmonious employment relationships.

 Reflective activity 9.6

Partnership agreements

Review this section in conjunction with what was said earlier in the chapter about the coexistence of conflict and cooperation in the employment relationship. List what you believe to be the benefits and drawbacks of formal partnership agreements to: the employer, the trade union and the employees of the organisation.

Each of the elements of partnership agreements justifies a little more explanation. The 'statement of intent' can be little more than empty rhetoric. However, if it genuinely reflects a greater level of trust between the parties, this is the key thing that may lead to improved employment relations. The development of communication and consultation processes can take different forms. Such processes may, for example, provide for trade unions to be more closely involved in the decision-making processes of the organisations, at least to the extent that union representatives are consulted on those matters that may have an impact on employees. Also, they may provide for representatives of all employees, not just those that are union members, to be informed and involved in business decisions.

The final two elements seek to meet the main needs of the employer and employees. Employees may be reluctant to be more flexible in their working arrangements if they believe that this could put jobs at risk. Thus flexibility comes if the employer is willing to agree to some level of employment security. Not, perhaps, a commitment that employees will keep those specific jobs as a result of organisational change, but that alternative jobs will be available – hence 'employment security'. These two components, then, combine to establish a degree of mutuality in the partnership agreement since each meets the respective key need of the employer and the employee.

It is important to note that, in the early 2020s, the principles of partnership working between government, employers and trade unions – in other words, on what is known as a tripartite basis – are increasingly being developed by the devolved government administrations in Scotland and Wales (Heery, Hann and Nash, 2020), although no parallel trends are evident in England. This illustrates that managers need to be aware of the social and political contexts in which employment relations operates. In Scotland, this momentum to develop the principles of 'fair work', and wider adoption by businesses of the so-called 'real living wage', results from the Scottish Government's Fair Work Convention to 2025; similarly, in Wales, there has been a Fair Work Commission, one of the consequences of which, at the time of writing, is a Social Partnership Bill going through the Welsh *Senedd*, which will put the principles of partnership in managing employment relations in Wales onto a more established legal footing.

 Case study 9.1

The implications of public sector pay restraint post-Brexit and -Covid-19

Successive UK Governments have tried to reduce public spending by controlling the wage bill in the public sector. They have, for example, reduced staff numbers, made changes to pension schemes and entitlements, introduced public sector pay freezes, imposed caps on government funding of annual pay increases, and attempted to restrict the practice of annual incremental pay progression, based on length of service and to relate pay progression within pay grades much more closely to individual performance. The pay limits have been applied both to those public servants whose pay is determined by collective bargaining and to those, such as teachers and most NHS staff, whose pay and conditions are supposed to be determined by recommendations to government from independent review bodies.

The various initiatives raise a number of issues for the recruitment, retention and motivation of staff in the public sector that are relevant to the subject matter of this text. Existing problems have been exacerbated, first, by Brexit, which has diminished the pool of EU migrants willing to staff UK public service positions, many of which require specialist training. Second, in the wake of the Covid-19 pandemic, many public sector workers at various skill levels can be classified as 'key workers', which implies that their jobs may have a particular public value worthy of recompense.

1 The relevant issues to consider include whether it is either possible or desirable for government to try to exercise such tight central control over public sector pay over such a long period of time, particularly when similar controls are not in place for the private sector. What, if any, incentives can be offered to attract staff as skill shortages in key areas start to emerge? Should pay be more closely related to performance, and how can one reliably define and measure what is meant by performance in the public sector anyway? Is annual incremental pay progression really just a second, 'hidden' pay rise, or is it an important way to retain the accumulated skill and expertise over time of staff? How realistic do you think it is for government to try to limit centrally the amount of pay increases in the public sector over a period of several years? What are the main objections that could be raised to this and what do you think could be the main unintended consequences of such a policy?

2 List the various arguments in favour of a) retaining annual progression pay increments, and b) making pay rises within grades more conditional on staff performance. Which case do you think is more convincing, and why? Draft out a case you could make in favour of your preferred alternative to try to convince someone who supported the opposite alternative?

3 As an HR manager, you have been asked to prepare a report that suggests ways of retaining and motivating hard to recruit staff in an era of low overall pay increases. What would be the main strategies and policies you would put in such a report?

9.5 Diversity at work

9.5.1 Individual differences and management styles

Management style also affects the way in which managers handle the individual characteristics of employees. We would expect those who have an 'investment orientation' towards employees to take account of individual differences to the benefit of the organisation. Such an approach is analogous with the management of diversity. Before examining the meaning of diversity, and contrasting the diversity approach with the 'equal opportunities' approach, we briefly consider the legal provisions on discrimination.

We noted earlier that statutory employment rights are an important source of an employee's terms, and that specific legislation makes for unfair discrimination if it is based on the grounds of sex, race, age, religion and belief, sexual orientation or disability. As we saw in Chapter 6, managers regularly discriminate between employees; for example in choosing between job applicants. The legislation prohibits discrimination which has no connection with the work to be done (in legal terms, which is not a 'genuine occupational requirement') and distinguishes between direct and indirect discrimination. An example of direct discrimination would be a job advertisement that states that only women can apply for the post. Indirect discrimination arises when a requirement or condition that cannot be justified is applied to a situation where members of one or more of the protected groups are disproportionately unlikely to be able to comply. An example of this was the previous requirement for applicants to the UK police force to be a minimum height; male recruits had to be 1.78m and female recruits 1.63m. These requirements were gradually phased out during the 1990s because height is no necessary requirement for the job and the policy was found to be discriminatory and unlawful to both individuals from certain ethic groups who were less capable of meeting the minimum height requirement, as well as to men. Legal provisions also exist safeguarding those believed to hold a protected characteristic from being harassed in the workplace because of it. It is worth noting that this applies whether or not the individual actually does hold the characteristic: there are a number of tribunal cases in favour of workers harassed for allegedly being gay, even though they were not, for example. The law also protects those who allege discrimination against victimisation, such as using having made a complaint as grounds for refusing a promotion.

9.5.2 Equal opportunities

The concept of equal opportunities (EO) underpins many organisational approaches to equality in the UK, which have been developed in response to the legislation introduced by successive UK Governments since the mid-1970s to address unfair discrimination in the pursuit, obtaining and retaining of employment, as well as other workplace practices. The result is a legal framework developed around a definition of inequality that draws heavily on the idea of indirect discrimination: 'discriminating against people on grounds that are irrelevant to the jobs they are doing or for which they are applying' (Chryssides and Kaler, 1996, p 89). To reduce the disparate treatment by managers, the HR profession has focused on establishing specific procedures to ensure legal compliance and demonstrate equal treatment (Harris, 2005). Thus, the 'neutral treatment' principle of much anti-discrimination legislation has become the cornerstone of organisational policies and procedures which are designed to achieve sameness of treatment in resourcing decisions (Foster and Harris, 2005, p 6).

An equal opportunities approach is seen as one of 'compliance' with the law. It typically focuses attention on groups that may be unlawfully discriminated against, and features such initiatives as target-setting, positive action and redressing past discrimination. A more recent manifestation of the EO approach at organisational level has been the legal requirement since 2017 for annual gender pay gap reporting in organisations with a headcount of 250 or more workers, and discussion of whether this requirement could or should be extended to protected characteristics such as ethnicity or disability (Brown, Rickard and Broughton, 2017). The EO approach's attraction for line managers is that it offers a certain simplicity and ease of application by reducing the scope for exercising discretion and providing the essential means of defending their decisions against claims of less favourable treatment (Wilson and Iles, 1999). Its limitation is that it has led HR specialists and operational managers alike to focus on consistency of process or procedural justice, even though consistency is a relative principle, whose pursuit alone will not act as a catalyst for progressive employment practice (Foster and Harris, 2005). At its worst, treating everyone the same can overlook the scope the law gives to treat disabled people more favourably than non-disabled people, precisely so that they can compete on a 'level playing field'. Relying on a principle of consistency is problematic as it does not require individuals to be treated well, only alike, and allows for situations where all employees are treated equally, but equally badly (Fredman, 2001).

Arguably, there are now two strands to equal opportunities issues that arise from different origins: we can call these a more collective 'equality' strand and a more individually-oriented 'flexibility' strand. We describe each briefly here, noting that the second strand will become more significant when we talk about diversity management later in this chapter. In the UK, the Equality Act 2010 extended anti-discrimination legislation to cover a broad range of groups who share so-called 'protected characteristics'. If one considers the case of age, for example, being discriminated against for being considered 'too old' or 'too young' for a particular job in the workplace could potentially affect any worker. In addition, other social and employment legislation, such as the Children and Families Act 2014, has introduced potential rights related to leave or flexible working that relate to personal circumstances rather than to protected characteristics: for example, parental leave rights. Starting from a somewhat restricted set of personal circumstances for workers to request flexibility in 2002, 20 years later the extension to all workers from day one of employment of the right to request flexible working is currently under consideration. The rapid progress of such initiatives has been given considerable impetus by the hasty enforced transformation of lives during the Covid pandemic as many workers were required to work from home. Some found this new freedom and adaptability to be at least equally productive as commuting to an office five days a week.

The resultant increased legal complexity has meant that managers need to be aware not only of individual rights, but – as we saw with an investment orientation to employees – a concern with individual needs at work. In other words, a managing diversity approach. Managing diversity in this context is framed as a strategic response arising from demographic change, and is differentiated from equal opportunities on the basis that organisations should focus on the individual rather than the potentially disadvantaged group to which the employee belongs. Thus, diversity encompasses a whole range of differences beyond those associated with disadvantage or covered by anti-discrimination legislation (Tomlinson and Schwabenland, 2010).

 Reflective activity 9.7

Equality and diversity in practice (1)

Pick an organisation that is required to report annually on its website its gender pay gap ratio. You can either use your own employer, if relevant, or choose another one. Research the gender pay gap revealed in its most recent report, and compare with the figures in previous years' annual reports. What reasons are offered for the persistence of a gender pay gap and what, if anything, does the organisation say that it is doing to reduce the gap? Do you think the rationales offered sound convincing?

9.5.3 *The nature of diversity*

Equal opportunities (EO) initiatives in the UK are aimed at developing a level playing field for disadvantaged groups, but it is claimed that they have failed to achieve the goal of greater organisational inclusion of minorities for two reasons. First, they do not cover adequately all disadvantaged groups: notably, social class is not a protected characteristic, although it is known that working class applicants are disadvantaged in certain occupations. The disadvantaged groups that are covered, such as women and Black, Asian and minority ethnic employees (often lumped together under the acronym BAME) are sometimes treated as homogeneous, often stereotyped, groups. Second, EO fails to generate the involvement and commitment of managers who perceive it simply as a compliance issue (Ahmed, 2007).

The managing diversity approach has been claimed to overcome these limitations, and to provide a powerful set of arguments with which to mobilise management interest in the needs of members of minority groups (Kandola and Fullerton, 1998). Rather like human resource management, the diversity paradigm originated in the context of the US in the 1980s, and then its principles spread to the UK and European countries. Kirton and Greene (2015, pp 127–28) summarise four basic tenets to the diversity approach. First, it aims to change the culture of the whole organisations to accept and celebrate greater diversity, rather than EO matters being the preserve of specialists. For managers, this means that the diversity approach will need to be driven (and led by example) by senior management and that it is likely to be a long-term process rather than a quick fix. Second, it makes a virtue of the idea of difference in organisations, instead of it being seen as a drawback. Third, the approach is rooted in the business case (also discussed further below). For example, writers such as Belbin (1991) found that culturally diverse teams were more effective than homogeneous ones, thus providing the basis of a business case for diversity. French (2015) summarises research showing that the performance of multicultural groups at work was typically either much better than that of monocultural groups, or significantly worse, highlighting the importance of careful management of such groups, if they are to be effective. Fourth, differences are largely individually based and therefore require individualised solutions. Unlike EO initiatives, a diversity approach recognises that everyone is different even though some may share certain characteristics such as ethnic origin, gender, etc. Diversity therefore consists of visible factors – for example, race and age – but also non-visible personal characteristics including background, culture, personality and preferred work style. Although there is no obvious dividing line, the diversity perspective is arguably more about *recognising* difference rather than *valuing* it, which is where the concept of inclusion comes into its own (CIPD, 2021s) (see Chapter 8). However, in principle, diversity management encourages the development of more innovative HR policies and practices, which offer greater reciprocity in the employment relationship by addressing individual needs. This HR approach appears more relevant to the flexible behaviour required of employees in the less predictable work roles that are a feature of contemporary working life (Foster and Harris, 2005). The problem for today's managers then is that there is no single best way of treating employees, because each one will have their own personal needs, values and beliefs.

9.5.4 *Organisational benefits of diversity*

Three main reasons are typically used to justify an organisational approach for making equality and diversity an important management issue:

- the business case
- the impact of demographic and social changes
- the social justice argument.

Social justice arguments are mainly discussed in more detail in Chapter 5. It is important not to lose sight of the wider social justice case for equality, as evidence suggests that this is a particular motivator for equality and diversity professionals who are charged with operationalising such issues in organisations, even if the 'sales pitch' for equality and diversity is made more frequently on business case grounds (Kirton, Greene and Dean, 2007). We consider the business case and demographic change below.

The business case for diversity

According to the CIPD (2010b), there are three business reasons for organisations exceeding legal requirements on discrimination: people issues, market competitiveness and corporate reputation.

1 *People issues* – creating an open and inclusive workplace culture in which everyone feels valued helps to recruit and retain good people. People aspire to work for employers with good employment practices and to feel valued at work. To be competitive, organisations need to derive the best contributions

from everyone. Skills shortages and difficulties in filling vacancies are forcing organisations to recruit from more diverse pools and to offer different working arrangements in the 'war for talent'. Managing diversity creates a recruitment pool that improves the chances of getting the right person for the right job. Diversity also creates engaged employees working in a climate of productivity and commitment, with low turnover and sickness absence rates. In turn, creativity and innovation are increased.

2 *Product market competitiveness* – a diverse workforce can help to inform the development of new or enhanced products or services, open up new market opportunities, improve market share and broaden an organisation's customer base.

3 *Corporate reputation* – healthy businesses flourish in healthy societies and the needs of people, communities and businesses are interrelated. Social exclusion and low economic activity rates limit business markets and their growth. Thus, businesses need to consider corporate social responsibility (CSR) in the context of diversity. The overall image of an organisation can be important in attracting and retaining both customers and employees.

Arguably, the business and social justice cases for diversity are complementary, because unless people are treated fairly at work they will feel less committed and may underperform. Despite many criticisms of the business case, researchers claim that it and social justice arguments can co-exist to produce a case for diversity that is capable of achieving greater social equality. In some organisations – for example, in the voluntary sector – the business case and social justice is largely the same thing (Tomlinson and Schwabenland, 2010).

Studies have found that not all HR diversity practices are associated with increased workforce diversity and that attitudes to diversity in large corporations have been, at best, mixed. For example, managers in some organisations have tended to see its value in recruitment and selection, but have not applied it to other working practices. There is also a wide recognition of the supposed value of workforce diversity, but mixed evidence on its impact on business performance. A report for the Department for Business, Innovation and Skills (2013) found that firms have reaped business benefits from equality and diversity practices including improved financial performance, but not all firms in all context at all times. Recent academic researchers in the US (Herring and Henderson, 2015) and Europe (Mensi-Klarbach and Risberg, 2019) have tended to adopt a more critical view of the diversity management paradigm and a more nuanced verdict on any association between the outcome of HR diversity practices and improved organisational performance.

 Reflective activity 9.8

Disability and diversity initiatives in the legal profession

Foster and Hirst's (2020) research with disabled lawyers identified a number of potential problems with diversity initiatives that organisations would do well to be aware of. These included what disabled lawyers described as compliance-oriented 'tick box' exercises that concentrated solely on disabled workers being employed at all, rather than how senior they were in their organisations. There were also attendant dangers of disabled lawyers being ghettoised in stereotypical areas such as personal injury or of organisations equating disability with highly visible symbols such as employing lawyers who were wheelchair users. Some also spoke of a perceived hierarchy of initiatives on inequalities in their organisations, with gender seen as the highest priority and disability as least prioritised.

Reflect on the above problems and consider how you think organisational diversity initiatives could be structured to avoid them.

A more recent question that needs to be asked of the managing diversity agenda is how well equipped its individualistic approach is to the increased influence of views that allege the systematic, institutional origins of discrimination. This would require organisations to look at their practices more holistically. The growth of movements such as Me Too and Black Lives Matter have shifted public focus and debate to concepts such as institutional sexism and racism. While still controversial, such ideas have become more mainstream in the early 2020s: the CIPD (2021t), for example, accepts the concept of institutional racism in its position statement on ending racism at work. In the wake of numerous news stories, organisations as varied as the National Health Service, Yorkshire County Cricket Club and the Metropolitan Police have become ensnared in accusations of being institutionally racist. It is an open question to what extent that more individualistic diagnoses and solutions of how to move the equality agenda forward will be able to prevail in this changing climate.

 Reflective activity 9.9

Equality and diversity in practice (2)

Go online and research the equality and diversity statements of your employer and one or two other employers. What indication do they give as to whether their approach is more focused on equal opportunities or on diversity? Identify some examples of the business case for diversity for your chosen organisations. What might be the drivers for taking a managing diversity approach?

Demographic and social changes

By the early 2020s it has become obvious that the UK labour market faces a number of resourcing problems, including in labour market participation rates, despite increasing vacancy rates after the pandemic. The UK workforce is ageing over time, a process accelerated by relatively low indigenous birth rates and reduced inward migration, and the likelihood is that the working population will have to support a growing proportion of economically inactive and retired persons. Since Brexit, the potential pool of overseas migrants to fill positions at different levels of the labour market has declined somewhat. More than one million people than one would have expected prior to the Covid-19 pandemic, among whom younger people in education and over-50s are disproportionally represented, have joined the ranks of those economically inactive in the labour market. This is indicative of both a long-term ill-health 'Covid effect' and 'long Covid effect' on the workforce (Institute of Employment Studies, 2022). Put simply, changing demographics means that employers need to consider broadening their search for employees.

 Case study 9.2

The use of non-disclosure agreements: covering up discrimination?

It is difficult to know the extent of potential discrimination or unacceptable behaviour within an organisation, in order to be able to tackle and to create a more congenial environment in which equality and diversity can flourish, unless one has some way of recording problematic behaviour. Unfortunately, widespread reports of the extension of the use of legally backed non-disclosure agreements (NDAs) to cover up toxic behaviour in organisations, sometimes accompanied by a pay-off to, and voluntary termination of the wronged employee, suggest that organisational reputation management can take precedence. A notorious case concerns the former President's Club charity fund-raising annual dinner in 2018, where hostesses hired for the occasion were required to wear skimpy clothing and to sign a non-disclosure agreement in advance of the event (Marriage, 2018). This suggests advance knowledge of the likelihood of sexually harassing behaviour of women in what was, after all, their workplace for the evening by the guests at the event. The reputational damage of the *Financial Times'* undercover investigation

of this event can be judged by the fact that the charity subsequently closed. A subsequent investigation by the House of Commons Women and Equalities Committee (2019) of the wider prevalence of the use of NDAs in discrimination cases and wider employment disputes found their use against complainants to be routine and often substituting for investigation and punishment of alleged wrongdoers – see also Pagan (2021).

1   In your view, in what circumstances (if any) is the use of NDAs by organisations acceptable in such problems and disputes?

2   Compare your view with that of a colleague or others in a small group, and debate how best an organisational environment can be created that maximises the likelihood that workers will feel safe to raise equality-related issues and have them adequately investigated. What are the respective roles in this for managers, HR professionals, and for workers themselves?

3   In both cases, what do you think would be the main likely unintended consequences, and how could you overcome them?

9.6 Conclusion: Reflections on managing the employment relationship

The management of the employment relationship is a complex task, characterised by balancing imperatives for conflict and cooperation in the workplace and managerial freedoms with external constraints. The external constraints include factors such as the market within which the business operates. Employers with tight product or service margins may decide that the costs of investing in employees cannot be afforded. They may try to avoid dealing with trade unions, in the belief that unions will limit managerial flexibility and add to labour costs. The legal and social environments also provide constraints, both in the body of employment law and expectations about how rigorously businesses may be expected to conform to laws and to wider social norms and values. This is evident in the increased profile of equality and diversity issues, including the reputational damage than can rapidly fall, in a more transparent, social media-driven world, onto organisations believed to transgress boundaries. Similarly, societal and political expectations about the extent that at least some organisations will work with their staff in a spirit of social partnership also imposes limits on managerial prerogatives.

Nevertheless, managers have had an increasing amount of choice in recent decades in the human resource strategies they can deploy to structure the employment relationship, including the extent to which they view employees as a resource, and how or whether to deal with trade unions as representatives of employees. Since the 1980s, power in organisations has flowed increasingly in the direction of management, aided by many years of a relatively benign economic environment underpinned by globalisation, governments supportive of reducing regulation as a 'burden on business', the seeming vanquishing of inflation and major industrial discontent as economic problems as trade union strength atrophied.

Looking at this paradigm from the vantage point of the early 2020s, the extent to which successive wheels have been removed from this seemingly virtuous rolling bandwagon is striking. Indeed, one could argue that the period from the 1980s to the onset of the financial crisis from 2007 onwards, Brexit and the Covid-19 pandemic constitutes the exception in the management of the employment relationship in the UK. Many of the UK's problems of the 1960s and 1970s have reappeared on the social and political agenda, although some have assumed a new guise, and some additional issues have materialised, all of which managers will be left to grapple with. These problems include the following.

- The reappearance of skill and labour shortages at many levels of the labour market, which are less capable of solution through immigration of ready-trained workers from overseas, in the wake of Brexit.

- Contrary to what one might expect, the pressures this would normally create for higher wages have only appeared to a limited extent, due to the relative weakness of trade unions and workers' bargaining power. Nevertheless, the consequences of Brexit and Covid have edged 'the worker question' firmly back towards the centre of public policy. There are signs that trade union decline has stabilised and that, at least at a rhetorical level, the need to address low wages and living standards has gained traction as a political issue, it remains to be seen if and how this might be translated into action. Certainly, there appears to be little governmental appetite for any serious expansion of employment regulation or enforcement of existing law that would cut into managerial freedoms.

- Instead of higher real wages, an era of relatively high levels of inflation appears to be returning, in the context of both a long-term decline, since the financial crisis, in real wages, deferred wages (i.e. pensions) and increased personal taxation to pay for the cost on public borrowing of the financial crisis, an ageing population and the temporary employment support measures taken during the Covid-19 pandemic.

- High levels of in-work poverty and the reappearance of social inequality have emerged as salient political issues. These have partially occurred because of the ways employers have tried to offload direct business risk, through such devices as offshoring work to countries with lower labour costs, precarious employment practices, zero hours contracts and the expansion of the so-called 'gig economy'. In combination, these factors have contributed to undermining the availability of long-term stable employment opportunities that formed an important part of the social glue holding the former UK employment model together.

- The uneven impact of Covid-19 in the workplace has exacerbated the above issues of relative poverty and inequality. Disproportionately dire economic consequences of the Covid-19 pandemic have been visited on older workers, disabled people and workers of certain ethnicities, adding to levels of economic activity. At the same time, many of those who have found themselves able to use technological advances to work remotely from home have experienced new levels of freedom that some will not want subsequently to relinquish. In such an environment, how best to motivate and control different sections of the workforce become more pressing dilemmas for managers.

- Comparatively low levels of state aid in the UK to support those unable to work or suffering from infectious diseases have been exposed as a further factor underlying poverty and inequality, particularly as such supports have declined since the worst of the Covid pandemic.

- Whatever might be said about 'culture wars', the widespread influence on the Anglo-American workplace of the issues raised by activist movements such as 'Me Too' and 'Black Lives Matter' in questioning what is regarded as acceptable behaviour has further shifted equality and diversity firmly towards the centre of concerns about how organisations should manage the employment relationship.

This is admittedly a fairly lengthy list for torrid times, but it serves to reinforce the myriad influences on those charged with managing the employment relationship. Many of these problems are likely to be endemic in determining the future directions of how employment matters will be managed. These factors also underline the personal responsibility that managers have, through their decisions and actions, in influencing the experience of work for those they manage.

KEY LEARNING POINTS

1 Beliefs shape management style and influence whether employees are seen as a resource or a factor of production, and whether trade unions are perceived to be legitimate representatives or a source of conflict.

2 To build a workforce that is trusting of management and committed to the success of the organisation requires managerial initiatives to develop an appropriate culture, supported by relevant policies and employment practices.

3 Two contemporary developments which reflect strategies to achieve the commitment of employees are partnership working and diversity management.

4 Potentially discriminatory decisions taken at work need to be made on factors relevant to the work itself and not on personal characteristics such as age, sex, race, etc.

5 An equal opportunities approach can be portrayed as one that seeks compliance with legislation, and typically focuses on identifying the groups who are more susceptible to unfair discrimination. It utilises procedures that are designed to meet legal requirements on equal treatment.

6 The managing diversity approach focuses on the individual with the aim of creating a work environment where everyone feels valued, where their talents are fully utilised and where organisational goals are met.

 Review questions

1 With regard to the following scenarios, identify what you consider to be typical features present in respect of the management of the employment relationship:

   a where employees are seen as a resource that can provide competitive advantage

   b where trade unions are recognised for collective bargaining

   c where employees are viewed as a 'factor of production'.

2 If possible, you should draw on your own work experience.

3 What action can an HR manager take to prevent conflict arising within an organisation? If it does arise, what options exist for its resolution?

4 A line manager has asked you to help her understand the importance of the contract of employment, and how far she can rely upon it to ensure she gets the best out of her staff. How would you reply?

5 Evaluate the evidence that managing diversity is good for business using examples from academic sources or from your experience. If you were an HR professional, what arguments could you make to your employer in support of the business case?

6 How might trade unions and other employee representative groups reconcile the needs of their collective body (equal treatment for all) with the needs of individuals (valuing individual needs)?

Explore further

Bennett, T, Saundry, R and Fisher, V (2020) *Managing Employment Relations*, 7th edn, CIPD, London. This is the CIPD text on the subject.

French, R (2015) *Cross Cultural Management in Work Organisations,* 3rd edn, CIPD, London.

Kirton, G and Greene, A-M (2015) *The Dynamics of Managing Diversity: A critical approach*, 4th edn, Routledge, Abingdon.

Mensi-Klarbach, H and Risberg, A (eds) (2019) *Diversity in Organizations: Concepts and practices*, Red Globe Press, London.

Williams, S (2020) *Introducing Employment Relations: A critical approach*, 5th edn, Oxford University Press, Oxford. Takes a thematic approach to the subject area.

WEBSITES

Department for Business, Energy and Industrial Strategy (BEIS): www.gov.uk/government/organisations/department-for-business-energy-and-industrial-strategy (archived at https://perma.cc/63K6-K9MT). This is the government department responsible for employment policy.

Trades Union Congress: www.tuc.org.uk (archived at https://perma.cc/D3WP-C6C7). The TUC is the umbrella organisation for most of the trade unions in the UK.

Confederation of British Industries: www.cbi.org.uk (archived at https://perma.cc/Q6K4-5V6N). The CBI is the national representative body for UK employers.

Advisory, Conciliation and Arbitration Service: www.acas.org.uk (archived at https://perma.cc/ZQ85-XGDK). ACAS provides a range of impartial advice and publications on employment relations. Its website includes both the Code of Practice and Guide on discipline and grievances.

CIPD: cipd.co.uk (archived at https://perma.cc/B7S2-3EJK). Contains research and other documents on employment relations and managing diversity.

Equality and Human Rights Commission: www.equalityhumanrights.com (archived at https://perma.cc/478F-LUBB). The Commission has responsibility for monitoring the effect of equality legislation.

10
Performance and reward: a strategic approach

GARY REES AND ALEX TYMON

LEARNING OUTCOMES

After reading this chapter, you should be able to:

- identify the different ways that performance management (PM) can be defined and interpreted by organisations
- understand the assumptions which underpin the application of PM
- recognise the contribution of organisational theory, industrial engineering and behavioural science systems to the development of PM
- understand the relationship between performance, motivation and reward
- evaluate the extent to which PM can assist in improving organisational effectiveness and efficiency
- consider the contribution that HR can make to PM.

10.1 Overview

Organisational effectiveness and efficiency is rarely, if ever, off the management agenda in work organisations, and assumes an even higher priority during times of economic difficulty. PM is one process that can enable organisations to produce greater quality of product or service. It is a potentially pivotal topic within the broader managing people area.

However, PM must not be regarded as the universal panacea for improving organisational effectiveness. This chapter places PM in context, and weighs up the pros and cons of adopting PM as a means to improve productivity or service by motivating employees to perform better and, at the same time, considers the arguments for the use of reward as a motivator.

Contemporary issues such as employee engagement and commitment are discussed as part of a focus on motivation theories and approaches, while we keep in view the underlying question of how HR can make a difference in adding value through PM.

10.2 Introduction

There is little doubt that most organisations in the twenty-first century share some common objectives in order to ensure their survival, so that by producing a consistent product and/or service – which raises more in revenue than it costs to provide – they will attract and retain customers and encourage them to keep spending. Not-for-profit organisations share some of these aims, such as the need for consistency and the requirement to minimise costs for the provision of their product or service – see also Chapter 4. What is also beyond doubt is the role of people in helping to meet these objectives. PM is all about managing employees effectively and there is a wealth of research which demonstrates that well-managed employees increase revenues and decrease costs (see, eg, Coombs et al, 2006 and Subramony, 2009, two meta-analytic studies). A very persuasive example from the not-for-profit sector is also provided by West et al (2002), who demonstrate the link between PM and patient mortality in hospitals.

The ongoing economic turmoil post-2007 further increased the spotlight on PM, with questions posed as to the robustness of PM in the light of the 'reward for failure' practices that accompanied the collapse of the banking industry. Wain (2009, p 17) cites the CIPD's research, which demonstrated that 92 per cent of its survey thought that closer scrutiny of poor performance accounted for the rising interest in PM. A preoccupation with PM has never really gone away: one recent survey (CIPD, 2021u) found that the trend to home working, greatly boosted by the Covid-19 pandemic, highlighted managing performance as a key challenge for HR professionals.

In this chapter we consider the concept of PM and the theories of motivation that underpin it, along with its implications for managing and leading employees.

10.2.1 What is performance management?

There are myriad definitions of PM, but one of the best known is that of Armstrong and Baron (2005), which has been adopted by the CIPD (2012d, p 1):

> *A process which contributes to the effective management of individuals and teams in order to achieve high levels of organisational performance. As such, it establishes*

shared understanding about what is to be achieved and an approach to leading and developing people which will ensure that it is achieved.

This definition informs us of two important factors: first, the all-encompassing nature of PM – it has been suggested that all activities within a business should be contributing towards better performance and that managing the performance of employees is 'running the business' (Mohrman and Mohrman, 1995); and, second, the implication that PM can be viewed as a 'continuous process' (Biron, Farndale and Pauuwe, 2011, p 1295), involving identifying, measuring and developing employees in line with organisation strategy.

The extent to which PM impacts upon performance is contingent upon the context and the interconnectedness and interlocking of various supporting mechanisms. The ultimate aim is to maximise organisational effectiveness, especially within the ever-changing context of the modern organisation (Budworth and Mann, 2011).

The all-encompassing nature of PM can be seen by examining the people–performance link. A classic approach is demonstrated by the Boxall and Purcell (2008) AMO model (see Figure 10.1), in which performance is a function of ability, motivation and opportunity.

Figure 10.1 The people and performance model

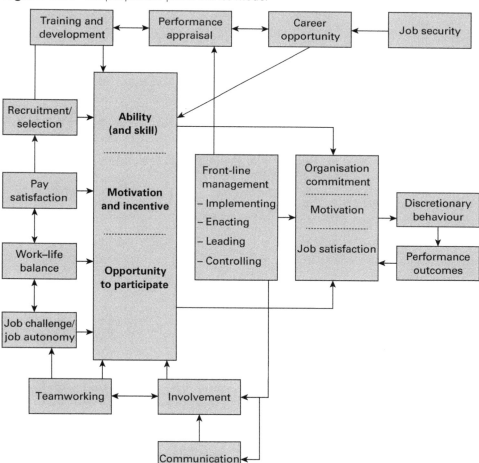

The role of the employer, their agent, or the manager has to be to maximise the three elements (ability, motivation and opportunity) in order to enhance performance. We see also in Figure 10.1 that certain HR policies and practices are shown to be particularly important in terms of influencing employee outcomes like commitment and motivation. However, it could be argued that the terminologies adopted by Boxall and Purcell (2011) need to be brought into line with current HR thinking and practice. Incorporating the elements of employee engagement (see Chapter 8) alongside employee commitment and job satisfaction allows us to expand the AMO model and recognise the increased complexity of high performance (see Figure 10.2). The nature of motivation will be discussed in more detail later in this chapter.

In the context of high-performance work organisations (HPWOs), research indicates that the activities presented in Figure 10.2 are representative of those demonstrated by top performing businesses. For example, Jamrog et al (2008) found that in a survey of 1,369 organisations, HPWOs have well-established values that are typically well understood by most employees and are key drivers of employee behaviour. They also report that HPWOs are clear about what behaviours employees need to exhibit in order to execute organisational and departmental strategies, and identified that managers need to:

- set clear goals
- understand employees' abilities
- guide and coach employees.

Although the relationship between these management activities and organisational performance is complex, and there are different levels of outcomes dependent on business sector and type of employee, there is evidence to show that PM is interpreted as an investment in staff, which leads to discretionary effort (McClean and Collins, 2011).

Figure 10.2 Some of the activities which could maximise ability, motivation, opportunity, satisfaction, commitment and engagement (AMOSCE)

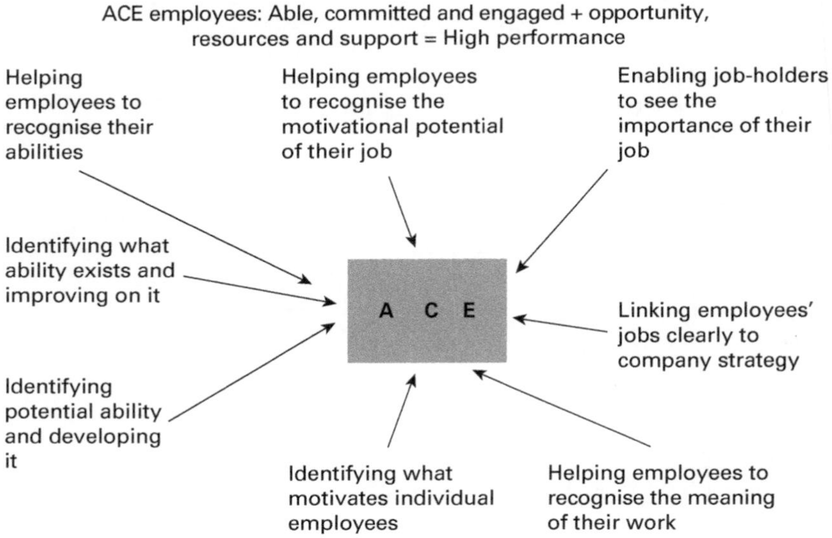

ACE employees: Able, committed and engaged + opportunity, resources and support = High performance

Helping employees to recognise their abilities

Helping employees to recognise the motivational potential of their job

Enabling job-holders to see the importance of their job

Identifying what ability exists and improving on it

Identifying potential ability and developing it

A C E

Linking employees' jobs clearly to company strategy

Identifying what motivates individual employees

Helping employees to recognise the meaning of their work

Figure 10.3 HR supporting mechanisms

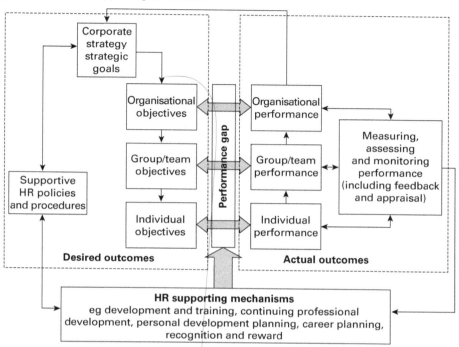

The PM process includes the alignment of objectives and performance through measurement, assessment and monitoring. Where there is a gap between objectives and performance, appropriate HR supporting mechanisms are required (Figure 10.3).

It could therefore be argued that HR as a function can add value through the range of supporting mechanisms that it can provide.

Another method of considering the strategic nature of PM is through the 'balanced scorecard', which attempts to link employee rewards to performance in the areas of finance, customers, internal business processes and innovation, learning and growth.

According to Chavan (2009, p 396), 'In some instances, companies see the non-financial measures as of such importance that a threshold level of performance is set for each of the non-financials. Only if an individual exceeds these threshold levels can they qualify for performance-related rewards linked to financial performance results.' The importance of organisational culture and vision also has a part to play in how the organisation considers and addresses performance.

10.3 Perspectives on performance management

From a managerialist perspective, where the manager has to ensure the most effective and efficient use of resources (including people) in achieving business objectives, PM can be seen as a tool to control and manipulate; very much a top-down process. The assumption underlying this perspective of PM is that the organisation, in the form of a controlling manager, can make a positive impact upon an individual's work performance. Within this assumption, managers are expected to demonstrate both general management skills as well as skills directly related to the PM process. The latter could include task skills such as objective-setting, understanding technical aspects of the job.

10.4 Monitoring progress and measuring results

General management skills, in contrast, could include leadership, mentoring, coaching (see Chapter 7) and interpersonal relationships. Managers may demonstrate strong task skills but have, over time, been regarded as lacking confidence in the softer interpersonal and social skills (Bowles and Coates, 1993).

The managerialist perspective also assumes a hierarchy of control, with a direct relationship between manager and subordinate. This is more difficult to achieve in complex organisational structures, such as multidimensional matrix structures. For example, a subordinate may report to several different line managers, who are all based in different locations. The control aspect of PM is legitimised through the perceived objectivity of the process. This objectivity then becomes the driving force for achieving performance outputs (Levinson, 1970, 1976).

10.4.1 The eternal triangle

Herzberg (1968) presents the eternal triangle perspective, in which there are three general philosophies of personnel (or HR) management: organisational theory; industrial engineering; and behavioural science.

The organisational theorist Weber (1947) believed that human needs are either so irrational or so varied and adjustable that personnel management has to be as pragmatic as the occasion demands. Herzberg cites the example of job design, where, if jobs are organised in a proper manner, the result will be the most efficient job structure, and the most favourable attitudes will follow. Alternatively, within the eternal triangle theory, the industrial engineer (Taylor, 1911) believe that humankind is mechanistically orientated and economically motivated, and therefore we need to attune the individual to the most efficient working process. Here we need to design the most appropriate incentive system and design the most appropriate working system for the human machine. Behavioural scientists, for example Schein (1984) focus on group sentiments, the attitudes of individual employees and the organisation's social and psychological climate, with the emphasis on instilling healthy employee attitudes and an appropriate organisational climate. This model illustrates a useful analogy for the use and possible misuse of PM as means to improve performance in organisations.

10.5 Performance management as a process

PM can also be viewed as a process by looking at the employee lifecycle and the management activities which could contribute to improved performance at each stage. The advantage of this approach is that it can provide guidance to organisations on which activities to introduce and when.

Before recruitment and during the selection process, some of these activities are understood and are embedded in many organisations, others less so. For example, how many organisations provide sufficient information to enable prospective employees to 'self-select' themselves out of the recruitment process, thereby potentially saving costs and effort of managing employees who cannot or will not be successful? How many organisations are explicit in looking for employees whose values are aligned to that of the business and are therefore more likely to be committed? How many organisations make the conscious effort to test for potential at the recruitment stage?

During formal induction or onboarding, when organisations run induction or orientation schemes, to what extent is the robustness of these schemes measured and subsequent action taken? Is there recognition that this is the stage at which employees learn both the formal and informal rules of behaviour and the difference between the overt or stated expectations of the organisation, and the reality of what will be tolerated in practice? A robust induction process can be invaluable in making performance standards and expectations explicit.

Research around the 'induction crisis' identifies problems which may manifest themselves in both the short term and long term. For example, the Reed Consulting Survey (2004) demonstrated that 4 per cent of new starters walk out of the job because of poor or non-existent induction programmes, and 93 per cent of the 5,700 respondents in their survey believed that a poor induction had a continuing adverse effect on their productivity at work.

During the period, to what extent do line managers appreciate the true value of the probationary period? All too often, it consists of a form-filling exercise initiated by the HR department. The manager signs to say that the new employee should have their position confirmed but without having any idea of how they are actually performing.

Then a few months later the manager may complain that the employee is under-performing, or worse still, is asking HR how they can remove them. During formal reviews and appraisals, how many managers recognise the value of constant feed-back, both positive and developmental? Behaviourist learning theory (Skinner, 1953, cited in French et al, 2015) demonstrates the power of positively reinforcing desired behaviours: employees are much more likely to repeat actions that gain them posi-tive recognition. Positive reinforcement has also been shown to increase employees' 'self-efficacy beliefs', which in turn, increases performance (Bandura, 1993).

However, there appears to be a blockage against recognising when an employee has performed to standard, a belief that employees should exceed before they receive recognition. A typical comment on supervisor training courses is: 'Why should I recognise an employee who has just reached the standard? That is their job.' But if we employ someone and ask them to reach a certain standard and they do, then this should be recognised and the danger of not doing so is that performance and standards will slide.

The power of positive feedback is the theory supporting appreciative inquiry (see below), but many managers appear to spend their time and effort looking for and acting on the 5 per cent of jobs that people do badly, whilst ignoring the 95% that they do effectively.

An excuse sometimes cited for lack of feedback is the idea that people learn from mistakes, and it is certainly true that allowing people to fail can be useful in some circum-stances. Control theory (Carver et al, 2000) indicates that failure can even motivate more than success. Learning organisation theory (Ellinger, 2004) suggests that freedom to fail is an important factor to enable an organisation to grow. But there is a lot of difference between giving employees space to experiment accompanied by constructive feedback and abdication management. According to Geal and Johnson (2002, p 26):

> *What do people learn from mistakes? What not to do, so they need to try something else. But, what else? A manager able and willing to give developmental feedback so they can improve is both necessary and motivating when handled well.*

So, using the excuse of allowing people to learn from mistakes could be viewed as lazy at best, and at worst could be incredibly costly for the organisation. In summary, the balance between allowing experimentation and providing appropriate feedback needs constant review.

At any time in the employee lifecycle, there may be the need to manage poor performance or conduct. This raises the question of how many managers are able and willing to manage poor performance or conduct in a positive way before it becomes a major issue. An organisation may well have a 'capability and conduct' procedure, which will undoubtedly espouse the wisdom of dealing with performance and conduct issues informally and early. But how many organisations train and support their managers to run these informal 'improving poor performance/poor conduct' discussions?

Table 10.1 Performance management as a process

Employee activity	Timeline and action		Manager/employer activity
Gains knowledge of expectations and culture Self-selects in or out	Before recruitments: Job descriptions, person specifications, adverts, company information		Gives signals of expectations on job performance standards, conduct standards and culture
Demonstrates ability and motivation Conscious or subconscious alignment with values Self-selects in or out	During selection process: Interviews/assessments, etc		Tests ability and motivation Checks values alignment Seeks potential
Learns conduct expectations Adapts to the culture	During formal induction/ orientation	At any time: Possible poor performance or poor conduct intervention	Formalises conduct expectations, terms and conditions/handbook, etc
Learns performance standards Develops knowledge and skills	During mandatory training		Provides standards of job performance Provides knowledge and skills Provides feedback
Becomes a productive employee Adapts to the culture	During probation period		Team briefing and communication Reinforces performance and conduct standards Provides feedback One-to-one reviews Provides ongoing training and coaching

(continued)

Table 10.1 (Continued)

Employee activity	Timeline and action		Manager/employer activity
Reviews performance Agrees objectives Identifies learning needs Considers aspirations Possibly gains reward	During formal reviews and/ or appraisals: Annual or more regularly		Reviews performance Sets objectives Agrees learning needs Identifies potential and aspirations Possible link to reward
Continuous improvement Develops self-feedback mechanisms Achieves potential	Ongoing: Business as usual		Team briefing and communication Reinforces performance and conduct standards Provides feedback One-to-one reviews Ongoing training and coaching

10.5.1 Appreciative inquiry

Drawn from research into positive psychology (Seligman, 1998), appreciative inquiry suggests that when employees are encouraged to focus on their strengths, then they are more likely to succeed and enjoy greater job satisfaction (Bryce, 2007). For a practical example, see Arkin (2005b).

 Case study 10.1

Performance appraisal at SodaStream

Operating in over 30 countries, SodaStream is the world's largest manufacturer, distributor and marketer of home water-carbonation systems. A change in HR personnel led to a project aimed at designing a new appraisal process. Focus groups were carried out to understand issues with the existing scheme and to answer a key question: what are the conditions that can make our performance evaluation process a success? The majority of employees described the existing system as an unpleasant and unhelpful experience; however, they also believed that it was crucial to have a performance appraisal process that was able to: positively energise employees; include follow-up; raise employee motivation; and be short and simple. As a result of this feedback, the HR team at SodaStream commissioned a new process building on the concepts behind appreciative inquiry and positive psychology, which was piloted with 64 employees and 26 managers.

Strength-based performance appraisal (SBPA) – the principles

The goals of the new system were: to improve organisational performance and business results;

focus on employees' strengths but without neglecting problems; to reflect the double meaning of appreciation, that is, valuing good performance and increasing value; and to support knowledge management within the organisation.

To this end, seven principles were adopted: feed forward; reflected best self-feedback; happiness research; developing strengths; the 3:1 positive to negative emotion principle; a win-win philosophy; positive organisational core; and collective efficacy.

The SodaStream performance appraisal

The SBPA system at SodaStream contains six steps:

- supervisor–employee meeting including success stories told by the subordinate and enthusiasm stories told by the supervisor
- a joint questionnaire and preparation of reports
- a second supervisor–employee meeting involving a strength-based evaluation discussion looking for new ways to use strengths and agree goals to achieve win-win outcomes
- creation of an organisational strengths map

- a celebration party to recognise strengths
- a follow-up process.

An initial evaluation

Benefits of the new system as reported by subordinates included: increased quality time with managers; a positive experience of performance evaluation; a focus on strengths; goal-setting; increased learning; and better matching of competencies to tasks.

For the organisation, reported benefits included: increased levels of motivation and performance; better goal-setting; improved organisational culture; increased collaboration; and improved manager–employee relationships.

1   How does the SodaStream performance appraisal process differ from ones you are familiar with?

2   What would need to be in place in an organisation in order to adopt this type of process?

SOURCE: Bouskila-Yam, O and Kluger, A (2011) Strength-based performance appraisal and goal setting, *Human Resource Management Review*, **21** (2), pp 137–47

 Reflective activity 10.1

Think about an organisation with which you are familiar. Using Table 10.1 as a guide, consider the evidence for a clear PM process being in place. What evidence exists that it has been implemented in an effective manner?

However, there is more to PM than just the actions involved. Effective PM is not only dependent upon *what* is done, but also upon *how* it is done. Purcell et al (2003) provide research evidence to support the proposition that no one particular HR practice is critical to organisational success, but rather that good management by line managers, applying various approaches effectively and appropriately according to the context, is the key factor. Committed and capable line managers are, therefore, essential to successful PM (Hutchinson and Purcell, 2003). These managers need to know the 'how' of PM as much as the 'what'; that is, the answers to questions such as:

- How can we define performance?
- Who should define performance?
- How can we measure performance?
- What is the link between motivation and performance?

10.5.2 Defining performance

For performance to be managed it has to be defined and measured. This demonstrates that what the organisation measures is indicative of what the organisation values (Johnson et al, 2011).

There is no single, universal definition of performance; it depends very much on the particular perspective adopted. For example, some definitions relate to the organisation and various expectations in terms of outputs: Performance should be defined as the outcomes of work because they provide the strongest linkage to the strategic goals of the organisation, customer satisfaction, and economic contributions (Bernadin, Kane and Ross, 1995).

Other definitions emphasise behavioural aspects, in addition to outputs or results: Performance means both behaviours and results. Behaviours emanate from the performer and transform performance from abstraction to action. Not just the instruments for results, behaviours are also outcomes in their own right – the product of mental and physical effort applied to tasks – and can be judged apart from results (Brumbach, 1988, p 389).

10.5.3 Who defines performance?

It is not only a question of *how* performance is defined, but also *who* within the organisation is, or are, responsible for defining performance standards. Often, it is the organisation itself that determines performance and how it will be measured. Performance requirements are often part of a strategic planning process, cascading top-down through the organisation from senior management (Humble, 1972). However, this does not have to be the case. Semler (1993) describes a bottom-up approach, where employees at Semco were allowed to set their own performance targets and define appropriate rewards. There is also the possibility of a combined top-down and bottom-up approach, with mutual adjustment of goals and objectives (Nonaka and Takeuchi, 1995).

Other stakeholders, such as shareholders, and customers, will have their own views on performance standards or achievements and their views may be contradictory. The parties involved have different perspectives, expectations and experience of performance. For example, shareholders are interested in long-term value of stocks and assets. Middle management may have an interest in protecting and advancing their own position, power and rewards. Customers are increasingly demanding high-quality, customised products and services. In addition, all these stakeholders may adopt different roles at different times or have multiple, simultaneous roles. Therefore, the agreement of what constitutes effective performance may be difficult to reach.

A more integrated approach may help to overcome some of the problems inherent in defining performance and performance standards. It is generally accepted that involving employees in the setting of objectives and targets is more likely to gain commitment to their achievement. Fundamentally, though, for the organisation to succeed, someone, somewhere needs to combine the targets to ensure that the organisational objectives are indeed being met. This is a line management responsibility, but HR might need to empower and ensure that the process is taking place.

10.5.4   *What aspects of performance can be measured?*

What an organisation chooses to measure, and when, depends on the PM framework adopted within the organisational context and on what the organisation values in its employees; for example, to what extent is learning valued as part of the PM process? But a robust PM process typically relies on the setting of definable and measurable goals and targets, which raises challenges as it is impossible to measure all aspects of an employee's performance. For example, how does an organisation measure knowledge-creation, creativity and innovation? PM too often assumes explicit performance measures and cannot always incorporate tacit inputs, throughputs and outputs at individual, group and organisational levels.

Similarly, there are temporal barriers. Performance targets are typically set in time and the timescale might in itself affect accurate measurement. How does one allow for long-term performance improvements and outcomes within an annual appraisal cycle, for example? The critical issue then becomes when we measure and record performance.

In addition, there is the challenge of the traditional PM emphasis on the individual, whereas the increasingly interdependent nature of work, and the consequent emphasis on team and groups, makes measurement more challenging. It is not just individual performance that is important, but also the contribution that the individual makes towards group effort, and the combined output of the group as a whole. So, team targets are an area that needs to be explored.

An example of these complexities can be seen in a study by Rosen et al (2011), who explore the challenges of managing and measuring adaptive performance in teams. This is potentially a very important aspect in the modern business environment; however, it can be difficult to measure behavioural dimensions over time, across groups of employees – as opposed to individuals.

10.5.5   *Pitfalls of defining performance targets*

There are many pitfalls with objectives and targets. Reeves (2008) used the term 'targetology' to describe the fixation of the then British Government and many organisations with targets. He agrees that targets can be helpful, citing the reduction in hospital waiting times as an example, but he questions the number of targets which are used:

> One or two clear targets can be powerful. A hundred targets is a recipe for confusion, stress and disaster... Just because targets are good, it does not mean that more targets are better.

Hall (2009, p 10) argues that 'Focusing organisation and individual activity on what really matters, through the use of targets linked to strategic aims, can be a powerful management "tool" but careful consideration needs to be given to what is targeted, how targets are applied and who targets are applied to.'

Research by Professor Yves Emery (2008) identifies some common issues with both defining targets and attaining them: policy deployment, quality versus quantity targets, goal displacement, individualisation effect, goal override and limited influence. An example of each is provided in Table 10.2.

 Reflective activity 10.2

Analyse the targets or objectives that you have been set during a PM process. To what extent do the pitfalls listed in Table 10.2 apply to these? How could your targets be improved upon?

Table 10.2 Pitfalls of target definition

	Example
Policy deployment The difficulties of translating strategic goals into meaningful bottom-line targets. Not all objectives are easily split and can become meaningless if broken down too much	A common strategic goal, such as 'increase market share', which may well translate into specific objectives for senior managers, but is almost impossible to be a meaningful objective for a back-office employee such as a payroll data entry clerk
Quality versus quantity targets Quantity targets are typically easier to set and therefore used in place of quality targets which may be more beneficial	An HR officer may be set a target to ensure 95% of employees who leave the organisation complete an exit interview: a very SMART target. But, actually, what is really wanted is quality of data from exiting employees about why they are leaving, so that meaningful decisions can be made
Goal displacement Where the measures become seen as the goal	In a call centre the goal may be to improve customer service and one measure of this is to answer calls more quickly. It is easy for employees to 'lose calls' – that is, drop them as soon as they are answered – in order to improve the call-answering statistics, which actually results in even worse customer service

(continued)

Table 10.2 (Continued)

	Example
Individualisation effect Where competing goals set up unintended competition between staff, especially competition for scarce resources	A cable TV sales team may be measured on the number of customers they sign up, and to ensure quality of sales the customers have to stay for a minimum time period of six months. However, the technicians who install the product in the customer's home are measured on speed of installation and the quicker the install, the more likely there will be a problem, which in turn leads to customers disconnecting
Goal override Where employees only focus on goal achievement and neglect other important responsibilities. It may become necessary to have a relatively complex measurement system in order to ensure that the 'day job' carries equal weight	A hotel maintenance team may be targeted on the completion of reported repairs and may go flat out to achieve these targets. As a result they may neglect the preventative maintenance jobs, which are a part of their job description, because they are not overtly measured
Limited influence Where employees have very little control over the targets set, or at least perceive this to be the case	In a retail environment where product range, price and advertising are all centrally controlled a shop assistant may easily perceive that they really have very little control over the actual sales they make and this perception may be the reality. It has also been argued that employees are just the delivery system and that 90% of the impact of their endeavours comes from the system!

10.5.6 *Measuring performance*

The PM process (Table 10.1) shows that measurement or performance review and feedback should be an ongoing activity, so that positive reinforcement or corrective action can be supplied as soon as it is justified. Normal management activities such as walking the floor and one-to-one reviews can enable this measurement to happen and ensure that one of the 'golden rules' of appraisals is followed: 'No surprises', that is, anything discussed in a period review or appraisal concerning performance should be expected by both parties.

This is important as 'surprised employees become angry employees, and angry employees sue' (Segal, 2010, p 76).

Another measurement technique, which is often overlooked, is self-measurement. Although different theorists may argue why, they do mostly conclude that participation in goal-setting can lead to improved performance. The research that supports the idea of autonomy and participation in goal-setting is also well known and includes the work of Herzberg (1968), Hackman and Oldham (1980) and Locke and Latham (1990), to name but a few. For example, Locke (1968) in Hollyforde and Whiddett (2002) identified the value of goals as a motivator and performance enhancer suggesting that specific rather than general goals and participation in goal-setting are important in improving performance. Locke also identifies self-regulation or self-measurement and management as being powerful enablers, an idea supported by Bandura (1993, p 128), who states that:

> Most human motivation is cognitively generated. People motivate themselves and guide their actions anticipatorily by the exercise of forethought ... Forethought is translated into incentives and appropriate action through self-regulatory mechanisms. This suggests that self-measurement is an everyday activity.

Latham (2007) provides a useful summary of some of the research around this area, but the message appears to be that although the effects are mediated and moderated by other factors, such as personality, involving employees in goal-setting and facilitating self-feedback can and does result in higher performance. This perhaps provides an argument for the use of more self-appraisal and for developing ways in which employees can access their own feedback on performance.

10.5.7 Appraisal as a performance management tool

The more recent literature (for example, Aguinis 2009), calls for a wide view of PM, including performance planning, assessment and review, identifying that it is more than simply appraisal. But some form of performance appraisal is nearly always incorporated with the aim of improving performance, motivating employees and/or allocating rewards.

An honest and accurate assessment of current performance can be a strong driver for further learning, development and performance improvement. As discussed earlier, feedback and the setting of improvement targets can itself be a strong motivator (Locke and Latham, 1990), and for there to be equitable distribution of rewards some fair method of comparing contributions between individuals is required. The potential impact of fairness is highlighted by Adams' equity theory – see 10.6.1 'Motivation theories' below.

The whole PM system should therefore ensure that employees perceive equity of treatment and fairness, none more so than in the appraisal process and distribution of rewards. This supports the argument that PM and reward policies need to be transparent. The role of perception means that extra attention must be paid to how the process is communicated so as to ensure that the message is clear and universally understood.

However, there is a wealth of evidence that points to negative aspects of performance appraisal and at least three writers have called for an end to them (Bouskila-Yam and Kluger, 2011). Bersin advocated back in 2007 the death of performance appraisal and a need to shift to more sophisticated methods of supporting employees, like coaching and development (Bersin, 2011). Very careful consideration is therefore needed when choosing a performance appraisal process and planning its implementation.

10.5.8 Types of appraisal

Different types of appraisal include: top-down, self-appraisal, peer appraisal, bottom-up and multi-rater, such as 360-degree and 720-degree feedback. The most common is a top-down approach with the inclusion of self-appraisal, usually as a preparatory activity for the employee. There are many benefits of a multi-rater approach, which in theory will produce a more rounded outcome, but the time and expense involved often rules this out as an option.

Appraisal methods can be divided into two main approaches: those oriented towards results (outputs); and those oriented towards competencies (inputs). Results-oriented appraisal is based on the setting of quantifiable, achievable and time-bounded objectives, most often agreed between manager and subordinate, and geared towards achieving organisational objectives. Competency-oriented appraisal is based on the demonstration of certain key skills and behaviours thought to be associated with high performance. These skills and behaviours, agreed by manager and employee, may also include the use of multi-rater instruments. The trend in recent years is towards combining both results and competency-based approaches in an attempt to deliver the dual benefits of achieving immediate performance targets and supporting longer-term development of key skills and capabilities.

Appraisals and the link to development and reward

PM systems differ in the emphasis they give to rewards or development. The trend is for increasing emphasis on development rather than reward, and de-emphasising the link between PM and pay (Armstrong and Baron, 2005). PM and development are overlapping and inter-dependent processes. Performance reviews, whether they are periodic appraisals or continuous day-to-day interactions between managers and employees, provide encouragement for learning and development. Development may take the form of informal training, self-managed learning by the individual employee, coaching by the manager, or more structured training and development interventions. Whatever the form, development is intended to have a direct impact on performance capabilities and can also have a powerful motivational effect (CIPD 2012d).

However, multiple perspectives on appraisals lead to conflicts. Reconciling PM as a developmental process and as a pay decision-making process is not straightforward. Linking performance appraisal to pay reduces the focus on development (Kessler and Purcell, 1992). An employee is less likely to highlight a development need if it might be seen as a weakness and therefore detrimentally affect their pay award.

10.5.9 Potential pitfalls when evaluating employees

Appraisals ask for evaluations to be made, and accordingly there are potential pitfalls, some of which are highlighted below.

Rating scale issues

In appraisal systems where a rating scale is used, there are constant issues with people being unhappy with the 'average' rating. Standard distribution dictates that not everyone will be at the top, some people will be at the bottom and most people will be in the middle. But being rated as 'competent', 'satisfactory', 'C' or '3/5' is unsatisfactory for people who can see 'exceptional', 'A' or '5/5' on the scale.

The Swiss Federal Administration trialled a new system with the following grades:

A++	Far beyond expectations
A+	Beyond expectations
A	Objectives fully reached
B	Objectives partially reached
C	Objectives missed

Although people psychologically still want to be A++, most employees will be rated as an A, which is psychologically better than a C (Emery, 2008). However, despite all the research into improving rating scales, there is little evidence that one is better than another, and recent focus has moved onto trying to minimise rater bias (Budworth and Mann, 2011).

Appraiser bias

Appraisers all have their own biases. Some have tendencies to rate everyone kindly or everyone harshly, which can raise issues, especially when rewards are linked and comparisons are made with other teams, whose managers have rated differently. In addition, there are those who struggle to differentiate between any employees, wanting something for everyone, known as the 'watering can effect'. Furnham (1997) identified 13 different 'perception errors', which he said could negatively influence an appraisal system.

These pitfalls can severely affect an employee's sense of equity and cause dissatisfaction with the system, which in turn is likely to diminish performance. Furnham's 13 systematic perception errors are:

1 First impressions – rather than how the appraisee has performed.
2 Halo effect – only focusing on one favourable behaviour or quality.
3 Horns effect – contrary to halo effect; a negative rating.
4 Contrast error – comparison with selected employees, often star performers.
5 Same as me – rating appraises highly due to sharing common attributes with appraiser.
6 Different from me – contrary to same as me.
7 Recency effect – judging only recent behaviour, then generalising.
8 Central tendency – rating everyone in the middle of the scale.
9 Leniency in rating – generous to everyone to avoid conflict.
10 Strict rating – consistently strict in appraising performance.
11 Performance dimension error – where two aspects of the appraisal follow, score two distinct qualities the same.
12 Spillover effect – based on previous appraisal.
13 Status effect – giving better ratings to higher-level employees.

Much of the training provided to appraisers attempts to reduce and minimise the impact of these types of rater bias.

 Reflective activity 10.3

Peter Cheese, CEO of the CIPD, argued in a blog article entitled 'Putting the human into HR' that managers who see established companies such as Accenture and Deloitte scrapping enshrined practices, like the annual performance review and performance rankings, would consider following suit. Cheese questions the validity and usefulness of long-established practices like PM, where there is now a need to remove the emphasis from control to enablement, which sounds plausible, but may not be so easy to bring about in practice.

1 During the 1980s, the concept of 'empowerment' was prevalent in some quarters and may have seemed to some managers to be the way forward. To what extent is Cheese's assertion of enablement simply a repetition of the notion of empowerment?

2 Consider the implications for management and leadership if we were to reduce or possibly abolish management tools, like the performance management system.

10.5.10 Reward pitfalls

While not all formal appraisal systems are overtly linked to rewards, there are many potential issues with appraisal systems being linked to rewards. Fixed quota systems, where evaluation is based on the amount of reward available and not on actual levels of performance, can lead to meaningless appraisals for employees, especially if the total amount of money available is limited. Evidence suggests that less than 10 per cent of annual salary has a very limited effect on motivating people to higher performance (Emery, 2008). In a turbulent economic climate, the question has to be asked as to how many organisations can make budgetary arrangements for this amount of money. If a smaller 'pot' is to be distributed in such a way as to offer more than 10 per cent to some employees, are managers willing or able to differentiate enough between their employees?

Dependent upon organisational structure and context, the practice of team reward may inhibit or adversely affect individual motivation (for further reading, see the CIPD website).

Do employees who are less confident and think they cannot achieve the standards to attain a bonus actually work less hard, so in effect the reward becomes a demotivator? Which leads to a fundamental question: do rewards such as pay and other recognition schemes actually motivate employees at all?

10.6 Motivated to perform?

It must be remembered that PM is, in itself, simply a process. Human beings don't always follow rules and do exactly what they are told. In order to maximise performance by employees themselves, we need to understand the human psyche by considering key aspects such as motivation, commitment and engagement.

10.6.1 Motivation theories

Content and process approaches

Content theories focus on what (outcome or reward) motivates people. Common examples of content theories include: existence-relatedness-growth (ERG) theory (Alderfer), achievement theory (McClelland), two-factor theory (Herzberg), and hierarchy of needs theory (Maslow). In contrast, process theories concentrate on how people are motivated, or the cognitive process used to connect effort with outcomes or reward. Goal-setting theory (Locke, 1968) is an example of a process theory, as are equity theory (Adams) and expectancy theory (Vroom), which are both discussed below. For an in-depth treatment of content and process motivation theories, see Mullins (2019). Effective management interventions combine both content and process motivation theories as they are complementary not opposites (Hollyforde and Whiddett, 2002).

Equity theory

Adams' (1965) equity theory contends that employees consider the inputs, for example abilities and effort they bring to work, in relation to the outputs (perceived rewards they gain as a result), and then go on to compare the ratio of these two factors with referent others, through the use of the distributive justice concept (see Chapter 5).

A perceived injustice motivates the individual to take action – they can increase or decrease their inputs, or seek to increase or decrease the inputs of others. Alternatively, they can seek to change the outputs for either themselves or others. In extreme circumstances they may choose to leave the organisation. Leaving the organisation may also include psychological withdrawal, for example turning up for work but spending all day on Facebook. It is important to note the critical part that perception plays in equity theory, so the injustice may not be perceived by others (Mullins, 2019).

All through the twentieth century, theorists argued about the capacity of money to motivate employees towards greater performance (Latham, 2007). Money, or what it can supply (money can be a status symbol or a sign of recognition), appears in all the 'content' theories of motivation and therefore it is implied that money is a motivator (see 'Reflection theory' below). Barber and Bretz (2000) suggest that money is among the most important factors for people when deciding on a job.

Reflective activity 10.4

Think about yourself and talk to others you know. What was it that would have made you and they think about looking for a new job?

This activity may give some insight into the complexity of the question as to whether money is a motivator. One only has to consider the 70,000 'games-makers' who volunteered to work during the Olympics and Paralympics of 2012 to recognise that money is not always the single motivator. These people were driven by other factors, and while without doubt some were driven by extrinsic drivers such as social or status needs, for many, the motivation would have been intrinsic, such as a sense of achievement or development and growth.

Expectancy theory

A process theory of motivation seeks to explain the cognitive process of how an individual is motivated to increase performance. A common example by Vroom (1964) is explained through the formula:

$$F = E \times I \times V$$

F is the force of motivation, ie how much effort will be applied ('how hard I am willing to work'). E is expectancy, ie the belief that extra effort will result in better performance ('if I work harder, my output will increase').

I is instrumentality, ie the belief that better performance will lead to a reward ('if my output increases, I will get a reward').

V is valence, the perceived value of the reward ('how much I want the reward'). Valence links back to content theories of motivation, which these tell us that individuals are motivated by a multitude of factors (needs and wants), including money, but also security, affiliation, power, achievement, status, growth and more.

SOURCE: Mullins (2019)

Contemporary views of motivation

Motivation theories never die, but some of them certainly age. Despite the ongoing criticism of Maslow's theory of the hierarchy of needs, many organisations still adopt this framework to unpick and understand human motivation. If we ignore the need to satisfy each level, starting with basic hygiene factors, then elements of esteem needs and self-actualisation may be associated with newer concepts, like 'employee engagement'. The 1990s saw the emergence of three psychological conditions (Kahn,

1990), which impacted upon engagement (and disengagement): psychological meaningfulness, psychological safety and psychological availability. These three terms can be interpreted as: firstly, feelings of worthwhileness, being values and useful to the organisation. Safety relates to carrying out work without losing face, and maintaining dignity and respect within working relationships. Psychological availability includes the sense of emotional, physical and psychological resources to engage at a given time.

Nohria, Groysberg and Lee (2008) argue that people are driven by four basic emotional needs or drives, which underpin everything that we do:

1 *The drive to acquire* – mainly physical goods, like money, which enhances our social status and then allows us to compare ourselves to others.

2 *The drive to bond* – people need to have a positive emotional bond to their organisation and people within it too.

3 *The drive to comprehend* – seeking meaning and contribution, seeking challenges and the scope to learn and grow.

4 *The drive to defend* – by promoting justice and feelings of security, as well as the need to maintain the status quo. Nohria's drives are not hierarchical in nature, but are relevant upon key 'levers' of motivation, namely: culture, job design, the reward system and performance management processes.

 Reflective activity 10.5

Review Maslow's (1943) hierarchy of needs model. Compare and contrast this with Nohria's four basic drives of motivation model. What are the key differences and do these reflect changes within a more contemporary society?

The importance of intrinsic motivation

The resurgence of interest in intrinsic factors such as meaning, purpose, spirituality and commitment and, more recently, engagement, has emphasised the importance of work as a motivator in the organisation (Fox, 1994; Lockwood, 2007; Meyer and Herscovitch, 2001). Intrinsic motivation is the spontaneous satisfaction individuals derive from the activity itself. Extrinsic motivation, in contrast, requires tangible or verbal rewards (Ankil and Palliam, 2012). Intrinsic motivation can lead to more engaged and committed employees and the four most critical intrinsic rewards are: a sense of meaning and purpose; a sense of choice; a sense of competence; and a sense of progress (Chalofsky and Krishna, 2009). In terms of meaningfulness, people with the highest levels of productivity and fulfilment view themselves as inseparable from their work, intrinsically motivated by the work itself and professionally committed to and engaged with the organisation (Chalofsky and Krishna 2009).

So, there is evidence to suggest money can reduce the effectiveness of intrinsic motivation and there are circumstances when it appears not to. The deciding factor, as is so often the case, is not what is done, but how it is done. Even if money is a motivational factor, it is commonly linked to equity theory (as discussed earlier in this chapter), that is, employees compare their rewards with colleagues and if they perceive unfair treatment, they are motivated to act. Transparency in how rewards such as pay are implemented is therefore very important. In addition, expectancy theories of motivation (see below) also provide potential guidelines on implementation of reward policies and practice.

Commitment and job satisfaction

Defined by Koster (2011, p 2838) as: 'the decision to participate', organisational commitment can be seen as the psychological bond between an individual and an organisation. Meyer and Herscovitch (2001) concluded that employees can be committed to different targets, including their occupation, team or manager in addition to or in place of their organisation. The positive benefits of increased employee commitment are well documented and include: increased performance outcomes; enhanced organisational citizenship behaviours; and reduced labour turnover (see, eg, Meyer et al, 2002).

Meyer and Allen (1991) expanded the concept of commitment to explain why it leads to positive outcomes, outlining three components: affective commitment – emotional attachment to the target; normative commitment – moral obligation to the target; and continuance commitment – a perceived lack of choice on whether to leave the organisation. Mayfield and Mayfield (2012) argue that affective commitment is the most powerful of the three components.

Job satisfaction, a more established concept, deals with how a person feels about their job or work experience (Locke, 1976). High levels of job satisfaction are not thought to increase performance directly; however, job satisfaction has been shown to increase commitment, reduce grievances, lower labour turnover and contribute to engagement.

Hackman and Oldham's (1980) job characteristics model in French et al (2015) links five job characteristics – skill variety, task identity, task significance, autonomy and feedback – with positive psychological states (see also Chapter 11). This model provides a platform for linking meaningful jobs with higher levels of job satisfaction.

10.7 The links between reward and performance

The topic of reward is in itself a significant area for research and debate. For further in-depth discussions, see Perkins and Jones (2021).

10.7.1 *Pay and intrinsic motivation*

According to Kuvaas (2006), the link between pay and performance is mediated and moderated by employees' personal levels of intrinsic motivation. It is suggested that money, an extrinsic motivator, may actually decrease long-term intrinsic motivation and so have a detrimental effect on performance.

Two conflicting meta-analyses were published in 2001, both trying to establish the link between extrinsic rewards and intrinsic motivation, and the results are mixed. According to Deci et al (2001), the use of rewards as a motivational strategy is a risky proposition, as this disengages interest and self-regulation. Cameron, Banko and Pierce (2001) counteracted this by stating that rewards are not harmful to motivation to perform a task (see Latham, 2007 for a summary of the debate). Interestingly, recent evidence from a multiple employer study showed that performance-related pay (PRP) was positively related to intrinsic motivation, which can shape the workforce. Employees for whom PRP is a motivator will self-select to work in organisations which offer this benefit (Fang and Gerhart, 2012).

10.7.2 Performance-related reward – expectancy theory in action

A classic use of expectancy theory is to define and execute a performance-related reward scheme, in order to improve short-term performance. An example could be an attempt to increase sales of sports shoes in a sports shop in the lead up to Christmas: the employer wants to increase the amount of effort (force) that employees will put in. For this to work employees need the following:

- A belief that putting in extra effort, talking to customers, learning about stock, etc will result in making extra sales. So, they need training, goal-setting and feedback to this effect (expectancy).

- A belief that the extra sales they make will be recognised by their manager and result in a reward. This could be extra pay, prizes, recognition, promotion, a permanent contract, time off, more interesting work, etc. There needs to be a system for individuals to record their sales that actually result in the promised reward being given (instrumentality).

- A belief that the reward is worth having to them. This is a good reason to offer a choice of rewards if possible (valence).

 Reflective activity 10.6

Why is pay important to an individual member?

Does pay provide the mirror by which an employee reflects images of power, status, value and succession? The meaning that pay holds is largely deduced from employees' personal characteristics (values), pay level (relative to others) and the level of familiarity the person experiences with the pay system (pay system knowledge). These meanings are expected to influence employee outcomes such as satisfaction, motivation and performance (Thiery, 2001, in Salimaki, Hakonen and Heneman, 2009).

This view is supported by anecdotal evidence of practitioners pointing to exit interview data and proclaiming that lack of money is the reason for demotivated people leaving an organisation. However, more detailed analysis may produce a different picture. People who have decided to leave an organisation may well quote the 'bigger and better' pay packet as the reason for joining a new organisation, but if a different exit interview question is asked – 'What made you start looking for another job to start with?'– then other factors begin to emerge. People become dissatisfied and demotivated with jobs due to poor management, lack of opportunities and boredom. Therefore, HR responding to management requests to match pay offers from competitors in order to retain employees seldom works, especially in the longer term.

Is performance-related pay right for your organisation?

As both performance and motivation are affected by many factors, PRP (or any other intervention) cannot be linked in a causal manner. Williams (1998, p 173) argues that managers' and employees' views need to be considered in order to analyse the effect of PRP on motivation and performance. While the debate around PRP continues, it is worth considering some of the operational difficulties that have been associated with reward practice.

The following set of questions has been raised by Williams (1998, p 176) and adapted to fit the categories provided.

With regard to organisational culture, teams and individual attitudes to PRP:

- Is PRP appropriate to all organisations?
- Is there a climate of trust (particularly in line manager–subordinate relations)?
- What effect does PRP have on team and co-operative building?
- Does a focus on individual performance lead employees to place self-interest ahead of those of the organisation generally?
- Does PRP create divisiveness?
- Does PRP encourage short-termism?

He similarly raises questions about the PM process itself:

- What criteria should be used for measuring performance? Outputs? Inputs? Both?
- Can individual performance be measured objectively and fairly?
- Can performance be defined comprehensively?
- Do line managers have the willingness and ability required to operate PRP?
- How much of performance is within the individual's control?
- How should average performers be treated?

Questions related to the value of rewards also need to be addressed:

- What amount of pay constitutes a significant increase in the eyes of employees?
- Will PRP diminish the value of intrinsic rewards?

It may be relatively simple to provide an answer to each of these individual questions. However, when considered together, the complexity of linking PRP to performance becomes much more evident. Thus simple, prescriptive solutions cannot be found.

So, the question of whether money is a motivator that can lead to improved performance is a very complex one and the answer is by no means clear (Latham, 2007). At best, it can be said that there is a connection between money and satisfaction, which may under certain circumstances increase commitment and perhaps performance. More important is the fact that all employees will be motivated by different factors, as highlighted by the 'content theories'. The effective manager will recognise this and work towards helping employees gain maximum motivation at work, using the principles of expectancy theories and equity theory to make this happen.

If a standard formal appraisal interview occurs with the appraisee, a range of actions or options is available to superiors and subordinates alike. As we have suggested already, there may be a portfolio of approaches that interact within the PM process, such as 360-degree feedback, self-appraisal, upward appraisal, coaching and mentoring interventions.

Companies may operate a system of forced ranking, or forced distribution, whereby groups of employees are compared against each other and ranked from best to worst, instead of being judged against independent performance standards. Although this approach is more common with appraising managers, it can be applied to any area of work. Employees who are placed in the lowest category (eg, the lowest 5 per cent) may be dismissed from the organization or given a fixed time to improve their current performance to the expected organizational standards. Conversely, the top-performing employees may be provided with significant learning opportunities, career growth and perhaps significant financial and personal rewards (Boyle, 2001).

10.7.3 How can performance be improved?

Dependent upon the source(s) of the performance problem, the organisation needs to decide on the type and scope of problem intervention. There may need to be consideration of the macro-level issues affecting the broader organisational context, or attention given to micro-level, individual issues.

Some of the techniques available include:

- learning
- development
- training
- coaching and mentoring
- team-building
- culture change programmes
- reward schemes
- structure, process, systems, job redesign, etc
- management approach.

10.7.4 Strategic reward

According to the CIPD (2021v), strategic reward 'takes a long-term approach to how an organisation's reward policies and practices can balance and support the needs of both the organisation and its employees'. Total reward by contrast 'covers all aspects of work that are valued by people, including elements such as development opportunities being rewarded fairly and flexible working, in addition to the pay and benefits package'.

Perhaps a focus upon the types of offering within strategic reward systems may shine more light on what can be done in using rewards as a means of increasing performance. Thorpe and Holman (2000) discuss a range of interventions including time-based pay, skills and competence-based pay, performance related pay, team-based pay, gainsharing (where groups of employees and managers meet regularly to discuss and review performance and plan how to improve it, leading to enhanced company performance), profit sharing and employee shared ownership, flexible plans for pay and benefits and occupational pension schemes. Each of these offerings has an obvious link to both short, medium and long- term planning and career development for employees, with some of these potentially ruled out because they have too long a time frame in terms of binding arrangements. Alternatively, if an organisation is looking to reap the benefits of an employee's labour over a relatively shorter period of time, many of these offerings could be adapted to a shorter time from if the organisation wishes to be flexible in making its reward packages attractive to the widest range of employees.

The question arises as to the ultimate purpose of having reward schemes – is it to attract suitable employees, to retain them, to get them to perform at a higher level, or something else. The question of fitness for purpose is critical in any strategic reward system. When we consider the HR literature, we may decide that focusing upon employee engagement (see Chapter 8) may be more productive than focusing completely on reward schemes.

 Case study 10.2

Total reward at Arup

Arup is a global design and engineering consultancy. The company employs around 10,500 people in 37 countries, around half of whom are based in the UK. At Arup, which is employee-owned, the reward package includes a global profit-sharing scheme as well as a range of other benefits.

Although the organisation did not formally publish a total reward policy until 2007, Arup has been practising a total reward strategy for much longer and offers online total reward statements to its employees around the world. Tony Hatton-Gore, director, group remuneration and benefits, joined Arup in 2001. At that time, there was an awareness of total reward within the organisation and, soon afterwards, Arup decided to adopt this approach.

There were three key reasons behind the decision to introduce total reward statements:

- total reward statements were seen as an effective way to ensure staff understood the make-up and the value of their employment package

- in line with its values of honest and fair dealings with staff, and in the interests of transparency, Arup wanted people to understand what was available within the organisation as an employee-owned firm

- as an engineering and design consultancy, the organisation wanted to take a holistic 'total design' approach to reward.

Total reward statements

Hatton-Gore explains that although there are some elements of the benefits package – such as the global profit-share scheme and global retirement policy – that are determined centrally, the benefits vary by country, and are based
on the company values in combination with what Arup needs to compete in the local labour markets.

The total reward statements are tailored for each individual employee. They include details of salary, profit-share payments and in some cases more than 20 items to which the employee is entitled. The items included are mainly those on which a value can be placed, and these are totalled to give a monetary value for the overall employment package.

Other benefits, such as holiday allowance or the availability of flu vaccinations, are included on the statement but not given a cash value.

Hatton-Gore notes that some of the benefits listed on the statement are included because the organisation wants to make sure that employees are aware of what is available: for example, the employee assistance programme.

He says: 'We have not attempted to put a monetary value on these things.'

However, while training and development opportunities are viewed as part of the employment package, these are not included on the total reward statement. Hatton-Gore explains that reward in a monetary sense is just one part of what working for the organisation is about; the career and personal development opportunities, and the chance to work on interesting projects, are part of the overall experience rather than another element in the reward list.

Arup's formal total reward policy combines both the monetary and the non-monetary benefits of working for the organisation. The policy was published in a company magazine when it was formally launched in 2007 and is also available to employees via the intranet.

Hatton-Gore says if somebody finds a way to put a value on some of the other, less tangible, elements of the employment package – such as career opportunities – this would be a 'very interesting idea', but says it is a challenge that has not yet been cracked.

1 To what extent can Arup's total reward strategy be truly transparent?
2 How will this reward approach be received across all 37 countries? What happens after PM?

SOURCE: Sharp, R (2009) Total reward at Arup. *IRS Employment Review*. (916), 19 February

10.8 Arguments against the use of performance management

There is increasing evidence that PM can have a positive impact on organisational performance (Armstrong, 2000; Molleman and Timmerman, 2003). However, evidence is not universally positive (Furnham, 2004; Hazard, 2004; Morgan, 2006). Some studies suggest performance appraisal and pay to be the least effective HR policies, as perceived by the employees (Hutchinson and Purcell, 2003). Pulakos (2009) reports that more than two-thirds of employees are dissatisfied with their PM system and believe it has no impact on improving their performance. This mixed picture may exist for multiple reasons: the spectrum of different PM approaches adopted across organisations; the issues of implementation, that is, the *what* may be right, but the *how* is neglected; and the difficulties of proving cause and effect between the use of high-performance work practices (HPWPs) and improved organisational performance (see, eg, Guest, 1997; Koster, 2011). So, PM should not be regarded as a simple 'best practice' solution. Rather than adopting mechanistic, off-the-shelf approaches or processes, organisations need to ensure their PM approach and processes are implemented in a way that suits their context, giving due consideration to organisational culture (Haines and St-Onge, 2012).

10.8.1 Measurement at what cost?

PM is not without potentially significant costs in terms of staff time and administration. Not only are implementation costs to be considered, but also the long-term maintenance costs of any PM system once established. To what extent do organisations consider the total costs of the PM system versus the impacts, both positive and negative, on performance outcomes? An example would be the internal focus of systems within the automotive manufacturing industry, where the needs of customers were ignored to the long-term harm of the organisation. Organisations may assume that a PM system will have a positive impact, but any improvement needs to be offset against the often substantial costs of running the system itself. Campbell and Wiernik (2015) suggest that we try and separate out specifications for performance content and specifications for performance process (the context in which the performance takes place and the manner in which performance develops and changes over time). It is easy to conflate the two and end up with spurious analysis and findings.

10.9 The role of HR and best practice within PM

Research suggests that world-leading companies adopt a more strategic approach to PM as opposed to a tactical one, and this linking of daily operations to strategy translates into increased employee commitment, engagement and performance (Biron, Farndale and Pauuwe, 2011). Therefore, although HR should support line managers in the implementation of PM processes, success is dependent on full involvement of senior managers within the organisation, requiring them to 'walk the talk', so that employees receive clear signals that this is important. Without this, PM can easily become a painful and negative form-filling exercise, with HR reduced to nagging line managers to complete what they see as a timewasting process. Therefore, perhaps the most important role for HR in PM is working with senior management to facilitate commitment so that they can model the required behaviours.

HR also has a key role in designing, communicating and training the PM process and there are interesting ideas emerging about how to improve this: for example, aligning the process to employment engagement strategies (see Gruman and Saks, 2011). In this way, HR managers can demonstrate the 'thinking performer' skills expected of the HR business partner. Another interesting stream of research looks at PM from the employee perspective (see, eg, Buchner, 2007), a valuable route for the increasing number of less hierarchical organisations employing knowledge workers.

Other important contributions that HR can make include: facilitating communication and training for both appraisers and appraisees, as this enables a more inclusive and positive process; communication of company strategy, which will lead to individual objectives; and helping employees see how their own values align with those of the organisation in order to build commitment and engagement.

10.10 Conclusion

The employment relationship continues to change in differing organisational contexts and climates. Performance remains at the centre of organisational strategies and plans, but what is expected of employees in terms of outputs has perhaps heightened. Talent management and developing future leaders remain key issues for organisations and these are undoubtedly (if not sometimes, subtly) linked to PM.

From an HRM and HRD perspective, the emphasis should be on developing people rather than the job itself. However, the challenge for employers may be in retaining employees for the duration of their most productive work (while they add value) and no longer. The choice of a global talent pool remains attractive for some organisations, but the reality for most organisations remains the need to drive down (not simply control) the cost of employment, with many public services in the UK enduring a pay freeze over much of the last the past decade, while manufacturing companies have been preoccupied with competing on cost with the rest of the world.

The HR (and HRD) strategy has to encompass all aspects affecting performance, at contextual, organisational, team and individual level. To do this, it has to be part of the main business strategy, closely aligned to organisational culture and supported by appropriate mechanisms – such as organisational structure, HR policies and procedures – and be strongly aligned to the HRD strategy.

More flexible and fluid arrangements will be necessary, within which there is a greater appreciation of the subjective, tacit, multi-stakeholder aspects of performance. From a more strategic perspective, the resource-based view of HR (Boxall, 1996; Boxall and Purcell, 2003) suggests ways in which organisations can build upon unique clusters or 'bundles' of human and technical resources in order to improve levels of performance and thereby achieve competitive advantage in the marketplace. The agility highlighted by Dyer and Shafer (1999) and adapted by Boxall and Purcell (2003) may provide an insight as to how organisations can use PM within a bundle of HR activities.

The HRD strategy could also be enhanced to incorporate ways in which HRD and HRD professionals can assist in motivating employees (Buchner, 2007), and move away from what is 'being done' to employees and move towards how the employees can grow in their capabilities, skills and competences.

PM may contribute to the success of the firm, but the vital issue is how the talents of employees can be retained, developed and utilised so as to add value to the organisation. Whilst we may concentrate on the output measurement from PM and deal with its consequences, the question to be answered is 'How do we increase performance?' The answer may take us back to developing and nurturing the organisation's greatest asset – employees: a theme we developed in Chapter 7.

 Case study 10.3

John Lewis Partnership

Highly praised and much loved, the John Lewis Partnership (JLP) has more than 80,000 partners in the best-known and arguably most successful example of employee ownership in the UK.

The partners (all permanent employees) co-own 276 Waitrose supermarkets and 36 John Lewis stores, an online and catalogue business, a production unit and even a farm. The workforce is retail-dominated, but also comprises distribution workers, head office staff and specialist buying, IT and finance functions. The workforce is stable, with lower turnover than its competitors and longer service. People who join JLP tend to go on to build careers through the organisation.

Andrew Clark, head of reward, is in no doubt that JLP's success is down to its partners and the competitive advantage they bring. They are, he says, 'what differentiates us from other organisations'. One of Clark's key priorities, however, is to further unlock the competitive advantage of partners to ensure JLP retains its successful position and, although this is an HR issue generally, he is certain that reward has a central role to play.

A key part of the reward strategy is pay and benefits positioning and Clark, along with the partnership council, has thought very carefully about where JLP positions itself in the market and how it rewards good performance through its PRP approach rather than reward basic levels of performance. JLP now pays above national minimum wage across the country regardless of local conditions that may allow them to pay minimum rates. And while there is, says Clark, pressure to be market-leading on recruitment rates, this is not the approach JLP has decided to take.

While some competitors may pay slightly higher starting rates, there is often very minimal pay progression beyond that point, whereas at JLP, through individual performance-driven progression, partners can, over time, achieve earning rates substantially ahead of their starting pay. So, for Clark it is about being competitive on base pay, market-leading on benefits, but being really distinctive on overall earning potential. By way of illustration, he says: 'What we want is to be distinctive on rewarding excellent performers and to allow earning potential without having to be promoted. So, if we've got an excellent furniture saleswoman who is of real value to the business, why shouldn't we be paying her a really great rate? Why should she need to go and be a section manager somewhere else, when actually her skills are best suited to her job and she can really drive her own earning potential?'

Getting these 'nuts and bolts' of pay right, says Clark, is the 'rock of solidity' underpinning the whole employee value proposition. In his view, if partners are paid right, they understand it, and if they think their pay is fair, consistent and equitable, this allows the organisation and partners to move on to discuss other things – from developing the benefits proposition to engagement and high performance.

As well as getting base pay positioned right and pay progression driving individual performance, JLP's total reward package is pretty exceptional.

Although it was lower in 2011, the universal partnership bonus was still 14% of salary (the equivalent of more than seven weeks' pay). There is a vast array of benefits on offer, from store discounts, subsidised holidays and leisure activities to life assurance and a final-salary pension scheme.

Innovative ways of presenting total reward statements – using QR codes so partners can access them via their smartphones, for example – are reaching those partners who may not engage with benefits through traditional media. Ultimately, though, Clark is unequivocal about the bigger picture: 'Customers keep coming back to us because of our partners. That is the key focus for the business, for HR and for reward.'

What JLP is executing in its reward strategy is all about putting the partners at the centre of this hugely successful business.

1 How does the concept of a 'partner' possibly change the employment relationship and attitude towards rewards?

SOURCE: CIPD (2012e) *Reward Management*, Annual survey report, CIPD, London

---

 KEY LEARNING POINTS

1 PM is only a process. The perspective that senior management adopts will impact significantly on how the process is implemented and the consequences of the process followed through.

2 Emphasis needs to be placed upon the employees' expectations throughout the whole PM and appraisal process. These expectations may link to the psychological contract and organisational culture influences.

3 When it comes to setting performance targets, there is a strong requirement to readjust to contextual changes and maintain a realistic perspective, or the targets themselves may negatively impact upon performance.

4 The question of who defines performance is a critical part of the PM process. The relationship between the appraiser and appraisee needs to be clearly defined and professionally maintained.

5 There needs to be a sensitive and pragmatic balance of PM, motivation and reward systems to affect appropriate performance outcomes.

6 Managers (including HR professionals) need to understand not just what motivates employees, but why they are motivated, and consider the strong links between employee engagement (see Chapter 8) and motivation.

Review questions

1 Critically assess the role and contribution that HR makes to the PM process.
2 What motivates you at work, and how would you classify these motivators in terms of content and process theories?
3 To what extent is 360-degree feedback a fad that is unsustainable as a true and workable practice (in relation to manager–employee interactions)?
4 Do you believe that everything surrounding and including PM places too much emphasis upon the individual, at the expense of teams, divisions, organisational cultures, etc?

 Explore further

Buytendijk, F (2008) *Performance Leadership: The next practices to motivate your people, align stakeholders, and lead your industry,* McGraw-Hill Professional, New York. This text provides a broader perspective on PM and is strong on highlighting its pitfalls.

Armstrong, M and Brown, D (2019c) *Armstrong's Handbook of Reward Management Practice: Improving performance through reward,* Kogan Page, London

Cokins, G (2004) *Performance Management: Finding the missing pieces (to close the intelligence gap),* Wiley, New York. This text provides a pragmatic approach to PM and introduces a range of techniques and approaches that HR professionals should find both interesting and useful.

Perkins, SJ and Jones, S (2020) *Reward Management: Alternatives, consequences and context,* 4th edn, CIPD, London. Read the latest edition of the CIPD Annual Reward Survey for insights as to what is changing and what is remaining the same in relation to benefits and reward available and adopted.

Jones, S and White, G (2021) Reward strategy and managing performance. In Rees, G and Smith, PE (2021) *Strategic Human Resource Management: An international perspective,* 3rd edn, Sage, London

11

Organisational design and effective working practices

RAY FRENCH AND EMILY YARROW

LEARNING OUTCOMES

After reading this chapter, you should be able to:

- assess the potential importance of organisational design and job design as part of the process of managing and developing people

- understand models and research findings which aid effective practice in organisational and job design

- recognise the contribution both concepts can make to the development of flexible and committed employees

- point to emerging trends in organisational and job design; for example, post-bureaucratic structures and polarised job realities within the twenty-first century global and post-pandemic workforce

11.1 Overview

In this chapter we examine organisational and work arrangements, in particular the ways in which organisations can be structured and jobs designed. These are core topics in people management. In an important sense they form part of the backdrop of working life and set the context within which workers' contributions are framed. As we will see, organisations and jobs can be designed in very different ways, and anyone involved in these activities can exercise a significant degree of choice. It is important therefore to understand contrasting models of structure and job design in order to make informed choices in these areas.

These topic areas contain insights derived from classical studies; some dating from early in the twentieth century. These, we argue, remain valid and influential so it is important to consider how they affect our understanding of the world of work today. However, thinking continues to evolve and there is a need to consider new and emergent thinking, as well as changes in the global context leading to the 'gig economy' model and increasingly flexible work practices. We address these terms in greater detail later in the chapter. Unanticipated events will also shape practice, as shown for example, by the focus on new working patterns in the post-pandemic workplace (CIPD, 2020a).

In practical terms there is evidence that structural arrangements and the design of jobs will have a strong influence on organisational performance (see also Chapter 10). Mullins (2019) summarises the classical work of Drucker (1989), who argued that a poor structure would diminish an organisation's performance – even where one found good managers. We will identify links between structure, job design and individual performance in this chapter.

The topics examined in this chapter can appear abstract, maybe even 'dry', and less engaging than areas such as talent management and ethical considerations. However, organisational and job design influence peoples lived experiences of work. If two friends, one working in a classical bureaucracy, the other in an 'creative cluster' (we will define these terms in more detail), compare their everyday experiences of work they will find that their working lives are indeed very different. Organisational and job design are core principles underlying strategies of people management, so they are of interest to existing and future HR managers as well. The links between organisational design, job design and flexibility will be further drawn out in this chapter, and it will be helpful for you to reflect on your own experiences of work as you consider the topics set out here in order to bring them to life.

11.2 Introduction

Effective working is underpinned by the infrastructure of work, including the ways in which organisations are set up and jobs designed. French et al (2015) put forward the concept of a 'performance equation'. This model states that in order to perform well workers must firstly have the requisite attributes (skills and abilities). High performance is, secondly, conditional on people wanting to excel (levels of motivation). However, workers' performance is also affected by a third dimension, namely the organisational support provided for them. It is this third dimension that we will focus on at this point.

In this chapter we deal with the backdrop to effective working on an 'everyday' workplace level. There are, however, wider moral, legal and ethical elements of the employment relationship – see Chapters 5 and 9. We should recognise that work is experienced very differently in different settings, particularly when we consider employment law and worker rights around the world. (Deloitte, 2022).

Much of the literature on job design posits a link between the ways in which people's jobs are designed and their productivity, attitudes and behaviour. These attitudes and behaviour will, in turn, have an impact on their motivation and engagement (CIPD, 2021q) – see also Chapters 8 and 10. Particular assumptions concerning worker motivation underpin work design models. So, for example, an approach which advocate breaking down work tasks into simple repetitive units, assumes that workers primarily seek ways of maximising their income rather than prioritise meaningful work. In contrast, an attempt to create more autonomy in people's working lives - seen for example in some professional roles – would only be successful if we believe that people would respond positively to this relative freedom at work.

At the time of writing there is significant debate around what the future of work and, in turn, organisational and job design may look like and how this will shape employees' lived experience, CIPD (2020e). Contemporary work in organisation and job design has frequently examined the notion of *flexible working* – highlighted as an important theme within people management in the twenty-first century. In 2013, Gilmore noted that flexibility as a theme had permeated discussion about employment in general terms, and labour utilisation more specifically. The emerging concept of post-bureaucratic organisation is also underpinned by the idea of flexibility. The same author also noted that flexibility is associated with interesting tensions arising in the employment relationship, something that in the contemporary post-Covid-19 context often underpins debates and writing around the future of work and the employment relationship. These are not neutral or anodyne concepts. The 2020 Covid pandemic led to rapid consideration of the options that may or may not be available around hybrid and or remote working and flexible working practices and these concepts rapidly became part of everyday vocabulary.

11.3 Key terms

11.3.1 *Organisational design*

Organisational design (OD) is defined as a planned activity in which designers, usually managers, maybe in conjunction with specialised consultants, attempt to adjust the formal shape of their organisation. There are many types of organisations and consequently many choices in organisational design. OD is defined by French et al (2015, p 189) as 'the process of choosing and implementing a structural configuration for an organisation'. We see therefore that organisational design and structure are not synonymous but in a fundamental sense are linked concepts. OD creates organisational structure, defined as the intended pattern of tasks, responsibilities, lines of authority and networks of communication in an organisation.

It can be seen from this categorisation of structure that we are in essence dealing with formalised features of organisations. The classic way to depict an organisation's structure is by viewing it as a chart or other diagram, in effect taking an impersonal view of what *should* happen in that organisation. The term 'informal organisation', contrastingly, denotes what *actually happens* in a workplace, which can deviate from what should occur within formal arrangements – for example, if people habitually ignore a bureaucratic rule or procedure.

'Organisation structure' as a term has several different sub-components within this overarching definition. These are set out below:

Formalisation

Formalisation refers to the extent to which an organisation stipulates the way work or particular roles comprising a job should be carried out. One guide to ascertain the degree of formalisation is the existence of procedural manuals or job descriptions pre-ordaining working styles and practices.

Specialisation

This aspect of structure refers both to the extent to which work roles involve a range of specialist activities and to the ways in which workers with similar or related roles and tasks are grouped together. Many organisations have historically operated in a highly specialised manner, typically by setting up discrete, functionally based departments, for example finance, logistics and distribution or, indeed, HR.

Vertical differentiation

This sub-set of structure links to power and authority. An organisation could specify many levels within a hierarchy, each with distinct reporting responsibilities, or it might be designed as a relatively 'flat' organisation, with few hierarchical levels. The concept of span of control in which the ratio of workers reporting to managers is prescribed is also relevant here.

Centralisation

This deals with decision-making, in particular whether responsibility in this regard rests with senior managers, rather than it being cascaded throughout the organisation. Closely associated with this central idea is the degree to which tight control is exercised by a head office or whether, contrastingly, greater autonomy is granted to operating units or divisions.

In the twenty-first century, outsourcing, franchising arrangements and self-employment models, have given an added dimension to this category, whereby workers may be 'remote' from the central organisation, although subject to prescribed standards and regulations. Russon (2021) outlines complexities affecting the Uber organisation in this regard – see also our discussion of the 'gig economy' later in this chapter.

Line and/or staff functions

In this element of structure there is a distinction between line functions, which are intimately connected with the primary purpose of the organisation, and contrasting (although complementary) staff functions, which supplement and further the aims of the organisation through the provision of ancillary services.

We have looked at the implications of this distinction for HR in Chapter 2. The relationship between line and staff (and their relative importance) raises issues of horizontal (as opposed to vertical) co-ordination and control. Later in this chapter we will examine the ways in which organisational design – and hence structure – can be utilised in a positive way within the overall project of managing and developing people.

 Reflective activity 11.1

Look again at the elements of organisational structure listed above. How formal, centralised and vertically differentiated do you imagine the following types of organisation should be? Give reasons for your responses.

- the British Royal Navy
- an animal welfare charity
- a web-design and social media agency.

11.3.2 Job design

Job design as defined by French et al (2015, p 244) is 'the planning and specification of job tasks and the work setting designated for their accomplishment'. The authors conclude that much contemporary writing on the subject views the objective of job design as facilitating meaningful, interesting and challenging jobs, with managers charged with responsibility to design jobs that will motivate an individual employee. This finding underpins much academic research in this area, which often posits a link between aspects of jobs and employees' psychological well-being.

We will examine several examples of work within this tradition in this chapter. However, job design, as we will see, does not presuppose the design of enriched jobs – it can also lead to the splitting of tasks into routine, repetitive and unskilled work.

There is a distinction between the terms 'job design' and 'work design'. The former refers to task patterns that could occur in any part of a work organisation, while 'work design' is underpinned by more broadly defined principles which could reflect that organisation's culture and structure (see also Chapter 3). This refining of terminology is useful in that it highlights the role of managerial choice in devising principles for organising work. Thus, job design, and beyond this, work design, can form part of a more strategic approach to managing people. Watson (2006) makes the distinction in this context between *direct* and *indirect* control principles. In the former case, there is a stress on prescribed task procedures with only a minimal level of commitment required from employees. In contrast, indirect control principles emphasise far greater discretion for employees in the way they perform tasks; this is in turn dependent on their higher levels of commitment, leading to mutual trust between members of the organisation in question.

It would be true to say that for much of its history job design, and the broader concept of work design, has been associated with principles of direct control. In reading earlier work on this subject, one finds particular resonance of these ideas in the work of Frederick Taylor (1911) and his model of Scientific Management, often subsequently referred to as 'Taylorism'. Taylor's work, together with principles associated with Henry Ford, tells us that jobs can be designed on a rational basis in order to maximise workers' efforts. The results of such an approach will be to quicken production, radically reduce costs and very significantly increase output. It can be argued that mass production and consumption patterns have been predicated on these principles, particularly when we consider 'McDonaldisation' (Ritzer, 1993), which refers to the rationalisation of production, consumption and work in the globalised context, where many organisations have adopted homogenised ways of working to maximise efficiency and profits. Ritzer asserted that there are four main components to 'McDonaldisation':

- *Efficiency*. This is achieved by gaining the maximum return from lower inputs. In a McDonalds restaurant staff do not serve at tables; rather the self-service model transfers cost to the customer.
- *Calculability*. Choice of 'product' is reduced, thereby ensuring low assembly costs.
- Predictability. A product or service would use standardised procedures so the customer 'knows what they are getting' in advance (although McDonald's menus do vary according to local setting, food and drink is cooked via set procedures).
- *Control*. This aspect seeks to minimise variability, in part through mechanisation and also by giving workers set procedures.

At the turn of the millennium several commentators promoted the case for Ford as one of the key influential figures of the twentieth century, in part because of his impact on social trends due to the production of affordable cars, but also because many millions of people worked in jobs that bore the stamp of his (and Taylor's) vision. The McDonaldisation thesis is interesting in that it points to the continuing prevalence of the model. Clegg, Pitsis and Mount (2022) suggest that McDonaldisation has in fact spread beyond the workplace into areas as diverse as dating.

Leach and Wall (2004) are among writers who located different views of job design over time, making the distinction between *traditional job design*, which emphasises the design of jobs in order to minimise skill requirements and training times, with more contemporary *job redesign*, which, contrastingly, recommends increasing the number of tasks carried out by an individual worker through job rotation and 'enlarging' and/or 'enriching' individual jobs. However, Huws (2013) claims that in Western societies the notion that work could and should involve some form of meaningful activity – prevalent since 1945 – had largely ended by the early twenty-first century due to a preponderance of routine process-driven or mechanised jobs. Whichever analysis – or combination of the two contrasting views – are correct, it is clearly important to take a historical developmental perspective.

Organisational design and job design are, in summary, broad concepts and we go on to explore them in greater detail later in this chapter.

11.3.3 Flexibility

We have referred to this concept on several occasions already in this book and here examine it in greater detail and depth. This broad term refers to several discrete areas of business operations. It can be applied firstly to flexible forms of organisational structure – implying a move away from a rigid bureaucratic form to one that can respond more speedily to demands emanating from its environment (Daft, Murphy and Willmott, 2016). At the same time, it refers to attempts to enrich workers' jobs through multiskilling, greater autonomy and responsibility with the general aim of fostering both better performance and greater commitment to the employing organisation. We will primarily examine the notion of flexibility with reference to these twin themes.

The term 'flexibility' is also, however, used in the area of employment itself, resulting in greater prevalence of such arrangements as part-time and fixed term working, casual employment, outsourcing and teleworking. For some commentators, such as Bratton and Gold (2017), increasing flexibility of employment has led to heightened distinctions between a core and peripheral workforce.

The field of human resources (HR) has itself been amenable to outsourcing, whereby employers choose to outsource parts of their employee resourcing activities, such as recruitment advertising and candidate sourcing and screening. Some of the more oft-cited reasons given for outsourcing include: increasing efficiency; reducing costs; freeing up HR managers to concentrate on more strategic activities; and increasing resourcing flexibility to meet peaks and troughs of demand. CIPD (2021w)

One can see that there are powerful reasons for outsourcing work beyond individual organisations. However, some of the same reasons given for outsourcing, particularly increasing efficiency and reducing costs, can equally be seen as a justification for keeping activities in-house. There are no right answers and individual circumstances intervene; for example, a particular relationship with an external provider might make it advantageous to outsource, but it is also important to think of the medium and longer-term impacts on employee engagement, equality, diversity and inclusion, as well as potential regional socio-economic effects, for example if an organisation is the biggest employer in an area, what might be the effects on that community and its people?

It is also very important to ensure that workers' knowledge and skills are deployed in ways that add value to the firm, and this will be discussed in further depth later in the chapter. For example, a recent CIPD report (CIPD, 2020e) found, drawing on a sample of 1,000 employers during the Covid-19 pandemic, that 'Some 19% of employers said they had cut the normal working week and another 11% said they planned to do so. A rather smaller share said they had increased hours (11%) or were planning to increase hours (9%)' (p 5) providing an example of how external forces also influence flexibility on the part of the employer, but which may have undesirable effects for employees for example where hours are reduced. Increasingly such 'flexibility' is built into contracts of employment, for example in zero-hour contracts whereby the employer is not obliged to guarantee any working hours, but rather can adjust them as and when the business requires, as well as fixed term contracts which end after a specified time frame. Flexibility is not only important because it is topical. It also offers scope to allow people to work when they like (time) where they like (location) and enables workers to engage with work in different ways, for example as permanent employees, agency workers or self-employed homeworkers. It has the potential to revolutionise the working lives of many people worldwide. However, we must also consider the potential ethical issues of such working, and the ways in which employers may exploit such flexibility to keep labour costs down for example.

Flexibility has been frequently identified as a key HR policy goal, along with strategic intention, quality and employee commitment, in order to ensure an adaptable organisation structure (Guest, 2004). These HR goals are in turn held to generate a range of positive organisational outcomes, such as high job performance, high quality problem solving, successful change, lower turnover, absenteeism and grievance levels and high cost-effectiveness' (CIPD, 2022h).

On the one hand employers, encouraged by governments and non-governmental bodies, such as the International Monetary Fund and the World Bank, press the case for workforce flexibility in the hunt for efficiency, and on the other hand it is claimed that individual employees look for flexibility in working hours as they attempt to juggle the demands of home and work lives. It seems that the two agendas might meet in a unitary, though stressful, work–life balance where employers' flexibility requirements can coincide well with the wants and needs of a great many employees, albeit increasingly there are many tensions, particularly surrounding workers' rights and employment law.

When the concept of flexibility emerged, four main types of flexibility were identified (Blyton and Morris, 1992):

1 Task or functional flexibility, where employees may be multiskilled.
2 Numerical flexibility, using different types of employment contracts and subcontracting concept.
3 Temporal flexibility, where the number and pattern of hours worked varies, for example zero hours, and annual hours.
4 Wage flexibility, where wages are individualised, and may be performance related.

This can provide us with an understanding of what the parameters of flexibility mean, though more contemporaneously we also need to consider that work may be allocated by algorithms, gig work and zero hours contractors may not be the choice of the worker themselves, and that there are deeply imbued equality and diversity issues in the various modes of working. The gig economy, which is now also an increasingly commonly used term in the media, and which includes various interpretations and definitions, is defined by the Department for Business, Energy and Industrial Strategy (BEIS) as:

> *The gig economy involves the exchange of labour for money between individuals or companies via digital platforms that actively facilitate matching between providers and customers, on a short-term and payment by task basis.* (BEIS, 2018)

Commonly, we think about delivery services including food, individual task solution services, task work and taxi services, though there are an increasingly widening range of the types of work that are conducted in the gig economy across the globe, with varying levels of algorithmic control over workers.

Case Study 11.1

Gig economy workers to get employee rights under EU proposals

Currently, at the time of writing, many gig workers both in the UK and many other parts of the world have limited, if any, employee rights, yet gig work is becoming an increasingly popular mode of working, with McKinsey, the global consulting house, estimating in 2016 that 'up to 162 million people in Europe and the United States—or 20 to 30 per cent of the working-age population' engage in some form of independent work or the gig economy (McKinsey, 2016).

Rankin (2021), discussing current debates about gig workers' rights in the EU, makes the extent of the issues clear: 'Companies that did not allow people to work for other firms, or had rules about appearance and how to carry out tasks, could be classed as employers, under the proposals, under criteria used to determine employment status. The new rules would not apply to genuinely independent contractors… In the EU's 27 member states, about 5.5 million workers are misclassified as self-employed, when they should be treated as employees with benefits and protection, such as accident insurance, according to the commission. Firms would only have to pay minimum wages, where they already exist. About 28 million people work for platforms in the EU, but this is expected to reach 43 million by 2025' (Rankin, 2021).

However, these regulations if passed, may not apply in the UK, due to Brexit (Britain's Exit from the UK), potentially leaving UK gig workers open to the ongoing employment issues. With regard

to the EU context, Rankin further explains: 'Under the directive, workers would also gain rights over algorithms, to stop situations where people are denied jobs, working hours or even fired as a result of machines' decisions. Instead, workers would have the right to receive explanations for and contest automated decisions, while companies would have to ensure access to a human contact for anything that would have a significant impact on the person.'

Given the rise of the gig economy, particularly during the Covid-19 pandemic when, for example, food delivery and other delivery services boomed, as well as the growth in overall numbers of people working in this way, such ways of working, via platforms under algorithmic control are becoming increasingly common, and as such greater legal protection for workers is required.

1. What are your thoughts on the lack of legal protection for gig or platform workers?
2. Have you worked within the gig economy or a digital platform? If so, how did this differ from other kinds of work?
3. How might knowing that if you are sick and unable to work, but knowing you have no legal protection as an employee make you feel?
4. Were your feelings towards flexible working positive or negative – or a mix of the two – and why?
5. Are there elements of job design that could ensure workers are better protected?

Having defined the key terms used in this chapter as well as having explored flexible working and gig work, we now turn to look more closely at the topic of organisational structure, which is an essential component of organisational design.

11.4 Models of structure

Bureaucracy has been a highly influential and long-lasting form of organisation structure: some writers see examples of it as far back as ancient Greek and Roman civilisations. In modern times, its key features were articulated by the sociologist Max Weber, who constructed an ideal type of bureaucracy, that is, what it would look like in an extreme or idealised form.

11.4.1 Weber's model of pure bureaucracy

- Tasks are allocated according to certified expertise, with resultant specialised (eg departmental) structure.
- Jobs are defined through clear and often simplified routine tasks.
- Control is exercised through a hierarchical structure, typically with many layers denoting levels of authority.
- Rules and procedures are clearly set out in the form of written documentation.
- There are pre-set formal systems of communication via specified channels with hierarchical authority paramount.
- Employees are appointed and, where appropriate, promoted on the basis of clear criteria often relating to their qualifications.
- Managers are salaried officials and do not have a financial stake in the organisation.
- Rules are set and all decisions made rationally in an attempt to eliminate non-rational elements such as emotional involvement or personal preference.

In the late nineteenth century Weber claimed that organisations (in Europe) came to lay particular stress on rational decision-making. It was claimed that this distinguished them from the ways in which previous communities' workplaces operated more on the basis of traditional authority.

The concept of bureaucracy has come under sustained criticism, and we will examine some of its documented disadvantages here. Indeed, the word 'bureaucratic' used in a non-technical sense has come to have an inherently negative connotation. This form of organisation has however had lasting relevance. In 2000 Paul Du Gay reiterated some powerful reasons for its enduring appeal:

- In a bureaucracy people know exactly what to do and how to do it.
- Career progression should be based on job performance.
- Everyone should follow the rules with nobody 'above the law.

One can summarise this line of reasoning by stating that bureaucratic structures hold the potential to be *predictable*, *stable* and *fair*, though nepotism, inequality, and exclusion remain in many organisations today.

It is very important to recognise that attempts to enhance performance through the application of design principles can founder through the law of unintended consequences. Watson (2012), for example, highlighted what are termed 'dysfunctions' of bureaucracy. Bureaucratic structures are intended to foster efficient working through stability, predictability and fair treatment (both of employees and clients or customers). Bureaucracy is thus essentially conceived as a rational system of organisation. The notion of a 'dysfunction' however, states that the very features which are supposed to *aid* efficiency can lead in reality to negative behaviours which hinder performance. For example, employees may always strictly adhere to rules resulting in defensive or even 'jobsworth' style behaviour. In a bureaucracy there are also typically rigid - and sometimes slow although fair - promotion procedures. If workers see limited scope for advancement they can revert to merely moderate or 'get-by' performance as a consequence.

11.4.2 Alternatives to bureaucracy: adapting to 'contingencies'

From the 1950s onwards, a wave of critical comment emerged centring on a perceived inability of bureaucratic structures to cope well in the face of changing circumstances. The underlying idea that organisation structures are influenced by 'external' factors, to which they must be adapted to ensure high performance, is commonly referred to as the contingency approach. Before examining the factors that have been identified as relevant situational events or contingencies, it is timely to look at some alternative structures which are either extensions of bureaucracy or radical alternatives to it.

Organic structure and 'adhocracy'

The organic model was originally put forward, in a classical and still relevant research finding, by Burns and Stalker (1961) as a viable alternative to the classic bureaucratic structure in certain contexts. As we shall see in the following section examining the impact of contingent factors on organisational form, Burns and Stalker found that this type of structure, or rather its component features, would be effective when organisations operated in a turbulent environment of rapidly changing technology, fierce competition and uncertain customer demand. The main features of the organic model of structure were:

- network (as opposed to hierarchical) structures of control and communication
- knowledge spread throughout the organisation (rather than located at the top)
- employee commitment to their tasks (compared with loyalty to the organisation)
- knowledge, skills and experience applied to diverse tasks (compared with long-term specialisation)

- communication flowing up, down and across the organisation rather than being essentially top-down.

Burns and Stalker's organic structure is overall characterised by informality and flexibility. Originally applied to the fast-changing microelectronics sector of the 1960s, it has increasingly been advocated in other areas of the private and public sectors because their environments are perceived as more turbulent as a result of economic, political and technological change.

The adhocracy shares important features of the organic form. However, it may go further in that it can be defined as an organisational type that is not planned in the first instance, rather it develops spontaneously or in an *ad hoc* manner, hence the name (Clegg, Pitsis and Mount, 2022).

Boundaryless organisations

We noted that the organic model identified by Burns and Stalker in 1961 represented a notable break from previous thinking in the area of organisational design both in terms of their stress on appropriate response to context and their advocacy of flexible structures. These insights continue to resonate at the time of writing. Bratton (2015) identifies four boundaries which organisations view as means of securing competitive advantage:

- vertical boundaries, which demarcate people in terms of seniority including through rank, status and title
- horizontal boundaries by which people are located by functional department or product group
- external boundaries separating the core organisation from its suppliers, customers, and other communities
- geographical boundaries, including the preceding three boundaries but, in addition, applied across time, countries and cultures.

Bratton proposes that the boundaryless organisation model has accelerated in influence since the mid-1990s and is associated with the spread of a neo-liberal business model and, in particular, the phenomenon of globalisation. For our purposes, the boundaryless organisation model points to a less hierarchical structure, with a need to share information and learn from 'followers'. It also implies effective working is dependent on sharing of risk and cost, so promoting the idea of outsourcing.

Virtual network structure

In defining types of structure above, it became evident that organisations may not simply structure their operations so that they are bounded within a single entity. Rather, as we saw in the case of divisional structure, individuals might operate separately from headquarters in important respects. Virtual network structures take this principle further with organisations 'farming out' activities to other companies. They link to the concept of the boundaryless organisation considered in the preceding section.

As we saw when considering the boundaryless model, this phenomenon is often referred to as outsourcing. Whole areas of activity can be outsourced to another organisation, including accounting, marketing, design and, interestingly for our purposes, HRM.

Virtual network structures may involve the 'hub' organisation imposing its own patterns of structure on its partners or, contrastingly, might enable partner organisations to devise their own structure and indeed ways of designing workers' jobs.

Key relationships in the network structure are those running *across* organisations and managing such relationships effectively becomes paramount. Relationships can be contractual in nature, with deterrents put in place to avoid betrayal and other negative behaviour, or might be based on trust-based links, underpinned by knowledge of the partner organisation. In some cases, the relationship can come to be based on goodwill and mutual obligation – akin to a successful personal relationship, albeit this can be exploited by an organisation.

Clegg, Pitsis and Mount (2022) put forward the notion of a *creative cluster* which they conceptualise as a new way of thinking about the linkages between organisations, rather than a form of organisation *per se*. In such a cluster there is a greater likelihood of planned or even random encounters that can spark innovation and creativity. This calls to mind explanations for the success and dominance of London as a political, media, cultural and financial centre, in contrast to other countries where these sectors are more spread out.

Please note that there are many models of structure included adapted rather than true bureaucracies. Please refer to our website (koganpage.com/spmad.) where we describe the important matrix, divisional and project team structures.

11.4.3 Contingent factors

As suggested earlier, the essence of the contingency approach is that particular types of structure should be designed in the light of the contingent factors affecting or potentially affecting the organisation in question. Although contingencies are by definition framed by and as unique circumstances, an organisation's 'environment' has been put forward as an overarching factor (Johns, 2006).

Organisational environments

As we have already noted, Burns and Stalker (1961) proposed their dichotomy of mechanistic and organic structures. The mechanistic category is very similar to Weber's model of bureaucracy, while the diametrically opposite organic form is flexible, is network-based and requires commitment – in addition to compliance and loyalty – from employees within this structure. The key contingent variable for Burns and Stalker was the particular environment facing the organisation. The more turbulent the environment, in terms of technological advance, competition and customer or client demand, the more organic the organisation should be, if it were to prosper and even survive in such a challenging milieu.

By 2020, there was a prevailing view that a very high proportion of organisations operated in turbulent environments with neo-liberal economic precepts and spread of globalisation creating an environment in which there was a relentless and accelerating drive for change. Grey (2021), Clegg, Pitsis and Mount (2022). This reinforced the general conclusion of contingency theory; namely that optimal structures depend upon the external context faced by organisations. Furthermore, the prevalence of turbulent environments pointed to a further push towards post-bureaucracy in many, although not all, organisations.

Please refer to our website (koganpage.com/spmad) for an overview of two other important contingent factors; namely an organisation's size and prevailing technology.

In conclusion, organisational design offers a degree of choice to decision-makers who should consider the contingent factors faced by their organisations before deciding on structural arrangements. Nonetheless, such choices are themselves constrained if we conclude that different structures tend to be more effective in particular circumstances, depending on factors such as size, technology and environment.

One should though be wary of assuming that organisations can only respond to contingent factors in a highly constrained way. There is a danger of interpreting the contingency model, which was conceived as a flexible idea, very much an antidote to the 'one best way' approaches of the 1950s, in an over-deterministic way. Child (1972) introduced the important idea of strategic choice, whereby managers or other senior figures within organisations make informed decisions about the conditions in which they chose to operate.

Child proposed that, in reality, large organisations could, and often do select and manipulate their environments. Daft, Murphy and Willmott (2010) use the example of the retailer Wal-Mart to illustrate this point, concluding that Wal-Mart had successfully lobbied the World Trade Organisation and UK and Chinese governments for a reversal of policies on large store openings. This enabled them to maintain their global structure, whereas if they had simply adapted to their environment, they might have merely complied with government diktat or conceivably not operated in those countries at all, but by active lobbying they influenced policies to their advantage. It is here where we must also consider and indeed critique the lobbying powers of profit-making organisations, particularly when the economic power of multinational corporations is deliberated. Large organisations are not only powerful economic actors that actively lobby government, but they are often afforded in turn, political influence to meet their own interests which is deeply problematic. An excerpt from a 2014 *Guardian* article succinctly frames this ongoing issue:

> Lobbyists operate in the shadows – deliberately. As one lobbyist notes: 'The influence of lobbyists increases when it goes largely unnoticed by the public.' But if the reasons why companies lobby are often obscured, it is always a tactical investment. Whether facing down a threat to profits from a corporate tax hike, or pushing for market opportunities – such as government privatisations – lobbying has become another way of making money. (Cave and Rowell, 2014)

Notwithstanding the validity of Child's work, the contingency view of organisational design remains dominant in management thinking and it contains many valid insights and can also be mobilised when thinking about business ethics, equality and diversity, and the role of businesses in society.

Case study 11.2

Taming a life-threatening illness

This is a story of a patient admitted to a UK hospital for transplant surgery. The operation was deemed lifesaving, so the oft-repeated cliché of work not being a matter of life and death did not apply. The ten-hour procedure was successful, and the patient embarked on a lengthy recovery, which began with being confined to his hospital bed. As one can imagine, this rest period afforded an opportunity for deep reflection on a range of topics.

Our patient was a Professor of Sociology, and his reflections came to encompass both his professional training and his deeply personal concerns. So, he began to ponder on how the human and social endeavour involved in saving his life had come to be. He could see: 'social acts of great learned skill and scientific knowledge, myriad social acts of humane and loving care, multiple social acts of practical activity – cleaning the floors, pushing trolleys with patients, providing food, keeping the plumbing going, welcoming the outpatients, organising beds, orchestrating a million little daily routines'.

1 In the course of its daily work, the hospital relied on so many roles: nurses, doctors, porters, ambulance drivers, social workers, phlebotomists, physiotherapists, transplant coordinators, administrators and ward managers. There are of course many more. Thousands of workers were organised through structure and job design in a massive division of labour in order to save people's lives. Hospitals are often categorised as bureaucratic organisations. What are the advantages of such a structure in a hospital setting?

2 Identify the contingent factors that impact on a hospital and show how they influence hospital structure. Could one ever envisage a non-bureaucratic hospital? Give reasons for your answer.

SOURCE: Plummer, K (2010) *Sociology: The basics*, Routledge, Abingdon

11.5 Approaches to job design

As we have seen, when job design emerged as a concept, early principles emphasised job simplification (Taylor, 1911), interpreted critically by some writers as deskilling, while more recent contributions to the subject area have typically recommended expanding jobs in order both to increase employee job satisfaction, or at least to reduce boredom, and to engender greater flexibility in a workforce (Hackman and Oldham, 1980). It is often proposed that such flexibility is desirable in view of changes in the wider business environment, and increasingly with worker wellbeing, employee engagement and equality, diversity and inclusion. In the UK context, it has been suggested that the country's fundamental economic structures have altered with significant growth in services built around knowledge, with a parallel reduction in sectors based on mass industrial production and 'raw muscle power' Hutton (2004). In this scenario work is becoming more 'intelligent', with a new workforce seeking greater autonomy and control.

One should be wary of assuming that there is, or will shortly be, a proliferation of 'intelligent' work. On the contrary, the emergence of increasing numbers of workplaces such as fast-food outlets, call centres and the rise of the gig economy have mainly been associated with standardised repetitive 'Taylorist'-style jobs. Beyond such work with its associated routine tasks, one also finds what Clegg, Pitsis and Mount (2022) refer to as 'grunge jobs' comprising both work carried out in the lower reaches of the supply chain supporting global business, and that performed by an underclass of marginalised workers operating in very poor conditions, as well as people working outside the formally recognised and regulated job market.

Nonetheless, there is also evidence that increasingly many workers will be required to act as thinking performers and this segment of the workforce will form the main focus in this chapter. In such an environment it is posited that organisations seeking distinctive high performance should be involved in job design which contributes towards a positive psychological contract between employer and worker. This, it is suggested, can also aid and reinforce successful organisational performance, as well as employee engagement. We have discussed this subject area in more detail in Chapter 8.

It is also necessary for all organisations to engage in job design as an 'infrastructure' task, to ensure that work is allocated into suitably sized role descriptions capable of being carried out effectively. At the same time, it is essential to ensure suitable demarcation of roles both vertically (in terms of skill, knowledge and hierarchical level) as well as horizontally (in functional terms). This aspect of basic job design is a prerequisite for minimal threshold standards of performance by organisations and is needed to avoid fundamental problems relating to the nature of work and roles.

 Reflective activity 11.2

Read the statement below which appeared recently on a well-known supermarket's corporate website and answer the question that follows.

Making our company a great place to work

We know that our people want four things from us:

- to be treated with respect
- a manager who helps me
- an interesting job
- an opportunity to get on.

This set of objectives is typical of those espoused by organisations in the retail sector (a major source of UK employment). They put forward a progressive vision of people management, incorporating recognition, support, opportunities for progression and also interesting work.

It might be thought, however, that the aim of securing interesting jobs in the supermarket context is the most challenging of the four aims set out above. In another section of the same website, we hear from a customer assistant who says: '… to be honest, I got a job [here] because I needed some money, but working here has been far more enjoyable and rewarding than I could ever have thought it could be.'

At the start of your study of this topic and without referring to material set out later in this chapter, suggest ways that supermarket managers could provide interesting jobs for store workers.

Answer from your knowledge of large supermarkets, as a shopper if you have no personal experience of shop work.

It is possible to locate key developments in the approach to job design, although while these have been developed in particular epochs, each can still be applied to current work situations. It is now time to look at these approaches in more detail. Increasingly, in the post Covid-19 era where more people are working from home, remotely, or more flexibly, there will be implications both for job design, as well as in employee demand. When we consider home working, remote working or more flexible forms of working, we must also consider the equality, diversity and inclusion implications, both for employees and organisational recruitment and retention strategies.

11.5.1 Scientific management

As indicated earlier, for its most famous proponent, Frederick Taylor, scientific management involved organising tasks into highly specialised jobs. Managers should take on responsibility for planning, co-ordinating and monitoring work, with the task worker restricted to the level of operative. Recruitment and training are simplified, and workers are grouped together in large units such as factories or, more recently, call centres, enabling a high volume of chiefly standardised goods or service provision. One example is the Fordist production line system, which, in addition to demarcating jobs, also controlled the speed of work. It is difficult to over-emphasise the significance of this model of job design on the world of work, even though the model is increasingly critiqued and not appropriate in many settings, particularly in contexts where worker autonomy and creativity are important. However, Henry Ford, in laying the conditions for mass production of cars, was able to reduce costs very substantially, which in turn led to greatly increased levels of car ownership in the USA.

Scientific management as a driver for job design has attracted much controversy and a good deal of criticism for the following reasons:

- it can lead to product inflexibility
- it has been criticised as dehumanising and for failing to recognise 'higher order' human needs such as self-actualisation
- it may foster compliance and an instrumental view of work as a means to an end, as opposed to engendering commitment and loyalty and in turn, also inclusion.
- monotony and boredom can result in reduced performance outcomes.
- Implications for worker wellbeing and ongoing training and development needs.

 Reflective activity 11.3

Scientific management is perceived by some commentators as a particular direct form of control of work and workers by management. Braverman (1974) is prominent among writers who go on to assert that this concept of job design is fundamentally associated with an attempt to deskill workers. The notion of deskilling derives from the work of Marx – see McLellan (2000) in which owners and managers seek to maximise surplus value from workers, in essence exploiting them. Managers as a group are, in the nature of their role, concerned to control and regularise jobs and work. Nonetheless, not all jobs have been subject to this version of job and work design and the ability of particular groups of workers to retain or even enhance skill levels remains an important factor in job design. How valid do you find the deskilling thesis, both as a theory and explanation of reality in work organisations?

11.5.2 Job redesign

Job redesign emerged in part as a reaction to the perceived negative effects of scientific management. Its academic roots lie in the so-called 'human relations' school, which emphasised people's social needs which, it was claimed, could and should be met in the workplace. Herzberg's two-factor theory of motivation, dating from the 1950s proposed that pure motivation derived from the content of work as opposed to hygiene factors such as pay, physical working conditions and quality of supervision. Hygiene factors, for Herzberg, were sources of dissatisfaction which could be lessened if, for example, pay was improved, though we know from recent research that a number of factors influence satisfaction or dissatisfaction, both from within and outwith the organisation. As an example, Bae (2021), drawing on a longitudinal data set from the public sector found that: 'that individual-based pay for performance has a significantly positive relationship with organizational and job satisfaction, but group-based pay for performance has a significantly negative relationship with pay satisfaction. Meanwhile, the results show that the perceived fairness of performance evaluations has significantly positive relationships with pay satisfaction, organizational satisfaction, and job satisfaction' (Bae, 2021, p 1). Given our earlier discussion of the role of the wider context on organisational behaviour, it is important to situate performance and satisfaction in the broader context.

However, workers would only be truly motivated if their job or work met their needs for recognition, autonomy and achievement. Herzberg's view was that virtually all human beings would respond to work which was rich in motivating factors, if they had the ability to do the job and the opportunity to carry out meaningful work. We will, however, question this near-universal perspective later in this chapter.

In a highly significant contribution to this topic area, Hackman and Oldham (1980) proposed, on the basis of research, that five key characteristics could be used to identify the extent to which a job would, in reality, be motivating:

- skill variety – if different and diverse activities demanded the exercise of a range of skills and abilities
- task identity – the extent to which a job involves a whole and identifiable piece of work with a tangible end result
- task significance – the perceived value and effect of a job on other people
- autonomy – where a worker is free to schedule the pace of his or her work, have some choice in how the work is carried out and is relatively independent of supervision

- feedback – the degree to which a worker gets information about the effectiveness of their performance. This feedback could be gained through observation of their work outcomes.

It is argued that each key characteristic is linked to a positive psychological state which, in turn, leads to desirable work outcomes. For example, task significance could result in a feeling of satisfaction in the meaningfulness of work undertaken, with positive outcomes of work motivation and effectiveness following on from this psychological state. In summary, Hackman and Oldham (1980) stated that intrinsic motivation is dependent on individuals experiencing three critical psychological states: experienced meaningfulness (as noted above); experienced responsibility for work; and knowledge of the results of work activities.

Hackman and Oldham (1980) recognise that individuals can respond to the characteristics differently; they are after all a function of the individual's perception, so the motivating potential of a job may vary between people. Several factors will influence the way any one individual will respond to changes in their job design:

- *Growth–need strength.* It is suggested that people vary in the extent to which they desire accomplishment and autonomy at work. People high in this category will therefore respond positively to enriched jobs; contrastingly, other workers might find newly enriched jobs a source of anxiety.

- *Knowledge and skill.* People who perceive they can perform adequately (known as a sense of self-efficacy) respond more positively to enriched jobs. This highlights the importance of individuals' perceptions and also the development of knowledge and skills at work.

- *Context satisfaction.* Hackman and Oldham (1980) found that employees who were more satisfied with contextual factors such as pay and working conditions would be more likely to respond positively to job enrichment than fellow workers dissatisfied on these measures.

However, despite recognising potential differences in the ways particular workers might respond to job enrichment, in overall terms Hackman and Oldham's model sets out a clear agenda for managers and others to devise meaningful and varied jobs.

 Reflective activity 11.4

How can Hackman and Oldham's model be applied to the following jobs?

- dentist
- train ticket inspector

- university lecturer
- tiler
- your current or previous job (assuming this is not one of the above).

The job redesign approach attempted to put forward a model which, through increasing the scope of jobs, could result both in greater efficiency and output (however defined) while also increasing the motivation of a workforce. Hackman and Oldham (1980), while stressing the importance of 'moderating factors' which depress levels of motivation (eg lack of knowledge or skill), 'low growth need strength' and other negative factors in the work context, clearly advocate the design of jobs which can lead to psychological well-being among the people who perform them.

It may be, however, that individual workers can also choose work that, although comparatively meaningless, may offer the prospect of other desired rewards including pay, for wider reasons based on their calculation of costs and benefits. Support for this notion is provided by the work of Goldthorpe et al (1968), who identified a category of workers who took an instrumental attitude or orientation to work. Formed outside the workplace and influenced by, among others, family and peers, the instrumental orientation regards work as a means to an end, and workers within this category often make a conscious decision to enter psychologically unfulfilling, but highly paid work. Thus, many workers meet their higher-order needs outside of work. However, with the rise of home working in the post-Covid-19 era, where there has been an increasing blurring of the home/work interface, as an extension of the work life interface, employees may seek other forms of satisfaction *from* their work.

This is not to say that decision-makers should make no attempt to design satisfying work for jobholders; there may be considerable practical benefits in so doing. It is useful, however, to adopt a contingency perspective in this area; that is to understand that the nature of job design may depend on a variety of factors including the work itself and the chosen orientations to work as well as the psychological needs of the workforce, as well as the organisational context and the wider macro context within which an organisation finds itself.

It should finally be noted that enriched work with its hoped-for concomitant high commitment can itself be regarded as a form of subjugation due to the demands it imposes on employees working within its precepts. Grey (2021) notes that it is viewed as normal for managers to work long hours, and do whatever it takes to get the job done. The assumption is that managers are motivated not just by the intrinsic interest of their work and the payment they receive. Underpinning their hard work is a deeply held sense of professionalism to which they are totally committed. Grey goes on, however, to paint a picture of managers stressed out by endless demands and locked into a particular set of corporate demands. While in many respects this may be preferable to stresses endured by workers in less enriched and self-managed jobs, there are considerable potential implications of high commitment and burnout is increasingly an issue.

Please refer to our website (koganpage.com/spmad) for details of three more important themes and approaches in job design: Influences from Japan and total quality management (TQM), Business process re-engineering (BPR) and Goal-setting.

11.6 Smart and agile working

At the start of this chapter, we noted that the topic areas of organisational and job design continue to be debated, with new thinking and research findings put forward for our consideration on a regular basis. A CIPD report (2008a) summarises several recent trends in these areas under the heading of smart working.

Smart working is defined as 'an approach to organising work that aims to drive greater efficiency and effectiveness in achieving job outcomes through a combination of flexibility, autonomy and collaboration, while optimising tools and working environments for employees' (CIPD, 2008a, p 7). Smart working is, furthermore, identified as a new paradigm in which a critical mass of workers (in the developed world) experience increasing autonomy at work. The report goes on to identify a collaborative work experience in many organisations in which a customised work experience is developed for groups of workers informed by their individual needs and aspirations.

Agile working, as summarised in a report (CIPD, 2014a) identifies a set of practices that enable the establishment of an optimal workforce. The notion of agile working reflects themes covered in this and previous chapters. Tools for agile working thus include an examination of work roles – with a recommendation to encourage multi-skilling and job rotation. They also, and importantly, deal with *when* people work and *where* they work, for example in co-working or remote setting (see Chapter 8). The question of *who* is employed, for example permanent core or outsourced peripheral workers, was also very important. The CIPD report concluded that while agile practices were associated with quick and effective responses to change, only some organisations were planning to implement them in 2014, CIPD (2014a, p 20). However, recently we have seen increasing and unprecedented numbers of organisations having to engage in both flexible working options and agile working as a response to the Covid-19 pandemic, and global market shocks, adopting maximum flexibility and agility in order to survive in the tumultuous world. In the context of Covid-19 and the post-pandemic world in which we now find ourselves, the debates around agile and more flexible modes of working have become even more important. The CIPD notes that home or remote working can mean people avoid lengthy commutes and have fewer distractions than in an office environment. These types of working arrangements can, however, result in people over-working and feeling isolated. It is important therefore to keep a focus on health and wellbeing. (CIPD, 2022h). It is clear that the contemporary world of work, and the future of work is set to change in a multitude of ways, and recent contributions to the literature identify trends in the wider work environment which have helped promote new forms of working. These include the advent of homeworking, enabled by developments in technology and a sense that with less expectation of long-term employment with an individual employer, workers are more prepared to switch jobs if they feel that job design is neglected or if more flexible or hybrid working options are not available.

This is an optimistic note on which to end the main body of this chapter and it is hoped that the experience of organisations and jobs will become a happier and more inclusive one for more and more of us – not just a fortunate few. Nonetheless, the smart working report records that the job characteristics model – outlined earlier in this chapter – in which people are subordinate to a pre-existing job (which may be more or less autonomous and responsible) is still relevant.

 Case study 11.3

Working at Capgemini

Capgemini is a global leader in consulting, technology, outsourcing and local professional services. Headquartered in Paris, the organisation operates in more than 30 countries with 82,000 people across the globe.

Capgemini's consultants need to be able to work effectively from any location. Therefore, all new recruits are provided with powerful lightweight laptops with wireless connectivity, mobile phones with email and internet capability, easy access to teleconferencing facilities and the ability to access the intranet remotely.

Although consultants are often based on-site with clients and – as we have seen – frequently work remotely, there is office accommodation too. However, this is intentionally unusual, and the Soho office in London comprises 'hot desks' and collaborative work areas and flexible zones intended to foster 'accelerated decision-making and open and honest discussion'. It is also noteworthy, that Capgemini has seen, like many organisations, an increase in 'the number of employees making use of flexible working options, jumping from 61% in 2016 to 78% in 2017' (Capgemini, 2022) and that this is set to increase further in the post-Covid-19 era, and in light of the organisation having taken the following actions:

- introducing new flexible working policies
- sharing employee stories on the benefits of flexible working

- training senior leaders in unconscious bias and inclusion
- engaging with clients around flexible options onsite (Capgemini, 2022).

Capgemini provides people with a great deal of autonomy in their daily work. Consultants are often responsible for the planning and definition of projects in line with customer requirements and operate as self-managed individuals.

Consultants refer to mentors and 'reviewers' (a colleague who is a grade above) on development matters.

Leaders should be approachable, know their people on a personal level and Capgemini aim for a 'low politics environment'.

Capgemini's structure complements this context of work. The business operates a flat structure with six grades of consultants throughout the business. Performance is assessed against defined objectives and client expectations. Each grade has a set of behavioural competencies aligned with learning interventions, feedback and self-analysis tools.

The way in which jobs and structures are set out at Capgemini is underpinned by a distinctive organisational culture. Values of fun, modesty, solidarity, freedom, trust, boldness and honesty are celebrated and reinforced through recruitment, performance, recognition, learning and other processes and role-modelled by leaders.

1 Would Capgemini's structure and work arrangements be suitable in your own job (or in one you are familiar with)? Explain your answer, what might work well and what might not work so well?

2 Which element of Capgemini's strategy is more important – its structure or its culture? Which facets of the organisational culture do you think are most effective? Why have you reached your conclusion?

11.7 Conclusion

The argument for linking principles of organisational design and job design to high performance and commitment workplaces can be summarised as follows:

- OD can achieve an organisational structure best suited to deal with that organisation's circumstances or contingent factors.
- A constantly changing and ever more competitive business environment means that work organisations in diverse sectors require multiskilled, proactive and customer-focused staff in order to be successful. These staff can be characterised as thinking performers – or possibly smart workers, who can respond to organisational changes.
- An increasingly educated workforce, used to exercising discretion and choice in other areas of their lives will, in any case, demand jobs which are psychologically fulfilling, and, increasingly in the post-Covid-19 era, offer more flexible or hybrid working options.
- High-performance work organisations will therefore increasingly need to design, or enable their workers to design, jobs that provide variety, flexibility, scope for initiative and autonomy and empower jobholders.

While acknowledging that many jobs have been 'upskilled' jobs, different models of job design continue to be the lived experience of many workers. We should critically address the proposition that work has become more meaningful for large numbers of the working population. A 2020 report by The Health Foundation showed that 36 per cent of UK employees of respondents taken from the UK Household Longitudinal Study perceived that they were in a low-quality job. This was defined as a job with two or more negative aspects including low pay and wellbeing. Low-quality jobs were also defined by perceived low levels of autonomy at work and everyday job dissatisfaction – our focus in this chapter. This not to say that no effort should be made to improve people's experience of their work and The Health Foundation concluded that with UK employment law potentially under review following departure from the European Union, there should be a particular focus on improving job quality.

Trends in job design are complex and non-linear, as well as being linked to external labour market forces and socio-economic changes, as well as market shocks and other unforeseen events such as the Covid-19 pandemic.

One can also put forward a view that organisational effectiveness can be achieved through different models and indeed conceptions of organisational design, which is both proactive and responsive to changes in the external operating environment. The fast-food sector provides a notable example of continuing simplification of tasks, albeit within a team-working framework, although job rotation within this setting is also not uncommon whereby employees rotate between different preparation and task areas, which enables elements of both job specialisation but also flexibility (also referred to as functional flexibility). Here, we have classical contingency principles operating – that is, the optimal structure of the organisation will all depend on the level of predictability required (both product and service), hierarchical relationships and the expectations of a workforce, many of whom in this case may have only short-term plans regarding their work and employment. In contrast, the nature of organisations and work in other sectors may lend itself far more easily to flat structures or even adhocracies, encouraging greater initiative and autonomy on the part of jobholders, which in itself may also function as a motivating factor.

Organisations should seek to implement and maintain functional flexibility, this concept encompassing job rotation, multiskilling and, where appropriate, team-working as part of an overall strategy of flexibility, agility or adaptability. Other aspects of flexibility included numerical flexibility, the precursor of many instances of downsizing, and financial flexibility, which, in an attempt to control salary costs, has seen numerous examples of sub-contracting work, zero-hours contracts and even the wholesale movement of jobs to other parts of the world, as well as the rise of the gig economy, with organisations such as Uber, Deliveroo and Task Rabbit growing exponentially. Such gig work is characterised not only by algorithmic control, whereby workers are allocated tasks in line with demand, and digitally, which for many can provide a highly flexible way of working, but also a way of working which lacks sufficient legal projection for workers. The way in which gig workers' jobs are designed and the way in which such organisations are set up and designed, influences almost every aspect of a gig workers work and critically, also how much they can or may earn.

To conclude, there are a range of strategic choices available to organisational decision-makers when approaching the area of both organisational and job design, but the role and importance of the context cannot be ignored. Organisational and job design may also be influenced by external contextual forces and or changes, as has become increasingly clear when we deliberate the emergent change around hybrid working, remote working and flexible working practices in the post-pandemic era.

> ## 🔒 KEY LEARNING POINTS
>
> 1 People's [lived] experience of work is affected by the organisational arrangements in which they operate and the nature of the work they do. The nature and future of work is changing in light of the Covid-19 pandemic in many contexts.
> 2 A variety of organisational structure models have been put forward in order to enhance performance, although how these are experienced will vary by organisational culture and context.
> 3 Job re-design emphasises increasing the scope of jobs in order to increase efficiency and foster high levels of worker motivation, as well as, increasingly, employee engagement.

4 Large numbers of people continue to work in jobs designed under principles of 'Taylorism' or scientific management, though this is an approach that needs to be problematised, particularly when employee wellbeing is considered.

5 A contingency approach, which acknowledges contextual changes, to both organisational and job design, stressing the importance of recognising situational factors, is recommended in order to foster strategic agility, and potentially in turn, organisational resilience.

 Review questions

1 List five advantages of the bureaucratic model of structure and five disadvantages. Do the advantages outweigh the disadvantages, or vice versa? How might these change depending on the nature of the organisation?

2 With reference to real-world examples, assess the usefulness of the contingency approach to organisational design.

3 Assess the importance of job design within the overall process of managing people. Give reasons for your answer.

4 How strong is the evidence that meaningful work will motivate a workforce? How would you define what meaningful work means to you?

 Explore further

Grey, C (2021) *A Very Short, Fairly Interesting and Reasonably Cheap Book About Studying Organizations*, 5th edn, Sage, London. This book provides a thought-provoking and entertaining account of the development and application of many of the principles dealt with in this chapter.

Hackman, JR and Oldham, GR (1980) *Work Redesign*, Adison-Wesley, New York. Read this source text for an in-depth discussion of how job characteristics can affect workers' attitudes.

Mullins, LJ (2019) *Organisational Behaviour in the Workplace,* 12th edn, Pearson, Harlow. This very comprehensive textbook is recommended for its detailed and extensive coverage so would provide a useful additional source.

12
Organisational development and change

GARY REES AND DAVID HALL

LEARNING OUTCOMES

After reading this chapter, you should be able to:

- explore the nature and types of change
- examine the context, process and content of change
- explore and examine various change interventions such as organisational development (OD) and systems theory of change
- examine change leadership and change capability
- examine the role of HR and change.

12.1 Overview

Change continues to take a front-of-stage role in both academic research and industrial practice. While it is difficult to pinpoint a universally accepted definition of change, we are reminded that change management is not a distinct discipline with rigorous and defined boundaries, but more that the theory and practice of change management draws upon a number of social science disciplines and traditions (Burnes, 2017). This chapter encapsulates the major theories in the field of change, adopting a strategic perspective, and considers how HR can impact upon change in organisations. In Chapter 1 we noted that there were enduring principles and models in the general area of managing people which have ongoing value. This is certainly true in the topic of change with several classical models which we will examine here – although we will also highlight contemporary issues and current thinking.

The appropriateness of change planning and intervention is dependent to some extent on how we fit theory into practice, and vice versa. Grint (1997, p 1) sums up the argument particularly well:

Theory is where you know everything and nothing works; Practice is where everything works,

But nobody knows why;

Here we combine theory and practice: Nothing works and nobody knows why.

While it is unlikely that any one change model fits perfectly, there is scope to consider a more hybrid approach to change. There needs to be a move away from 'static' models of change, which stress the content and substance of change (Nelson, 2003), to the dynamics of change, with the expectation that change occurs within a less certain environment, where flexibility is required to maintain or enable competitive advantage. These issues are explored throughout this chapter.

12.2 Introduction

12.2.1 Defining change and change management

Small-scale and relatively simple change, typically categorised as 'hard' problems, are usually managed within day-to-day operational management activity. This type of change is not usually referred to as 'change' by managers, and the process of managing it is not described as 'managing change' or 'change management' within organisations.

Managers have to consider the many factors involved in a complex and dynamic situation before making decisions that implement actions that will influence the effectiveness, efficiency and ultimately the sustainability of their organisations.

Brech (1975, p 19) defines management as:

A social process entailing responsibility for the effective and economic planning and regulation of the operations of an enterprise, in fulfilment of given purposes or tasks, such responsibility involving:

(a) Judgement and decision in determining plans and in using data to control performance and progress against plans;

(b) The guidance, integration, motivation and supervision of the personnel composing the enterprise and carrying out its operations.

Brech characterises four main elements of management namely; planning, control, co-ordination and motivation. Fayol (1949) describes the function of management in similar terms, proposing five elements of management: planning, organising, commanding, co-ordinating and controlling.

Management can be described as, essentially, an intervention for controlling operational performance outcomes in line with an organisation's purpose and objectives.

In carrying out their responsibilities, managers deal with change on a day-to-day basis, which raises an interesting question: when does management become 'change management'? Is this purely an academic question (it will be for many managers), or is it helpful from a management and organisational perspective to understand what, if anything, differentiates the two?

Change may be defined simplistically as making things different, but this needs to make explicit mention of actual and perceived change(s). Mullins (2019) notes that if change is to work it must involve altering perceptions attitudes and behaviour of people, while at the same time recognising that people often become defensive and more generally negative towards change. Mullins proposes, therefore, that one of the most important elements in successful organisational change is the style of managerial behaviour. The Society for Human Resource Management (SHRM, 2022) defines change management as: 'The systematic approach and application of knowledge, tools and resources to deal with change.' Change management means defining and adopting corporate strategies, structures, procedures and technologies to deal with changes in external conditions and the business environment.

Therefore, managing change or 'change management' is a form of management control through the application of systematic management interventions that involve people to achieve a desired future state with defined performance outcomes in line with the organisational strategy.

From this definition, it is clear that there is a strong and inextricable link between organisational change, performance and strategy.

12.3 Types of change

Dependent upon the perspective that has been adopted, a variety of models and concepts can be utilised in order to consider types of organisational change. This chapter will consider the level of change, the size and scope of change, the nature of change and the momentum of change.

12.3.1 *The level of organisational change*

Carnall and Todnem By (2014) suggest that there are three levels of strategic change. First, organisation-specific changes, such as a new information system. Second, generic organisation-wide change programmes, such as business process engineering (BPR). Third, generic multi-organisational change programmes, for example mergers and acquisitions.

Figure 12.1 Child's approaches to organisational change

Approaches to organisational change

	Planned	Emergent	
Radical	BPR	Organic development (eg. start-up company)	Whole org.
	Merger of departments	Changes to selection of new members made by teams	part org.
Incremental	Annual targeted improvements	Organisational learning	Whole org.
	Changes agreed in staff performance plans	Continuous improvement through project teams	part org.

12.3.2 The size and scope of change

Child (2005) provides a useful model on how to differentiate between the scope of change and type of change – see Figure 12.1.

It must be borne in mind that whilst radical and incremental change may be defined and measured, it is often the perceived scale of change that may be more important than the 'actual' scale of change.

12.3.2 The nature of change – planned or unplanned?

While it may be assumed that all organisational change is both rational and planned, with control of nearly all processes and resources, there may be occasions when a less planned and logical method may be adopted. A parallel argument is one of adopting an organic approach to change (Burns and Stalker, 1994) versus an expected mechanistic approach. If it is assumed that change can emerge, then one approach by management may be to throw a metaphorical hand grenade into the organisation, and then see what emerges.

For example, an organisation may deliberately set about rumour-mongering around restructuring and job cuts, then formally notify employees that all jobs have been red circled and that employees have to make applications for new posts. During this time, communication and consultation is deliberately kept to a minimum. Management then see what emerges after a period of time. A less contentious scenario could also be envisaged, where the management of an organisation simply let things run, without obvious intervention.

Change models tend to centre around planned change, which in itself will determine the various factors or characteristics that are then compared to, for example: strategic/tactical and operational change; radical, transformational and incremental change; the rate of change (change momentum); and hard versus soft change.

However, complex large-scale change, usually driven by external factors and having a significant 'soft' change element, are planned and co-ordinated. The terms 'managing change' or 'change management' can be used to describe the application of systematic interventions to implement a planned change within organisations to achieve a desired future state. In the following section, several key change management models are considered.

The nature of change – hard and soft change

The 'hard' elements of change are the tasks within change management, which are defined and measured. 'Soft' factors, such as culture and motivation, may be more difficult to assess. Emphasis may be placed upon managing task factors at the expense of soft factors during change interventions; however, Sirkin, Keenan and Jackson (2005) argue that four hard factors correlate to the outcome of change interventions, namely: duration (length of time); integrity (reliance on managers); commitment (of all involved in change); and effort (within the opportunity of time allowed).

When characterising change, we have considered the speed and magnitude of change, and related this to the problem of complexity. The problems that change presents to an organisation can be perceived by managers as 'difficulties', which are 'bounded' in that they can be well defined (specified) and can be dealt with without involving or impacting on the wider organisation.

Another category of problems is those which cannot be well defined and are 'unbounded' in the sense that the wider organisation is implicated and needs to be involved in dealing with these types of problems.

The nature of change – top-down versus bottom-up

Top-down change can stem from a managerial prerogative for maintaining control throughout the change. Change can be driven through by management, and resistance controlled and eliminated. Here change can become more of a political issue (Gioia and Thomas, 1996). Lupton (1991) argues that a bottom-up approach has its benefits in that employees at all levels have skills and expertise that are often lost in change processes. A third option is a combination of top-down and bottom-up approaches.

Change momentum: magnitude and speed

The momentum of change, that is the combination of speed and magnitude of change, is a useful concept to analyse and characterise different types of change. As we have seen, change momentum is not always easy to predict, but if it can be anticipated (which is often the case) interventions to manage change may be considered from the options available. In other words, if managers are able to characterise the type of change an organisation will experience, this can be helpful in considering appropriate interventions to manage change in an effective way. We will consider change management interventions later, but let us return to characterising change. Figure 12.2 represents a model of change momentum based on the two key variables of speed and magnitude.

'Smooth' and 'bumpy' change are both characterised by relatively small (and less complex) change, but differ in speed of implementation, with 'smooth' change happening over a longer period of time than the latter. Smooth change happens in small steps and is often described as being 'incremental', being barely noticeable in the day-to-day

Figure 12.2 Model of change momentum

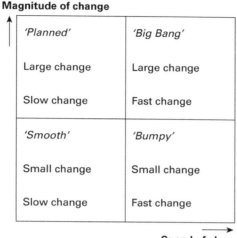

Magnitude of change

'Planned' Large change Slow change	*'Big Bang'* Large change Fast change
'Smooth' Small change Slow change	*'Bumpy'* Small change Fast change

Speed of change

business of an organisation. Relatively minor changes to policies and procedures would be examples of this type of change. It is typically driven by internal factors.

'Bumpy' change is more noticeable, as the speed of change is fast and therefore requires a quicker response time by managers and employees in dealing with it. It is typically driven by external factors which require an organisation to move quickly to respond. Examples of this would include organisations responding to crisis, which require significant investment and/or changes in practice, for example health, safety and the environment, regulatory reform or legal proceedings. Companies involved in fast-moving markets often have to manage this type of change as consumer opinion and tastes quickly change.

Grundy (1993) describes three types of change related to speed of change. The first is 'smooth incremental change' as change that evolves slowly in a systematic and predictable way. He also describes 'bumpy incremental change' as periods of relative calm, that is, little or no change that is punctuated by accelerated change. The third type of change described by Grundy is 'discontinuous' change, which he defines as 'change which is marked by rapid shifts in strategy, structure or culture, or in all three' (Grundy, 1993, p 26). This equates closely to 'Big Bang' change in terms of change momentum.

Grundy's 'discontinuous change' and 'Big Bang' change describes many of the characteristics of what has become known as 'transformational' change – a type of change that involves the values, attitudes and behaviours of people that contribute towards shaping the culture of an organisation. This form of complex change focuses on the motivation and commitment of employees and their contribution towards performance outcomes. Leadership which emphasises these employee attributes in managing change is described as 'transformational leadership' (Bass, 1985), to which we shall return later.

In conclusion, a range of differing variables have been used to examine the different types of change. However, there may be other more relevant comparators than the ones presented. It is necessary to examine the context of change as well in order to assess whether the most appropriate comparators have been used.

12.4 Analysing the change context

The question as to why organisations change is often determined by a combination of push and pull factors. Organisations sometimes have choices as to whether they want to change, or are sometimes forced to change, because of legal or other reasons. The importance of why organisations change is linked to the timing of change. Whilst there may be a range of comparators with which to analyse change dimensions, a potential metaphor is one which considers a combination of change interventions running concurrently – see Figure 12.3. The metaphor shows a range of change interventions, some of which start anew, some end, and all of which may impact upon each other.

While classic change models may posit a start, middle and end part of the change process, it is important to have to start at some point in terms of determining where the organisation is now and where it wants to arrive at in terms of change. Change models can either adopt a reactive approach ('this is why we need to change'), or adopt a proactive approach ('where do we want to get to as an organisation?'). Figure 12.4 demonstrates the iterative nature of change, and planning for change.

With strategic change, we may start with a strategic plan, or possibly a vision or mission statement, which leads to a strategic plan. When analysing why organisations change, there is often a trigger for change. The following factors are proposed here as triggers for change – see also CIPD (2021x):

- growth opportunities, especially new markets
- economic downturns and challenging trading conditions
- shifts in strategic objectives
- technological developments
- competitive pressures, including new entrants, mergers and acquisitions

Figure 12.3 Combination of concurrent change interventions

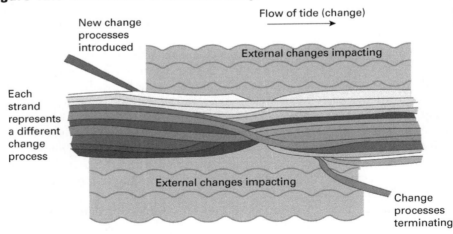

Combination of change interventions running concurrently

Figure 12.4 The iterative nature of change and planning for change

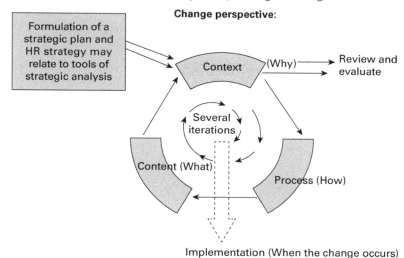

- customer or supplier pressure, particularly shifting markets
- learning new organisation behaviour and skills
- Government legislation/initiatives.

In 2021 the CIPD change management factsheet referred to above also noted the exceptional impact of the Covid-19 pandemic which created a situation of rapid change, significant in terms of its near universal impact, plus the fundamental areas of operations that it affected. This type of very dramatic change trigger can be added to the perennial factors listed in the above bullet points.

When it comes to analysing the strategic context, a range of models can be utilised. Both the internal and external context need to be analysed.

Caldwell (2013) argues that change should be understood from a 'changing organisation' perspective, which places multiple, simultaneous adaptive demands upon individuals (employees) from many forces within the organisation, which in themselves may be planned or possibly unplanned.

12.4.1 External drivers of change

A useful tool to examine the external drivers of change involves the PESTLE taxonomy. The earliest known reference to a framework for describing the external business environment is by Aguilar (1967) who presents 'ETPS' as a mnemonic to represent the four sectors: Economic, Technical, Political, and Social. Variations of this include 'PEST' and 'PESTLE', which add the Legal and Environmental dimensions – see Table 12.1.

The PESTLE taxonomy provides a useful external environment scanning framework and a methodology for identifying and analysing factors that shape the external business environment. When combined with a SWOT (strengths, weaknesses,

Table 12.1 PESTLE framework

Factor or driver	Typical considerations
Political	Taxation and other policies Current and future political support Funding, grants and initiatives Trade organisations Internal and international relationships
Economic	Economic situation Consumer spending Levels of government spending Interest rates, inflation and unemployment Exchange rates
Social	Demographics and social mobility Lifestyle patterns and changes People's attitudes and actions Media perception and influence Ethnic and religious differences
Technology	Research, technology and innovation funding Consumer behaviour and processes Intellectual property Global communication technological advances Social networks
Legal	Legislation in employment, competition and health and safety, etc Changes in legislation Trading policies Regulatory policies International protocols
Environmental	Clean technologies and processes Waste management and recycling Attitudes of government, media and consumers Environmental legislation Global warming and emission protocols

opportunities and threats) analysis, this evidence-based approach provides valuable information for strategic decision-making.

The external environmental factors identified from a PESTLE are typically considered as opportunities or threats in a SWOT analysis. Strengths and weaknesses are usually regarded as internal organisational factors which can be considered against the external opportunities and threats. This 'looking out' and 'looking in' approach provides a basis for internal–external organisation analysis and is an important part of the strategic management process, if carried out in a purposeful and rigorous manner.

12.4.2 *Internal drivers of change*

Not all organisational change can be attributed to managers responding to a business environment comprising external factors. Internal drivers of change can also play a major role in initiating change and these include:

- new leadership
- new strategy
- new structures
- new business model
- organisation growth
- redesign of jobs
- redesign of business processes
- outsourcing
- change of location
- installation of new technology and systems
- changes to employees' terms and conditions
- being acquired or merged with another organisation
- redundancies.

These changes can be and often are influenced by external factors but they can also be triggered by decisions which are not made as a response to changes in the business environment.

Pettigrew and Whipp (1993) argue that environmental assessment is only one of five factors that determine the success of managing change. The other four factors are leading change, linking strategic and operational change, considering human resources as both assets and liabilities, and a central factor in all of this – coherence – pulling together the other four factors.

 Reflective activity 12.1

Duty of care

Change has been equated to bereavement (Marris, 1986). Constant change may not allow employees time to grieve. It could be argued that organisations have a duty of care to ensure that the welfare of their employees is paramount and thereby limit constant and dramatic change.

Johnson (2016) argues that there are three key elements of excessive change – change frequency, extent and impact. If an organisation does not constantly seek employee feedback and make an assessment through an organisational stress thermometer, then how will it know how much employees can take? Acas (2010) recommends that employees' emotions are taken into account when managing change, by including the following within every change process:

- create a vision
- lead (the change)
- consult (with employees)
- engage (employees)

- reflect upon the change process (including employees' views).

1 What are the implications for organisations when deciding upon the nature and type of change, and how change should take place?

SOURCE: Johnson, K (2016) The dimensions and effect of excessive change, *Journal of Organizational Change Management*, **29** (3), pp 445–59

It is important to differentiate between external and internal factors when considering change, with the key difference being that organisations and managers may have little, if any, control over the external factors. However, internal factors are typically management decisions which are designed to exert some form of control aimed at achieving certain performance outcomes.

Organisations lobby governments on many issues in an attempt to influence politicians' decisions and the outcomes that define the external factors which ultimately shape the business environment in which they operate. Climate change and the environment are examples of contemporary issues that continue to attract the lobbyists in the early part of this century.

Control is the primary motivation for doing this because if organisations can be a factor in shaping their business environment, this enables them to predict more accurately what this environment will look like. This, in turn, puts these organisations in a stronger position to be able to make informed strategic decisions to control their future direction and performance.

The then UK Government's 'modernisation programme' of public services described in a 1999 White Paper set out a 10-year change programme aimed at delivering more responsive and high-quality public services which can be measured by better results. The NHS is probably the most widely publicised example of this modernisation agenda, having been subjected to a plethora of change initiatives and performance targets, which have continued in to the 2020s. A combination of external and internal factors typically drive this type of change in organisations.

12.5 Choice of change intervention

After the context has been analysed, the choice of change intervention needs to be considered. A range of differing change interventions are discussed below in order to provide an understanding of how the organisation can manage change.

12.5.1 TROPICS test

The Open University (1985) described two types of problems as 'difficulties' and 'messes'. Paton and McCalman (2000) use the terms 'hard' and 'soft' respectively to describe these same sets of problems, and devised the 'TROPICS' test as a guide to help determine the nature of change in terms of a continuum from hard to soft (see Table 12.2).

Table 12.2 The TROPICS test

Hard	Soft
Timescales clearly defined/short- to medium-term	Timescales ill-defined/medium- to long-term
Resources needed identified	Resources uncertain
Objectives specified and quantified	Objectives subjective and ambiguous
Perceptions of the problem shared by all	No consensus of problem
Interest in problem limited and defined	Interest in problem is widespread and ill-defined
Control within managing group	Control is shared with people outside of managing group
Source of the problem lies within organisation	Source of the problem is from outside the organisation

This test provides a useful reference framework to help characterise and understand the parameters involved when facing change. It is important to recognise that this is a continuum, and many change programmes will combine elements of hard and soft change.

When managers have knowledge and understanding of the issues involved in a change scenario, they are in a better position to be able to assess the situation and decide on an appropriate course of action to help control and manage the change process.

12.5.2 Lewin's three-phase change model

One of the earliest known models applied to managing change is a three-phase model by Kurt Lewin (1951) which focuses on the psychological aspects of behaviour modification:

- *Unfreezing* – lowering resistance to change by recognising and accepting the need for change.
- *Movement* – developing new attitudes to encourage behaviours necessary for change to occur.
- *Refreezing* – stabilising, supporting and reinforcing the new change conditions.

This model presents a systematic approach to change management, describing a sequence of well-defined and interrelated processes. The premise for this model is that by identifying and understanding the key stages involved in the change process, the likelihood of effective change management is increased – by managers making better informed decisions about which interventions to use in managing change.

Lewin (1947) was also responsible for developing the force-field analysis, a diagnostic technique which considered the forces or 'drivers' for and against change.

Figure 12.5 Lewin's force-field analysis

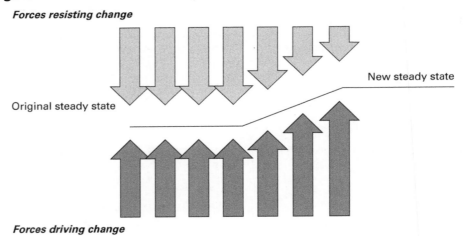

At any time, there will be a number of forces in play that resist change and support the status quo, and forces that encourage change. These can be internal or external forces, or, as is usually the case, a combination of both.

When the sum of the forces 'for' and 'against' change are equal, they cancel each other out, resulting in equilibrium, that is, a steady state. However, when the forces driving change are greater than the forces of resistance (either by the driving forces increasing or the restraining forces decreasing) then change will occur, and the organisation will inevitably change and move to a new state, as shown in Figure 12.5.

Although Lewin's model is criticised for over-simplifying change by describing a sequential linear process, its three stages of change are reflected in other more contemporary change-management models. French et al (1985) list eight components of a planned-change effort, which can be related to Lewin's model. The other main criticism of Lewin's model and other linear change models is that they describe the process of change transforming from an initial state to a final stage. Today, change is widely recognised as being a constant and continuing phenomena for all organisations, albeit at a faster rate for some compared to others.

12.5.3 Resistance to change

A multitude of factors could contribute to resistance to change. Prahalad, quoted in Allio (2008), cites three primary reasons for resistance to change in organisations. First, the logic of management actions and behaviours is not always obvious. Secondly, if change occurs, the accumulated intellectual experience of the players becomes devalued and change is taken as a personal threat (so a safety net is needed). Thirdly, managers need to have their hand held while they are learning. Prahalad emphasises the need for managers to be constantly learning new skills.

French et al (1985) suggest that in order to minimise resistance in such cases, the change agent should make sure that the people affected by the change know specifically how it satisfies the following criteria:

- *Benefit.* The change should have a clear relative advantage for the individuals being asked to change; ie it should be perceived as 'a better way'.
- *Compatibility.* The change should be as compatible as possible with the existing values and experiences of the people being asked to change.
- *Complexity.* The change should be no more complex than necessary. It must be as easy as possible to understand and use.
- *Triability.* The change should be something that people can try on a step-by-step basis and make adjustments throughout the process.

Frahm and Brown (2005) argue that one of the key aspects of creating strategic change is the receptivity of employees to organisational change. They argue that organisational communication can significantly help alleviate problems often associated with change fatigue and change resistance.

 Reflective activity 12.2

Your organisation (or an organisation of your choice) has decided to introduce job evaluation and performance management organisation wide. It is also operating a recruitment ban and pay freeze. As the HR business partner, use Lewin's change model to identify some of the potential forces acting for and against this change initiative.

12.5.4 Kotter's eight-stage change model

John Kotter (1996) described an eight-stage change process for managing change in large organisations following his research into US organisations that had failed to manage change effectively:

1 Establish a sense of urgency – the need to change.
2 Create a guiding coalition – with authority and credibility.
3 Develop a vision and strategy – a clear aim and way forward.
4 Communicate the change vision – promote understanding and commitment.
5 Empower broad-based action – enable people to act and overcome barriers.
6 Generate short-term wins – to motivate and ensure further support.
7 Consolidate gains and produce more change – maintain change momentum.
8 Anchor new approaches in the culture – new values, attitudes and behaviours.

This model appears to be a linear and sequential set of processes, and has been criticised for these reasons. However, in the final two steps, Kotter attempts to address the problem of the 'refreezing' stage in Lewin's model by encouraging organisations and their employees to develop attitudes and values which help to promote the behaviours required to encourage and support further change. Developing an organisational culture that is proactive to change helps to create a feedback mechanism which transforms a linear change model into a continuous process.

Many change management programmes applied in organisations are based on systematic change management models comprising sequential processes similar to the examples outlined above. However, a common modification to these models in practice is to introduce an additional process at the end, which provides a feedback step from the final to the initiating stage. With this modification, these models describe a cyclical and continuous change management system.

A significant feature of Kotter's model is the role of leadership, particularly in developing and communicating the vision for change, which is critical to effective transformational leadership, and management of change in large-scale organisations (Bass, 1985).

This type of approach to change tends to be effective for change that is predominantly 'hard' by nature, that is, as characterised in terms of the TROPICS test. Objectives, milestones and performance can be quantified and applied within the boundaries of a specific change programme, thereby offering a means to assess progress of the managed change programme.

12.5.5 *Organisational development*

There is another approach for intervening to improve organisational performance through managing change called organisational development (OD) that offers appropriate solutions to the 'softer' aspects of change. We must remember that hard and soft change is part of a continuum, and that the majority of change scenarios involve both aspects.

When managing change, organisations will apply a range of interventions often using both approaches described in this chapter. These different approaches are not mutually exclusive.

There are many definitions of OD, but the following definition is particularly useful in helping to develop understanding of the context, content and processes involved in OD as a change and organisational performance intervention.

French and Bell (1999) define OD as: a long-term effort, led and supported by top management to improve an organisation's visioning, empowerment, learning and problem-solving processes, through an ongoing, collaborative management of organisation culture – with a special emphasis on the culture of intact work-teams and other team configurations, using consultant-facilitator role and the theory and technology of applied behavioural science, including action research.

CIPD (2009) offers the following succinct definition of OD: 'planned and systematic approach to enabling sustained organisational performance through the involvement of its people'.

OD emphasises the management of culture and employee behaviour as the central interventions for sustaining organisational capability to deal with long-term change and improve performance. An examination of several definitions of OD reveals a number of common features which highlight the distinguishing characteristics of the OD approach to change:

- It has top management support and involvement – it is participative.
- It deals with change over the medium- to long-term – it is strategic.

- It applies to an entire organisation and its component parts – it is systematic within institutionalising change.
- It draws on the theory and practice of behavioural science – such as leadership, group dynamics and work design.
- It emphasises the transfer of knowledge and skills through training and developing people – using action-research and organisational learning methods.
- It is concerned with planned change but is adaptable to new situations – rather than prescribing a rigid process which must be followed.
- It is uses data to inform decision-making and progress – it is 'evidence-based'.
- It often makes use of change agents or OD practitioners to facilitate the OD process.
- It is aimed at facilitating planned change and improving organisational performance over the longer term.

The roots of OD can be found in the motivation theories of the 1940s and 1950s, which gave rise to the human relations school of management and organisation. It became popular towards the end of the last century as an alternative approach to the hard systems approach shaped by the models which flourished in the 1980s and 1990s. These models struggled to deal with the complexities and often unknown factors that were common components of the 'unbounded' soft and messy problems organisations faced as their environments rapidly changed.

OD focuses on managing organisational culture by promoting values and attitudes associated with personal and professional development, problem-solving, openness, engagement and commitment. The premise of this approach is that if an organisation's employees share such common values, this will manifest in desirable and normative behaviour at all levels: individual, team and organisation.

An example of where the application of the OD approach would be particularly relevant is in developing a 'high performance culture' within an organisation. By establishing a shared set of values which employees, particularly managers, agree to adhere to in the work environment, this provides a guide for what is regarded as acceptable employee behaviour, which, over a period of time, becomes regarded as normal behaviour by most employees.

The set of values would typically include values related to learning and improvement, working with others, being honest and respectful, etc, which ultimately influence an individual and group behaviour to enable performance improvement. These values would typically be applied in performance management interventions, recruitment and selection, career development and progression, reward schemes and leadership development, to facilitate and embed an evasive organisational culture that encourages and supports high levels of commitment to performance.

This is a sophisticated and complex form of organisational control based on influencing normative behaviour which is acceptable to managers and employees. The principles of OD also facilitate management of the psychological contract, which is defined by Guest and Conway (2002) as 'the perceptions of the two parties, employee and employer, of what their mutual obligations are towards each other'.

Guest and Conway propose in their model of the psychological contract that the implicit nature of contract is moderated by the employees' and employer's sense of fairness and trust, and the belief that the employer will honour the unwritten arrangement between them. It is suggested that a healthy psychological contract will promote employee commitment and satisfaction and have a positive influence on performance.

How employees experience and perceive the workplace, and their relationship with managers and colleagues, will play a role in shaping their attitudes and consequent behaviour. OD, with its emphasis on values and attitudes as a means of managing culture and change, also presents an opportunity for employers and employees to develop positive psychological contracts to the benefit of both parties.

Although OD is an intervention for managing change and improving performance, because it focuses on the culture of an organisation influencing the attitudes and values (and ultimately behaviour), it pervades all areas and activities of an organisation. With an emphasis on learning and improvement, at individual, group and organisational levels, through techniques such as action learning, it develops and sustains the performance capability of an organisation through its people asset (human capital) and prepares an organisation for dealing with continuous change, ie it develops a state of enduring readiness for change.

In doing this, OD shapes the culture of an organisation to encourage managers and employees not to resist change but to be accepting and even embrace change, and approach it in that way. In other words, OD influences the ethos of an organisation and its people in dealing with change. It is an approach which addresses the soft and often intangible aspects of managing change which, because of the complexity involved, the rationality-based linear change models do not adequately accommodate.

Organisations that take the OD approach towards managing change tend to rely less on specific and explicit change programmes, but approach change as a normal part of everyday business. In the UK, the NHS has attempted to take this approach, having undergone radical change since inception of the modernisation programme (see 12.4.2 'Internal drivers of change').

The OD approach implies that normal business is about change and that dealing with change is implicit in what organisations and their people do – it is 'business as usual'. This makes a lot of sense because if we accept that organisational change is a permanent phenomenon, employees will soon become exhausted and demotivated if they are presented with one change programme after another, and sometimes multiple change programmes at the same time.

That is not to say that organisations that adopt the OD approach cannot and do not roll out specific projects for introducing change. This would be a particularly appropriate approach for managing when hard changes which are specific and contained, and lend themselves to being managed as a project with clearly defined and measurable objectives.

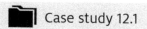 Case study 12.1

How Coca-Cola HBC transformed its company culture during Covid

Thorsten Klein claims to be a big fan of Mr Drucker's statement: 'Culture eats strategy for breakfast.' With 77 per cent of people saying they would consider a company's culture before applying for a job and more than half considering it more important than salary, this statement never gets old.

Evolving company cultures is not easy, especially when you work with nearly 30,000 people across 28 diverse markets on three continents. With a global pandemic in the mix and remote working from one day to the next, things become even more challenging.

Let's take a few steps back. I joined Coca-Cola HBC two years ago, with an ambitious plan to unlock a new culture of sharing and learning where people radiate and activate purpose. What I found when I arrived was already solid – a culture of performance, with passionate and resilient people, driven and energised by results. The feeling of being a family with a 'work hard, play hard' attitude complemented the picture. We began our transformational journey with unlearning and relearning behaviours and mindsets, together with our leaders, focusing on more cross-functional collaboration and on how we achieve our results.

When the pandemic struck, our culture faced the ultimate test. For everyone's safety, we asked our colleagues who could work from home to do so and most of them still are. We implemented strict health and safety measures for our colleagues in production and those working in the markets, and secured a constant supply of protective equipment for them.

Our focus on employee wellbeing also had to change from one day to the next. In line with that, we shifted fully to digital working across all domains, while enabling networking and collaboration and maintaining productivity at the same time. Ongoing dialogue and listening, as well as constant check-ins with team members and their personal situations, helped us to get through 2020.

Our employee assistance programme, which is available for all our people and their families, continues to offer additional 24/7 professional, free and confidential support to our colleagues, and has helped many through personal challenging situations.

Maintaining visible and engaging leadership to take care of our people in a transparent and authentic way was crucial. We held regular virtual meet-ups with senior management, reinforced messages from our senior leaders, and supported our managers to support their teams.

We constantly stayed in touch by running pulse surveys to see how people were doing and how we could help them. And we acted upon their pulse feedback in real-time. Our mobile feedback app also became prominent as it allowed teams, colleagues and everyone to stay connected and provided an additional opportunity to ensure we offered the right level of support.

We provided a range of virtual opportunities for our colleagues to interact and learn in the new normal. With summer festivals being cancelled, we set up our own first virtual learning festival (10 days, three stages, 40+ inspirational speakers and more than 5,000 participants). All participants also contributed to a good cause, which led to a €20,000 charitable grant for an NGO.

The strength of our culture shift also showed in many other creative ways: colleagues setting up cooking classes for others, and organising virtual coffee meetings and after-work drinks, as well as supporting each other throughout the year one to one. We also celebrated the holiday season by creating our first virtual Christmas festival, thanks to our amazing people. This was culture live in the making.

We digitised the entire employee experience and activated new digital learning platforms, available anytime and on any device across all our 28 markets. We also introduced a digital platform for mentoring and coaching, which we scaled up and democratised. This enabled us to make it accessible to everyone virtually and support our 30,000 staff through the pandemic and beyond. As a result, we received the 2020 CIPD People Management award for the best mentoring initiative, and are the subject of a Gartner case study as proof that our approach is working.

With Opportunity Marketplace, an online platform where people publicise and support short-term projects, we further encouraged cross-country and cross-functional collaboration and helped our people acquire new skills through projects, enhance their personal network and learn new skills. For our new colleagues, we have digitised and fully automated onboarding, aiming to provide a great employee experience from the very start to connect to our culture.

Despite all initiatives, the biggest culture shift was that we empowered our people and trusted them to make the right decisions. At the end of 2020, our sustainable engagement index remained high. Collaboration scored high, with almost 90 per cent of people saying colleagues are willing to help each other even if this means doing something outside their usual activities.

Despite a challenging year, more than 90 per cent of our employees feel proud to be part of Coca-Cola HBC, indicating the strength of the culture we build together.

Upon reflection, 2020 was a truly unique year. Despite all the tragedies and challenges we had to experience, it also helped us in new ways – we experimented and we reinvented ourselves, and we continue to do so. The key thing we learned was that nothing is set in stone and any crisis can easily be turned into opportunity if you are up for it. Everything we co-created in 2020 shifted our culture, thanks to our amazing leadership and culture team and the Coca-Cola HBC HR teams that have made this all happen. They've built strong foundations for the future of work – a fine achievement.

1 To what extent could it be argued that this was a planned culture change programme at Coca-Cola?
2 Why were the changes successful?

SOURCE: Klein, T (2021) How Coca-Cola HBC transformed its company culture during Covid, *People Management*, 11 February

Figure 12.6 A systems approach to change

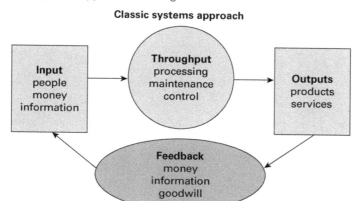

12.5.6 A systems approach to change

While the concept of a systems approach may on the face of it appear simplistic, systems models allow for a great deal of complexity and data to be analysed. Figure 12.6 demonstrates the key components of a process model of change

While there is a range of systems models available to the change agent, Mayon-White (1993) highlights the example of systems intervention strategy (SIS) as a useful tool for undertaking change. The diagnosis phase asks 'Where are we now?' (the description), then 'Where do we want to be?', which evolves the identification of objectives and constraints.

The question 'How will you know when you get there?' is addressed by the formulation of measures to achieve the objectives. In the design phase, we ask 'How can we get there?' in order to generate a range of options, then ask 'What will it be like?', where we can model options selectively. During the implementation phase, we consider whether we will like it, and then evaluate options against measures. Finally, we ask 'How can we carry it through?' then consider the design of implementation strategies and carry through the planned changes. Figure 12.7 demonstrates how the 'problem owners' fit within this model. While McCalman and Paton (1992) argue that the problem owner may clearly define the nature of change, those affected by the change, the boundary and scope of the change and the relationships affected by the change, it could be contested that establishing who is affected by the change is not always apparent. 'Affected' could be considered in terms of job, role, task, function etc, but may not account for emotional or cultural ties, etc.

Mayon-White (1993, p 136) provides a chart showing the types of action and tools and techniques that are used in systems intervention strategy (see Table 12.3).

A range of models have been presented, some of which show signs of overlap; for example, systems intervention strategy includes Lewin's force-field analysis. The choice of model(s) is up to the change agent and key stakeholders. It is possible to combine aspects of different models, for example having a combination of OD and SIS, but caution needs to be expressed so that there is no confusion as to what the process actually involves.

Figure 12.7 Systems intervention strategy

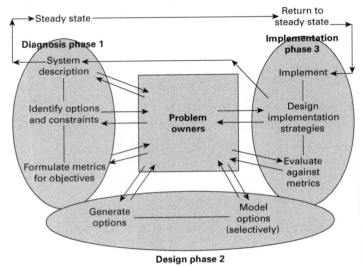

Design phase 2

Table 12.3 The key features and methods of SIS

The three phases of the strategy	The steps of the strategy phases	What kinds of actions are appropriate to each step?	What tools and techniques are available to help?
Diagnosis	Entry	Start by recognising that change is a complex process.	Make use of the concepts of 'mess' and 'difficulty'.
	1. Description	Structure and understanding the change in systems terms. Get other points of view on the change problem or opportunity.	Use diagrams. Set up meetings (NGT, Delphi, etc). Create a model of things as they are.
	2. Identify objectives and constraints	Set up objectives for the systems that you are examining. Think of the objectives of the change itself.	Set up an 'objective tree'. Prioritise your objectives for change.
	3. Formulate measures for your objectives	Decide on ways of measuring if an objective is achieved.	Use '£s' or quantities where possible. Scaling or ranking methods elsewhere.

(*continued*)

Table 12.3 (Continued)

The three phases of the strategy	The steps of the strategy phases	What kinds of actions are appropriate to each step?	What tools and techniques are available to help?
Design	Generate a range of options	Develop any ideas for change as full options. Look at a wide range of possibilities. Your objectives may suggest new options.	Brainstorming. Idea writing. Interviews and surveys. Comparisons with best practice in other organisations.
	5. Model options selectively	Describe the most promising options in some detail. Ask of each option: what is involved? Who is involved? How will it work?	Diagrams are simple models. Cost–benefit analysis. Cash flow models. Computer simulations.
Implementation	6. Evaluate options against measures	Test the performance of your options against an agreed set of criteria.	Set up a simple matrix to compare the performance of your options. Score each option against the metrics.
	7. Design implementation strategies	Select your preferred options and plan a way of putting the changes into place.	Look for reliable options. Check back to 'problem owners'. Plan time and allocate tasks.
	8. Carry through the planned changes	Bring together people and resources. Manage the process. Monitor progress.	Sort out who is involved. Allocate responsibility. Review and modify plans if necessary (CPA, etc).

SOURCE: Mabey and Mayon-White, 1998

12.5.7 The ADKAR model

This model was developed by Hiatt (2006) and is useful in that it is designed to guide both individual and organisational level changes. It includes the following – awareness of the nature of the issue, desire to change (the status quo), knowledge in terms of how to change, ability to implement the changes that are needed, and, finally, reinforcement to maintain the change. The acronym for this process resulted in the ADKAR title. The model is useful both in terms of its analytical approach as well as its predictive nature and its ability to identify the root cause of people change failure (Ali et al, 2021).

12.5.8 THE Burke–Litwin model

When it comes to organisational performance and change, a useful model is posited by Burke–Litwin (1992), where the three long-term levers of transformational factors are mission and strategy, leadership and organisational culture, and these interact with three operational transformational levers – namely structure, management practices and systems (policies and procedures) – together with work unit climate. In addition, there are three individual and personal short-term levers in the form of motivation, individual needs and values, and task and individual skills. All of the factors above sit within the context (the external environment) and individual and organisational performance. The Burke-Litwin is a causal model of change and potentially too complex and difficult to analyse, and sometimes gives rise to greater complexity when this produces further sub factors when drawing analysis of the specific change scenario.

When used in practice, this can be a useful model when analysing a range of factors, and allows us to examine in detail organisational climate and culture. It also allows us to traffic light the 12 key elements. So, a red shading (eg leadership) is something that needs urgent attention and perhaps a green shading (eg systems) may be something that we don't need to consider as urgent. This leaves us with an amber shading (eg motivation) as an area under consideration and one that we may intervene and act upon shortly. This model focuses on both process and contend allows for consideration of both transactional and transformational factors.

Reflective activity 12.3

Many modern organisations operate within stringent financial controls and exercise both lean thinking and lean management principles. In simple terms, organisations need to do more with less. Classic work undertaken by Womack and Jones (1996) placed particular emphasis upon the needs of the customer, with five key lean principles:

- *Value* – specifying what creates value from the customer's perspective.
- *The value stream* – identifying all the steps along the process chain.
- *Flow* – making the value process flow.

- *Pull* – make only what is needed by the customer (short-term response to the customer's rate of demand).
- *Perfection* – strive for perfection by continually attempting to produce exactly what the customer wants.

While these principles may be particularly suitable when applied to production processes, consider how this model could be applied to a charitable organisation or perhaps a small local authority organisation. In particular, consider who the 'customer' is and how the particular organisation (charity of authority) could change in order to meet the needs of the customer.

12.6 Leading change

The choice of change agent is critical to the success of any change intervention. While a universal definition of a change agent proves impossible to locate, characteristics, competences and skills can differentiate across change agents. In simple terms, Rosenfeld and Wilson (1999, p 294) define change as 'the individuals or groups of individuals whose task it is to effect change'.

What does a change agent look like? While the determination of choice of change agent will be determined by a range of factors, Lessem (1989) provides a range of change agent characteristics:

- You are professional, with an in-depth knowledge and experience in a particular field, and often with greater loyalty to your profession than to your organisation.
- You learn from change, by observing, conceptualising, experimenting and validating. Also, by accommodating through flexible communications.
- You troubleshoot, rapidly identifying opportunities for change, and coming up with alternative courses of action to exploit them.
- You adapt to change, by mapping out the internal and external environment, and by creating systems and procedures for dealing with change.
- You experiment with change, by continually forming temporary project groupings and solving ongoing problems in interdisciplinary teams.
- You plan for change, by constructing long-term plans with contingencies built in, monitoring changes and adapting plans accordingly.
- You embody the spirit of change and are respected as a free thinker. You also embody the organisation's cause.

 Reflective activity 12.4

To what extent can the HR function adopt Lessem's seven characteristics and demonstrate these during a change process?

The historical nature of the role and significance of change agents has varied, from 'change masters' and 'transformational leadership experts' in the 1980s to 'catalysts of change' in the 1990s (Caldwell, 2003). A useful model that progresses the definition and nature of change agents is provided by Caldwell (2003), who posits that a fourfold classification expands our understanding of change agency. His four descriptors are:

1 *Change leadership* – typically through identifying various traits and magical qualities associated with change leaders (akin to some leadership theories).

2 *Managers as change agents* – focusing on the role of managers (particularly middle management) in implementing change.

3 *Management consultants as change agents* – with particular emphasis on the role of project managers, often pitched at strategic co-ordination of complex and large-scale multiple change projects.

4 *(The emergence of) change teams* – facilitated by flatter structures and self-managed teams which combine knowledge and specialist expertise of internal and external consulting teams.

While attempts to define what a change agent might look like appear plausible, the intentionality and integrity of this agent might determine their nature and subsequent actions and behaviour. Beckett (1999) highlights the notion that change agents seek to bring about change in order to enhance their own interests, and some of these actions could result in entrepreneurial activities and outcomes. While no value judgement is made about undertaking entrepreneurial activities, the debate around change agents pushing boundaries beyond those expected of project managers could provide opportunity for further discussion and research.

 Reflective activity 12.5

As an HR professional, consider Caldwell's fourfold classification when applied to the process of recruiting and selecting a change agent for a complex change scenario. To what extent would this model help you to narrow down the type of change agent(s) required for the task?

Assuming that there is no singular and simple definition of a change agent, another approach to understanding what a change agent is and what they do may consider how change agents operate and, in particular, what tools they use when carrying out change.

Doz and Prahalad (1988) cite a range of tools that change agents can select from and use. First, data management tools concern the manipulation of information, systems, resource allocation procedures, strategic planning and budgeting arrangements. These tools are used to guide decision-making. Second, management tools are a combination of hard and soft approaches. 'Hard' tools involve manipulation of key appointments, career planning and reward systems. 'Soft' tools include changes to management development and socialisation patterns. These tools dictate the rules of the game. Third, conflict management tools involve relocation of decision responsibility, formation of business teams, task forces and co-ordination committees, the appointment of 'integrators', and establishment of procedures to resolve issues. These tools may be used more predominantly at different stages of a change intervention, where data management tools may prove most useful at the early stages of change, but conflict management tools may be used throughout some change interventions or perhaps during the 'movement' and 'refreezing' stages of a change process.

Buchanan and Boddy (1992) identified 15 competences that change agents adopt, clustered into five areas, namely: goals, roles, communication, negotiation and managing up. These competences sit within a framework that emphasises the political dimension.

The importance of both frontstage and backstage activity emphasises how the change agent has to manage their position continuously so as ensure their tenure and

Figure 12.8 The expertise of the change agent

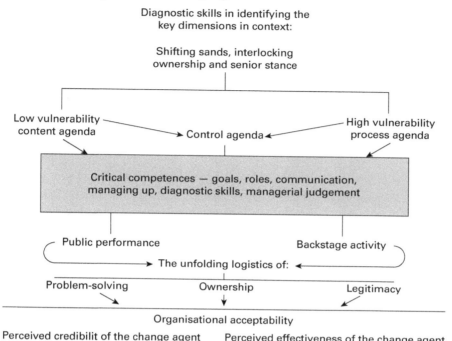

SOURCE: Buchanan and Boddy (1992)

sustainability through the change intervention. Figure 12.8 displays the three critical agendas that may impact upon the determination of the change agent, where the content agenda relies upon technical competence (similar to Doz and Prahalad's data management tools), and the process agenda matches implementation skills, where communication, consultation, team-building, influencing and negotiation skills are key (similar to Doz and Pralahad's conflict management tools).

It could be argued that the more strategic the change, the more politically charged it will be and thereby draw upon more power bases. Balogun et al's research (2005) supports Hardy's argument (1994, 1996) that change agents address and engage the 'power of the system', mobilising existing power to negotiate power interdependencies to enrol staff to their cause. This parallels with Kotter's (1999) notion of forming powerful coalitions so as to effect a change agenda. Kotter argues that managers typically form powerful coalitions through network building and setting both business and personal agendas.

When making an assessment as to whether change agents could be recruited internally within an organisation, it might be useful to conduct an evaluation of whether there is a critical mass of the various skills within this context. If not, perhaps the necessary skills can be bought in.

The choice of who leads the change is a critical one and should not rely purely on technical expertise. Endemic to this change process may be the setting of a vision or visioning statement by key player(s). If HR is to remove its reputation of being the bridesmaid, rather than the bride, then it needs to adopt strategic positioning, understand the business completely (business partnership), and adopt a leadership role (business leader).

Case study 12.2

How Foxtons overhauled its people practices

Walk down a high street anywhere in London and you'd struggle to avoid a branch of Foxtons. Famed for its yellow and green branding, glowing glass box offices and sharply dressed staff zipping around in liveried Minis, the estate agency is ubiquitous in England's capital, with 59 branches spanning Camden to Canary Wharf and Woolwich to Wood Green.

But the company's prestigious almost 40-year history has not been without its controversies. Partly renowned for its reportedly aggressive sales tactics, in 2008 it found itself at the High Court defending some of its business practices against the Office of Fair Trading. And with its reputation for upmarket properties, for several years the firm's Brixton office was the focus of anti-gentrification protests in the formerly deprived area, with local people claiming rising prices were forcing them out. Several instances of vandalism at the branch culminated in 2015 with protestors smashing the trademark floor-to-ceiling windows.

And although not one but two dedicated Twitter accounts exist for Foxtons customers to vent their frustrations against the company, it seems this is very much only half the story. The firm currently boasts a 4.7-star rating out of five on customer review site Trustpilot and, despite 'a hint of sharp practices in the past', things have moved on in recent years, according to chief people officer Sarah Mason. Having joined the company in 2018, Mason is all too aware of the link between employer and customer brands: 'I'm very focused on one driving the other – we get our people practices right; that will drive a great customer experience.'

The business is certainly closer to getting its people practices right since the start of Mason's tenure. With her role being newly created and three separate recruitment, training and personnel teams previously reporting to different departments, her main focus has been uniting the people team. What was 'recruitment' is now a talent acquisition team, previously focused on a high volume of entry-level hires to cope with the demands of the high-growth housing market, but now using an evidence-based approach to bring the right fit of people into the business. 'If we don't get the right people in at the start, the rest of the people practices fall over,' explains Mason.

The former 'training' team has been rebadged as L&D too. Although not wanting to dispense completely with the rigorous induction that has won the business awards and given it a reputation in the industry for being akin to National Service, Mason instead wanted to 'spread out' the team's remit with the introduction of digital learning and coaching platforms. 'Their purpose should be enabling learning to drive performance, and we want everyone to have development opportunities,' she says.

Mason has also changed the remit of the former 'personnel' department, which mainly spent its time on 'processes and red tape', as well as sending out birthday cards to every member of staff, to one that is more advisory focused and uses data to drive outcomes. 'Two of our advisers have done their Level 5 CIPD qualification, and another is completing it at the moment,' says Mason. 'We want them to be experts in their field and have a real advisory focus, rather than just being the people that send out cards,' says Mason.

Such mammoth changes might seem daunting to some, but Mason – who has a master's in organisational change – actually found the firm was more receptive than most. 'I've worked in other companies where you finally launch an initiative and hit a brick wall,' she says. 'But here, people say 'you've been brought in as an expert – tell us what you need and we'll do it'.'

The newly refreshed and empowered team was, then, in a strong position when the Covid-19 pandemic hit. For Mason and her senior colleagues, the most important part of the company's reaction was being responsible, and doing more than was required. When government guidelines after the first national lockdown allowed estate agents to reopen their doors with a day's notice, Foxtons instead took two weeks to ensure the right health and safety measures were in place, and that staff were comfortable with them. 'We knew that would be at the cost of losing business for doing the right thing, but it just couldn't happen,' she says. 'And we're OK with that.'

But as well as bringing its own set of challenges, Covid also pushed back other projects Mason had planned for 2020, including building on her already-successful I&D strategy. While the company is an unusually diverse industry 'outlier' – 43 per cent of its employees have an ethnic minority background, and it has close to a 50/50 gender split – engagement surveys revealed staff thought it fell short on inclusion. To rectify this, as well as actively listening to those in minority groups, educating leaders and putting in place processes to support inclusion, Mason and her team focused on employee networks for different groups, including black, female and LGBT+ staff, with senior employees running each one. The company has seen a three-fold increase in involvement, as well as recent surveys revealing that 93 per cent of staff now believe Foxtons supports a diverse, inclusive workplace. And, pandemic permitting, Mason has plans to expand these efforts into disability inclusion too. 'Like so many HR people, lots of resource has been dedicated to Covid this year,' she says. 'But hopefully it's something we can look at in 2021.'

1 To what extent did Mason adopt an organisational development approach in changing Foxtons?
2 Is there an argument to be had that Covid added to the enablement of change at Foxtons?

SOURCE: Whitehouse, E (2020) How Foxtons overhauled its people practices, *People Management*, 10 December

12.7 HR value added and change

Can HR establish and maintain a strategic-level involvement in organisations? The danger of pigeonholing functions is that some form of reductivism may result. If strategy was determined at a resource and capability level, then HR could perhaps fit more readily within strategic decision-making in organisations. However, Warren (2009) argues that OD needs to start with the business and HR's role is to facilitate it. HR and OD should be one and the same. It depends upon the level of importance that OD has within organisations as to whether OD impacts (and possibly guides) upon strategic planning.

For HR partners to take a leadership and proactive role, they will need to contribute towards key strategic decisions, and to do this, understanding of strategic change and change interventions is critical.

When bridging the strategic and tactical level, we can identify various ways in which HR professionals can endeavour to secure a successful role in the contribution made to change projects, namely:

- involvement at the initial stage in the project team
- advising project leaders in skills available within the organisation – identifying any skills gaps, training needs, new posts, new working practices, etc
- balancing out the narrow/short-term goals and broader strategic needs
- assessing the impact of change in one area/department/site on another part of the organisation
- being used to negotiating and engaging across various stakeholders
- understanding stakeholder concerns to anticipate problems
- understanding the appropriate medium of communication to reach various groups
- helping people cope with change, performance management and motivation.

There are perhaps many other areas where HR should impact upon change in organisations, such as learning from change, capturing appropriate knowledge and knowledge-sharing. Similarly, HR can facilitate teambuilding. Arrata, Despierre and Kumra (2007) argue that three critical elements are crucial to any change programme: thoughtful design; careful recruitment and development of personnel; and close integration between the change agent team and the organisational areas targeted for change. Successful communication underpins the effectiveness of the change team.

 Reflective activity 12.6

Concepts such as engagement and communication are vital within strategic and organisational change. It could be argued that HR has a central role in the day-to-day running of both of these concepts. In some cases, HR takes a leading role in implementing a range of change initiatives.

1 To what extent are there tensions for HR when managing change at both strategic and operational levels?

2 As a counter-argument, should line managers be largely responsible for engagement and communication within their respective divisions or departments?

12.7.1 Evaluating success

Successful change may be very much value judgemental. Beer and Nohria (2000) provide a useful framework when considering the perspective of change and how it may be judged. Their model included theory E and theory O when considering organisational change. Theory E is all about economic value to the organisation, with an emphasis upon economic returns in the form of shareholder returns. On the other hand, theory O change focuses upon corporate culture and human capability being developed. Aligned to this is the building of trust and emotional commitment through employees and teams. Beer and Nohria (2000) argue that the balance of these two approaches is critical. They differentiate the appropriateness of the two models using six key dimensions of change: goals, leadership, focus, process, reward system and the use of consultants. Dependent upon the context, both theory E and theory O may have a part to play in bringing about successful change. On a word of caution, there is a need to consider the extent to which the two theories are focusing on input measures or output measures alone.

12.8 Change and performance

Ordinarily, organisational development will include a range of strategic objectives and measures so that a 'before and after' can be scientifically measured in order to assess the actual impact of the change. When we consider that there is a high percentage of failure in change initiatives, any success measure may be welcomed. Higgins (2005) refers to 'Strategic performance' by extending the McKinsey 7S framework (see Chapter 3) into an eighth element on strategic performance and argues that both the context (7 S's) and strategic performance are aligned. The significance of this eigth element is that it provides both focus and closure of the change intervention. Ultimately it is the result that will count.

 Case study 12.3

Managing change through marginal gains in sport and business

A concept known as 'marginal gains' came to prominence during the London 2012 Olympics when the GB cycling team won a record eight gold medals. This outstanding performance followed similar success at the 2008 Beijing Olympics, and is attributed to the management approach adopted by Sir Dave Brailsford, the British Cycling Performance Director at the time of the 2008 and 2012 Olympic Games.

The concept of marginal gains can be neatly summarised in the following quote from Brailsford: 'Put simply... how small improvements in a number of different aspects of what we do can have a huge impact on the performance of the team' (Slater, 2012). In other words, it is the aggregation of a number of small gains that result in a large gain in overall performance that can be significant in terms of outcomes and achievement. The application of marginal gains in sport is not confined to cycling and it has been adopted by across many sports by individuals and teams. Well-known examples of sports that use marginal gains as an intervention to improve performance include Formula 1 racing, rugby, athletics, swimming and golf.

Marginal gains are typically presented and discussed in terms of performance improvement, particularly when the context is competitive sport. However, the essence of marginal gains is change and the recognition of marginal gains as an intervention for managing change is often shadowed by the focus on performance and results. Many elements of marginal gains are key components of managing change, particularly in terms of continuous improvement and the application of metrics, such as statistical process control and quality management, are fundamental to the effective application of marginal gains. This case study highlights marginal gains as change intervention and discusses how this approach is applied in non-sport organisations with specific examples from a UK public sector organisation.

A strategy for change

To compare the use of marginal gains in sport with performance in business, it is helpful to consider the principles which underpinned the team's 2012 Olympic success. Sir Dave Brailsford provides insight into the systematic management approach applied at the GB cycling team: 'Firstly, you need a team with the skills and motivation to succeed. Secondly, you need to understand what you want to achieve. Thirdly, you need to understand where you are now. Then, you need to put a plan in place to see how you can get from where you are now to what you want to achieve' (*BBC Breakfast*, BBC1, 7 August 2012). This quotation captures the strategic and systematic management approach taken by Brailsford and his team. Understanding where the GB cycling team is now and planning future performance is based on the sophisticated application of

metrics to track marginal performance gains. Marginal gains are sought from every aspect of the team's activities that that contribute towards performance, including the technology that enables collection and analysis of real-time performance data. Performance improvement across such a range of areas demonstrates the holistic management approach taken by the team.

Theories in performance management and high-performance teams/organisations suggest that people need to be highly skilled and motivated to perform well (Katzenbach and Smith, 2005). Brailsford states that the first requirement is a team with the skills and motivation to succeed. Elite sports teams are high-performance teams that are shaped by a high-performance organisational culture. The HRM literature describes the application of specific and integrated ('bundling') of high-performance work practices (HPWPs) in high-performance work organisations (HPWOs) to aggregate gains (Lawler, 2005). Team GB cycling has successfully embedded continuous improvement practices in all aspects of its operation to realise aggregated marginal gains and, in doing so, is effectively managing change and performance.

Marginal gains at a UK fire and rescue organisation

To respond effectively to business challenges, major (destabilising) change may be required, but this type of change can be complemented by small evolutionary change ('incremental') that focuses on marginal gains. However, the goal of marginal gains may be obscured by the revolutionary strategic debate, rendering continuous change aimed at improvement through marginal gains passive rather than being driven by strategic intent. It is this context that sparked an interest in the concept of marginal gains at a UK Fire and Rescue organisation as an intervention opportunity to empower a more proactive approach towards organic change and improving organisational performance.

Specific examples of change and performance improvement at this organisation through a marginal gain approach include allowing on-call firefighters to text in their availability rather than having to visit the station, resulting in a significant increase in fire and rescue coverage across the area. Another example is the application of barcode readers to manage the organisation's assets, which has led to significantly improved legal compliance and management of over 30,000 traceable pieces of equipment. Changing station shift systems in tandem with increased managerial flexibility has led to a more productive working day. Less prescription over work routines has allowed adaptable and responsive services to be applied to changing community needs. All of these examples in isolation are small, incremental changes, but the accumulative effect through the aggregation of the marginal gains led to considerable improvements to community and firefighter safety.

Based on the success of marginal gains as a change and improvement intervention, this organisation has progressed to consider a more strategic management approach that identifies and connects marginal gains activities into larger programmes that are more strategically focused. Three key areas have been identified as a focus for discussion to take this forward:

- *Leadership gains*: small changes in overall strategic leadership and management that provokes new thinking in managers, and innovation within and between departments that improve efficiency, effectiveness and increased morale.

- *Technological gains*: introducing low-cost, undisruptive ICT or equipment changes that improve customer and service delivery experiences.

- *Process gains*: changing processes through lean thinking and application, along with the improved use of metrics to focus resources on the things that really make a difference and from which marginal gains can be determined.

To take a more strategic and proactive position on marginal gains, the organisation's management team believe that there are a number of common challenges to organisations. There may also be some that are more relevant to public sector organisations where the bottom line is more complex than profit, or in the case of sport, quickest time or points accumulated on the board.

Enabling organisation culture

One of the key challenges is to mindfully recognise margin gains within the overall strategic discussion and debate regarding continuous improvement. This must start with a discussion on the cultural norms that an organisation wishes to develop and promote. The focus needs to be on 'we're good, how do we get better?' and 'our people are good, how do we make them better?' Adopting this position sets a fundamentally different starting position from one that may often be focused on gaps and weaknesses. Although both approaches are focused on continuous improvement, the former is more likely to positively inspire, support higher levels of trust and allow empowerment to flourish. An example could be adoption of a strengths-based leadership approach to the development and management of our leaders that could produce the marginal improvements in personal performance and maximise talent.

Consider the intangibles

It is important that resources are fully accountable and used to their full potential: metrics are clearly important when indicating areas for marginal gains and measuring their success. However, while organisations can often sleepwalk into an approach whereby gains need to be fully justified and accounted for or, potentially, may be dismissed. Introducing measurement frameworks and metrics may lead to innovation more focused on meeting targets (because individuals are held to account) than a more creative culture where managers are encouraged to innovate and to find marginal gains in all areas of their work.

This may be particularly relevant in the public sector where outcomes and outputs are sometimes less tangible and often intangible; it may need to be accepted that not everything can or needs to be measured. There is the danger that intended marginal gain may be quickly eroded by the bureaucracy needed to measure it. Sometimes it may take courage to allow the gain to be ill-defined: irrational, but emotionally valid. For instance, a feeling of self-efficacy in managers through greater empowerment is essential in creating improved performance is extremely difficult to measure.

Conclusion

This case study proposes that a marginal gains approach to managing change offers a proactive and empowering approach to strategy for achieving continuous improvement. The incremental approach of marginal gains offers advantages for managing change, including encouraging and supporting employee involvement resulting in less resistance. This approach facilitates an organisational culture that supports high-performance behaviours in individuals and groups, which is essential to manage continuous improvement. Key to this approach is the recognition that many marginal gains can accumulate to deliver significantly greater in terms of individual and group performance for an organisation.

1   Can you identify where you could make marginal gains in the tasks you undertake (in work and out of work), and how would you prioritise these?
2   How would you monitor the gains you identified in Question 1 to determine your improvement?
3   What would need to be in place to support you in taking a marginal gains approach to your individual work and the teams you are a member of?

SOURCE: Hall, D, James, D and Marsden N (2012) Marginal gains: Olympic lessons in high performance for organisations, *Human Resource Bulletin: Research and Practice*, **7** (2), pp 9–13

12.9 Conclusion

Lloyd and Maguire (2002, p 149) argue that, 'In future, the critical focus for sustainable organisational success will build on what the organisation knows about itself and its environment, and not on the transient structure and detailed processes. The successful organisations of the future will not be managing change but rather facilitating conversations for organisational learning and individual responsibility.' Hence, the emphasis here is upon individual and team development, which sits comfortably within the scope and domain of HR.

'Change is ultimately about people – if they do not change, nothing significant happens' (Miller, 2004, p 10). Perhaps the argument for organisations having stronger and more sophisticated OD processes can never be understated. A positive employee attitude towards change is vital to a successful outcome. Tan and Tiong (2005) found that the highest correlated success factor was optimism, which they define as attitude towards change. HR, in partnership with line management, need to ensure that organisational change is planned, communicated and executed successfully on an ongoing basis in order to sustain business survival.

🔒 KEY LEARNING POINTS

1 There are numerous ways in which change can be analysed as far as the scope and nature of change is concerned.

2 HR professionals need to have an appreciation of the complex nature of several (sometimes contradictory) change interventions operating concurrently.

3 The context of change needs to be analysed in order to decide upon whether and which type of change intervention is needed or appropriate.

4 OD is a change intervention particularly suited to changing employees' values and organisational culture.

5 HR has a significant contribution to make to strategic change interventions, particularly when collating knowledge and learning emanating from change interventions, which can then be used on subsequent change interventions.

6 Change agents typically have to exhibit a range of skills and competences in order to demonstrate their credibility as a change agent, and simultaneously be aware of the political context within which they operate.

❓ Review questions

1 Discuss the extent to which a vision and mission statement is important when an organisation is going through cultural changes.

2 Consider a change intervention with which you are familiar and consider what some of the barriers to change were, and where resistance to change was encountered. Try and classify these barriers and resistance factors into key categories.

3 What are some of the key skills that a change agent needs to exhibit? To what extent are these skills context specific?

4 Think about how you could apply Lewin's change model to a change scenario of your choice. To what extent were there critical moments that defined the unfreezing, movement and refreezing?

Explore further

Cameron, E and Green, M (2019) *Making Sense of Change Management: A complete guide to models, tools and techniques of organisational change*, 5th edn, Kogan Page, London

Cheung-Judge, M and Holbeche, L (2021) *Organisational Development, A practitioner's guide for OD and HR*, 3rd edn, Kogan Page, London

Hayes, J (2018) *The Theory and Practice of Change Management*, 5th edn, Palgrave Macmillan, London

Hughes, M (2019) *Change Management: A critical perspective*, 2nd edn, CIPDLondon. A sound textbook presenting a range of approaches to change.

PART FOUR
Conclusion

13

Summary themes and future trends

GARY REES AND RAY FRENCH

LEARNING OUTCOMES

After reading this chapter, you should be able to:

- identify some of the key challenges and themes impacting on HR/people management
- indicate some possible future HR considerations and developments
- highlight key research findings that impact upon HR (this learning outcome is embedded throughout the chapter).

13.1 Overview

Material contained throughout this book aims to strengthen readers' understanding of strategic people management by reviewing major research findings and theories and linking these to effective practices and positive outcomes.

In Chapter 1 we set the scene by showing how key chapters align with CIPD module 7C002 *People Management and Development Strategies for Performance*.

We also set out the range of pedagogic features, which we hope have enabled the reader to reflect on the various topic areas and also engage with review questions, case studies and other useful sources intended to set the HR debate alive. Chapters 2 and 3 adopted a strategic approach and linked key areas together in formulating our understanding of the potential scope and role of HR and how HR practitioners can align strategy culture and values. Chapters 4 and 5 broadened debates beyond a simple functional approach towards understanding HR by examining theory and practice globally, questioning the vital questions around ethical and professional practice and, in so doing, taking one step back to consider not just the way in which organisations *do*, but *should* operate. Chapters 6 to 10 considered applied aspects of HR/people management in practice and the core areas in which HR typically operates within organisations. Following this, Chapters 11 and 12 focused the debate on to modern day effective working practices by aligning structure and change.

In this final chapter, we will revisit and highlight recurrent themes from earlier sections of the book, in order to identify the key challenges facing the 'people management function' in the contemporary de-globalised workplace. The concept of deglobalisation is emerging from the changing way in which the planet has operated post-pandemic, with major shifts in supply chains and how businesses operate significantly worldwide (eg Amazon and Google).

13.2 Key trends

While not wishing to introduce an exhaustive list of important themes for the people profession moving forward, this section aligns with the CIPD module 7002 on People Management and Development Strategies for Performance. Digital technologies continue to advance at great pace, leading us to question whether the people management function is keeping up with digitalisation, let alone utilising digitalisation in making additional advances in the workplace. The advancement in artificial intelligence (AI) and sophistication of big data collection draws significant demands upon the people management function too. The increased global competition for talent and competitiveness raises questions around high performance work and working practices. Ultimately, the people profession has to pay its way, demonstrate clear business value and play a key role in strategic decision-making in organisations.

13.2.1 Digital age people management

'Taking the Strategic out of Strategic HR in the new Digital Age.' This controversial headline from Ram Charan in 2014 and his announcement that it was 'time to say goodbye to the Department of Human Resources' probably needs revisiting post Covid-19 and other global events between 2020 and 2022. (See also Dave Ulrich's (2014) response to this.) This headline suggested that the HR function be split between operational and strategic lines, which is still manifest in many organisations today. It could be argued that HR has expanded itself through stronger corporate agendas around wellbeing, EDI (equality diversity and inclusivity), values driven business and so on.

In an article in *Work* (2021), two opposing views are presented. Toby Peyton-Jones argues that the HR function is already fragmented, with the HR function having become more digitalised with the role of line manager changing dramatically so that line managers carry out much of the decision-making work. He argued that with the proliferation of the HR business partner role, and greater use of data and metrics, the HR Director role allows for greater attention and actions around business strategy. However, Danny Harmer puts forward a counter-argument for an integrated HR function, requiring the correct set of experts. HR needs to represent all aspects of the business at board level, and advise accordingly on critically important issues such as equality, diversity and inclusivity.

While the debate continues, questions arise as to who is drawing down the data and making the critical analysis leading to sound recommendations and subsequent decisions and actions. Harmer argues that the HR function showing added value continuously is of significant importance to businesses. The difficulty of these discussion pieces lay within their reach, with cash rich multinational companies being able to make structural and other significant related changes, whereas small to medium-size enterprises may struggle with economies of scale and maximising the use of data analytics and enhanced technologies. These economies of scale may be critical when evaluating the rise of digitisation in the workplace, and this is echoed in research carried out by Eurofound (2021), which highlighted some interesting data around European practice. In terms of key findings:

- Of organisations with 10 employees or more, 28 per cent are highly digitised, with an association between company size and digital intensity.
- Digitalisation in EU establishments coincides with innovation, internationalisation and job creation.
- Digital technologies are reaching both high levels of sophistication and affordability. However, data from the ECS (European Company Survey) (2019) showed that only 5 per cent of EU establishments used data analytics for employee monitoring before the Covid-19 crisis.
- Digital technology has enabled greater home working and organisational flexibility.
- As digitalisation spreads, there remains a 'human in the loop' so that task assignment, management and surveillance are not entirely left to algorithms.

However, there were several critical challenges presented too.

- Digitalisation was stymied by lack of available financial resources. Also, the lack of required skills created significant bottlenecks.
- Polarisation and shortages expected in the labour market due to the spike in demand for high-skilled white-collar workers.
- Digitalisation disrupts the continuity of employment relationships leading to increasing concerns about the quality of employment.
- If digitalisation does not take into account workers' interests, then negative consequences like increased exposure to physical and psychosocial risks arise from long working hours and increased stress may also occur.
- Social dialogue and collective bargaining may struggle to represent and mobilise workers within the digital age.

With regards to a public sector perspective on AI within the UK, work by The Mind Foundry (2022) drew data from 334 public sector organisations and revealed some very interesting results.

First, when asked whether they have an effective data strategy, only 26 per cent admitted that they had. Second, 38 per cent of respondents stated that they struggled to integrate different data sets. Third, only 3 per cent stated that they excel in their own data strategy. Fourth that only 21 per cent of respondents were spending significant resources to curate data, and, finally, 12 per cent of respondents mentioned that they find it hard to maintain data and that they are unsure how to evaluate its data. This possibly highlights the level of sophistication needed to have an appropriate Data Strategy and supportive Information Systems infrastructure that allows the big data to be mined, let alone looking to add value at more of an operational level.

 Case study 13.1

VIVID Housing Association: Leading with data to improve workforce wellbeing

VIVID is a Housing Association that employs around 900 staff and is based in Portsmouth, Hampshire. When VIVID was formed from a merger of two housing associations in 2017, Cathryn Gee (Head of People) knew that the changes would cause stress to some people. There was a lot to do, including service offerings and processes to align, new values to embed and so on. Gee then turned to people data to form their strategy on dealing with stress, and to gain support and investment for their initiatives. They collected data from their HR systems, staff surveys and benefits providers. They used Excel to analyse what happened, when, to whom and, where possible, explore why it happened, as this would help understand the repercussions of certain decisions and actions. This exercise showed them the state of their people's mental health and wellbeing at different points in time.

VIVID signed the 'Time to Change' pledge to remove the stigma attached to poor mental health. Colleagues volunteered to become 'Stigma Busters' and in doing so shared their personal stories of dealing with mental health issues in blogs and drop-in sessions. Gee argues that 'A real turning point for us was when a male, senior leader who was an ex-builder came forward to talk about his own struggles. He was not the sort of person who would ordinarily be confident to talk about this. But he did. It was so powerful it resonated with many other people across the organization.'

VIVID also introduced new employee benefits: a new wellbeing app with 300 programmes and updated their Employee Assistance Programme to provide counselling and cognitive behavioural therapy (CBT) as a standard offering. They also trained their managers on how to recognise the signs of someone who's struggling, and how to have those conversations.

In terms of outcomes and lessons learnt, their key metrics improved as more people participated in their mental health and wellbeing initiatives and staff became more used to the new work culture. Over the 12 months to March 2020, engagement rose from 66 per cent to 85 per cent, mental health sickness fell by 1.5 days to 2.2 days, and labour turnover reduced by 4.8 percentage points to 9.8 per cent. Seventy per cent of people used the new wellbeing app. With fewer people off sick and fewer leavers, VIVID have avoided around £100,000 in costs.

Their people's health and wellbeing improved and their approach to supporting people has stood them well during the Covid-19 pandemic. 'It's the actions that are taken after analysing the data that create real strategic impact – the people initiatives – not the numbers on the spreadsheet,' says Trevor Rawlins (HR Manager). VIVID won the People Management Awards for the Best Health and Wellbeing Initiative in 2020.

1 Trevor Rawlings said that the numbers led to insights and stated that actions led to impact. Why do you think was this the case?

2 To what extent were the events set out here simply an example of culture change bringing about positive outcomes?

SOURCE: VIVID www.youtube.com/watch?v=hoM4bVs7du8&t=4s

13.2.2 The rise of the robots?

For more than 70 years, films and television have portrayed robots taking over the Earth and posing a major threat to humankind. Contemporary writers suggest that robots are useful for replacing tedious and unnecessary tasks performed by employees, Ford (2021). Automation and artificial intelligence (AI) have increased in size and complexity, with a 2019 CIPD Report 'People and Machines: From hype to reality' 'CIPD, 2019a) arguing that AI and automation is more likely to create jobs than eliminate them. This report also argues that 'They tend to make jobs more skilled and interesting and give employees more autonomy and control over their work, not less. And far from weakening job security for employees, AI and automation can actually help strengthen job security' (p 4).

The proliferation of data together with other innovative technologies in cloud processing and computing power means that AI is growing faster than ever. In an Accenture report of 2019, 84 per cent of C-suite executives believe that they must leverage AI in order to meet growth objectives, but at the same time, 76 per cent admitted that they struggle when it comes to scaling AI across the business, and, importantly, 75 per cent of these C–suite executives believe that if they don't scale AI in the next five years, then they risk going out of business entirely.

The need for an integrated strategy that seamlessly blends both the people strategy as well as plans for technology is paramount when it comes to success. So, the question lies as to what is holding companies back here? Boston Consulting Group (BCG, 2022) suggest that while scaling AI can lead to significant competitive advantage, this may not be enough to invest within cutting-edge technologies and algorithms and that organisations need to rewire decision-making and extract value, and more critically invest in human capabilities to make it stick. This investment in AI leads to much greater agility of ways of working. BCG go on to say that without the correct approach and focus on change management strategies, then it is nearly impossible to achieve AI at scale across the business (see Chapter 12 on organisational change). Perhaps there are analogies then between the problems of change and how successfully AI can be introduced and maintained in organisations.

13.2.3 Revisiting high performance working practices, teams and organisations

- While there remain several definitions of what constitutes high performance working organisations (HPWOs), much emphasis is placed upon the inclusion of engaged and empowered employees and high-quality goods and services. It could be argued that this definition is somewhat tautological. According to Messersmith and Guthrie (2010, p 242), high performance work systems (HPWS) are defined as 'a set, or bundle, of human resource management practices related to selection, training, performance management, compensation, and information sharing that are designed to attract, retain, and motivate employees'. Critically, HPWS need to be consistent with organisational culture (Hartog and Verburg, 2004) and convey the core competence of the organisation. The culture needs to be integrated seamlessly with the strategy and structure of the organisation through its talent pipeline – see also Chapter 7.

Questions remain as to whether HPWOs are the result of high-performance work practices that lead to greater performance and critical success factors in organisations. Huselid and Rau (1997) found HPWPs to be associated with the following:

- Companies in more profitable industries were more likely to adopt incentive and performance measures of high-performance working systems.
- Those organisations in more volatile or dynamic environments were more likely to shift risk onto employees through variable compensation schemes.
- Adoption of performance management and incentive systems is negatively correlated with unionisation and a unionised workforce associated with the adoption of staffing development practices (but the USA context may play a part here).
- There was some support for an association between high performance working practices and business strategies, with companies who pursue a differentiation strategy more likely to adopt high performance working practices than those adopting a cost leadership strategy (see also Chapter 3), but there was little evidence of what kinds of HR policies and practices might be appropriate.
- External factors have a greater impact on reward management than others.

Critical elements such as, trust, building trust, creating and maintaining enthusiasm and commitment to working processes through organisational culture remain critical.

In terms of how organisations develop high performance working teams, the building of human capital is critically important. In simple terms, Schultz (1961, p 140) defines **human capital** as 'knowledge, skills and abilities of people employed in an organisation'. Ployhart et al (2014) extend the concept of human capital by broadening the definition to include the context of organisational/unit level outcomes, see Table 13.1.

Table 13.1 Human capital at multiple levels

Individual characteristics	Individual capabilities Heterogeneous
KSAOs	Knowledge, skills, abilities and other capabilities
Human capital	Individual KSAOs relevant for achieving economic outcomes Performance related Individual or unit level capacities that are based upon individual KSAOs.
Strategic human capital resources	For unit relevant competitive advantage

SOURCE: Houghton, 2017

This model distinguishes between human capital resources and strategic human capital resources, with the significant distinction between these two facets relating to the outcome of the resource, with best practice versus competitive advantage enabling a more strategic approach to being adopted. Questions then arise as to how much organisations are aware of the potential leverage for strategic advantage using human capital and high performance working cultures, and at the same time ensure that trust, creativity and performance focus are paramount.

Holbeche (2018) emphasises the need for organisations to also ensure organisational agility and resilience within a crowded and faster marketplace that has embraced more advanced technologies. In addition, Holbeche (2018) stresses that organisational efficiency requires a strong future focus (particularly in respect to change), strong customer collaboration and an experimental, innovative and empowering culture.

In summary, whist manage core HR aspects and activities have remained relatively stable (training and development, performance appraisal, etc), the context in which HR operates and continues to operate is extremely dynamic and unpredictable and links strongly with technological advances and their impact upon working practices.

 Case study 13.2

Google

Googleplex is the company's headquarters in Silicon Valley, adapted in 2004 by architect Clive Wilkinson, who redesigned the previous house of Silicon Graphics, creating a radical new space that reflects Google's culture, aiming to foster creativity, social interaction and innovation (Jakobsson and Stiernstedt, 2010; Vise, 2005).

Google's organisational culture has three major characteristics – geek culture, vision to change the world, and selective recruitment – that shape its unique identity (Iyer and Davenport, 2008, p 67). 'Geek culture' refers to a university-like atmosphere in the company, as well as to the extended knowledge of programming by

Googlers, who promote a 'do it on your own' mentality (Konzack, 2006).

Google's organisational culture largely affected the design of the 'living environment' at Googleplex, which reminds one more of a university than a 'conventional work environment' (Chang, 2006).

Office design is crucial, placing 'three or four people into an office, a configuration that the co-founders liked from their Stanford grad-school days' (Chang, 2006), while the creation of social spaces aims to facilitate knowledge exchange and social talk. Informatisation reflects on Google's norm to consider every aspect of organisational life and performance as information on a continuous flow that is evident to statistical analysis and control (Iyer and Davenport, 2008). An example of this norm is Google's 'experiment in using mathematical modelling for personnel management' (Carr, 2008, p 203). In 2006, Google launched a 300-question questionnaire that tracked the personality of Googlers, measuring both in-work and out-of-work characteristics. In 2007, based on this information, the company created algorithms that might predict performance, which are used for employee selection.

In contrast to Google's centrality in ICT business worldwide, Googleplex has been designed to promote *decentralisation and self-organisation* as key principles of organisational life. Social media plays a vital role in decentralisation and self-organisation in terms of 'small groups of Googlers working independently on their own projects' (Jakobsson and Stiernstedt, 2010, p 121), and sharing knowledge and information through social media platforms.

Decentralisation is also reflected in its architecture, which includes both public and private spaces which encourage collaborative work at some times, and secure privacy and isolation at other times (Chang, 2006). The rise of data scientists has, in turn, driven data-driven human resource practices.

Lorraine Twohill, Google's senior vice president of global marketing, comments that 'Google has a very data-led culture.' For instance, human resource practices are led by the People Analytics Department, which is responsible for recruiting, training and organising activities across the organisation. According to Prasad Setty, the Vice President of People Analytics and xCompensation, the goal of people analytics is to 'complement human decision makers, not replace them' (Setty claims that people analytics has contributed towards limiting the number of interviews required from 100 to four per position). Based on analysing data across the organisation, the People Analytics team has identified the optimal size and shape for each department, improved the retaining of female employees by better managing their needs during maternity leave, helped new employees to better adapt at the beginning of their employment at Google, and *'produced an algorithm to review rejected applications and hire talent otherwise missed'*.

Recently, Google has announced its plans for recreating its Mountain View headquarters. The new Googleplex is planned to be an urban village, equipped with robotic technologies that physically transform the building according to the changing needs and configurations of its teams. As Mangalindan (2015) reports for Mashable UK, 'small cranes and robots will reconfigure the corporate buildings by moving around floors, walls and ceilings, in just a few hours', adding that 'the make-it-yourself design also seems like a nod to Google's open-source approach'. Glass-canopy structures will create a space in harmony with the natural environment of the area and open to the public.

Finally, the use of big data and social media at Google appears as best practice that is closely tied with the management of human resources and the firm's performance. It seems that there is a strong belief within the organisation and, specifically, the People Analytics Department, that big data can resolve important problems and lead the way to the future.

Interestingly, this demonstrates and foretells a departure from the typical human resource approach into data-driven human resources, considering each employee and team as data-generator. The plans of Google to integrate robotics with its new architecture reveal its intention to create a media-enriched organisational space. A pioneer of the new office paradigm, Google is now implementing the data-driven office, blending science with human resources, while leading the way to the intelligent office.

Implications for human resource practice

Organisational spaces such as the Googleplex stimulate a culture of creativity (Amabile, 1983), play (Statler, Roos and Victor, 2009) and collaboration (Perry-Smith, 2006). The new office paradigm emerged to challenge bureaucratic and mechanistic views on organisational culture – see also Chapter 11. For instance, artistic intervention is hailed as a catalyst for organisational renewal, as 'neo-avantgarde art practices which show a renewed interest in [intervening into] the everyday production of public space' (Beyes and Steyaert, 2011, p 100). As a consequence, the metaphor of a glass cage challenges bureaucratic rules in organisations, but at the same time increases transparency and surveillance (Gabriel, 2005). Although embracing iconic architecture, Googleplex encapsulates a paradox of organisational creativity. On the one hand, it purports to distribute power and promote a 'be-yourself' ethos at work, amplifying cultural diversity and openness (Fleming and Sturdy, 2009; Zhang et al, 2008). On the other hand, increased transparency which supposedly deconstructs previous norms may introduce new ones as delicate means of control, increasingly blurring the line between work and life (Dale, 2005; Gabriel, 2005; Fleming and Sturdy, 2009; Randle and Rainnie, 1997; Sennett, 1998).

The question is whether HPWS are best practices, or customised approaches required to fit better with the conditions and needs of an organisation (Guest, 2011). HPWS lead to the development of standardised practices, which aim for long-term committed employment that reflects on stability, retention and development of employees (Messersmith and Guthrie, 2010). By embracing big data and social media, human resource management strategies aim for supporting an agile organisation (Atkinson and Moffat 2005). In this malleable context, the HPWS approach is particularly useful in maintaining high commitment of human resources towards long-term employment, stability and job satisfaction.

However, HPWS are required to shift from static systems into coupled and recoupled situations. In this way, the design of HPWS is not expected to aim for best practices, but for customised policies that couple the core competences with the needs of the firm. HR practitioners are required to transcend the boundaries of their departments and, working closely with data scientists, instilling the vision of the firm. Hence, HR in the age of the data driven organisation, and in the future, the intelligent office, is expected to play an interdisciplinary role translating the needs of the firm across departments, while contributing to the social construction of big data implementation within the firm (Leonardi and Barley, 2010).

The data scientist is a relatively recent role that emerged from the need to analyse the vast amount of data HR managers need to extract meaningfully ordered information, and then exercise their judgement and creativity (Sowe and Zettsu, 2014). Consequently, this causes a reconfiguration of the organisation of human resources which should aim for nurturing lateral thinking by distributing leadership across the organisation (Bolden, 2011). HR should thus find appropriate use of social media to facilitate coordination across divisional and organisational boundaries (Nielsen, 2013).

Empowerment, in this case, takes place through 'job crafting', enabling individuals in organisations to develop a set of skills and roles which are unique, and in some cases, unexpected (Nielsen, 2013). At Google, social media, as well as the 20 per cent rule dedicated to autonomous projects, led to product and service innovations, including the creation of Gmail, Google News and the Google Art Project, among others (Vise, 2005; Proctor, 2011). Social media and big data in the 2020s can accelerate the process of innovation, and the role of HR is to design HPWS that promote job satisfaction through job crafting.

HPWS could facilitate building an agile workforce as a source of competitive advantage (Harvard Business Review, 2015). Especially in the field of software development, agility is crucial in order to deliver products and services faster than the competition. Agility in this case not only refers to flexible working, but to a creative process in which the stages of product development (planning, design, development, testing and implementation) run in circles instead of sequentially. Specifically, HR should concentrate on changing the most difficult factor for creating an agile organisation – the culture – in order to accelerate the creative process (*Harvard Business Review*, 2015).

The designers of HPWS should couple agility with long-term planning. In addition, there is a need to slow down which explains why a technological giant such as Apple, Google or Facebook, who rely on speed, design organisational spaces that aim to comfort employees. In the creative process, slowing down is as important as speeding up, providing social time and space for knowledge exchange and collaboration (Baird, Griffin and Henderson, 2003).

Human resources managers now have more tools available in their hands than ever (space, social media, big data) to create a working environment that balances velocity and slowness, and their role is to 'master the clock of business'.

The role of human resource management evolves in tandem with technological change and the needs of the information society. While aiming for collecting rich information for the individual customer in order to provide a customised instead of standardised experience (Pine and Gilmore, 1998), human resources should provide and 'curate' the context of individuals' work experience. By curating is meant the increasingly hybrid physical and media-enriched space that mediates the HPWS and organisational performance. Finally, those transformations feed back into the role of HR managers and the skills they require to lead this process. As new media gradually inserts itself into organisational life, shifting the vertical organisation into a horizontal form, HR managers are expected to develop a new set of interdisciplinary skills (Sennett, 1998), integrating data analytics with HR practices.

1 Social and environmental engineering seems to be part of Google building HPWS's, but to what extent is creativity and innovation part of corporate culture or part of a socially constructed milieu?

2 There is a distinct lack of emphasis upon leadership and management in this case study. Why is this the case?

SOURCE: Samdanis, M and Lee, SH (2015) Big data, social media and HPWS for the intelligent office, CIPD Applied Research Conference on The Shifting Landscape of Work and Working Lives www.cipd.co.uk/Images/big-data-social-media-hpws_2015_tcm18-15586.pdf

13.2.4 The great resignation and generational differences

While the Microsoft sponsored research headline that more than 40 per cent of all employees were thinking about leaving their jobs at the beginning of 2021 caused raised eyebrows (Microsoft, 2021), we await the longer-term ripple of workforce movements and changes. The anticipated trends identified in this report were that flexible (hybrid) working is here to stay, therefore leaders have to adapt to the new world of working. Secondly, employees are struggling and leaders must support them. Third, that productivity remains high, but with a human cost, with digital intensity being a key factor. Fourth that Generation Z is at risk and in need of re-energising. This last point is of significant concern. For the 18- to 25-year-old category of employees, struggling with work life balance and feeling exhausted is of massive significance.

According to Sull, Sull and Zweig (2022), there are five key issues that explain attrition then how employees assess their compensation and these are (in order of importance from first to fifth: toxic corporate culture (this includes failure to promote diversity, equality and inclusion and employees feeling disrespected together with unethical behaviour), job security and reorganisation (both of these are linked to culture as well as poor career prospects), high levels of innovation (with innovation in itself not being a factor, but innovative companies see employees working very long hours as well facing a fast-paced environment and culture), failure to recognise employee performance (from high performing employees to laggards) and, finally, poor response to Covid-19. The necessary HR practices needed to avoid or reduce the issues above sit with employee engagement and wellbeing being strategic imperatives moving forward. Reward strategies by themselves may help a little, particularly with short-term solutions (see Chapter 10) but may not stop the employee attrition. Tessema et al (2022) cite strategies for minimising employees' resignations as: providing flexible work arrangements (hybrid working and the contracted scheduling of hours and days), providing attractive compensation (pay, benefits and incentives), providing proper employee support (work/life balance, employee assistance programmes, social networking, wellness programmes etc.). Tessema et al (2022) provide a two-fold solution, by the organisation eradicating some traditional HR practices (like work schedules, leave policies etc.) and integration, by assimilating new HR practices that enhance employee retention.

Perhaps working more within the 'fit the job to the person' rather than 'fit the person to the job' managerial philosophy is the way forward. Also, the real war for talent may have truly be started by the impact of Covid-19. The concept of employee value proposition (EVP) is not a new one, with Minchington (2006) defining EVP as a set of associations and offerings provided by an organisation in return for the skills, capabilities and experiences an employee brings to the organisation. This employee-centred approach could itself act as the magnet in attracting and recruiting employees as well as retaining existing talented employees who may easily take up an employment offer elsewhere (see also employer branding in Chapters 3 and 6).

13.3 Conclusion

The Covid-19 pandemic in 2020 and its continuing aftermath has had a major impact on work organisations, with fundamental questioning of workplace location and working patterns, for example hybrid working, corporate decisions around what work was more essential than other work, the introduction of furloughs and much more.

Perhaps, more critically, every aspect of work was scrutinised in all functions, including marketing, finance, HR and all others. Employee wellbeing raised itself up the corporate ladder of importance and the resultant movement and exiting of employees had significant impact upon talent acquisition. Employee retention, like wellbeing, worked itself up the corporate ladder too, and critically led to significant changes in behaviour from line managers and the HR function alike. The skill shift mentioned throughout this textbook will continue to alter and this could heighten the need to be more highly business engaged, understand the HR role from a global perspective and embrace modern technologies, including artificial intelligence, big data and emerging technologies. The shifting nature of global communications and feedback means that the HR function must maintain its role as the bastion of virtues and values for the organisation as well as integrate corporate social responsibility, employee wellbeing and equality, diversity and inclusivity as fundamental pillars of HR policy and practice. The criticality of corporate values, how these are exhibited (by senior management and the HR function) and alignment to employees' values will become more important over time and employers of choice will have attractive company cultures, leadership and employee engagement initiatives to both current employees and potential candidates (employee) alike. One thing is certain – people management will remain the key strategic imperative and focus moving forward.

 Explore further

Throughout this book we have stressed the importance of keeping abreast of current research. Indeed, this is one important theme within the CIPD People Management and Development Strategies for Performance unit. You are recommended to search appropriate websites in order to be aware of emerging reports and data surveys.

Suitable websites include those listed below:

- Chartered Institute of Personnel and Development: cipd.co.uk (archived at https://perma.cc/B7S2-3EJK)

- CIPD magazine: www.peoplemanagement.co.uk (archived at https://perma.cc/ESA3-Y5DE)

- Institute for Employment Studies: www.employment-studies.co.uk (archived at https://perma.cc/SKA4-GJ9D)

- International Labour Organization: www.ilo.org (archived at https://perma.cc/RXJ2-42KT)

- Department of Business, Innovation and Skills: www.bis.gov.uk (archived at https://perma.cc/EHM4-R3XH)

- Office of National Statistics: www.ons.gov.uk (archived at https://perma.cc/M3JA-LGTA)

- European Union Employment and Social Affairs: ec.europa.eu/social/home.jsp (archived at https://perma.cc/5CBM-LBWR)

- Chartered Institute of Management: www.managers.org.uk (archived at https://perma.cc/6WFU-2XFK)

- Trades Union Congress: www.tuc.org.uk (archived at https://perma.cc/42AS-VXYK)

- *Independent* newspaper: www.independent.co.uk (archived at https://perma.cc/742J-7YM2)

- *Daily Telegraph* newspaper: www.telegraph.co.uk (archived at https://perma.cc/PL5E-L9ZY)

- The BBC: www.bbc.co.uk/news (archived at https://perma.cc/H7S2-9PMM)

- CNN business news: www.cnn.com/business (archived at https://perma.cc/V5JB-JLBZ)

- *WORK* by CIPD.

BIBLIOGRAPHY

ABBETT, L, COLDHAM, A, and WHISHNANT, R (2010) *Organizational Culture and the Success of Corporate Sustainability Initiatives: An empirical analysis using the competing values framework*. A project for the degree of Master of Science, University of Michigan. https://seproject.org/wp-content/uploads/2019/10/SGMOrganizational-Culture-Sustainability.pdf (archived at https://perma.cc/9LH2-UNCM)

ACAS (2010) *How to Manage Change: ACAS guidelines*, January www.acas.org.uk (archived at https://perma.cc/3W2D-A869)

ACAS (2015) *Code of Practice on Disciplinary and Grievance Procedures, Code of Practice 1*, The Stationery Office, London

ACAS (2020) *Discipline and Grievances at Work: The ACAS guide*, ACAS, The Stationery Office, London

ACCENTURE (2014) *Career Capital 2014 Global Research Results*, Accenture, London https://wearethecity.com/accenture-career-capital-2014-global-research-results/ (archived at https://perma.cc/7BHW-EGFU)

ACCENTURE (2019) *AI: Built to scale*, 14 November www.accenture.com/gb-en/insights/artificial-intelligence/ai-investments (archived at https://perma.cc/89PT-MHA5)

ACKERS, P (2002) Reframing employment relations: The case for neo-pluralism, *Industrial Relations Journal*, 33 (1), pp 2–19

ADAIR, J (1983) *Effective Leadership*, Pan Books, London

ADAIR, J (2003) *The Inspirational Leader: How to motivate, encourage and achieve success*, Kogan Page, London

ADAMS, JS (1965) Inequality in social exchange. In Berkowitz, L (ed) *Advances in Experimental Social Psychology*, Academic Press, New York

ADLER, PS (1999) The emancipatory significance of Taylorism. In: Cunha, MPF and Marques, CA (eds), *Readings in Organisation Science – Organisational Change in a Changing Context*, Instituto Superior de Psicologia Aplicada, Lisbon

ADLER, PS (2001) Market, hierarchy, and trust: The knowledge economy and the future of capitalism, *Organization Science*, 12 (2), 215–34

AGUILAR, FJ (1967) *Scanning the Business Environment*, Macmillan, New York

AGUINIS, H (2009) *Performance Management*, 2nd edn, Pearson Prentice Hall, New Jersey

AHMAD, MI, FIRMAN, K, SMITH, HN and SMITH, AP (2018) Psychological contract fulfilment and well-being, *Advances in Social Science Research*, 5 (12), pp 90–101

AHAMMAD, MF, GLAISTER, KW and GOMES, E (2020) Strategic agility and human resource management, *Human Resource Management Review*, 30 (1), p 10070, https://eprints.whiterose.ac.uk/149891/3/Strategic%2520Agility%2520and%2520Human%2520Resource%2520Management.pdf (archived at https://perma.cc/7T8H-VNVL)

AHMED, S (2007) The language of diversity, *Ethnic and Racial Studies*, 30 (2), pp 235–56

ALDOSSARI, M and ROBERTSON, M (2018) Repatriation and the psychological contract: A Saudi Arabian comparative study, *The International Journal of Human Resource Management*, 29 (8), pp 1485–512

ALFES, K, ANTUNES, B and SHANZ, AD (2017) The management of volunteers – what can human resources do? A review and research agenda, *The International Journal of Human Resource Management*, 28 (1), pp 62–97, www.tandfonline.com/doi/abs/10.1080/09585192.2016.1242508 (archived at https://perma.cc/3WXN-3JZN)

ALFES, K et al (2010) *Creating an Engaged Workforce: Findings from the Kingston Employee Engagement Consortium Project*, CIPD, London

ALI, MA et al (2021) The Power of ADKAR change model in innovative technology acceptance under the moderating effect of culture and open innovation, *Scientific Journal of Logistics*, **17** (4), pp 485–502

ALIMO-METCALFE, B (1995) An investigation of female and male constructs of leadership and empowerment, *Women in Management Review*, **10** (2), pp 3–8

All Party Parliamentary Group On Wellbeing Economics (2019) *A Spending Review to Increase Wellbeing: An open letter to the Chancellor* https://wellbeingeconomics.co.uk/wp-content/uploads/2019/05/Spending-review-to-increase-wellbeing-APpG-2019.pdf (archived at https://perma.cc/HX8J-W755)

ALL PARTY PARLIAMENTARY GROUP ON WELLBEING ECONOMICS (2022) *Home Page* https://wellbeingeconomics.co.uk/ (archived at https://perma.cc/U6MX-LQF3)

ALLEN, MR and WRIGHT, P (2007) Strategic management and HRM. In Boxall, P, Purcell, J and Wright, P (eds) *The Oxford Handbook of Human Resource Management*, Oxford University Press, Oxford

ALLEN, WC and SWANSON, RA (2006) Systematic Training – Straightforward and Effective, *Advances in Developing Human Resources*, **8** (4), pp 427–29

ALLIO, RJ (2008) CK Prahalad heralds a new era of innovation, *Strategy and Leadership*, **36** (6), pp 11–14

ALVESSON, M and WILLMOTT, H (2002) Identity regulation as organizational control: producing the appropriate individual, *Journal of Management Studies*, **39** (5), pp 619–44

ALVI, FH (2021) How global business could be the unexpected COP26 solution to climate change, *The Conversation* https://theconversation.com/how-global-business-could-be-the-unexpected-cop26-solution-to-climate-change-172133 (archived at https://perma.cc/FUZ8-SQAX)

AMABILE, TM (1983) *The Social Psychology of Creativity*, Springer-Verlag, New York

AMES, J (2022) Banker who had witch's hat left on her desk awarded £2m, *The Times*, 31 January www.thetimes.co.uk/article/banker-who-had-witchs-hat-left-on-her-desk-awarded-2m-hm36dpqfd#:~:text=A%20high%2Dflying%20woman%20City,unequal%20pay%20based%20on%20gender (archived at https://perma.cc/VU9W-SFBY)

ANDERSEN, C (2022) Shattering talent taboos: Five steps to an entrepreneurial culture, HRZone, 28 February https://hrzone.com/talent/retention/shattering-talent-taboos-five-steps-to-an-entrepreneurial-culture (archived at https://perma.cc/HHU2-RJ7L)

ANDERSEN, M, BIEMANN, T and PATTIE, MW (2015) What makes them move abroad? Reviewing and exploring differences between self-initiated and assigned expatriation, *The International Journal of Human Resource Management*, **26** (7), pp 932–47

ANDERSON, M (2015) *A History of Fair Trade in Contemporary Britain: From civil society campaigns to corporate compliance*, Palgrave Macmillan, Basingstoke

ANDERSON, N, BORN, M and CUNNINGHAM-SNELL, D (2001) Recruitment and selection: Applicant perspectives and outcomes. In Anderson, N, Ones, D and Sinagil, HK (eds) *Handbook of Industrial Work and Organizational Psychology*, Vol 1, Sage, London/New York

ANDERSON, V (2007) *The Value of Learning: From return on investment to return on expectation*, CIPD, London

ANDERSON, V and BOOCOCK, G (2002) Small firms and internationalisation: Learning to manage and managing to learn, *Human Resource Management Journal*, **12** (3), pp 5–24

ANDERSON, V and SKINNER, D (1999) Organisational learning in practice: How do SMEs learn to operate internationally?, *Human Resource Development International*, **2** (3), pp 235–58

ANELL, B and WILSON, T (2000) The flexible firm and the flexible co-worker, *Journal of Workplace Learning: Employee Counselling Today*, 12 (4), pp 165–70

ANKIL, E and PALLIAM, R (2012) Enabling a motivated workforce: Exploring the sources of motivation, *Development and Learning in Organizations*, 26 (2), pp 7–10

ANSOFF, HI (1988) *Corporate Strategy*, Penguin, London

ARGYRIS, C (1960) *Understanding Organizational Behaviour*, Tavistock, London

ARKIN, A (2005a) Power play, *People Management*, 11 (5), pp 40–2

ARKIN, A (2005b) Mr Bright Side, *People Management*, 5 May, pp 28–30, www.cipd. co.uk/pm/peoplemanagement/b/weblog/archive/2013/01/29/mrbrightside-2005-05.aspx (archived at https://perma.cc/C2GQ-D8LR)

ARMSTRONG, M (2000) *Performance Management Practice: Key Practices and Practical Guidelines*, Kogan Page, London

ARMSTRONG, M and BARON, A (2005) *Managing Performance: Performance management in action*, CIPD, London

ARMSTRONG, M and BROWN, D (2019a) Strategic human resource management: Back to the future, *Institute of Employment Studies Reports*, pp 1–36

ARMSTRONG, M and BROWN, D (2019b) Strategic Human Resource Management: Back to the future, *Institute for Employment Studies Reports*, pp. 1–36

ARMSTRONG, M and BROWN, D (2019c) *Armstrong's Handbook of Reward Management Practice: Improving performance through reward*, Kogan Page, London

ARMSTRONG, M and TAYLOR, S (2020) *Armstrong's Handbook of Human Resource Management Practice*, 15th edn, Kogan Page, London

ARNOLD, J (1996) The psychological contract: A concept in need of close scrutiny?, *European Journal of Work and Organisational Psychology*, 5 (4), pp 511–20

ARNOLD, J, COOPER, CL and ROBERTSON, IT (2005) *Work Psychology: Understanding human behaviour in the workplace*, 4th edn, FT/Prentice Hall, Harlow

ARNOLD, J, COOPER, CL AND ROBERTSON, IT (2010) *Work Psychology: Understanding human behaviour in the workplace*, 5th edn, FT/Prentice Hall, Harlow

ARNOLD, J et al (2020) *Work Psychology: Understanding human behaviour in the workplace*, 7th edn, Pearson, London

ARNTZ, M, GREGORY, T and ZIERAHN, U (2016) The risk of automation for jobs in OECD countries: A comparative analysis, *OECD Social, Employment and Migration Working Papers*, 189, OECD Publishing, Paris

ARRATA, P, DESPIERRE, A and KUMRA, G (2007) Building an effective change team, *McKinsey Quarterly*, 4, pp 1–4

ARSTEIN, V (2015) Number of workers relying on zero hours contracts rises to 700,000, *People Management*, 26 February www.cipd.co.uk/pm/peoplemanagement/b/ weblog/archive/2015/02/26/number-of-workers-relying-on-zero-hours-contracts-rises-to-700-000.aspx (archived at https://perma.cc/4TKD-2FHR)

ARTHUR, M (2008) Examining contemporary careers: A call for interdisciplinary enquiry, *Human Relations*, **61** (2), pp 163–86

ASHFORD, S and DERUE, S (2012) Developing as a lLeader: The power of mindful engagement, *Organizational Dynamics*, **41** (2), pp 146–54

ASTON CENTRE FOR HUMAN RESOURCES (2008) *Strategic Human Resource Management: Building research-based practice*, CIPD, London

ASTON, L (2013) Time to address the engagement deficit, *People Management*, 7 January www.cipd.co.uk/pm/peoplemanagement/b/weblog/archive/2013/01/07/timeto-address-the-engagement-deficit.aspx (archived at https://perma.cc/Q5W8-NGEV)

ATKINSON, C (2002) Career management and the changing psychological contract, *Career Development International*, 7 (1), pp 14–23

ATKINSON, J (1984) Manpower strategies for flexible organisations, *Personnel Management*, **16** (8), pp 28–31

ATKINSON, SR and MOFFAT, J (2005) *The Agile Organization*, CCRP Publication Series, Chicago

AVEN, HB and ANDREASSEN, TA (2020) Trustee professionalism transformed: Recruiting committed professionals, *Current Sociology*, pp 1–19 https://oda.oslomet.no/oda-xmlui/bitstream/handle/10642/9761/0011392120969759.pdf?sequence=1&isAllowed=y (archived at https://perma.cc/D2M2-TR2H)

AVOLIO, BJ, KAHAI, S and DODGE, GE (2000) E-leadership: Implications for theory, research and practice, *The Leadership Quarterly*, **11** (4), pp 615–68

AVOLIO, B, WLUMBWA, F and WEBER, T (2009) Leadership: Current theories, research and future directions, *Annual Review of Psychology*, **60**, pp 421–49

BACH, AS, LOKKE MOLLER, AK and VILLADSEN, AR (2021) Perceived red tape and recruitment and selection practices in the public sector, *Academy of Management Proceedings*, **2021** (1), p 113–29

BACKHAUS, K (2003) Importance of person–organisation fit to job-seekers, *Career Development International*, **8** (1), pp 221–26

BAE, KB (2021) The differing effects of individual-and group-based pay for performance on employee satisfaction: the role of the perceived fairness of performance evaluations, *Public Management Review*, 1–19

BAIRD, L, GRIFFIN, D and HENDERSON, J (2003) Time and space: Reframing the training and development agenda, *Human Resource Management*, **42** (10), pp 39–52

BAKAN, I, SUENSO, Y, PINNINGTON, A and MONEY, A (2004) The influence of financial participation and participation in decision-making on employee job attitudes, *International Journal of Human Resource Management*, **15** (3), pp 587–96

BAKER, K (2009) Whitehall HR business partners get skills refresher to deal with cuts, *Personnel Today*, 17 November

BAKER, S, PONNIAH, D and SMITH, S (1999) Survey of risk management in major UK companies, *Journal of Professional Issues in Engineering Education and Practice*, **125** (3), 94–102

BALLANTYNE, I (2009) Recruiting and selecting staff in organizations. In Gilmore, S and Williams, S (eds) *Human Resource Management*, Oxford University Press, Oxford

BALOGUN, J et al (2005) Managing change across boundaries: Boundary-shaking practices, *British Journal of Management*, **16** (4), pp 261–78

BANDURA, A (1977) *Social Learning Theory*, Prentice Hall, Harlow

BANDURA, A (1993) Perceived self-efficacy in cognitive development and functioning, *Educational Psychologist*, **28** (2), pp 117–48

BANO, Y, OMAR, SS and ISMAIL, F (2021) Revitalising organisations' emergency succession planning in the face of the Covid-19 outbreak, *The European Journal of Social & Behavioural Sciences*, **30** (1), pp 5–20

BARBER, A and BRETZ, R (2000) Compensation, attraction and retention. In Rynes, SL and Gerhart, B (eds) *Compensation in Organizations*, Jossey-Bass, San Francisco

BARNEY, JB and HESTERLY, WS (2008) *Strategic Management and Competitive Advantage*, 2nd edn,: Pearson/Prentice Hall, Harlow

BARTRAM, T, CAVANAGH, J and HOYE, R (2017) Special issue: Human resource management in the Ngo, volunteer and not-for-profit sector, *The International Journal of Human Resource Management*, **28** (14), pp 1901–11

BARUCH, Y (2004) The desert generation, *Personnel Review*, **33** (2), pp 241–56

BARUCH, Y (2006) Career development in organisations and beyond: Balancing traditional and contemporary viewpoints, *Human Resource Management Review*, **16** (2), pp 125–8

BARUCH, Y and ROSENSTEIN, E (1992) Career planning and managing in high tech organisations, *International Journal of Human Resource Management*, **3** (3), pp 477–96

BASS, BM (1985) *Leadership and Performance Beyond Expectations*, Free Press, New York

BBC (2022) Law firm says staff can work from home – for 20 per cent less pay, 2 May www.bbc.co.uk/news/business-61298394 (archived at https://perma.cc/9RBD-V22L)

BEARD, CM and WILSON, JP (2006) *Experiential Learning: A best practice guide for trainers and educators*, Kogan Page, London

BEARDWELL, J and CLAYDON, T (2017) *Human Resource Management: A contemporary approach*, 8th edn, Pearson, Harlow

BEARDWELL, J and COLLIN, A (2014) Talent management. In Beardwell, J and Thompson, A (eds), *Human Resource Management: A contemporary approach*, 7th edn, Pearson, Harlow

BEARDWELL, J and THOMPSON, A (eds) (2014) *Human Resource Management: A contemporary approach*. 7th edn, Pearson, Harlow

BEAUMONT, P and HARRIS, R (2002) Examining white-collar downsizing as a cause of change in the psychological contract: Some UK evidence, *Employee Relations*, **24** (4), pp 378–88

BECKER, B and HUSELID, MA (2006) Strategic human resource management: Where do we go from here?, *Journal of Management*, 32 (6), pp 898–925

BECKETT, J (1999) Agency, entrepreneurs and institutional change. The role of strategic choice and institutional practices in organisations, *Organisation Studies*, **20** (5), pp 777–99

BEECROFT, A (2011) Report on Employment Law www.gov.uk/government/publications/employment-law-review-report-beecroft (archived at https://perma.cc/27RA-XCTF)

BEER, M and NOHRIA, N (2000) Cracking the code of change, *Harvard Business Review*, 78 (93), pp 133–41

BEER, M and SPECTOR, B (1989) Corporate-wide transformations in human resource management. In: Walton, RE and Lawrence, PR (eds) *Human Resource Management, Trends and Challenges*, Harvard University School Press, Boston

BEER, M et al (1984) *Managing Human Assets*, Simon & Schuster, Free Press, New York

BEEVERS, K, REA, A and HAYDEN, D (2019) *Learning and Development Practice in the Workplace*, 4th edn, Kogan Page, London

BEIS (2018) The characteristics of those in the gig economy, Final Report https://assets.publishing.service.gov.uk/government/uploads/system/uploads/attachment_data/file/687553/The_characteristics_of_those_in_the_gig_economy.pdf (archived at https://perma.cc/57WM-ESET)

BEIS (2021) *Trade Union Statistics 2020*, Department of BEIS, London

BELBIN, MR (1990) *Team Roles at Work*, Butterworth-Heinemann, Oxford

BELBIN, MR (1991) *Management Teams – Why They Succeed or Fail*, Butterworth, Oxford

BELBIN, MR (1993) *Team Roles at Work*, Butterworth-Heinemann, Oxford

BELOVICZ, MW and FINCH, FE (1971) A critical analysis of the 'risky shift' phenomenon, *Organizational Behaviour and Human Performance*, **6** (2), pp 84–6

BENNETT, N and LEMONINE, GJ (2014) VUCA Really Means for You, *Harvard Business Review*, January/February https://hbr.org/2014/01/what-vuca-really-means-for-you (archived at https://perma.cc/VE7V-5BCJ)

BENNETT et al (2003) *Distributed Leadership*, National College for School Leadership, Nottingham

BENNETT, T, SAUNDRY, R and FISHER, V (2020) *Managing Employment Relations*, 7th edn, CIPD, London Bentley, R (2008) Where did the business partner model go wrong?, *Personnel Today*, 31 March

BERGMAN, S (2012) Open thread: What are the best methods to recruit staff?, *The Guardian*, 22 November

BERNADIN, HK, KANE, JS and ROSS, S (1995) Performance appraisal design, development and implementation. In: Ferris, GR, Rosen, SD and Barnum, DJ (eds) *Handbook of Human Resource Management*, Blackwell, Cambridge, MA

BERNHARD, F and O'DRISCOLL, MP (2011) Psychological ownership in small family-owned businesses: Leadership style and nonfamily-employees' work attitudes and behaviors, *Group & Organization Management*, **36** (3), pp 345–84

BERSIN and ASSOCIATES (2011) *UK Talent Acquisition Factbook 2011: Benchmarks and Trends in Spending, Staffing and Key Recruiting Metrics*, Report

BERSON, J (2021) The death of performance appraisal – redefining performance management, 8 July https://joshbersin.com/2007/09/redefining-performance-management/ (archived at https://perma.cc/6N2K-RGPE)

BERRY, M (2007) Cadbury-Schweppes launches UK graduate recruitment campaign with a new online chatroom, *Personnel Today*, 7 November www.personneltoday.com (archived at https://perma.cc/D6MR-P2Y9)

BEYES, T and STEYAERT, C (2011) The ontological politics of artistic interventions: Implications for performing action research, *Action Research*, **9** (1), 100–15

BIGGS, D and SWAILES, S (2006) Relations, commitment and satisfaction in agency workers and permanent workers, *Employee Relations*, **28** (2), pp 130–43

BIRD, A and MENDENHALL, ME (2016) From cross-cultural management to global leadership: Evolution and adaptation, *Journal of World Business*, **51** (1), pp 115–26

BIRON, M, FARNDALE, E and PAUUWE, J (2011) Performance management effectiveness: Lessons from world leading firms, *International Journal of Human Resource Management*, **22** (6), pp 1294–311

BJORKMAN, I and YUAN, L (1999) The management of human resources in Chinese–Western joint ventures, *Journal of World Business*, **34** (2), pp 1–19

BLAKE, R and MCCANSE, AA (1991) *Leadership Dilemmas – Grid Solutions*, Gulf Publishing, Kaur

BLAKE, RR and MOUTON, JS (1964) *The Managerial Grid*, Gulf Publications, London

BLANCHARD, PN and THACKER, JW (2004) *Effective Training: Systems, strategies and practices*, Pearson/Prentice Hall, New Jersey

BLANCO, MR and GOLIK, MN (2021) Mind the gap: Line managers as effective or non-effective talent spotters, *International Journal of Training and Development*, 25 (1), pp 23–42

BLOISI, W, COOK, CW and HUNSAKER, PI (2003) *Management and Organisational Behaviour*, McGraw-Hill, London

BLOISI, W, COOK, CW and HUNSAKER, PI (2007) *Management and Organisational Behaviour*, 2nd edn, McGraw-Hill, London

BLOOM, BS (ed) (1956) *Taxonomy of Educational Objectives Handbook 1: Cognitive domain*, Longman, New York

BLYTON, P and MORRIS, J (1992) HRM and the limits of flexibility. In Blyton, P and Morris, J (eds), *Reassessing Human Resource Management*, Sage, London

BOATRIGHT, JR (2000) *Ethics and the Conduct of Business*, 3rd edn, Prentice Hall, London

BOEKHORST, JA (2015) The role of authentic leadership in fostering workplace inclusion: A social information processing perspective, *Human Resource Management*, 54 (2), pp 241–64

BOLDEN, R (2011) Distributed leadership in organizations: A review of theory and research, *International Journal of Management Reviews*, **13** (3), pp 251–69

BOLLAERT, H and PETIT, V (2010) Beyond the dark side of executive psychology: Current research and new directions, *European Management Journal*, 28 (5), pp 362–76

BONCORI, I, SICCA, LM and BIZJAK, D (2019) Transgender and gender non-conforming people in the workplace: Direct and invisible discrimination. In Nachmias, S and Caven, V (eds) *Inequality and Organizational Practice*, Palgrave Macmillan, Basingstoke

BONNETON, D et al (2022) Do global talent management programs help to retain talent? A career-related framework, *The International Journal of Human Resource Management*, 33 (2), pp 203–38

BOSELIE, P, BREWSTER, C and PAAUWE, J (2009) In search of balance – managing the dualities of HRM, *Personnel Review*, 38 (5), pp 461–71

BOSELIE, P and THUNNISSEN, M (2018) Talent management in the public sector: Managing tensions and dualities. In Collings, DG, Mellahi, K and Cascio, WF (eds), *The Oxford Handbook of Talent Management*, Oxford University Press, Oxford

BOSTON Consulting Group (BCG) (2022) Artificial Intelligence and AI at scale www.bcg.com/capabilities/digital-technology-data/artificial-intelligence?utm_source=search&utm_medium=cpc&utm_campaign=digital&utm_description=none&utm_topic=ai&utm_geo=global&utm_content=ai-in-action&gclid=Cj0KCQjwjN-SBhCkARIsACsrBz7eoX2Emu57XGA8OmrmvKkZK3A0Bilzpck78n46DaL19qNuIv1S_rgaAn1HEALw_wcB (archived at https://perma.cc/9FMP-8JTM)

BOUSKILA-YAM, O and KLUGER, A (2011) Strength-based performance appraisal and goal setting, *Human Resource Management Review*, 21 (2), pp 137–47

BOWLES, ML and COATES, G (1993) Image and substance: The management of performance as rhetoric or reality?, *Personnel Review*, 22 (2), pp 3–21

BOXALL, P (1996) The strategic HRM debate and the resource-based view of the firm, *Human Resource Management Journal*, 6 (3), pp 59–75

BOXALL, P and PURCELL, J (2000) Strategic human resource management: Where have we come from and where should we be going?, *International Journal of Management Review*, 2 (2), pp 183–203

BOXALL, P and PURCELL, J (2003) *Strategy and Human Resource Management*, Palgrave Macmillan, Basingstoke

BOXALL, P and PURCELL, J (2008) *Strategy and Human Resource Management*, 2nd edn, Palgrave Macmillan, Basingstoke

BOXALL, P and PURCELL, J (2011) *Strategy and Human Resource Management*, 3rd edn, Basingstoke: Palgrave Macmillan

BOXALL, P and PURCELL, J (2015) *Strategy and Human Resource Management*, 3rd edn, Palgrave Macmillan, Basingstoke

BOYLE, M (2001) Performance reviews: Perilous curves ahead, *Fortune Europe*, **143** (11), p 87

BRADSHAW, D (1985) Transferable intellectual and personal skills, *Oxford Review of Education*, 11 (2), pp 201–16

BRAMLEY, P (1996) *Evaluating Training Effectiveness*, McGraw-Hill, Maidenhead

BRATTON, J (2015) *Introduction to Work and Organizational Behaviour*, 3rd edn, Palgrave, London

BRATTON, J and GOLD, J (2007) *Human Resource Management Theory and Practice*, 4th edn, Palgrave Macmillan, London

BRATTON, J and GOLD, J (2017) *Human Resource Management Theory and Practice*, 6th edn, Palgrave, London

BRAVERMAN, H (1974) Labour and Monopoly Capital: The degradation of work in the twentieth century, *Monthly Review Press*, New York

BRECH, EFL (1975) *Principles and Practice of Management*, 3rd edn, Longman, Harlow

BRIMHALL, KC et al (2016) Increasing Workplace Inclusion: the promise of leader–member exchange, *Human Service Organization Management*, **41** (3), pp 222–39

BRIMHALL, KC (2019) Inclusion is important ... but how do I include? Examining the effects of leader engagement on inclusion, innovation, job satisfaction and perceived quality of care in a diverse non- profit health care organization, *Nonprofit and Voluntary Sector Quarterly*, **48** (6), pp 716–37

BRINT, S (2015) Professional responsibility in an age of experts and large organizations. In Mitchell, DE and Ream, RK (eds), *Professional Responsibility: The fundamental issue in education and health care reform*, Springer International, Cham, pp 89–107

BRISCOE, J and HAll, D (2006) The interplay of boundaryless and Protean careers: Combinations and implications, *Journal of Vocational Behaviour*, **69**, pp 4–18

BROCKETT, J (2010) See HR as a professional services firm, says Ulrich, *People Management*, 14 (25 March), p 11

BROMLEY, P and MEYER, JW (2017) They are all organizations: The cultural roots of blurring between the nonprofit, business and government sectors, *Administration and Society*, **49** (7), pp 939–66

BROOKS, B (2021) *Are You Developing Employees to Succeed in Hybrid, Remote Work?* https://hrexecutive.com/are-you-developing-employees-to-succeed-in-hybrid-remote-work/ (archived at https://perma.cc/VML5-GLCM)

BROUGH, P, GARDINER, E and DANIELS, K (eds) (2022) *Handbook on Management and Employment Practices*, Springer Live Reference https://link.springer.com/referencework/10.1007/978-3-030-24936-6 (archived at https://perma.cc/26JB-ZCBY)

BROWN, AD (2015) Identities and identity work in organizations, *International Journal of Management Reviews*, **17** (1), pp 20–40

BROWN, D (2021) Former Malone Souliers Boss Jailed for £500,000 Expenses Fraud, *The Times* www.thetimes.co.uk/article/former-malone-souliers-boss-jailed-for-500-000-expenses-fraud-08wvkgv76 (archived at https://perma.cc/A35S-BJGJ)

BROWN, D, RICKARD, C and BROUGHTON, A (2017) *Tackling Gender, Ethnicity and Disability Pay Gaps: A progress review*, Research Report 100, Equality and Human Rights Commission, London

BROWN, RL and MOLONEY, ME (2019) Intersectionality, work, and well-being: The effects of gender and disability, *Gender & Society*, **33** (1), pp 94–122

BROWN, W (2017) The toxic politicising of the national minimum wage, *Employee Relations*, **39** (6), pp 785–9

BRUMBACH, GB (1988) Some ideas, issues and predictions about performance management, *Public Personnel Management*, Winter, pp 387–402

BRYCE, V (2007) Give me strength, *People Management*, 8 February, p 7 www.cipd.co.uk/pm/peoplemanagement/b/weblog/archive/2013/01/29/givemestrength-2007-02.aspx (archived at https://perma.cc/2KEM-J7B5)

BUCHANAN, D and BADHAM, R (1999) *Power, Politics and Organizational Change: Winning the turf war game*, Sage, London

BUCHANAN, D and BODDY, D (1992) *The Expertise of the Change Agent*, Prentice Hall, London

BUCHANAN, D and HUCZYNSKI, A (2007) *Organizational Behaviour*, 6th edn, FT/Prentice Hall, London

BUCHANAN, D and HUCZYNSKI, A (2010) *Organizational Behaviour*, 7th edn, FT/Prentice Hall, London

BUCHANAN, D and HUCZYNSKI, A (2019) *Organizational Behaviour*, 10th edn, Pearson, Harlow

BUCHANAN, DA and WILSON, B (1996) Next patient please: The operating theatres problem at Leicester General Hospital NHS Trust. In Storey, J (ed) *Cases in Human Resource and Change Management*, Blackwell Business, Oxford

BUCHNER, TW (2007) Performance management theory: A look from the performer's perspective with implications for HRD, *Human Resource Development International*, **10** (1), pp 59–73

BUCKLEY, R and CAPLE, EJ (2009) *The Theory and Practice of Training*, Kogan Page, London

BUDRIA, S (2012) The shadow value of employer-provided training, *Journal of Economic Psychology*, **33** (3), pp 494–514

BUDHWAR, P et al (2022) Artificial intelligence – challenges and opportunities for international HRM: A review and research agenda, *International Journal of Human Resource Management*, **33** (6), pp 1065–97

BUDWORTH, M and MANN, S (2011) Performance management: Where do we go from here?, *Human Resource Management Review*, **21** (2), pp 81–4

BULLER, PF, and MCEVOY, GM (2012) Strategy, human resource management and performance: Sharpening line of sight, *Human Resource Management Review*, **22** (1), pp 43–56

BURNES, B (2017) *Managing Change*, 7th edn, Pearson, Harlow

BURNS, J (2008) Informal learning and transfer of learning: How new trade and industrial teachers perceive their professional growth and development, *Career and Technical Education Research*, **33**, pp 3–24

BURNS, T and STALKER, GM (1961) *The Management of Innovation*, Tavistock, London

BURNS, T and STALKER, GM (1994) *The Management of Innovation*, 3rd edn, Oxford University Press, Oxford

BURTON, P (2022) Why the new hybrid working approach is a win–win, *People Management*, 21 March

Business Roundtable (2019) Business Roundtable redefines the purpose of a corporation to promote 'an economy that serves all Americans www.businessroundtable.org/business-roundtable-redefines-the-purpose-of-a-corporation-to-promote-an-economy-that-serves-all-americans/ (archived at https://perma.cc/XCU2-DZ86)

BUTLER, MG and CALLAHAN, CM (2014) Human resource outsourcing: Market and operating performance effects of administrative HR functions, *Journal of Business Research*, **67** (2), pp 218–24

BUYTENDIJK, F (2008) *Performance Leadership: The next practices to motivate your people, align stakeholders, and lead your industry*, McGraw-Hill Professional, New York

CALDWELL, R (2003) Models of change agency: A fourfold classification, *British Journal of Management*, **14** (2), pp 131–42

CALDWELL, R (2008) HR business partner competency models: Recontextualising effectiveness, *Human Resource Management Journal*, **18**, pp 275–94

CALDWELL, SD (2013) Are change readiness strategies overrated? A commentary on boundary conditions, *Journal of Change Management*, **13** (1), pp 19–35

CALIGIURI, P and TARIQUE, I (2012) Dynamic cross-cultural competencies and global leadership effectiveness, *Journal of World Business*, **47** (4), pp 612–22

CALIGUIRI, P, LEPAK, D and BONACHE, J (2010) *Managing the Global Workforce*, Wiley, Chichester

CALLAGHAN, G and THOMPSON, P (2002) 'We recruit attitude.' The Selection and Shaping of Routine Call Centre Labour, *Journal of Management Studies*, **39** (2), pp 233–54

CAMERON, E and GREEN, M (2019) *Making Sense of Change Management: A complete guide to models, tools and techniques of organisational change*, 5th edn, Kogan Page, London

CAMERON, J, BANKO, KM and PIERCE, WD (2001) Pervasive negative effects of rewards in intrinsic motivation: The myth continues, *The Behaviour Analyst*, **24** (1), pp 1–44

CAMERON, KS and QUINN, RE (2011) *Diagnosing and Changing Organizational Culture: Based on the competing values framework*, 2nd edn, John Wiley, Chichester

CAMPBELL, JP and WIERNIK, BM (2015) The modelling and assessment of work performance, *The Annual Review of Organizational Psychology and Organizational Behaviour*, **2**, pp 47–74

CANTRELL, S and BENTON, JM (2007) The five essential practices of a talent multiplier, *Business Strategy Series*, **8** (5), pp 358–64

CAPGEMINI (2022) Work Life Harmony: Achieving balance between work and home, www.capgemini.com/gb-en/careers/life-at-capgemini/work-life-harmony/ (archived at https://perma.cc/35GZ-LSQR)

CAPPELLI, P (2000) A market-driven approach to retaining talent, *Harvard Business Review*, **78** (1), pp 103–11

CARNALL, C (2003) *Managing Change in Organizations*, 4th edn, FT/Prentice-Hall, Harlow

CARNALL, C and TODNEM BY, C (2014) *Managing Change in Organizations*, 6th edn, Pearson, Harlow

CARR, N (2008) *The Big Switch: Rewiring the world, from Edison to Google*, WW Norton and Company, New York

CARVER, C, SUTTON, S and SCHEIER, F (2000) Action, emotion and personality: Emerging conceptual integration, *Personality and Social Psychology Bulletin*, **26** (6), pp 741–51

CASSELL, C, NADIN, S and GRAY, M (2002) Exploring human resource management practices in small and medium-sized enterprises, *Personnel Review*, **31** (6), pp 671–92

CAULKIN, S (2003) How to catch a rising star, *The Observer*, 9 November

CAVE, D (2022) How Ukrainian HR is working through war, *People Management*, 6 April

CAVE, T and ROWELL, A (2014) The truth about lobbying: 10 ways big business controls government, *The Guardian*, 12 March www.theguardian.com/politics/2014/mar/12/lobbying-10-ways-corprations-influence-government (archived at https://perma.cc/6F3Q-NFKD)

CBI (2009) *Education and Skills Survey* www.cbi.org.uk/ndbs/content.nsf/ b80e12d0cd1cd37c802567bb00491cbf/e83f616f81370ce880256dc60047ede9 (archived at https://perma.cc/38SA-55AC)

CBI (2015) *Inspiring Growth: CBI/Pearson education and skills survey 2014* www.voced.edu.au/content/ngv:69086 (archived at https://perma.cc/CY4D-ND9Q)

CERVERO, R (2001) Continuing professional education in transition 1981–2000, *International Journal of Lifelong Education*, **20** (1/2), pp 16–30

CHALOFSKY, N and KRISHNA, V (2009) Meaningfulness, commitment and engagement: the intersection of a deeper level of intrinsic motivation. *Advances in Developing Human Resources*, 11 (2), pp 189–203

CHANG, J (2006) Behind the glass curtain: Google's new headquarters balances its utopian desire for transparency with its very real need for privacy. *Metropolis Magazine*. www.metropolismag.com/cda/story.php?artid=2123 (archived at https://perma.cc/ 7BEM-6M9N)

CHAO, J, KAETZLER, B, LALANI, N and LYNCH, L (2020) *Talent retention and selection in M&A*. www.mckinsey.com/business-functions/m-and-a/our-insights/talent-retention-and-selection-in-m-and-a (archived at https://perma.cc/Y97N-XHW7)

CHARAN, R (2014) It's time to split HR, Harvard Business School, Jul–Aug, https://hbr. org/2014/07/its-time-to-split-hr (archived at https://perma.cc/T8M3-UH8H)

CHARLWOOD, A, and GUENOLE, N (2022) Can HR adapt to the paradoxes of artificial intelligence? Human Resource Management Journal DOI:10.1111/1748-8583.12433 (archived at https://perma.cc/GEB2-F9QH)

CHAUDHURI, S and GHOSH, R (2012) Reverse mentoring: a social exchange tool for keeping the boomers engaged and millennials committed, *Human Resource Development Review*, 11 (1), pp 55–76

CHAUDHURY, A, COYLE-SHAPIRO, J and WAYNE, S (2011) A Longitudinal Study of the Impact of Organizational Change on Transactional, Relational, and Balanced Psychological Contracts. *Journal of Leadership & Organizational Studies*, 18 (2), pp 247–59

CHAUDHRY, A, WAYNE, S and SCHALK, R (2011) A Sensemaking Model of Employee Evaluation of Psychological Change Fulfilment: How and When Do Employees Respond to Change? *The Journal of Applied Behavioural Science*, 45 (4), pp 498–520

CHAVAN, M (2009) The balanced scorecard: a new challenge. *Journal of Management Development*, 28, (5), pp 393–406

CHEESE, P (2015) *Putting the human into HR* www.cipd.co.uk/podcasts/look-ahead-to-2015#gref (archived at https://perma.cc/VC2B-KWQT)

CHEETHAM, G and CHIVERS, G (2001) How professionals learn in practice: an investigation of informal learning amongst people working in professions. *Journal of European Industrial Training*, 25, pp 250–88

CHEUNG-JUDGE, M and HOLBECHE, L (2021) *Organisational Development, A practitioner's guide for OD and HR*, 3rd edn, Kogan Page, London

CHHOKAR, JS, BRODBECK, FC and HOUSE, RJ (eds) (2007) *Culture and Leadership Across the World*. New Jersey: Lawrence Erlbaum Associates

CHILD, J (1972) Organizational Structure, Environment and Performance: The Role of Strategic Choice. *Sociology*, 6 (1), pp 1–22

CHILD, J (2005) *Organization: Contemporary Principles and Practice*, Oxford: Blackwell

CHILD, J(2015) *Organisation: Contemporary Principles and Practice*, 2nd edn, John Wiley & Sons, Chichester

CHO, Y, CHO, E and McLEAN, GN (2009) HRD's role in knowledge management, advances in developing human resources. Online First, published 14 July 2009 as doi: 10.1177/1523422309337719 (archived at https://perma.cc/7T9F-FHAE)

CHO, S CRENSHAW, KW and McCALL, L (2013) "Toward a field of intersectionality studies: Theory, applications, and praxis." *Signs: Journal of women in culture and society*, 38 (4), pp 785–810

CHON, KKS and ZOLTAN, J (2019) Role of servant leadership in contemporary hospitality. *International Journal of Contemporary Hospitality Management*, 31 (8), pp 3371–94

CHRYSSIDES, G and KALER, J (1996) *Essentials of Business Ethics*, McGraw-Hill, Maidenhead

CHUNG, KL and D'ANNUNZIO-GREEN, (2018) Talent management practices in small- and medium-sized enterprises in the hospitality sector. *Worldwide Hospitality and Tourism Themes*, 10 (1), pp 101–16

CHURCHARD, C (2015) Zero hours contract workers 'as happy as permanent staff'. *People Management. Online edition* 4 December. www.cipd.co.uk/about/media/press/041215-zero-hours#gref

CHYNOWETH, C (2015) The public sector faces terrifying challenges, *People Management Online edition September 23* www.cipd.co.uk/pm/peoplemanagement/b/weblog/archive/2015/09/23/the-public-sector-faces-terrifying-challenges.aspx (archived at https://perma.cc/9V3N-YBZ2)

CIPD (2004a) *Human Capital Reporting: An Internal Perspective*, CIPD, London

CIPD (2004b) *Graphology*. Factsheet, CIPD, London

CIPD (2005) *Managing Diversity: People make the difference at work – but everyone is different*, CIPD, London

CIPD (2007a) *Leadership and Management Standards*, CIPD, London

CIPD (2007b) *Diversity in Business: A Focus for Progress.* Survey report, CIPD, London

CIPD (2008a) *Smart Working: The Impact of Work Organisation and Job Design.* Research Insight, CIPD, London

CIPD (2009) *Organisation Development*. Factsheet, CIPD, London

CIPD (2010a) *HR Business Partnering*. Factsheet, CIPD, London

CIPD (2010b) *Diversity: An overview*. Factsheet, CIPD, London

CIPD (2012a) *HR and its Role in Innovation, Part 1, November 2012: Innovative forms of organising: Networked working*, CIPD, London

CIPD (2012b) *Managing for Sustainable Employee Engagement: Developing a Behavioural Framework*, CIPD, London

CIPD (2012c) *Game On! How to Keep Diversity Progress on Track*. Policy report, CIPD, London

CIPD (2012d) *Performance Management: An Overview*. Factsheet, CIPD, London

CIPD (2012e) *Reward Management*, Annual survey report, CIPD, London

CIPD (2013a) *The role of HR in corporate responsibility*. Research report. February 2013, CIPD, London

CIPD (2013b) *HR Outsourcing*. Factsheet, CIPD, London

CIPD (2014a) *HR: Getting smart about agile working*. Research Report. November 2014, CIPD, London

CIPD (2015a) *HR Business Partnering*. Factsheet. www.cipd.co.uk/hr-resources/factsheets/hr-business-partnering.aspx (archived at https://perma.cc/FF4F-R795)

CIPD (2015b) Research Report - Leading transformational change: Closing the gap between theory and practice). www.cipd.co.uk/hr-resources/research/landing-transformational-change-gap-theory-practice.aspx (archived at https://perma.cc/78N2-WTQC)

CIPD (2015c) Human Capital Management Factsheet, CIPD, London

CIPD (2015d) *From best to good practice HR: developing principles for the profession*, CIPD, London

CIPD (2015e) *HR Outlook: Winter 2014–15*. Survey report. London: CIPD www.cipd.co.uk/binaries/hr-outlook_2015-winter-2014-15-views-of-our-profession (archived at https://perma.cc/4CGP-654M)

CIPD (2017a) *HR Professionalism: What do we stand for? Research Report*, CIPD, London

CIPD (2017b) How to conduct a strengths-based interview. *People Management* editorial 16 August 2017 www.cipd.ae/news/stregths-based-intervew (archived at https://perma.cc/EZ5U-TCSW)

CIPD (2017c) *The future of technology and learning*. www.cipd.co.uk/knowledge/work/technology/future-technology-learning#gref

CIPD (2018a) *Diversity And Inclusion At Work: facing up to the business case*. Report June 2018, CIPD, London www.cipd.co.uk/Images/diversity-and-inclusion-at-work_2018-facing-up-to-the-business-case-1_tcm18-44146.pdf (archived at https://perma.cc/P3UA-PYU9)

CIPD (2018b) *Labour Market Outlook; views from employers*. Summer 2018. www.cipd.co.uk/Images/lmo-survey-summer2018_tcm18-45850.pdf (archived at https://perma.cc/B6RU-8QS2)

CIPD (2019a) People and Machines: From hype to reality, Executive Summary April, www.cipd.co.uk/Images/people-and-machines-exec-summary_tcm18-56971.pdf (archived at https://perma.cc/2VFS-6YHB)

CIPD (Sep 2019b) *Building Inclusive Workplaces: Assessing the Evidence* www.cipd.co.uk/Images/building-inclusive-workplaces-report-sept-2019_tcm18-64154.pdf (archived at https://perma.cc/X4TR-6XAT)

CIPD (2019c) *Five actions you can take to foster inclusion* www.cipd.co.uk/knowledge/fundamentals/relations/diversity/five-actions-fostering-inclusion (archived at https://perma.cc/PA7H-BYMB)

CIPD (2020a) *People Profession 2030: A collective view of future trends*. Report, CIPD, London

CIPD (2020b) *Code of Professional Conduct*, www.cipd.co.uk/code-of-professional-conduct-april-2020_tcm18/ (archived at https://perma.cc/Y6AD-YJU2)

CIPD (2020c) *Workplace technology: the employee experience*, Report, CIPD, London www.cipd.co.uk/knowledge/work/technology/workplace-technology-employee (archived at https://perma.cc/B49P-73X3)

CIPD (2020d) *Line managers' role in supporting the people profession: learn about the role of line management and its relationship to an organisation's people practices*. www.cipd.co.uk/knowledge/fundamentals/people/hr/line-managers-factsheet (archived at https://perma.cc/ULU3-QCLA)

CIPD (2020e) *Embedding new ways of working* Report, CIPD, London www.cipd.co.uk/Images/embedding-new-ways-working-post-pandemic_tcm18-83907.pdf (archived at https://perma.cc/S9U2-4DNK)

CIPD (2021a), *Strategic human resource management*, Factsheet. 3 June 2021, CIPD, London www.cipd.co.uk/knowledge/strategy/hr/strategic-hrm-factsheet (archived at https://perma.cc/D9FL-LXL5)

CIPD (2021b) Labour Market Outlook, CIPD, London www.cipd.co.uk/Images/labour-market-outlook-autumn-2021_tcm18-103227.pdf (archived at https://perma.cc/9NB3-YSWZ)

CIPD (2021c) People Profession survey report www.cipd.co.uk/knowledge/strategy/hr/people-profession-survey (archived at https://perma.cc/4FF9-MAGA)

CIPD (2021d) Embedding new ways of working: implications for the post-pandemic workforce www.cipd.co.uk/Images/embedding-new-ways-working-post-pandemic_tcm18-83907.pdf (archived at https://perma.cc/A3V6-25FZ)

CIPD (2021e) Learning and development evolving practice www.cipd.co.uk/knowledge/strategy/development/evolving-practice-factsheet (archived at https://perma.cc/9JFX-98D5)

CIPD (2021f) *Coaching and Mentoring*, Factsheet 14 June 2021 www.cipd.co.uk/knowledge/fundamentals/people/development/coaching-mentoring (archived at https://perma.cc/VWB6-RE28)

CIPD (2021g) *Guide to environmental sustainability* www.cipd.co.uk/knowledge/strategy/corporate-responsibility/sustainability (archived at https://perma.cc/83BB-TYST)

CIPD (2021h) *Technology and the future of work*. Factsheet 6 January 2021 www.cipd.co.uk/knowledge/work/technology/emerging-future-work-factsheet (archived at https://perma.cc/PH7C-5DB8)

CIPD (2021i) *Resourcing and Talent Planning Survey 2021*, Report, CIPD, London, www.cipd.co.uk/Images/resourcing-and-talent-planning-2021-1_tcm18-100907.pdf (archived at https://perma.cc/8KED-8E2C)

CIPD (2021j) *Recruitment: an introduction*, Factsheet 28 October 2021, www.cipd.co.uk/knowledge/fundamentals/people/recruitment/factsheet (archived at https://perma.cc/8ZEQ-JR4K)

CIPD (2021k) *Competence and competency frameworks*, Factsheet 15 December 2021 www.cipd.co.uk/knowledge/fundamentals/people/performance/competency-factsheet (archived at https://perma.cc/BLV9-G2AM)

CIPD (2021l) *Talent management: understand the changing context and benefits of talent management, and the key features of a talent management strategy.* www.cipd.co.uk/knowledge/strategy/resourcing/talent-factsheet (archived at https://perma.cc/N6K2-TZZA)

CIPD (2021m) *Talent management.* www.cipd.co.uk/knowledge/strategy/resourcing/talent-factsheet#gref

CIPD (2021n) *Using technology to improve hiring and onboarding.* www.cipd.co.uk/knowledge/work/technology/digital-transformation-insights/improve-hiring-onboarding (archived at https://perma.cc/GC4B-T9EX)

CIPD (2021o) *Learning methods.* www.cipd.co.uk/knowledge/fundamentals/people/development/learning-methods-factsheet#6679 (archived at https://perma.cc/7TTV-EGPM)

CIPD (2021p) *Management development.* www.cipd.co.uk/knowledge/strategy/development/management-factsheet (archived at https://perma.cc/F7M3-QPEG)

CIPD (2021q) *Employee engagement and motivation* www.cipd.co.uk/knowledge/fundamentals/relations/engagement/factsheet (archived at https://perma.cc/75KL-QP5W)

CIPD (2021r) *Health and wellbeing at work survey 2021*, CIPD, London www.cipd.co.uk/knowledge/culture/well-being/health-well-being-work (archived at https://perma.cc/UJS5-EHH5)

CIPD (2021s) *Inclusion and diversity in the workplace* www.cipd.co.uk/knowledge/fundamentals/relations/diversity/factsheet (archived at https://perma.cc/6FVK-8SR6)

CIPD (2021t) *End Racism at Work – Position Statement.* 19 July, CIPD, London

CIPD (2021u) *Planning for hybrid working* 30 September 2021 www.cipd.co.uk/knowledge/fundamentals/relations/flexible-working/planning-hybrid-working#gref (archived at https://perma.cc/9TZU-PWQZ) LEW

CIPD (2021v) *strategic reward and total reward*, Factsheet 18 May 2021 www.cipd.co.uk/knowledge/strategy/reward/strategic-total-factsheet#gref (archived at https://perma.cc/K26X-AUZR)

CIPD (2021w), *HR Outsourcing*, Factsheet September 22. www.cipd.co.uk/knowledge/fundamentals/people/hr/outsourcing-factsheet#gref (archived at https://perma.cc/UVT7-VMZN)

CIPD (2021x) *Change management*, Factsheet September 6 www.cipd.co.uk/knowledge/strategy/change/management-factsheet (archived at https://perma.cc/2GZA-AUML)

CIPD (2022a) *Explore the Profession Map: Face the challenges of today and the future with confidence.* https://peopleprofession.cipd.org/profession-map#gref (archived at https://perma.cc/3YXA-GWX3)

CIPD (2022b) *Talent management roles: maximising the potential of those working in an organisation.* www.cipd.co.uk/careers/career-options/talent-management-roles (archived at https://perma.cc/YR63-KETN)

CIPD (2022c) *Mencap: Recruiting from the heart* https://peopleprofession.cipd.org/get-started/case-studies/mencap (archived at https://perma.cc/3PLF-873U)

CIPD (2022d) *Itsu: Cutting-edge engagement* https://peopleprofession.cipd.org/get-started/case-studies/itsu (archived at https://perma.cc/6WUA-FE5H)

CIPD (2022e) CIPD In a Nutshell (January 2022) *Changing our minds about work* www.cipd.co.uk/news-views/nutshell/issue-113/changing-mind-work (archived at https://perma.cc/W6RH-U27M)

CIPD (2022f) *The psychological contract.* Factsheet 9 February 2022. www.cipd.co.uk/knowledge/fundamentals/relations/employees/psychological-factsheet#gref (archived at https://perma.cc/L627-28PT)

CIPD (2022g) Viewpoint. *Employee health and wellbeing* www.cipd.co.uk/news-views/viewpoint/employee-health-well-being (archived at https://perma.cc/K6HK-JAUY)

CIPD (2022h) An update on flexible and hybrid working practices 26 April 2022 www.cipd.co.uk/knowledge/fundamentals/relations/flexible-working/flexible-hybrid-workingpractices#gref (archived at https://perma.cc/XB42-TAPT)

CLARK, J (1993) Full flexibility and self-supervision in an automated factory. In CLARK, J (ed) *Human Resource Management and Technical Change*, Sage, London

CLARKE, C and PRATT, S (1985) Leadership's four-part progress, *Management Today*, March, pp 84–86

CLARKE, M and SCURRY, T (2020) The role of the psychological contract in shaping graduate experiences: a study of public sector talent management programmes in the UK and Australia. *The International Journal of Human Resource Management*, 31 (8), pp 965–991

CLEGG, S, KORNBERGER, M and PITSIS, T (2008) Managing and Organisations. Sage, London

CLEGG, S, KORNBERGER, M and PITSIS, T (2011) *Managing and Organisations.* 3rd edn, Sage, London

CLEGG, S PITSIS, TS and MOUNT, M (2022), *Managing and Organizations: An Introduction to Theory and Practice*, 6th edn, Sage, London

CLERKIN, RM and COGGBURN, JD (2012) The dimensions of public service motivation and sector work preferences. *Review of Public Personnel Administration*, 32 (3), pp 209–35

COGIN, J (2012) Are generational differences in work values fact or fiction? *International Journal of Human Resource Management*, 23 (11), pp 2268–94

COHEN, A, FETTER, M and FLEISCHMANN, F (2005). Major change at Babson College: Curricular and administrative, planned and otherwise. *Advances in Developing Human Resources*, 7 (3), pp 324–337

COHEN, TR, PANTER, AT and TURAN, N (2012) Guilt Proneness and Moral Character. Current Directions in Psychological Science, 21 (5), pp 355–59

COKINS, G (2004) *Performance Management: Finding the missing pieces (to close the intelligence gap)*, Wiley, New York

COLLINGS, DG, SCULLION, H and DOWLING, PJ (2006) Global staffing: a review and thematic research agenda. International Journal of Human Resource Management, 20 (6), pp 1253–72

COLLINGS, DG, MCMACKIN, J, NYBERG, AJ and WRIGHT, PM, (2021) Strategic human resource management and COVID-19: Emerging challenges and research opportunities. *Journal of Management Studies*. doi:10.1111/joms.12695 (archived at https://perma.cc/8NZC-UJ7H)

COLLINGS, DG and ISICHEI, M (2018) The shifting boundaries of global staffing: Integrating global talent management, alternative forms of international assignments and non-employees into the discussion, *The International Journal of Human Resource Management*, 29 (1), pp 165–87

COLLINGS, DG, MELLAHI, K and CASCIO, W (2017), *The Oxford Handbook of Talent Management*, Oxford University Press, Oxford

COLLINGS, DG and MELLAHI, K (2009) Strategic talent management: a review and research agenda. *Human Resource Management Review*, 19 (4), pp 304–13

COLLINGS, DG, VAIMAN, V and SCULLION, H (2022) *Talent Management: A decade of developments*, Emerald Publishing, Bingley

COLLINS, CJ (2021) Expanding the resource based view model of strategic human resource management. *The International Journal of Human Resource Management*, 32 (2), pp 331–58 https://doi.org/10.1080/09585192.2019.1711442 (archived at https://perma.cc/6UND-3NXC)

COLLINS, H, EWING, K and MCCOLGAN, A (2012) *Labour Law*, Cambridge University Press, Cambridge

CONFESSORE, SJ and KOPS, WJ (1998) Self-directed learning and the learning organisation: examining the connection between the individual and the learning environment. *Human Resource Development Quarterly*, 9, pp 365–75

CONGER, J (1999) Charisma and how to grow it. *Management Today*, December, pp 78–81

CONGER, J (2002) Danger of delusion. *Financial Times*. 29 November

COOMBS, J, LIU, Y, HALL, A and KETCHEN, D (2006) How much do high-performance work practices matter? A meta-analysis of their effects on organizational performance. *Personnel Psychology*, 59 (3), pp 501–28

COOPER, C (2005) The future of work: careers, stress and wellbeing. *Career Development International*, 10 (5), pp 396–99

COOPER, C L, LIU, Y and TARBA, SY (2019)' Resilience, HRM practices and impact on organizational performance and employee well-being, *The International Journal of Human Resource Management Special Issue*, 30 (8), pp 1227–38

COWELL, C, HOPKINS, PC, McWHORTER, R and JORDEN, DL (2006), Alternative Training Models. *Advances in Developing Human Resources*, 8 (4), pp 460–75

COYLE-SHAPIRO, J and KESSLER, I (2000) Consequences of the psychological contract for the employment relationship: a large-scale survey. *Journal of Management Studies*, 37 (7), p 903

CRAIL, M (2007) Online recruitment delivers more applicants and wins vote of most employers. *Personnel Today*. 20 November. Available online at: www.personneltoday.com (archived at https://perma.cc/FQ8H-WN93)

CRANE, A and MATTEN, D (2010) *Business Ethics*. 3rd edn, Oxford University Press, Oxford

CRANE, A, MATTEN, D, GLOZER, S and SPENCE, L (2019) *Business Ethics: Managing corporate citizenship and sustainability in the age of globalization*, 5th edn, Oxford University Press, Oxford

CRANET (2011) *Cranet survey on comparative human resource management: International executive report 2011*, Cranfield University, Cranfield

CROOK, C (2005) The good company. *The Economist*. 22 January, pp 3–4

CROWLEY, E and OVERTON, L (2021) Learning and Skills at Work Survey, CIPD, London

CROWLEY-HENRY, M, O'CONNOR, E and SUAREZ-BILBAO, B, (2020) Self-Initiated Expatriates' Experiences in SMEs. In: Andresen, M, Brewster, C, and Suutari, V (eds) *Self-Initiated Expatriates in Context: Recognizing Space, Time, and Institutions*, pp 153–72, Routledge, New York

CRUSH, P (2013) Parental Leave Mums v Dads. *People Management*. 8 January, p 20

CRUSH, P (2015) Government backs name-blind CVs' to end discrimination. *People Management*. 26 October. www.cipd.co.uk/pm/peoplemanagement/b/weblog/archive/2015/10/26/government-backs-name-blind-cvs-to-end-discrimination.aspx/ (archived at https://perma.cc/2864-GCXD)

CSIKSZENTMIHALYI, M (1990) Flow: The psychology of optimal experience, Harper Perennial, New York

CULLY, M, WOODLAND, S and O'REILLY, A (1999) *Britain at Work, as depicted by the 1998 Workplace Employee Relations Survey*, Routledge, London

CUNNINGHAM, I (2008) A race to the bottom? Exploring variations in employment conditions in the voluntary sector. *Public Administration*, 86 (4), pp 1033–53

CUNNINGHAM, I and JAMES, P (2017) Analysing public sector outsourcing: The value of a regulatory perspective, *Environment and Planning C: Government and Policy*, 35 (6), pp 958–74

D'ARCY, C and GARDINER, L (2014) *Just the job – or a working compromise? The changing nature of self-employment in the UK*. The Resolution Foundation. May. www.resolutionfoundation.org/wp-content/uploads/2014/05/Just-the-job-or-a-working-compromise-FINAL.pdf (archived at https://perma.cc/KLD8-BVF5)

DAFT, RL MURPHY, J and WILLMOTT, H (2010) *Organization Theory and Design*, Cengage, Andover

DAFT, RL, MURPHY, J and WILLMOTT, H (2016) *Organization Theory and Design*. 2nd edn, Cengage, Andover

DALE, K (2005) Building social materiality: Spatial and embodied politics in organizational control. *Organization*, 12 (5), 649–78

DANY, F, GUEDRI, Z and HATT, F (2008) New insights into the link between HRM integration and organizational performance: the moderating role of influence distribution between HRM specialists and line managers, *International Journal of Human Resource Management*, 19 (11), pp 2095–112

DAVENPORT, TH (1993) *Process Innovation: Re-engineering work through information technology*, Harvard Business School Press, Boston, MA

DAVENPORT, T, HARRIS, J and SHAPIRO, J (2010) Competing on Talent Analytics. *Harvard Business Review*. October, 88 (10), pp 52–8 https://hbr.org/2010/10/competing-on-talent-analytics/ (archived at https://perma.cc/2D2V-UM4Y)

DAVIES, ME (2013) *Women on Boards*. Cranfield, Bedford: Cranfield School of Management

DAY, D and SIN, HP (2011) Longitudinal Tests of an Integrative Model of Leader Development: Charting and Understanding Development Trajectories. *The Leadership Quarterly*, 22 (3), pp 545–60

DCSF (2009a) *14–19 Briefing: Making change happen*. www.dcsf.gov.uk/14-19 (archived at https://perma.cc/BLW9-UZWJ)

DCSF (2009b) Quality, Choice and Aspiration. Report. http://webarchive.nationalarchives. gov.uk/20130401151715/www.education.gov.uk/publications/eOrderingDownload/IAG-Report-v2.pdf (archived at https://perma.cc/CU46-QDCA)

DECI, EL, RYAN, M and KOESTNER, R (2001) The pervasive negative effects of rewards on intrinsic motivation: response to Cameron. *Review of Educational Research*, 71, pp 43–51

DE GAMA, N, MCKENNA, S and PETTICA-HARRIS, A (2012) Ethics and HRM: Theoretical and Conceptual Analysis. *Journal of Business Ethics*, 111 (1), pp 97–108

DEL GIUDICE, M, NICOTRA, M ROMANO, M and SCHILLACI, CE (2017) Entrepreneurial performance of principal investigators and country culture: Relations and Influences, *The Journal of Technology Transfer*, 42 (2), pp 229–35

DELOITTE (2009) *Shaping Up: Evolving the HR function for the 21st century*, Deloitte MCS Limited, New York/London

DELOITTE and BERSIN (2014) *Global Human Capital Trends 2014: Engaging the 21st-century workforce*. http://dupress.com/wp-content/uploads/2014/04/GlobalHumanCapitalTrends_2014.pdf (archived at https://perma.cc/T7CD-E4RG)

DELOITTE (2021) *Global Shared Services and Outsourcing Report* www2.deloitte.com/us/en/pages/operations/articles/shared-services-survey.html (archived at https://perma.cc/Q4EH-RM3S)

DELOITTE (2022) International Employment Law Guide. Source: www2.deloitte.com/global/en/pages/legal/articles/IELG/international-employment-law-guide.html (archived at https://perma.cc/QD9L-T3QK)

DE MENEZES, L and KELLIHER, C (2011) Flexible Working and Performance: A Systematic Review of the Evidence for a Business Case. *International Journal of Management Reviews*, 13 (4), pp 452–74

DENCKER, JC, JOSHI, A and MARTOCCHIO, JJ (2008) Towards a theoretical framework linking generational memories to workplace attitudes and behaviours, *Human Resource Management Review*, 18 (3), pp 180–87

DEPARTMENT FOR BUSINESS INNOVATION AND SKILLS (2013) *The Business Case for Equality and Diversity: A survey of academic studies*. BIS Occasional Paper No 4. Department for Business Innovation and Skills, London

DEPARTMENT FOR BUSINESS, INNOVATION AND SKILLS (2015) *Trade Union Membership 2014: Statistical Bulletin*. Department for Business Innovation and Skills, London

DE STEFANO, F, BAGDADLI, S, and CAMUFFO, A (2018). The HR role in corporate social responsibility and sustainability: A boundary-shifting literature review. *Human Resource Management*, 57 (2), pp 549–66

DEVANNA, MA, FOMBRUN, CJ and TICHY, NM (1984) A framework for strategic human resource management. In: FOMBRUN, CJ, TICHY, MM and DEVANNA, MA (eds) *Strategic Human Resource Management*, John Wiley, New York

DE VOS, A and MEGANCK, A (2009) What HR managers do versus what employees value. *Personnel Review*, 38 (1), pp 45–60

DE WIT, B and MEYER, R (2004) *Strategy: Process, content and theory*. 3rd edn, Thomson Publishing, London

DILLARD, N and OSAM, K (2021) Deconstructing the meaning of engagement: An intersectional qualitative study, *Human Resource Development International*, 24 (5), pp 511–32

DIMBLEBY, D (2012) The BBC Has Throttled Itself With Its Own Bureaucracy. Daily Telegraph. 12 November. www.telegraph.co.uk (archived at https://perma.cc/X5F2-D5R5)

DINH, JE, LORD, RG, GARDNER, WL, MEUSER, JD, LIDEN, RC and HU, J (2014) Leadership theory and research in the new millennium: Current theoretical trends and changing perspectives. *The Leadership Quarterly*, 25 (1), pp 36–62

DOBSON, J (2007) Applying virtue ethics to business: The agent-based approach. *Journal of Business Ethics and Organization Studies*, 12 (2), p 1

DOHERTY, N (2013). Understanding the self-initiated expatriate: A review and directions for future research. *International Journal of Management Reviews*, 15 (4), pp 447–69

DOHERTY, NT and DICKMANN, N (2012) Measuring the return in investment in international assignments: An action research approach. *International Journal of Human Resource Management*, 23 (16), pp 3434–54

DONALDSON, T and PRESTON, L (1995) The stakeholder theory of the corporation: concepts, evidence and implications. *Academy of Management Review*, 5, pp 265–69

DOWLING. PJ, FESTING, M and ENGLE, AD (2008) *International Human Resource Management*. 5th edn, Thomson, London

DOZ, YL and PRAHALAD, CK (1988) A process model of strategic redirection in large complex firms: the case of multinational corporations. In: PETTIGREW, AM (ed) *The Management of Strategic Change*, Blackwell, Oxford

DRIES, N (2013). The psychology of talent management: a review and research agenda. *Human Resource Management Journal*, 23 (4), pp 272–85

DRIES, N and PEPERMANS, R (2008) Real high-potential careers. *Personnel Review*, 37 (1), pp 85–108

DRUCKER, PF (1989) *The Practice of Management*, Heinemann Professional

DRUCKER, PF (1993) *Post-Capitalist Society*. Oxford: Butterworth-Heinemann

DRUCKER, PF (2005) Managing Oneself. *Harvard Business Review*, 8 (1), pp 100–09

DTI (2001) Diversity Best Practice in the Corporate World: A guide for business. London: Department of Trade and Industry, Women and Equality Unit

DTI (2005) *High Performance Work Practices: Linking strategy and skills to performance outcomes*. London: DTI in association with the CIPD

DU GAY, P (2000) *In Praise of Bureaucracy*, London: Sage

DUPRE, R (2014) Strategies to Address the Energy Industry Talent Gap www.rigzone.com/news/oil_gas/a/133221/strategies_to_address_the_energy_industry_talent_gap/ (archived at https://perma.cc/6WP7-25TE)

DUTTA, D, MISHRA, S K, and VARMA A (2021) Predictors of job pursuit intention across career stages: a multi-phase investigation. *The International Journal of Human Resource Management*, 32 (20), 4215–4252. doi.org/10.1080/09585192.2019.1651376 (archived at https://perma.cc/2YYD-G5JF)

DYER, L and SHAFER, R (1999) Creating organizational agility: implications for strategic human resource management. In WRIGHT, P, DYER, L and BOUDREAU, J (eds) *Research in Personnel and Human Resource Management* (Supplement 4: Strategic human resources management in the twenty-first century), JAI Press, Stamford, CT

EDGELL, V HUSSEIN, R HARRISON, D BADER, AK and WILSON, R 'I Find it Daunting... That I'm Gonna Have to Deal with This until 60': Extended Working Lives and the Sustainable Employability of Operational Firefighters' *Work, Employment and Society* (2021), 19 (1), pp 1–19

EDUCATION and TRAINING (2006), 48 (8/9)

EDWARDS, MR (2010) An integrative review of employer branding and OB theory", Personnel Review, 39 (1), pp 5–23. Emerald Publishing Group

EDWARDS, P (2003) The employment relationship and the field of industrial relations. In: EDWARDS, P (ed) *Industrial Relations*. 4th edn, Blackwell, Oxford

EGAN, J (2009) HR Roles and Responsibilities. IRS Employment Review survey (2nd edition, January). www.xperthr.co.uk/searchresults.aspx?s=egan (archived at https://perma.cc/CP3J-MCT8)

EGLIN, R (2004) Cash is not king in holding on to staff. *Sunday Times* Appointments. 15 February, p 7

EHNERT, I (2014) Paradox as a lens for theorizing sustainable HRM. In EHNERT, I, HARRY, W, ZINK, KJ (eds) *Sustainability and Human Resource Management.* Berlin Heidelberg: Springer

EIKHOF, DR, WARHURST, C and HAUNSCHILD, A (2007) Introduction: What work? What life? What balance? Critical reflections on the work-life balance debate. *Employee Relations,* 29 (4), pp 325–33

ELLEHAVE, C and ULRICH, D, (2021) Above and Beyond the Yearly Wheel: Anticipating and Realizing the Ever-Evolving Contribution of HR *Journal of Human Resource Management,* 9 (3), p 88. doi: 10.11648/j.jhrm.20210903.15 (archived at https://perma.cc/28GE-DHQK)

ELLESWORTH, RE (2002) *Leading with Purpose: The new corporate realities* Stanford University Press, Palo Alto, CA

ELLINGER, A (2004) The concept of self-directed learning and its implications for human resource. *Advances in Developing Human Resources,* 6, p 158

ELLIOTT, L (2004) Job flexibility can tie you up in knots. *Guardian Weekly.* 25–31 March, p 16

EMERY, Y (2004) Rewarding civil service performance through team bonuses: findings, analysis and recommendations. *International Review of Administrative Sciences,* 70 (1), pp 157–68

EMERY, Y (2008) Lecture presentation at Portsmouth University, based upon three research articles by Emery, Y and Glauque, D (2005) *Paradoxes de la gestion publique.* Paris: L'Harmattan

EMERY, Y and GONIN, F (2007) *Dynamiser la gestion des resources humaines.* Lausanne: Presses polytechniques et universitaires romandes

ENGLE, AD, DOWLING, PJ and FESTING, M (2008) Globalisation of SMEs and implications for international human resource management research and practice. *European Journal of International Management,* 2 (2), pp 153–69

ENTWISTLE, N (2001) Styles of Learning and Approaches to Studying in Higher Education. *Kybernetes,* 30 (5), pp 593–603

ENZ, CA (2009). Human resource management: a troubling issue for the global hotel industry. *Cornell Hospitality Quarterly,* 50 (4), pp 578–83

EUROFOUND (2021) The digital age: Implications of automation, digitisation and platforms for work and employment, Challenges and prospects in the EU series, Publications Office of the European Union, Luxembourg

EUROPEAN FOUNDATION FOR THE IMPROVEMENT OF LIVING AND WORKING CONDITIONS (2013a) *Work organisation and innovation in Ireland. Case study: Medtronic Galway.* www.eurofound.europa.eu/sites/default/files/ef_publication/field_ef_document/ef1348en2.pdf (archived at https://perma.cc/HE59-K4B4)

EUROPEAN FOUNDATION FOR THE IMPROVEMENT OF LIVING AND WORKING CONDITIONS (2013b) *United Kingdom: GlassEco, case study* www.eurofound.europa.eu/observatories/emcc/case-studies/the-greening-of-industries-in-the-eu/united-kingdom-glasseco-case-study (archived at https://perma.cc/TJ85-KST6)

EVANS, J (2008) Leaders need to be humble, not heroes. *People Management.* 17 April. www.peoplemanagement.co.uk (archived at https://perma.cc/TXB2-GC5L)

EVANS, P, PUCIK, V and BJORKMAN, I (2012) *The Global Challenge: International Human Resource Management.* 2nd edn, McGraw-Hill, London

EVANS, P, SMALE, A and BJORKMAN, I (2019) Macro talent management in Finland: Contributing to a rapidly evolving knowledge economy. In Vaiman, V, Sparrow, P, Schuler, R and Collings, DG (eds.). *Macro Talent Management on Managing Talent in Developed Counties*. Routledge

EVETTS, J (2013) Professionalism: Value and Etiology. *Current Sociology Review*, 61 (5–6), pp 778–96

FAN, D, ZHU, CJ, HUANG, X and KUMAR, V, (2021) Mapping the terrain of international human resource management research over the past fifty years: A bibliographic analysis. *Journal of World Business*, 56 (2), p.101185. https://doi.org/10.1016/j.jwb.2020.101185/ (archived at https://perma.cc/M3BR-F9WR)

FANG, M and GERHART, B (2012) Does pay for performance diminish intrinsic interest? *The International Journal of Human Resource Management*, 23 (6), pp 1176–96

FARNDALE, E and BREWSTER, C (2005) In search of legitimacy: personnel, management associations worldwide. *Human Resource Management Journal*, 15 (3), pp 33–48

FARNDALE, E, PAUUWE, J, MORRIS, SS, STAHL, G, STILES, P, TREVOR, J and WRIGHT, P (2010) Context-bound Configurations of Corporate HR Functions Across the Globe. *Human Resource Management*, 49 (1), pp 45–66

FARNDALE, E, SCULLION H and SALLOW, P (2010) The role of the corporate HR function in global talent management. *Journal of World Business*, 45 (2), pp 161–68

FARNDALE, E, SPARROW, P, SCULLION, H and VIDOVIC, M, (2018) Global talent management: New challenges for the corporate HR function. In *Global talent management* pp 90–109 https://api.ngampooz.com/images/107438/Global-Talent-Management-Routledge.pdf#page=109 (archived at https://perma.cc/R53R-ZJK3) [1 March 2022]

FARNDALE, E, HORAK, S, PHILLIPS, J and BEAMOND, M, (2019) Facing complexity, crisis, and risk: Opportunities and challenges in international human resource management. *Thunderbird International Business Review*, 61 (3), pp 465–70 https://doi.org/10.1002/tie.22037 (archived at https://perma.cc/49ER-LQPD)

FARNHAM, D and PIMLOTT, J (1995) *Understanding Industrial Relations*. 4th edn, Cassell, London

FARNHAM, D and STEVENS, A (2000) Developing and implementing competence-based recruitment and selection in a social services department. *International Journal of Public Sector Management*, 13 (4), pp 369–82

FAYOL, H (1949) *General and Industrial Management*. London: Pitman

FESTING, M and HARSCH, K (2019) Macro talent management in Germany: A strong economy facing the challenges of a shrinking labor force. In: Vaiman, V, Sparrow, P, Schuler, R and Collings, DG (eds.). *Macro Talent Management on Managing Talent in Developed Counties*. Routledge

FESTING, M, SCHÄFER, L, and SCULLION, H (2013) Talent management in medium-sized German companies: an explorative study and agenda for future research. *The International Journal of Human Resource Management*, 24 (9), pp 1872–93

FINDLAY, P, LINDSAY, C, McINTYRE, S, ROY, G, STEWART, R and DUTTON, E (2021) CIPD *Good Work Index 2021: survey report*. London: Chartered Institute of Personnel and Development

FITZGERALD, C and HOWE-WALSH, L (2008) Self-initiated expatriates: an interpretative phenomenological analysis of professional female expatriates. *International Journal of Business and Management*, 21 (3), pp 156–75

FLAMINI, G, PITTINO, D and VISINTIN, F, (2021) Family leadership, family involvement and mutuality HRM practices in family SMEs. *Journal of Family Business Strategy*, p. 100468. https://doi.org/10.1016/j.jfbs.2021.100468 (archived at https://perma.cc/AG98-FDQK)

FLEMING, P (2015) There's nothing good about zero-hours contracts – ban them now. *The Guardian* 7 September

FLEMING, P and STURDY, A (2009) 'Just be yourself!' Towards neo-normative control in organizations. *Employee Relations*, 31 (6), 569–83

FLETCHER, C (2007) Appraisal, Feedback and Development: Making performance review work. 4th edn, Taylor & Francis, London

FLETCHER, C and WILLIAMS, R (1996) Performance management, job satisfaction and organisational commitment. *British Journal of Management*, 7, pp 169–79

FOMBRUN, CJ, TICHY, MM and DEVANNA, MA (eds) (1984) *Strategic Human Resource Management*. John Wiley, New York

FOLDY, EG (2019) Employee Resource Groups: What We Know about Their Impact on Individuals and Organizations, In *Academy of Management Proceedings*, (1), p. 10633

FOOT, M and HOOK, C (2005) *Introducing Human Resource Management*, 4th edn, FT/Prentice-Hall, Harlow

FOOT, M and HOOK, C (2011) *Introducing Human Resource Management*, 6th edn, FT/Prentice-Hall, Harlow

FOOTE, D (2001) The question of ethical hypocrisy in human resource management in the UK and Irish charity sectors. *Journal of Business Ethics*, 34, pp 25–38

FOOTE, E, HANCOCK, B, JEFFREY, B and MALAN, R (2021) *The key role of dynamic talent allocation in shaping the future of work. Report.* www.mckinsey.com/business-functions/people-and-organizational-performance/our-insights/the-key-role-of-dynamic-talent-allocation-in-shaping-the-future-of-work (archived at https://perma.cc/YWE9-74KY)

FORD, M (2021) Robots: stealing our jobs or solving labour shortages, *The Guardian*, 2 October 2021 www.theguardian.com/technology/2021/oct/02/robots-stealing-jobs-labour-shortages-artificial-intelligence-covid (archived at https://perma.cc/Y293-HKT4)

FOSTER, C and HARRIS, L (2005) Easy to say, difficult to do: diversity management in retail, *Human Resource Management Journal*, 15 (3), pp 4–17

FOSTER, D and HIRST, N (2020) *Legally Disabled? The Career Experiences of Disabled People Working in the Legal Profession*, Cardiff University, Cardiff

FOSTER, D and WILLIAMS, L (2011) The past, present and future of workplace equality agendas. In: BLYTON, P, HEERY, E and TURNBULL, P (eds) *Reassessing the Employment Relationship*. Palgrave Macmillan, Basingstoke, pp 318–41

FOURNIER, V (1999) The appeal to 'professionalism' as a disciplinary mechanism. *Sociological Review*, 47 (2), pp 280–307

FOX, A (1966) *Industrial Sociology and Industrial Relations*. Research Paper No 3. Royal Commission on Trade Unions and Employers' Associations, HMSO, London

FOX, A (1974) *Beyond Contract: Work, power and trust relations*. Faber & Faber, London

FOX, M (1994) *The Reinvention of Work: A new vision of livelihood for our time*. HarperCollins, New York

FRAHM, J and BROWN, K (2005) First steps: linking change communication to change receptivity, *Journal of Organisational Change Management*, 20 (3), pp 370–87

FRANCIS, H and KEEGAN, A (2006) The changing face of HRM: in search of balance. *Human Resource Management Journal*, 16 (3), pp 231–49

FRANK, E (1991) The UK's Management Charter Initiative: The First Three Years, *Journal of European Industrial Training*, 17 (1), pp 9–11

FRANKIEWICZ, B and CHAMORRO-PREMUZIC, T (2020) The post-pandemic rules of talent management. *Harvard Business Review*. https://hbr.org/2020/10/the-post-pandemic-rules-of-talent-management (archived at https://perma.cc/QAK4-53DM)

FREDMAN, S (2001) Equality: a new generation? *Industrial Law Journal*, 30 (2), pp 145–68

FREEMAN, RE (1984) *Strategic Management; A stakeholder approach.* Pitman, Boston MA

FREEMAN, RE, HARRISON, JS, WICKS, AC, PARMAR, BL, and DE COLLE, S (2010) *Stakeholder Theory: The state of the art.* Cambridge University Press, Cambridge

FREEMAN, R E, PHILLIPS, R, and SISODIA, R (2020) Tensions in stakeholder theory, *Business & Society*, 59 (2), 213–231

FREEMAN, R E, MARTIN, K, and PARMAR, B (2007) Stakeholder capitalism, *Journal of Business Ethics*, 74 (4), 303–314

FREER, T (2011) Social media gaming – a recipe for employer brand success, *Strategic HR Review*, 11 (1), pp 13–17

FREIFELD, L (2009) Brain sells, *Training*, 46 (6), p 9

FRENCH, J and RAVEN, B (1968) The bases of social power. In: CARTWRIGHT, D and ZANDER, A (eds) *Group Dynamics: Research and theory.* Harper & Row, London

FRENCH, R (2010) *Cross-Cultural Management in Work Organisations*, 2nd edn, CIPD, London

FRENCH, R (2015) *Cross-Cultural Management in Work Organisations*, 3rd edn, CIPD, London

FRENCH, R, RAYNER, C, REES, G and RUMBLES, S (2011) *Organizational Behaviour.* 2nd edn, John Wiley & Sons, Chichester

FRENCH, R, RAYNER, C, REES, G and RUMBLES, S (2015) *Organizational Behaviour.* 3rd edn, John Wiley & Sons, Chichester

FRENCH, WL and BELL, CH (1999) *Organizational Development: Behavioural science interventions for organizational improvement.* 6th edn, Prentice Hall, Upper Saddle River, NJ

FRENCH, WL, KAST, FE and ROSENZWEIG, JE (1985) *Understanding Human Behaviour in Organizations.* Harper & Row, London

FRIEDMAN, M (1970) The social responsibility of business is to increase its profits. *New York Times Magazine.* 13 September. p 32ff

FULLILOVE, C (2020) *Intersectionality and the employee experience* www.adp.com/spark/articles/2020/09/intersectionality-and-the-employee-experience.aspx (archived at https://perma.cc/Y2LX-R3UY)

FURNHAM, A (1997) *The Psychology of Behaviour at Work.* Psychology Press, Taylor & Francis, Hove

FURNHAM, A (2004) Performance management systems. *European Business Journal*, 16 (2), pp 83–94

FURNHAM, A (2005) Where egos dare. *People Management*, 11 (3), pp 40–2

GABRIEL, Y (2005) Glass cages and glass palaces: Images of organization in image-conscious times. *Organization*, 12 (1), pp 9–27

GAL, U, JENSEN, T B, and STEIN, M K (2020) Breaking the vicious cycle of algorithmic management: A virtue ethics approach to people analytics. *Information and Organization*, 30 (2), 100301. https://doi.org/10.1016/j.infoandorg.2020.100301 (archived at https://perma.cc/Y49R-KFMA)

GALLARDO-GALLARDO, E, DRIES, N and GONZALEZ-CRUZ, TF (2013) What is the meaning of 'talent' in the world of work? *Human Resource Management Review*, 23 (4), pp 290–300

GALLARDO-GALLARDO, E and THUNISSEN, M (2016) Standing on the shoulders of giants? A critical review of empirical talent management research. *Employee Relations*, 38 (1), pp 31–56

GALLARDO-GALLARDO, E, THUNNISSEN, M and SCULLION, H, (2020) Talent management: context matters. *The International Journal of Human Resource Management*, 31 (4), pp 457–73

GARAVAN, TN (2012) Global talent management in science-based firms: an exploratory investigation of the pharmaceutical industry during the global downturn, *The International Journal of Human Resource Management*, 23 (12), pp 2428–49

GARAVAN, T, WATSON, S, CARBERY, R and O'BRIEN, F (2015) The antecedents of leadership development practices in SMEs: The influence of HRM strategy and practice, *International Small Business Journal*, January, pp 1–21

GARAVAN, TN MCCARTHY, A and CARBERY R (2019) An Ecosystems Perspective on International Human Resource Development: A Meta-Synthesis of the Literature, *Human Resource Development Review*, 18 (2), pp 248–88

GARCIA, MF, POSTHUMA, RA GARAVAN, T, WATSON, S, CARBERY, R, and O'BRIEN, F (2015) The antecedents of leadership development practices in SMEs: The influence of HRM strategy and practice, *International Small Business Journal*, 0266242615594215

GARCIA, MF POSTHUMA, RA and COLELLA, A (2008) Fit perceptions and the employment interview: the role of similarity, liking and expectations, *Journal of Occupational and Organizational Psychology*, 81 (2), pp 173–89

GARR, SS, GANTCHEVA, I, YOSHIDA, R and WE, M (2017) *Talent Matters: How a Well-designed Talent Experience Can Drive Growth in Emerging Markets*, Deloitte University Press, Westlake

GARRARD, J (2021) *The three pillars of engaging organisational talent*. www.forbes.com/sites/forbeshumanresourcescouncil/2021/05/06/the-three-pillars-of-engaging-organizational-talent/?sh=3a57c66d4a5d (archived at https://perma.cc/X2KU-TXD9)

GEAL, M and JOHNSON, B (2002) Management performance: a glimpse of the blindingly obvious, *Training Journal*, October, pp 24–7

GHOSHAL, S, BARTLETT, C and MORAN, P (1999) A new manifesto for management. *Sloan Management Review*, 40 (3), pp 9–22

GILES, C, GUHA, K and ATKINS, R (2010) At the sharp end – the failings of flexibility. *Financial Times*, 22 January, www.ft.com (archived at https://perma.cc/3ZGP-P7FL)

GILLILAND, SW (1993) The perceived fairness of selection systems: an organizational justice perspective, *Academy of Management Review*, 18, pp 694–734

GILMORE, S (2009) 'Conclusions', in Gilmore, S and Williams, S (eds) *Human Resource Management* Oxford University Press, Oxford

GILMORE, S (2013) Introducing Human resource management, in Gilmore, S and Williams, S (eds) *Human Resource Management*, 2nd edn, Oxford University Press, Oxford

GILMORE, S and WILLIAMS, S (2003) Constructing the HR professional: a critical analysis of the Chartered Institute of Personnel and Development's professional project, *Third International Critical Management Studies Conference*. Lancaster University Management School

GILMORE, S and WILLIAMS, S (2007) Conceptualising the 'personnel professional': a critical analysis of the Chartered Institute of Personnel and Development's professional qualification scheme, *Personnel Review*, 36 (3), pp 398–414

GILMORE, S and WILLIAMS, S (eds) (2009) *Human Resource Management* Oxford University Press, Oxford

GILMORE, S and WILLIAMS, S (2013) *Human Resource Management*, 2nd edn, Oxford University Press, Oxford

GIOIA, DA and THOMAS, JB (1996) Identity, image and issue interpretation: sense making during strategic change in academia, *Administrative Science Quarterly*, 41, pp 370–403

GLAISTER, AJ (2014) HR outsourcing: the impact on HR role, competency development and relationships, *Human Resource Management Journal*, 24, pp 211–26

GLAISTER, AJ, KARACAY, G, DEMIRBAG, M and TATIGLU, E (2018) HRM and performance– The role of talent management as a transmission mechanism in an emerging market context, *Human Resource Management Journal*, 28 (1), pp 148–66

GLASGOW TOURISM AND VISITOR PLAN (2021) New Talent Development Programme Launched https://glasgowtourismandvisitorplan.com/news-and-media/2021/february/tourism-and-hospitality-talent-development-programme/ (archived at https://perma.cc/8SCN-H3GX)

GLENN, T (2012) The state of talent management in Canada's public sector, *Canadian Public Administration*, 55 (1), pp 25–51

GLOVER, L and BUTLER, P (2012) High-Performance Work Systems, Partnerships and the Working Lives of HR Professionals, *Human Resource Management*, 22 (2), pp 199–215

GMAC. (2008) www.expatica.co.uk/hr/story/Reporting-on-global-relocation-trendsin-2008.html/ (archived at https://perma.cc/X6PH-8ZZ2)

GOLD, J, HOLDEN, R, ILES, P, STEWART, J and BEARDWELL, J (2013) *Human Resource Development: Theory and Practice*, 3rd edn, Palgrave Macmillan, Basingstoke

GOLD, J, THORPE, R and MUMFORD, A (2010) *Leadership and management development*, 5th edn, CIPD, London

GOLDTHORPE, JH, LOCKWOOD, D, BECHHOFER, F and PLATT, J (1968) *The Affluent Worker: Attitudes and behaviour*, Cambridge University Press, Cambridge

GOLEMAN, D (1999) *Emotional Intelligence: Why it can matter more than IQ*, Bantam, New York

GOULD-WILLIAMS, J (2003) The importance of HR practices and workplace trust in achieving superior performance: A study of public sector organizations, *The International Journal of Human Resource Management*, 14 (1), pp 28–54

GRATTON, L (2000) *Living Strategy: Putting people at the heart of corporate purpose*, FT/Prentice Hall, Harlow

GREEN, M PETERS, R, and YOUNG, J (2020) People Profession 2030, a collective view of future trends, CIPD, pp 1–40, www.cipd.co.uk/Images/people-profession-2030-report-compressed_tcm18-86095.pdf (archived at https://perma.cc/C7C9-HF3P)

GREENLEAF, R (1977) *Servant Leadership: A Journey into the Nature of Legitimate Power and Greatness*, Paulist Press, New York

GREENWOOD, M and FREEMAN, RE (2011) *Ethics and HRM. Business and Professional Ethics Journal*, 30 (3/4), pp 269–92

GREGORY, M and HAWKES, C (2022) Can you use artificial intelligence to sack workers? *People Management*, 30 March

GREINER, L (1972) Evolution and revolution as organizations grow. *Harvard Business Review*. July–August. 78.63.254.76/Organizations.pdf https://hbr.org/1998/05/evolution-and-revolution-as-organizations-grow (archived at https://perma.cc/S52M-WQ3S)

GRELLER, M (2006) Hours invested in professional development during late career as a function of career motivation and satisfaction, *Career Development International*, 11 (6), pp 544–59

GREY, C (2009) *A Very Short, Fairly Interesting and Reasonably Cheap Book About Studying Organizations*, 2nd edn, Sage, London

GREY, C (2013) *A Very Short, Fairly Interesting and Reasonably Cheap Book About Studying Organizations*, 3rd edn, Sage, London

GREY, C (2021) *A Very Short, Fairly Interesting and Reasonably Cheap Book About Studying Organizations*, 5th edn, Sage, London

GRINT, K (1997) *Fuzzy Management*, Oxford University Press, Oxford

GRUMAN, J and SAKS, A (2011) Performance management and employee engagement, *Human Resource Management Review*, 21, pp 123–36

GRUNDY, T (1993) *Managing Strategic Change*, Kogan Page, London

GUBBINS, C and GARAVAN, TN (2009) Understanding the HRD role in MNCs: the imperatives of social capital and networking, *Human Resource Development Review*, 8, pp 245–75

GUEST, D (1997) Human resource management and performance: a review of the research agenda, *International Journal of Human Resource Management*, 8 (3), pp 263–76

GUEST, D (1998) Is the psychological contract worth taking seriously? *Journal of Organizational Behaviour*, 19, pp 649–64

GUEST, D (2004) Flexible employment contracts, the psychological contract and employee outcomes: an analysis and review of the evidence, *International Journal of Management Reviews*, 5/6 (1), pp 1–19

GUEST, DE (2011) Human resource management and performance: still searching for some answers, *Human Resource Management Journal*, 21 (1), pp 3–13

GUEST, DE and CONWAY, N (2002) *Pressure at Work and the Psychological Contract*, CIPD, London

GUEST, DE and WOODROW, C (2012) Exploring the Boundaries of Human Resource Managers' Responsibilities, *Journal of Business Ethics*, 111 (1), pp 109–19

GUO, C, BROWN, WA, ASHCRAFT, RF, YOKISHIOKA CF and DONG, HKC (2011) Strategic human resource management in non-profit organizations, *Review of Public Personnel Administration*, 31 (3), pp 248–69

HAAK-SAHEEM, W, HUTCHINGS, K, and BREWSTER, C (2021) Swimming ahead or treading water? Disaggregating the career trajectories of women self-initiated expatriates, *British Journal of Management*, https://doi.org/10.1111/1467-8551.12465 (archived at https://perma.cc/CYV3-QUZ6)

HACKMAN, JR and OLDHAM, GR (1980) *Work Redesign*, Adison-Wesley, New York

HAINES III, V and ST-ONGE, S (2012) Performance management effectiveness: practices or context? *The International Journal of Human Resources Management*, 26 (6), pp 1158–75

HAKIM, C (2011) Feminist Myths and Magic Medicine: The Flawed Thinking Behind Calls for Further Equality Legislation. Centre For Policy Studies. eprints.lse.ac.uk/36488/1/ Feminist_myths_and_magic_medicine_the_flawed_thinking_behind_calls_for_further_ equality_legislation_(lsero).pdf (archived at https://perma.cc/J45A-8SBS)

HALL, D (1996) *The Career Is Dead, Long Live the Career*, Jossey-Bass, San Francisco, CA

HALL, D (2004) The Protean Career: A Quarter-Century Journey, *Journal of Vocational Behaviour*, 65 (1), pp 1–13

HALL, D (2009) How Smart are Targets? *HR Bulletin: Research and Practice*, 4, pp 8–10

HALL, D, JAMES, D and MARSDEN, N (2012) Marginal gains: Olympic lessons in high performance for organisations, *Human Resource Bulletin: Research and Practice*, 7 (2), pp 9–13

HAMILTON SKURAK, H MALINEN, S NASWALL, K and KUNTZ, J (2018) Employee wellbeing: The role of psychological detachment on the relationship between engagement and work-life conflict, *Economic and Industrial Democracy*, 42 (8), pp 2–26

HAMILTON, SH, MALINEN, S NASWALL, K and KUNTZ, JC (2021) Employee wellbeing: The role of psychological detachment on the relationship between engagement and work–life conflict, *Economic and Industrial Democracy*, 42 (1), pp 116–41

HAMMER, M and CHAMPY, J (1993) *Re-engineering the Corporation: A manifesto for business revolution*, Nicholas Brealey, London

HANCOCK, B and SCHANINGER, B (2020) *HR says talent is crucial for performance – and the pandemic proves it.* www.mckinsey.com/business-functions/people-and-organizational-performance/our-insights/hr-says-talent-is-crucial-for-performance-and-the-pandemic-proves-it (archived at https://perma.cc/8WEQ-9W4A)

HANDY, C (1976) *Understanding Organisations*, Penguin Books, London

HANDY, C (1989) *The Age of Unreason*, Business Books, London

HANLON, G (1998) Professionalism as enterprise: service class politics and the redefinition of professionalism, *Sociology*, 32 (43)

HARDY, C (1994) *Managing Strategic Action: Mobilizing change – concepts, readings and cases*, Sage, London

HARDY, C (1996) Understanding power: bringing about strategic change, *British Journal of Management*, 7 (special issue), pp S3–S16

HARNEY, B and ALKHALAF, H (2021) A quarter-century review of HRM in Small and Medium-Sized Enterprises (SMEs), Capturing what we know and exploring where we need to go, *Human Resource Management*, 60 (10), pp 5–29

HARRINGTON, S, RAYNER, C and WARREN, S (2012) Too Hot to Handle? Trust and Human Resource Practitioners' Implementation of Anti-Bullying Policies, *Human Resource Management Journal*, 22 (4), pp 392–408

HARRIS, JG, CRAIG, E and LIGHT, DA (2011) Talent and analytics: new approaches, higher ROI, *Journal of Business Strategy*, 32 (6), pp 4–13

HARRIS, L (2005) Employment law and human resourcing strategies. In: LEOPOLD, J, HARRIS, L and WATSON, TJ (eds) *The Strategic Managing of Human Resources*, Pearson Education, Harlow

HARRISON, R and KESSELS, J (2003) *Human Resource Development in a Knowledge Economy*, Palgrave Macmillan, Basingstoke

HARRISON, R (2005) *Learning and Development*, 3rd edn, CIPD, London

HARRISON, R (2009) *Learning and Development*, 5th edn, CIPD, London

HARRY, W and COLLINGS, D (2012) Localisation, Societies, Organisations and Employees. In: STAHL, GK, MENDENHALL, ME and ODDOU, GR (2012) *Readings and Cases in International Human Resource Management and Organisational Behaviour*, 5th edn, Routledge, London

HARTOG, DN and VERBURG, RM (2004) High performance work systems, organisational culture and firm effectiveness, *Human Resource Management Journal*, 14 (1), pp 55–78

HARVARD BUSINESS REVIEW ANALYTIC SERVICES REPORT (2015) https://hbr.org/resources/pdfs/comm/atlassian/atlassian2015.pdf (archived at https://perma.cc/D7H9-XDN3)

HASE, S and KENYON, C (2007) Heutagogy: a child of complexity theory, *Complicity: An International Journal of Complexity and Education*, 4 (1), pp 111–8

HASSON, J (2007) Blogging for talent, *HR Magazine*, 52 (10), pp 65–8

HAYES, J (2018) *The Theory and Practice of Change Management*, 5th edn, Palgrave Macmillan, London

HAYS (2022) *Why company values matter*, www.hays.net.nz/employer-insights/management-issues/why-company-values-matter (archived at https://perma.cc/8NVU-YY4P)

HAYS-THOMAS, R (2004) Why now? The contemporary focus on managing diversity, in Stockdale, MS and Crosby, FJ (eds) *The Psychology and Management of Workplace Diversity*, Blackwell, Oxford

HAZARD, P (2004) Tackling Performance Management Barriers, *Strategic HR Review*, 3, pp 3–7

THE HEALTH FOUNDATION (2020) *One in three employees report being in low-quality jobs*, February 4 2020

HEENAN, D and PERLMUTTER, H (1979) *Multinational Organizational Development: A social architecture perspective*, Addison-Wesley, Reading, MA

HEERY, E, HANN, D and NASH, D (2020) Political devolution and employment relations in Great Britain: the case of the Living Wage, *Industrial Relations Journal*, 51 (5), pp 391–409

HENDERSON, S (1997) Black swans don't fly double loops: the limits of the learning organisation, *The Learning Organisation*, 4 (3), pp 99–105

HENDRICK, H (1983) Pilot Performance Under Reversed Control Stick Conditions, *Journal of Applied Psychology*, 56 (4), pp 297–301

HENDRY, C (1995) *Human Resource Management*, Butterworth-Heinemann, Oxford

HENEMAN, RL (1992) *Merit Pay: Linking pay increases to performance ratings*, Addison-Wesley, Reading, MA

HERMAN, ER and GIOIA JL (2001) Helping Your Organisation Become an Employer of Choice, *Employment Relations Today*, 28 (2), pp 63–78

HERRING, C and HENDERSON, L (2015) *Diversity in Organizations: A Critical Examination*, Routledge, Abingdon

HERSEY, P, BLANCHARD, K and JOHNSON, D (2001) *Management of Organisational Behaviour: Leading human resources*. 8th edn, Prentice Hall, London

HERZBERG, F (1968) One more time: how do you motivate your employees? *Harvard Business Review*. January–February, pp 109–20

HESKETT, J (2022) Author Talks: How to gain a competitive edge with organizational culture, McKinsey & Company, Columbia Business School Publishing, www.mckinsey.com/featured-insights/mckinsey-on-books/author-talks-how-to-gain-a-competitive-edge-with-organizational-culture?cid=other-eml-alt-mip-mck&hdpid=1b9a121d-6c2d-43cf-b56a-7e4e63004c6c&hctky=2872684&hlkid=23001334a3ba4871bf3be093293115ee (archived at https://perma.cc/J7NC-VCS9)

HEWETT, R and SHANTZ, A, (2021) A theory of HR co-creation. *Human Resource Management Review*, 31 (4), pp 100823. https://doi.org/10.1016/j.hrmr.2021.100823 (archived at https://perma.cc/GXS8-W2YM)

HI BOB (2022) What is people management? www.hibob.com/hr-glossary/people-management/ (archived at https://perma.cc/K46W-LTCS)

HIATT, J (2006) What is the ADKAR Model? Retrieved from www.prosci.com/adkar/adkar-model (archived at https://perma.cc/2DEQ-Q9HX)

HIGGINS, JM (2005) The Eight 'S's of successful strategy execution, *Journal of Change Management*, 5 (1), pp 3–13

HILTROP, J-M (1996) Managing the changing psychological contract. *Employee Relations*, 18 (1), pp 36–49

HIRSCH, PB (2021) "The great discontent." *Journal of Business Strategy*, 42 (6), pp 439–442

HIRSCHI, A (2012) The career resources model: an integrative framework for career counselors. *British Journal of Guidance and Counselling*, 40 (4), pp 369–383

HIROKAWA, R, GOURAN, D and MARTZ, A (1988) Understanding the Sources of Faulty Group Decision Making: A Lesson from the Challenger Disaster, *Small Group Behaviour*, 19, p 423

HIT SCOTLAND (2022) Learn today, Shape Tomorrow: Welcome to the tourism and hospitality talent development programme – Phase 2 https://hitscotland.co.uk/talent-development-programme (archived at https://perma.cc/PV77-X32Y)

HM Treasury (2004) Gershon Efficiency Review www.hm-treasury.gov.uk/spend_sr04_index.htm/ (archived at https://perma.cc/G9S3-TZLQ)

HOBSON, J (2009) Bullying in the workplace, *Personnel Today*, 5 March

HM GOVERNMENT (2018) *The Good Work Plan*, Cm 9755, The Stationery Office, London

HOCHSCHILD, AR (2012) *The Managed Heart: Commercialization of Human Feeling*, University of California Press, Berkeley

HOFSTEDE, G (1991) *Cultures and Organizations*, McGraw Hill, Maidenhead

HOFSTEDE, G (2001) *Culture's Consequences: Comparing values, behaviours, institutions and organizations across nations*, Sage, London

HOLBECHE, L (2008a) *Aligning Human Resources and Business Strategy*, Butterworth-Heinemann, Oxford

HOLBECHE, L (2008b) Where is Leadership Going? *Impact*, Issue 22, February, pp 16–17

HOLBECHE, L (2013) The Future of HR. In REES, G and SMITH, PE (eds) *Strategic Human Resource Management: An International Perspective*, Sage, London

HOLBECHE, L (2018) Organisational effectiveness and agility, *Journal of Organizational Effectiveness: People and Performance*, 5 (4), pp 302–313

HOLBECHE, L and MATTHEWS, G (2012) *Engaged: Unleashing your organisation's potential through employee engagement*, Wiley/Josey Bass, Chichester

HOLDEN, N (2002) *Cross-Cultural Management: A knowledge management perspective*, Pearson, Harlow

HOLLAND, D and SCULLION, H (2021) Towards a talent retention model: mapping the building blacks of the psychological contract to the three stages of the acquisition process. *The International Journal of Human Resource Management*, 32 (13), pp 2683–2728

HOLLYFORDE, S and WHIDDETT, S (2002) *The Motivation Handbook*, CIPD, London

HOLST, JD (2009) Conceptualizing training in the radical adult education tradition. *Adult Education Quarterly*, 59 (4), pp 318–334

HONEY, P (1998) *101 Ways to Develop Your People Without Really Trying: A manager's guide to work-based learning*, Peter Honey Publications, Maidenhead

HOOK, C and JENKINS, A (2019) *Introducing Human Resource Management*, 8th edn, Pearson, London

HOSKING, P (2022) Phoenix Group bans the word energetic from job ads to lure older workers, *The Times*, 17 January 2022

HOUGHTON, E (2017) May Research Report, Human Capital Analytics and reporting: explaining theory and evidence, www.cipd.co.uk/Images/human-capital-analytics-and-reporting_tcm18-22281.pdf (archived at https://perma.cc/YYZ9-ARVV)

HOUSE Of COMMONS WOMEN AND EQUALITIES COMMITTEE (2019) *The Use of Non-Disclosure Agreements in Discrimination Cases*, HC1720, House of Commons, London

HOUSTON, J and KESTER, B (2014) *Talent analytics in practice: go from talking to delivering on big data*. www2.deloitte.com/us/en/insights/focus/human-capital-trends/2014/hc-trends-2014-talent-analytics.html (archived at https://perma.cc/NSE8-MJYF)

HOWE-WALSH, LJ and KIRK, S, (2020) Self-initiated expatriates and the role of international human resource management (pp 195–213). In ANDRESEN, M, BREWSTER, C and SUUTARI, V (eds), *Self-initiated Expatriates in Context*, Routledge, New York

HOWE-WALSH, LJ and SCHYNS, B (2010) Self-Initiated Expatriates: Implications for HRM, *International Journal of Human Resource Management*, 21 (2), pp 260–73

HOWELL, WS (1982) *The Empathetic Communicator*, Wadsworth Publishing, University of Minnesota

HR OUTLOOK (2015) *Views of our profession*, Winter 2014–5, CIPD, London www.cipd.co.uk/hr-resources/survey-reports/hr-outlook-winter-2014-15-views-profession.aspx (archived at https://perma.cc/BBS3-2MQ4)

HSIEH, YH and CHEN, HM, (2011) Strategic fit among business competitive strategy, human resource strategy, and reward system, *Academy of Strategic Management Journal*, 10 (2), pp 11–32

HUBNER, S, RUDIC, B and BAUM, M, (2021) How entrepreneur's leadership behavior and demographics shape applicant attraction to new ventures: the role of stereotypes. *The International Journal of Human Resource Management*, pp 1–36 https://doi.org/10.1080/09585192.2021.1893785 (archived at https://perma.cc/G2FX-LMEP)

HUCZYNSKI, A and BUCHANAN, D (2013) *Organisational Behaviour*, 8th edn, Pearson Education, Harlow

HUGHES, JC and ROG, E (2008) Talent management: a strategy for improving employee recruitment, retention and engagement within hospitality organizations. *International Journal of Contemporary Hospitality Management*, 20 (7), pp 743–757

HUGHES, M (2019) *Change Management: A critical perspective*, 2nd edn, CIPD, London

HUMBLE, J (1972) *Management by Objectives*, Management Publications, London

HUNT, B (2007) Managing equality and cultural diversity in the health workforce, *Journal of Clinical Nursing*, 16, pp 2252–2259

HUO, M-L, BOXALL, P and CHEUNG, G W (2020) How does line manager support enhance worker wellbeing? A study in China, *The International Journal of Human Resource Management*, 31 (14), pp 1825–1843, DOI: 10.1080/09585192.2017.1423103 (archived at https://perma.cc/TL57-ZXEM)

HUONG, L ZHENG, C and FUJIMOTO, Y (2016) Inclusion, organisational justice and employee well-being, *International Journal of Manpower*, 37 (6), pp 945–964

HUSELID, MA (1995) The impact of human resource management practices on turnover, productivity and corporate financial performance, *Academy of Management Journal*, 38, pp 635–672

HUSELID, MA and Rau, BL (1997) *The determinants of High Performance Work Systems; Cross Sectional and Longitudinal Analyses*, Academy of Management Meetings Division. In: TAMKIN, P (2004) High Performance Work Practices, Institute of Employment Studies, Brighton, https://citeseerx.ist.psu.edu/viewdoc/download?doi=10.1.1.1072.283&rep=rep1&type=pdf (archived at https://perma.cc/TWK7-EWRF)

HUSSAIN, K, AHMAD, AM, RAGAVAN, NA and LEONG, QL (2020) Raising standards for hospitality and tourism education in Malaysia. *Worldwide Hospitality and Tourism Themes*, 12 (2), pp 199–206

HUTCHINSON, S (2018) *Performance Management: Theory and Practice*, Kogan Page, London

HUTCHINSON, S and PURCELL, J (2003) *Bringing Policies to Life: The vital role of front-line managers in people management*, CIPD, London

HUTTON, W (2004) Got those old blue-collar blues, *Observer*, 22 August

HUWS, U (2013) Capitalism's Zero Hour, *Times Higher Education*, 15 August

HUWS, U and O'KEEFE, B (2008) *EMCC company network - Managing change in EU cross-border mergers and acquisitions - Case example: Impress: Meeting company goals through strategic acquisitions*. www.eurofound.europa.eu/publications/htmlfiles/ef08043.htm (archived at https://perma.cc/N66B-5V2G)

IBHARRA, H (2004) Working Identity: *Unconventional strategies for reinventing your career*, Harvard Business School Press, Boston, MA

IBM (2013) *IBM Graduate Scheme*, www-05.ibm.com/employment/uk/graduate-programmes/index.shtml (archived at https://perma.cc/FB99-72CJ)

IDS (2006) *Online Recruitment*, IDS study 819, April, Incomes Data Services, London

ILES, P, FORSTER, A and TINLINE, G (1996) The changing relationships between work commitment, personal flexibility and employability: an evaluation of a field experiment in executive development, *Journal of Managerial Psychology*, 11 (8), pp 18–34

INKSON, K and ARTHUR, M (2001) How to be a successful career capitalist. *Organisational Dynamics*, 30 (1), pp 48–61

INSTITUTE OF BUSINESS ETHICS (2014) Collaboration Between the Ethics Function and HR, *Business Ethics Briefing*, Issue 40, April, Available: www.ibe.org.uk/userassets/briefings/b40_hr.pdf (archived at https://perma.cc/9J4R-URSD)

INSTITUTE OF BUSINESS ETHICS (IBE) (2022) Innovating Business Ethics: The power of stories, www.ibe.org.uk/resource/innovating-business-ethics-the-power-of-stories.html (archived at https://perma.cc/EA65-89FZ)

INSTITUTE OF EMPLOYMENT STUDIES, (2022) *Labour Market Statistics*, February 2022, IES, Brighton

IQBAL, M and KHAN, R (2011) The growing concept and uses of training needs assessment, *Journal of European Industrial Training*, 35 (5), pp 439–466

IRS (2000) Measuring intangible assets. IRS Management Review. Issue 19. www. xperthr.co.uk/article/6106/measuring-span-span-classhighlightintangible-spanspan-classhighlightassets.aspx (archived at https://perma.cc/GK4J-YQBC)

IRS (2008) Line managers' role in people management. IRS Employment Review. Issue 894. www.xperthr.co.uk/article/84008/survey--line-managers-role-in-peoplemanagement.aspx (archived at https://perma.cc/9HNM-PY2J)

IRS (2009) IRS flexible working survey 2009: availability, take-up and impact. IRS Employment Review. Issue 92. www.xperthr.co.uk/article/93627/irs-flexibleworking-survey-2009--availability,-take-up-and-impact.aspx (archived at https://perma.cc/A5YT-8DGS)

IRS (2010) *Evaluation of training: the 2010 IRS survey*. IRS Employment Review. www. xperthr.co.uk/article/100298/evaluation-span-of-spanclasshighlighttraining--the-2010-irs-survey.aspx (archived at https://perma.cc/J4JV-79DV)

IYER, B and DAVENPORT, HT (2008) Reverse engineering Google's innovation machine, *Harvard Business Review*, April, 59–68

JAKOBSSON, P and STIERNSTEDT, F (2010) Googleplex and Informational Culture. In: Ericson, S and Riegert, K (eds), *Media houses: architecture, media and the culture of centrality*, Peter Lang Publishing, New York, pp 111–32

JAMALI, DR, EL DIRANI, AM and HARWOOD, IA (2015) Exploring human resource management roles in corporate social responsibility: the CSR-HRM co-creation model. *Business Ethics: A European Review*, 24 (2), pp 125–143

JAMROG, JJ and OVERHOLT, MH (2004) Building a strategic HR Function: Continuing the evolution, *Human Resource Planning*, 27 (1), pp 51–62. https://web.s.ebscohost.com/ehost/pdfviewer/pdfviewer?vid=1&sid=a8fa200e-ea80-4ff5-8580-f782df313419%40redis (archived at https://perma.cc/X3YL-7X5D)

JAMROG, JJ, VICKERS, M, OVERHOLT, MH and MORRISON, CL (2008) High-performance organizations: finding the elements of excellence, *People and Strategy, The Human Resource Planning Society Journal*, 31 (1), pp 29–38

JANIS, I (1972) *Victims of Groupthink*, Houghton Mifflin, Boston MA

JANIS, IL (1982) *Groupthink: Psychological studies on policy decisions and fiascos*, Free Press, New York

JARRETT, T (2011) *The Equality Act 2010 and Positive Action*. Standard Note SN/BT/6093. London: House of Commons Library

JEHN, K (1994) Enhancing effectiveness: an investigation of advantages and disadvantages of value-based intragroup conflict optimising performance by conflict stimulation. *International Journal of Conflict Management*, 5 (3), pp 223–238

JENNER, S and TAYLOR, S (2007) *Employer branding – fad or the future for HR?* Research Insight Paper, CIPD, London

JENNINGS, C and WARGNIER, J (2010) Experiential learning – a way to develop agile minds in the knowledge economy? *Development and Learning in Organizations*, 24 (3), pp 14–16

JOHNS, G (2006) The essential impact of context on organizational behavior. *Academy of Management Review*, 31 (2), 386–408

JOHNSON, G and SCHOLES, K (2002) *Exploring Corporate Strategy* 6th edn, FT/Pitman, London

JOHNSON, G, SCHOLES, K and WHITTINGTON, R (2007) *Exploring Corporate Strategy*, Texts and cases. 7th edn, FT/Pitman, London

JOHNSON, G, SCHOLES, K and WHITTINGTON, R (2011) *Exploring Corporate Strategy*. 8th edn, FT/Pitman, London

JOHNSON, G, SCHOLES, K, WHITTINGTON, R, ANGWIN, D and REGNER, P (2019) *Exploring Strategy, Text and Cases*, 12th edn, Pearson Education

JOHNSON, K (2016) The dimensions and effect of excessive change, *Journal of Organizational Change Management*, 29 (3), pp 445–59

JONES, S and WHITE, G (2021) Reward Strategy and Managing Performance. In Rees, G and Smith, PE (eds) *Strategic Human Resource Management: An international perspective*, 3rd edn, Sage, London

JONES, S and WHITE, G (2021), Reward Strategy and Managing Performance. In REES, G and SMITH, PE (2021), *Strategic Human Resource Management: An International Perspective*, 3rd edn, Sage, London

JONES, TW (1995) Performance management in a changing context. *Human Resource Management*, Fall, pp 425–442

JONSEN, K POINT, S KELAN, EK and GRIEBLE, A (2021) Diversity and inclusion branding: A five-country comparison of corporate websites, *International Journal of Human Resource Management*, 32 (3), pp 616–49

JOOSS, S, BURBACH, R and RUEL, H (2021) Examining talent pools as a core talent management practice in multinational corporations. *The International Journal of Human Resource Management*, 32 (11), pp 2321–2352

JUDGE, TA and CABLE, DM (1997) Applicant personality, organisational culture and organisation attraction. *Personnel Psychology*, 50 (2), pp 359–394

JUDGE, WQ, NAOUMOVA, I and DOUGLAS, T (2009) Organizational capacity for change and firm performance in a transitional economy. *International Journal of Human Resource Management*, 20 (8), pp 1737–1752

KABWE, C and OKORIE, C (2019) The efficacy of talent management in international business: the case of European multinationals. *Thunderbird International Business Review*, 61 (6), pp 857–872

KAHN, WA (1990) Psychological conditions of personal engagement and disengagement at work. *The Academy of Management Journal*, 33 (4), pp 692–724

KAKABADSE, A, MYERS, A, McMAHON, T and SPONY, G (1997) Top Management Styles in Europe: Implications for Business and Cross- National Teams, in Grint, T *Leadership: Classicals, Contemporary and Critical Approaches*, Oxford University Press, Oxford

KALYVAS, S (2020) *How to reverse the brain drain*, www.ekathimerini.com/opinion/248292/how-to-reverse-the-brain-drain/ (archived at https://perma.cc/Q43W-YUZK)

KANDOLA, R and FULLERTON, J (1998) *Diversity in Action: Managing the mosaic*, 2nd edn, CIPD, London

KANG, D and STEWART, J (2007) Leader-member exchange (LMX) theory of leadership and HRD, *Leadership and Organization Development Journal*, 28 (6), pp 531–551

KAPLAN, RS and NORTON, DP (2005) The Office of Strategy Management, Harvard Business Review, October, https://hbr.org/2005/10/the-office-of-strategy-management (archived at https://perma.cc/DXP9-Q3L9)

KAPTEIN, M, and SCHWARTZ, M S (2008) The effectiveness of business codes: A critical examination of existing studies and the development of an integrated research model, *Journal of Business Ethics*, 77 (2), pp 111–127

KATOU, AA and BUDHWAR, PS (2009) Causal relationship between HRM policies and performance: evidence from the Greek manufacturing sector, *European Management Journal*, 28, pp 25–39

KATOU, AA, BUDHWAR, PS and PATEL, C, (2021) Line manager implementation and employee HR attributions mediating mechanisms in the HRM system—Organizational performance relationship: A multilevel and multipath study, *Human Resource Management Journal*, 31 (3), pp 775–795. https://doi.org/10.1111/1748-8583.12327 (archived at https://perma.cc/5UZ3-UJD6)

KATZENBACH, JR and SMITH, DK (2005) *The Wisdom of Teams: Creating the High Performance Organisations*, McGraw-Hill Professional, New York

KAUR, J and FINK, AA (2017) *Trends and practices in talent analytics*, www. shrm.org/hr-today/trends-and-forecasting/special-reports-and-expert-views/ Documents/2017%2010_SHRM-SIOP%20Talent%20Analytics.pdf (archived at https:// perma.cc/D259-H7A6)

KEARNS, P (2005) *Evaluating the ROI from learning: how to develop value-based training*, CIPD, London

KELLIHER, C and ANDERSON, D (2010) Doing more with less? Flexible working practices and the intensification of work, *Human Relations*, 63 (1), pp 83–106

KESSLER, I and PURCELL, J (1992) Performance-related pay: objectives and application, *Human Resource Management Journal*, 2 (3), pp 6–33

KETCHEN, D J, Jr, and HULT, G T M (2007) Bridging organization theory and supply chain management: The case of best value supply chains, *Journal of Operations Management*, 25, pp 573–580

KHAPOVA, S and ARTHUR, M (2011) Interdisciplinary approaches to contemporary career studies, *Human Relations*, 64 (1), pp 3–17

KHILJI, SE and SCHULER, RS (2017) Talent management in the global context. In DG Collings, K Mellahi and WF Cascio (eds), *The Oxford Handbook of Talent Management*, pp 399–420, Oxford University Press, Oxford

KIER, L (2020) *Remote work: the ultimate equalizer for talent acquisition and employee experience*, www.forbes.com/sites/forbescommunicationscouncil/2020/08/10/ remote-work-the-ultimate-equalizer-for-talent-acquisition-and-employee-experience/?sh=10083b47986f (archived at https://perma.cc/L96A-6844)

KIERAN, S, MACMAHON, J and MACCURTAIN, S, (2021) Simple rules for sensemaking praxis: How HR can contribute to strategic change by developing sensemaking capability in organisations, *Human Resource Management Journal*, https://doi. org/10.1111/1748-8583.12404 (archived at https://perma.cc/T84C-XVYY)

KIM, W and MAUBORGNE, R (2005) Blue Ocean Strategy: From theory to practice, *California Management Review*, 47 (3), pp 105–21

KING, KA (2019) Macro talent management in Canada: A review of the national context, competitive strengths and future opportunities to attract, develop and retain talent. In VAIMAN, V, SPARROW, P, SCHULER, R and COLLINGS, DG (eds). *Macro Talent Management on Managing Talent in Developed*, Routledge, London

KING, Z (2004) *Guide to Career Management*, CIPD, London

KINNIE, N, SWART, J, HOPE-HAILEY, V and VAN ROSSENBERG, Y (2012) *Innovative forms of organizing: Networked working in HR and its role in innovation, Part 1*, CIPD, London

KINNIE, N, SWART, J, KUND, M, MORRIS, S, SNELL, S and KANG, SC (2006) *Managing people and knowledge development in professional service firms*, CIPD, London

KIRTON, G and GREENE, A-M (2015) *The Dynamics of Managing Diversity: A critical approach*, 4th edn, Routledge, Abingdon

KIRTON, G, GREENE, A-M and DEAN, D (2007) British diversity professionals as change agents – radicals, tempered radicals or liberal reformers, *International Journal of Human Resource Management*, 18 (11), pp 1979–1984

KISSLER, G (1994) The new employment contract. *Human Resource Management*, 33 (3), pp 335–352

KLEIN, T (2021) How Coca-Cola HBC transformed its company culture during Covid, *People Management*, 11 February

KNIES, E, BOSELIE, P, GOULD-WILLIAMS, J and VANDENABEELE, W, (2018) Strategic human resource management and public sector performance: context matters, *The International Journal of Human Resource Management*, pp 1–13. https://doi.org/10.108 0/09585192.2017.1407088 (archived at https://perma.cc/WE9U-HTWW)

KNOWLES, M (1990) *The Adult Learner: A neglected species*, Gulf Publications, London

KOLB, DA (1984) *Experiential Learning: Experience as the Source of Learning and Development*, Prentice-Hall

KONTOGHIOrGHES, C (2016) Linking high performance organizational culture and talent management: satisfaction/motivation and organizational commitment as mediators, *International Journal of Human Resource Management*, 27 (16), pp 1833–53

KONZACK, L (2006) *Geek culture: the 3rd counter-culture*, Presented at FNG2006, Preston, England. www.academia.edu/3808704/Geek_Culture_The_3rd_Counter-Culture (archived at https://perma.cc/7679-UZHH)

KOOPMAN, R, ENGLIS, PD, EHRENHARD, ML and GROEN, A (2021) The chronological development of coaching and mentoring: side by side disciplines, *International Journal of Evidence Based Caching and Mentoring*, 19 (1), pp 137–51

KOSTER, F (2011) Able, willing, and knowing: the effects of HR practices on commitment and effort in 26 European countries, *The International Journal of Human Resource Management*, 22 (14), pp 2835–2851

KOTTER, JP (1996) *Leading Change*, Harvard Business School Press, Boston, MA

KOTTER, JP (1999) *What Leaders Really Do*, Harvard Business School Press, Boston, MA

KOUKPAKI, ASF and ADAMS, K (2020) Enhancing professional growth and the learning and development function through reflective practices: an autoethnographic narrative approach, *European Journal of Training and Development*, 44 (8/9), pp 805–827

KRAMAR, R (2014) Beyond strategic human resource management: is sustainable human resource management the next approach? *The International Journal of Human Resource Management*, 25 (8), pp 1069–1089

KRAVARITI, F and JOHNSTON, K (2020) Talent management: a critical literature review and research agenda for public sector human resource management, *Public Management Review*, 22 (1), pp 75–95

KRAVARITI, F, ORUH, ES, DIBIA, C, TASOULIS, K, SCULLION, H and MAMMAN, A (2021) Weathering the storm: talent management in internationally oriented Greek small and medium-sized enterprises, *Journal of Organizational Effectiveness: People and Performance*, 8 (4), pp 444–463

KRAVARITI, F, TASOULIS, K, SCULLION, H and ALALI, KM (2022a) Talent management and performance in the public sector: the role of organisational and line managerial support for development, *International Journal of Human Resource Management*, www.tandfonline.com/doi/full/10.1080/09585192.2022.2032265 (archived at https://perma.cc/P5D5-SCLV)

KRAVARITI, F, VOUTSINA, K, TASOULIS, K, DIBIA, C and JOHNSTON, K (2022b) Talent management in the hospitality industry: a critical review and research agenda, *International Journal of Contemporary Hospitality Management*, 34 (1), pp 321–360

KRISHNAN, TN and SCULLION, H (2017) Talent management and dynamic view of talent in small and medium enterprises, *Human Resource Management Review*, 27 (3), pp 431–441cip

KUBOVCIKOVA, A and van BAKEL M (2022) Social support abroad: how do self-initiated expatriates gain support through their social networks? *International Business Review*, 31 (1), 101894

KULIK, CT, RYAN, S, HARPER, S and GEORGE, G (2014) Aging populations and management, *Academy of Management Journal*, 57 (4), pp 929–935

KUVAAS, B (2006) Performance appraisal satisfaction and employee outcomes: mediating and moderating roles of work motivation, *International Journal of Human Resource Management*, 17 (3), pp 504–22

KWAN, A and LIAKOPOULOS, A (2011) *Talent edge 2020: Building the recovery together: What talent expects and how leaders are responding*, www2.deloitte.com/us/en/insights/topics/talent/talent-edge-2020-building-the-recovery-together.html (archived at https://perma.cc/2G7L-B2EG)

LAASCH, O, and CONAWAY, R (2017) *Responsible Business: The textbook for management learning, competence and innovation*, Routledge

LADKIN, D (2008) Leading Beautifully: How Mastery, Congruence and Purpose Create the Aesthetic of Embodied Leadership Practice. *The Leadership Quarterly*, 19 (1), pp 31–41

LADKIN, D and TAYLOR, S (2009) Enacting the True Self: Towards a Theory of Embodied Authentic Leadership. *The Leadership Quarterly*, 21 (1), pp 64–74

LAGERVELD, SE ET AL (2012) Work-focused treatment of common mental disorders and return to work: A comparative outcome study, *Journal of Occupational Health Psychology*, 17 (2), pp 220–234

LASHLEY, C (1995) Towards an understanding of employee empowerment in hospitality services. International Journal of Contemporary Hospitality Management, 7 (1), pp 27–32

LATHAM, G (2007) *Work Motivation: History, theory, research and practice*, Sage, London

LAWLER, E (2005) Creating high-performance organisations. *Asia Pacific Journal of Human Resources*, 43 (1), pp 10–17

LAWLER, E (2009) The knowing-doing gap. Conference Board Review, 46 (3), pp 29

LAWRENCE, P and LORSCH, J (1967) *Organisation and Environment*, Harvard Business School Press, Boston, MA

LEACH, D and WALL, T (2004) *What is Job Design?* Institute of Work Psychology, Sheffield

LEANNA, C and BARRY, B (2000) Stability and change as simultaneous experiences in organizational life. *Academy of Management Review*, 25 (4), pp 75–9

LEDET, E, McNULTY, K, MORALES, D and SHANDELL, M (2020) *How to be great at people analytics.* www.mckinsey.com/business-functions/people-and-organizational-performance/our-insights/how-to-be-great-at-people-analytics (archived at https://perma.cc/E79N-FASD)

LEGGE, K (2000) HRM in a Critical Analysis. In: STOREY, J (ed) *Human Resource Management: a Critical Text*, Thomson, London

LEGGE, K (2005) *Human Resource Management: Rhetorics and realities*, 2nd edn, Palgrave Macmillan, Basingstoke

LEICHT-DEOBALD, U, BUSCH, T, SCHANK, C, WEIBEL, A, SCHAFHEITLE, S, WILDHABER, I, and KASSPER, G (2019) The challenges of algorithm-based HR decision-making for personal integrity. *Journal of Business Ethics*, 160 (2), pp 377–392

LEMMETTY, S and COLLIN, K (2020) Self-directed learning as a practice of workplace learning: interpretative repertoires of self-directed learning in ICT work, *Vocations and Learning*, 13, pp 47–70

LENGNICK-HALL, ML, LENGNICK-HALL, CA and RIGSBEE, CM (2013) Strategic Human Resource Management and Supply Chain Orientation, *Human Resource Management Review*, 23, pp 366–377

LEONARDI, PM and BARLEY, SR (2010) What's under construction here? Social action, materiality, and power in constructivist studies of technology and organizing. *Academy of Management Annals*, 4 (1), pp 1–51

LESSEM, R (1989) *Global Management Principles* Prentice Hall, Harlow

LEVINSON, H (1970) Management by whose objectives? *Harvard Business Review*. July–August, pp 125–134

LEVINSON, H (1976) Appraisal of what performance? *Harvard Business Review*. July–August, pp 30–46

LEWIN, D (2001) IR and HR perspectives on workplace conflict: what can each learn from the other? *Human Resource Management Review*, 11 (4), pp 453–85

LEWIN, K (1947) Frontiers in group dynamics, *Human Relations*, 1, pp 5–42

LEWIN, K (1951) *Field Theory in Social Science*, Harper & Row, New York/London

LEWIS, G (2015) *Obsessive email checking damaging productivity and family life* www.cipd.co.uk/pm/peoplemanagement/b/weblog/archive/2015 (archived at https://perma.cc/4SCX-2RHG)

LEWIS, RE and HECKMAN, RJ (2006) Talent management: A critical review, *Human Resource Management Review*, 16 (2), pp 139–154

LINSTEAD, S, FULLOP, L and LILLEY, S (2009) *Management and Organisation: A critical text*, 2nd edn, Palgrave Macmillan, Basingstoke

LIU, H (2020) *Intersectionality in the Workplace: Creating Justice, Not Diversity* https://disorient.co/intersectionality-in-the-workplace/#why-intersectionality-in-the-workplace-matters (archived at https://perma.cc/6WZP-AVQM)

LLOYD, M and MAGUIRE, S (2002) The possibility horizon, *Journal of Change Management*, 3 (2), pp 149–157

LOCKE, EA (1968) Towards a Theory of Motivation and Incentives, *Organizational Behaviour and Human Performance*, 3 (2), pp 157–189

LOCKE, EA (1976) The nature and causes of job satisfaction. In: DUNNETTE, MD (ed) *Handbook of industrial and organizational psychology*, Rand McNally, Chicago, pp 1297–1349

LOCKE, EA and LATHAM, GP (1990) *A Theory of Goal-Setting and Task Performance*, Prentice Hall, Englewood Cliffs, NJ

LOCKWOOD, NR (2007) *Leveraging employee engagement for competitive advantage: HR's strategic role*, Society for Human Resource Management, Alexandria, VA

LÓPEZ-COTARELO, J (2018) Line managers and HRM: A managerial discretion perspective, *Human Resource Management Journal*, 28 (2), pp 255–271

LOWRY, C (2006) HR Managers as Ethical Decision Makers: Mapping the Terrain, *Asia Pacific Journal of Human Resource Management*, 40 (20), pp 211–221

LUPTON, T (1991) Organisational change: top-down or bottom-up management? *Personnel Review*, 20 (3), pp 4–10

MABEY, C -WHITE, B (eds) *Managing Change*, 2nd edn, Open University/Paul Chapman Publishing, Buckingham

MACDONALD, DJ and MAKIN, PJ (2000) The psychological contract, organisational commitment and job satisfaction of temporary staff, *Leadership and Organization Development Journal*, 21 (2), pp 84–91

MACFARLANE, F, DUBERLEY, J, FEWTRELL, C and POWELL, M (2012) Talent management for NHS managers: human resources or resourceful humans? *Public Money & Management*, 32 (6), pp 445–452

MACKAY, M (2015) Identity formation: professional development in practice strengthens a sense of self, *Studies in Higher Education*, 40 (8), pp 1–15

MACKIE, JL (1977) *Ethics – Inventing Right and Wrong*, Penguin, Harmondsworth

MACLEOD, D and CLARK, N (2009) *Engaging for Success: Enhancing performance through employee engagement*, Office of Public Sector Management, London

MAGUIRE, H (2002) Psychological contracts: are they still relevant? *Career Development International*, 7 (3), pp 167–180

MAHONEY J (1994) How to be ethical: ethics resource management, In: Harvey, B (ed) *Business Ethics – A European Approach* Prentice Hall, Hemel Hempstead

MAMMAM, A, AKURATIYAGAMAGE, VW and Kubo, CJ (2006) Managerial perceptions of the role of the human resource function in Sri Lanka: a comparative study of local, foreign-owned and joint venture companies, *International Journal of Human Resource Management*, 17, pp 2009–2020

MANGALINDEN, JP (2015) Plan for futuristic Googleplex raises hopes, fears, *Mashable UK*. http://mashable.com/2015/02/27/google-plans-newheadquarters/#ZnQkjtAzpsq5 (archived at https://perma.cc/H6YX-5Z5Z)

MANROOP, L, MALIK, A, CAMP, R, and SCHULZ, E (2021) Applicant reactions to social media assessment: A review and conceptual framework. *Human Resource Management Review*. https://doi.org/10.1016/j.hrmr.2021.100853 (archived at https://perma.cc/D8G6-9PTL)

MARCHINGTON, M (2015) Human resource management (HRM): Too busy looking up to see where it is going longer term? *Human Resource Management Review*, 25 (2), pp 176–187

MARCHINGTON, M, CARROLL, M, GRIMSHAW, D and PASS, S (2009) *Managing People in Networked Organizations*, CIPD, London

MARCHINGTON, M, GRIMSHAW, D, RUBERY, J and WILLMOTT, H (2005) *Fragmenting Work: Blurring organizational boundaries and disordering hierarchies*, Oxford University Press, Oxford

MARCHINGTON, M, RUBERY, J and GRIMSHAW, D (2011) *Alignment, integration and consistency in HRM across multi-employer networks*, CIPD, London

MARCHINGTON, M, VINCENT, S and COOKE, FL (2005) The role of boundary-spanning agents in inter-organizational contracting. In: MARCHINGTON, M, GRIMSHAW, D, RUBERY, J and WILLMOTT, H (eds) *Fragmenting Work: Blurring organizational boundaries and disordering hierarchies*, Oxford University Press, Oxford

MARINAKOU, E and GIOUSMPPASOGLOU, C (2019) Talent management and retention strategies in luxury hotels: evidence from four countries, *International Journal of Contemporary Hospitality Management*, 31 (10), pp 3855–3878

MARKS, A (2001) Developing a multiple foci conceptualization of the psychological contract, *Employee Relations*, 23 (5), pp 454–469

MARKS & SPENCER (2008) About Plan A Company website: plana.marksandspencer.com (archived at https://perma.cc/A6WC-67L2)

MARRIAGE, M (2018) Men only: Inside the charity fundraiser where women are put on show, *Financial Times*, 23 January, www.ft.com/content/075d679e-0033-11e8-9650-9c0ad2d7c5b5 (archived at https://perma.cc/ZG5Q-6BV9)

MARRIS, P (1986) *Loss and Change*, 2nd edn, Routledge & Kegan Paul, London

MARSDEN, D and FRENCH, S (1998) *What a Performance: Performance-related pay in the public services*, Centre for Economic Performance, London

MARTIN, G (2012) *Lens on Talent, a collection of Next Generation HR Thought pieces. Part 2, August*, CIPD, London

MARTIN, G (2007) Employer Branding – time for some long and "hard" reflections? in Employer Branding – The latest fad or the future of HR? *CIPD Research Insight report*, https://silo.tips/download/employer-branding-the-latest-fad-or-the-future-for-hr (archived at https://perma.cc/J3U9-7LJL) on the 5th May 2022

MARTIN, MJ (2006) That's the Way We Do Things Around Here: An Overview of Organizational Culture, *The Journal of Academic and Special Librarianship*, Spring, https://digitalcommons.unl.edu/cgi/viewcontent.cgi?article=1060&context=ejasljournal (archived at https://perma.cc/AN8L-J2X4)

MASLOW, AH (1943) A theory of human motivation, *Psychological Review*, 50 (4), pp 370–396

MAURER, T and CHAPMAN, E (2013) Ten years of career success in relation to individual and situational variables from the employee development literature, *Journal of Vocational Behaviour*, 83 (3), pp 450–465

MAYFIELD, M and MAYFIELD, J (2012) Logo leadership: breathing life into loyalty and putting meaning back into work. *Development and Learning in Organizations*, 26 (2), pp 11–15

MAYON-WHITE, B (1993) Problem-solving in small groups: team members as agents of change. In: MABEY, C and MAYON-WHITE, B (eds) *Managing Change*, 2nd edn, Open University/Paul Chapman Publishing, Buckingham

McCALMAN, J and PATON, RA (1992) *Change Management*, Paul Chapman Publishing, London

McCLEAN, E and COLLINS, C (2011) High-commitment HR practices, employee effort, and firm performance: Investigating the effects of HR practices across employee groups within professional services firms, *Human Resource Management*, 50 (3), pp 341–363

McDONNELL, A, COLLINGS, DG, MELLAHI, K and SCHULER, R (2017) Talent management: a systematic review and future prospects, *European Journal of International Management*, 11 (1), pp 86–128

McKINSEY, (2016) Independent work: Choice, necessity, and the gig economy. Report, October 10, 2016. Source: www.mckinsey.com/featured-insights/employment-and-growth/independent-work-choice-necessity-and-the-gig-economy (archived at https://perma.cc/4PDQ-PW5J)

McKINSEY (2022) *Addressing the unprecedented behavioral-health challenges facing Generation Z* www.mckinsey.com/industries/healthcare-systems-and-services/our-insights/addressing-the-unprecedented-behavioral-health-challenges-facing-generation-z (archived at https://perma.cc/V2TY-WCTQ)

McINTYRE, K (2021) *Why wellbeing in the workplace is so important* www.peoplemanagement.co.uk/voices/comment/why-wellbeing-workplace-important (archived at https://perma.cc/HR6X-8CQL)

McCLERNON, T (2006) Rivals to systematic training, *Advances in Developing Human Resources*, 8 (4), pp 442–459

McCRACKEN, M and WALLACE, M (2000) Towards a redefinition of strategic HRD, *Journal of European Industrial Training*, 24 (5), pp 281–290

McDONALD, P, BROWN, K and BRADLEY, L (2005) Have traditional career paths given way to Protean ones? Evidence from senior managers in the Australian public sector, *Career Development International*, 10 (2), pp 109–129

McDOWALL, A and SAUNDERS, M (2010) UK managers' conceptions of employee training and development, *Journal of European Industrial Training*, 34 (7), pp 609–630

McGUIRE, D and GUBBINS, C (2010) The Slow Death of Formal Learning: A Polemic, *Human Resources Development Review*, 9 (30), pp 249–265

McKINSEY & COMPANY (2021) Back to Human: Why HR leaders want to focus on people again. www.mckinsey.com/business-functions/people-and-organizational-performance/our-insights/back-to-human-why-hr-leaders-want-to-focus-on-people-again (archived at https://perma.cc/39UJ-27PW)

McLELLAN, D (ed) (2000) Karl Marx: Selected Writings, Oxford University Press, Oxford

McMACKIN, J and HEFFERNAN, M, (2021) Agile for HR: fine in practice, but will it work in theory? *Human Resource Management Review*, 31 (4), pp 100791 https://doi.org/10.1016/j.hrmr.2020.100791 (archived at https://perma.cc/K6N8-E35J)

McNAIR, S (2012) *Older People's Learning in 2012: A survey*, National Institute of Adult Continuing Education, London

McNULTY, Y, LAURING, J, JONASSON, C, and SELMER, J (2019) Highway to Hell? Managing expatriates in crisis. *Journal of Global Mobility: The Home of Expatriate Management Research*, www.researchgate.net/publication/334425200_Highway_to_Hell_Managing_expatriates_in_crisis (archived at https://perma.cc/XX43-EWXU)

MEGGINSON, D and WHITAKER, V (2007) *Continuing Professional Development*, 2nd edn, CIPD, London

MEIREHANS, J (2022) Law firm says staff can work from home – for 20 per cent less pay, 2 May 2022, www.bbc.co.uk/news/business-61298394 (archived at https://perma.cc/K35P-V4SS)

MEJIA, C and TORRES, EN (2018) Implementation and normalization process of asynchronous video interviewing practices in the hospitality industry, *International Journal of Contemporary Hospitality Management*, 30 (2), pp 685–701

MENSI-KLARBACH, H and RISBERG, A (eds) (2019) *Diversity in Organizations: Concepts and practices*, Red Globe Press, London MENTZER, JT, DeWITT, W, KEEBLER, JS, MIN, S, SMITH, CD (2001) Defining supply chain management, *Journal of Business Logistics*, 22, pp 1–25

MERCER SURVEY (2008/9) www.employeebenefits.co.uk/item/7971/23/319/3 (archived at https://perma.cc/8AKC-564B) www.cos-mag.com/human-resources/hr-stories/2009-pay-increases-vary-greatly-by-industry-mercer-survey-finds.html (archived at https://perma.cc/Z9UL-Q6RH)

MERRICK, L (2022) *How coaching & mentoring can drive success in your organisation.* https://chronus.com/resources/summary-how-coaching-mentoring-can-drive-success-in-your-organization (archived at https://perma.cc/35UL-7SE2)

MESSERSMITH, JG and GUTHRIE, JP (2010) High performance work systems in emergent organizations: Implications for firm performance, *Human Resource Management*, 49 (2), pp 241–264

MESSERSMITH, JG PATEL, PC LEPAK, DP and GOULD-WILLIAMS, J (2012) Unlocking the black box: exploring the link between high-performance work systems and performance, *Journal of Applied Psychology*, 96 (6), pp 1105–18

MERRICK, L (2022) *How coaching & mentoring can drive success in your organisation.* https://chronus.com/resources/summary-how-coaching-mentoring-can-drive-success-in-your-organization (archived at https://perma.cc/76DP-KSUJ)

METCALFE, B D, MAKAREEM, Y, and AFOUNI, F (2021) Macro talent management theorising: transnational perspectives of the political economy of talent formation in the Arab Middle East, *International Journal of Human Resource Management*, 31 (4), pp 562–588

MEYER, JP and ALLEN, NJ (1991) A three-component conceptualization or organizational commitment. *Human Resource Management Review*, 1, pp 61–89

MEYER, JP and HERSCOVITCH, L (2001) Commitment in the workplace: towards a general model, *Human Resources Management Review*, 11, pp 299–326

MEYER, JP and HERSCOVITCH, L (2002) Commitment to organizational change: extension of a three-component model. In: *Journal of Applied Psychology*, 87 (3), pp 474–487

MEZIROW, J (1997) Transformative learning: theory to practice. In Cranton, P (ed.). *Transformative Learning in Action: Insights from Practice - New Directions for Adult and Continuing Education*, pp 5–12. Jossey-Bass

MICROSOFT (2021) *The Next Great Disruption Is Hybrid Work — Are We Ready?* Microsoft, March 22, 2021, www.microsoft.com (archived at https://perma.cc/3H9T-RHR6)

MIHELIC, KK (2020) *Global talent management best practices for SMEs.* https://ec.europa.eu/research/participants/documents/downloadPublic?documentIds=080166e5cb9a876a&app Id=Pp GMS (archived at https://perma.cc/888Y-EJEK)

MILLER, D (2004) Building sustainable change capability. *Industrial and Commercial Training*, 36 (1), pp 9–12

MILLS, C (2010) HMRC running out of time to regain its sense of purpose. *The Times.* 14 January

MILLWARD, N, BRYSON, A and FORTH, J (2000) All change at work: British employment relations 1980–1998 as portrayed by the Workplace Industrial Relations Series, In: BLYTON, P and TURNBULL, P (eds) *The Dynamics of Employee Relations*, 3rd edn, Palgrave Macmillan, Basingstoke

MINCHINGTON, B (2006) *Your Employer Brand*, Hyde Park Press, Torrensville

MISHRA, D, KUMAR, S, SHARMA, RRK and DUBEY, R, (2018) Outsourcing decision: do strategy and structure really matter? *Journal of Organizational Change Management*, 31 (1), pp 26–46, DOI 10.1108/JOCM-04-2017-0144 (archived at https://perma.cc/2T2N-2PXZ)

MLITZ, K (2021) *Remote work frequency before and after COVID-19 in the United States 2020*, www.statista.com/statistics/1122987/change-in-remote-work-trends-after-covid-in-usa/ (archived at https://perma.cc/ZX3S-VM99)

MOERSCHELL, L (2009) Resistance to technological Change in Aacademia. *Current Issues in Education*, 11 (6), pp 1–10

MOHDZANI, H (2021) *Operating efficiency: implementing HR information systems in SMEs*, CIPD, London 11 June 2021

MOHRMAN, AM and MOHRMAN, SA (1995) Performance management is 'running the business', *Compensation and Benefits Review*, July–August, pp 69–75

MOLLEMAN, E and TIMMERMAN, H (2003) Performance Management When Innovation and Learning Become Critical Performance Indicators, *Personnel Review*, 32 (1), pp 93–113

MORGAN, R (2006) Making the Most of Performance Management Systems, *Compensation and Benefits Review*, 38, pp 22–27

MORRIS, TH (2019) Self-directed learning: a fundamental competence in a rapidly changing world, *International Review Education*, 65, pp 633–653

MORRISON, J (2015) *Business Ethics: New Challenges in a Globalised World*, Palgrave Macmillan, Basingstoke

M'PELE (2015) PM Flexible Working: A win-win situation or a recipe for disaster? *People Management*, www.linkedin.com/grp/post/4004145-65045126590180917 (archived at https://perma.cc/TMA5-C3JR)

MULLINS, LJ (2007) *Management and Organisational Behaviour*, 8th edn, FT/ Prentice Hall, Harlow

MULLINS, LJ (2010) Management and Organisational Behaviour, 9th edn, FT/ Prentice Hall, Harlow

MULLINS, LJ (2013) *Management and Organisational Behaviour*, 10th edn, FT/ Prentice Hall, Harlow

MULLINS, LJ (2019) *Organisational Behaviour in the Workplace*, 12th edn, Pearson, Harlow.

MUMFORD, E (1995) Contracts, complexity and contradictions: the changing employment relationship. *Personnel Review*, 24 (8), pp 54–70

MURPHY, N (2008a) Line manager's role in people management. IRS Employment Review survey, Issue 894, 3 April. www.xperthr.co.uk/article/84008/survey--linespan-span-classhighlightmanagers-span-span-classhighlightrole-span-in-people-spanclasshighlightmanagement.aspx?searchwords=murphy_2008_line_managers_role (archived at https://perma.cc/8PLV-WB6H)

MURPHY, N (2008b) HR roles and responsibilities. IRS Employment Review survey. www.xperthr.co.uk/searchresults.aspx?s=murphy_2010 (archived at https://perma.cc/YKA8-WSRE)

MURPHY, N (2008c) Trends in recruitment methods in 2006 and 2007. IRS Employment Review, Issue 893. www.xperthr.co.uk (archived at https://perma.cc/LMP6-XGPp)

MWILA, NK and TURAY, MIS (2018) Augmenting talent management for sustainable development in Africa, *World Journal of Entrepreneurship, Management and Sustainable Development*, 14 (1), pp 41–49

NATIONAL AUDIT OFFICE (2021) Efficiency in government, Report. HM Treasury

NDUBISI, NO and NYGAARD, A (2018) The ethics of outsourcing: when companies fail at responsibility, *Journal of Business Strategy*, 39 (5), pp 7–13

NEEDLE, D (2015) *Business in Context*, 6th edn, Cengage, Andover

NELSON, D and BERGMAN, D (2013) Bangladesh dispatch: the miracle of Rana Plaza gives way to grief as body count rises, *Daily Telegraph*, 25 April

NELSON, L (2003) A case study in organisational change: implications for theory, *The Learning Organization*, 10 (1), pp 18–30

NHS Employers (2017) *Eight Elements of Workplace Wellbeing* www.nhsemployers.org/articles/eight-elements-workplace-wellbeing (archived at https://perma.cc/NRB3-H9U7)

NICKSON, S (2001) The human resources balancing act, *Risk Management*, 48 (2), pp 25–29

NIELSEN, R (2006) Introduction to the special issue. In search of organizational virtue: moral agency in organizations, *Organization Studies*, 27 (3), pp 379–404

NIELSEN, K (2013) Review article: how can we make organizational interventions work? Employees and line managers as actively crafting interventions. *Human Relations*, 66 (8), pp 1029–50

NIMMO, J (2022) War for talent hots up as workers rate firms on their morals. *Sunday Times*, 20 February 2022, www.thetimes.co.uk/article/war-for-talent-hots-up-as-workers-rate-firms-on-their-morals-dgnxjcsx6 (archived at https://perma.cc/B7K3-6M66)

NIJSSEN, M and PAAUWE, J (2012) HRM in Turbulent Times: How to Achieve Agility. In: *International Journal of Human Resource Management*, 23 (16), pp 3315–3335

NOHRIA, N, GROYSBERG, B and LEE, L (2008) Employee motivation. *Harvard Business Review*, 86 (7/8), pp 78–84

NONAKA, I and TAKEUCHI, H (1995) *The Knowledge-Creating Company*, Oxford University Press, Oxford

NOON, M and BLYTON, P (2002) *The Realities of Work*, 2nd edn, Palgrave Macmillan, Basingstoke

NOORDEGRAAF, M (2016) Reconfiguring professional work, *Administration and Society*, 48 (7), pp 783–810

NORRIS-GREEN, M and GIFFORD, J, (2021) *CIPD Good Work Index 2021*, Chartered Institute of Personnel and Development, London

NORTH, MS, (2019) A GATE to understanding "older" workers: Generation, age, tenure, experience. *Academy of Management Annals*, 13 (2), pp. 414–443. https://doi.org/10.5465/annals.2017.0125 (archived at https://perma.cc/G3GH-JY58)

NYE, J (2008) *The Powers to Lead: Soft, hard, and smart*, Oxford University Press, Oxford

NYFOUDI, M and TASOULIS, K (2021) Effective coaching for high-potentials: a talent management approach. In Tarique, I (eds). *The Routledge Companion to Talent Management*. Routledge

O'BOYLE, E JR and AGUINIS, H (2012) The best and the rest: revisiting the norm of normality of individual performance. *Personnel Psychology*, 65 (1), pp 79–119

OECD (2016) Be Flexible! Background brief on how workplace flexibility can help European employees to balance work and family www.oecd.org/els/family/Be-Flexible-Backgrounder-Workplace-Flexibility.pdf (archived at https://perma.cc/GTW5-ZPRT)

OECD (2019) *SME and entrepreneurship outlook*, Paris

OECD (2021) *Teleworking in the COVID-19 pandemic: trends and prospects*. Report. https://read.oecd-ilibrary.org/view/?ref=1108_1108540-p249kho0iu&title=Teleworking-in-the-COVID-19-pandemic-Trends-and-prospects (archived at https://perma.cc/Z9WD-L999)

OLSON, M (2014) *The Business Partner Balancing Act: An Analysis of Alternative Employee Advocacy Practices in the Modern HR Function* http://digitalcommons.ilr.cornell.edu/chrr/73 (archived at https://perma.cc/W5AM-7ZTN)

OSLAND, JS (2022) An Interview with Paula Caligiuri, Pioneer in Global Leadership Effectiveness Research. In *Advances in Global Leadership*, Emerald Publishing Limited, Bingley

ONS (2010) Office for National Statistics. www.statistics.gov.uk (archived at https://perma.cc/4EFL-ZYHH)

ONS (2014) *An Analysis of Employee Contracts That do not Guarantee a Minimum Number of Hours*, Report, ONS, London

OPEN UNIVERSITY (1985) Block 1. Managing and Messy Problems. Course T244. *Managing in Organizations*, Open University, Milton Keynes

PAAUWE, J (2009) HRM and performance: achievements, methodological issues and prospects. *Journal of Management Studies*, 46 (1), pp 129–142

PAAUWE, J and BOSELIE, P (2005) HRM and performance: what next? *Human Resource Management Journal*, 15, pp 68–83

PAGAN, V (2021) The murder of knowledge and the ghosts that remain: non-disclosure agreements and their effects, *Culture and Organization*, 27 (4), pp 302–317

PAGÁN-CASTAÑO, E, MASEDA-MORENO, A and SANTOS-ROJO, C (2020) Wellbeing in work environments, *Journal of Business Research*, 115 (1), pp 469–74

PALUCK, E PORAT, RONI, R CLARK, C and GREEN, D (2020) Prejudice Reduction: Progress and Challenges. *Annual review of psychology*. https://static1.squarespace.com/static/5186d08fe4b065e39b45b91e/t/601766eb09286e6fda49d962/1612146411820/PaluckPoratClarkGreen_2020.pdf (archived at https://perma.cc/WN3C-TD6T)

PAPAVASILEOU, EF and LYONS, ST (2015) A comparative analysis of the work values of Greece's 'Millenial' generation. *The International Journal of Human Resource Management*, 26 (17), pp 2166–2186

PARA-GONZÁLEZ, L, JIMÉNEZ-JIMÉNEZ, D and MARTÍNEZ-LORENTE, ÁR (2019) Do SHRM and HPWS shape employees' affective commitment and empowerment?, *Evidence-based HRM*, 7 (3), pp 300–324. https://doi.org/10.1108/EBHRM-01-2019-0004 (archived at https://perma.cc/TNS7-GUV6)

PARKES, C, and DAVIS, AJ (2013) Ethics and social responsibility – do HR professionals have the 'courage to challenge' or are they set to be permanent 'bystanders?' *The International Journal of Human Resource Management*, 4 (12), pp 2411–2434

PATEL, C, BUDWHAR, P, WITZEMANN, A and KATOU, A, (2019) HR outsourcing: The impact on HR's strategic role and remaining in-house HR function. *Journal of Business Research*, 103, p 397–406. https://doi.org/10.1016/j.jbusres.2017.11.007 (archived at https://perma.cc/F7SL-Z9R2)

PATEL, P, BOYLE, B, BRAY, M, SINHA, P and BHANUGOPAN, R, (2019) Global staffing and control in emerging multinational corporations and their subsidiaries in developed countries: Indian IT EMNCs in Australia. *Personnel Review*, 48 (4), pp 1022–1044. https://doi.org/10.1108/PR-07-2017-0211boxall (archived at https://perma.cc/2U6U-G6TX)

PATON, G (2010) Exploited work experience students forced to make tea. *Daily Telegraph*, 11 January

PATON, RA and MCCALMAN, J (2000) *Change Management: Guide to effective implementation*, 2nd edn, Sage, London

PATTERSON, M, WEST, M, LAWTHORN, R and NICKELL, S (1997) Impact of People Management Practices on Business Performance. *Issues in People Management*, 22, Institute for Personnel and Development, London

PECCEI, R and VAN DE VOORDE, K, (2019) Human resource management–well-being–performance research revisited: Past, present, and future. *Human Resource Management Journal*, 29 (4), pp 539–563, https://doi.org/10.1111/1748-8583.12254 (archived at https://perma.cc/Q637-977B)

PELSTER, B (2013) *Talent 2020: surveying the talent paradox from the employee perspective*, www.deloitte.com/us/en/insights/topics/talent/talent-2020-surveying-the-talent-paradox-from-the-employee-perspective.html?id=us:el:dc:redirect (archived at https://perma.cc/KJ5J-GYDX)

PERKBOX (2021) *20 employee wellbeing initiatives to implement at work* www.perkbox.com/uk/resources/blog/employee-wellbeing-initiatives (archived at https://perma.cc/34PE-NYQA)

PERKIN, H (1989) *The Rise of Professional Society – England since 1880*, Routledge, London

PERKINS, SJ and SHORTLAND, SM (2006) *Strategic International Human Resource Management*, 2nd edn, Kogan Page, London

PERKINS, SJ and JONES, S (2020) *Reward Management: Alternatives, consequences and context*, 4th edn, CIPD, London

PERLMUTTER, HV (1969) The tortuous evolutions of the multinational corporation. *Columbia Journal of World Business*. January–February, pp 9–18

PERRY, M (2001) Flexibility Pays, *Accountancy Age*. In: *Human Resource Management International Digest*, 10 (4), pp 13–15

PERRY-SMITH, JE (2006) Social yet creative: The role of social relationships in facilitating individual creativity. *Academy of Management Journal*, 49 (1), pp 85–101

PESTON, R (2007) Rose Goes Green in Pursuit of Profit. BBC News website, 15 January. news.bbc.co.uk (archived at https://perma.cc/QQF2-GYKT)

PETERS, TJ (1999) *The Brand You 50; Or: Fifty ways to transform yourself from an 'employee' into a brand that shouts distinction, commitment, and passion!* Knopf Publishing, New York

PETTIGREW, A (1985) *The Awakening Giant: Continuity and change at ICI*, Blackwell, Oxford

PETTIGREW, A and WHIPP, R (1993) Understanding the environment. In: MABEY, C and MAYON-WHITE, B (eds) *Managing Change*, 2nd edn, Paul Chapman Publishing, London

PIAGET, J (1964) Part I: cognitive development in children: Piaget development and learning. *Journal of Research in Science Teaching*, 2 (3), pp 176–186

PILBEAM, S and CORBRIDGE, M (2006) *People Resourcing: Contemporary HRM in Practice*, 3rd edn, FT/Prentice Hall, Harlow

PILBEAM, S and CORBRIDGE, M (2010) *People Resourcing and Talent Planning: HRM in Practice*, 4th edn, FT/Prentice Hall, Harlow

PINE, BJ and GILMORE, JH (1998) Welcome to the experience economy. *Harvard Business Review*, 76, pp 97–105

PISANO, P PIRONTI, M RIEPLE, A and CILLO, V (2021) In: REES, G and SMITH, P (eds) Human resource management Through a Strategic perspective in: *Strategic Human Resource Management: An International Perspective*, 3rd edn, Sage, London

PITCHER, G (2008) Backlash against HR business partner model. *Personnel Today*, 29 January

PLOYHART, RE NYBERG, AJ REILLY, G and MALTARICH, MA (2014), Human capital is dead; long live human capital resources! *Journal of Management*, 40 (2), pp 371–398

PLUMMER, K (2010) *Sociology: The Basics*, Routledge, Abingdon

POLLERT, A (1991) The orthodoxy of flexibility. In: POLLERT, A (ed) *Farewell to Flexibility?* Blackwell, Oxford

POOCHAROEN, OO and LEE, C (2013) Talent management in the public sector: A comparative study of Singapore, Malaysia, and Thailand. *Public Personnel Review*, 15 (8), pp 1185–1207

PORTER, M (1985) *Competitive Advantage: Creating and sustaining superior performance*, Free Press, New York

PORTER, M (1998) *Competitive Strategy: Techniques for analyzing industries and competitors*, Free Press, New York

PORTER, ME (2004) *Competitive Advantage: Creating and Sustaining Superior Performance*, Free Press, New York

PORTER, ME and KRAMER, MR (2006) Strategy and society: the link between competitive advantage and corporate social responsibility. *Harvard Business Review*, 84 (12), pp 78–92

POVAH, L and SOBCZAK, K (2010) A Context-oriented Approach to Leader Selection: A Strategy for Uncertain Times. *People Strategy*, 33 (4), pp 40–47

POWELL, C (2022) Covid enabled Severn Trent to supercharge its strategy, *People Management* www.peoplemanagement.co.uk/voices/case-studies/covid-enabled-severn-trent-supercharge-strategy (archived at https://perma.cc/S5MS-Y7C8), 28 February 2022

PREECE, D (2012) HRM in an Organizational Context. In GILMORE, S and WILLIAMS, S (eds) *Human Resource Management*, 2nd edn, Oxford University Press, Oxford

PRICE, A (2004) *Human Resource Management in a Business Context*, 2nd edn, Thomson, London

PRICE, D (ed) (2009) *Principles and Practice of Change*, Palgrave Macmillan, Basingstoke

PRITCHARD, K and SYMON, G (2011) Identity on the line: Constructing professional identity in a HR call centre. *Work, Employment and Society*, 20 (2), pp 175–188

PROCTOR, N (2011) The Google art project: a new generation of museums on the web? *Curator: The Museum Journal*, 54 (2), pp 215–221

PUGH, DS and HICKSON, DJ (1976) *Organizational Structure in Its Context*, Saxon House, Farnborough

PULAKOS, E (2009) *Performance management: A new approach for driving business results*, Wiley-Blackwell, Malden, MA

PURCELL, J and AHLSTRAND, B (1994) *Human Resource Management in the Multi-Divisional Company*, Oxford University Press, Oxford

PURCELL, J and HUTCHINSON, S (2007) Front-line managers as agents in the HRM performance causal chain: theory, analysis and evidence. *Human Resource Management Journal*, 17 (1), pp 3–20

PURCELL, J, KINNIE, N, HUTCHINSON, S, RAYTON, B and SWART, J (2003) *Understanding the People and Performance Link: Understanding the Black Box*, CIPD, London

PWC (2012) *Delivering better business results through talent: talent management*, Report, www.pwc.com/gx/en/hr-management-services/assets/pwc-strategic-talent-management.pdf (archived at https://perma.cc/AW74-A4QK)

PWC (2014) *The talent challenge: adapting to growth*. www.pwc.com/gx/en/hr-management-services/publications/assets/ceosurvey-talent-challenge.pdf (archived at https://perma.cc/EP3F-BXGW)

PWC (2020a) COVID-19 The impact on Global Mobility and the mobile workforce. www.pwc.co.uk/human-resource-services/assets/EMRS/impact-on-global-mobility-mobile-workforce-survey.pdf (archived at https://perma.cc/N2XG-4BXX)

PWC (2020b) Talent Mobility 2020. www.pwc.com/gx/en/managing-tomorrows-people/future-of-work/pdf/talent-mobility-2020.pdf (archived at https://perma.cc/944P-3WKF)

PWC (2020) *Talent trends 2020: upskilling: building confidence in an uncertain world*. www.pwc.com/gx/en/ceo-survey/2020/trends/pwc-talent-trends-2020.pdf (archived at https://perma.cc/JTK5-9ZZ7)

QUINN, R E and J ROHRBAUGH. (1983) A Spatial Model of Effectiveness Criteria: Towards a Competing Values Approach to Organizational Analysis. *Management Science*, 29 (3), pp 363–377

RAMBHAI, J (2021) Blood Cancer UK implemented a truly flexible culture in order to better retain talent, *People Management*, 9 December, www.peoplemanagement.co.uk/article/1746561/blood-cancer-uk-implemented-truly-flexible-culture-better-retain-talent (archived at https://perma.cc/6P2W-YBDK)

RANDLE, K and RAINNIE, A (1997) Managing creativity, maintaining control: a study in pharmaceutical research. *Human Resource Management Journal*, 7 (2), pp 32–46

RANKIN, J (2021) Gig economy workers to get employee rights under EU proposals, *The Guardian* 9 December. www.theguardian.com/business/2021/dec/09/gig-economy-workers-to-get-employee-rights-under-eu-proposals (archived at https://perma.cc/ME39-W8KT)

RAO, TV and VARGHESE, S (2008) Trends and challenges of developing human capital in India. *Human Resource Development International*, 12 (1), pp 15–34

RAYNER, C and ADAM-SMITH, D (eds) (2009) *Managing and Leading People*, 2nd edn, CIPD, London

REES, C ALFES, K and GATENBY, M (2013) Employee voice and engagement: connections and consequences. *The international journal of human resource management*, 24 (14), pp 2780–2798

REES, D and MCBAIN, R (2004) *People Management*, Palgrave Macmillan, Basingstoke

REES, G and SMITH, P (eds) (2021) *Strategic Human Resource Management: An international perspective*, 3rd edn, Sage Publications, London

REEVES, R (2008) The trouble with targets. *Management Today*. 8 January. www.managementtoday.co.uk/news/774435/the-trouble-with-targets (archived at https://perma.cc/5Q4F-NNU2)

REICHEL, A and LAZAROVA, M (2013) The effects of outsourcing and devolvement on the strategic position of HR departments. *Human Resource Management*, 52 (6), pp 923–946

REID, M, BARRINGTON, H and BROWN, M (2007) *Human Resource Development*, 7th edn, CIPD, London

REILLY, H and SVENSSON, R (2021) *Talent management in the new reality*. https://home.kpmg/uk/en/blogs/home/posts/2021/08/talent-management-in-the-new-reality--why-talent-philosophy-need.html (archived at https://perma.cc/CZ98-EQG9)

REISSNER, S and IZAK, M (2017) How Mobile Working Ruins Work–Life Balance – Unless You've Got a Good Manager, *The Conversation*, https://theconversation.com/how-mobile-working-ruins-work-life-balance-unless-youve-got-a-good-manager-89182 (archived at https://perma.cc/G3E8-YXPA)

REISSNER, S and IZAK, M (2021) *Swimming Rather than Sinking? Flexible Working (more than) a Year into the Covid-19 Pandemic*, Workwise UK www.workwiseuk.org/blog/2021/5/15/guest-blog-swimming-rather-than-sinking-flexible-working-more-than-a-year-into-the-covid-19-pandemic-by (archived at https://perma.cc/Y5NJ-67PT)

REISSNER, S and PAGAN, V (2013) Generating employee engagement in a public–private partnership: Management communication activities and employee experiences, *The International Journal of Human Resource Management*, 24 (14), pp 2741–59

REVANS, RW (1982) What is Action Learning? *Journal of Management development*, 1 (3), pp 64–75

REZAI, Mana. KENDALL, K Bui, S and LINDSAY,S. (2020) Measures of workplace inclusion: a systematic review using the COSMIN methodology, *Journal of Occupational Rehabilitation*, 30 (3), pp 420–454

RICHARDSON, J and McKENNA, S (2014) Towards an understanding of social networks among organizational self-initiated expatriates: a qualitative case study of a professional services firm. *The International Journal of Human Resource Management*, 25 (19), pp 2627–2643

RICKLEY, M and STACKHOUSE, M (2022) Global Leadership Effectiveness: A multilevel review and exploration of the construct domain, in OSLAND, JS, REICHE, BS, SZKUDLAREK, B and MENDENHALL, ME (Eds) *Advances in Global Leadership* (*Advances in Global Leadership*, Vol. 14), Emerald Publishing Limited, Bingley, pp 87–123

RIDDER, HG, PIENING, EP and BALUCH, AM (2012) The third way reconfigured: how and why non-profit organizations are shifting their human resources management, *Voluntas*, 23 (3), pp 605–625

RIEGEL, B (2013) I lived the high life as a Pan Am air stewardess, 15 April 2013, www.mirror.co.uk/news/real-life-stories/lived-high-life-pan-am (archived at https://perma.cc/Z5WW-9ND5)

RITZER, G, (1993) *The Mcdonaldization of society*. Thousand Oaks, Calif

ROBERTS, P (2006) Analysis: The defining phase of systematic training. *Advances in Human Resource Development*, 8 (4), pp 476–491

ROBBINS, S (1993) *Organisational Behaviour: Concepts, controversies and applications*. 6th edn, Prentice Hall, Englewood Cliffs, NJ

ROCHE, WK and TEAGUE, P (2012) Do recessions transform work and employment? Evidence from Ireland. *British Journal of Industrial Relations*, 52 (2), pp 261–285

RODWELL, JJ, NOBLET, AJ, STEAN, P, OSBORNE, S and ALLISEY, AF (2008) Investigating people management issues in a third sector health care organisation – an inductive approach. *Australian Journal of Advanced Nursing*, 27 (2), pp 55–62

ROPER, I and HIGGINS, P (2020) Hidden in plain sight? The human resource management practitioner's role in dealing with workplace conflict as a source of organisational–professional power. *Human Resource Management Journal*, 30 (4), pp 508–524

ROPER, J (2020) Why Swiss Re put HR front and centre of its change programme, *People Management*, 20 February www.peoplemanagement.co.uk/voices/case-studies/swiss-re-put-hr-front-centre-change-programme (archived at https://perma.cc/N44H-SJZQ)

ROSE, S (2007) Back in fashion: how we're reviving a British icon. *Harvard Business Review*. May, pp 51–58

ROSEN, M, BEDWELL, W, WILDMAN, J, FRITZSCHE, B, SALAS, E and BURKE, C (2011) Managing adaptive performance in teams; Guiding principles and behavioral markers for measurement. *Human Resource Management Review*, 21 (2), pp 107–122

ROSENER, J (1990) Ways women lead. *Harvard Business Review*. November–December, pp 119–125

ROSENFELD, R and WILSON, D (1999) *Managing Organisations: Texts, readings and cases*, 2nd edn, McGraw-Hill, London

ROTHWELL, A (2005) How HR professionals rate 'continuing professional development'. *Human Resource Management Journal*, 15 (3), pp 18–32

ROUSSEAU, D (1995) *Psychological Contracts in Organizations: Understanding written and unwritten agreements*, Sage, London

RUSSON, M-A (2021) Uber drivers are workers not self-employed, Supreme Court rules, BBC News February 19 2021

SADLER-SMITH, E, ALLINSON, C and HAYES, J (2000) Learning preferences and cognitive style: some implications for continuing professional development. *Management Learning*, 31 (2), pp 239–256

SALIMAKI, A, HAKONEN, A and HENEMAN, R (2009) Managers generate meaning for pay. *Journal of Managerial Psychology*, 24 (2), pp 161–177

SAMDANIS, M and LEE, SH (2015) Big data, social media and HPWS for the intelligent office, CIPD Applied Research Conference on The Shifting Landscape of Work and Working Lives www.cipd.co.uk/Images/big-data-social-media-hpws_2015_tcm18-15586.pdf (archived at https://perma.cc/EQB3-BPLL)

SARABI, A, HAMORI, M and FROESE, FJ (2019) Managing global talent flows. In COLLINGS, DG, SCULLION, H and CALIGIURI, PM (eds). *Global Talent Management*. Routledge

SARGEANT, M and LEWIS, D (2014) *Employment Law*, 7th edn, Pearson, Harlow

SARGEANT, M and LEWIS, D (2020) *Employment Law*, 9th edn, Taylor and Francis, Abingdon

SARIDAKIS, G, LAI, Y and COOPER, CL, (2017) Exploring the relationship between HRM and firm performance: A meta-analysis of longitudinal studies. *Human resource management review*, 27 (1), pp 87–96, https://doi.org/10.1016/j.hrmr.2016.09.005 (archived at https://perma.cc/Z3DQ-VG94)

SARVAIYA, H, EWEIE, G, and ARROWSMITH, J (2018) The roles of HRM in CSR: strategic partnership or operational support? *Journal of Business Ethics*, 153 (3), pp 825–837

SAUNDERS, MNK and THORNHILL, A (2006) Forced employment contract change and the psychological contract. *Employee Relations*, 28 (5), pp 449–467

SCHAUMBERG, R and FLYNN, F (2012) Uneasy Lies the Head That Wears the Crown; The Link Between Guilt Proneness and Leadership. *Journal of Personality and Social Psychology*, 103 (2), pp 327–42

SCHEIN, E (1978) *Career Dynamics: Matching the individual and organisational needs*, Addison-Wesley, Reading, MA

SCHEIN, E (1984) Coming to a new awareness of organizational culture. *Sloan Management Review*, 25 (2), pp 3–16

SCHEIN, E (1992) *Organizational Culture and Leadership*, Jossey-Bass, San Francisco

SCHEIN, E (2009) *The Corporate Culture Survival Guide*, Jossey-Bass, San Francisco

SCHULER, RS, DOWLING, PE and DE CIERI, H (1993) An integrative framework of strategic international human resource management. *Journal of Management*, 19 (2), pp 419–59

SCHULTZ, TW (1961) Investment in Human Capital, *American Economic Review*, 40 (2), pp 1–17

SCOTTISH TOURISM ALLIANCE (2021) *Press release – Tourism and hospitality talent development programme funded for second year*. https://scottishtourismalliance.co.uk/press-release-tourism-and-hospitality-talent-development-programme-funded-for-second-year/ (archived at https://perma.cc/CD5V-2YRF)

SEARLE, R (2003) *Selection and Recruitment: A critical text*, Palgrave Macmillan in association with the Open University, Milton Keynes

SEARLE, RH and SKINNER, D (2011) New Agendas and Perspectives. In SEARLE, RH and SKINNER, D (eds) *Trust and Human Resource Management*, Edward Elgar Publishing, Cheltenham

SEARS, L (2010) *Next Generation HR: Time for change – towards a next generation HR*, CIPD, London

SEGAL, J (2010) Performance management blunders. *HR Magazine*. November, pp 75–78

SEIBERT, S, KRAIMER, M and LINDEN, R (2001) A Social Capital Theory of Career Success. *Academy of Management Journal*, 44 (2), pp 219–237

SELDEN, SC and SOWA, JE (2015) Voluntary turnover in non-profit human service organizations: the impact of high-performance work practices. *Human Service Organizations Management Leadership and Governance*, 39 (3), pp 182–207

SELIGMAN, M (1998) *Learned Optimism*, Simon & Schuster, New York, NY

SEMLER, R (1993) *Maverick: The success story behind the world's most unusual workplace*, Arrow Books, London

SENGE, P (1993) *The Fifth Discipline: The Art and Practice of the Learning Organisation*, Random House, New York

SENIOR, B and SWAILES, S (2010) *Organisational Change*, 4th edn, FT/ Prentice Hall, Harlow

SENNETT, R (1998) *The corrosion of character*, WW Norton & Company, London, New York

SHARP, R (2009) Total reward at Arup. *IRS Employment Review*. (916), 19 February

SHARP, R (2015) *Public-sector pay 2014/15: pay restraint continues* www.xperthr.co.uk/survey-analysis/public-sector-pay-201415-pay-restraint-continues/154029 (archived at https://perma.cc/35DQ-5FEP)

SHAW, JD, (2021) The resource-based view and its use in strategic human resource management research: The elegant and inglorious. *Journal of Management*, 47 (7), pp 1787–1795, https://doi.org/10.1177/0149206321993543 (archived at https://perma.cc/36AM-DPS7)

SHEN, J, CHANDRA, A, D'NETTO, B and MONGA, M (2009) Managing diversity through human resource management: an international perspective and conceptual framework. *International Journal of Human Resource Management*, 20 (2), pp 235–251

SHRM (2022) *Managing for employee retention.* www.shrm.org/resourcesandtools/tools-and-samples/toolkits/pages/managingforemployeeretention.aspx (archived at https://perma.cc/F9JW-TQNA)

SIMMS, M (2019) *What Do We Know and what Should We Do about the Future of Work?* Sage, London

SINHA, P PATEL, P and PRIKSHAT, V eds, (2021) *International HRM and Development in Emerging Market Multinationals*, Routledge, Abingdon

SIRKIN, HL, KEENAN, P and JACKSON, A (2005) The Hard Side of Change Management. *Harvard Business Review*, 83 (10), pp 108–118

SKINNER, BF (1974), *About Behaviorism*, Knopf

SKUZA, A, McDONNELL, A and SCULLION, H (2015) Talent management in the emerging markets. In HORWITZ, FM and BUDHWAR, P (eds), *Handbook of Human Resource Management in Emerging Markets.* Edward Elgar Publishing, Cheltenham

SLATER, D (2020) The imperatives of customer-centric innovation, https://aws.amazon.com/executive-insights/content/the-imperatives-of-customer-centric-innovation/ (archived at https://perma.cc/FG5R-8RL7)

SLATER, M (2012) *Olympic cycling: Marginal gains underpin Team GB dominance* www.bbc.co.uk/sport/0/olympics/19174302 (archived at https://perma.cc/DW3C-BVML)

SLOMAN, M (2007) *The Changing World of the Trainer*, Routledge, London

SOARES, ME and MOSQUERA, P (2019) Fostering work engagement: The role of the psychological contract, *Journal of Business Research*, 101, pp 469–476

SOGA, LR BOLADE-OGUNFODUN, Y MARIANI, M NASR, R and LAKER, B (2022) Unmasking the other face of flexible working practices: A systematic literature review, *Journal of Business Research*, 142, pp 648–662

SOWE, SK and ZETTSU, K (2014) Curating big data made simple: Perspectives from scientific communities. *Big Data*, 2 (1), pp 23–33

SPARROW, PR (2005) *Global human resource management*, in SHAMS, M and JACKSON, P (eds) *Developments in Work and Organizational Psychology: Implications for international business*, Elsevier, London, New York and Amsterdam

SPARROW, PR (2012) Globalising the international mobility function: the role of emerging markets, flexibility and strategic delivery models. *International Journal of Human Resource Management*, 23 (12), pp 2404–2427

SPRINGETT, N (2002) The impact of corporate purpose on strategy, organisations and financial performance. *Human Resources and Employment Review*, 2 (2), pp 117–124

SPRINGETT, N (2004) Corporate Purpose as the Basis of Moral Leadership of the Firm, *Strategic Change*, 13 (6), pp 297–307

STAHL, GK, BJORKMAN, I, FARNDALE, E, MORRIS, SS, PAAUWE, J, STILES, P, TREVOR, J and WRIGHT, P (2012) Six principles of Effective Global Talent Management. *MIT Sloan Management Review*, 53 (2), pp 25–32

STATLER, M, ROOS, J and VICTOR, B (2009) 'Ain't misbehavin': Taking play seriously in organizations. *Journal of Change Management*, 9 (1), pp 87–107

STERNBERG, E (2000) *Just Business*, 2nd edn, Oxford University Press, Oxford

STEVENS, M (2013) Employers are from Mars, Young People are from Venus. *People Management.* www.cipd.co.uk/pm/peoplemanagement/b/weblog/archive/2013/04/25/employers-are-from-mars-young-people-are-from-venus.aspx (archived at https://perma.cc/5MT7-AVF6)

STEWART, J (2009) Developing managers and managerial capabilities. In Leopold, J and Harris, L (eds). *The Strategic Managing of Human Resources*, 2nd edn, FT Prentice Hall, London

STEWART, J and CURETON, P (2014) *Designing, Delivering and Evaluating L & D*, CIPD, London

STEWART, J and MCGOLDRICK, J (eds) (1996) *Human Resource Development: Perspectives, strategies and practice*, Pitman, London

STOCK, K (2021) Statement Read in Absentia, 'Hate, Heresy and the Fight for Free Speech', Battle of Ideas https://kathleenstock.com/statement-read-in-absentia-h/ (archived at https://perma.cc/P2RD-QKM7)

STOKES, P, DIOCHON, PF and OTTER, K (2021) Two sides of the same coin? Coaching and mentoring and the agentic role of context. *Annals of the New York Academy of Sciences*, pp 142–152

STOREY, J (1983) *Managerial Prerogatives and the Question of Control*, Routledge, London

STOREY, J (1989) From personnel management to human resource management, in Storey, J (ed.) *New Perspectives on Human Resource Management*, Routledge, London

STOREY, J (1992) *Developments in the Management of Human Resources*, Blackwell, Oxford

STOREY, J (1995) *Human Resource Management: A critical text*, Routledge, London

STOUT, L (2012) *The Shareholder Value Myth*, Berrett-Koehler, San Francisco

STUBBINGS, C and SETHI, B (2020). *Talent Trends 2020: Upskilling: Building Confidence in an Uncertain World*. PwC

STUDENROTH, J (2022a) 5 Tips on building intersectionality at work, www.understood. org/articles/en/5-tips-building-intersectionality-work?_sp=48dec231-6076-4ef7-804f-3d3bc94ad978.1645544535834 (archived at https://perma.cc/GA6D-W98C)

STUDENROTH, J (2022b) What's intersectionality in the workplace, www.understood. org/articles/en/whats-intersectionality-in-workplace (archived at https://perma.cc/D77D-KUDN)

SUBRAMONY, M (2009) A Meta-analytic investigation of the relationship between HRM bundles and firm performance. *Human Resource Management*, 48 (5), pp 745–768

SUFF, R (2008) Business partnering at the AA. *IRS Employment Review*. Issue 908

SUFF, R (2012a) Recruiting and selecting graduates: 2012 XpertHR survey. *IRS Employment Review*. www.xperthr.co.uk/article/114836/recruiting-span-andspan-classhighlightselecting-span-span-classhighlightgraduates--2012-xperthrsurvey. aspx?searchwords=recruiting+and+selecting+graduates (archived at https://perma.cc/G2A5-2LEE)

SUFF, R (2012b) XpertHR recruitment trends survey 2012: activity picks up. IRS Employment Review. www.xperthr.co.uk/article/112441/xperthrrecruitment-span-span-classhighlighttrends-span-span-classhighlightsurvey-2012--activity-picks-p.aspx?searchwords=recruitment+trends+survey (archived at https://perma.cc/4SLN-2HA8)

SUFF, R (2013) Using corporate websites for recruitment: 2013 XpertHR survey. www. xpertHR.co.uk/article/115260/usingcorporatewebsitesforrecruitment (archived at https://perma.cc/TQE2-ZS9E)

SULL, D SULL, C and ZWEIG, B (2022) Toxic Culture is Driving the Great Resignation, *MIT Sloan Management Review*, 11 January 2022, www.sloanreview.mit.edu/article/toxic-culture-is-driving-the-great-resignation/ (archived at https://perma.cc/8VH6-4GSR)

SULLIVAN, S and BARUCH, Y (2009) Advances in Career Theory and Research: A Critical Review and Agenda for Future Exploration. *Journal of Management*, 35 (6), p 1542

SULLIVAN, J, WONG, W ADUSUMILLI, D, ALDER, A, BLAZEY, L, HUGGETT, M and PARKIN, J (2009) Deal or no deal? An exploration of the modern employment relationship. The future of HR Working Paper, The Work Foundation, London

SULLIVAN, S (1999) The changing nature of careers: a review and research agenda. *Journal of Management*, 25 (3), pp 457–484

SUROWIECKI, J (2004) *The Wisdom of Crowds*, Doubleday, New York

SUTHERLAND, J (2009) WERS Report. Training and employee use of skills in Scotland: some evidence. *Fraser Economic Commentary*, 33 (1), pp 60–64

SUUTARI, V and BREWSTER, C (2000) Making their own way: international experience through self-initiated foreign assignments. *Journal of World Business*, 35 (4), pp 417–436

SWART, J, KINNIE, N, RABINOWITZ, J, LUND, M, SNELL, S, MORRIS, S and KANG, SC (2007) *Managing across boundaries: human resource management beyond the firm*, CIPD, London

SZYDLO, J and GRZES-BUKLAHO, J (2020) Relations between National and Organisational Culture – Case Study, *Sustainability*, 12, pp 1522

TAKEUCHI, R, LEPAK, D and SWART, J (2011) How organizations evaluate and maintain fit of human capital with their needs. In: BURTON-JONES, A and SPENCER, JC (eds) *Oxford Handbook of Human Capital*, Oxford University Press, Oxford

TAMKIN, P, BARBER, L and HIRSH, W (1995) *Personal Development Plans: Case studies of practice*, Institute for Employment Studies, Brighton

TAMS, S and ARTHUR, M (2010) New directions for boundaryless careers: Agency and Interdependence in a Changing World. *Journal of Organizational Behaviour*, 31 (5), pp 629–646

TAN, V and TIONG, TN (2005) Change management in times of economic uncertainty. *Singapore Management Review*, 27 (1), pp 49–68

TANNENBAUM, R and SCHMIDT, WH (1973) How to choose a leadership pattern. *Harvard Business Review*. May–June, pp 162–180

TARIQUE, I (2021) *The Routledge Companion to Talent Management*, Routledge, Abingdon

TAYLOR, FW (1911) *Principles of Scientific Management*, Harper, New York

TAYLOR, R (2002) The future of work–life balance. *Human Resource Management International Digest*, 10 (4), pp 13–15

TAYLOR, S (2019) *Resourcing and Talent Management*, 7th edn, Kogan Page, London

TESSEMA, MT TESFOM, G FAIRCLOTH, MA TESFAGIORGIS, M and TECKLE, P (2022), The 'Great Resignation': Causes, Consequences, and Creative HR Management, *Journal of Human Resource and Sustainability Studies*, 10, pp 161–178

THAU, S DERFLER-ROZIN, R PITESA, M MITCHELL, MS and PILLUTLA, MM (2015) Unethical for the sake of the group: risk of social exclusion and pro-group unethical behavior, *Journal of Applied Psychology*, 100 (1), pp 98–113

THE ECONOMIST (2009) Talent on tap: the fashion for hiring temps has reached the executive suite. 10 December

THEEBOOM, T, BEERSMA, B and Van VIANEN, AE (2014) Does coaching work? A meta-analysis on the effects of coaching on individual level outcomes in an organisational context, *Journal of Positive Psychology*, 9 (1), pp 1–8

THE MIND FOUNDRY (2022) Unlocking the value of AI in the Public Sector https://learn.mindfoundry.ai/report/unlocking-the-value-of-ai-public-sector?hsLang=en-gb (archived at https://perma.cc/2SAG-9GTH)

THE NEXT GENERATION OF MARCOMS EUROPEAN REPORT (2013) European Communications School, London

THOMAS, RM (2001) *Recent Theories of Human Development*, Sage, Thousand Oaks, CA

THOMAS, R (2009) The business environment of human resource management. In GILMORE, S and WILLIAMS, S (eds) *Human Resource Management*, Oxford University Press, Oxford

THOMSON, P (2008) The business benefits of flexible working. *Strategic HR Review*, 7 (2), pp 17–22

THOMPSON, P and MCHUGH, D (2009) *Work Organisations: A critical approach*, 4th edn, Palgrave Macmillan, Basingstoke

THOMPSON, P, WILLIAMS, R and KWONG, C, (2017) Factors holding back small third sector organizations' engagement with the local public sector, *Nonprofit Management and Leadership*, 27 (4), pp 513–531. https://doi.org/10.1002/nml.21260 (archived at https://perma.cc/WL5S-83NQ)

THORPE R and HOLMAN, G (2000) *Strategic Reward Systems*, Prentice-Hall, London

THUNNISSEN, M, BOSELIE, P and FRUYTIER, B (2013) A review of talent management: 'infancy or adolescence? *International Journal of Human Resource Management*, 24 (9), pp 1744–1761

TOMLINSON, F and SCHWABENLAND, C (2010) Reconciling competing discourses of diversity? The UK non-profit sector between social justice and the business case. *Organisation*, 17, pp 101–121

TOMPROU, M ROUSSEAU, DM and HANSEN, SD (2015) The psychological contracts of violation victims: A post-violation model, *Journal of Organizational Behavior*, 36 (1), pp 561–581

TORRINGTON, D, HALL, L and TAYLOR, S (2002) *Human Resource Management*, 5th edn, FT/Prentice Hall, Harlow

TORRINGTON, D, HALL, L and TAYLOR, D (2008) *Human Resource Management*, 7th edn, FT/Prentice Hall, Harlow

TORRINGTON, D HALL, L TAYLOR, S and ATKINSON, C (2014) *Human Resource Management*, 9th edn, Pearson, Harlow

TORRINGTON, D, HALL, L, ATKINSON, C and TAYLOR, S (2020) *Human Resource Management*, 11th edn, Pearson, Harlow

TREVINO, LK and NELSON, KA (2014) *Managing Business Ethics: Straight Talk about How to Do It Right*, 6th edn, John Wiley & Sons, Chichester

TROMPENAARS, F and HAMPDEN-TURNER, C (2004) *Managing People Across Cultures*, Capstone, Chichester

TRUSS, C and GILL, J (2009) Managing the HR function: the role of social capital. *Personnel Review*, 38 (6), pp 674–695

TRUSS, C, SOANE, E and EDWARDS, C (2006) *Working life: employee attitudes and engagement 2006*. Research report, CIPD, London

TURSUNBAYEVA, A, PAGLIARI, C, Di LAURO, S and ANTONELLI, G (2021) The ethics of people analytics: risks, opportunities and recommendations. *Personnel Review*, 53 (3), pp 900–21

ULRICH, D (1997) *Human Resource Champions: The next agenda for adding value and delivering results*, Harvard Business School Press, Boston, MA

ULRICH, D (2014) Do not split HR – at least not Ram Charan's way, *Harvard Business Review*, July 30, https://hbr.org/2014/07/do-not-split-hr-at-least-not-ram-charans-way (archived at https://perma.cc/PN4B-UDTL)

ULRICH, D and BROCKBANK, W (2005) *The HR Value Proposition*, Harvard Business School Press, Boston, MA

ULRICH, D and SMALLWOOD, N (2004) Capitalizing on Capabilities. *Harvard Business Review*, 82 (6), pp 119–127

ULRICH, D, YOUNGER, J and BROCKBANK, W (2008) The twenty-first-century HR organization, *Human Resource Management*, 47 (4), pp 829–850

UMPHRESS, E, BINGHAM, J and MITCHELL, M (2010) Unethical behavior in the name of the company: the moderating effect of organizational identification and positive reciprocity beliefs on unethical pro-organizational behavior, *Journal of Applied Psychology*, 95 (4), p 769

UNILEVER (2020) Unilever Celebrates 10 Years of the Sustainable Living Plan www.unilever.com/news/press-and-media/press-releases/2020/unilever-celebrates-10-years-of-the-sustainable-living-plan/ (archived at https://perma.cc/3T9P-PL5H)

VAIMAN, V, CASCIO, WF, COLLINGS, DG and SWIDER, BW (2021) The shifting boundaries of talent management, *Human Resource Management*, 60 (2), pp 253–257

VAIMAN, V, HASLBERGER, A and VANCE, C M (2015) Recognizing the important role of self-initiated expatriates in effective global talent management, *Human Resource Management Review*, 25 (3), pp 280–286

VAIMAN, V, SCULLION, H and COLLINGS, DG (2012) Talent management decision making. *Management Decision*, 50 (5), pp 925–941

VAIMAN, V, SPARROW, P, SCHULER, R and COLLINGS, DG (2019) *Macro Talent Management in Emerging and Emergent Markets: A Global Perspective*. Routledge, London

VAN BUREN, HJ, GREENWOOD, M and SHEEHEN, C (2011) Strategic Human Resource Management and the Decline of Employee Focus. *Human Resource Management Review*, 21 (30), pp 209–219

VAN DIERENDONCK, D (2010) Servant Leadership: A Review and Synthesis, *Journal of Management*, 37 (4), pp 1228–1261

VAN WANROOY, B, BEWLEY, H, BRYSON, A FORTH, J, FREETH, S, STOKES, L and WOOD, S (2013) *Employment Relations in the Shadow of the Recession*, Palgrave Macmillan, Basingstoke

VERBRIGGHE, J and BUYENS, D (2015) Adding Value and HRM Practice: Evidence-based HR. *Human Resource Management Practices*, pp 15–30

VILANOVA, M, LOZANO, M and ARENAS, D (2009) Exploring the nature of the relationship between CSR and competitiveness, *Journal of Business Ethics*, 87 (1), pp 57–69

VISE, AD (2005) *The Google Story*, Pan Macmillan, London

VISSER, W (2012) *The Quest for Sustainable Business: An Epic Journey in Search of Corporate Responsibility*, Greenleaf Publishing, Sheffield

VLAJČIĆ, D, CAPUTO, A, MARZI, G and DABIC, M, (2019) Expatriates managers' cultural intelligence as promoter of knowledge transfer in multinational companies, *Journal of Business Research*, 94, pp 367–377, https://doi.org/10.1016/j.jbusres.2018.01.033 (archived at https://perma.cc/5ELE-WXZS)

VON BERGEN, CW, SOPER, B and PARNELL, JA (2005) Workplace diversity and organisational performance, *Equal Opportunities International*, 24 (3/4), pp 1–16

VODAFONE BUSINESS (2020) *The Vodafone Business Future Ready Report* www.vodafone.com/business/news-and-insights/white-paper/future-ready-report-2020 (archived at https://perma.cc/C3E7-6MSJ)

VOEGTLIN, C and GREENWOOD, M (2013) CSR and HRM: A review and conceptual analysis. *Academy of Management Proceedings*, Issue 1

VROOM, V (1964) *Work and Motivation*, John Wiley, New York

WAHRENBURG, M, HACKETHAL, A, FRIEDRICH, L and GELLRICH, T (2006) Strategic decisions regarding the vertical integration of human resource organizations: evidence for an integrated HR model for the financial services and non-financial services industry in Germany, Austria and Switzerland, *International Journal of Human Resource Management*, 17 (10), pp 1726–1771

WAIN, D (2009) Command performance. *People Management*, 15 (23), p 17

WAINWRIGHT, S, CLARK, J and GRIFFITH, M (2006) *The UK Voluntary Sector Almanac*, NVCVO Publications, London

WALUMBWA, F, AVOLIO, BJ, GARDNER, WL, WERNSING, T and PETERSON, S (2008) Authentic leadership: development and validation of a theory-based measure, *Journal of Management*, 34 (1), pp 89–126

WANG, C, INDRIDASON, T and SAUNDERS, M (2010) Affective and continuance commitment in public private partnership. *Employee Relations*, 32 (4), pp 396–417

WANG, D and SHYU, C (2008) Will the strategic fit between business and HRM strategy influence HRM effectiveness and organizational performance? *International Journal of Manpower*, 29 (2), pp 92–110

WANG, GG and SUN, JY (2009) Clarifying the boundaries of human resource development. *Human Resource Development International*, 12 (1), pp 93–103

WARECH, M and TRACEY, JB (2004) Evaluating the impact of human resources: identifying what matters. *Cornell Hotel and Restaurant Administration Quarterly*, 45, pp 76–87

WARREN, C (2009) HR and OD 'should be one and the same'. *People Management*, 20 November

WATERMAN, R, WATERMAN, J and COLLARD, B (1994) Toward a career resilient workforce, *Harvard Business Review*, July–August, pp 87–95

WATKINS, MD (2013). What is organizational culture? And why should we care? *Harvard Business Review*, May 15. Available online: https://hbr.org/2013/05/what-is-organizational-culture (archived at https://perma.cc/94F8-MRTN)

WATSON, TJ (2006) *Organising and Managing Work*, 2nd edn, FT/Prentice Hall, Harlow

WATSON, TJ (2012) *Sociology Work and Organisation*, 6th edn, Routledge, Abingdon

WEBBER, A (2020) NHS boss who lied about degree receives prison sentence. *Personnel Today*, 24 January 2020.

WEBER, M (1947) *The Theory of Social and Economic Organization*, Oxford University Press, Oxford

WELCH, M (2011) 'The Evolution of the Employee Engagement Concept: Communication Implications,' Corporate Communications, 16, 328–46

WEST, MA, BORRIL, C, DAWSON, J, SCULLY, J, CARTER, M, ANELAY, S, PATTERSON, M, and WARING, J (2002) The link between the management of employees and patient mortality in acute hospitals. *International Journal of Human Resource Management*, 13 (8), pp 1299–1310

WHAT WORKS CENTRE FOR WELLBEING (WWCW) (2020) *Question Bank* https://whatworkswellbeing.org/resources/workplace-wellbeing-question-bank/ (archived at https://perma.cc/H53H-LMAJ)

WHAT WORKS CENTRE FOR WELLBEING (WWCW) (2022) *About Us* https://whatworkswellbeing.org/about-us/ (archived at https://perma.cc/BRJ9-ZJX5)

WHITEHOUSE, E (2021) How VisitBritain/VisitEngland devised a new people strategy during Covid. *People Management* www.peoplemanagement.co.uk/article/1742321/how-visibritain-visitengland-devised-a-new-people-strategy-during-covid (archived at https://perma.cc/K327-4RCQ)

WHITFORD, A (2003) *Why You Can't Ignore Internet Recruitment: One-stop guide* www.xperthr.co.uk/commentary-and-analysis/online-recruitment-why-you-cant-ignore-internet-recruitment/38314/ (archived at https://perma.cc/Y2RD-29B4)

WHITMORE, J (2017) *Coaching for Performance*, 5th edn, Nicholas Brealy, London

WIBLEN, S and MARLER, JH (2021) Digitalised talent management and automated talent decisions: the implications for HR professionals. *International Journal of Human Resource Management*, 32 (12), pp 2592–2621

WIBLEN, S and McDONNELL, A (2019) Macro talent management in Australia: Balancing industrial relations, isolation and global competitiveness. In Vaiman, V, Sparrow, P, Schuler, R and Collings, DG (eds) *Macro Talent Management on Managing Talent in Developed Counties*, Routledge, London

WILEY, C (2000) Ethical standards for human resource management professionals: a comparative analysis of five major codes, *Journal of Business Ethics*, 25, pp 93–114

WILKINSON, T, BOOHAN, M and STEVENSON, M (2014) Does learning style influence academic performance in different forms of assessment? *Journal of Anatomy*, 224, pp 304–308

WILLIAM, N (2008) Competency-based interviews and online psychometric tests are best for choosing candidates. *Personnel Today*, 10 March

WILLIAMS, RS (1998) *Performance Management: Perspectives on employee performance*, International Thomson Business Press, London

WILLIAMS, S (2014) *Introducing Employment Relations: A critical approach*, 3rd edn, Oxford University Press, Oxford

WILLIAMS, S (2020) *Introducing Employment Relations: A critical approach*, 5th edn, Oxford University Press, Oxford

WILSON, D (2022) FTSE Womens leaders Review www.ftsewomenleaders.com (archived at https://perma.cc/6UQF-X6MS)

WILSON, E (2000) Inclusion, exclusion and ambiguity–The role of organisational culture, *Personnel Review*, 29 (3), 274–303

WILSON, E and ILES, P (1999) Managing diversity – an employment and service delivery challenge. *International Journal of Public Sector Management*, 12 (1), pp 27–48

WILSON, FL (2006) *Organizational Behaviour and Work: A critical introduction*, 2nd edn, Oxford University Press, Oxford

WOMACK, JP and JONES, DT (1992) *Lean Thinking: Banish waste and create wealth in your corporation*, Simon and Schuster, London

WOOD, J, ZEFFANE, R, FROMHOLTZ, M, WIESNER, R and CREED, A (2010) *Organisational Behaviour*. 2nd edn (Australasia), John Wiley & Sons, Milton, Queensland

WOODALL, J and GOURLAY, S (2004) The relationship between professional learning and continuing professional development in the United Kingdom. In WOODALL, J, LEE, M and STEWART, J (eds) *New frontiers in HRD*, Routledge, London

WOODALL, J, SCOTT-JACKSON, W, NEWHAM, T and GURNEY, M (2009) Managing the decision to outsource human resources. *Personnel Review*, 38 (3), pp 236–52

WOODS, D (2011) UK talent acquisition costs rise to £5,311 per hire, compared to £2,226 in US. *HR Magazine*. www.hrmagazine.co.uk (archived at https://perma.cc/KE68-LXN5)

WOODWARD, J (1965) *Organisation and Technology*, Oxford University Press, Oxford

WOLGAST S, BACKSTROM, M and BJORKLUND, F (2017) Tools for fairness: Increased structure in the selection process reduces discrimination. PLOS ONE 12(12): e0189512. https://doi.org/10.1371/journal.pone.0189512 (archived at https://perma.cc/YZG6-UQDV)

WORK, (2021) Spring, pp 57–59, www.cipd.co.uk/Images/work-magazine-march-2021_tcm18-92449.pdf (archived at https://perma.cc/SH9L-TSW9)

WORKFORCE MANAGEMENT (2004) www.workforce.com/section/09/feature/23/85/39/index.html (archived at https://perma.cc/SN4H-YKF2)

WORK FOUNDATION (2003) The Missing Link: From productivity to performance. Work and enterprise panel of inquiry, The Work Foundation, London

WORK FOUNDATION (2009) Quality People Management for Quality Outcomes: The future of HR review on evidence on people management. Report. July, The Work Foundation, London

WORK FOUNDATION (2010) *Employability and Skills in the UK: Redefining the Debate*. www.bl.uk/britishlibrary/~/media/bl/global/business-and-management/pdfs/non-secure/r/e/a/reading-counts-why-english-and-maths-skills-matter-in-tackling-homelessness.pdf (archived at https://perma.cc/ZE5K-3J53)

WRIGHT, C (2008) Reinventing human resource management: business partners, internal consultants and the limits of professionalization. *Human Relations*, 61 (8), pp 1063–1086

WRIGHT, PM and HAGGERTY, JJ (2005) Missing variables in theories of strategic human resource management: time, cause and individuals, *Management Review*, 16, pp 164–173

WRIGHT, PM and McMAHAN, G (1992) Theoretical perspectives for strategic human resources management, *Journal of Management*, 18 (2), pp 295–320

XPERT HR (2008) International HR: the People Agenda. *Personnel Today*, 24 November

XPERT HR (2012) How employers align HR with the business: 2012 XpertHR survey. *Employment Review*, 30 July

YORKS, L, LAMM, S and O'NEIL, J (1999) Transfer of learning from Action Learning programs to the organizational setting, *Advances in Developing Human Resources*, 1, p 56

ZHANG, L, VAN IDDEKINGE, C H, ARNOLD, J D, ROTH, P L, LIEVENS, F, LANIVICH, S E, and JORDAN, S L (2020) What's on job seekers' social media sites? A content analysis and effects of structure on recruiter judgments and predictive validity, *Journal of Applied Psychology*, 105 (12), pp 1530–1546, https://doi.org/10.1037/apl0000490 (archived at https://perma.cc/2KJF-DPTC)

ZHELTOUKHOVA, K (2015) Are business ethics HR's business? Blog. www.cipd.co.uk/community/blogs/b/research-blog/archive/2015/09/30/are-business-ethics-hr-s-business (archived at https://perma.cc/2FCQ-ZFAB)

INDEX

Note: Page numbers in *italics* refer to tables or figures

ACAS code 10
Accenture 236
Accountancy Cloud 131
achievement theory (McClelland) 237
Ada 169
Adams, John Stacey 237
The Advisory, Conciliation and Arbitration
    Service (ACAS) 201, 285–86
agile working 51, 271–73
Aguilar 283
Ahlstrand, B 204–05
Alderfer, Clayton 237
Aldossari, M 189
Alexander Mann Solutions (AMS) 42
Alfes et al 170, 173
algorithmic decision-making (ADM) 8
Allen, NJ 240
ALLIO, RJ 288
All-Party Parliamentary Group 175
American luxury hotels 146
AMO model 222
Andersen, M 135
Anderson, D 173, 176–77
anti-bullying policy 94
anti-gentrification 302
Apple 322
appraisal
    potential pitfalls 234–36
    types of 234
Arden, Elizabeth 32
Arend, Gabriele 32
Aristotle 100–01
Arkin, A 227
Armstrong, D 220–21
Arrata, Despierre and Kumra 304
artificial intelligence (AI) 7, 8, 106, 314,
    315–16, 317, 324
    case study 8
Arup 244–45
Asda 101
Asos 6
Atkinson, J 190
Aurora 75
Australia 55, 145, 189
Australian luxury hotels 146
AVEgreen 131

Baby Boomers 143–44, 175
Backhaus, K 135

Backstrom, M 129
Badley, Jessica 51–52
Bae 268
Bahrain 150
Bahraini ministry 161
Balogun et al 301
Bandura, A 233
Bangalore 99
Banko, KM 241
Barber, A 237
Baron, A 220–21
Bartle, Philip QC 100
Bath model (HRM) 27
BBC 59
    journalist 158–59
Beardwell, J 25
Beckett, J 300
Beer, M 26, 27–28, 304–05
Behaviourist learning theory 225
Beijing Olympics (2008) 305–08
Bell, CH 290
Benton, JM 36
Bersin 35, 233
Beyoncé 100
'Big Bang' change 281
big data 316, 321–23, 324
Biggs, D 173
'Bike on the Boat Tour' (concept) 33
Bingham, J 92
Bjorklund, F 129
Bjorkman, I 134
Black Lives Matter 213, 216
Blue Ocean strategy 47, 69
Boatright, JR 104
Boddy, D 300–01
Boekhorst, JA 189
Boncori et al 185–86
Bonneton et al 146
Boston Consulting Group (BCG) 317
Bourneville 159
Boxall, P 22, 23, 43, 74, 182, 221, 247
BP Group 144
Brailsford, Dave 305–08
brand image 54, 128
Branson, Richard 158
Bratton, J 257, 262
Braverman, H 267
Brech 277–78
Bretz, R 237

Brexit 68, 116, 197, 198, 207, 214, 215
  gig economy 259
BRIC countries (Brazil, Russia, India and
    China) 145
Briggs, Andy 133
Brimhall, KC 189
British Cycling Performance Director 305
British government 230–31
British Royal Navy 255
Brixton office 302
Brockbank, W 31, 73
Brown, K 289
Brown, RL 177
BT Group 158
Buchanan 300–01
'bumpy incremental change' 281
Burke–Litwin model 297–98
Burns 261–62, 263
Burton, Perry 9
Business process re-engineering (BPR)
    270–71, 278
business
  automation and artificial intelligence 317
  business ethics 96–97
  customer and organisation 59–60
  Global/international HRM and SME 85–86
  Google (case study) 319–23
  HR function 35–37
  HR in different contexts 68–73
  HR, shape of 30–34
  HRD and strategic HRD 27–30
  HRM 25–27, 25
  HRM and HCM 38–40
  HRM and HRD 23–25
  Impressit (case study) 5–6
  internationalization 77–78
  job design, approaches to 265–70
  purpose 95–96
  scope and nature of strategy 46–49
  SIHRM 79–82
  SMEs 73–77
  strategy and culture 53
  see also change management; employee en-
    gagement; employment relationship; ethics;
    inclusion; organisational design (OD);
    performance management; recruitment and
    selection; talent management; wellbeing

Cable, DM 135
Cadbury 159
Caldwell, R 283, 299–300
Cameron, J 241
Cameron, KS 56, 241
Campbell, JP 246
Canada 145
Canadian civil servants 147
candidates 10, 63, 104, 128, 129, 151–52, 160
  attracting 120–21

  selection 121–22
  selection methods 122–24
Cantrell, S 36
Capgemini (case study) 272–73
Carnall, C 278
Cassell, C 132
Caterpillar 158
change agent 289, 295, 298–301, 301, 304
change management 279–80, 295
  ADKAR model 297
  analysing 282–86, 282, 283, 284
  change, types of 277–81, 279, 281
  Lewin's three-phase change model
    287–88, 288
change management factsheet (CIPD) (2021) 283
Change models 282
change momentum 280–81, 281
Chartered Institute of Personnel and Development
    (CIPD) 13–15, 90–92, 93–95, 106–07,
    126, 128, 129–30, 175–76
  CIPD (2020e) 253
  CIPD (2010b) 211–12
  CIPD (2017c) reports 155
  CIPD (2019c) 185
  CIPD (2021a) 25
  CIPD (2021l) 141
  CIPD (2021q) 168
  CIPD (2021s) 183
  CIPD (2021t) 213
  CIPD (2021v) 244
  CIPD (2021w) 257
  CIPD (2021x) 282
  CIPD (2022b) 149
  CIPD (2022f) 166–67
  CIPD Profession Map 22, 157
  CIPD report (2008a) 271
  CIPD report (2013) 133–34
  CIPD Report (2019) 317
  CIPD report (2020e) 257
  CIPD survey (2004b) 134–35
  employee wellbeing 179–82, 181
  factsheet 32, 38, 283
  Good Work 56–59
  Labour Market Outlook survey 68
  Learning and Skills at Work Survey 28
  organisational development 290–95, 295
  People Profession survey (2021) 77
  People Profession 2030 41, 102
  People Profession 2030: A collective view of
    future trends 4
  People Profession survey 70–71
  performance management 220–23, 221,
    222, 223
  research report 31, 34
  Resourcing and Talent Planning Survey
    (2021i) 116, 120, 121, 125, 132, 133, 157
  survey 30–31
Chavan, M 223

Cheese, Peter 236
Chen, HM 47
Cheung, G W 182
Chicago School economists 95
Chief People Officer (CPO) 22
Child 264, 279, 279
Children and Families Act (2014) 209
China 129, 134, 145, 182, 264
Chronus Corporation 156
CIPD People Management award (2020) 294
CIPD People Management Awards (2021) 33
CIPD Profession Map 157
CIPD qualification (Level 5) 302
Citi India 148
Citi Woman Leader Award 148
Citibank 148
Citigroup 148
Clark, Andrew 248–49
Claydon, T 25
Clegg, S 256, 264, 266
clients 9, 21, 42, 69, 74, 91, 162, 179, 261
     Capgemini (case study) 272–73
Coalition Government (2010–15) 198
Coca-Cola HBC (case study) 293–94
Cochrane, David 150–51
Code of Practice 201
cognitive behavioural therapy (CBT) 316
Cognitive learning theory 154
Collings, DG 141
'Comms Cells' 33
competing values framework (CVF) 46, 56
conflict management tools 300
contingency theory 264
continuing professional development (CPD) 92,
     140, 142, 159–60
continuous professional development (CPD) 92,
     140, 142, 159–60
Control theory 225–26
Convention prohibiting child labour (ILO) 197
Conway, N 292
Cooper, Cary 177, 180
Corbridge, M 120–21, 123
corporate social responsibility (CSR) 90, 212
Covid-19 pandemic xiv, 4, 8, 23, 28, 75, 153,
     157, 160–62, 175, 207, 209, 253, 303,
     315, 323
     agile working 271
     Blue Ocean and Red Ocean strategy 47
     Capgemini (case study) 272–73
     CIPD survey 133
     Coca-Cola HBC (case study) 293–94
     employment relationship 215–16
     employment rights 198
     gig economy 259
     Good Work Index 58–59
     HRM and 61–63
     job design 265–70

labour market 213–14
and managing employee 142
online recruitment 128–29
people strategy 54–55
PM 220
Porter's generic analysis 48
Scottish hospitality and tourism industry
     150–51
and Severn Trent 32–33
UK government 133–34
VIVID (case study) 316–17
see also human resources (HR); organisational
     change
Crothall, Marc 150–51
Crowley, E 28–30
Crozier, Adam 158
C-suite 317
customers 24, 69, 96, 115, 143, 152, 162, 223,
     229–30, 246
     Aurora (case study) 75
     customer alignment 60–61
     employee wellbeing 179–82, 181
     internationalisation 77–78
     and organization 59–60
     performance standards 229–30
     Schein on 50
     Severn Trent (case study) 32–34
     Stock (case study) 104–05
     Strategy, HR and 46–47
     supply chain orientation 48–49

Daft 264
Daily Telegraph (newspaper) 158
De Wit, B 24
decentralisation 320
Deci et al 241
Deliveroo 274
Deloitte 35, 99, 142, 161, 236
Deloitte Consulting LLP 35
Deloitte report 32
Department for Business, Energy and Industrial
     Strategy (BEIS) 258
Department for Business, Innovation and Skills
     (2013) 212
Devanna et al 26
digital innovation 29
digital learning 28, 302
digital skills 143
digital talent pools 161
digital technology 9, 69, 70, 315
digital transformation 143
digitalisation 63–64, 162, 314–15
Dillard, N 169
disabled people 209
'discontinuous' change 281
diversity 208–14
diversity management 22, 194, 209, 211, 212

Dobson, J 101
Donaldson, T 95
Doz, YL 300
Drucker, PF 252
Du Gay, Paul 260–61
Duchess of Sussex 100
Duke University 53
Durham University 130
Dyer, L 247

Eastern Europe 26, 81
ECS (European Company Survey) 315
Edgell et al. 179
EDI (equality diversity and inclusivity) 314
Edwards, MR 53–54
Eikhof, DR 177
Elite sports teams 306
Elle 169
EMEA 39–40
Emery, Yves 231
Employee Assistance Programme (VIVID) 316
employee engagement 33, 55, 69, 142, 167–70,
      184, 200, 238–39, 244, 249, 274, 323–24
  defining 167–69
  generating 170–72, 204–05
  job design, approaches to 265–70
  outcomes of 172–74
  outsourcing 257
  talent management 142
  see also employees
employee engagement strategies 69
employee lifecycle 224, 226
employee performance 140, 323
employee retention 61, 179–80, 323, 324
employee value proposition (EVP) 324
employees experience 32–33, 167, 168, 185,
      292, 294
employees
  artificial intelligence 8
  automation and artificial intelligence (AI) 317
  business ethics 96–101, 106–09
  competing values framework (CVF) 56
  conflict and employment relationship 203–07
  customer alignment 60–61
  employee engagement 32–34
  employment, contract of 195–202, 195
  flexibility 257–60
  Google (case study) 319–23
  Hays on 53
  HRD 27–30
  HRM and HRD 23–27, 25
  human resource development, definitions
      of 22
  human resource management (HRM)
      function 3–4
  human resource management, definitions
      of 21–22

inclusion 182–90, *185–86*, *188*, *189*
IRS survey 37
job design 255–56, 265–70
learning and development 154–60, *156*
organisation, strategy of 78–86
organisational design (OD) 253–55
personnel management, definitions of 21
PM 220
recruitment and selection 114–16
recruitment and selection, candidates 118–22
Schein on 50
strategy and culture 53, 64
sub-cultures 52
wellbeing of 174–82, *181*
work diversity at 208–14
see also change management; Chartered Insti-
      tute of Personnel and Development (CIPD);
      employee engagement; human resource
      management (HRM); human resources
      (HR); organisational culture; performance
      management; recruitment and selection;
      talent management
employer brand 54, 133
employer branding 53–54, 120, 128, 142, 151
employers 7, 57, 58–59, 187–88, 201–02,
      203–04, 257–58, 324
  artificial intelligence 8
  candidates attracting 120–21
  collective bargaining 201–02
  continuing professional development
      (CPD) 159–60
  data, technology and ethics 106–07
  diversity, benefits of 211–14
  employee engagement 167–70
  employee selection methods 114–16
  employment, contract of 195–99, *195*
  gig economy 259
  online recruitment 128–29
  partnership working 205–07
  personnel management 21
  recruitment and selection 134–35
  recruitment and selection challenges 133
  self-initiated expatriate 84–85
  wellbeing 174–82
  see also employees
Employment Appeal Tribunal (EAT) 195–96
Employment Relations Act (1996) 196, 200
employment relationship 5, 22, 168, 215–16,
      247, 253
  conflict and 203–07
  employment, contract of 195–202, *195*, *199*
  nature of 194–95
  work, diversity at 208–14
employment rights 197–98, *195*, 208
employment, contract of 195–99, *195*
  employment relationship management
      199–202, *199*

England xiv, 54–55, 99, 132, 206
EnterpriseAlumni 131
Equality Act (2010) 209
Equality and Human Rights Commission 130
equity theory (Adams) 237, 240, 243
ethics
    approaches to 97–101
    business ethics 96–97, 264
    business, purpose of 95–96
    data, technology and 106–07
    embedding 108
    equal opportunities and 103–05
    see also employee engagement; inclusion;
        recruitment and selection; wellbeing
'ETPS' (Economic, Technical, Political, and
        Social) 283
EU nationals 133
Eurofound (2021) 315
Europe 55, 145, 212, 259
European countries 145
European Union (EU) 4, 133, 197–98, 207, 259,
        273, 315
Europeans 153–54
Evelyn 169
Evetts, J 91
Evviva Brands 129
existence-relatedness-growth (ERG) theory 237
expectancy theory (Vroom) 237, 238, 241–43
Experiential learning theory 155

Facebook 51, 123, 129, 178, 237, 322
Fair Work Commission 206–07
Fair Work Convention 206–07
Fayol 278
FDM 6
Fernon, Deborah 133
Fielden, Paul 42
Financial Times (newspaper) 214
Finland 145
force-field analysis (Lewin) 295
Ford 256
Ford (2021) 317
Ford, Henry 256, 267
Fordist production line system 267
Foster, D 212–13
Four Seasons 100
4IR (4th Industrial Revolution) 106
Fox, A 203
Foxtons (case study) 302–03
Frahm, J 289
Freidman, Milton 95
French et al 134, 172, 240, 252, 253, 289, 290
    change, resistance to 288–89
    job design 255–56
Friends (television sitcom) 32
FTSE Women Leaders Review 105
Furnham, A 235

Gal, U 107
gamification 128
Garavan, TN 27
Gartner case study 294
Geal, M 226
Gee, Cathryn 316–17
'Geek culture' 319–20
gender diversity 148
Generations X 143–44, 172, 175
Generations Y 172
Generations Z 175, 323
Germany 145
Gershon Efficiency Review 23
Gherkin building 39
gig economy 259
gig workers 274
Gill, J 69
Gilmore, S 190–91, 253
Gioia, DA 27
Gioia, JL 54
Glassdoor 130–31
Global Data Protection Regulations (GDPR) 106
global economic recession (2007/2008)
        142, 143, 145
global GPD 146–47
Global human capital trends (2014) 35
Global North 142
Global staffing 78
globalisation 43
gmail 322
Goal-setting theory (Locke) 237
Gold, J 257
Goldman Sachs 101
Goldthorpe et al 270
Good Work Index (CIPD) 46, 56–59
Good Work Plan 198
Google 319–23
Google Art Project 322
Google News 322
Googleplex 319–23
Grant Thornton 9
graphology 134–35
Gray, M 132
Greece 145
Greek civilisation 260
Greek government 145
Greek luxury hotels 146
Green Inc. 83
Greene King 6
Greiner, L 74–75
Grey, C 264, 270
Grint, K 92, 277
GROW model 157
Groysberg, B 239
Grundy, T 281
Grzes-Buklaho, J 49–50
Guardian, The (newspaper) 264

Gubbins, C 27
Guest, DE 292
Gulf Cooperation Countries (GCC) 150
Guthrie, JP 318

Hackman and Oldham's model 269–70
Hackman, JR 233, 240, 268–70
Hall, David 25, 231
Hamilton Skurak et al 180
Hampden-Turner, C 50
Hampshire 316–17
hard models (HRM) 26
Harmer, Danny 315
Harrison, R 30
Hartley, James 39–40
Harvard economists 95
Harvard school 74
Hatton-Gore, Tony 244–45
Haunschild, A 177
Hays 53
The Health Foundation (2020 report) 273
Heckman, RJ 141
Henley Business School 31
Herman, ER 54
Herscovitch, L 240
Herzberg, Frederick 224, 233, 237
Heutagogy 155
Hiatt, J 297
hierarchy of needs theory (Maslow) 237,
        238, 239
Higgin, P 94, 305
high performance work systems (HPWS) 114,
        318, 321–23
high-performance work organisations
        (HPWOs) 222, 306, 318
high-performance work practices (HPWPs) 246,
        306, 318
high-performance working practices
        (HPWPs) 246, 306, 318
Hilton Group 158
Hirst, N 212–13
Holbeche, L 127, 170, 319
Hollyforde, S 233
Holman, G 244
Holy Grail 49
horizontal integration 25
Hospitality Industry Trust (HIT) 150–51
host-country nationals (HCNs) 80–81
House of Commons Women and Equalities
        Committee (2019) 214
Howe-Walsh, LJ 84
HR business partnering relationship 32
HR management strategy 115
HR manager. See human resources (HR)
HR Market Outlook report 114
HR professionals. See human resources (HR)
HR transformation 38

HSBC 78
Hsieh, YH 47
Hult, G T M 48–49
human capital 27, 318–19, 319
human capital investment 76
human capital management 22, 35, 38
Human Capital Reporting survey (CIPD) 26–27
human resource development (HRD) 20, 44,
        71–72, 109, 247–48
    Harrison work 30
    HR function 35–37
    HRM and 23–25
    human resource development 21–22
    scope and nature 23–25
    SMEs 73–75
    strategic 27–29
human resource development, definitions of 22
human resource information systems (HRISs) 132
human resource management (HRM) 20–22,
        94–95, 103, 109, 180, 318, 322
    capability building 35–37
    changing nature of 34
    definitions of 21–22
    equal opportunities and ethics 103–05
    Harrison work 30
    HR roles 73–77
    HRM practices 131–34
    international HRM and the SME 85–86
    models and strategic 25–30, 25
    and risk 61–63
    scope and nature 23–25
    Small and medium-sized enterprises 131–34
    strategic and human capital management
        38–40
    strategic HRM 48–49
    see also strategic international HRM (SIHRM)
human resource management theory 203–04
human resources (HR) 223
    artificial intelligence 8
    capability building 35–37
    and change 303–05
    CIPD report 4–5
    embedding ethical practice 108
    employment, contract of 195–99, 195
    ethics 97–101
    flexibility 257–60
    future trends 41–42
    Google (case study) 319–23
    HR function 68–73
    Impressit (case study) 5–6
    improving performance 10
    John Lewis Partnership (case study) 248–49
    learning and development theories 154–55
    managing and developing people (case
        study) 5–6
    organisation, globalisation of 77–78
    organisation, strategy of 78–86

roles 73–77
shape of 30–34
strategy 24–25, 46–49
sustainability and 102–03
Swiss Re (case study) 39–40
Tawse (case study) 10–11
VIVID (case study) 316–17
see also employment, contract of; ethics; human
  resource development (HRD); human
  resource management (HRM); inclusion;
  organisational culture; organisational
  design; performance management; talent
  management
Huo, M-L 182
Huong et al 189
Huselid and Rau 318
Hutchinson, S 172–73
Huws, U 256
hybrid working 9
hybrid working model 50–51

IBM 42, 80
IKEA 117, 135, 136
Impellam group 6
Impressit 5–6
inclusion 4–5, 178, 182, 185–86, 188,
  189, 191, 257, 323
  appraisal 234
  Capgemini (case study) 272–73
  customer alignment 60–61
  defininition 183–84
  Foxtons (case study) 302–03
  inclusion-centred approaches 185–90
  job design, approaches to 265–70
  Severn Trent (case study) 32–34
  Stock (case study) 104–05
  strategy and culture 53
  Unilever (case study) 102–03
  work, diversity at 208–14
  workplace dynamics 165–67, 166
  see also recruitment and selection
inclusive talent management programme 145
'inclusivity at work' 9
India 42, 99, 129, 145, 148
Indian School of Business 148
'induction crisis' 225
Instagram 123
Institute of Business Ethics (IBE) 96, 108
international HRM (IHRM) 68
The International Journal of Human Resource
  Management 180
International Labour Organisation 197
International Monetary Fund 258
IRS survey 36–37
Itsu 153–54
ITV 158
Izak, Michal 178

Jackson, A 280
Jamrog et al 222
Jamrog, JJ 60–61
Janis, I 52
Japan 270–71
Jenner, S 43
Jensen, TB 107
job design 255–56
  agile working 271–73
  approaches 265–70
John Lewis Partnership 158, 248–49
John Lewis stores 248
Johnson et al 48
Johnson, K 285–86
Johnson, B 226
Jones, J 241, 298
Jope, Alan 102–03
Judge, TA 135

Kahn, WA 168–69
Kahn, William 167–68
Kant, Immanuel 97–98
Kaplan, RS 46
Keenan, P 280
Kelliher, C 173, 176–77
Kenya 160
Ketchen, D 48–49
Kim, W 47, 69
Kiverska, Maryana 5–6
Klein, Thorsten 293–94
Kolb's experiential learning cycle 155
Koster, F 240
Kotter, John 289–90, 301
Kotter's eight-stage change model 289–90
KPIs 33
KPMG 161
Kraft 159
Kramar, R 103
Krishnan, TN 132
Kuvaas, B 240–41
Kwarteng, Kwasi 101

labour market 35, 68, 104, 131, 133–34, 177,
  198, 201, 315
Lang, Debra xiv, 54–55
Latham, GP 233
LBC radio 101
Leach, D 256
lean management principles 298
learning and development (L&D) 28, 29, 30,
  40, 54, 73, 102, 133, 153, 155–56, 157,
  234, 302
Learning organisation theory 226
Lee, L 239
Lessem 299
Lewin, Kurt 287–88, 288, 289–90
Lewin's three-phase change model 287–88, 288

Lewis, Angela 62–63
Lewis, G 177
Lewis, RE 141
line managers 5, 29, 30, 43, 51, 68–73, 94, 108,
    114–15, 158, 225, 246–47, 315
  business partnership describing 31
  devolution to 85–86
  employee engagement 167–70
  employment, contract of 195–99, 195
  engagement (case study) 171–72
  equal opportunities 208–10
  HR policies and practices 191
  HR practice 229
  inclusion-centred approaches 185–86
  IRS survey 36–37
  psychological contract 166–67
  talent management and 148–50
LinkedIn 121
Lloyd and Maguire 308–09
Locke, EA 233
Locke, Edwin 237
London 39, 59, 263, 272, 302–03
  marginal gains (case study) 305–08
London 2012 Olympics (case study) 305–08
London Heathrow Airport 42
London Olympic Park 42
Lufthansa 127
Lupton 280
Lush 6
Luwolt, Roy 100
Lyons, ST 172

MacDonald, DJ 173–74
Machiavelli 100
Mackie, JL 99
Maguire, H 166
Makin, PJ 173–74
Malone Souliers 100
Mangalindan (2015) reports 320
Marchington et al 170
marginal gains 305–08
Marks & Spencer 6
Marriott Hotel Group 128
Martin, G 54
Martin, MJ 49
Mashable (media) 320
Maslow, Abraham 237, 238, 239
Mason, Sarah 302–03
Matthews, G 170
Mauborgne, R 47, 69
May, Theresa 198
Mayfield, J 240
Mayfield, M 240
Mayon-White (1993) 295
MBA 148
McBain, R 43

McCalman 286–87, 287, 295
McClelland, David 237
McCracken, M 28
'McDonaldisation' 135, 256
McDonalds 256
McGoldrick, J 22
McHugh, D 124
McIntyre, K 179
McKinsey 140, 152–53, 175, 259
McKinsey 7S framework 305
McLellan 267–68
Me Too 213, 216
Mediterranean countries 81, 145
Meierhans, Jennifer 59
Mellahi, K 141
Merrick, L 156
Messersmith, JG 318
Meyer, JP 240
Meyer, R 24
Microsoft 128, 160–61, 323–24
Milan 100
Millennials 143–44, 172
Minchington 324
The Mind Foundry 316
Mintel 187–88
Mitchell, M 92
Mncube, Bongiwe 39
Modern Slavery Act 2015 98
Mohdzani, H 132
Moloney, ME 177
Morrison, Neil 33–34, 96
Morrisons 6
motivation theories 237–40
Mount, M 256, 264, 266
Mullins, LJ 115, 237, 252, 278
multinational enterprises (MNEs) 78, 82,
    85–86
Mumbai 148
Murphy, J 264
My Marriott Hotel 129

Nadin, S 132
NASA 52
National Health Service NHS (UK)
    147, 213
National Transition Training Fund
    (Scotland) 150–51
Nestlé 158
Netflix 135
New Public Management 147
New York 100, 153–54
New Zealand 33
NHS foundation trust 118, 147, 182, 286, 292
Nissim, Gillian 187
Nohria, N 239, 304–05
Nokia 145

non-disclosure agreements (NDAs) 214
Nordegraaf 92
Norton, DP 46
Norwegian government 105

OCAI measurement tool (Cameron) 56
OECD report (2019) 130–31
Oldham, GR 233, 240, 268–70
Olympics and Paralympics (2012) 238
Optiweb 147
Organisation for Economic Co-operation and
        Development (OECD) 114
organisation structure
    flexibility 257–60
    models of 260–65
organisational change 62, 94, 279, 282, 283, 295
    analysing 282–86, 282, 283, 284
    definition 278
    HR value added and 303–05
    leading 298–303, 301
    and performance 305–08
    resistance to 288–89
    systems approach 295–97, 296, 296–97
    types 278–81
organisational citizenship behaviour (OCB) 173
organisational culture
    blood Cancer (case study) UK 50–52
    competing values framework 56
    customer and 59–60
    definition of 49–50
    Google (case study) 319–23
    Kotter's eight-stage change model 289–90
    marginal gains (case study) 305–08
    organisational development 290–92
    recruitment and selection 135
    SodaStream (case study) 227–28
    strategy and 53
organisational design (OD) 253–54, 255, 260,
        273, 289–95, 303–04, 309
Osam, K 169
'Our Little Book of Why' 40
outsourcing 76–77, 86, 99, 190–91,
        254, 257, 262–63
    Capgemini (case study) 272–73
Overholt, MH 60–61
Overton, L 28–30

Pagan, V 214
Paltrow, Gwyneth 100
Pan American World Airways 127
pandemic. See Covid-19 pandemic
Papas, Elena 75
Papavasileiou 172
parental leave rights 209
parent-country nationals (PCNs) 80–81
Paris 100, 272–73

Patel, C 77
Patel, P 84
Paton 286–87, 287, 295
Pedigree Petfood (Mars) 158
Pedini, Elaine 118
people analytics 57, 161, 320
people analytics team 320
People Profession survey (2021) 77
performance improvement 306
performance management 23, 40, 108, 126, 151,
        221, 222, 223, 226–27, 289, 318
    definitions 220–23
    dissatisfaction 246
    HR and 246–47
    HR, role of 246–47
    and measuring results 224
    motivation theories 237–40
    perspectives on 223–24
    as a process 224–36, 226–27, 231–32
    reward and 240–45
performance management tool 233
performance-related pay (PRP) 241,
        242–43, 248
Perkbox 180, 182
Perkins, SJ 241
Perlmutter, H 80–81
personnel management, definitions of 21
PESTLE taxonomy 283–84, 284
Peterborough 130
Pettigrew, A 285
Peyton-Jones, Toby 315
Phoenix Group 133–34
Pierce, WD 241
Pilbeam, S 120–21, 123
Pisano et al 46–47
Pitcher, G 32
Pitsis, TS 256, 264, 266
Ployhart et al 318–19, 319
Pollert, A 190
Porter, Michael 47, 48, 68–69
Portsmouth 316–17
Prahalad, CK 288, 300
presenteeism 9
Preston, L 95
PricewaterhouseCoopers (PwC) (case study)
        179–80
Prikshat, V 84
private sector 23–24, 70–72, 144, 147, 194, 207
    work intensification and wellbeing (case
        study) 176–77
professionalism 30, 90–95, 109, 270
ProFinda 161
'psychological contract' 26, 159, 165, 166–67,
        166, 170, 174, 189–90, 191
    organisational development (OD) 290–92
psychological safety 57, 239

public sector 23–24
    Blood Cancer UK (case study) 50–52
    HR in different contexts 68–73
    job redesign 268–70
    marginal gains (case study) 305–08
    post-Brexit (case study) 207
    private sector vs. 146–48
    talent management agendas 160–62
    talent management stakeholders 148–51
Pulakos, E 246
Purcell et al 182, 229
Purcell, J 22, 23, 43, 74, 172–73,
    204–05, 221, 247
PwC reports (2020b) 153
PwC survey 81–82

Quinn, RE 56

Raffles 100
Ram Charan 314
Ramrachia, Ashley 131
Rankin, J 259
Rao, TV 36
Rashid, Wes 131
Rawlins, Trevor 317
recruitment and selection 114–17
    challenges 133–34
    contemporary themes 125–29
    contingency approach 134–35
    effective 118–22
    fairness in 129–31
    selection methods 122–25
    see also candidates
Red Ocean strategy 47, 69
Reed Consulting Survey (2004) 225
Rees, D 43
Reeves, R 230–31
refugees 4, 6
Reinforcement learning theory 155
Reissner, Stefanie 178
Resourcing and Talent Planning Survey
    (2021i) 132, 157
'resourcing cycle' 120, 124
RetailCo 151–52
Rezai et al 185
Ritzer, G 256
Robert Walters 6
Robertson, M 189
Rolls-Royce 108
Roman civilisation 260
Roper, I 94
Rose, Stuart 101
Rosen et al 230
Rosenfeld 299
Ross Geller (fictional character) 32

Royal Mail 158
Royal Mencap Society 152
Russia 158–59
Russon, M-A 254

Saatchi & Saatchi 158
Sainsbury's 6
SAP 161
Saudi Arabia 189
Saunders, MNK 174
'scattergun' applications 134
Schein, E 50, 224
Schuler et al 79
Schultz, TW 318
Schyns, P 84
Scientific Management 256, 267–68, 275
    job redesign 268–70
The Scotch Whisky 151
Scotland 150–51, 206–07
Scottish Government 150–51, 206–07
Scottish Tourism Alliance 150–51
Scullion, H 132
Searle, RH 126
self-initiated expatriate (SIE) 84–85
Semco 229
Semler, R 229
Senedd 207
Setty, Prasad 320
7S framework (McKinsey) 53
Severn Trent 32–34
sex discrimination 10–11
shadow boomers 172
Shafer, R 247
shareholders 24, 71, 95–96, 229–30
    theory E and 305
Shell (oil company) 158
Silicon Graphics 319
Silicon Valley 319–23
Sinclair, Emma 6, 131
Sinha, P 84
Sirkin, HL 280
skills gaps 29, 304
Slater, D 59
small and medium-sized enterprises (SMEs) 78,
    85, 131–32, 146–47, 153, 162
Smallwood, N 36
'smooth incremental change' 281
Social learning theory 155
Social Partnership Bill 207
Society of Human Resource Management
    (SHRM) 92, 152–53, 161, 278
SodaStream 227–28
soft models (HRM) 26
Soho office 272
South Africa 39–40, 80

Spector, B 27–28
Sri Lankan public banking sector 161
stakeholders 5, 67, 90, 93–94, 147, 163, 229–30,
    295, 304
    and HRD managers 36
    HRM goals 23–24
    line managers, devolution to 85–86
    people management 58–59
    stakeholder theory 95–96
    talent management and 148–50
    wellbeing 175–76
Stalker 261–62, 263
Stanton, Marc 98
Stein, MK 107
Stephenson Harwood 59
Stewart, J 22
Stock, Kathleen 104–05
Storey, J 21
strategic international HRM (SIHRM) 78–86
    definition 79–82
strategic plan 282
strategy
    branding and organisational values 53–55
    business strategy 38, 71
    and culture 53
    customer alignment 60–61
    and HR 24–25, 25
    HR strategy 70–71, 126
    HR, role of 246–47
    HR, shape of 30–34
    HRD and strategic HRD 27–30
    HRM and strategic HRM 25–27
    internationalization 77–78
    PricewaterhouseCoopers (PwC) 179–80
    scope and nature 46–49
    SIHRM 78–86
    small and medium-sized enterprises 131–34
    SMEs 73–77
Strength-based performance appraisal
    (SBPA) 227–28
Studenroth, Jamie 186
Sull and Zweig 323
Sun, JY 28
supply chain orientation (SCO) 48–49
Swailes, S 173
Swiss Federal Administration 235
Swiss Re 39–40
SWOT (strengths, weaknesses, opportunities and
    threats) analysis 283–84
systems intervention strategy (SIS) 295
Szydlo, J 49–50

talent acquisition 140, 142, 151, 162, 302, 324
talent acquisition team 302
Talent development 151
talent gap 144
talent management scholarship 141

talent management
    approaches 140–41
    developed vs. developing countries 144–45
    importance 142–43
    key element 154–60, 156
    performance management 247–48
    private sector vs. public sector 146–48
    reshaping 160–62
    talent management cycle 151–54
    talent management stakeholders 148–51
    see also recruitment and selection
talent retention 152–53
Tan and Tiong 309
targeted investment 29
Task Rabbit 274
Tawse, Natalie, 10–11
Taylor, Frederick 256, 267
Taylor, Matthew 198
Taylor, S 43
'Taylorism'. See Scientific Management
Technologies Inc. (TI) 82
technology
    agile working 271–73
    Blood Cancer UK (case study) 50–52
    data, technology and ethics 106–07
    HR in different contexts 68–73
    internationalisation 77–78
    learning technologies 155–56
    learning technologies and self-directed
        learning 155–56
    organisational development 290–95, 295
#TellOurStory initiative 39–40
Terminal 5 (London Heathrow Airport) 42
termination 200
Tesco 6
theory E 305
theory O 305
third-country nationals (TCNs) 80, 83
Thomas, JB 27
Thompson, P 124
Thornhill, A 174
Thorpe, R 244
Todnem BY, C 278
Tokyo 100
total quality management (TQM) 270–71
Tourism and Hospitality Talent Development
        Programme (Scotland) 150–51
Tracey, JB 35–36
Trades Union Congress website 202
'transformational leadership' 281
'transformational' change 281
Transformative learning theory 155
Trompenaars, F 50
TROPICS test 286–87, 287
Truss, C 69
Trustpilot 302
23rd Annual Global CEO Survey

(PwC) 143
Twitter 123, 178, 188, 302
two-factor theory (Herzberg) 237, 268
Twohill, Lorraine 320

Uber 274
Uber organisation 254
UK driving test 122
UK Fire and Rescue organisation 307
UK governments 9, 98, 133, 264, 286
    equal opportunities 208–10
    wage bill (case study) 207
UK hospital 265
UK Household Longitudinal Study 273
UK law 194
UK luxury hotels 146
UK police force 208
UK public sector organisation 306
UK. *See* United Kingdom (UK)
Ukraine 4, 5–6, 158–59
Ulrich, D 21, 30, 31, 36, 43, 67, 73
Umphress, E 92
Unilever (case study) 102–03
Unilever Sustainable Living Plan [USLSP] 102–03
UNITE 72
United Kingdom (UK) 4, 9, 62–63, 120, 129–30,
    147, 153–54, *195*, 201–02, 204, 316
    Arup (case study) 244–45
    CIPD 90, 92
    CIPD *HR Market Outlook* report 114
    employment relationship 215–16
    employment, contract of 195–99
    equal opportunities 208–10
    Good Work Index 58
    IBE 96
    job design, approaches to 265–70
    John Lewis Partnership (case study) 248–49
    marginal gains (case study) 305–08
    Modern Slavery Act 2015 98
    outsourcing 99
    Severn Trent (case study) 32–34
    SIHRM, definition 79–82
    Swiss Re (case study) 39–40
    UK public sector 69
    wellbeing 175–80, *181*
    wellbeing, dimensions of 175–78
    work, diversity at 208–14
    see also recruitment and selection
United States of America (USA) 55, 80, 92, 134,
    160, 169, 212, 259, 267, 289
    HR practices 26
    self-directed learning 155–56
University of Alberta 157
University of Sussex (case srudy) 104–05
US organisations 289–90

vandalism 302

Varghese, S 36
vertical integration 25
Virgin Group 158
VIVID (Housing Association) (case study)
    316–17
Vodafone 6
Vodafone Business 161–62
The Vodafone Business Future Ready Report
    (2020) 153
Vroom, Victor Harold 237, 238

'wage–work bargain' 177–78, 194–200, *195*, 202
Wahrenburg et al 77
Wain, D 220
Waitrose supermarkets 248
Wales 206–07
Wall, T 256
Wallace, M 28
Wal-Mart 264
Wang, CG 28
Warech, M 35–36
Warhurst, C 177
Warren, C 303
water services regulation authority (Ofwat)
    142–43
Watkins, MD 49
Watson, TJ 255, 261
Weber, Max 224, 260
Weber's model 260–61
wellbeing
    dimensions of 175–78
    employee wellbeing 179–80, *181*
West et al 220
Whiddett, S 233
Whipp, R 285
Whitbread 158
Wiernik, BM 246
Wilkinson, Clive 319–23
Williams, RS 242
Williams, S 199
Willmott 264
Wilson, E 189, 299
Wolgast, S 129
Womack 298
'work design' 255–56, 291
workforce 21, 55, 62–63, 126, 168, 187
    agile working 271–73
    diversity organisational benefits 211–14
    employment relationship 215–16
    engagement generating 170–72
    flexibility 257–60
    Google (case study) 319–23
    HR function 35–37
    inclusion 182–90, *185–86*, *188*, *189*
    internationalization 77–78
    job design approaches 265–70
    John Lewis Partnership 248–49

private sector vs. public sector talent
    management 146–48
selection methods 122–25
talent management agendas 160–62
UK workforce 177, 201
VIVID (case study) 316–17
Zielinska (case study) 130–31
workforce agility 29
workforce interchange network and shadowing
    (WINS) portal 55
Working Mums 187–88
workplace 314–15
    artificial intelligence 8
    Covid-19, impacts of 58
    data, technology and ethics 106–07
    employment relationship 215–17
    engagement 167–74
    Foxtons (case study) 302–03
    inclusion 183–84
    inclusion and gender 185–86,
        185–86
    job design approaches 265–70
    online recruitment 128–29

organisational design (OD) 253–55,
    290–95, 295
PricewaterhouseCoopers (PwC)
    (case study) 179–80
Severn Trent (case study) 32–34
wellbeing, dimensions of 175–78
work, diversity at 208–14
Working Mums 187–88, 188
workplace culture 124, 165
workplace dynamics 165–67, 166
Works Centre for Wellbeing 175
World Bank 258
World Trade Organisation 264

Yorkshire County Cricket Club 213
Younger, J 31
Yuan, L 134

zero hours 258
Zielinska, Chloe 130–31
ZNF Bank 10–11
Zomko, Roman 5–6
Zurich 39